THE ☉ MANUSCRIPT

To my mother
Alice

Books in english by Lars Muhl:

The Aramaic Mystery (Book & DVD) 2009

Books in danish by Lars Muhl:

Soul at Fire, 1993
Zoé, 1995
The Eye of Freya, 1996
Shadowtravels, 1998
The Stillness of The Heart, 1999
The Celestian Way, 2000
The Forgotten Language, 2001
The Andalusian Seer, 2002
Mary Magdalene, 2004
Grail, 2006
The Wisdom of The Broken Heart, 2007

LARS MUHL

THE ☉ MANUSCRIPT

THE SEER   THE MAGDALENE   THE GRAIL

 LEMUEL BOOKS

The ☉ Manuscript
Translated from Danish by Bent Abkjer Hansen
Annette Armstrong & Jane Helbo

Copyright © 2008 by Lars Muhl
Lemuel Books ApS

First published in Danish 2002, 2004, 2006
by Lindhardt & Ringhof

Cover design by Lars Muhl & Lemuel Books
Typeset in Trajan Pro, Centaur Pro (11/ 13,2)
Text design and layout by Kirsten Puggaard

Printed and bound in Denmark by Narayana Press

Library of Congress Cataloging-in-Publication Data
Muhl, Lars, 1950-
The ☉ Manuscript: The Seer, The Magdalene, The Grail
Includes bibliographical references and index.
ISBN 978-87-991820-7-7 (hbk.)
I. Religion/ Mind Body Spirit (51795)

Lemuel Books ApS
Mejlgade 28, gaarden
DK-8200 Aarhus N
Denmark
(Ph. +45 21831447)

www.larsmuhl.com
www.lemuelbooks.com

CONTENTS

PUBLISHER'S INTRODUCTION

Already as a 10 year old, Lars Muhl had experienced glimpses of another reality. The shock, following the sudden death of his younger sister, caused painful kundalini-like experiences, giving access to the ethereal worlds and a hypersensitive insight into other people's pain. This lasted for three years.

A turning point came when Lars was 15 and received a book anonymously in the post. Hazrat Inayat Khan's *Gayan, Nirtan, Vadan*, became the start of a lifelong esoteric study.

Like Paulo Coelho, Lars was for many years a successful singer/songwriter who, concurrently with his music, studied the world's religions and esoteric knowledge. Then in 1996, he was struck down by an unexplained illness, which neither doctors nor alternative therapists could diagnose. For three years he lay in bed without being able to move or think straight.

Through a close friend's intervention, Lars was put in touch with a seer who, via the telephone, brought him back to life. That was the start of a completely new existence and the beginning of that quest he has so grippingly described in *The ☉ Manuscript*.

This is the trilogy you, dear reader, now hold in your hand. Don't let yourself be misled by the three subtitles. This is NOT another book about the Holy Grail, Jesus and Mary Magdalene based on the usual theses and theories that, over the years, have become trivialised. Instead *The ☉ Manuscript* is the result of one man's moving journey into "another reality" towards a more genuine and authentic way of being. A journey that engages from the outset and, unlike most of the other books in this genre, doesn't mislead with irrelevant who-done-it riddles. Instead *The ☉ Manuscript* opens up to the very centre of man's true mystery. The insight one gets through the author's meeting with another reality is mirrored synchronistically in the epic and dramatic story of the forgotten feminine power: the uniting of eros and agape, being recounted parallel to the author's story. Book I mirrors the masculine principle, while Book 2 portrays the feminine. Book 3 is dedicated to the mystery of the bridal chamber, where the masculine and the feminine become united as an isogenic entity.

When Book I, *The Seer*, came out in the author's homeland in 2000 it didn't awaken all that much interest, but despite that the trilogy has since reached cult status in Scandinavia and sold in ever greater numbers. The book also came out at an early date in a Russian translation and is now, with this English translation, on its way out into the wider world.

Book I, *The Seer*, takes as its starting point Lars' illness, his meeting with the Seer and their work on the holy mountain of Montsegur in the southern French Pyrenees. The book is not only a spell-binding introduction to the ancient gnosis of everything's interconnectedness, but also a critical evaluation of a long list of limiting new age dogmas.

When Lars and the Seer part, the latter hands an old manuscript into the author's care; a manuscript that, surprisingly, turns out to be a doorway to the events that take place in the following two books of the trilogy.

Book 2, *The Magdalene*, came out at the same time as "The Da Vinci Code", and unfolds along two themes: the author's continuing work with and parting from the Seer and his glimpse into the collective Akasha, where he is confronted with Mary Magdalene as the feminine force's most outstanding archetype and also as a historic person. Among the book's high points is the moving description of Jesus and Mary Magdalene's time together and their mutual initiation in the bridal chamber.

Book 3, *The Grail*, which on its publication and without any publicity whatsoever, flew straight into first place on the bestseller list, deals with the author's fateful meeting with Sylvia, an old priestess in *The Order of The World Mother*. It's the story of the quest she decrees he must take. We follow him on his twofold path where he meets his own feminine counterpart/anima and at the same time recognises things that bring him to understand the feminine archetype's significance for our present time.

Among the book's many high points are the author's meeting with a nameless Being of Light in a hidden cave on the holy mountain of Montsegur and in Mary Magdalene's secret cave near Périllos in the southern French Pyrenees.

During the first meeting with this Being of Light Lars gets the chance to travel with *The Chariot of Fire (Merkabah)* and, during this and the second meeting, receives answers that challenge many of today's spiritual dogmas.

The books distinguish themselves by being written in such a way that, in spite of their complicated subject matter, they are suitable for a wide readership. The many layers to be found in the texts mean that both beginners and the more initiated in these themes are struck by the authenticity of the words and the author's ability to bring "heaven down to earth" or "the reader nearer heaven".

The ⊙ Manuscript is not just another spiritual sweetener but the beginning of a most exciting journey for anyone who reads it. The books are not to be read merely to be "understood", but to be absorbed into the very texture of your conscious being and your higher Self.

Kirsten Puggaard
Publisher

Dear unknown Friend, dear Sister, dear Brother.

There was once a monastery-like religious community. Each day when the congregation celebrated Mass, the monastery cat disturbed the holy ritual. The abbot therefore asked someone from the congregation to tie the cat up so that Mass could continue in peace.

This went on for many years.

When the abbot died they continued tying up the cat up each day just before Mass.

Then the cat died. The new abbot immediately ordered that a new cat should be acquired to be tied up before Mass. Everybody rejoiced since this was what they had always done.

However, one day a newcomer asked why they tortured the poor animal in this way. The question raised a great commotion and the man who asked the question was immediately expelled from the monastery. In order to make sure that something like this would never happen again, some of the scholars among them began writing theological treaties about the necessity of tying up a cat before each and every Mass.

Religions and theology as well as interpretations of historical events have often been the cause of very funny misunderstandings. But usually such misunderstandings have lead to catastrophic results. Usually because both religion and history are expressions of the limitation of those who wrote it.

Throughout time, historiography and religion have been used as a means for power. The truth about the many troubles of the world, e.g. the holocaust, as well as the truth about the many wonders of the world, e.g. Christ, may at any time be seen and read in the great cosmic memory, the Akasha-field, by those who tune in to it. Insight into the flow behind the so-called historical events may be gained through two channels: Either through the horizontal, time-related one, or through the vertical, transcendental, visionary one, which dissolves time and place.

Transcendental visions may always be understood in more than one way. When they are written down it isn't necessarily because they should be taken literally, or because they claim to be expressions of so called historical facts. They are, first and foremost, allegories about life's true secrets. They represent the most profound wisdom of the heart that opens us to possibilities that blow to pieces any kind of habitual thinking, all cold facts and all limited ideas of reality with its crushing tyranny. Visions are priceless echoes from the Akasha-field.

The vision about the Grail is first and foremost the story about all that we seem to have forgotten. The Grail is neither a secret, worldly treasure in the shape of a cup, a specific mortal woman, nor a hidden, chosen family somewhere in the world.

The Grail is a state of heart and mind!

A multidimensional consciousness accessible to all who dare: to let go of time's cosy little crime mysteries; to get up from the soft couch of comfort; to find the courage to set out on the quest for the Grail and to take the quantum leap most people only dare dream about.

I am myself simply an itinerant errand boy who is only just awakening and beginning to understand the language of transcendence, which is accessible to all who are prepared to make the effort to learn it.

This book is a personal document that attempts to describe some personal experiences and acknowledgements. But the chronological order of events has had to give way to the truth, which may be seen between the lines only. It is only in the gaps, where words do not get in the way that the true quest for the Grail and ⊙ may begin.

I wish you a pleasant journey.

Lars Muhl

BOOK I

THE SEER

To the memory of
Calle Montségur
(1934 – 2007)

Those who dance are often condemned
by those who cannot hear the music

I

It was an ice cold day in February. The kind of day where the Copenhagen Central Station is anything but inviting. I dragged my suitcases up the stairs to get out of the chilling wind from the platform and quite deliberately ignored the beggars and the down-and-outs squatting on old newspapers and waving their blue coffee-pots at the passers by. My own budget was more than over the limit, and, furthermore, I felt dizzy. I felt nauseated. I wasn't myself at all. Had I misunderstood something, since I lost my balance to such a frightening degree? And then just now, when I was about to embark on what was probably the most important journey of my life.

I drank a bottle of club soda at the cafeteria and found a corner where I could sit relatively undisturbed in order to recover. I had a couple of hours before the night train for Cologne was scheduled to depart. In spite of how far I thought I had come, I still sat there and felt like a totally abandoned novice. Unsuccessfully, I had tried to sell the account of my journey to a major newspaper just two days earlier. But how were they to know that a train journey to southern

15

Spain could be more exotic in this day and age, than an aeroplane trip to the Antarctic Continent, simply because it takes longer? They knew better at the DSB travel agency. It was the first trip of this kind that they had sold for several years.

"Are you sure?" the woman asked wonderingly and slightly curious as I booked the ticket.

I chose not to start a major explanation about my having stopped flying many years ago, but couldn't help smiling at the paradox that I was about to begin a 48 hour train journey to Spain, in principle, in order to fly. Well, not by plane, but still ...

The characteristic, greasy smell of today's special: meat, cabbage, gravy and potatoes, mixed with too much smoke and nicotine, made my stomach turn and I had to concentrate in order not to be sick. I was cold in spite of the heat, had sweat on my forehead, and I shivered so much that I had to hold on to the bottle with both hands. I drank some soda and tried to think about something else.

"But isn't this Lars Muhl?" A far too optimistic voice cut through the noise from the plates and cutlery. I looked up and nodded automatically. A man handed me a paper napkin and a pen: "Could I please have your autograph?"

He smiled at the girl standing next to him, who seemed to be his daughter. I was just about to be sick. Beads of sweat trailed down my face as I grabbed the pen and wrote my name while getting up from my seat. I then ran as fast as I could towards the men's room.

When I got back, the man and his daughter had disappeared. It was the first autograph I had written for ages. A middle-aged woman who was hanging on to a strong beer at the neighbouring table scowled disapprovingly at me through a black eye and I could almost hear her thinking: "Who the hell do you think you are?" Well, I would really like to know that myself. I closed my eyes and tried to concentrate on the present situation. But somehow, my thoughts automatically went back. Back to the day when my career as a singer categorically ended, and my present journey started. Back to all that went before the NOW.

I had always known that a person is more than his or her mere personality. I had always known that the real person is to be found somewhere behind all the defences and the protective shields of titles, careers and jobs. I had always been aware that no matter how well known, how rich and how celebrated you are, there aren't enough fans, money and attention in the world to close the gap and ease the pain which all the hullabaloo carries with it. I have always known that notwithstanding your living conditions and social position, ultimately, all this seems strangely illusory, seen in the perspective of eternity.

Since childhood I have been familiar with another reality. From my tenth to my twelfth year, each evening before I fell asleep, I had some unfamiliar and painful kundalini experiences with the result that I hardly slept at all during this period. Since I wasn't able to share these experiences with anyone I became more and more introvert and unable to function. I found social situations difficult to handle and did badly at school. However, this didn't stop me reading on my own. When I was fifteen years old I received the sufi-mystic Hazrat Inayat Khan's book *Gayan, Vadan, Nirtan* by mail. I don't know who sent it. But the book was a revelation and inspired me to read other books by Khan. The problem was, however, that what I read and studied all somehow connected to my knowledge of the other reality and thus stood out in sharp contrast to all my school learning. When finally I left the school in 1966 to throw myself into the intensity of life as a musician, I was hoping that this once and for all would cut out the reality which had made me so damned lonely and which no one else seemed to care about.

My attempt seemed to succeed, when destiny brought the band I was playing in to Israel in 1969, where we were supposed to tour for a couple of months. We played for the soldiers at the army summer camps, for the students at the universities and for the young people at the clubs and the discotheques. Drugs were more or less compulsory but unfortunately also banned in Israel at the time. Thus, when we were taken with cannabis and amphetamine during a raid at the hotel, we were forced to spend about a week at the notorious remand prison in Jaffa just outside of Tel Aviv. It thus took a stone bench to sleep on, a cold water faucet to wash by, a hole in the middle of the cell for the necessary relief and a very primitive form of communication between prisoners and guards, – to wake me from my magic sleep.

During one of the exercise rounds one of my fellow prisoners showed me the holes in the ground measuring two by two meters, where they kept the insane, the murderers and the rapists each in his hole with an iron grid over their heads: in the daytime a burning oven, at night an icy refrigerator. Each time a prisoner passed by and spat or threw a rock at the miserable creatures, they reacted with inarticulate and hysterical howls and an infernal noise from the shackles, which they banged against the iron grids. It was hard to accept, that almost at the same time the American astronaut Armstrong put his foot on the moon with the words: "One small step for man – one giant leap for mankind." I for one didn't understand it. What did it mean? Was this a cosmic joke or a part of civilized man's catering to the ultimate duality dividing life into black and white, heaven and hell.

It was as if everything that happened during the three months in Israel simply sharpened my psychic senses, which up and until that time I had frantically tried to hide. Whether it was due to the ancient, historical surroundings with all their myths and religious traditions, I do not know; however, I nevertheless started getting sporadic visions from ancient times and heard voices from a strange and yet familiar world. Furthermore, for the first time in my life I also met another person with the same experiences. Simon. A Jewish boy, thirteen years old, who also knew about this other reality.

One day sitting on our terrace facing the street, he happened to pass by. Even seeing him at a distance as he was approaching I immediately knew who he was. Having reached the terrace he stopped. He also recognized me. I invited him in for tea and from that day on we met almost daily. One day he gave me a necklace with a piece of jewelry on which he had done some filigree work. A round globe with a piece of cedar wood inside it and a spiral shaped cone fastened to it. The globe symbolized the earth. The little piece of cedar wood symbolized *King Solomon's* Ginkgo Maidenhair Tree, The Cosmic Tree, which possessed a magical power. The spiral symbolized the eternal, death and rebirth and the transformation of matter to spirit.

As I put it on, a large, affirmative YES sounded through me and it felt like a blessing.

Meeting Simon combined with the psychic experiences made me believe that I had now found the place where I belonged and in my euphoria I forgot the realities of my life. Maybe there is some truth in the saying that a chain is never stronger than its weakest link since one day I found out, that the necklace with the piece of jewelry was gone. It was like a bad omen. And yet another awakening. This time an awakening to the unavoidable fact, that it was time to go home. Immediately prior to my departure I had my first out-of-body experience.

Now, more than thirty years later, I was sitting at the Copenhagen Central Station feeling out-of-the-body in a different way; well, more like out-of-place. What had summoned me here? Was it time – my time – which finally was about to reach its point of eternity, where ends meet and two realities become one?

Each life is a journey and mine was no exception. But had I come to a cul-de-sac or was the journey almost over? Seen from the point of view of the traditional idea of what constitutes a good life, mine seemed in many ways to be a failure. For more than thirty years I had been fighting a losing battle with a career as a musician and later as a singer. I had had decent results, but each time it got really serious something in me pulled in the opposite direction. Away from the public eye and the surface, promotion and duties. As time went by this something seemed to take over more and more of my reality.

Here I was watching it all from a distance. Watching the lie with which I had betrayed myself and which had kept me in a condition that finally had become unbearable, simply because it made me ill. Far too long did I believe that it was possible to walk in two opposite directions. To be part of the music scene with all that it entailed and at the same time to live quietly in contemplation as some kind of mystic. To relate to a static, unified, strictly intellectual and materially focused world while at the same time I was really rediscovering and getting to know the other hidden and totally different reality – it simply wasn't possible. Finding myself on stage in the big tent at the Roskilde Festival in 1991 the question suddenly struck me in the middle of a song, "What are you doing here?" I could suddenly see myself from outside of myself, I could hear myself talking to the audience, trying to regain my composure with a lame, "hey, hey, hey" and to get in contact with the reality of the festival, which was slowly disappearing in a fog of beer and senseless drunkenness. It was totally surreal and of course impossible, since you cannot get out of the boat once it is launched. That same evening I decided to end the tour, and that same year I left my hometown and moved to a small island.

"The train for Cologne with an estimated departure of 6.45 p.m. will arrive at platform three in about 30 minutes," a metallic voice proclaimed through the loudspeakers.

I checked the time on my own wristwatch. I myself felt like an island in the middle of the steaming sea of people dining at the cafeteria. The place was filling up. I bought yet another club soda. The nausea and the dizziness were disappearing. In the arrival hall the beggars sat freezing and shaking on the benches trying to keep warm. The passers by didn't notice them at all. All in all it didn't seem as if anyone noticed anything. Buttoned up, eyes ahead. Apparently, all were sufficient to themselves. What were they thinking? Where were they going? What about me? Wasn't I sufficient to myself? Had my ability to partake in social activities improved since I withdrew to the island? Hardly! But I did it because I had to.

Had I not frequently heard people expressing their wishes to be sufficiently wealthy to be able to retire to a rural idyll in order to focus on themselves. But it wasn't like that at all. I was not wealthy. On the contrary. The material renunciation caused by the collapse in my career would have given most citizens in a Welfare State nightmares. The process I had been through was a paradoxical mixture of an existential stripping down and a mental breakdown.

Having settled down on the island I started writing as a natural part of the process of tidying-up. Slowly I began to realize that language constituted an important part of my change and after the publication of my first book, more followed. My fascination by the first Taoist and Buddhist writings turned into further extensive, comparative studies of religion, the Christian mystics, Sufism, various occult and Christian heresy schools. Lately I had started studying Aramaic on my own, the language that Yeshua (Jesus) is supposed to have spoken. A daily practice of various forms of quietude and meditation only distanced me further from my former life. But something or other in me kept me vainly clinging to a small, final and stubborn part of what was left of my diversified show biz career.

Until the day when circumstances helped me make the decision that I myself had hesitated making. During the recording for "Mandolina," which would turn out to be my last album, the record company suddenly informed me that after fusing with a multinational company they had decided to cease our business relationship (before it really started) for reasons unknown to me. This meant that the contract we had just signed and which included yet another album, was now cancelled. Only reluctantly did the company accept that I could finish what I was in the middle of doing. A lot of work, if not directly wasted, was certainly published in an unfinished condition. It was very frustrating in every way.

The recording companies didn't treat me kindly anymore. The commercial expectations for my songs had not paid off and from one day to the other I had no access to my income.

Was it all an element of the irony of fate or was it the efforts of a growing commercialization of the industry trying to clean the recording trade of the last alien substances? I couldn't help thinking about a conversation I once overheard between two managing directors of recording companies, one of whom dryly remarked, that apart from having to work with the artists, the music business wasn't bad at all.

It seemed as if an extensive part of my life was over. It just happened. Like snapping my fingers. It was not until later, that I understood that you are not easily forgiven when you move out of the limelight, when most artists feel that, more or less, it is this limelight that is giving them their livelihood. However, my problem was that I didn't belong there. From then on, my down hill drive went faster and faster. The intervals between phone calls widened and finally the phone didn't ring at all. When I found out that I also didn't have anyone to call, I pulled the plug and cancelled my phone subscription. I was where I wanted to be. Wasn't this what I wanted? Also when apparently my economic situation went from the acceptable to the more than strained? Maybe, finally, I had reached the point of no return. Perhaps I had started to realize that it was time to take care of my real self. Was I finally beginning to understand that life is too short for mere trivialities?

"The train for Cologne will arrive at platform three in a few minutes."

Bending over to lift my suitcases, I felt dizzy. But while crossing the arrival hall I sensed a slight electric current running through my spine. It felt like a very fragile current slowly spreading its energy through my whole body removing any sign of dizziness. I flicked a coin of twenty kroner into a coffee pot and went down to the platform and the waiting train.

2

I placed my suitcase on the upper shelf. It was covered by a worn, woollen blanket and a sheet, which smelt powerfully of an indefinable but very strong disinfectant.

Travelling on a 2nd class sleeper is only for those who travel light. All dimensions are created from a diminutive and ascetic picture of the world. The size of the berth, washing facilities and lavatory indicate that travelling is just a short phase, a discreet intermezzo, emphasized yet again by the long series of arrivals and departures, hellos and good-byes, absences and expectations, kisses and hugs, tears and sadness, which you witness along the way and which mark out the ephemeral station of any train journey and any life. Paradoxically it is also proof that man and his life is more than just a haphazard complex of unstable qualities and unpredictable influences.

Life is an expression of unity no matter how fragmented it may seem to be. It had taken me many years to realize that. It was not until my own life felt reduced and limited that I needed more space. It was not until I had lost all that which I thought was important and impossible to live without, in fact everything that makes life complicated and impossible, – not until then did I begin to have an inkling of how magnificent and unlimited life can be in all its simplicity. But such recognition was not painless.

Hinting at the possibility of another, more open and much freer reality – that for example a musical note could be shaped like a pyramid and that forgiveness could happen faster than the speed of light – was asking to be burned at the stake of an anaesthetized time of roaring silence and patronizing sarcasm. I am telling you!

The sleeper was full as the train grindingly started to roll. A businessman on the opposite berth, wearing blue and white striped pyjamas, completed his evening toilet with great difficulty and according to a meticulously planned ritual. Below him a stout German was wrestling his equally stout luggage and on the lower berth two young men from Copenhagen were exchanging canned beer and bad jokes, while an elderly gentleman in the berth below my own was snoring loudly. I slowly let go and allowed myself to float into the clear, frosty and starry night, over the sleepers and into unknown tunnels and the black holes of foreign universes, back to the year where I found myself stuck in the furthest corner of the maze, the shabby cul-de-sac of my own life.

It was the year when I fell into the dark night of the soul. It happened through a series of attacks, which physically meant that the back of my neck hurt like hell, I felt nauseated, lost all energy and had to stay in bed for days on end. It was like being caught in a no-mans land between the conscious and the unconscious, between being awake and asleep, the feeling of iron. To be locked into an almost hermetically sealed torture chamber, where everything was heavy and slow and blown apart. Every thought disappeared in a lethargic stupor almost before it was begun. The thought of having to reach for a glass of water seemed such an insurmountable obstacle that I usually gave it up. Once in a while when I came to, I managed to think that this must be hell before sinking back into bottomless darkness. I had only tried something similar in 1962, when I started my first book, which was written in a trance-like state similar to this one.

For two months I stayed in the same room, living on coffee and aspirin, clacking away at my old typewriter or lying unconscious on my equally old couch. Night and day disappeared in a monotonous fog and only my writing changed it into something like euphoria; an unreal, psychosomatic condition which didn't stop until I had written the last dot in the book.

Now the condition came back and made me unfit for work for longer and longer periods of time. A number of visits to the doctor, examinations at the hospital and at several specialists and alternative healers had no effect at all. At one time I was almost unconscious in my bed for about two weeks without getting anything to eat and drink but biscuits and water. They didn't even manage to find the reason for my condition when one day I fainted at my neighbour's house and had to spend the rest of the day in hospital supported by oxygen and a drip. As time went by I experienced more and more that I had to let go of the music since it had given way to this other thing. My crisis was total. After more than two years like this I didn't want to live anymore.

And then it happened – the unavoidable. It happens at least once in every man's life, although you may not notice it. The condition you are in is such that all too easily you disappear into the no man's land of pain and self-centredness, where all is lost and immovable. But the time was ripe because I was ripe, since I didn't have any other way out and nowhere to go. Was it a sign or was it an angel? In my case it was the latter. The angel came in the shape of a colleague from the slowly growing but still very small and invisible family. She gave me the telephone number that was going to turn everything upside down.

"Call the Seer and let him help you," she said before disappearing into thin air. I just stood there alternately staring into the hole in the air left by the angel and at the note she had pressed into my hand. "Only between 8 and 9 a.m." it said in the parenthesis following the phone number.

The Seer?

That evening I took a long walk along Frederiksberg Allé before going to bed in my room at Weber's Hotel, totally exhausted.

During the night I had a dream. In it I am walking down a long, deserted road. It ends abruptly and I'm standing at the edge of a precipice looking out into the universe. The quiet is underlined by an almost inaudible but very beautiful, deep and continuous note. The sound of matter. The sound that holds everything together. Touching and unutterable. I hear myself speaking in Aramaic: *Nehwey sibyanak aykana d'shmaya aph b'arab.* I remember. *Thy will be done on earth as it is in Heaven.* I now understand what these words really mean. *Let that happen on earth which is written between the stars. Unfold the light of the universe through each and everyone of us according to the laws of the universe.*

It was half past eight when I woke up. Again this dull feeling of iron at the edges of my consciousness. It took some time before I remembered what had happened the day before. Then I remembered the dream, the angel and the phone number. I got up feeling quite dizzy and started going through the pockets of my jacket and trousers. No such luck. Panic. It was as if already then I had realized what I was about to lose if I let this slip through my fingers. Finally. The slip of paper was in the breast pocket of my shirt. I dialled the number and held my breath. I waited and waited. I could follow the slow shift from the hotel telephone system to the phone company's by the sound of the series of changing notes. I was just about to hang up when I was finally connected, just to hear that the number was engaged. A lifetime of butterflies in my stomach. Looked at my watch. Almost nine, waited and tried again.

Still busy. Ten past nine, connection. I sat thinking that my telephone call was making a sound in the house of an unknown person, and that at the end of this ring tone that person had decided not to answer my call. I let it ring for a while and hung up.

Back at the island my condition improved and I found my usual rhythm alternating between my work with the Aramaic, which by now had really caught my attention, and periods of dizziness. Several times I was tempted to call the number again but for some reason or other I postponed it.

Getting further and further into the Aramaic language a totally new world opened to me. As early as 1989 Dr. Edith R. Stauffer from Psycho Synthesis International had sent me a copy of an Aramaic excerpt from The New Testament, *The Khaboris Manuscript*. This made it clear that the Aramaic is able to express the transpersonal psychology to such a degree, that the syntax at the same time can describe the correlation between thought, acknowledgement, perception, reason, the ability to dream, the structure of mind, understanding, human attitudes and behaviour. It does not distinguish between the mental, the physical, the emotional and the spiritual. Between cause and effect. This means that each word and each idea is totally neutral in its root, but that it is activated through the suffixes "-ta" or "-oota." To me this was a revolutionary discovery, which suddenly gave the words of Yeshua a new and deeper power and meaning than I got from the Greek translation of The New Testament. And slowly it dawned on me, that not only the meaning of the words but also the sound of them have an effect on the physical as well as on the spiritual level.

At that time I had no idea how much these studies would mean later on.

During this period, when I was mainly studying Leshana Aramaya, I had a fit one morning, which was so severe that I could hardly get out of bed. But I knew that it was now or never. The small slip of paper with the phone number was attached to the wall of my study with a pin. All my reservations and all the butterflies were gone as I lifted the receiver and dialled the number.

"Yes," an articulate and neutral voice replied.

I introduced myself.

"What can I do for you?" the voice continued.

"I'd like to make an appointment," I replied.

"Well, it'll be another 6 months before I can fit you in. What is your problem?"

I explained my condition as well as I could.

"Just a moment, I'll see what I can do."

It sounded as if he had put the receiver down. I listened to the sound of silence in the room at the other end of this connection; a kind of soft, white noise which seemed to continue indefinitely. I don't know for how long I sat like this but suddenly the voice was back:

The Night
(Mask made by Anne Maria Galmez, 1989 – Photo: Jan Jul)

"You'll be okay until we meet again."

He gave me the address and hung up.

I sat for a long time with the receiver in my hand, completely overwhelmed, before I could replace it. My thoughts wandered across the fields outside my window. I was suddenly struck as if by a hammer and I knew I had to get back to bed before I fainted. I just managed to think that the Seer was just another quack before sliding down into a deep, dreamless sleep.

"Cologne in half an hour," a voice boomed in the corridor.

I opened my eyes. On the shelf opposite me I only saw the businessman's well organized luggage. A heavy cloud of aftershave and toothpaste told me that he had been up for quite a while. I looked at my watch. It was half past six. The elderly gentleman, who had been snoring loudly during the night, was also up. The German must have got out in Hamburg, since he and all his luggage were gone. The two young people from Copenhagen were still sleeping heavily. I dressed lying down, and put my shoes on. The businessman was in the corridor, well groomed and smoking a cigar. There was a queue at the bathroom door. When it was finally my turn, I decided not to use it when I saw the condition it was in. Someone had plugged the toilet bowl with toilet paper and then apparently had shit in the sink. The floor was a lake of urine and the stench was unbelievable. The shower wasn't much better. I packed my bags and stood watching the lively activity and couldn't help thinking which one of all those nice people was so self-centred that he literally didn't give a shit about other people.

Cologne Central Station was, if possible, even more cold and inhospitable than the Central Station in Copenhagen. There was heavy traffic everywhere. People in all degrees of sleepiness were on their way to work. I just had time for a quick visit to the bathroom and a cup of coffee before catching the train for Paris. I sat down at a table in an espresso bar and wondered why we are so busy that we don't notice what is going on around us. In fifty years all these people would be gone or be in nursing homes thinking back over their busy lives, while the train station would be just as filled with people, the only difference being, that it would be other busy people. And when they were gone, others would follow. The stage set would outlive the actors. The extras and the stars in an everlasting staff turnover, one team after the other. Forward, forward, don't look up, never look back, as if no one dared to stop, fearing that they might lose face and perhaps end up as the homeless in the corner or the beggar on his bench. Perhaps it was better to cling to the illusion of eternal material comfort,forgetting all until that one day, when we all have to leave. An eternal escape from the hour of truth.

Was it this hour that had finally caught up with me? The day when I thought I had called just another quack. If someone had told me that I was going to die during my sleep, I would certainly have accepted this as a sensible solution. But this was not to be. After half an hour's sleep I woke up to a new world. Immediately I felt that all had changed but could hardly believe it. Did I really wake up to a new life? Was the more than two years of nightmare really over?

For the first time I felt close to something peaceful. But although the pain was gone I had not forgotten it. On the other hand, I probably had a deeper sense of gratitude. My thoughts kept returning to the voice on the phone. It had easily pierced my armour, opening up to a painful spot in me which far too long had been locked. After this miraculous improvement of my condition, this spot now lay open and vulnerable, waiting for my own awakening that I might heal the wound. I saw the beauty and the ugliness of the pain. I saw that it was as much beast as it was human. I saw that I could pet it the way you might pet a cat. The nature of pain is as ruthless as a cat seems to be, when it plays with a mouse just before it kills it. But just as it is impossible for an animal to be evil, since it is just following its natural instincts, pain will follow its laws until people understand, that these laws are not static but flexible, and that the one suffering from it may heal and transform. As early as the year 630 John Climacus wrote: "A man having received the sentence of death is not concerned with the repertoire of the theatre."

I began to understand the role that pain had played in my life. I began to understand how, at another level than the level of reason, it had opened my eyes to the suffering of others. I began to understand that any kind of pain is a tool in the hands of a higher cause, since in the long run it undermines any kind of judgement and any kind of half-heartedness, in fact, that it quite literally cuts to the bone. In the most effective way it transforms self-pity and selfishness to compassion and attention. Seeing and understanding this with both my body and soul wasn't possible before the pain had disappeared, and it was all due to a person that I did not know and had never met.

There were some distinctive patterns in me that started to dissolve. During all the time I had lived on the island I had started to experience the external appearances such as nature, the forest, the sea and the elements, more intensely, which opened my eyes to the same nature – the elements – within myself. I didn't see another person for long periods of time. Not that I wanted to isolate myself or to be without the company of others, but because it was necessary to find my way into that which for far too long had been hiding behind a career in the limelight. I had experienced a new kind of simplicity, which at times could be so intense that I felt as if I was disappearing. I started to practise focusing my thoughts. I practised controlling them, ignoring them or letting them have their way. It was almost frighteningly easy to give in to the temptation of letting go. Just to leave everything and disappear into silence. It was a condition that didn't make it any easier for me to function. On the other hand, I also knew that there was no going back. Although in some ways alarming, I felt that the underlying gratitude became a deeply felt reality to a degree that I had always known existed, and which now gave me a new kind of openness. It was neither particularly melancholy nor melodramatic. It just happened. Like that. Like an old summer bee buzzing around in a window in slow motion knowing that it was soon going to die. It was not that it couldn't get through the glass. But why should it? It could see everything through the window pane. I was not a bee, but a part of me knew about the cycle of bees. It happened one day as I was walking into the forest. I suddenly hovered across a clearing and found a treetop. I just sat there and fell out of time. Into the universe. Into the centre. I saw how beautiful life can be. Without any commotion, without any filters. But I soon sensed that I shouldn't stay in that openness too long. Not as a human being. Because you might forget your purpose and get lost, so that you wouldn't be able to find your way back.

Sitting in the treetop not thinking at all, it was as if I were in an inner room. There must have been an opening in it since a mild and warm light shone in. The appearing shadows turned into an understanding and were no longer an obstacle. I sat quite still. No effort. No wishes. I felt the walls dissolve and disappear. As if a veil had been drawn away. Everything happened in one single movement. Nothing else existed. I was in the middle of it, was part of it as a slight shivering. I slowly opened my arms. From above, the light fell over me like glittering rain filling me with something. Beyond words. Silence is a part of truth. The only word that might cover it is the word – certainty. I sank into certainty, where everything is united and where we come from and are at home. There was no *inside* and no *outside*, no *I want to* or *I shall*, just this quiet certainty. At a distance I saw my old spent self, hanging on a cross-like tree. No pain. Not pathetic. No guilt. No sin. No shame. All was in unity. In light. Here! At the same moment I was aware that right now an old summer bee was dying on my windowsill. I slid down from the tree. I could see everything. Life flowed unimpeded through me. I came round in the forest. Tears flowing freely.

So this was freedom. I had now seen it. Been in it. Although a glimpse only. I was ecstatic, although in a strange, quiet way in spite of my pounding heart. I was not for a moment in any doubt that I had been at the centre of my being, totally devoid of the endless series of big and small needs that normally make us blind.

After a few days of peace I suddenly got disorientated and this soon turned into sadness. Concurrent with tangible reality moving closer, the deep abyss between the two states became painfully clear and it was hard to see how they could ever be united.

It was during this period that the last sliver of interest in the superficial circus of show business disappeared. I simply didn't have the strength anymore to relate to it. It had been like this for a long time, but not until now did I understand it in a physical sense. The many years in solitude on the island, without newspaper, radio and television, had made it easier for me to relate to the basics of life. It was much easier to get rid of all the masks. It was now easier to see, that the pure and the vulnerable in me, which I wrongly had thought were mistakes or weaknesses not to be seen, in reality were the only true prerequisites for my existence. Having lived outdoors for a long time had robbed me of all the escape routes that normally occupy man. I knew from my own life that far too often I partook in the endless and nervous chase for surrogates to sweeten my life and to keep me from looking at it. We had always been told that the pain would cease if quite literally we would move away from the spot where we were at a specific time. That the party was somewhere else. This attitude, more or less, was the birthplace of the whole social structure of The Western World. On the basis of this it had been possible to maintain the illusion that it was morally acceptable to continue an unlimited growth and an overproduction of unnecessary goods and deadening entertainment. And I understood that even the apparently meaningful illusions still and maybe even first and foremost, were considered to be entertainment. That even though it may make the illusion more acceptable, it was just and yet another self-increasing alibi.

I was of course very much aware that I wasn't the first person to realize this. I knew that I had to get through the crises, which arose when the rug is pulled away from under our old life patterns. If I wasn't supposed to live by my music, what then? If I no longer was a singer, what was I then? It was frightening suddenly being without an income. It was frightening not knowing how to find money for the next rent. It was the more frightening since it became absolutely clear how important this kind of security had been in my life. That the fear of losing the little I had, all the time had been lurking in the wings like an invisible force, which had run my life. It was the year that I took the decision to completely let go. It was the year where the album appeared that would mark the end of my career. The sinking feeling in my stomach – the great hole in my heart.

On the day the album was released, I went to the beach to watch the announced eclipse of the sun and had the very extraordinary experience of seeing that all the rocks as far as I could see, big and small, were standing upright as if pointing to the sun. A sign? Perhaps a sign that the night was almost over. I ran as fast as I could. The voice from the loudspeaker had just announced that the train for Paris would be leaving in a few minutes. I heaved my suitcase through the door and managed to jump on board the moment the wheels started turning.

3

Within half a year the last of the remains disintegrated. The claustrophobic condition which had been a firm part of the old world, was now replaced by the open and edifying air sickness, which attacks you when you stand at the edge of an old abyss looking into the universe, very much aware that within a minute or so you will take that step forward and disappear into the blue. The six months seemed like an eternity. Never had I been so poor and felt so rich. Once in a while the past still caught up with me and I had to take a major roller coaster trip. An agreement about writing a musical was cancelled without warning and it began to look like more than a coincidence that what seemed to be my last door to the music business was slammed shut with a bang. At the same time I received a letter from the newspaper for which, off and on, I reviewed literature. They regretted to inform me that they no longer needed my services. I felt persona non grata in every possible way. During these periods it was still difficult to realize and accept that my time as a singer was over and that it would never come back, since my work with music had somehow always been an illusion. I now had to realize that I could not let myself be lured into believing the same thing about being a writer, just because a few of my manuscripts had been published. And this was what could still hurt so terribly much: to realize that I was nothing, and even worse, to accept that I would never be anything, – I would just be.

Soon, however, it became very clear that *to be* wasn't something I could just practise, this was something I had to learn. My neurotic fear of the abyss was now mixed with a fascination for it. I cautiously moved close to the edge. It started to dawn on me. Everything I thought had been a conspiracy against me I now saw was just a mirage created by my own projections. I had split a whole universe into bits and pieces by letting them grow. For the sake of my own convenience I had placed all my own defects in others. The defects that I quite self-righteously refused to see in myself. I now had to learn to function in the empty space that was left. It was during this process that I understood, that in spite of all our rules and systems and intentions of peace and tolerance, we usually only managed to produce chaos, noise and pollution. We arrive in this world screaming noisily we walk through it, just to leave a boundless mess behind, as we leave it again.

It was an art form to let go. Each day had its challenging renunciations. One veil after the other lifted, and along with them the most persistent of my prejudices. One by one I left my mistaken beliefs behind, which had held me in a vice most of my life. I even had to let go of the sadness and the shame. When finally the day came that I had waited for, there wasn't much left of the one I once thought was me. The day of the appointed consultation with The Seer.

A misty rain fell as I walked along Store Kongensgade. I walked in a daze. And still I remember everything. A couple wearing matching sailor shoes and pulling their bikes. A mother with a red pram; her parchment like transparency and the heartbreaking cries from the child. Two policemen crossing the road, one of them looking as if he had been crying. An old man entering a bus at a bus stop, his curved hand full of wisdom and death. A girl on a green bicycle in the opposite direction; burning eyes and the well shaped posterior in a pair of jeans on a saddle. A green messenger. A taxi which had just rammed into the rear end of a car; broken glass from a tail light and angry voices and hysteria too long repressed. A woman's mysterious smile and lazy walk; maybe because she had just left her lover's bed. A green door in the house opposite from the police station; the dryness of my mouth.

I opened the door and stepped into a stairway that still smelled from the past like a luxurious home for a well-to-do family. From far above I heard the sound of shuffling feet going upwards. I followed. A door opened and closed again and for a short moment I heard voices speaking in a foreign tongue. There were echoes of my own feet. On a landing a stubborn cactus in a pot with dried out soil. I rang the bell at the floor above and looked through the black square on the door, where the name sign had been. From somewhere in the building I heard the sound of a toilet being flushed and some blurred voices disappear into the maze of muffled sounds running into the river of noise from the cars in the street. I pressed the doorbell again. I heard it ringing in a room somewhere in the apartment. No reaction. I looked at the note again: "2nd left." I looked at my watch. Two minutes to three. I waited. Tried again. Not a sound. Five minutes past three. The front door slammed shut down below. Light steps were on their way up. They got closer. I turned around and looked into a pair of black eyes. She handed me an envelope. I took it and was about to say something, but her shoes danced a flamenco on her way down at top speed. I looked at the envelope. My name was on it. I then followed the flamenco dancer. As I got to the street I just managed to see the posterior in jeans getting on to the green saddle and disappear in the traffic. Behind me I heard the lock of the door clicking shut. A cold wind blew around the corner and pushed at the heavy smell of diesel. I opened the envelope and took out a sheet of paper, "Libraire 'Le Galois' Montségur-Village N 19, September 30th, 7 a.m." was the laconic message. It was signed, "Crede Et Vicisti – C de M."

It had stopped raining. Across the city roofs the sun was disappearing behind a black cloud. A well known critic with dark rings under his eyes was eating a bun outside a baker's shop. On the other side of the street a mother was scolding her child, who was happily jumping up and down in a puddle. Behind the windows in an apartment a poet might at this moment be writing a poem about it all. *Crede et Vicisti!* Believe and win! I walked towards Kongens Nytorv.

The train was filled with businessmen in Hugo Boss suits, sitting with laptop offices on their knees and talking on cell phones. They looked like a painting by Magritte. I had obtained a window seat and looked out on a bleak landscape dotted over with equally dismal villages. A row of colourless, artificial pearls on strings of power lines strung between whole forests of electricity pylons which became more and more chaotic and impenetrable the closer we got to Brussels. I couldn't help thinking that these power lines somehow symbolized the financial and political energies merging here to become a river of capsized expectations, stranded in over-administration and bureaucracy, just like Brussels itself looked like a suburb of a metropolis that did not exist at all. A pipedream? A dream? A nightmare?

There was a nervous and hectic energy in the carriage, where cell phones produced the same digital waltzes and marches in endless monotony. Some of the Magritte-men had been exchanged with other Magritte-men who did their best to look just as important as their predecessors. This was a reality where no wobbling about was tolerated. Brussels Central Station seemed as neat and cleansed of social riffraff as the European conscience had to be full of glittering repressions. As the train rattled through the forest of power poles, destination Paris, it was a reminder that the vision of economic security that was constantly thrown at us, in reality is identical with the lie that only creates losers and sick people.

Standing at Kongens Nytorv, the note from the Seer in hand, I decided to take the decisive step toward the abyss. Well, I really told myself that I could hear his voice calling me to the edge. Based on the motto that the one who has nothing, also has nothing to lose, I spent the following months preparing for my journey.

I knew a little about Montségur beforehand. I knew that it was a small town and a mountain with a fortress, situated in the French part of the Pyrenees. I knew the tale about the southern French heretics, the Cathars, the *bons hommes*, and their fateful deaths on the inquisition stakes at the foot of Montségur as a culmination of the Albigensian Crusade in the year 1244.

The Cathars considered themselves to be the true Christians. Part of their learning rested on primitive Christian, Gnostic, Jewish and Islamic ideas, which at all decisive points differed from the Roman Church. The daily bread was for the Cathars the spiritual bread, and both women and men could become priests, *perfecti*, in their community. The Cathar movement had wide support among the Languedoc population and when this support tended to spread to all of France the Pope, Innocence III, sent a monk, Bernhard of Clairveaux, to preach against the heretics. He saw, however, that their services and morals were far more Christian than those of his own corrupt Church. He also admitted that he could find no fault with the *parfaits* of the Cathars. They only practised what they preached. This was not to the liking of the Pope and thus he implemented the crusade resulting in the massacre at Montségur.

Legend has it that the Holy Grail had been in the possession of the Cathars and that maybe they succeeded in getting it to safety before they surrendered to the executioners of the inquisition. But legend did not say what the Holy Grail actually was. The general opinion was that the Grail was the cup that Yeshua had used during the last supper and in which later Joseph of Arimathea is supposed to have collected Yeshua's blood, as he was hanging on the cross. Legend went on to say, that at one time the Grail had been in Spain, where a Moor and sufi master, Kyot of Toledo, had written about it. The first real tale of the Grail was written by Chrétien de Troyes in the 12th century, while the most well known was written by Wolfram von Eschenbach in the epic poem *Parzival*, in which the legend of King Arthur and the Knights of the Round Table was mentioned.

A common legend which had been retold for generations by the descendants of the Cathars, was told by a shepherd from Montségur as late as 1929:

"When the walls of Montségur were still intact, the Cathars, the pure ones, guarded the Holy Grail there. Montségur was in danger. The armies of Lucifer lay in a circle around the walls. They wanted the Grail, so that they could mount it in the emperor's tiara, from where it had fallen to the ground when the angels were banned from Heaven. When peril was at its highest a white dove descended from Heaven and split the mountain in two with its beak. Esclarmonde, the female guardian of the Grail, threw the precious, holy treasure into the mountain. It then closed again. In this way the Grail was saved. When the devils forced their way into the fortress, they were too late. Filled with anger they burned all the pure ones at the foot of the cliffs under the fortress on the *camp des crémats*, on the field where the stake was built."

Two hundred and five Cathars, men, women and children, chose by their own free will to be burned at the stake. According to an oral tradition, they had promised to return after seven hundred years.

Early in the morning on the 29th of September I got on the train in Aarhus bound for the south of France. At half past four the next morning I got off at the small railway station in Foix. The moment I stepped down from the train and into the dense fog I realized that my reality would be changed forever. I stood still in order to find my bearings in the silence. I thought that I saw a human shape moving on the fringes of the cold, unreal light from a single lamp, only to disappear into the shadows at the end of the platform. However, I wasn't certain. All in all I wasn't certain about anything. The waiting room was empty and I couldn't see anyone as I stepped out into the sleeping town. The white, ghostly fog seemed to be the only thing alive and through a hole in it I saw what looked like a bridge. I walked that way, thinking that it may lead to the centre of the town. The sound of turbulent water assured me that I moved in the right direction. I had not gone far, however, when I was blinded by a white light, which was suddenly switched on in front of me. Then the sound of a car door being opened. I stepped out of the light and caught a faint glimpse of a person behind the wheel of a car. The person signalled to me to come closer.

"Do you need a lift?" a voice asked in beautiful English from inside the car. It was a woman. I leaned forward and muttered a "Yes, thank you."

"There aren't any buses at this hour," she said. Hesitantly I got in, placed my suitcase on my lap and closed the door. In the faint light from the dashboard I saw what seemed like a smile. She then put the car into gear and swung out into the night. The headlights danced in the fog and it was like being in a spaceship on its way into an unknown universe. Neither of us spoke and I could feel that there was no need for more words. It wasn't expected. And for the first time in a very long time I felt totally relaxed and strangely free. I do not remember how far we drove. I could have continued like this forever. It was as if time disappeared and dissolved in the fog. I did notice, however, that we drove upwards and around one hairpin bend after another, as if the car found its way all by itself. Suddenly the veil was pulled away. It was an overwhelming sight as we drove out of the fog. In the light from the full moon I could now see how far up we were. Below us the mountain peaks went up through the clouds and in front of us loomed the shadow of an impressive mountain. It looked like a gigantic runic stone.

"Montségur," she said.

I could actually sense the pride in her voice.

"This is where you get off."

She pointed to a sideroad winding through some rocks.

"Just follow that."

I was a bit confused and just managed to say thank you and goodbye as she set the car in motion. It wasn't until I was standing in the ghost-like lunar landscape, watching the car disappearing around a corner further ahead, that I realized she had not asked where I was going. How did she know that I was going to Montségur?

And what was I really doing here, since actually I could have stayed in my warm bed back home on the island? Wouldn't any normal person consider this an insane project?

The air was just as pure and cold as the moonlight. I shivered and started walking. Normal or insane – did it matter? Would it be possible to find anyone who could define the one in relation to the other? The road wound its way between the rocks. Up and up and up. At times I literally walked on the edge of the abyss. Far below the milk white carpet was spread across the valley. Ahead was Montségur. Off and on I could see the fortress on top of the mountain in the moonlight. It seemed as if the road was situated on a ridge circling the mountain. Something moved in the shrubs. The sound of animals disturbed by my steps, which echoed in the ice-cold air. I must have walked for about an hour when the road turned and straightened out away from the cliffs at the foot of the mountain. Below me the village of Montségur was bathed in a surreal light looking like the set in an adventure movie. From where I was I could see that, apparently, there was only the one road leading to the town. It would seem this was not a town you just travelled through. You either had business there or there was no need to make the effort of taking the road all the way around the mountain. I started the descent. The road fell in tight hairpin bends. After three quarters of an hour I finally got clear of the mountain and walked the rest of the way on the straight stretch.

The house was situated at the first corner as you came into town and you could not miss it due to the sign over the shop: Librairie "Le Gaulois." From the road it looked as if it was a one story house only. It seemed totally closed. A road continued downwards away from the town alongside the mountain and a long row of houses, which each leaned on the other. Another road turned down by another mountain also with houses built together on sloping terraces. I turned a corner and saw that the house had two and a half storeys. A few steps down was a half open gate. A leaning figure one, followed by a nine in cracked enamel was fastened to the wall under a lamp with no light in it. The gate opened into a garden behind the house. I followed the steps. From the back the house looked more inviting. A window and a folding door with windowpanes, where the shutters were open. The door was locked. I then noticed another door to the right of the folding door. I knocked and turned the handle.

The door opened with a prolonged squeaking. Once inside I stood still in order to get used to the darkness. There was a faint smell of eucalyptus and roses. A raincoat was hanging on a peg. In a corner a cane and hiking boots. A flight of stairs at the end of the hall. Above it a clock and I could see that it was just past seven. I cleared my throat. I then tried with a somewhat louder hello and stood waiting in the darkness. Through an open door I could see a moonbeam shining through the window of the next room. The only sound was an electric drone from a refrigerator. I found a switch by the doorframe. It was a genuine French country kitchen with a large table in the middle of the room. Next to the kitchen sink a plate and a glass, and knives and forks in a dish drainer. Otherwise no sign of life. I went back into the hall and found another door leading into a room which most of all looked like a small banqueting hall. The outside light shone through the windows of the folding door. An enormous fireplace was the natural focal point. Two swords hung crosswise on the wall. In the middle of the room a refectory table with a bench on each side. Over the door a Cathar cross with a white dove. I went back into the hall and up the staircase. From the landing I saw a light under one of the four doors, two on each side of a long corridor. I knocked. Waited. No reaction. I opened the door. The window was ajar and here also the moon stretched its pale arms into the room, lighting it up. The room was empty except for a single mattress. There was a note on the eiderdown. "Prat des crémats, 12 noon." I was tired enough to sleep in a bush of thorns and my considerations whether or not to undress before going to bed were quickly done with. The last thing I remember was the mattress hitting me in the face. Then all went black.

It was a great relief when the train arrived at Gare du Nord. I had had enough of Magritte-men and digital waltzes. I had almost 8 hours to find Gare du Austerlitz, where I was supposed to catch the night train for Madrid. Although the air was cool you could sense the first smell of a Parisian springtime. Outside Gare du Nord the sun stood pale and low over Boulevard de Denain, where I usually visited Brasserie "La Consigne." If you have only a few hours in Paris, Brasserie "La Consigne" is the perfect place to spend them. It is as if all variations of Parisians meet here, from the retired pimp with his boxer's conk and the bleached blonde deep in conversation across two large Pernod at a table to the rear, to the young teenage girls with too much eyeliner, pigtails, peeping bellybuttons, coffee, fags, a pout and eloquent looks in the glassed-in lounge facing the boulevard. In the middle of the room the smooth dinnertime bustle with office staff, tradesmen and a single tourist who are busy eating their lunch meal of mussels or fish soup, chocolate cake or home-made creme de fromage, before the next group arrives.

I found a small table in the midst of the bustle and ordered sardines with ginger and a glass of pastis. In the background Jaques Brel was singing: *Je ne sais pas pourquoi la plui, quitte lá-haut ses oripeaux* ... *I do not know why the rain is leaving its point, the heavy, grey clouds in the sky, in order to lay down and rest in our vineyards. I do not know why the wind is having fun spreading the laughter of the children — the frail glockenspiel of winter — in the clear mornings. I know nothing about all this; but I do know that I still love you* ...

And my thoughts danced in and out between Brel's lines. Like a very old memory, which could only be set free now. Because I knew this rain with its point and the heavy clouds in the sky, because this sky was inside of me. *Je ne sais pas pourquoi la route, qui me pousse vers la cité* ... *I do not know why this road is pushing me towards the town from one poplar to the next, into the warm air of the confused, or the icy cold veil of fog, which is accompanying me, — why it makes me think of the cathedrals where we pray for the dead loves. I know nothing about all this; but I do know that I still love you* ... Because I knew that I had sat in this brasserie and looked at all these faces so many times before. If not there, then somewhere like it. I knew that I had been there and listened to their voices talking about defeats and lies, hectic screws, infidelity and jealousy so often, that perhaps my own heart had grown distant and hard. And I had thought that I had put all this behind me. Perhaps I was finally looking towards another kind of future, unused and new. And then it happened. *Je ne sais pas pourquoi la ville* ... *I do not know why the town is opening up its suburban ramparts in order to let me slide quietly under the rain between its lovers — in all my frailty. I do not know why all these people have their noses glued to the windowpanes in order better to celebrate my defeat — in order better to follow my funeral procession. I know nothing about all this; but I do know that I still love you.*

Maybe now I finally understood that all these destinies were not merely stories taking place in a fictitious world outside of me. They were all me. The masks and the characters. The streets and the towns. The beggars and the train stations. The songs and the wind. The longing. *Je ne sais pas pourqoui ces rues . . . I do not know why these streets are opening up in front of me one by one, virginal and cold, cold and naked. Nothing is there but my own steps and there is no moon. I do not know why the night has forced me to come here in order to cry in front of this train station, by strumming me like a guitar. I know nothing about all this; but I do know that I still love you.*

This was everything I thought I had forgotten – the memory of longing – which had finally caught up with me. And at the end of the galled and hardened voice of Jacques Brel, right at the edge of this world's amusement park, the terminal station of everything, I let go of all the artificial finery, since I was just travelling through and perhaps I did not need to remember anything else. *Je ne sais rien de tout cela, mais je sais que je t'aime encore.*

The House

4

I woke from my dream because the rain was beating against the window pane. The water trickled in the gutter and sang in the down pipes outside. A grey light moved lazily across the cracked ceiling. In the corner a small porcelain clown sat smiling in his cream-coloured eternity. In my dream I had been giving a concert for my fellow patients at the asylum for the mentally ill, where I was admitted. I had built the piano I was playing on from conches and I had tuned it with a ladle. When I played, the notes turned into drops of water and the music into rain, which could make you psychic if it got into your eyes. Just before the finale the concert was interrupted because the professor had just found out that the piece I was playing wasn't written by anyone. Then I woke up.

I stayed in bed hoping to hear the sound of people; but I only heard the rain. Then I got up and went downstairs. It was just before eleven. There was a toilet and a shower in a corridor behind the banqueting hall. I took a badly needed shower. Afterwards I found a kettle in the kitchen and boiled some water. Someone had placed freshly baked bread on the table. Under it a map of the area. A red line marked the road to "Prat de crémats." I found a piece of goat's cheese in the refrigerator. I cut a few slices of bread, made tea and noticed that the dish drainer was empty. In the hall both the raincoat and the boots were still there. I was not surprised to find that they fitted me perfectly. I pulled the hood over my head as I walked out into the pouring rain.

The town seemed ghostlike. Many houses were closed for the winter, but smoke came out of several chimneys and fused into the grey clouds. A wet cat was licking itself in an open shed. The beat from a hammer echoed from the cliff wall in the cold air. Craftsmen were putting a new roof on a house situated on the slope of the mountain. An old Citröen stood on a ledge leaking oil, which mixed with the rain and made purple stripes on the tarmac. A dog barked in the vicinity. I passed the cemetery and started walking along the same winding road by which I had arrived.

It took about twenty minutes. I began feeling the rigours of the night. Every step hurt. When I reached the parking place at the foot of the mountain, a granite stairway lead up to some bushes and a few trees. According to the map this was the only path leading to the fortress. It had stopped raining. Making my way through the bushes I suddenly felt something cold in my face. An impulse? The presence of an invisible power? A whisper? *Give me your heart!* A flicker of light between the trees. A soft vibration in front of me. A movement in the air. I stopped. Closed my eyes and took a deep breath. It felt as if I was being carried by invisible hands. I then stepped into an open space. *Prat des crémats!*

A man was standing in the middle of the meadow facing me. He was too far away for me to see his features. But I had no doubt at all that this was the Seer. Behind him the mountain was waiting. At the top the fortress was waiting. In the fortress ... ?

It was as if all the corners of the world moved towards the figure at the centre. Like a centripetal force whirling everything around. I had stopped noticing my steps, but I felt that I floated towards him. I could now see his face. His beret. The white beard. The mysterious smile. The eyes! The eyes that sucked me into the power of the eternal centre. And in that moment I knew that there was no going back and that everything was exactly as it was supposed to be.

"Do you always make such a commotion when you arrive somewhere?" he said with a smile and stuck his cane into the ground in front of him.

"One might think that you were expected."

He waved his arms about:

"Welcome to Prats place. It was here that two hundred and five men, women and children voluntarily went to the stake. If you can imagine that?"

He pointed to the fortress.

"What is up there is important. But not until you understand what happened down here."

He pointed to the ground in front of him. I was watching him. It was impossible to see how old he was. He might be sixty or one hundred. But his movements were agile like those of a young man. There was an aura of calm about him. As if he himself was a mountain. All my tensions and reservations were gone like morning dew. There was an openness in his voice which made me feel safe. A solicitude that went right through you and into your core. It was as if it restored everything that had been upset in you and removed everything that shouldn't be there.

"Why am I here?" I heard myself asking. The question hovered in the air like a bird shot in its flight. He smiled. He knew that I knew the answer even before I had put the question to him.

"It was just a matter of time before we met," he said.

"The time has come, and this is where it should happen."

He looked at me and my eyes melted into his. It seemed totally unreal. It was like looking into an endless universe where time was no more. The black eyes were illuminated galaxies that had been travelling since time immemorial to manifest here in a meadow in southern France. All this lasted for just a moment. But a moment which had been forever. Like throwing a glance and this glance sees everything. I could see a shape mirrored in his eyes, and I realized that it was me. Flames reached towards the sky from an enormous bonfire behind me.

"What happened?" I asked.

"A decision was made. It is the traditional understanding of what death is that blurs our understanding. We see nothing but the fear in the faces of those pushed towards the flames, we hear nothing but the screams of the condemned. But this is not what is essential. The Cathars made a choice. They might have returned to their villages and continued to live their lives as usual, if they'd been willing to renounce what they knew to be true and then convert to the Church of Rome. But they refused to do that. They chose the stake. Apparently, they had a knowledge that went further than the traditional meaning of what life and death meant."

His words were muffled and came directly at me. They made me remember. I myself had once been tied to the stake surrounded by flames. That is why I knew that the stake was just an external manifestation of the limitations connected with mortal life. That the pain and the transition from one situation to another last for a short moment only. That there was another meaning to it.

"Now it's your turn to make a decision. That is why you have come. You have been studying for twenty years. You have been thinking and writing. You know all the mystics, all the various traditions. You've experienced flashes of the other reality. But until now, it has all been like a lifelong flirtation. You didn't know how to make any use of it. It's high time that you made your choice. There is still time to go back to the comfort of your spiritual and religious fascination. You'll probably learn to be happy as time goes by. But then again, you may as well start collecting stamps."

A bird screeched close by.

"You can also choose to take the path."

He pointed to the path disappearing between the bushes and continuing its way up the mountain.

"If you choose that, you choose the stake."

He hesitated and continued more quietly:

"I shall start you on your path and show you your possibilities. Hand you your freedom. But before you make your choice you must know, that if you follow me now you must be ready to learn

The Mountain

everything over again. Do not believe that walking the path is the same as living a carefree life. Quite the opposite."

For the first time he looked away. It was as if a chasm opened between us. It was my choice and mine alone. He turned around and started walking. I looked at him while thoughts were spinning in my head. He stopped fifty meters away. I could almost feel the flames. I was thinking that if I was to tell anyone about this it would seem totally absurd. Sparks flew in the air. They were everywhere. They looked like angels and they danced above the Seer's head. The whole place was filled with them. Suddenly I was in doubt. In all the accounts I had read about mystics, they warned about these kinds of experiences. They thought that they were the work of the devil – illusions created to lead people to believe that they had seen something divine. That at worst it might make them arrogant and make them feel above others.

It looked like a firework display. And in the middle of everything stood the Seer smiling his unfathomable smile. Illusions or not, I took a step forward.

"This is where you may meet Prat, the female guardian of nature." he said when I got close to him.

"She is standing in front of you and is saying that she's been waiting for you a long time. Your time has come, and you must acknowledge that you must accept your task and that you must complete it. She says that she is your guardian."

He stepped aside. I was looking into space. I tried to squint but didn't succeed. She wasn't there. I closed my eyes. I made the greatest effort. Where were the angels now? It was completely quiet. Most of all, I wanted to open my eyes and disappear into the wonderful fireworks around me, but I forced myself to keep standing there looking into the darkness. I don't know for how long I stayed like this. My thoughts went in all directions. It felt like coasting down a very long and steep hill on a bicycle without knowing if the brakes were working. Then I also let go of the bicycle that disappeared under me and left me floating in a different form of wakefulness. I thought I spotted the outline of a girl in front of me but it was vague and it disappeared before I could maintain it. The moment the picture disappeared I felt something cool similar to my experience when I walked through the bushes. I opened my eyes and looked around. The Seer had gone and so had the fireworks. I spotted a figure well on its way up the mountain. It was him. He was waiting in the same agile, alert and relaxed way, his cane in front of him but now about half a kilometre away. This was impossible! I started walking. The beginning of the path went in a straight line. Bare and steep with a sandy and lose surface which made it even more difficult to walk on. I was completely exhausted when I reached him.

"How did you get up here so fast?" I asked him out of breath. But, the question that really burned in me was more what was I doing here. He stood for a while looking at Prat des crémats below us. Then he looked at me. He totally ignored my question and instead answered what was on my mind.

"You are here to set foot where most people dare not go. It is your task to travel into the unknown, to penetrate into the mystery about eternity in man, to reveal new possibilities and to write home about it. You are a kind of explorer, if you like."

He saw right through me. Perhaps I ought to have felt frightened, but I didn't. It seemed quite natural.

"But you still have to make up your mind about a few things and to put them behind you, before you can travel freely."

He stepped in among the bushes and pulled out a backpack and gave it to me.

"Put it on."

I looked at him questioningly. What was going on?

"Just do what I say," he said with an encouraging smile.

Slightly bewildered I took it and began strapping it onto my back. He bent down and picked up a stone. It was the size of a fist.

"This stone symbolizes your reluctance to accept your right place in life."

He put the stone into the backpack and bent down to pick up another, which he showed me.

"This represents your reservations in regard to other people."

He bent down once more.

"This, your unclarified relationship to your parents."

And yet another one.

"This, your unclarified relationship to women."

He then searched carefully until he found one that seemed right. He showed it to me and it was quite a bit bigger than the others:

"This one symbolizes all your unimportant and unnecessary worries."

It was added to the others and I could feel the straps cutting into my shoulders. He bent down again and came up with a stone that was even bigger than the previous one:

"This one is for all the mistakes you have ever made and all the shortcomings you feel are still a part of you."

I had to lean forward to compensate for the backward pull and was about to protest as he handed me another couple of stones:

"There are only three more to go. They all represent the guilt and the fear of life expressed in you as cowardice – arrogance – and self-righteousness."

One by one he placed them on top of the others pondering each word carefully. I could feel the anger boiling inside of me. What did he know about all this? It was exactly this that I felt I had been working so intensely with. I really wanted to stop this circus and walk away. Instead I set my teeth, leaned forward stubbornly in order to get a better grip on the straps of my backpack, which by now was very heavy. Deep down I knew that he was right.

"Now, focus your thoughts on the burden you carry on your shoulders. Think about each and every stone and what it symbolizes. Each one is a part of what holds you in chains and restricts your freedom. They represent all that keeps you from moving freely about to do what you came to do.

Before coming to Monségur you worked with these things on an intellectual level, but were unable to let them go. That is the reason for your illness. You have to relate to your problems in a truer way. You are now going to carry them for the last time. Together we will climb this mountain to find the spot where you will let all of it go"

He turned around and started climbing. I followed him.

The path narrowed. Further up it began winding its way between rocks, scrubs and bushes. The stones we walked on were slippery from the rain and I had to concentrate on each step. In front of me the Seer almost floated upwards while my own boots became more and more heavy. Off and on, the path almost disappeared because of the rain, and I had to press against the face of the cliff and hold my balance from ledge to ledge. At other places it widened again and became fairly safe and stable to walk on. My burden became more and more real. By now, I was bending over so far, that I almost crawled upwards. I was sweating profusely. As promised by the Seer, I now felt the physical weight of all that had been the psychological burden of my life. Carrying them up the mountain, all the shortcomings, reservations and projections were made real in a way that forced me to look at them. It was impossible to repress them now, because they quite literally cut into my shoulders, bent my back and made my legs wobble beneath me. And crawling forward I began to understand the meaning of this apparently pointless task. I suddenly felt responsible for all these ailments. It all of a sudden became important to me that they were brought safely to wherever they were supposed to go. I was totally soaked with sweat and reeling when finally we made a halt on a wide ledge.

"No more today," the Seer said.

I was about to take off my backpack; but he stopped me.

"Wait, – come over here and enjoy the view."

I went over to the edge. The cliff wall went straight down. The valley spread out below us looking like a fairy tale. On the other side the Spanish part of the snow topped Pyrenees showed itself. An eagle soared across the sky. The Cathar landscape spread beautifully on both sides as far as we could see. I could see the fortress high above us. It was still far away. He reached across my shoulder and into the backpack and took out a stone, which he handed to me:

"Now, take your self-righteousness. Hold it in your hand. Feel it. What do you want with it? It is totally unimportant. Forget it! Drop it!"

He pointed to the edge. I closed my eyes holding it and feeling its smooth surface. Feeling its weight. I could suddenly understand what had nurtured it and why I had felt it necessary to hide behind it.

"Your self-righteousness has now served its purpose. Although it will reappear in a new disguise you'll be able to recognize it and know what to do with it. Today you have decided to let it go forever. You have made a choice."

I opened my hand and let the stone fall from it. It hit a protruding piece of cliff and fell into the deep chasm.

"And here is your arrogance."

He handed it to me. This one was also smooth and cold. It was round as a ball and I put it up to my cheekbone like a shot-putter. I blessed it and sent it out into nothingness forever.

"Your cowardice."

He handed me a big and dry one with edges, which felt blunt and unwieldy. A shapeless monument of infamy to my equally shapeless feelings of guilt and fear which had caused so much chaos.

"You have dissolved it by finding the courage to carry it up here in the first place. You can let it go now."

I let it fall.

"Here are all your shortcomings."

It was a big and warm stone, which was both angular and round. It felt right in my hand and it had a nice feel to it.

"Those are the shortcomings that are the reason you are here today. Without them you would have experienced nothing and learned nothing. There's a lot to be grateful for. But now you have outgrown them and you must let them go."

I stood for a long time with the stone in my hand. In a way it represented what until now had been a stabilizing factor in my life. But it had also been a pleasant possibility of escape. I kissed it and threw it over the edge. It drew a fine curve in the air and disappeared.

"Your unimportant and unnecessary worries."

The stone was cold with sharp edges. This one also represented escape and fear. I made a run-up and threw it with all my force.

"Your crippled way of relating to women." he said with a smile.

I now saw that this stone more or less looked phallic. This apparently, was a kind of graphic education, where the point quite literally was carved in stone. I held it at arms length. It was funny.

The Seer

Screamingly funny. I couldn't help laughing, and we both laughed with tears running down our cheeks.

"A so called stand-up-comedian!" he said when I kissed the petrified phallus and, still laughing, threw it into the abyss.

I knew, of course, that it was more serious than that. But our laughter somehow gave it all the proper perspective. It became clear that my way of relating to women had something to do with a track or a power in me, that I had not yet acknowledged. Once more it seemed as if the Seer could read my mind.

"Tomorrow you may meet Prat. Then you will know," he said and reached for yet another stone:

"This stone represents your unclarified relationship with your parents."

I took it, and although it was scarred after many beatings, it was also warm and a perfect work of art.

"You must now forgive them all the shortcomings that you've quite consciously blamed them for, and hope that they'll also forgive you your silent accusations and rejections."

The words went straight to my heart. Suddenly I could see it all quite clearly. My parents and the circumstances they acted from. Their relentless battle to build a life matching all the expectations and all the standards they felt they had to live up to. All their losses and disappointments. And in the middle of it all, their care and stubborn will to get there, in spite of it all. I let go and watched the stone slide down the mountainside until it was out of sight.

"Finally, these two. Your relationship to other people and the way you relate to your present task."

I took the stones one in each hand, and weighed them against each other. They were about equally heavy. It would be a waste of time to hold on to them. I let go of them at the same time and heard the echo as they struck the cliff wall further down.

"Well, that's it," I said and looked across the valley.

It was completely quiet. Only the whisper of the wind was heard between the cliffs like the sound from a conch that you hold against your ear. The sound of heaven and of freedom. The impossible had happened. Not only did I feel liberated and relieved, but for the first time ever I felt no guilt for having these feelings. It was not a practical joke. This was serious. It worked. It was through the manifesting of all my problems as physical burdens, which I could change or discard, that the sense of liberation and relief was able to reach my inner self. No matter how I looked at it, no matter how many excuses came to mind, it was impossible to deny that on a completely tangible level I had now made peace with deeply distressing elements from my past. In spite of severe pains in my joints and muscles I was filled with a well-being that I had never known before. I turned around to offer my thanks, only to find that he was gone. I listened. But heard only the wind and the silence. I thought I could see a tiny shape at the outskirts of Prat des crémats far below, but was unsure. Under normal circumstances I would have sworn it was impossible he could have gone that far. But now, I didn't know what to believe.

The descent from the mountain was as long and as difficult as the ascent had been, and when finally I got back to the village it was getting dark. I was totally exhausted. Someone had turned the light on in the kitchen. I practically fell into a chair and had to sit for quite a long time before I felt myself again. I barely managed to have some bread and goat's cheese. I do not remember how I got into bed.

5

The tube under Gare du Nord was like a silent, unrelenting sea. Endless rivers of individuals kept appearing, tumbling up and down stairs, flowing between ticket counters and turnstiles and splitting into smaller rivers heading for various destinations: Bobigny, Pablo Picasso, Place d'Italie, Porte de Clignancourt, Porte d'Orleans, Orly or Aéroport de Gaulle. I remembered everything from my trip to Montségur half a year earlier and followed the river and the signs to the platform for Place d'Italie. Everywhere masks of despair, downcast and expressionless eyes, brief, silent and haunted looks. Legions of boots and shoes hammering through ice cold passages, sometimes to the right, sometimes to the left and others straight ahead. The last, long passage towards the platform was black with people. Black with black people. I was the only white person in sight. Had it been six months earlier then I would have kept step, since I myself was black in my soul. I now stepped out of the river, pressed against the wall and stayed there. Maybe to break or underline the apparent symbolism.

Se tiennent par la main et marchent en silence ... They are holding hands and are walking in silence in these extinct cities brought into an equilibrium by the drizzle of the rain. Nothing can be heard except their singing steps, step by step. *They walk silently, the broken-hearted.* Who else but Jacques Brel could have written this song for the film "Les Désespérés?"

Ils ont brûlé leurs ailes ils ont perdu leurs branches ... They have scorched their wings, they have lost their branches, shipwrecked to a degree that death seems white. They return out of love, they have been awakened, they march in despair, the broken-hearted. I wonder if Brel was conscious about this picture when he created it? Did he know that death here in the tube at Place d'Italie, quite literally, was white, because he himself once stood here pressed against the wall?

Et je sais leur chemin pour l'avoir cheminé ... And I know their road because I have walked it myself, by now more than a hundred times, a hundred times more than halfway, less aged or more bruised they would have ended it. *They walk in silence, the broken-hearted.*

The train was packed. People standing and sitting – almost on top of each other. I was sucked in when they whistled for departure and the doors slid to. Turned away faces. Downcast eyes. Eyes shut. The smell of clothes and coins. Skin and anger. Poverty and sex. Violence and longing. The rocking of the train. Gare l'Est, Jacques Bonsergent, République. Like a river that kept overflowing. At Oberkampf a mass of tributaries, the last downfall of the lonely, the iron fist of disappointment, the losing dance, a falling shadow in the long chorus of oblivion. Richard Lenoir, Bréguet Sabin. Bastille. Stanza after stanza – man's endless and short-sighted song to destiny. Or was it destiny's short but endlessly repeated song to us? A stranger in transit got off at Gare d'Austerlitz and went up to get a cup of coffee and a glass of pastis at Saint-Germain-des Prés. *Ils marchent en silence les désespérés.*

It rained all morning. I woke up while it was still dark. Down in the kitchen I lit a candle and sat watching the day being born. Perhaps I finally understood that *being* was only possible when you can accept that it doesn't entail being anything in particular. That this really is the most beautiful way of being anything at all. That the abandonment of the eternal chase for recognition and confirmation is a decisive condition for the gaining of peace. To be able to be out of sight and therefore to be unnoticed by others. To be able to sit quietly in an unknown darkness far away from the attention of other people. To be able to focus on yourself without being egocentric, and then expand your consciousness to a degree that it may contain something other than your own self, which is convinced it is the master of the world. A condition where the ideas of subjectivity and objectivity begin to dissolve.

Everything that the Seer had helped me to let go on the mountain had opened up to something else. As he told me, anyone can get up and publicly air lofty ethics and a fine sounding morality. Saying one thing and doing something else is a part of the lie and psychological make-up accepted by humanity. But what thoughts and what ethics move the same person in solitude and without an audience? Is it at all possible to stay alive without being seen and being heard?

What I had let go on the mountain had opened up to a condition, where it became possible to be satisfied with just sitting unnoticed in the dusk, listening to the blessed monotony of the rain. Without any other need than just remaining there. Perhaps this condition was part of what the Seer had told me to study and write about. Simply because otherwise people would not know it existed. Perhaps it didn't seem like much. It was probably nothing. Not very fascinating. It could not be bought or sold. But, precisely because of that, it might be important – that you might to find peace by doing nothing. Not necessarily as a permanent condition, but a kind of state from where you might reach something important. Maybe it was the house? Maybe it was the village or the mountain? Maybe it existed in another time or outside of time? Somehow, I had always lived there and always known that it existed, because it had always been there as a possibility in me. It was the same with the Seer. Although I had spent one day only with him, it felt as if I had always known him. The fact that I had met him just now was simply an expression of the perfect timing of an age old yet timeless Andalusian manuscript.

After a shower, as I was drying myself, I thought I heard sounds from the kitchen followed by the front door being closed. I quickly tied the towel around me and ran to the glass door in the great hall. I was just in time to see a woman disappearing through the garden gate. Returning to the kitchen I found a parcel on the table containing freshly baked bread and some goat's cheese. Apparently there was no end to the fairy tale.

Outside the wind started to blow. I made breakfast and began writing in my diary. The shutters moaned on their hinges. I had written a couple of pages when I felt this strange, cold wind touching my face. I looked up but no one was there. At this moment one of the shutters hit the window with a bang and left the kitchen in darkness. I stayed in my chair listening intensely, but the only sound was the wind playing with the open shutters in my room upstairs. I nevertheless felt that someone was in the room. I groped for the matches on the table, but overturned my cup splashing tea over everything. The chair fell over backwards when I got up to reach for the matches, which I knew were on the kitchen range. I lit a candle and was just in time to save my diary before it became soaked in tea. I was startled when I saw him. He sat at the end of the table almost outside the circle of light, smiling his subtle smile.

"How did you get in?" I asked open-mouthed.

I must have looked ridiculous as it was very difficult for him to keep his laughter back. I took a dishcloth and wiped the table.

"Let us say that I wanted to test your elegance," he said and continued, "I wanted a cup of coffee and thought that because of the weather you might want a lift to the mountain."

He got up and poured boiling water into a cup with instant coffee. Outside, we could hear the fury of the elements. I was thinking that if this house, this town, well, the whole area didn't exist in another reality, then it might not exist at all.

"Don't worry. This is more real than you can imagine."

Once more he had read my thoughts, and once again he did not answer the question I had put to him.

"But how's it possible that you suddenly appear in this kitchen without any sound and without being seen?"

This time I wasn't going to let him off the hook. He hesitated and then said "It is all a matter of balance. But you'll soon know."

He opened the window and pushed the shutters open. The grey light filled the kitchen.

"You have already started on this part of it. You're contemplating to what degree you'll be able to just *be* and do nothing. A part of you finds it is appropriate, while another part is protesting loudly. There is a little man inside you who feels you can't live unless you fill your life with a cornucopia of intense and nervous activity. Since this activity must have another purpose than just fulfilling the needs of this little man, he invents a series of positive purposes to work towards. But they constitute nothing except his alibi for continuing his escape and maintaining a high degree of consumption. Of course he also finds it's important to help the poor of the Third World and abolish wars and all that. That's one of the reasons he's so busy. He's not considering the fact that it is precisely his own over consumption, that's is indirectly causing most of the wars. And also that it's impounding most of the resources which otherwise could have benefited the Third World."

He rinsed his cup and placed it in the dish tray. I felt that I had to protest and had a strange urge to play the Devil's Advocate:

"You can't just sit down and just *be*, and then leave everything alone."

"You can't?"

He turned towards me and looked into my eyes.

"But who's going to keep the wheels turning, and where is everything going to come from?" I asked.

"You wait and see."

We drove in his car. A dark green Chrysler Vision. I couldn't help thinking that this also represented some kind of extravagance and was about to comment on it. But he got in first.

"Well, I'm sorry," he said, – "I'm probably a romantic, but a realistic kind of romantic. You only see the items. You see the brand of the car. Today this car is ours. Tomorrow somebody else may drive it. It has been a part of my home for a couple of months now. It is useful when you work at great altitudes."

He smiled and continued:

"It's all a matter of balance. At any given moment to be able to let go. Not to let yourself become attached to anything. To be able to distinguish. To be flexible."

It took only ten minutes. He parked the car between some bushes. The wind had died down, but the sky was black and it looked as if it might open its floodgates at any moment.

"You'd better take this," he said and handed me a black cane with an interlacing pattern.

"Today we take it one step further up."

He didn't waste any time.

"Today I want to show you Prat, and we can only hope that she also wants to see you. I'll go through the thicket first and you follow immediately. When you feel a slight, electric like shiver down your spine, you'll know that she's present.

But you won't be able to see her. Instead, you must tell yourself that you want to be isogynic. Do you understand? It is important that you do understand this. The isogynic condition is, in a way, a neutral condition. Don't be afraid if you feel you are beginning to dissolve. When you get through the bramble, stand still and concentrate on being isogynic. It is a mind leap. It is an icon. In the isogynic state you are free from being either man or woman, you are not one or the other, you are both and none of them. It has got nothing to do with the androgynous or sexuality. It is a beautiful condition. Open, free, transcendent and flexible. It's not enough to imagine the condition, you must become it. I'll let you know when you can move on from there. Do you understand?"

He looked directly into me. The light played in his black eyes. I nodded. He turned around and walked towards the bramble. Suddenly he seemed very serious, which I had not noticed before. I followed him until he was out of sight.

The bramble closed around me. The branches seemed alive. I walked with my eyes closed and concentrated as much as possible. But my thoughts were all in shambles and went this way and that. I kept repeating: I am isogynic, I am isogynic. A gust of wind went through the thicket. I stopped, had doubts. Was this her? A movement? A whisper? *Give me your heart!* It felt like a slight touch. I recognized this feather light touch. In a series of very quick movements layer after layer was removed inside me. I tried instinctively to fight it, but I couldn't. It happened as fast as the last drop of water sucked from the plughole of a bathtub. You notice it, but you are not sufficiently fast with the plug, before the water is gone. In a flash I realized that I was neither the bathtub nor the water running out. I was the *emptiness* in the bathtub, the empty space, the openness that the water had filled just a moment ago.

He was standing in the middle of the open space. Exactly as the day before. I stayed at the outskirts and waited for a sign. The wind had died down. There was a hypnotic silence everywhere. Then the lines started drawing towards him. Slowly at first, in a gliding movement, but then faster and faster without any sound. Once more I felt the sense of floating as I moved closer to him.

"Very well." he said as I stood in front of him looking into an endless universe.

His seriousness apart, I felt that he was now also very determined.

"Please listen very carefully, I have no intention of repeating this. There is so much to show you here. Prat tells me that you are well known to her. You are a lonely wanderer. You have been misunderstood and mistreated. You don't want that anymore. You are standing here, beaten and perplexed. But if this was not so, you would not have come. There is a connection between everything. You have just now, without any seeming difficulty, moved in and out of the isogynic condition. Your time has come. It is totally up to you if you want to go all the way. Prat tells me that you have the opportunity now, but you must seize it now if you are serious. You may not get another."

The galaxies shone. I could feel his eyes all the way into empty space. Then he stepped aside. I stood still with my eyes closed but felt right away that this wasn't right. When I opened them again she stood directly in front of me. Prat. The quintessence of compassion. This universal being represented the essence of womanhood in all its various shapes and ages. I saw her as the girl on a throne. The feminine force. The guardian of the Grail, Esclarmonde? She got up, walked towards me and embraced me. She took my heart and filled it with tenderness. A kind of tenderness that I did not know existed. Here is your heart! I saw a sparrow sitting on the ground in front of me. It hopped back and forth for a while. Then it flew away. She was gone.

It took but a few moments. Still, I wasn't surprised to see that the Seer, like the day before, had already passed the initial, steep part of the climb. He waved at me. I started thinking how helpful it would be if I also could learn to fly.

We began the ascent. Although I no longer had a backpack heavy with stones, it was still an exhausting climb. The Seer walked upright and effortless in front of me, and I concentrated on the heels of his boots, just to keep up. Getting up part of the way, I could see black clouds hovering towards us. Lightning flashed now and then and you could hear the thunder getting louder and louder. We were about halfway up when the rain fell and, apparently, there was nowhere to seek shelter. The Seer signalled to me that we should carry on, but further ahead he stepped away from the path and found his way under a ledge hidden behind a few bushes.

"We can find shelter here," he said shaking the water off.

We sat down on two pieces of rock and admired the landscape stretched out in front of us. The rain poured down as he broke the silence:

"Are you hungry?"

Before I had time to answer he pointed behind me, where I saw two bottles of water and a metal box filled with biscuits between the rocks.

"They are very far-sighted – the Norns," he said when I handed him a bottle of water and a few biscuits.

"The Norns?"

I must have looked quite foolish considering his familiar smile.

"Didn't you notice them?" he replied drinking from the bottle.

I looked around but couldn't see anyone. He laughed noisily and I tried again.

"Urd, Verdante, Skuld?" I asked.

He nodded. Of course I knew the Fatal Sisters from the Nordic Mythology, Past, Present and Future. The Norns who spin, measure and cut the thread of life for each individual. But what were they doing here?

"Who do you think supply breakfast for strange fugitives visiting as remote a place as Montségur?" he asked teasingly. "Or meet strange persons like yourself at the railway station of Foix in the middle of the night? Or hide supplies between the rocks for two madmen like us on a mountain during a thunderstorm?"

He flung his arms about, but became serious again.

"Urd is saying that your past has contained a lot of fear. Your life has been marked by a deep sense of feeling abandoned and lonely. You've never been able to feel at home anywhere. Neither here nor there. Verdante says that you have now left the spiral fog in order to manifest your true qualities."

His eyes were like needles.

"Skuld is saying that you will be ready for the task in the future, because you know how to work in solitude and how to work secretly. She also says that you must retreat if anyone pushes you too far or exceeds your personal barriers. You are here to offer new possibilities. It is, however, very important that you work freely and without any kind of limitations."

He emptied his bottle and got up. The rain had stopped and the air was fresh and cool.

"I'm glad I don't have to tell anyone about all this," I said and followed him.

"Who says that you don't?" He walked to the edge and looked across the valley. He then brushed his hands against each other and made a sign for us to continue. The path was even more slippery now after the rain and we progressed only slowly. I was considering what he had just said. But how was I to tell anyone about this. Most people would think that I had lost it. On the other hand, what did that matter? I would almost certainly be dismissed as it was. And why should I take this into consideration anyway, just to look good in the eyes of others? Wasn't life too short to keep silent and to hide things?

Girl on Throne
(Thomas Gotsch, 1894)

We struggled upwards and rested on a ledge further up. He turned to me:

"This is where we find the Oracle. This is where you may ask your question and receive the answer yourself. You might as well learn it now. I'll ask the same question and we'll see if I get the same answer."

He motioned me forward.

"You must ask your question loud and clear."

I took a step forward with my eyes closed and was just about to start, as he interrupted:

"No, you must open your eyes. This is important."

I opened my eyes and stood still and tried to concentrate. I then noticed an eagle soaring ahead of me. It was on the lookout for prey. Then I asked:

"How do I continue from here?"

I hadn't thought much about the question. It just seemed to come into my mind. I followed the eagle with my eyes. It circled and circled, ready to strike. I sensed the intensity around it. It was totally concentrated on its task and would soon unite with its prey. Then it swooped down and at that moment I received the answer. Like lightning.

"Did you get an answer," he asked.

"I think so," I replied.

He nodded with a satisfied look on his face:

"Good, here is my version."

He stood for a while looking straight ahead, then continued:

"You must travel alone and without any unnecessary luggage. At this present stage of the voyage you must not visit anyone, not even those similarly disposed. The process of dissolution that you have experienced over the last years is at an end. You must now travel freely, work in silence and develop your powers of thought. You must write about it later on."

I was totally dumbfounded. This was exactly the answer I had received myself. Maybe not precisely in the same wording, but there was no doubt about the contents. He looked at the sky. It still looked black and menacing. He said:

"We will not walk further today. Tomorrow we'll take it yet another step higher."

I looked up at the fortress. Then I spotted the eagle. It soared through the air, circled once and settled in a tree on a ledge next to ours. It was carrying something. A sparrow.

We had our supper at Gilbert's. Gilbert was the proprietor of the Hotel Costes, a small business, which had been in the hands of the family for generations. It was a humble place with a few rooms upstairs and a few tables in the restaurant, which was run on very simple principles: Gilbert's wife, Maurisette, in the kitchen, Gilbert himself serving the meals each day, eight months a year. Full satisfaction or your money wasted.

At one of the tables two middle-aged couples were having trout. A smell of vinegar and aniseed. An old radio was playing a scratched version of old, French dance hall music, interrupted by a voice trying to get through from a time long forgotten. We were greeted with open arms. Gilbert took the Seer's hands in both his, squeezed them and shook them over and over while words and laughter filled the room. He called Maurisette into the restaurant so that she could also welcome us. We had hardly sat down at the table before two glasses of pastis and a carafe of water were placed in front of us. The Seer raised his glass to me:

"Such a welcome is rare even among the closest of friends."

We drank.

Maurisette and Gilbert understand the simple and the uncomplicated. You may have meat and vegetables or fish and vegetables or just vegetables. That's the menu. Simple all the way. All eight months. This is the essence of respect. This they show by making certain that one feels at home. They do that by the quality of the food and the very reasonable prices. All the primary produce is from the local area. It is first and foremost a way of life, the business is secondary.

We drank to each other again. Gilbert behind his table, beaming like the sun. Nobody should be in doubt that tonight he had a very important and highly treasured guest.

Gilbert served fish. The Seer had brought wine from Don Cesar in Spain. He gave Gilbert several bottles. More guests arrived. The arthritic dance music boomed like a fun fair filled with bustle and noise. Maurisette appeared and turned it down. As soon as she was out of sight, Gilbert turned it up again. They laughed and drank to each other. The Seer said:

"Every perfection has its flaw. No system is infallible. Even great truths know about the little white lie! He pointed to his plate:

"Here, even the fish can fly."

6

I walked in the drizzle along Jardin des Plantes on my way to Boulevard Saint-Germain. I was thinking whether or not I had the time to visit 14 Rue Abbe de l'Epee, where the Danish author Herman Bang used to stay, when Paris was his second home. I knew the place and had been there several times, but for some reason I decided against it. Perhaps because I suddenly and for no apparent reason had found myself in the songs of Brel. Although in many ways they resembled the writings of Bang, they belonged to another era. Or maybe I had lost that particular thread because I was presently reading the collected works of Georges Simenon. Perhaps I was descending into a far deeper memory which had not necessarily anything to do with Paris but which, for reasons unknown, could only be redeemed here. I had experienced such situations since childhood, but I never knew beforehand when they would arise. They were kind of holes in time, openings to another reality or to a parallel universe. As a child I had experienced transcendence into other eras. I had seen deceased persons come alive. I had seen past and future incidents played out in front of me, without realizing what it was until much later. I had felt other people's sorrows as my own just by looking at them. Many times had I seen the reasons for them. Through these openings I often wandered unnoticed out of time and into other worlds. I could never tell what activated the memory and what created the opening. It might be a person, a pair of eyes, a mouth, a scent or a sound. It might be an item, a letter or the way in which the rain fell. It might be a place, a street, a house, or the way the light shone. It might be a word, a song, or the way two people passed each other. I could be walking down a street when suddenly I had the choice either to continue towards the destination I had set out for or follow a sudden impulse, which might lead through a gate and into a backyard, or to getting on a bus going in the opposite direction. It has always been like this with me and books, that if I didn't find them, they found me. In a bookstore, for example, I might walk directly to a bookcase and pull out the exact book that I needed at that moment. If it didn't seem like it at the beginning, I could be quite certain that somewhere in the book there would be references to the one I needed. At other times they might quite literally fall on my head or arrive by mail. I had never considered it to be particularly unusual at all. It was just a part of the things that one didn't talk about. Little by little I learned to keep those things to myself. It was downright embarrassing when someone bent forks and made clocks stop by the simple power of thought on television. It was very strange when someone wanted to upset the two most important inventions of man, utensils for eating and time. I supposed that no one had seen the same person straightening the forks out again or making the clocks go again. All such showmanship made people with the same kinds of abilities play them down or keep silent about them.

It was not until Montségur that the Seer showed me how these time holes could be used as convenient escape routes, through which I could disappear each time reality became too insistent. They might also be linked to the periods of time when I was ill. He had shown me how these loopholes, which usually lead to the lower astral conditions, could instead be transformed into openings to a present reality, openings, so to speak, turning inward towards the now of things instead of outward and away from them. By sharpening my attention and intensifying it, every time these situations arose, I would eventually come to master them. In this way I would eventually be able to develop the inner resonance and the inner sight, which was a prerequisite to being able to move freely through other dimensions. But as things were right now, I didn't feel that I could master anything.

Then it happened. I was walking along one of the narrow streets in the 5th arrondissement, not far from Bang's place. I spotted an Algerian bar and felt compelled to go inside. It was one of those bars that once had been so plentiful on the left bank of the Seine but which had now been replaced by more fashionable bistros and shops. Dimly lit, Arabian music, primitive furniture and a smell of incense, shish kebab and cannabis. I could barely make out a row of smiling, white teeth in the darkness behind the bar and ordered a pastis. When my eyes got used to the poor light, I spotted him. In the mirror behind the bar I saw him sitting at one of the tables. The Seer. I turned around. The room was empty, and so was the mirror. But it was this unmistakable smile. I sipped my pastis and closed my eyes. Then I realized that there was something about this bar that belonged to a past era and another place. I saw something that looked like a bazaar with a large square. I knew that it was somewhere in Spain. I went out into the scorching heat and the piercing sunlight. The street was swarming with people, but my attention was caught by two men in deep conversation in the square. There was something disturbingly familiar about them. They seemed to be totally preoccupied with each other. I went closer until I could hear their voices, and although I did not understand the language they were speaking, I could use my eyes. I became aware that one was the learned one and the other was an itinerant singer. The learned one had a fair complexion and blue eyes. The singer was dark and had brown eyes. Suddenly, the singer looked in my direction. The other had also spotted me. At first they seemed surprised but then they smiled. The dark one lifted his arm as if he wanted to wave me over, but the learned one stopped him. Something in his eyes made me turn around. I started running. In and out between traders, snake charmers and fortune tellers. A door slammed when I returned to the bar. I opened my eyes. A man with a dark complexion had let the door slam behind him and he disappeared behind the counter and into a back room. I drank my pastis and paid for it. I still had an hour before my train would leave from Gare du Austerlitz.

The wind had died down and it had stopped raining. I had been awake many times during the night but had apparently dropped off again since I woke up when someone called me. When I opened my eyes the Seer was in the doorway.

"What time is it?" I asked a bit confused and reached for my shirt.

"A few hours past elegance or five minutes before silliness. It's all up to you."

I got up. He had boiled some water and put bread on the table while I had my shower. He watched me while I had my breakfast.

"If you want to be in touch with reality you must know what real timing is. If you know that, you'll always be on time. Not five minutes before or five minutes past, but the exact moment where any given situation will have the best possible chance of success."

He poured hot water into my cup and pushed the jar with instant coffee across the table.

"The time has come for you to replace the theories with practice. Try to watch one of your thoughts. Apparently, it rises out of nothing, and before you know it another has taken its place. It happens, and you can't do anything about it. If your "I" is also a thought, who is thinking then?"

The question was vibrating between us.

"When you have experienced your "I" dissolving, who was it that experienced this?"

Suddenly I was wide awake since these were questions I had asked myself many times without getting the slightest bit closer to an answer.

"That is why we have to move away from the level of behaviourism. We cannot deny the "self". But we must understand that there is a "self" that solely relates to the world, and another, higher "Self" which is without limitations and in perfect balance with all the aspects of life. While the little "self" is busy counting its money and planning the future, creating strategies and nurturing its career, shopping and consuming, worrying and looking for confirmation, the higher "Self" is simply concerned with *being*. While the little "self" feels that it needs all its activities in order to function, the higher "Self" *is*, because it is totally free of any excess luggage. That is why people sometimes experience that there are two different worlds. Such an experience, of course, is a beginning, but you should have passed that stage long ago. When you lose your timing it is simply because you aren't present. Most people think that if they really apply themselves and concentrate to the point of exhaustion, then they've got it. But it is really the other way round. You first have to loosen up and let go. You must be willing to let things be and to leave opportunities alone. No matter how obvious they may be. Then you must learn to sharpen your attention without any effort. This way you'll train your ability to be really present. Such presence is an extension of a deeper intuition. Do not confuse this with the traditional understanding of female intuition. The real intuition is more like a kind of omnipresence and omniscience, if you like. It is because of the certainty that this "Self" is able to *be*."

"What kind of knowledge is this? What is really the point?"

"If we only relate to the level of behaviour, we soon find that everything we do and everything we seek is based on fear. As long as we remain at this level and refuse to see that there are other levels, we shall basically think and act from fear for the rest of our lives. This fear is based on the little self's knowledge that there isn't enough of anything for everybody, that it will be burgled if it doesn't hide behind thick walls and is insured against every kind of threat, that war shall break out if we do not rearm etc. The knowledge of the true Self is based on trust. It knows that its origin is universal. Since it is not interested in property or status, there is nothing to lose. The true Self knows where it comes from, why it is here and where it is going. When you forget this knowledge in all the commotion, you may only regain it by giving up everything the little self appreciates and adores."

The words organized themselves in order like the cards in a game of solitaire, which had just worked out. I still sensed that he had left something out. That there was more behind the sentences. Something deeper, something, which might be so decisive and irrevocable that it neither ought nor could be said.

It cannot be said in any simpler way than in Shakespeare's immortal words: "To be or not to be, that is the question." Unfortunately, these words have lost their power as time has gone by, and we have forgotten what they really mean.

He got up, indicating that it was time to go. Outside the sun had now climbed over the mountaintop. The wet earth began to steam, and it looked as if it was going to be a clear day. On the slope workers had almost finished laying tiles on the roof of a building. Two cats were licking a ray of sunshine that fell on them. There was a golden glow over the town.

"It seems like a good day for flying," the Seer said as he swung the car between the bushes and into the parking place.

We walked through the bramble. The sense of dissolving that I had felt the previous days, I now experienced as a natural and neutral state, which appeared the moment I whispered the word isogynic. We walked directly into the middle of Prat's meadow and the Seer turned towards me and asked:

"Who are you?"

The question was direct and surprised me. I hesitated. I had lulled myself into what I thought was a pure and neutral state, but realized right away that it was more an expression of a lack of responsibility, telling me that I was not really present. My mind was spinning. One concept followed another, but I could not decide which one would be appropriate here. How did I want to look? Who did I want to be? And while I was worrying about that I realized, that this was exactly the reason that I, in relation to his question, was exactly as far off as I had been when he woke me up in the morning. I could now see all the pretentious notions I had had about myself. All the masks I had been hiding behind passed me by on an inner screen, like a film running off its reel at high speed. Then just the white light from the projector. Nothing! He didn't wait for my answer but continued:

"What do you want here?"

I knew that if my answer was "nothing" it wouldn't be true and he would know it. I was also aware that he didn't ask the question in order to get an answer. He knew them already. It was just a way to help me sharpen my alertness. Everything happened so fast. I noticed how my ability to think clearly came to life through his intervention. Everything happened without delay and easily in his presence. Before I was able to find an answer I realized that they were all connected to the kind of basic fear he had mentioned earlier. There was nothing to add.

We began the ascent. I walked determinedly, leaning forward and jabbing my cane into the sand over the first, straight, steep stretch. The Seer walked upright with a light step, carrying his cane over his shoulder. The moment I saw that, I was immediately aware that this was part of his purpose, and that he wanted to show me that it was all a matter of attitude on both the physical, mental and spiritual levels. It was his way of telling me to straighten up and to regain my dignity. There was no reason to make it more difficult than necessary.

I straightened up and right away felt the agility of my back. We passed the first ledge. The air was bright and space was endless. The sun shone directly on the mountainside. The Seer was again in the lead and increased his speed. Once again I saw only the heels of his boots. Left, right, left, right. I was sweating and not till later did I notice that I had lost my posture. When we reached the second ledge I was not focused anymore, and ascending towards the third ledge, all of a sudden a series of thoughts appeared and I knew that they must come from him. *Illness comes from resistance! Resistance to change!* Above the abyss the eagle soared. It was now difficult for me to keep up. My breath was short and gasping, my legs heavy as lead. I took off my jacket and slung it over my shoulder. When we reached the fourth ledge I was convinced that he would stop. I had reached the end of my tether. But he continued without a word. He was now more than ten metres ahead of me and I only continued because I didn't want him to witness me throwing in the towel. In principle he could have been my father.

The path wound its way up and up and in and out between bushes
and rocks, and suddenly he was out of sight. I hurried along the best
I could. *Give up your resistance!* I partly crawled and partly walked.
He was still out of sight when I turned the corner where he had
disappeared. I went on. My lungs felt like a pair of bellows filled
with sand. When finally I passed a section of the path full of bushes
I saw him waiting further up. This gave me a new strength. He was
standing at the edge of the ledge. I approached slowly. My legs gave
way under me. All was quiet. Silent. I only felt the sense of floating
that I had felt earlier at Prat des crémats. *"Come on!"* He called
me over to the edge. I was no longer in control of my movements.
Something came up from deep down in my memory. I could now see
the abyss. I had a sinking feeling. An enormous chasm lay before me
and somewhere in the dark I sensed my panic. *Let go now.* The voice
was calm and precise. I was standing right at the edge. *I am with you.*
My stomach contracted. *Show me your true Self.* He took my hand.
Now! I closed my eyes and took one step forward. My hand squeezed
his. It was like two electric leads touching. Like two flames freed from
wax and wick, merging into one.

The flame burned with a bright glow in the clear, blue air.

*Floating. Two persons on the ledge. The silver thread connecting us
to ourselves. Endless rows of ideas and words like dominoes tumbling
over one by one and burning in the air as far as one can see. Read
them yourself.*

I opened my eyes and saw that I was standing one step away from
the abyss.

"What was that?"

He smiled. But not his usual smile. He was very clear and glowing.
The sight of him made my question completely meaningless. He had
also taken off his jacket. I could see beads of sweat on his forehead.
He seemed somehow changed, or maybe it was my way of looking at
everything that had changed. There was now a totally different basal
tone resonating. It was purer. Filled with a new kind of humour, far
beyond puns and permissiveness. There was no longer a distance
between us. In a split second two flames became one. The climb
had been fierce and strenuous. The transference itself undramatic,

quiet and easy. Everything I myself had pondered over, everything that had almost developed into a kind of existential pastime or a convenient hiding place, everything that I hitherto had understood on an intellectual and emotional level, was only a shadow of the reality he had just shown me. It had all just taken a short moment. Now I also knew that in each and every one of us there is more than one alternative. That we do have a choice and that we must be willing to make that choice. That immediately next to the fearful and the worried, the unhappy and the hateful, the self-asserting and the fraudulent, the envious and the greedy, there is always another kind of being, undivided and embracing, uncomplicated and whole. A flame, which will always burn, be it ever so small and thus placed in the remotest nook.

The Seer walked ahead of me on the way down. I couldn't help watching him. His relaxed ease filled with presence and care. Never before had I met anyone like him. He was of another world. But still there was something about him, which was very familiar. I was contemplating the thought that he had suddenly entered my life at a time where everything was black and disintegrating. If this was not an example of perfect timing, what kind of divine intervention might then be responsible? Why me? Why this mountain?

We made a short break on a ledge further down. We looked at the valley and the mountain in silence. This enormous, breathtaking and inexplicable view, which constantly found new ways of surprising me.

We arrived in town in time for a visit to the small, local bookstore *Libraire "Le Gaulois,"* which lay facing the street. The owner, Thierry Salles, served wine since it was the last shopping day of the season. The small room was filled with books. I walked over to a shelf and pulled out a book. *Massacre at Montségur* by Zoé Oldenbourg. On the slope the workers were putting their tools away. Outside one of the houses an elderly woman was taking her laundry in from an unsteady clothes rack. The sun brushed its long and golden rays across the Pyrenees. The three of us standing on the street watched it disappear. Somewhere nearby a child laughed. I just stood there and felt that life was benign.

The night train for Madrid left Paris at 7.45 p.m. I had entered the wrong carriage and was moving through the train in order to find the right one. The curtains were drawn in my compartment. I opened the door and stepped inside. A thin man sat squeezed into a corner. He was wearing a Nike T-shirt, a pair of thin, stained gabardine trousers and a short imitation leather jacket. I nodded and placed my suitcase on the floor between the seats. A sign on the wall told us that we were not allowed to pull out the cots. The staff would come and do that at 10 p.m. I sat down diagonally opposite the thin man. He was in his mid thirties and undernourished. The greasy hair and the stubble told their own story. It was clear that he was not Spanish and did not look French either. He was fumbling with his bag placed on the seat next to him. When finally the zipper gave in, the compartment filled with the spicy smell of salami. He was rummaging in the bag and finally found what he was looking for. He placed a whole bottle of vodka on the small table by the window.

"From Ukraine," he said in broken English. "You want?"

My first thought was to decline his offer, but there was something about him, which made it difficult. I nodded hesitatingly. He was already emptying the sealed cup for brushing your teeth, which was filled with disinfected water, so that it may be used for the vodka. I protested when he filled it with vodka, but he cut me short with a: "Vodka from the Ukraine, best in the world."

He emptied yet another cup and filled it with vodka.

"Ukrainian vodka much better than Russian vodka. Russian vodka very bad."

He raised his cup and touched mine. He emptied his at a single draught. I was sipping mine.

"Drink, drink," he said elated.

He filled his cup once more. His movements and his whole demeanour told me that he had a problem. I took a bigger draught in a failed attempt to be polite, which made me cough it all up again.

"Drink, drink!" he yelled.

Although he was smiling, I could tell from his glassy stare that this was not a happy man.

"Where are you going?" I asked him.

"Madrid. Last week I go from Ukraine. I go Germany, I go Paris. Paris I stay two days. Now I go Madrid. Friend have bar in Madrid. He rich."

I couldn't help wondering how he had managed in Paris for two days at this time of year. He didn't look as if he could afford a hotel. On the other hand, I wouldn't embarrass him by asking.

"Ukraine and Europe, friend – yes!"

He lifted his cup and emptied it. The effect was showing now. He leaned slantingly towards me:

"Europe kaput. Black people no good. Everywhere black people and Asian people. No good."

The corners of his mouth now drooped condescendingly, underlining his scorn.

"Ukraine and Europe, good, yes. White people, good, yes!"

He could hardly control his movements as he poured himself another drink. Time dragged heavily by. He poured, we lifted our cups. I tried to make my sips look convincing, but it really didn't matter anymore. He didn't take any notice but became more and more angry with the world, which he blamed for the misery that had befallen the country he came from. If someone had offered him an armband with a swastika it would probably not cost them more than a glass of vodka. It was very difficult to like him. Suddenly I could see him. I could look through the layers of loss, abuse, pain, inferiority and hatred. It didn't take a degree in psychology to see that. But there was something else as well.

He is five years old. Together with his smaller sister he is bending over his mother, who is on the floor in an awkward position. They are trying to wake her up. Later, the neighbour comes in to help, but the mother doesn't wake up. He is walking along the main street in the village where he used to live many years ago. There are no other people in the street. All the houses are empty. There is a grey light all over. In an enclosure a few cars are parked in front of a grey building. Power plant. He walks to the other end of the village. He is standing in front of a garden gate leading up to a big, dilapidated wooden house. Orphanage. Night-time. He is running towards a tall fence. Factory. A dog is chasing him. Behind him a guard in a pool of blood. The spoils do not even come to half a day's wages. He is walking along a street in a city. It is cold and people are busy. At a square, where you can buy anything, he is exchanging his warm overcoat for a posh leather jacket that will make him look more respectable in Europe.

When the steward came to prepare for the night he was already sleeping heavily. His head had sunk onto his chest and he was drooling. The cup was turned over and a small river of vodka was running across the floor. I wiped his face, got the jacket off him and managed to get him to bed. As I tugged the blanket around him, he opened his eyes and mumbled:

"Ukraine, best place in the world."

Far into the darkness I saw a light. The flame was not very clear, but it was there.

7

Day by day we worked our way closer and closer to the top of the mountain. At the same time the Seer helped me to get further and further past the edge of the conceivable. We repeated the same steps every day, and I felt my ability to focus and to concentrate getting better and the feeling of being present intensifying. As the days went by it became clear, that everything he did had a higher purpose and was part of a lager plan. Together with him life became an instrument of change where we were playing on all its keys. It was a symphonic process of cleansing and realization. As he put it:

"How can you move if you are not willing to let go of everything that blocks the way? Man is an instrument that has to be tuned in order to play in tune."

When he thought that a day had passed particularly well we celebrated with Gilbert at the Costes. We were dancing on the ruins of all the miseries that had been laid to rest that day, so to speak. This was a way of showing our respect for every single item that had now served its purpose.

The evening prior to the last workday we set the table in the banqueting hall and lit a fire. I prepared a simple meal. The Seer put a bottle of Don Cesar on the table. Outside, it had started to rain again. Gusts of wind made the shutters bang against the window frames.

"We have actually finished this round. You have found the way. But this is only a beginning. A totally new way of life is beginning for you here. As I told you on the first day, life will not necessarily become easier from now on. But you will now know why the problems arise and you will have the tools to overcome them if that is what you want. Tomorrow we shall ascend all the way to the fortress. There are no more tests for you. You are just going to see what is ahead. *The Shaft of the Soul*, the Gate of Time and the Grail. Consider this the crowning glory of the work you have done until now."

It was a sad feeling that I was going to leave him and this place. Never before had I felt such intense meaning in life. Probably because I had met a man who dared take it seriously. He changed the fragmented and the physical into unity and spirit. Life was movement. A fairy tale. He showed me that there was a way, a purpose and a way to fulfil it. He lifted his glass:

"Let us toast the Norns. Here's to Urd, Verdande and Skuld. They have been your guardian angels here. They did a good job."

The wind came up, became powerful and whispered through doors and cracks. The shadows danced a final dance in the banqueting hall by the light of the flickering candles and the flames from the open fireplace. Peace was beyond time.

The train arrived at Madrid Chamartin just before nine a.m. Nikolai looked even more pale and ill in the glaring sunlight on the platform. He looked around slightly confused as if he expected to be met by someone, and stalled a bit when we parted. I watched him as he disappeared in the crowd. I then spent half an hour looking for the tube for Atocha, from where I was to continue by train to Malaga. I could already smell the scent of my Spain. This strange conglomerate of a country, which had made me return again and again since I set foot here for the first time twenty five years ago.

Breakfast at Atocha Renfe. Fried eggs and toast. Bustle and light. Conversation with a young, Italian girl who asks me if I can spare a bit of money for a cup of coffee. She is on her way to Seville to try her luck as a dancer. Big smile on the surface. Sad and lonely. Tells me that Italy is no-future. Rootless and restless and far too young to be an existential refugee. Offer her breakfast and moral support.

Did we recognize each other because we were both refugees? What kind of future did she expect to find there, that she couldn't find anywhere else? I then remembered Itálica to the north of Seville, the first town that the Romans established in Spain. Here they built the biggest amphitheatre outside of Rome. This was the spot where the gladiator fights had become so cruel, that Marcus Aurelius finally banned them. *Those who are about to die — salute you!* This was the way that gladiators saluted emperors and consuls before going into battle. She waved and smiled valiantly as she disappeared in the direction of Seville. A quarter past twelve, I started the final lap of the journey.

The wind had died down and it had stopped raining. Instead, the fog thickened in the valley. Walking through the thicket the certainty of the natural condition was underlined. No worries, no trouble. In the meadow he asked me to walk out to meet Prat alone. She was already waiting. *Here is a square. Walk into each of the corners and give each one a quality. Then collect them into your own force in the middle. One by one they came from the upper right corner and moved clockwise. Care. Strength. Courage. Compassion. They dissolved in one single movement and met in a single point: Silence!*

We walked side by side along the first, difficult part. I walked with my cane across my shoulder and walked with a light step. We moved slowly upwards. I walked ahead. I turned around on the first ledge. Although I was slowly getting used to this it still took me by surprise that he was gone. I was going up alone.

The air was full of oracles. *A man is walking along a long road. He is lost. He gets very happy when he meets another human being.* The Norns were there. The visions floated in and out of the fog. *An encouraging word doesn't cost much, and the price of a little support doesn't necessarily have to be high.* I walked empty handed through the void and was filled up.

They were everywhere. They made the trees and the bushes come alive. Each and every pebble on the path became a star in the universe. I knew every turn and every boulder. My breath fell into harmony with the shape of the mountain. Point by point and ledge by ledge I moved upwards with ease.

I had passed all the well known places. The path grew narrower towards the end and seemed more and more like a maze. Pulling free of the thicket I got a glimpse of the fortress through the fog. The Seer stood waiting outside of it. This was how it had to be.

"Perfect." he said, – "Perfect."

His words struck a chord, clear as a bell, in my mind.

"I'm now going to show you *The Shaft of the Soul.* The bridge between life and death. On the walls of that shaft you'll see many pictures from your own life. Once in a while you'll see a dark square. One day, when you become familiar with this condition, you may go in and exchange the dark square with a window. You may then open it and make it golden. Walk through it and push your way further and further in. But today I'll only show you the shaft to give you an indication of what it is. Stand there."

I stepped in front of him. It lasted a moment only and was totally undramatic.

I am standing in a tube with nondescript walls. Many pictures of situations, people and places are seen in one single, indescribable picture. There is a golden light streaming down from above. It has no shape. All the places are one place. All pictures are one picture. All persons are one person. I rush upwards through the shaft at top speed and get born with a sound like a cork being pulled out of a bottle.

The Norns had put out water and biscuits for us. I was watching the fortress. It wasn't very big. It seemed quite impossible that two hundred and five people should have lived here for a longer period of time. He got up and called me to the gate of the fortress.

"This is the gate of time. You must stand in it."

I did as he told me.

The Gate of Time: The Castle seen from The Castle

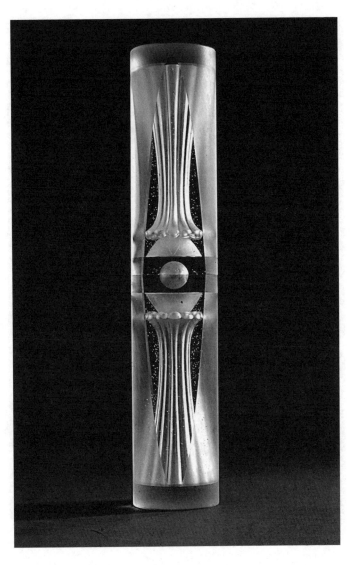

The Grail in its fundamental thoughtform as seen by The Seer

"This is the shapeless opening where all of time becomes eternity. The past, the present and the future all become one. There is no division.

Everything *is* in the same moment. If you become accepting, then you will always be the person you were supposed to be."

The tone vibrated. The reverberation mixed with the silence and became endless, it was like an echo of the one moment that contained everything. *You were not caught by time, it was you who dissolved it.* I stepped into the courtyard. It was almost pentagonal. There was an unreal atmosphere, which was enhanced by the dense fog. Something drew me into the middle of the courtyard. I was facing the tower, which was situated to the north. To my left the gate of time through which I had just passed. Opposite, to my right, a smaller gate opened to the east. I wanted to see what was on the other side, but I couldn't move. I was held firmly to the spot by an inexplicable power. Any kind of resistance was unimaginable. I gave up my thoughts and remained quiet.

While I was standing like this a veiled woman came through the big gate. She walked softly closer leaning slightly forward, as if she didn't want to disturb. She passed me closely by and looked at me from her awkward pose with an indefinable smile. She had no age. She greeted me silently, walking softly on and disappearing through the small gate. A short time after another woman appeared from the fog and repeated the same pantomime, and after her yet another.

"Come closer."

It was the Seer. I stepped forward.

"I'm now going to show you the Grail. Or rather its basic thought form. You will be able to see it and touch it, but it is up to you to see it in its variable form, which it has right now. But the basic form is always the same, and this is what you'll see in a little while. It is true that the Cathars possessed it. No one managed to take it from them, since it did not exist as a physical thing, it was pure spirit. A higher form of consciousness."

He held both his arms in front of him as if he wanted to conjure up something or other from the earth. He guided my hand to the same place in the air where he had just formed the invisible sculpture.

There were no words, just a confirmation. *"You can do it. Do it!"*

Standing like this we suddenly heard female voices singing. In a corner of the fortress the three women from before were holding each other's hands. More human shapes appeared from the fog. A small group of five tourists wearing macs and cameras. The Norns waved me closer. We all took each other's hands. Then we began singing:

"O Signore, fati me, un instrumentum, della tua pacem."

The voices fused into a tone, which had been struck ages ago. I recognized the words from the prayer of St. Francis of Assisi. The Seer was standing in the middle of the courtyard. Around him a weak fluorescent light was visible. We stood still and listened in silence to the tune that surrounded the fortress, as the song ebbed away. What had made us come here? As we introduced ourselves to each other it struck me. One woman was from Romania, one from Sweden and one from England. One man was Jewish and from the USA, the last one was from Italy. They all worked in Brussels. I looked at the Seer. He was standing in the fog in front the gate of time smiling inscrutably.

In the evening we drove to Villeneuve D'Olme to dine at "Le Castrum," far outside of Ariége, well known for its food and good service. Here as well, the Seer was welcomed like royalty. We were the only guests. We were placed at a lavishly set table in the middle of the room. Behind the Seer a young and beautiful female waiter was standing. Behind me her twin brother. Opening the menu the head waiter signalled the two, and, as if conjured out of nothing, they poured the wine we had ordered. The three of them worked in the same rhythm. Not one unnecessary movement, everything fully co-ordinated and in tune with each other. They anticipated every wish and fulfilled them almost before we had had the thought ourselves.

"I love to come here. It is a study of timing and precision that one can never grow tired of."

The Seer nodded approvingly towards the beautiful woman as she served the first course. When she leaned over to pour the wine, he whispered a gallant aside, which made her blush. He turned to me and said:

"From now on you must practise becoming invisible. That way you'll get rid of the last remnants of old traumas that you didn't remove here. Try as much as possible to avoid publicity. Do not waste too much attention on the world but go into your inner sanctity and prepare yourself there. You must sharpen your precision and your timing. You must learn to fall into the cosmic flow of life. Concentration is not the same as attention. Concentration separates and excludes. Attention sees everything as one, without any resistance or reservation. Instinct is not the same as intuition. And intuition is not the same as *intuition!* When you get home things will begin to happen. Do not despair when you find that worldly opportunities pass you by. Remember the old saying that if you think only one single, noble and unselfish thought in a mountain cave, then it will form vibrations throughout the universe and will do what must and can be done."

He raised his glass. There were so many things I wanted to ask him.

"But how am I to integrate everything you showed me. How do I use it in my everyday life?"

"Don't worry about that. It will all merge into a higher synthesis."

We raised our glasses and it was time for the main course. The Seer was at his best. The flirtation he had started with the young girl developed into a dance with their eyes, hidden movements, a well chosen word and an accidental touch, all the time balancing between innocence and sensuality. It was breathtakingly beautiful to watch his virtuosity in showing her his appreciation without it ever becoming awkward. On the contrary, it placed the moment in a beautiful perspective. Lifted it out of timeliness. Her eyes were radiant and her movements became more and more graceful. Everything had gained a new meaning. Everything was exactly as it was supposed to be.

Suddenly something flew through the air. I got a shock. It all happened so fast. One single movement. Across the table and without toppling one single glass. It was the Seer. To this day I do not know how it was done, but suddenly he was standing next to me with a forefinger against my chest.

"Allow me to remind you of the things I have taught you. Be vigilant. Dance! Also when you are sitting down quietly. Be present. Here! Now!"

Before I had collected myself he was again sitting in his own seat. Behind him the woman had difficulty keeping her composure. He said a few words to her in his usual, elegant way. Then she couldn't hold back anymore and broke into uncontrollable laughter. This started an avalanche. In one split second all behaviour exploded and everything dissolved into laughter. But as if by magic all went back to normal. The waiters disappeared and shortly after they returned and served the dessert. The Seer raised his glass:

"Come back to Andalusia next year, and we shall begin the real work!"

The next morning he drove me to Foix. We drank a pastis in a bar in the town square. We were both silent. We shook hands outside the train station. I wanted to say something, mumbled a thank you but couldn't really find any other words.

"See you in Spain," he said.

He then turned around and walked towards the town without looking back.

Sitting in the train heading for home and looking in my bag for my diary I found an envelope. I opened it and found a large silver ring inside it. Something was engraved on it. "Crede Et Vicisti." Inside the ring, my name.

Home again life became just as difficult as the Seer had predicted. After a series of nocturnal dreams which culminated in a dream taking place in a baronial castle where I acknowledge, that I am who I am, I am handed a hand-woven rug by a caliph. It is embroidered with Arabic letters telling me that I have passed the exam.

After this dream I felt totally out of touch with my old reality. Over and over again I had to remind myself of the inscription of the ring, "believe and you'll win." Instead of getting closer to the world, I felt that the distance had grown. I was back in a vacuum. My financial situation was still in shambles. All my extrovert, work related activities failed. Only when I walked into the forest did the world become whole again. Once in a while I experienced the basic simplicity so intensely that I stayed there all day long. I would sit with my back against the trunk of a tree at the edge of the forest facing the beach and listen to the sea and watch the clouds slowly drifting across the sky. I then began to understand what deep layers the Seer had opened in me. I began to understand that the time of the trees, the sea and the clouds were that of the rhythm of the heart and the breath and totally in contrast with the kind of Cronus that man normally uses. I could just *be*. But could I live with that? It seemed like an insoluble paradox until the day I finally remembered:

"You are not going to live from it. You are going to *be* it and to write about it." That was what he had said.

"Thus shall everything fall into place. What must happen will happen."

When, a few weeks later, I was heading a three-day workshop about the creative process for songwriters and composers, I experienced for the first time a new level that I had brought with me from Montségur. On the last day of the workshop, whilst I was writing comments for each of the participants in my hotel room, I suddenly received some inexplicable pictures in my head, and I immediately wrote them down. I told the team on the following day that I wasn't quite sure what these pictures meant, and that they should disregard them if they didn't make any sense. However, if they did, I would certainly like to know. It turned out that some of the pictures and some of the comments were so precise that they went straight to the core of the personal space of the particular individual.

The inspiration from the presence of the Seer's personality was unmistakable. I felt that he wanted to show me, that when you are willing to set yourself and your own wishes aside, you may then become a flawless mirror for other people. I myself experienced that I could see the participants in a clear light, devoid of any kind of assessment or judgement. Teacher or student, what difference did it make?

I also felt his inspiration in my everyday life. During the months leading up to my fiftieth birthday I started to have nocturnal dreams, which apparently had something to do with my past. The dreams were so intense that it affected me for several days. In the beginning I didn't understand what they tried to tell me. But then I woke up one morning after having dreamt about meeting the Seer in one of them.

"Acknowledge your mistakes." He said with his familiar smile.

"I thought that was done at Montségur," I objected.

"Well, apparently that wasn't enough."

He spoke directly to my conscience. I then understood that just like that time on Montségur I had to relate directly to his words. But for how long should this cleansing continue?

"As long as it takes," I heard him saying.

"Be willing always to unmask the motives of the little self. That is the only way to deal with them."

In the following days I searched my memory for unconsidered episodes and actions in my life, which until now had been veiled in the darkness of oblivion. I wrote everything down as it appeared. Page after page of situations where I had hurt someone or had acted on the basis of my own, selfish needs. All my lies. Black as white. The little "innocent" theft many years ago. The smarting remark. The unsympathetic attitude. The unworthy manipulations. Women. Everything. It was shocking how much I could still find in the nooks and crannies of my mind and which I had ignored or repressed with a shrug of the shoulders as time went by. I now had to relate to everything once again. It was not just embarrassing it was an inevitable, naked pain.

At the same time I started sorting through my personal documents. A large part of a whole life's correspondence, notes, scraps of paper, photos etc. were put into cardboard boxes. It wasn't your regular birthday party. Instead I started a bonfire in the garden. At exactly twelve noon my shabby and glorious past went up in flames.

"Are you sure about this?" Asked one of my friends who happened by.

"Apart from this," I replied, "I'm not sure of anything at all."

On the same day I received a letter headed 25 Gammel Kongevej September 26th, 1905:

"Dear . . .

No, I'm sorry, I cannot offer the service of reciting anything any more. The curtain has come down — the Iron Curtain. It is so sad not to be able to help any longer. But it is over.

Many kind regards

Herman Bang."

Bang was fifty-one when he wrote this letter. I read the lines over and over. The well known, spidery writing stood out on the paper and became legible.

He is sitting at the window looking at St. Joergen's lake across the road. There is a wind coming up. Why write anymore? Here? Dizzy. On his hand a stain of soya which he removes with some difficulty. The truth? The stain of shame on the heart cannot be removed. Travel. Yes, travel. Away. Forever. Being nothing at all. A tired fly buzzes in the otherwise so quiet rooms at Gammel Kongevej ninety-nine years ago.

It was an ice-cold day in February. The kind of day where Copenhagen Central Station is anything but inviting. I dragged my suitcases up the stairs to get out of the chilling wind from the platform and quite deliberately ignored the beggars and the down-and-outs squatting on old newspapers and waving their blue coffee pots at the passers by. My own budget was more than over the limit, and, furthermore, I felt dizzy. I felt nauseated. I wasn't myself at all. Had I misunderstood something, since I could lose my balance to such a frightening degree? And just now, when I was about to embark on what was probably the most important journey of my life.

8

The rails sang as the train rushed into a curve at high speed and disappeared into the darkness. I was dozing off but woke up for a minute as my head hit the window. The afternoon sun flickered into the compartment shortly after. We had left Sierra de Almijara and were on the last straight lap towards Malaga. Forty-eight hours of travelling were coming to an end. I was now embarking on another kind of travel. I closed my eyes and sank into the rocking movement of the train. Into the wordless language. Into the black hole of memory. Into Patio de los Leones. Into the singer who for the first time leaned against the pillars at the courtyard of the Lions at Alhambra in Granada in order to let himself be perpetuated there, and without any hesitation lead the photographer through to the residence of the emperor. Into the reception room Mexuar. Into the Myrtle garden and his beloved Sala de los Embajadores. What had made me go to Spain at that time? What was it that kept drawing me there? Behind it all I seemed to see a glimpse of the Seer and his familiar smile as a watermark on the veil that was slowly being withdrawn. A dying summer bee on a windowsill. A buzzing fly in an apartment on Gammel Kongevej. The *Old* King's Road? *King of* ... what? An ephemeral person on his way out of showbiz? *Store* Kongensgade. The Grand King's road. Alhambra and Montségur. Memory. Apparently, it was no coincidence that the lines seemed to meet in Andalusia in order to be transformed into the invisible red thread of their own history. What kind of manuscript was it? Who wrote it and where was it hidden?

The three dimensional papier mâchiér reproduction of Picasso's "Guernica" was still hanging over the descent to the coastal railway exactly the way it did when I was here the last time. The Seer waited at the bar under one of the surrealists' invisible clocks at the far end of the train station.

"Well, have you regained your elegance?" he asked smilingly, as if he wanted to indicate that time was not operating here.

I looked at him slightly puzzled and was about to ask him what he meant.

"The Central Station in Copenhagen," he continued.

"Oh" I replied and stood on one leg with open arms á la Edie Sedgewick.

I had happily forgotten all about dizziness and nausea. The electrical impulse in my spine. That had been a greeting from him then!

His car was parked outside. We drove along the coast on the motorway, which quite appropriately was nicknamed "Death road." I couldn't help thinking what had made him settle down here in the middle of a touristy cesspool of deep frying smells, plastic and concrete slum. I didn't ask him.

"I live in Switzerland. I live in Italy. I live in Alpha Centauri. Omega Centauri. What difference does it make? I live everywhere and nowhere. Right now, I am living here. Let me tell you something. Years ago I met a man who had been in jail for ten years. In order not to lose his mind while inside, he began studying. He read everything he could put his hands on, all the philosophers, works of natural science, the old religious scriptures, simply everything. I think he also took a degree in philosophy. At the same time he kept a strict account of the days, the weeks, the months and the years. He was convinced that the world would have changed when he re-entered society. When finally the day arrived and he impatiently walked out of the prison gate in his own suit, he experienced that the expected feeling of freedom failed to come. Several weeks of partying didn't change anything. He simply realized that his idea of freedom had been linked to an illusory idea of "freedom" being outside the prison walls, and "imprisonment" inside. He could go wherever he wanted. But on another level he was still a prisoner and a slave of his own expectations and those of others, of the prejudices, imaginings, habits, dreams and desires. Even ten years of studying all forms of knowledge did not change the simple fact that he did not feel in the least free.

He left the motorway.

The house was situated in a square in the old part of town. The church bells were tolling for evensong. The sun disappeared behind the houses and the guests in front of the cafes went inside. A boy on a moped without a silencer was circling the square with a girl sitting behind him. The one-legged lottery vendor looked at himself in the reflection of the fountain and got ready to pack up, while the horns of the cars gave a concert in the main street under the haze of petrol. A beautiful, mature doña dressed in black greeted the Seer as we crossed the square. The balconies were overflowing with blazing geraniums. He lifted his white straw hat. A soft wind in an old figtree. The entrance was halfway down Don Quixote. We took the elevator to the fifth floor. There were five rooms in the apartment. It was furnished in a simple style. A view of the town and the Mediterranean. I unpacked my suitcase in the guest room and prepared the tape recorder. We had water and a single pastis on the terrace facing the square. Ben Webster was playing. Everything was deeper and more clearly outlined. It was like coming home.

"We'll start tomorrow. We'll be busy in the next few days. When my telephone consultation hour finishes at 9 a.m. you'll see how I work and how the energies work. You may ask all the questions you need to ask after lunch. Similar to the days on Montségur we shall dissolve all limitations. Have you brought a crash helmet?"

It was dark as we went out for dinner. The streets were closely lined with restaurants. The waiters moved about restlessly. It was out of season. However, there was still a hint of nauseating sun oil and the tourist's menu mixed with the smell of Mediterranean salt and desert wind. We had Chinese.

At exactly 8 a.m. the first client phoned. The door to the Seer's study was ajar. He listened, spoke a few words that I couldn't hear and then placed the receiver on his writing desk. I could now see the kind of silence I had experienced at the other end of the line and that I heard as a kind of white noise. He lifted his hand and let it hover over something that I couldn't identify. He sat like this for a long time. He then picked up the receiver, spoke a few words and hung up. They called from far and near. He spoke English then German, French then Italian. This continued for an hour. Every time he hung up it started ringing. I sneaked into the kitchen to prepare tea and toast. He looked tense coming out of the study. He was somewhere else. We ate our breakfast standing up.

"Something bothering you?" I asked.

"Well, an Italian ambassador had a stroke in the Far East. This was his wife. I told her that I couldn't go on repairing him this way. I first told him to retire many years ago, but he never wanted to listen. Each time he has a stroke, his wife calls me because it is faster than calling the emergency. But some day even I shall not be able to help him. He is holding on to life with his fingertips. If he falls this time there is no way back. I have already given him one treatment, but he needs another."

I followed him into his study. He started right away. Lifted his hand and let it hover over his desk.

"What are you doing?" I asked.

"I am visualizing a picture of him and then sending it the relevant energies. I can see that one of his heart valves doesn't function properly. His blood circulation isn't very good either. I now check all the other organs and I see that something is wrong with his digestion. All in all he is not in balance. It looks as if he needs the whole package. Organs, blood circulation, chakras and aura. Follow me."

The Seer at work in his study

He signalled to me that I should be quiet. The grail sculpture was on the desk in front of him refracting the light. I concentrated and tried to sense his reality. He wasn't there. He was looking far into the distance. His eyes saw something that others couldn't see. The galaxies moved through unknown universes. I sat completely still with a straight back. I thought I saw something like very small glimpses of light in the air. I felt electrical impulses. I closed my eyes.

Through a thin haze of grey light something bluish shone through at the edges.

A flame-like thought. The Seer is bending over a stoutly built man on a cot. He is working in deep concentration and very determined. The man's breathing is very poor. The light changes and turns blue. The Seer is taking one of the luminous particles in the air. It shines with a golden light like a star. He is placing the crystal where the heart used to be and closes.

"*Îkhal!*"

Complete. Activated. The reinstatement of the original condition. He blows on his hands and moves them over the sick body.

"*Ephatah!*" — *In one single instant he opens the man's blood circulation, the chakras and the aura. He then whispers something to the sleeping man. A long line unfolds and becomes endless. It is a whole life but it lasts a short while only.*

"Done!"

I opened my eyes. The Seer was standing up.

"Could you follow that?"

I was still shaken.

"It felt like eternity and yet like a single moment."

"Well, we are working with powerful energies."

He looked more relaxed now. He smiled relieved.

"Our friend can go another round. It might be the last one. I'm not so sure that there'll be another. And I told his wife. It is up to him."

"What did you whisper to him?"

"I didn't whisper anything. If that is what you experienced it is because you were in the psychic or astral area. Since in this case I had no possibility of giving the client an option to his present situation by word of mouth. I transferred it directly with the healing itself. Hopefully, it is going to manifest and become expressed in another way of living and another attitude. But sometimes it is easier to move a rock than a human being. Even the gods fight in vain against this kind of inertia."

He seemed to be surprised at the way I had experienced this.

"It's fine that you are able to see anything at the psychic/astral level, but I'd like you to be able to see clearly. If this had been the case you would have seen the client's incarnation picture. You would then have seen that the cause for his present condition is spread out over a longer period of time than this single life. Furthermore, you would immediately have seen the connection between his poor heart and the star Rigel in the Orion constellation, and you would have known that this is where you had to seek help. You would have seen the connection between micro- and macro cosmos. When it is a matter of treating physical diseases it is an advantage to operate on the ethereal level. But it is still limited in itself. The astral level has a tendency to become flighty and is also limited. Both the astral and the mental level are more or less tied to the personal level. But there is a higher aspect of all three levels, a universal, creative area which dissolves all limitations. In order to see clearly it is absolutely necessary to be able to let go of everything that is connected to yourself. In such a condition there are no pictures as we normally understand the word. Instead of a linear, horizontal way of looking it is more of a circular, vertical concentration, which is immediate. You have a long way to go and you might as well start right away and properly. Tonight I'll show you a simple but effective exercise that you may use. I shall now take you to the Tolox Mountain. Later, we'll have lunch at the town of Tolox."

Tolox was situated about 50 kilometres into the mountains. For a long time it felt like driving in a virtual reality of cardboard stage set wings with one hastily erected holiday apartment complex after the other, broken only by just as stereotypical and hastily built golf courses and hotels. Not until we got up further did the architectonic horrors change into citrus groves and blooming almond trees. The hairpin bends got tighter and the road more and more bumpy. We were at an altitude of 1800 meters and followed the last gravel road until it came to an end. He parked the car and we started climbing along the path. Similar to Montségur we went through the initiation points. So that I did not forget them, as he said! I sensed that this was about something else. We sat down further up. I unpacked my tape recorder and we got started on the questions of the day. When we finished we sat quietly and watched the endless view. I was slowly realizing that this was one of the Seer's qualities that I appreciated the most. To be present without words, without expectations and without any judgement. These were the times when I felt that he could communicate his thoughts and visions through his presence alone. Looking out became looking in. It was an undramatic kind of transmission, which would move you almost imperceptibly and silently. At these moments I felt my body relax completely. Each fibre, each muscle and every single cell found its correct place. An empathetic vigilance grew from this relaxed condition, a vigilance, which saw people and things as they were on their own merit. This was not about acceptance anymore, since there was nothing to accept. Everything was as it was. It was a long forgotten language. He showed me how almost all communication between people, the spoken and the written word, is nothing but our desperate attempts to cling to illusory personalities and identities tainted by prejudices, fear and vanity. A language which did not allow any room for listening, which focused on itself, which was excluding and only lived due to its attack and defence system was, according to him, a poor and inhumane one. Although the users of this language were usually very good at repartees and were able to write infinitely, they were really only good at maintaining and communicating limitations without end. It was this maintaining of limitations which was one of the main reasons that the great paradigm change, which all were waiting for, did not happen. He did not judge. He simply looked at and worked for the release of limitations wherever he met them. Not until the dissolution of all mental noise would it be possible to practise the transmission of stillness as a transforming kind of communication between people. It was not possible to enter this condition with a limited attention. The road to the transpersonal and the related level might seem difficult, because it demanded an obligation, which included the complete human being. It was not enough to be just a little bit pregnant. You either were or you were not. And the paradoxical difference between the one and the other was the simple fact that the sleeping person decided to open his eyes, to wake up and become conscious of his wakeful condition. The fact that such a seemingly simple decision could seem so difficult lay in the fact that it entailed the release of more or less everything that you have ever learned and gained, and which you erroneously have interpreted as a true realization.

He presented all these considerations to me on the mountain. In one single thought, without words, without judgement.

On our way back to the car he suddenly stopped.

"Do you feel it?"

I stopped in my tracks. He pointed to the shadows in front of us and then into the distance. The sun stood at an angle behind us. I looked at the horizon and then down the mountainside. Now I saw it. The shadows moved. The mountain moved. The earth moved. And we were standing on it. It was a magnificent experience. For one single moment I experienced that we were standing on a globe that moved forward majestically. Moving around a sun in a galaxy in the universe. The silence. The clouds. The grass. The shadows. The pulse. The breathing. Unity. Gravitation. The whisper of the universe in the wind.

"Quite moving, isn't it?" he said smiling.

We drove down to Tolox and had our siesta at the local *venta*. We continued working on our questions and answers after lunch. We then started talking about art and the role of the artist:

"When artists receive something from the universe they are able to transform it into something beautiful. Not beautiful in the ordinary sense, but beautiful in a universal sense so that the power is expressed in work. But almost everyone is taken in by their egotism. Therefore art does not play the role it was meant to play. Artists are generally small children who like to play without understanding the power they are playing with. And the more art is personified the lesser art it is. The artists, then, are no longer the mouthpiece of the universe. The gifts that are given to them are not given for their own sake.

A good writer, poet, painter, musician, filmmaker, singer, dancer etc. is an interpreter of the universal language, the impressionable language, words, pictures and music which moves. It is not their inspiration, not a gift for their personalities, but something they are obligated to interpret and to pass on. Then it becomes beautiful. The Seer sees and – moves. The painter paints out of the universal, not out of himself and not for his own sake or for the sake of money. Leonardo da Vinci was formidable. He was able to transform things in the same spirit as he received them. He was the mouthpiece of visions. It was a kind of clear-sightedness. He understood that it was his task to develop a prophetic sense.

It was clear that he wanted to emphasize this.

There is no true art apart from the ability to see and to listen at a super sensitive level. To be receptive to cosmic impulses. An artist must be willing to sharpen his consciousness and his intuition in order to see and to liberate the humane and the cosmic in even the most insignificant, the banal, the superficial and the mediocre. He must never let himself sink to the level of simple reproduction. The task of the artist is transformation. Unfortunately, only very few are willing to give up their personal ambitions, their egotism, the strategies of which are always blocking the way to a higher realization.

It grew dark before we got back to the apartment.

He placed a burning candle in front of me.

"This lesson moves us right back to the beginning. It is solely about concentration. Nothing else. Sit down in front of the candle. Relax and concentrate on your natural breathing. Do not force anything. Concentrate on all the stages of breathing in and breathing out. The short break between the breath's transition from the inner to the outer. Feel your coexistence with the world, with the universe. The energies which run through your breathing connecting you to the air and the atmosphere, the universe and the cosmos. Now, look at the flame and concentrate on the wick itself, then the visible light and finally the aura of heat that the flame radiates. Now, close your eyes and visualize these three dimensions of light in front of your inner eye. Bring the flame inside and let it lighten your innermost room. Feel how you are fused together. You are one. The flame is you and you are it. See how frail it is. The slightest breath of air may blow it out. But it should not be hidden under a bushel. Later, when you master this lesson, you may expand it and move to the beginning so to speak."

He put his hands together and opened them shaping the wings of a butterfly.

"In this lesson, looking at the flame, you must at the same time consider the consciousness which is looking at the flame."

I fell asleep with a thousand flames dancing in front of my eyes. Later, in a dream, they all became one.

9

"Ask your question through all the universes."

The voice came from the flame. There was a face in it. A Greek philosopher. The face changed and took on Roman features. The wick in the flame disappeared. Only the pure flame remained. It had a totally golden and clear aura with a cool, blue centre. It was burning clearly in the air. A new face appeared. It was the Seer.

"Now you are present," the voice said.

Then I woke up.

I got up and got ready for the task of the day, which started with an hour of stillness. The Seer was already seated in his consulting room. His eyes were only partly open. They didn't see anything. They saw everything. Outside a storm was brewing. A sunshade on a balcony on the opposite side of the street overturned and was being blown over the edge. I sat down in the living room and tried to find my way into an inner silence but was constantly disturbed by the noise from the street. Then I noticed one of the pictures on the wall. It was an old engraving depicting Marcus Aurelius.

Next to it was a small painting. It showed the interior of a room in semidarkness. A person was dimly to be seen in one corner of the room. A vague notion made me stand up in order to study the picture more closely. Standing in front of it I could see that it was a picture of a Moorish building. Tiles decorated with braided ribbons made out of twelve-pointed stars formed the friezes around the closed and arched windows. In between them was a door. Above it calligraphed, ornamental ribbons. The person in the corner seemed to be a woman dressed in a traditional dress with a veil. Memory.

The first client phoned at exactly eight a.m. Each time the connection was interrupted a new one called. I cleaned the kitchen and prepared breakfast so that it would be ready as soon as the Seer had finished the consultations of the day. He was bustling with energy as he sat on the kitchen table with a cup of coffee.

"Today I'll tell you about healing. When I talk about being willing to move out into the universe in order to find an answer, you must understand that man is himself a part of this universe. When you open yourself to the cosmic energies then we are dealing with a sort of dual attention. It is directed both inwards and outwards. Things are united. As it is inside, so is it outside. Physically, mentally and spiritually. When you obtain harmony with the universal laws you fulfil your purpose. It is an all inclusive level where you cannot talk about the outer space without including the inner space. That which lies beyond man. When I heal I return freedom to the person in question. This is the case in all its simplicity. I try to remove the concept of power in a person. Remove the criteria for success, everything that is crippling to a human being. In this way I can, maybe, remove the diseases of the body and of the mind. But I must move in order to move others. I must be able to see the connections and the deeper meaning. Ask the question: "What can I do?" This way you make yourself available. Unlimited. This is the only true way in which to be present. It is the prerequisite to seeing. When you turn your back on the underlying reality then you turn your back on your finest qualities. When I see I can move – I then have a responsibility. When I do not see, then I'm irresponsible. We can ask any question of the stars and the galaxies and they will all answer us.

The Isogynic Being

It is sad when we do not use this potential. It is so essential, so simple that most people do not know what I'm talking about. But if man knew, if man only knew how things are connected and how much influence they have on their own destiny. Think – come on!"

The light crawled slowly across the wall behind him. The sounds from the street grew faint and disappeared between the words.

"It might be that as a practising Buddhist you might have to turn your back on Buddhism for a while in order to reach the true level. It might be that as a Christian you may have to turn your back on Christianity in order to unite with the Christ-energy, free of all dogma. Maybe the seeker within both Islam and Judaism will have to look past religion in order to get to know the true power behind Allah and Elohim? Yes, maybe we have to be ready to deny every fundamentalist idea about God and the divine in order to be able to recognize the basic energy as purely as possible?

All of his personality radiated openness and compassion.

"Imagine that there is no more power. No limitations. You have all thought forms inside of you, everything, all. You are not a static organism. The prerequisite for seeing is that you do not cling to anything. That you understand, that everything moves. There are no final answers. There are two ways to live – consciously or unconsciously. Most people live on an unconscious level. Stagnated robots, living dead who may be able to uphold a career and support a family, but who basically may be compared to zombies without a choice. Being consciously present means to open your eyes and to see. The moment you start focusing your attention on the right place, the energies will be with you. They need you. They need your thought forms. You become a conscious servant. You say: "I am present and I am available." This is the first step towards healing. This is how you communicate with the universe. Pure thought forms. Do you see?"

He raised his hand and drew a horizontal figure eight in the air. He then kept on moving one finger in a circle until a luminous, electric current appeared. It was breathtaking. It moved.

"You see. The reaction. The pictures. Do you think all this comes from nowhere? The universe must have access to man, and that is what questions are – access. You will be recognized by them. It is a kind of cosmic, genetic material. It is totally uncomplicated. See — do you see it?"

He drew a line of pulsating light through the air.

"Movement, movement, movement. See how simple it is, how beautiful it gets."

It was quite incredible. I could feel the same kind of ease that I had felt on Montségur, and I understood that it was possible to suspend gravity.

"Everything is so simple. The stars, the galaxies. They consist of the same minerals as we do. The same basic elements. They are our family. Ask them anything. But not: Help me, help me! That is the imperative, that doesn't work. See the beauty in taking the opposite direction. Here I am. I'm available. Then things happen. That is freedom. There is no hocus-pocus here. As a seer and a healer you do not say, this is what it looks like, this is how it is. You offer a choice. The choice of freedom. When I treat someone from afar, I simply activate or set free the clients own, forgotten knowledge of his well-being. What most people cannot decide about themselves, I help them decide. I activate the options. In this connection distances are irrelevant. It takes elegance. It is a responsibility I take upon myself. It is my task to re-establish the harmony between an unhealthy organ and the universe. A closed person is no good for anyone or for the universe. I try to transform ways of thinking, karma and the purpose of life. At that moment I must dissolve myself, that which is me, everything. I'm a traveller. An ambassador of stillness. I ask my way through forty-eight universes and receive the answers. This is how my consultations have been for thirty-five years."

"Why do we get sick?"

"Accumulation of unresolved thought forms. Not just in a single life but through one incarnation after the other. It is not necessarily the specific bad thought in itself, but it is the sum of all the bad thoughts of the person in question, which causes the breakdown. Just as it is not the specific slice of nitrite-filled salami, which kills the person, but the sum of all nitrite filled food which eventually makes the person ill. One-sidedness and being closed up creates diseases."

The telephone rang. The Seer went to the office to take it. He came back half an hour later.

"It was a woman from Germany. Her husband died yesterday. She wants me to guide him to the other side. I cannot do this until tomorrow, since three days should preferably pass to allow the higher bodies to be fully liberated. It's a journey that requires preparation."

"How is this journey?"

"Beautiful. Death is not death. It is the liberation of everything you have thought in a lifetime. That is what death is."

"When I watched you heal the Italian ambassador from afar yesterday you took light crystals from the universe, what happened?"

"The various universes contain elements of the diseases that people are confronted with during the earthly refinement process, and that is why a mirror image of the person may be seen out there. Through his journey, through his incarnations on the earthly plane, man must go through a series of sufferings, sort of cosmic children's diseases. A kind of cleansing. As I said before, I am trying to reawaken the client's dormant qualities. I use the thought forms or energies of the universe, if you like. I move into Creation. It is a very beautiful kind of energy, which is constantly moving. In this case, creation in Orion's Belt. Creation uses neutrinos which are very small amounts of energy with the strange quality that they can get into all of the body, all of the planet, get out on the other side and still contain the same amount of energy. They are the carriers of the creating energy. Since they are thought forms it is possible to stop them. Just as mediation is a kind of relaxation, then this is more of a process of becoming conscious. You don't make yourself empty in order to stay empty, but in order to get filled with the power. The kind of creation I'm talking about happens every day. It is present as a possibility every day. That is the beauty of it. Then comes the Builder. The actual thought containing all thoughts. We carry that within us. And then, finally, the Accomplisher comes into force."

"This sounds like the Father, Son and Holy Spirit?"

He nodded.

"The Accomplisher or the Holy Spirit, the conscious, cosmic breath, is an option which is always present wherever there are living creatures. But it does not function until it is activated. That is what is activated when healing happens over a distance. All people contain and are surrounded by this quality. It is outside of time and space. But it is still present everywhere. You just have to be willing to receive it. This is what I do. I wake people up and activate them. No problem. But we must always remember that it must be preceded by ethics. Unlimited man carries in him a crystallized and pure ethic, which is movable in the sense that it is made stronger concurrent with the conquering of mental limitations. It doesn't necessarily come into force automatically, but it becomes a very clear option. Demanding a choice. A prerequisite for this is that you refrain from any thought of power. This is also the prerequisite for the unlimited. It is very important to understand this. This is valid in all circumstances, big as well as small. And the one in power is always more limited than the subjugated. Since the one who wants to control others always ends up losing control over himself. It may even be felt as a threat having to give up your mental limitations, because they are locked into place and have become habitual. It takes courage. We always carry the ethical along with us and basically we all know what is right or wrong. It lies below that which is basic; by this I mean behaviour. It is part of the essential centre. When the ethic is given up, when you turn your back on it, it is a mistake. That is when diseases occur. Diseases, thus, are a mistake. But a mistake may be corrected."

I could feel his energy directly. I experienced once more how it had a relaxing effect, which made every atom in my body fall into place.

"In order to be able to correct errors you must practise communication as purely and as directly as possible. The records and the answers you receive may not always be what you expect, but you must remember that pure energy is neutral. It is neither good nor bad. Such ideas do not exist in this context. The usual concept of being neutral does not cover the idea here.

Universal neutrality is an active energy however, it is not tied to emotionally charged ideas. It is neither sentimental nor religious. Each person has his records within him. Your questions are situated in micro cosmos. A copy of your records are situated in the universe. Your answers are situated in macro cosmos. Answers and questions.

You are situated somewhere in between, in the middle of the bridge between the one and the other, at the point of balance between inhaling and exhaling, expansion and contraction, this is where the '*you*' is, here and now. And now. And now. Do you see it? It is an eternal movement."

The particles of light practically danced around him. He then snapped his fingers and they disappeared as fast as they had arrived.

"The existence of cosmic genetics is as common as physical genetics. The higher you get the more sensitive it is. Do not think that creation isn't sensitive. It is. At a cosmic as well as an intellectual level. All great energies are vulnerable. This is what makes them great. It can be quite frightening when you see it. The same with people. Man must find his strength in his vulnerability. Through the acknowledgement of his vulnerability and not by projecting it out as a defence. This is the way that man may break down walls. May loosen up. Make himself sensitive, increase the speed of vibration and become a cosmic being."

He was like an age-old lotus flower. Slowly, slowly I watched it unfolding. Majestically and filled with poetry he unfolded his vulnerability, shining in golden light, and I saw that this was a spontaneous moment from which pure joy springs. He opened his hands in a welcoming gesture: "This is happiness. A total experience of being, a total experience of NOW! As you can see, it is not comparable to winning the lottery or getting a new car. This is something totally different. It is important to understand the difference. This is where you'll find the answer to all diseases and all healing. Happiness is a deep and much more all-embracing condition which happens when we acknowledge all our being. Realization brings certainty. And certainty is knowing that we are connected to the universe. And the universe is NOW, and NOW is happiness. Happiness is healing."

It is impossible to describe the feelings that rushed through me. It was a completely new and free energy, a quiet sparkling power of unfathomed dimensions, perhaps the kind of creation of which he had just spoken. It filled my breathing and renewed itself every time I breathed. I started to understand, that all the things he had showed me on Montségur had only been a necessary introduction, a therapeutic prerequisite for much higher layers of consciousness. This was the time where the decisive introduction to the hidden reality was beginning. It was now that I could begin to feel the fire under me of which he had spoken, and I realized that I had to stop running away. If for no other reason, then because there were no other places to hide. I realized that there was nothing to be afraid of. That that which would be devoured by the flames was merely the remains of all that had held me locked into long worn-out patterns. I had mistaken flight for movement. He looked into the air for a long time, then he said:

"Through all your incarnations you have been present on certain conditions. You never wanted to be here. You were here without being present. You saw a mountain and you climbed it. Standing on the top and recognizing that it was artificial you said: "Was this all? This is not for me." Since then everything has been a matter of unlearning. Your economy is practically nonexistent. You do not want to sing anymore. You do not want to be here. You have given up everything and withdrawn more and more from the world. You have really entered what is called *the small death*, which is not really death, but you do not live. I know all your studies. All your books. This is now opening up. That is why we are here. We are into a third principle called: *You are!* The moment you understand this, things will happen. You are the one moving the universe. It is not the other way round. You have been brought to the bottom of the hole of existence. You were never allowed to talk about everything you brought with you, your enormous, collected knowledge, everything you knew to be true. We are now going the other way and you'll now start talking about it. That is why we met. You have found the true mountain."

His voice brought me further and further into realization:

"Your elegance was totally out of balance that day at the Central Station. Suddenly, there was no elegance. You couldn't tear yourself away. You were afraid to travel alone. Both literally and metaphorically. But you wanted to come down here. There was no doubt. You might say that your voyage through Europe in a sense was your body's message to the universe, that in spite of all the complications, you really wanted to be here. That for the first time in your life you have a sincere wish to be present as a human being."

He got up.

"Let's go and have lunch."

The desert wind rushed through the town, throwing tiles and flowerpots into the almost empty street. We walked further into the old part of town and found a restaurant in a small square where the wind couldn't get in. The Seer asked for a jug of water. I couldn't help thinking about the kind of pressure he must have experienced through all his years as a healer. The responsibility he had taken upon himself for thousands of people, most of whom had found their way to him only when their doctors had given up and they had nowhere else to go.

"The time has come. The moment is here. We shall dissolve the old. Forget everything about making money for tomorrow. It doesn't matter at all. When you have expressed the thought that you are going to make money, you have already limited yourself. Forget it. That is not the way it works. That is the kind of thing you find within the New Age milieu, you know: money is chakra-energy, make your first aura-million before your neighbour and all that. Limitations. Pseudo. And every time you feel you have made some progress you feel happy, and that is fine. But if you rest for too long on your laurels you get stuck. That doesn't work. It is not the gain that matters but the effort. Not the answer but the question. Not the prize but the deed. None of my abilities matter, since they are not ascribable to me as a person. All that matters is that one is available and willing to question everything. One may not reach new conclusions, one may not get new answers, but one will obtain a new consciousness. A more embracing consciousness. One won't get a medal for it, no prizes, no Nobel prize. It simply isn't essential. That is why we haven't developed further. Man thinks about profit even before he has done the job. Thus, the job gets all too limited. He is willing to sell a new consciousness for a conclusion, a prize cup, money, prestige, anything. It doesn't work. Existence is free-flowing. When it is limited by personal ambitions, the world gets smaller. If people would realize to what extent they are connected to everything else, they would act and build their lives quite differently. It is completely indescribable what happens when the universes come back to one and say: "Finally, someone who believes." The experience that one may do something for the universes and thus for other people. That one can move somebody. Not sentimentally, not personally. Not at all – don't think that. But really move. Everything, then, becomes unbelievably beautiful and simple. One then experiences what real intuition means. What really great things are like. It is certainly not a question of making money. Never. The great thing in a specific person's development process is who he is and what he can do, seen from a universal perspective. Those are totally different criteria for success than those we know today. This is the new kind of freedom. Give me somewhere to be and I shall move the universe. This has been my life for many years. The tough years as a healer are almost over. Now, I must start helping, out there. Meanwhile, let us see what we can make of you."

The waiter brought us sardines and a salad. My brain was like an overloaded and enormous net, in which my thoughts were racing around. I knew from Montségur that he didn't say one superfluous word, that everything had meaning and had to be considered. I knew from several experiences in his vicinity, that he made things happen, tensions and locked thoughts loosened up, the incomprehensible suddenly became understandable, the vague became clear, obvious and transparent. He transmitted the most complicated questions without a word, while the more simple, basic rules were formed in glowing sentences, word by word, materialized into earth, fire, air and water. Thus, I slowly started comprehending some of his meaning, when he talked about the fact that we and the universe have the elements in common. But one thing was how much of everything he said I was able to understand and accept. Another was everything he only hinted at and which could only be read between the lines. This was where logic and intellect failed. That's where you had to mind your P's and Q's. Shaking his head, he showed me again and again that the greatest obstacles to understanding what he tried to tell me, was my all too good manners, my dry intellect and the arrogance which followed. Luckily, his patience with me was unlimited.

After lunch we went back to the apartment. After an hour's silence we continued with questions and answers. He kept his answers simple but left it to me to decide which topics we should consider. We ended the afternoon with a breathing exercise.

"The universe is shaped like a pyramid. The equilateral triangle is the basic matrix of everything. The universe has been expanding through this form for billions and billions of years. After comes a short silence and then the inhalation. Exactly like breathing. Expansion and contraction, inhalation and exhalation. In connection with the discovery of further universes I experienced the importance of freedom of movement. Passing beyond the universe means being unlimited. This is the way our breathing should be. But notice the short silence between the in- and exhalation. This is the moment where all problems are solved. This is where you fuse into the NOW!"

The wind had died down outside. I was in the kitchen making one of my simple meals. The Seer went and got a bottle of Don Cesar. After dinner I was overcome by a pleasant tiredness. Frank Sinatra's Rat Pack was swinging in the background. There were no hindrances. The day had settled down and I don't know what made me ask:

"Have we met each other in another life?"

The question didn't seem in the least to take him by surprise. He was warming his glass in his hands the way you do with brandy.

"We have met at a specific level of understanding. Both of us have always been aware, that although we live here on earth there is something else we have access to. Some very pure records that, unfortunately, we have not been able to use until now. It is unbelievably beautiful, but it has also been very difficult to apply and has lead us along different roads to the place we are now, to this very moment in this very living room. Access to the universal level has made us shy and somehow unsuited to be here. Lonely beings since during most of our incarnations we have not been able to transform the universal to the level of the earth. When through one life after another you have been isolated with your knowledge and your ideas, a deep loneliness will arise in you as an earthling. And this has been rather difficult for the two of us. It hasn't been very pleasant but now it seems that things have started to crystallize a bit. There is an opening. Other types of consciousness. My luck is that this time I have had the great good fortune to be allowed to use my abilities to the full. It therefore looks as if I'm approaching the end. The exit is at hand. I know what it is but it is difficult to describe. This is where you come in. Otherwise it is in the interplay with my clients that I find my language. And it doesn't get any more beautiful than that. The clients and their healing is my guarantee that I'm here and that my métier is the right one. It is the basis of my studies and my research. It stimulates me to move people. My work is constantly disproved or confirmed. When I work outside the universes and am accepted by the energies, I get permission to take them back to the earth and to use them here. To transform them. And since I can transform them into something tangible, such as healing others, they open for me on a personal level. Following all my incarnations I now know that I'm allowed to be here."

"Who are you? Where do you come from?"

A smile crept slowly over his face and disappeared in a shadow. I thought I saw him change his character in a flash. It surprised me. Suddenly, he wasn't the one I expected him to be. Did I sense a change in his voice also?

"I'm from a time before the beginning. I transcend. It was quite a shock for me when for the first time as a seer I began to understand some of my early thought forms and saw how I had abused my power. Until I acknowledged and accepted it. Then I could move on. I was present in a room where twenty-four energies were also present, each with its own thought form. I was the twenty-fifth energy and possessed two. Apparently I couldn't control them. At any rate, something went terribly wrong. But I changed that later on. That is why I'm now in the process of phasing out. I used to be power. Now I'm freedom."

The last two sentences kept hanging in the air like two snakes intertwined. A sudden impulse made me point to the two engravings I had been looking at earlier that day. It was more than a feeling. They were a part of the invisible text that had to be seen between the lines.

"How do these two pictures relate to you?"

"When I'm reading Marcus Aurelius' *Meditations*, some very familiar thought forms appear. I found that out a few years ago. I feel very close to that thought form, and it might have been an earlier incarnation. I'm not saying that I was him, but I do have a very close knowledge of the thought form Marcus Aurelius. I can even feel it in my body. The great separation he felt. The emperor who had to wage the necessary wars in order to maintain the Roman Empire, while at the same time absorbing himself in meditation. But this is *my* experience and I shall keep this to myself."

I pointed to the painting of the Moorish room next to the other two pictures.

"You'll know that soon enough. I want to sleep now. We have a busy day tomorrow. Goodnight."

I couldn't sleep although I was totally exhausted. Everything he told me, all the exercises we had been through, met in a whirling tornado which kept turning around in my head until everything slowly disappeared into a soft light, which grew more and more dark. I was losing my grip. Then I let go and slipped into the reality of the dream. It was totally quiet. The Moorish room with the white figure. I do not know what made me do it. Maybe it was the narrow streak of light under the door from outside. Neither do I know how it happened, but suddenly I was at the door, opening it. The hinges creaked. The door was heavy and slow as if it hadn't been opened for a long time. I opened it wide. The noise

from outside was deafening and the sunlight blinding. A big square filled with stalls. I stepped into the scorching sun and tried to find my bearings. It was overwhelming and I almost panicked. Then I started to run.

10

Everything was quiet when I woke up. My alarm clock showed half past five. I stayed in bed and listened to the silence. Then I remembered the dream and tried to recall what had happened after I stepped into the Andalusian marketplace. What had made me run? Where did I run to?

I got out of bed and walked out on to the balcony into the no-man's-land between night and day where the gritty light made everything look as if it were made of marzipan. Through an opening between the houses I could see the misty, white waves of the light green Mediterranean Sea, silently and monotonously massaging the pale, ghostlike beach. Somewhere close, a woman was singing the same note, almost chant-like, spellbindingly and manically repeating it over and over again as if she wanted to warn the still sleeping town of a destiny beyond their control, which on this specific morning had disguised itself as a tall, stooping shadow desperately floating through the streets unable to find its way home. A fire was burning in that voice. A fire, which once and for all made it clear that singing is older than language. Once again I was standing at the edge of the endlessness of memory not knowing if it was mine, if it belonged to eternity or whether it was just another Andalusian mirage twirling in the wind behind the numbing veil of oblivion. I went inside in order to participate in the first quiet lesson of the day.

The telephone rang precisely at eight a.m. The Seer was deeply concentrated. I was in the kitchen but had been told not to make breakfast, neither tea nor coffee. It was the day of fast. Only water was allowed. It looked like a tough day. He had planned on using most of the afternoon for bringing the dead German man to the other side. Before that, he insisted that there should be time for me to receive the instructions for the day. He was pale when he returned from his consultations. I was ready with the glass of salt water that he had requested. I considered suggesting that we take the afternoon off so that he could save his strength for later, but realized that it wasn't necessary to say this aloud. He nevertheless ignored it.

"The kind of movement of the inner spheres that I'm talking about has been absent from human beings far too long. Man can be intellectual, spiritual, political, artistic, highly educated, rich or anything really. These aspects only tell you something about the degree of limitation the specific person is living under, more than it is telling you anything about who this person is. When manager this or professor that comes to me, and he is dying and he doesn't know where else to go, it gets very clear that these titles and these medals and all these ambitions are often part of the disease. I must then make some radical corrections. At that moment all the external and vain imaginings are seen in sharp contrast to the essential, to that which really matters, such as who this person really is at his very core. Real liberation cannot happen before such a time. But you see, not many people want to acknowledge that. They cling to the medal and to their illusory estimation of their own selves as a shipwrecked man clings to the sinking ship."

He was watching me. The sounds from the street seemed unreal as if they belonged to another world. Then he continued:

"That is why you must know the power of thought. Thoughts do have consequences. Thoughts do create form. Considering pollution and the greenhouse effect, people forget that the flow of polluting thoughts is far greater and even more poisonous than the amount of greenhouse-gas. We have surrounded ourselves with so many layers of polluting thoughts that we have created a shield, which prohibits us from communicating purely with the universe. Instead, we are getting our own old and useless thought forms thrown back at us over and over again. It is developing into an evil circle. The movement is misdirected since it corrects the degree of the negative output only, which is reflected from all the unresolved, negative thought forms that are limiting our ability to see. We must change that. An enormous amount of parallel work lies ahead of us on both the personal and the collective level. Be always vigilant as to your motives. Be always willing, quite unprejudiced, to ask yourself why you do this and why you do that. Remember that everything you do, any thought, any action, will be followed by a reaction. *You* may not see it, but rest assured that someone somewhere will, and that you eventually must face the consequences. Not many people are aware of that. That is why someone throughout a whole lifetime may act on the basis of his or her own concept of good intentions without knowing that eventually, they will create negative results. In general, people do not think very much about their actions. So here is rule number one: Be conscious about your motives. Rule number two says: Let go of any kind of power. When you let go of any ambition demanding: *I want this! This is mine!* The doors will open. You will then automatically take the next step into the true, universal flow. It really hurts to notice all the limitations that man's idea of happiness, money and prestige bring forth. It is very sad. Abundance will always be present in the universe, but what does it help if man misses his opportunities and refuses to see them? The universe is on the lookout for the thoughts of man. Here is our option. All it requires is our openness. In spite of man's sophisticated way of life he still reacts primitively, but in such a specialized way that, without realizing it, he escapes the openness that I'm talking about. He sees enemies everywhere since he is projecting his unresolved thought forms onto his surroundings. The universe is looking for friends. The universe is neutral. Pure, living, moving. It contains everything. Therefore: renounce everything that implies a demand for power. Then the universe will open up."

He got up and nodded casually towards the painting of the Moorish room which I visited in my dream:

"I see that there is already an opening."

He went into the kitchen to get more water.

Now I also noticed what I didn't see earlier. Something had changed. Something was missing. The woman in white was gone. I got up to have a closer look at the painting. I let my finger slide across the paint where the figure had been. I saw that the door was now ajar and that a ray of light fell on the Arabian tile floor in the foreground of the painting. I felt dizzy. Did I forget to close the door properly after me? It had just been a dream. Or? Had I lost my way and not returned yet? I sat down on the sofa before he returned from the kitchen. He smiled his familiar smile.

"You look as if you could use some water."

He poured from a large carafe before continuing his lecture.

"The concept God is a metaphor for the highest awareness, the highest form of energy which we are all part of. Therefore we are all gods or the children of God if you like. We are created to move others. But, of course, this depends on the fact that we are aware of our true origins and true purpose. Time is ripe to let go of our old concepts. The used-up myths. The worn-out time. Time is ripe to leave the heavy thought forms behind us in return for some much faster vibrations. This is done partly by cleansing our present thought forms and by changing the old. We originate from basic matter, we were created from the first picture, primordial matter. It is everywhere but has its origin outside the universe."

"What does the matter consist of?"

"Consciousness. Pure consciousness. It contains unconditional, unsentimental and pure love. The energy form above all energy forms."

"You showed me how it works, but when I try to activate the energies myself nothing happens. I do have my moments, my loopholes and all that which I can't master by myself. How do I control the process myself?"

"First of all by letting go of your wish for control. That is why I keep returning to the most basic practices and ideas. If you think that the lessons become more and more difficult, you are wrong. It is the basic work, such as everything that most people skip, which is the most difficult part because it demands more renunciation, more concentration, more patience, more courage, more strength and more humour than most people are able to muster. There are no shortcuts to paradise. There are no other solutions that are easier or more simple than these. If only people would realize that. When finally we understand this, I mean really understand, then it is the simplest thing ever. Because it is universal. Cosmic. And this is what the practices are for. Liberating the universal, cosmic man from all the traumas, the neuroses, projections and all other unnecessary luggage that we are carrying with us. You are beginning to understand. That is why you are here now. When you resolve the old patterns you also resolve time. Time and space are thought forms. Time doesn't necessarily extend. It is not necessarily horizontal. And the concept of space is man's beautiful but impossible attempt to encircle and secure *something*. Imagine that there are seven levels each with seven steps, then imagine that the level of vibration rises for each step, while at the same time, time as we know it is disintegrated. The way you yourself experienced it on Montségur when we experimented with time as we passed through the Gate of Time. Try to remember how heavy you felt before we started, and how day by day you felt lighter and lighter, how your vibrations became faster and faster. This was where you experienced the disintegration of time. When you get back to your daily routine it becomes difficult to be present. But it is an act of balance that you have to learn. It is the art of being here. It can be a very hard job to stay grounded when you have started to loosen up and to let go. Time doesn't exist on the seventh level. Then, you simply *are*. Man transcended.

We strolled along the promenade. The wind had died down. It had started to drizzle instead. We passed one depressing concrete hotel after the other. At the end of the promenade we stood for a long time looking out across the sea. Far out to sea we saw something that looked like a small ship being lifted and then disappearing into a trough of the waves just to appear again a moment later. I remembered the tale about the world traveller in a small steam-driven ship who had run out of fuel in the middle of the ocean and who had to stoke the boiler with wood from the hull of the ship. Was this traveller me, I wondered? We turned and walked toward the town. The Seer was silent and I knew that he was preparing for the task ahead. But I sensed that this moment was important, like everything else that he was a part of. We walked in the same rhythm. I sensed that I was part of a larger cycle. A common breathing forming a circle, a free area, an opening where the energies were flowing freely. Even the simple task of walking became an act of the universe. We walked and we walked. Across the town, around it and back again through unknown streets and quarters. With my inner eye I saw the world traveller in his boat, which by now had been reduced to a few planks that barely could keep him and the steam engine afloat. The dissolution of self?

We stopped in front of the bullring of the town, Plaza de Toros. I followed the Seer through the gate and the corridor into the arena. No one to be seen. Raindrops made fine, dotted patterns on the dark yellow dirt of the arena. As if it was the most natural thing in the world he opened a small gate and walked into the arena of death.

"Come on." he said, and started walking.

The sound of his voice echoed back from the empty auditorium. I followed. He stopped at the centre of the arena.

"If you'll just stay here, I'll leave the stage to you."

I looked at him uncomprehendingly. I had no idea what he was talking about. He kept walking toward a gate at the other end of the arena. Something was pushing against the gate from the other side. Something which made disconcerting noises. I couldn't help smiling. I simply refused to finish the thought. Although he might be unpredictable and although with him I always had to expect the unexpected, it couldn't be this. I watched him as he pulled the chains from the iron rings holding the gate in place. He slowly pushed the gate against the balustrade. I was staring into the dark shade of the opening and thought that something was moving. I couldn't believe it. The arena disappeared around me and left me floating in a yellow room.

A huge, black and shining bull was standing in the gateway. I was about to call out to the Seer but it didn't really matter now. I couldn't see him. I was frozen to the spot. My brain worked at full speed. Automatically I was considering the odds. Would I be able to find cover behind the barrier or was this giant faster than I could imagine? Would it refrain from attacking if I stood stock still? The situation was totally surreal. Insanely ridiculous. It defied any sound reasoning. It almost looked like a cartoon without the redeeming text, which might put the craziness into perspective. The bull took one step forward. Now I could really see how big it was. A beautiful animal, which in these circumstances and in a man's mind suddenly became a symbol of evil incarnated. Now it smelled me. I shivered. Suddenly, nothing mattered. Montségur, the Grail, the Seer and all his games. Right there, at this moment, I would have given anything to get out of there in order to save my hide. The bull lowered his head and scraped with one front leg in the gravel. I looked around for the Seer in despair, but he wasn't there. That was when it took off. I watched the wide open and snorting nostrils, I watched the gravel spraying from his hooves as they dug down, leaving secret and momentous signs. Everything happened in slow-motion. I could see every muscle on the bull's neck, tense and resilient, spreading over its broad chest where the sweat formed an armour of white foam. My scream got stuck in my throat. I closed my eyes. Then I reacted, turned my body around but far too slowly. My shoes slipped on the gravel as I wanted to take off. At that moment I heard a voice in my head wordlessly saying: "Walk towards me. Have no fear. Walk towards me!" I opened my eyes. Thousands of years of projections came at me, thundering and snorting, with flaming eyes and lowered horns. NOW! — NOW! I took one step forward. The bull ran straight through me. I felt nothing.

I turned around in order to see where it had gone, but it had disappeared like morning dew. In the auditorium a single figure was applauding me.

"Olé."

It was the Seer.

"Olé."

I sank slowly down onto the arena floor. Among the dots of rain in the dirt only the Seer's and my own footprints could be seen.

We sat down under an awning at a bar across from the bullring. The Seer asked for water and salt. I could feel that he paid more attention to my reactions than usual.

"Many years ago somewhere in Italy the thought form of Yeshua came to me. He said: "Why didn't you help me?" It was so simple and pure, so free of any accusation and judgement that it made me cry. You see, I was completely aware of what he meant. It was a reminder of all my major failures over the years. It was not an accusation but more of a cleansing. At that moment I realized how I had turned my back on him then, thinking that he had to deal with this himself. Yeshua was both a superhuman and an intensified force. His energies and the thought forms were so pure that his presence alone was sufficient to make things happen. He was pure. Completely pure. Showing himself to me I could see that he knew that I had known but had still not helped him. I then understood that there is nothing wrong with Yeshua or Christ, but with the church and Christianity. They have twisted everything. We must help him, it is not up to *him* to help us. He is carrying the pure energy. That is why. Yeshua has no message as such. He was just pure. This was his single message. He had no special abilities as such, but things happened around him *because* he was pure. He was also purely isogynic. An example to be followed. *Ecce homo.* Look – this is how man can be. Yeshua was an earthly incarnation. Christ is a universal, cosmic consciousness. Christ is a choice. Christ is man's access to earthly life, a gate of consciousness. Christ consciousness is in us all. Just like the Grail."

He sprinkled salt into his glass of water and drank.

"Also many years ago in Switzerland I experienced the thought form of Adolf Hitler appearing. He asked to be understood. He had misunderstood his task but had performed it nevertheless. Do you remember that you describe something like that in one of your books, where you experience that Adolf Hitler comes to you in a dream asking you for help? He is just a small, orphaned boy. A victim himself. Some of that was dissolved through you. Some of the thought form was cleansed through you. We all take part in the cruelty of the world. Even when we think that we know nothing about it. We all carry a Hitler and a Yeshua in us. At one time or another each person must stop and face his own failures and cruelties. Otherwise they are just projected on. It has to stop somewhere. It has to stop where forgiveness starts. All the world's dictators, whatever their names, all the concepts that we have decided are identical with evil, just like the bull today, are simply expressions of our own projections. It doesn't make sense. It doesn't justify anything, it simply tells us about our common heritage. We all take part in the cruelties. You have taken your part upon you today. You have moved from fear to freedom.

Walking back along the promenade we looked across the sea. The waves had settled down. The small ship was nowhere to be seen.

After our quiet hour the Seer prepared to guide the deceased through *The Shaft of the Soul.* I followed him into his office. As usual he started without any hesitation. I knew that I had to be wide awake and that my total attention was required if I should have any hope of being present through this. The Seer let one of his hands hover over his desk. I closed my eyes. Inside myself the sea was like a well-waxed floor polished by an eternal breath. The exhalation spread out and flowed into nothingness inventing the corners of the world and the lines and shapes of everything. It filled the void with sounds and presence for aeons. At the end of darkness light was born. In the beautiful void the eternal NOW. Then inhalation poured back through endless time filling space with memory and new life. A golden sea of light. The memory of the initial state. The dense sound of the universe. The harmonic principle of all notes.

A single, tall, stooping figure is waiting on the beach. It is the deceased. He is almost lost in the dense fog and seems confused and scared. A burning compassion for this person. I want to call out to him, that there is no need to be afraid, help is on its way. Then a shushing finger touches my mouth. A boat approaches through the fog. The Seer is standing upright in it. He says something to the deceased, which I cannot hear, and helps him onboard. They disappear in the fog.

I then hear a new note being struck. Îkhal — Ephatah a voice chants.
Îkhal — Ephatah! The voice grows clearer. I recognise the insistent
sound with the same light green colour as the sea, the same pale colour
as the beach, the same prickly sensation as rain against the skin, the
same spellbinding element of prayer as the woman I heard singing in
the morning.

I opened my eyes. The Seer was in deep concentration. I could
now hear that the voice of the singing woman came from outside. I
tried to repress it and to find my way through the fog, back to the
memory in the great breath, but in vain. I gave up and slipped out
of the office.

Two hours later the Seer had ended his work. He was pale but
clearly relieved.

"Did you come along?" he asked.

I explained what I had experienced and he nodded
understandingly.

"There is progress. Your sight is clearer than the last time. I'll try
to explain the process as well as it may be done in words."

He drank the glass of salt water, which I had prepared for him.

"It is important that the deceased is left in peace for sixty eight
hours after dying so that the person in question has discarded all
his bodily elements. Then you are ready for moving through the
shaft. Before leaving I ask if there is anything unfinished, something
that has not yet been realized and accepted and therefore cannot be
resolved. It is not an easy process. It demands great care, empathy
and poise. On the walls of *The Shaft of the Soul* you see pictures
of the life, recently ended. We stop and look at the pictures that
call for special attention, pictures of conflicts and trials from this
incarnation. I ask if the deceased understands the pictures and is able
to acknowledge the motives he acted from in the various situations.
When the picture is understood I ask if the deceased is ready to let it
go. Major things only are pictured in the shaft. Working our way up
there are fewer pictures. There both is and isn't any sense of space in
the shaft. It is very difficult to describe. You experienced this yourself
at Montségur. It is a kind of picture gallery where you are turning
and watching the various pictures. It is in a way holographic. When

the process of acknowledgement is finished and has turned into acceptance, you rise into a fantastic, intense light just before reaching the spiritual levels. Here the Collector is waiting, a ball-like thought form, collecting everything that you didn't bring with you, everything that wasn't redeemed. When I accompany the deceased we usually deal with it on the way. The deceased and I together correct the unresolved pictures and neutralize all the obstacles. If a helper isn't present, or if people do not know what is going on in *The Shaft of the Soul* before they die, they may react to the pictures they are presented with without understanding, and do not do what is necessary before moving on. All pictures are collected in what I call the Collector. This is where one is met with a light more intense than the sun, but with a softness that enables us to see it. Here you meet the two pillars of light – guardians – about the same height as a human being. Then the voyage goes on to the spiritual levels. We do not bring the pictures there. There is no need for them. On the contrary. Later, on the way back to the level of earth we pass the Collector again, going down into another *Shaft of the Soul*, confronting the pictures, which were not resolved in the former life. We bring them with us into the new incarnation, where they influence us in one way or another. If we realize this here, we may practise in the sense that everyday we may ask if there is anything we should have done which we didn't do, or if we did something that we shouldn't have done. As far as I am concerned it is a part of my daily work to look at my own pictures in order to correct and hopefully to constantly be in harmony with the universal principles and the work I'm here to perform. It is a guarantee for me to be precise in my work with other people. And there is always something that needs calibration. Everything is in eternal motion so that the pictures, which were calibrated in the morning, may need a new calibration in the evening. It is quite unbelievable how little it takes for things to tilt one way or the other. The idea that the wing of a butterfly should have an effect on the weather on the other side of the globe is thus very descriptive of my point. When we have redeemed all our pictures we have finished incarnating here on earth. The earth level is a school. We are talking about a refinement process where we must learn to be conscious co-workers in this universe, so that later we can do the same in the others."

"Where does man originate?"

"The earth is a half-way-house. Man originates in the universe. The process of evaluation is firstly and lastly about consciousness and awareness. We are on the earth right now, but we belong to primordial matter, the universal consciousness, the eternal thought form."

The Seer went to bed early. I stood for a long time in front of the painting of the Moorish room before I turned in as well. There was no sign of the figure in white. The door was still ajar.

II

It was daylight when I woke up. The rays of the sun fell through the wide-meshed curtains and formed arabesques on the wall. Listening to the sounds outside I knew that I had slept too long. Slightly confused I got up and took a bath. The Seer had already started his consultations. When he finished we had our compulsory stand-up breakfast in the kitchen. All morning he drummed the principles of distant healing into me. It was difficult for me to concentrate and my thoughts flew here and there. This just made him intensify his teaching. It was a relief when the clock struck twelve.

"You look as if you could do with a change. Let us have some lunch."

We drove towards Marbella along *la Carretera de la Muerta*. He parked in a multi-storey car park situated near one of the many fashionable malls, where designer goods and prizes competed for the impertinence award. If material poverty existed in Marbella it was very well hidden. The only person apart from the two of us who stuck out like a sore thumb in these surroundings was a young gipsy woman in a washed-out, flowery dress walking down the main street. She was so beautiful, and moved with such grace, that everyone had to stop and turn to admire her. We continued towards Puerto Banús.

"This is where some of the richest people meet. The Spaniards call it the playground of the rich. Almost everyone here is a foreigner. The Andalusians come here only to work in the bars and the restaurants."

An impressive marina was spread out as far as you could see. One enormous vessel next to the other. Onboard some of them were uniformed crewmembers of North African descent busy varnishing masts, scrubbing decks or polishing brass. Red carpets covered the gilded gangways. Cars worth millions were parked side by side along the pier. Well-groomed and sun-tanned men and women in expensive fashion clothes were having lunch outside six-star restaurants. We found a table under an awning in front of a small Moroccan bar at the outskirts of the promenade. The Seer asked for pastis and water.

"Look around. Look at all the yachts. Some of them the size of ferry boats. Look at the cars. All this represents energy. But they are locked forms of energy. They have no value in and of themselves. It is just money. A dead weight without any use. The ships are seldom out sailing. They simply stay moored at the pier as a symbol of the wealth of the owner. Just like the cars. Look at the one getting out of the Ferrari. This is the moment that matters to those who come here. We are the ones who at this moment may watch this man walk from his extremely expensive car to an even more expensive yacht, just to give a silent command to one of the uniformed crew in order to be seen by us and others here. He is not going anywhere. He is certainly not going sailing. He is only confirming his own and our insatiable need for confirmation and material security. The irony is, that on the other side of the Mediterranean on the northern coast of Africa, they really want to go sailing. So much so that they are quite satisfied even with a battered rubber dingy. Every night they come ashore along the Spanish Riviera, if they get that far, only to be sent back. It may cost them as much as their life savings. Or their lives. At the same time we are sitting here with our drinks contemplating life."

"What are we doing to change all this?"

"Well, you can't do it just like that. We must follow the universal laws. We must let go of sentimentality and try to live up to our own dignity, or what is left of it. What we consider a social privilege and an imbalance is connected to karma. This of course, doesn't mean that we should refrain from reacting to other people's misfortunes, since this is our dharmic challenge, considering the fact that we are well off materially. The thought forms of greed are the greatest curse of the Western World. Therefore, money must also be transformed into a universal means in order to represent real values to be used in the service of good causes. Everything may be misused. When you let go of the power of money, when you refuse to be obsessed by it, when you work in harmony with the universe, you will never lack anything. When in the beginning I charged people for my treatments, I sometimes thought that I should increase the amount, since I didn't charge very much. I thought that since people are willing to pay three thousand for a bicycle, they should be willing to pay something to improve their health. But no. I was immediately told from above that I shouldn't do that. I only needed enough money to sustain a living. That's how it was. The moment I accepted this I never needed anything. And it has been like that ever since. This is how I understand the energy of money. This is how it works. Let all your worries about money go. Life is too short to waste on things like that. Establish your life so that you are not burdened with the dead weight of material things. Do not make yourself a slave of consumption and expensive habits. Always be ready to let go of material possessions. Everything on earth is borrowed. This way you will always be able to move and be free."

He pushed the brim of his straw hat up with the point of his finger. We ordered fried eggplants.

"In this way you become one with the universal pulse. In this way you may be one hundred percent present without being burdened by heavy trivialities. The beautiful dona in the main street a minute ago, the one that everybody turned around to see, was a good example of being present unconsciously. There was an incredible ease in her bearing, while at the same time she conquered the space and the sidewalk in a very feminine and earthly way. It was obvious, that the way she walked, the swinging of her hips, her agility, the bearing of her back and the back of her neck, was a song to the present. She was present in the moment. As soon as she was seen, everything artificial, all illusions and all the props came tumbling down. All the fashion clothes and all the expensive jewellery lost their value. Her mere presence cancelled out all that was false. It was pure art."

The waiter served the grilled eggplants covered with a layer of minced garlic and parsley stirred in olive oil. On the side we had homemade humus and pita bread with fresh salad.

"When you are imprisoned by money and material slavery and feel down, it can be very difficult to imagine a way out. Instinctively you know that it involves a good deal of problems because it demands a confrontation with personal pride and the masks you hide behind. But it doesn't have to be either painful or difficult. It takes humour to be a spiritual person. Humour is elegant. It transforms and opens up. Sarcasm, however, freezes up and closes. Sarcasm is just an extension of the smallness of limited man. Humour comes from the heart. When I started out as a healer I always diagnosed the clients the day before they were to arrive. One day I had diagnosed a client as suffering from some kind of problem in the right ovary. When next morning I found out that the client was a man I nearly collapsed with laughter. When I told the client why, he also fell about laughing, and I do believe that this is the only client I have had where the problem was solved with the help of humour alone. It was a very liberating and worthwhile experience. Humour is first and foremost the ability to look at oneself in a disarming light. It takes humour to be able to go out into the universes and ask questions. And it takes elegance to be here. It's like a dance. A cosmic dance. The higher the levels the more dance and humour you need. This is how you can be present, moving and dancing."

"What happens in this dance?"

"You leave your personality behind. Otherwise you cannot communicate through energies."

"You are neutral then?"

"Oh, I wouldn't call it that. It is more like a state of nonpersonality."

His warm laughter made people turn around.

"It's a fantastic feeling. It is like touching your transpersonal consciousness, looking at this consciousness while you are looking. It is indescribably beautiful and it makes me laugh every time. Sometimes I really must make an effort. I reach an edge, and I must say, OK, this is humour. I like that. At this level all the heavy stuff, all the slow stuff is resolved and you feel so relieved."

He beamed like the sun. I could see that here was a direct line to his innermost being.

"It is deeply serious but in a light and elegant, dancing and humorous way." Beyond all words and concepts. To move *along with* the energies. In spite of all the dark matter, which I call complementary matter, the universe is full of humour and lightness."

I was thinking that what he had just said was similar to the words of a Christian mystic: "I now see that the eyes through which I see God are the same eyes through which God sees me." I understood that the isogynic condition to which the Seer had introduced me might be identical to the words of Yeshua in *The Gospel of Thomas*: "When you make the two into one, and when you make the inner like the outer and the outer like the inner, and the upper like the lower, and when you make male and female into a single one, so the male will not be male and the female will not be female ... then you will enter the Kingdom."

The Seer continued:

"You're an elegant person. You claim your right to move. In order to be able to do that, you are aware that you must phase out your personality, such as your ambitions to be someone in the musical field. All the outer stuff. If you are going to open completely and uncompromisingly to the energies, there is no room for a personality which first and foremost is tied to worldly ambition. I've also been phasing out for a long while. It really takes humour. This is how you become a cosmic dancer. That's the way it is with the writing you are going to do. You won't write for anyone or to gain anything. You will be writing a book. You won't tell people how they are but simply give them an option. Your task is to tell about the options that are available. Without setting conditions. Man – think! That's all."

He became silent and looked at me with the long glance that I had come to know so well. He looked right through me. The galaxies rotated.

"You never belonged to anyone. Because your thoughts were extraordinary, you didn't want to limit yourself. You have always known, through your observations which were crystal like, that you had access to some thought forms which were extraordinary. Then the abhorrence of other people's opinions arose. Opinions that you couldn't accept. Their battle to become something special didn't interest you at all. You were used by others during the incarnations immediately preceding this one. Your abilities were exploited, until the day you stated that you didn't have any money, no dignity, nothing. Going back before the incarnations it gets a bit more vague since we are talking about some very extreme thought forms. In the first picture of you time does not exist. You *knew*. Your sophistication then, before all the incarnations, was not of the earth. You have always been a stranger here. The refined being who didn't want to communicate. You knew then that you wouldn't be understood if you opened up your potential. Thus your loneliness increased through the incarnations. You were not allowed to tell. You have always been on the lookout for your own language. But that language has never been accepted. Nobody understood. That is why you are a cripple on this earth. You have now found your forgotten language. The language that can move. You are getting close to a state of mind where you are able to be present. Of course you have taken drugs. I would have done the same in your place. In order to get back, in order to start all over again. You have been used through all your incarnations. You were an itinerant singer here in Spain. During this incarnation you have been a singer in Denmark and have tried to be present in this way, but without success. You are too extreme. You didn't get close to a common consciousness. You are not plain. Your elegance is in your thought forms, and not very many have been able to fathom and accept those. You have never been present."

He ordered more water and pastis.

"The new man knows what it means to be a non-personality. This is the point when you are willing to ask the question: "Who am I not?"

Assuming of course that you know who you are, and which masks you have been hiding behind at a behavioural, psychological level. True being can only come from non-being, the same way that sound can only come from silence and light from darkness. The concept of the great emptiness of non-existence is simply an illusion, just as personality is, seen in a universal perspective. The emptiness you experience in connection with the phasing out of your personality is in reality the fullness from which all living things are created."

He stopped talking in order to make sure that I knew what he was talking about. I nodded and he continued:

"It is both beautiful and touching when a person, for the first half of his life, fights his own battle in order to fulfil all his dreams and ambitions of being someone. But in a way it is also sad, because this battle takes him away from his real destiny. The ambitions and the dreams are in command. If they are fulfilled they simply create further, transient dreams. If they remain unfulfilled they bind the person. That is why I always recommend that young people realize or phase out the ambitions of the "I," before they get too old. Such a development is in fact a prerequisite to all that I'm talking about and all that we are working with. The most efficient way of breaking that kind of power is to say: "I am not!" This is an enormous quantum leap. Imagine the freedom when you are nobody and you do not want to be anybody, you are simply present, freed from all demands and illusions. Do not confuse this with escape. On the contrary, it is a higher state, a state where your consciousness is expanded, the perfect way of being present. Through my work I can see how much of the known medicine is not working anymore, and therefore I have the feeling that a new human being is on its way. The energies of man have moved somewhat. I see it in the electromagnetic fields. All the energies in the universe are moving closer. Thus, it is my opinion that basic matter will play a decisive roll in the lives of the new human being, since basic matter is found both in man and in the universe. Man must also find out how to be present in a new way. He must transform the backlog of old energies and thought forms which are imprisoning him. Man is so busy *being something* in order to be able to say that he has a personality with these or those qualifications, one who has made a lot of money has done this or that etc. This insistence on your own space and all your illusions and the artificial jewels is static and limiting. Thus, man is reducing himself to merely a survivor, one who is clinging to life like a dead weight. Then he doesn't dance. Man must be willing to step out into the unknown and risk himself where he cannot hide behind his own prejudices and projections, but, totally clean, make himself available to the universal principle. Man is a transformer, a channel for the universal, where the energies are transformed. This is his destiny. When man understands that, he becomes free and pliant and he thus transforms himself into *one big open moment.*"

He raised his glass as a sign that the lecture was over.

"Pastis!"

Coming back to the apartment we practiced an hour of silence. I sat down in the living room and tried to connect to the concentration of energies that the Seer had activated. I knew that the ability to disregard any imagination, any demand and any prejudice was the first prerequisite for it to happen. Oppenheimer once said that it was easier to split an atom than our prejudices. The Seer said that we must distinguish between the instinctive level, where we are driven by our needs and our egocentricity, and the intuitive level, where we are sympathetic and compassionate. The difference between the two levels is a question of to what degree you master your own thoughts. When the hour had passed the Seer came in with a bottle of red wine and a single glass. He must have read my thoughts as usual as he began the lesson for the afternoon:

"I have mentioned the importance of the correct use of the power of thought earlier. We shall now conduct an experiment which will show you the practice of my theory."

He pulled the cork and poured some wine into the glass standing in front of me.

"Please taste it."

I lifted the glass, took a sip, then nearly spat it out again – it was that sour. It tasted like straight vinegar. He smiled teasingly.

"Well, this may not be the most exquisite wine you can imagine.

To tell you the truth it is a kind of cheap wine they use in the making of a kind of marinade that I do not know. But put the glass down and let me see if I can do something about that."

I did as I was told. He sat for a while piercing the glass with his long glance.

"Now taste it!"

Lifting the glass to my mouth I immediately sensed that the wine had changed its scent. I tasted it. It was soft and rounded like a vintage wine of the best quality.

It was amazing. Still, I had stopped being surprised by anything that was to do with him. Instead I just said the first thing that came into my mind:

"Water to wine, or vinegar to wine!"

"More like wine to you," he said laughing.

"What you have witnessed here is a refinement process. As you see, it was very simple. The power of thought works. You can do this with all foodstuffs. This is how you bless a meal. By giving it energy. It is a good idea to get used to giving everything you eat the same energy as your own. This way your body gets no surprises. Then there are no toxins. Poison is also thoughts. That's the way it is. That is why it can be influenced. Instead of saying grace it is a good idea to ask the food you are about to eat to be with you. No matter what it is. You just send your thought into it and visualize a gas blue colour. Thus you make sure that the energies harmonize with your body. The gas blue colour belongs to the physical part. To the organs. Then follows the superior part, the spiritual part, the golden colour. These are the two colours that definitely work for the new man. The old chakra colours have lost their value. The problem is, that although we understand intellectually what is good and what is bad for us and can decide that we want to change things, centuries of influences are locked into the memory of the body, each and every cell, which may result in various diseases if we do not make the proper corrections. There are two colours, which are completely safe: the gas blue for the physical part in every chakra and the golden for the spiritual part. You can mix them or alternate between them. Then see what happens. See how the vibrations get going."

We worked the rest of the afternoon with visualization exercises. From neutralizing acids in coffee and removing tensions in the back of the neck to sending noticeable energy to the chakras. It was incredibly simple when you took it seriously. Over and over he pointed out how important it is that you set yourself aside in order to connect one hundred percent purely with the matter or the person to whom you want to send energy.

"Fear is the basic concept which blocks pure communication. Fear arises from ignorance. The unconscious thought forms have a tendency to run amok, and then all hell breaks loose. Fear is an expression of limitation. Fear may also be a basic condition in the universal archives. But only because an individual, through his various incarnations, has not been able to dissolve this thought form. Then it grows, builds up and gets out of control. It is a widely spread disease of our time. But what is there to be afraid of? What is the worst that can happen? That you are going to die? We all have to die it is just a matter of time. At the cosmic level it may be a matter of a build-up of energies, which haven't been dealt with. It may be energies, which need attention and help. In the cosmos there is no judgement over light and darkness. Good and evil are qualities that we give the energies. They do not express an either-or principle but they are always mutually interactive. Some thought forms may be linked to a specific basic matter belonging to certain types of star which may therefore interact with humans. We are counterparts of the stars."

It was late before we had supper. Although I was tired it was a kind of tiredness that felt more like being relaxed. I was not at all in doubt that this was also part of the Seer's work with me. It was not strange therefore, that after supper he suggested that we should go to a jazz club.

The club was situated in an alleyway in the tourist area of the town. There were hardly any visitors because of the time of year. A single couple was sitting at the long, narrow and dimly lit bar looking deeply into each other's eyes. The bartender polished the glasses for the umpteenth time. A piano player was playing jazz standards on a grand piano on a raised platform to the rear of the room. We sat down at a table near the exit. The Seer asked for water only but paid for it as if it were alcohol. After an hour there were about ten, fifteen guests in the room. The Seer smiled but said nothing. I didn't suspect any mischief. We were just listening to the music. The air in the room was getting thick with smoke. There was a lazy yet tense atmosphere. Suddenly he leaned across the table:

"Are you at all interested in being present?"

The question hovered threateningly in the air. I sensed that something was coming. If I didn't know that there was a deeper meaning behind the question it would have made me insecure, the way I had experienced it when he confronted me with similarly challenging questions at Montségur.

"Yes," I said.

"Quite sure?"

"Yes!"

"There's a microphone on the piano. It's switched on. Why don't you go up and sing a song?"

I was more or less paralyzed. He could move at the speed of lightening, materialize bulls and make them disappear again, change vinegar into wine and all kinds of things. It was fantastic but it didn't surprise me anymore. This, however, was totally outrageous. This was crossing a line, which now became embarrassingly clear. On the other side of that line was a whole life of stage fright, the fear of not being sufficiently good, the fear of competition, the fear of failure, the fear of the little I and its false understanding of itself. Everything that I had tried to repress. I had counted on him to respect the fact that this subject would never be up for discussion. I knew now, that from the moment he had made the suggestion, nothing could change the fact that in a few minutes I would rise up, go forward, take the microphone and sing for these people. I knew that this was the only way to break the curse of fear.

It was like a dream. When I got up on the stage the piano player was already playing an intro. I was nobody. Just a man who happened to pass by. I took the microphone and sang into the corridor of oblivion:

My funny Valentine, sweet comic Valentine, you make me smile with my heart. Your looks are laughable, unphotographable, yet you're my favourite work of art. Is your figure less than Greek? Is your mouth a little weak, when you open it to speak? Are you smart? Don't change your hair for me. Not if you care for me. Stay, little Valentine, stay! Each day is Valentine's day ...

12

Each day is Valentine's day . . .

I put the microphone back on the grand piano. No reaction. The guests stared at me with empty eyes. I thanked the piano player, stepped down from the stage and walked through the narrow room. The Seer was no longer at the table. I walked towards the exit, pushed the door open and stepped into the burning heat.

I stood still in order to let my eyes get used to the sharp sunlight. The smell of cinnamon and roses mixed with the dancing dust swirling in the air over the bustling marketplace. I was at the square just outside Isathar's house. The door was ajar. I spotted her in the crowd. She smiled and gave me her most confident and passionate look. I wanted to take her in my arms and make love to her there and then, but I withstood the temptation. I turned my back on her and looked at the multicoloured view in front of me instead, in order to find a place to sing. People had come from the remotest corners of the Moorish kingdom to participate in the festivity. Even the Caliph of Granada had announced his arrival. All kinds of artists were to be seen: fortune-

tellers, animal trainers, female dancers, storytellers, singers, writers and calligraphers. I walked along stalls with all kinds of magnificent merchandise and commodities: beautifully woven materials from Mecca, spices from Cairo, sables and swords from Toledo, valuable things of gold and silver, beautifully bound manuscripts from Cordoba with the poetry of the prophets. Then it all fused into one. I do not remember anything else.

One day followed the next. But no two of them were alike. The further into the universe the Seer took me, the closer to the ground I got. However, it was not comparable to anything I had tried or even been close to before. It was a totally new way of being present. It opened me up to another kind of perception, a sharpened form of attention, which until now I had only experienced as holes in reality. The holes that I, on and off, had fallen through and sought shelter in. Thanks to the Seer these moments were now turning into tools that I could consciously make use of. The time was getting close where I would have to take over and bring everything he taught me into a new world. The teaching about the isogynic human being. But there was still something indefinable just below the surface. A memory. Something which for a long time had been in hiding behind an impenetrable veil, but, which was now unveiling and becoming visible in dreams and visions. An infinite number of small streams uniting into a river, which moved slowly toward the open sea.

I woke up early one morning and was sitting on the terrace. It had just stopped raining and the air was fresh and clean. I was just sitting there being present, when I noticed a raindrop hanging from the edge of a folded sunshade, shining like a diamond in the growing morning light. Getting close to it I noticed that it was reflecting everything around it, one hundred and eighty degrees. Looking into the raindrop I could see the wealth of microscopic life in it. It was a whole universe in itself, while at the same time it was connected to the larger universe it was reflecting. In a little while when the time was ripe it would fall and mix with the water forming a small pool at the foot of the sunshade. At that moment the drop of rain would stop being a drop. But it would still exist as water. During the day the sun would cause the water to evaporate and form a small cloud. Tonight the cloud would dissolve and fall like dew or like rain. And tomorrow morning I might once more be watching a drop on the edge of the Seer's sunshade. This was the working of the simple law of the disappearance and reappearance of everything that is. The cosmic cycle. *Gravity and grace.*

The clouds above me were opening up. The clouds which I knew contained the rain of memory. A drop here and drop there. The river was growing and becoming more and more majestic.

Indeed, he had met a stranger. He was right about that. But never in his life had he met anyone like this stranger. He had never heard anyone speaking in such simple and understandable terms about inconceivable things. The words that came out of this man's mouth tugged at his heartstrings. Right where the blood was dripping with all the new and incomprehensible things which had been so decisive, but which also in some inscrutable way had also brought him hope about another kind of life, hope that he might break through the fatal horizon. The words of this man had brought him to a state of tranquillity which he hadn't known since his earliest childhood. Like a mother breast-feeding her child, after which the child falls asleep in her arms full and tired.

"Perfect!" the man had said, — "just perfect!"

He didn't remember for how long he had stayed in this small community but it had been a staggering experience. He didn't understand. But he could feel it.

People who wanted to help. Generous people. People with no other weapons than the words they had at their disposal. He didn't understand them, but he felt them, and shortly after the pains in his chest had disappeared as suddenly as they had come.

But the day came when he had to move on, and they told him about the paradise he was looking for and that he might be able to find it among the Moors at Alhambra, but that the paradise he was really looking for would always be within his reach and that he didn't have to travel to get to it. But, since this was the way it seemed to be, they would have to let him go and they told him in what direction he should go. He then left the Pyrenees and travelled to the land of Spain.

This is what I wrote in one of my books three years before an angel sent me into the arms of the Seer. And there was more. Much more. I began to see that a major part of what I had written was not just about things that had happened, but also very much about things that were to come. I then remembered the Seer telling me that it was a matter of being it and writing it, furthermore he had suggested that, by accessing the memory I had to reinvent my forgotten language and I had to learn to see. I had to find a way of being present. A way back to life. This left only one last question. If life was the paper and man the pen, whose hand then was to take the pen and do the writing?

One day when the Seer and I were walking along the promenade, we continued our walk past the last of the hotels and building sites with only partly finished *appartementos* and into the poor part of the town, which more or less looked like a suburb. Washing was hanging from clothes-lines across the streets. A couple of prostitutes were offering their services at a street corner. Dogs roamed freely and behind the houses cockroaches the size of mice were scurrying in and out of the garbage piles. The sweet smell of rat poison mixed with the unmistakable stench from the overloaded sewer system. The houses moaned with euro disco and fandango. The sunlight was broken by a forest of TV aerials and satellite dishes and made the shadows flicker and dance a grotesque fandango in the narrow streets. We had walked for a while without talking. I had the feeling of walking next to myself – further and further into an unreal state of mind.

A dark skinned man crossed the street and disappeared into a small bar. I could hear Arabian music. The atmosphere of a repressed life within this maze-like quarter of the town somehow resembled the blacked out maze of my memory.

"This is the place in your memory you keep returning to without understanding or seeing the connection."

I didn't understand what he was talking about.

"What does this mean?"

We stepped into an old square filled with shaky tables and stalls. The sun was scorching. I squinted in order to see better. For a moment I thought I saw people dressed in foreign clothes, women in veils and flowing oriental robes, men in capes and turbans. The Seer walked into the throng of people. I followed. He stopped in the middle of the square.

"Take note of this place," he said.

The sun stood right above us. At the same moment, out of the corner of my eye, I saw the man from before coming out of the Arabian bar.

The Seer saw right through me. The black galaxies were turning through the universe. His voice was quite clear. But still, it felt as if he was talking to me from another era.

"We have stood here before, you and I."

The sentence echoed through the endless corridors of my memory. *We have stood here before, you and I — we have stood here before, you and I.* Something made me turn my head toward the bar. The rays of the sun reflected in a shining object and blinded me. I could just glimpse a dark figure standing outside.

"I have been waiting for this moment for a long time."

The voice ricocheted off the walls of the corridor. *This moment — this moment — this moment — this moment!* I had my doubts at first. But then I saw that it was true. The dark man was watching us. My eyes met his for a fraction of a second. In this fraction of a second I looked into a burning desert of stars and loneliness. Looked into … It was impossible. It couldn't be. Slowly he began moving towards us. I was about to signal to him when the Seer took my arm. Everything stood still. Like a held breath. Like a raindrop suspended in mid-air before disappearing into the sea. Then the man turned around and ran back towards the bar. He almost overturned a jewellery stall before disappearing through the door he had emerged from a little earlier. A young gypsy woman shouted after him. I wanted to say something but the words stuck in my throat. Then I lost sight of her. The Seer was quietly watching me. Everything happened so fast. Life continued around us. Then he pointed to a stall where a man was selling antique haberdashery and old bits and pieces, and said as if nothing had happened:

"I'm almost certain that this metal box contains something belonging to me."

We walked over to the stall. The man opened the metal box and took out an old silver coin and gave it to the Seer. They negotiated for a while. The Seer paid him. A little later he handed me the coin. On it was the image of a man crowned with laurels, a Roman. I could hardly believe my eyes. It was Marcus Aurelius.

"It looks as if everything is going to join here and now. It seems as if those up there are speaking quite loudly – and at the same time. And you really look as if you could do with a pastis."

I was still shaken when we returned to the apartment. On the wall of the living room, next to the old engraving of the emperor Aurelius, was the picture of the Moorish room. The woman dressed in white was still nowhere to be seen. Had she ever existed? Or was she Zoé the isogynic one, Prat the guardian of nature, Isathar the gypsy or the incarnation of all three? The mother, the earth mother, the maiden. The incarnation of the feminine principle. The Norns Urd, Verdante, Skuld? The isogynic duplicate in every human being?

The Seer placed a carafe of water on the table.

"The sexes find each other in their hidden half. A relationship between man and woman must first and foremost work as a mirror, in which both parts mutually integrate with each other, thus getting close to the isogynic state. Seen from a universal point of view, man has unfortunately reduced the relationship to a playground game called mum, dad and children. There are much more powerful forces at stake. If you look at the chakras, man is still stuck at the second chakra connected with sexuality. But according to the evolution and the cosmic laws man should really be at the thought form of the third chakra. We are still stuck in the remains of the previous millennia. That is why sexuality goes berserk so that man cannot control the sexual energy but ends up letting it control him. The result is that too much egotism is expressed and this is pulling in the wrong direction. Man has turned sexuality into a party game to fight off boredom. Our culture has worn out the concept of love. It is eradicated daily by the media, in commercials, songs, novels, movies and anywhere one can get away with it. Love doesn't get deeper just because it speaks with big, pink, lisping letters, does it now? Since we are so focused on this, more and more unclean thought forms are produced binding man instead of setting him free. Probably because it is so easy to lose yourself in sexuality. But losing oneself is not the same as transforming oneself. And this is the purpose of the union between woman and man."

I then turn around to look for Isathar but I cannot see her. At one of the stalls I spot a manuscript so beautifully made that I linger for a while admiring it. As I'm about to pick it up I am overwhelmed by a strong feeling. An inexplicable certainty makes me leave it where it is and walk on. Driven by unknown forces I'm moved along by the throng of people into a state of mind, which suddenly changes everything. Two men are talking to each other at a distance from me. It is as if my reality is torn apart. I am rooted to the spot. I have a feeling that I know them but I don't know from where. Now, one of them turns and spots me. His eyes shine like the sun and burn with fire. He is pointing at me. Are they men of the Inquisition? I feel panic spreading in me. I have no intention of waiting to find out who they are. I start running. Back to Isathar's house. I see nothing. Bump into everything. I hear a voice calling out my name. Isathar's voice? I cannot even calm down when I'm in Isathar's cool room with the door closed behind me. My heart is beating like mad. A sound at the door. A shadow in the opening. Isathar, Thank God. She looks at me, surprised.

"What happened?"

"Nothing," I said.

I don't want to talk about it. I want to forget everything. Maybe it is really just my own senses playing a trick on me? She doesn't look convinced. I walk over and hold her. She puts her arms around my neck. Slowly I loosen the hidden strings in the top of her white dress. She smiles in the darkness and lets me do what I want. I kiss her on the mouth. It is not easy to undress a woman. I touch her breasts lightly. Let my hands slide down along her back. Then she is standing in front of me as God created her. Shining. Vibrant. I let my cape fall to the floor and we both slide down together. I hold her close, I kiss her and sense her secretive scent of cinnamon. How could I ever forget that? How could I forget this creature opening herself so generously like a rose in bloom? I bow down and break the seal of the rose. Slowly we ride through a primitive land, heavy and bursting, towards distant horizons. Later the landscape opens up. It is summer and we are travelling through endless, foreign lands. I see a boy and a girl bathing in a stream. See the boy following the girl toward a lake. See them merge into each other, becoming one. See them lying side by side after growing old. Smiling very much aware that they are about to die. I look into the burning eyes of Isathar. She dissolves all my mistakes and all my deceits. I see the black galaxies glimmering. I arm the bow of the blue moon with the golden arrow of the sun. I let go and let myself fall. I fall freely and eternally through her timeless universe. To the secret of pain and light in her innermost being ... Zoé, Prat, Isathar.

Sophia — Hokhmah.

Nehwey sibyanak aykana d'shmaya aph b'arah. Let that happen on earth, which is written in between the stars. Unfold the light of the universe through us in harmony with universal laws. Never again shall anything keep us apart. From this moment on I shall always be free.

A few days later the Seer drove me to the railway station in Malaga. Waiting on the platform, he gave me a parcel. It was relatively heavy.

"This may be the answer to the questions you have been asking yourself for a long time."

The words were burning in the air. I knew that he saw me the way I am. I, on the other hand, saw the galaxies in his eyes floating quietly through the universes, hovering on the breath of timelessness. A memory disappearing in a grand, open moment. Liberated from any kind of limitation. He left without saying good-bye and without looking back. Elegant as always, dancingly present, moving everything. I had a lump in my throat and a tear in the corner of my eye. If he had seen this he would jokingly have told me that I was sentimental. I leaned out of the window of the compartment and saw him disappearing in the throng of people. A stream in a flood. A drop in the ocean.

The train lurched forward with a jerk. I opened the parcel. It contained a manuscript almost four hundred pages long. The main title was, "Kansbar, the Protector of the Grail."

Zoé, Prat, Isathar
What is hidden must be unveiled

And below, "Alhambra 1001." Then a small introduction. I started to read:

"Kansbar is not my real name. But due to the secrets I have been chosen to guard, I have taken this old, Persian name. Kansbar the Chosen One. Kansbar the Wise. Kansbar the Seer. Kansbar, the Protector of the Grail. I am getting old. For many years I have been searching for the one who is to take over this duty after me. But in vain. Not until now do I remember the day I met Flegetanis, an itinerant Moorish singer, at a marketplace in a small town on the coast of Andalusia. This manuscript is for him. This is the story of the Grail."

I put the manuscript down. A slight electric current ran up my spine. It felt like a fine tension slowly spreading its energy all through my body. I just saw the sun setting behind the mountains before the train roared into the endless tunnel of memory. *Rukha d'koodsha — malkoota d'shmaya, Rukha d'koodsha — malkoota d'shmaya, Rukha d'koodsha — malkoota d'shmaya.*

BOOK II

THE MAGDALENE

To my beloved
Githa

The heights that the climb may lead you to
are in proportion to the depths to which
you are willing to delve

0

The train started with a jerk. I opened the parcel. It contained a manuscript almost four hundred pages long. The main title was, "Kansbar, the Protector of the Grail." And below, "Alhambra 1001." Then a small introduction:

"Kansbar is not my real name. But due to the secrets I have been chosen to guard, I have taken this old, Persian name. Kansbar the Chosen One. Kansbar the Wise. Kansbar the Seer. Kansbar, the Protector of the Grail. I am getting old. For many years I have been searching for the one who is to take over this duty after me. But in vain. Only now do I remember the day I met Flegetanis, an itinerant Moorish singer, in a marketplace in a small town at the coast of Andalusia. This manuscript is for him. This is the story of the Grail."

Back in Denmark I immediately started to write the manuscript, which later became the book: *The Andalusian Seer.* I was so occupied with this task for the first few months that I forgot all about the old Andalusian manuscript, which the Seer had left in my care. If the sun one day hadn't sent its rays onto my bookcase and more or less pointed to the manuscript with an insisting finger, it is hard to say how long it might have stayed there collecting dust. Now I took it, opened it with a pounding heart and started to read:

"There once was a king's daughter who came from far away, and no one knew whence she had come but they saw that she was unique, beautiful and wise in everything she did, and they were astonished when they saw that she was surrounded by 32 rays of golden light. They said, "She is truly born by the light since the world is enlightened through her deeds." They asked her, "Where do you come from?" She answered, "From my own place." They said, "Then your people must be blessed. Blessed be you and blessed be your place." She said, "Let those who desire this blessing follow me. I have come to establish true balance in the world." But most of them hesitated for they had no faith in a woman. Not until she had disappeared and no longer enlightened the world did they repent and look for her, but in vain. Then they visited the wisest man in the country and asked him, "What are those 32 rays of golden light?" He answered, "These 32 are paths. They are like the king in the innermost chamber of his palace, and the number of chambers was 32, and there was a path leading to each of the chambers. Did the king allow anyone access to his chambers along those paths? No! Did he allow that these pearls, hidden treasures and divine things were shown? No! What did the king do? He took his daughter and collected all the paths in her and her gown, and any one who desired to set foot in the innermost chamber had to see her. The king in his endless love for her called her "My daughter," and she is his daughter. At other times he calls her, "My mother" or "My sister," but at all times did he call her, "My beloved one.""

I

It had been raining all that Sunday and also throughout the night. It was as if the floodgates of the Flood itself had been opened. I was in my study lost in the endless rain and the soaked landscape outside. The air was tense with static electricity. Something indefinable was gathering across the sea, a series of dark shadows of breaking clouds filled with unanswered questions.

I had just finished the manuscript for "The Seer," when the phone rang.

"Now is the time," a familiar voice stated.

It was the Seer.

"Meet me at Montségur Friday next week."

I wanted to say something but the words got stuck in my throat. A deep, warm sense of happiness flowed through me. Maybe I had given up hearing from him again. He had been in my dreams and I had experienced the presence of his inspiring power from afar. What else could I want? Now I was sitting here afraid that he would disappear from my life again.

"Be vigilant," he said, "it is close to quarter day."

The connection was cut off and I was left with the world's loneliest note in my ear. Quarter day? What was all that about? Was it just another example of the Seer's well-known sense of drama or his equally precise sense of timing?

The mere sound of his voice once more activated the invisible language, with which I was slowly becoming familiar and which I was aware was only used when something unavoidable was to be communicated. A sound which could be received only by one who had been initiated to it. The ominous and no-nonsense undertone was unable to dampen my joy at having heard from him again.

"See. Wake up and SEE!" a voice whispered.

On the following day the catastrophe struck, which was to change the sense of reality for a whole generation on several continents. The day was September 11th, 2001. The day that the Tower of Babel, the Twin Towers came crashing down. The generation was called fear and the part of the world was the Western World.

Quarter day!

It was a rude awakening. Finally, the abscess burst and we now stood paralyzed and staring blindly into our own self made darkness. But instead of a willingness to see, the leaders of the world once more chose the destructive escape route of repression and fear: Projection. The hopeless result of a one-sided, rigid and masculine desire for power.

"Only immature leaders need external enemies." a voice whispered.

I couldn't help thinking what the world would look like if the Tibethan-Buddhist monasteries in India, the Greek-orthodox monasteries at the Athos Mountain in Greece, Medjugorje in Bosnia, Monitou in Crestone, USA, the spiritual descendants of Black Elk in the Black Mountains and the Seer's office in Andalusia, did not intensely work to uphold the paper thin balance between earthly insanity and a universal order, in co-operation with the higher powers. Where would we be?

Everything surges with a deep sense of pain in this time and age.

It is the old usedup powers turning and twisting in their death throes in a last, desperate attempt to maintain the status quo of their power. Deep beneath the ice cap of repression the earth and every soul is trembling in labour, foreshadowing that soon something new and long awaited is about to be born. A cosmic power that people have not been able to recognize before because they are just now learning to open up to it. *Realization!*

In my childhood home we had one of these strange ornaments, which today we might call a hate-gift, a miniature, marble sundial with a plaque saying, "do as I do – count the bright hours only." One day while studying this small monument to the repressions of humanity, I suddenly thought, "What are we going to do with all the dark hours?" It was not till I met the Seer and started working with him, that I understood that what we call darkness is only hidden qualities waiting to be illuminated and activated.

"I'm glad I live in a country like Denmark," the taxi driver said just as we arrived at the Aarhus Central Station, "something like that could never happen here."

I nodded in agreement, mainly to be polite, and paid for the trip. The sky was leaden and closed. There was a sleepy, trance-like bustle in the arrival hall. Next to the news about "Islam's attack on the West" on the front page of a newspaper, I saw a headline saying, "The Sale of Prozac explodes." In a dark corner smelling of urine a number of flies circled around a huddled, dirty bundle, which I assumed was a human being.

Somewhere inside me a landscape was becoming more and more visible. Sometimes it showed itself as a large meadow with a foggy, milk-like horizon which had no beginning and no end. No people were to be seen. The cry of a raven cut the air as if it wanted to announce the ensuing silence, which made everything vibrate in what I could only describe as an ominous emptiness. Maybe it was our most basic and most feared state of life, the loneliness, which thus manifested itself as an inner, endless and surreal setting like a bridge between perdition and transformation. The beginning of a nightmare or a new life. The choice was up to the lonely one. A choice which had to be made every day well, every second.

Everything had changed since I got home from Andalusia and the Seer. As I gave up my old worries and practised the difficult art of *being*, I started a whole new life.

A voice was coming alive: *You are a leaf in the wind. A leaf falling through the air and landing exactly where it belongs. Not haphazardly but unpredictable. You are a leaf in the wind. But you are also the wind. The leaf is transient. The wind is eternal.*

In the same way I was the urine-smelling bundle in the darkest corner of the railway station. But I was also the one who passed him by. I convinced myself that it was not a lack of compassion. No. I recognized a brother in an impossible situation. But I also knew that somehow it was also an illusion, and that it was neither meaningless nor without hope, but rather the most certain possibility of change. It was a confrontation with all my rigid ideas about humanity's deepest obligation: helping a fellow human being in need. The understanding that the apparent arrogance in such a way of thinking might really be the first step towards a deeper understanding of the word respect. A key to the simple lecture from that Voice about being a leaf in the wind. On the other hand it was also a challenge to move into the unknown darkness, where only the most hopeless beings wander restlessly about, in order to see that those beings are really hidden aspects of ourselves. *Being the wind that carries the leaf through the air.*

From the moment I put pen to paper it was like getting on a train that thundered into a tunnel where time ceased to be. Not going backwards, nor forwards. But into the now in which I was writing.

Everything I had learned thus became an unlimited reality. Writing was in itself an act of expansion of consciousness. A transformation of consciousness through which I finally, although carefully, might confirm the magic words: *I make myself available. I accept my responsibility.*

While I was writing "The Seer" an episode occurred which marked a final shift in my apparently insoluble, financial problems. It happened on the day when an enticing voice tried to lure me into taking a tailor-made role as a seedy pop-singer in the tv-series "The

Hotel." The answer to my financial problems or the final temptation? Suddenly I knew. I knew that if I accepted the offer it would just be an escape back to all that I tried to free myself from. I politely declined. I declined the enticing salary, which might have saved my frail economy, but couldn't give me the new life I so desperately yearned for. I said no to the seedy pop-singer who did not exist anymore. Just like that! In exactly that moment another door opened. A debt which had been paid several times due to the compound interest was suddenly waived. Unexpected incomes arrived by mail. Offers of lectures. Zap! As easy as snapping your fingers.

How was this possible?

Could the answer be that I had given up nurturing the problems with my worries? Could the reason be, that finally, I showed some confidence in that which really mattered, the métier that was mine? Was this the visible result of following the Seer's simple teaching about stepping into the flow? Maybe the Board upstairs had not given up on me yet?

The train slid silently into the bleak landscape. I was looking at the fields and the trees, which continuously disappeared and reappeared. The window misted up a little and in its fog-like reflection I thought that I could discern a vaguely familiar face. At first I thought it was my own reflection, but then I saw that it belonged to a much older man. A woman appeared behind this face. I turned around.

"New passengers?"

The conductress smiled. Slightly confused, I found my ticket and gave it to her.

"Foix – isn't that the Town of the Virgin?" she said casually, the way she might have commented on the weather. It was more of a statement than an actual question.

She punched my ticket and gave it back to me without waiting for an answer.

Did I hear correctly?

"Excuse me," I said rather confused, "what did you say?"

"Have a pleasant journey," she said smilingly with a raised voice as if talking to a deaf person. She disappeared down the aisle.

I changed trains in Hamburg and again in Cologne.

Twenty-five kilometres outside Paris the train stopped in the dark. Panic spread throughout the train. Bomb threat. Shortly after, we were told to leave our seats and go outside. Serious faces. A child cried inconsolably. In the carriage where I was sitting they had stopped looking secretively at an Arabian looking man – now they looked directly and accusingly at him. I froze to the core of my being.

An hour later we were on our way again. The delay meant that we had just missed being caught in an explosion on the outskirts of Toulouse. A gunpowder factory had been the target of terrorism – or maybe it was just one of those accidents that will happen? An hour after the explosion we slowly moved through a charred suburb filled with crumpled cars, melted street lamps and houses without windows. It was like travelling on the edge of a volcano.

The Seer met me at the railway station at Foix. He seemed taciturn and distant. Only the patriarchal aura around him gave its familiar glow to the surroundings. We pushed our way through the throng of people. The Seer's car was parked outside.

We didn't talk. Instead I was watching the mountains as we drove through the pass onto the plateau leading to the village. After half an hour's driving I could see the Mountain of Montségur between the trees. I felt something warm flowing through me. Deep inside I sensed something indefinable loosening up. We passed the mountain and descended through the hairpin bends towards the village. The house was right in front of me and seeing it I realized how much I had missed it.

"What do you want here?"

In spite of the fact that I knew his style pretty well by now, I was still taken aback. He took a large pitcher and poured water into two glasses with pastis in them. Then I heard myself saying:

"You asked me to come. I was afraid that I should never hear from you again."

He looked straight at me for the first time.

"Have you forgotten everything I taught you? Tell me, how on earth could it ever happen that you and I would lose each other? We, who have never been apart."

He lifted his glass and touched mine. I sipped at mine. I didn't like it. Inside me the foreign voice continued the sentence, which had been cut short:

"What you experience as separation is yet another escape into the illusion which believes in dividedness. From this another disease grows: longing."

What did I long for?

"Tell me, do you think it was me who asked you to come? Do you think it was you who heard it and obeyed? Or could you imagine that such a way of thinking was just an expression of your limited understanding of the beautiful confirmation, that you and I are one."

He emptied his glass and poured more water before continuing:

"But if I repeat it enough times I suppose you'll end up understanding."

He seemed distracted. Once more the mystical voice continued to speak:

"Only the one who is sleeping knows the surprise in waking up. And now that we are on the subject, which shadow of yourself, allowed itself to be so arrogantly lead astray by his own laziness thus leaving a brother in need at the Central Station in Aarhus?"

What kind of voice was this, where did it come from and why was it so insistent right now?

My confusion was not helped by the fact that the Seer didn't seem to be himself. He seemed strangely excited and frantically poured more pastis into his glass.

"I plan to break the autocracy of the Church and Christianity. It has outlived itself and is a limitation which has been in power far too long."

He was sincerely indignant. I had no doubt that this was something that meant a lot to him. It was not the first time he had touched on this subject.

"If people knew what kind of lie they have been sold, they would abolish the Church right away. If I told you that Yeshua was a peasant boy who knew nothing and couldn't do anything, what would you say?"

His voice sounded sharp. I wondered whether this was another test, or whether he really meant it. There was nothing new in his statement. Anyone with the slightest knowledge of the actual history behind the making of The New Testament would know that part of its contents should be taken with quite a large grain of salt. Not just because of the obvious corrections which clearly had been made, but also in the light of all the new findings of scrolls which saw the light in Qumran at the Dead Sea and Nag Hammadi in Upper Egypt about fifty years ago. This being said, there are scripture passages in the New Testament that are, to my mind, simple and irrefutably true whose secrets only a few Christian Churches are aware of.

"Yeshua was nothing," he repeated harshly, "he was manipulated and used in the struggle for power. It was the apostles who ran the show."

I didn't necessarily disagree with him on this latter part, but I felt that I had to protest against his statements about Yeshua. At a deeper level I knew that the Seer's ability to see at this moment was decided by his own personal opinion, which again had something to do with his past, an earlier life. This wasn't something I reached by way of a mental process, it was pure certainty. Within this certainty, Yeshua was not the only son of the Power (God), as the gospels said, but a role model for all of us, his brothers and sisters. Exactly like the multitude of wise men and women filling our history.

At that moment I realized that this subject from then on would be a stumbling-block between us. And this fact, together with the indignation sounding from his words, filled me with a very deep feeling of loneliness, which made me sad. Also since there didn't seem to be any mediating factor which could loosen the conflict looming ahead of us.

"Remember," the voice said within my chest, "the energy follows the thought."

I wanted to say something but there was no sound. There was nothing else to say. I felt that something was brewing. Something was about to open up. The Seer was bustling about with his boots in the hall. I was sitting in the kitchen lost in the silence and sensing that the air was active with creatures, momentarily showing themselves as sparks, as fire, jumping about in the pulsating light. I closed my eyes and slipped into another state of being. At that moment it became clear that this condition reached much further than the reality we experience with our normal senses. It is very difficult to explain, and since I'm still trying to do that, it is with the reservation that the act of trying in itself constitutes the greatest limitation. In this state there are no pictures, no ideas, by which the state may be communicated. But it doesn't matter now. There was no doubt that this was the beginning of a new chapter, not just in my spiritual upbringing, but also in the subject, for better or for worse, of trying to be a human being with a task to fulfil here on earth. The voice spoke to me from my inner core:

"It is important that you realize what kind of change is coming. It will turn all that you previously took for granted and considered to be true, upside-down. Humanity's limited imagination, all its thoughts and ideas, all the fear and anxiety causing energies to be imprisoned within illusions, materialism and misunderstood religion, have created more anger and bitterness than they have created love and forgiveness. The kind of religion that men and women have created is usually a limitation of the eternal. Fear keeps people in a state where they may be controlled. Once, it may have been necessary and in many ways even beautiful. However, the time has come for the energies to be set free. If humanity understood the concept of trust and the power it represents, it would have no need to limit reality."

The voice softly fused into the silence, turning into small particles of light dancing out from my heart. It was quite physical my body told me that this was true.

"When you give in to fear you are doing the exact opposite of what you have come to do, which is changing matter into spirit, darkness into light, demons into useful possibilities. Any lie eventually turns into a ghost or a demon. And this is exactly what the Church has made out of the message. Whether the lie is born in the unconscious or in ignorance, it is still a lie. No one is to blame. It is not a kind of sin. It is more a sad fact. But luckily a fact which may be changed. Do not take this as an opportunity to make more enemies. We have enough of those. Transform and set free. You may experience the journey you are

about to take as a journey through yet more pictures and apparently new illusions. But imagine that the contents of the cauldron, which at the dawn of time was placed over the fire, become smaller by the second, because all the slag is burned away and only the purest and the simplest necessities remain — then you will begin to understand what is being talked about. And when even the picture is burning and both the cauldron and the fire do not exist anymore, neither physically nor as an idea, when even the idea of empty space and the great silence is gone, then all is one in the One."

It was as if the words turned the silence inside out and it seeped into the walls, which lost their solidity and opened outwards in waves — or maybe they opened inwards?

When finally I let go of the picture and opened my eyes, the candle in front of me had burned down and the smoke from it tickled my nostrils. A strange paradoxical feeling of rebellion and gratitude flowed through me. Everything the voice had said struck my own basic tone so clearly that all my previous ideas of what love is, were reduced to what it was — a limp copy of a unique masterpiece. And this masterpiece manifested itself in the Voice:

When humanity realizes that it cannot go on exclusively identifying love with emotions and sensations, and sees that love is much more than that, then people are given a new kind of flexibility. Emotions alone are far too unstable to build on. This doesn't mean that you should make yourself insensitive, but simply that you should set your feelings free. It means awaking to reality and starting "to see". There are more and more so-called clairvoyant people advertising and swindling just because they are able to look into the sub-astral mess. But that doesn't move anything and has got nothing to do with real freedom. Instead, humanity is caught up in new ideas and illusions that form the basis for new churches, hierarchies and careers, which become a repetition of the old and well known institutions which were the cause of your wish to be free to begin with. One doesn't make the lie less of a lie by calling it the truth. A dirty mind doesn't become clean by putting on a clean coat. Words are easy. Attitude and action mean change. The responsibility for yourself is yours and yours alone. No sage or seer can take it upon themselves. There are no shortcuts to Paradise. And all roads lead through what limited man sees as hell. That is why people do not want to take it upon themselves but project it onto a guru, another human being or their surroundings. When it comes down to it, there may be only one out of a million who really has the courage to free himself and take on responsibility for himself.

I got up and walked over to the window but the voice continued:

"Arise, take up your bed and walk — you are healed," someone once said. He might as well have said, "Arise and be responsible for yourself. It is now you yourself who changes things. It is now you yourself who must wake up and do what you have come to do. No more and no less. This is the option given to all people, right now!"

The particles of dust danced in a sunbeam falling through a kitchen window. The sound of the bells from the sheep on their way to the field at the other side of the road was a signal that the lesson was over. I went to my room to unpack and to get ready for the reunion with the mountain — my beloved Montségur.

It was a clear sky the light was sharp and the air clean and pure as we walked through the thicket towards the female guardian of nature Prat's meadow. Whispering beings danced around us for every step we took, and I had the sensation that they came alive because of the Seer and were busy welcoming us. Oddly enough, it didn't strike me as strange that such a sight now seemed quite natural. Maybe because it hadn't dawned on me yet that in the words of the Voice this was a step into a new sphere that had not yet settled in my consciousness, and I was once more satisfied with the fascination itself and not the symbolic content behind it.

Prat was expecting us. The Seer and I walked side by side and it felt as if we were drawing all the vertical and horizontal lines after us into the centrifugal force which was prevalent at this place, until they formed an equilateral, rotating cross, which was centred here and offered to our beautiful friend by invisible hands.

I saw her faintly in the empty square, her transparent, graceful movements and embracing, radiating nature, hovering and vibrating in the air in front of us. I took one step aside and stared into the melting pot of the sun, into the essence of fire — the eternal re-melting process of matter and form — into the flowing glass of billions of years, into the dying mastodon of pain and life – into the limited cleansing dance of shadows. All of it limiting, pathetic words, pictures and ideas only. All of it nothing but a monument to the transience of form. But also a beautiful memory of the seed and the earth, the mustard seed growing and growing until it finally shatters the frozen crystal of the heart. A galactic explosion of timeless visions, predictions and prophesies, which fell like a redeeming rain in an age old consciousness at this moment.

"Lars!"

The voice was inside and outside. There was no distance. The figure in whom I recognized the Seer was only an empty shell. Within the glowing square I saw Prat and an unknown consciousness united in a smile full of warmth and compassion radiating towards me. I was just about to throw myself into the fire in order to let myself be destroyed by fire as I felt a hand on my shoulder shaking me gently, and the voice of the Seer reaching me from outside:

"Lars!"

We walked across the meadow. I followed him closely and thought that this was the reality he had talked so much about. It wasn't a dream.

We passed the steep and straight part with ease and stopped at the stone erected to commemorate the death of the Cathars at the stake of the inquisition.

"Something decisive has happened."

The Seer watched me closely as he continued:

"I've got permission to show you the hidden path to the fortress."

He pointed sadly towards a white fence of thin undressed spruce stems blocking what had once been a path, but which was now overgrown and had almost disappeared under bushes and tall grasses. Boulders were lying helter-skelter between overturned trees which had once been part of a forest which had later crawled up along the side of the mountain where it now spread around it like the hair around the bald pate of a monk.

We sat down in the grass.

"We'll start tomorrow morning early. This is just the beginning.

You must prepare yourself. Prepare yourself to be one hundred percent present. This is a chance that you may never get again. If you do this, you can do anything."

I nodded without hearing what he was saying, but I simply got lost in the aftermath of all the fantastic experiences I had just had, content in the thought that now I could see. Momentarily, I was smitten by the disease, which is a basic challenge in any kind of spiritual work: *vanity* – and I must have looked rather like a blithering idiot.

I do not know for how long this lasted. Maybe it was the handful of sparrows hopping about in the grass that woke me up. I straightened my back, and inside me someone else was straightening his back. One who got up and took his up bed – and got ready to walk.

"Well, now you have tried this also."

The Seer was gentle and full of understanding:

"It is one of the children's diseases that you must get over in a hurry."

Getting back to the valley the sun was on its way down behind the mountains, leaving a soft, pink hue swaddling the village and rendering a surrealistic gleam to the houses. The smell of sheep and pressed grapes mixed with the smell of burnt hawthorn coming from the village chimneys. A flight of white doves swung across the roofs like a live cloud and settled at the pigeon-house where they belonged. We sat in the garden enjoying the last few minutes of twilight. Then the cold crept up from the ground and it was time to go back inside.

The Seer was cooking while I was setting the table in the banqueting hall and lighting a fire in the open fireplace. We found ourselves in a place other than the one we knew, maybe on another planet in another universe. I don't know what – only that we were on a journey of change through eternity.

While I was lighting the candles it struck me that the words of the Seer, when he called me, turned out to be true in every way. I now had no more doubts about what he meant by the word "quarter day." The journey from Aarhus to Montségur had been a journey from one kind of reality to another. Almost without the participation of myself I had been guided through a transformation so radical that

I was just beginning to understand that the lesson for the day was about giving up the most steadfast kind of resistance, that is – *my own!*

I was slowly beginning to understand that the distance from one reality to the next as well as the shift between them could happen as easily as snapping my fingers. That the invisible basic steps in the cosmic dance with no effort at all could revoke every lead-filled step in the gravitational dance of death – if only you knew the score.

However, had I known what lay ahead, I would not have been as self-satisfied and confident.

After dinner I cleared the table and did the dishes. Getting back to the banqueting hall I saw the Seer lost in deep thought and staring into the fire. I was about to sit down as he turned towards me:

"Tonight you'll sleep at Coste's."

The words fell quietly and precisely.

"I have booked a room for you."

I was about to argue the point, but it was clear that this was not a subject for debate.

"We'll meet here tomorrow at 7 a.m."

"Is something wrong?"

He shook his head:

"No, this is just the way it must be."

"Have I done anything wrong?"

"Just go – tomorrow you'll know why."

He walked towards the staircase leading upstairs:

"Good night."

In the gleam from the open fire reflecting its light in the glass door I saw a shadow of an unfamiliar being which seemed to smile laconically and almost fatalistically. I cannot say for sure, but it seemed as if the features were jackal-like. From far away I heard my own voice answering him:

"Good night."

2

She was twelve years old when, for the first time, she saw the man that her parents had promised her to. It was just a glimpse. She saw him from a balcony at her parent's palace in Bethany. He was received in the courtyard by the servants who washed the dirt from the traveller's feet as was the custom in this country.

She shivered from excitement at the sight of this handsome young man, eighteen years of age, whom she had heard so much about. The excitement spread to her small breasts and made the blood rise in her cheeks and quickened her breath.

This was *her* great day. Proof that she was now a fully matured woman who was able to love a man and to give birth to his children. She wanted most of all and right away to throw her arms around his neck, but she knew that she had to be patient and that she would probably have to wait for a year, at the most two years, before her dream would come true. This was not a regular wedding. Much more was at stake than the whimsical love of a young girl. The whole nation nourished the hope that from this occasion, once and for all, the age old wound would be healed, that the dismembered people would be whole again and that Israel once more would become an autonomous nation beyond the reaches of Roman tyranny. And all of this depended upon the union between the tribes of Benjamin and Judah.

One of her two older sisters, Martha, together with a maid, helped her to get ready for the engagement party. They teased her in their playfulness by exaggerating their movements when washing her in the most intimate places, while they giggled and told her about all the terrible things a man would do to a woman when finally she belonged to him.

There were already rumours about her amazing beauty. Rumour had it that without any doubt, she would develop into the most beautiful woman Jerusalem had ever nurtured. Hope-filled wooers had asked her parents for her hand in marriage, but all of them had been forced to leave the palace without having accomplished their object. Even Teutilus the mighty Roman merchant and a close friend of Herod Antipas, had thrown out a feeler. This had caused a great uproar among the Jews, who quite unreservedly had expressed their anger over such an insult. Who did he think he was? Not only was he a Roman, he was also a very old man. This was a violation of all rules – written as well as unwritten.

After a week, however, the anger had died down and Teutilus instead became the butt of Jerusalem's most biting sarcasm. The man had simply made a fool of himself.

Her father, Zerah, had calmly and quietly refused any offer. He was from Benjamin's tribe but grew up in exile in Egypt just like Moses. Later, he had served under a Syrian king and had been rewarded with property in Jerusalem and Bethany.

He and his wife, Jezebel, who came from a wealthy, Jewish family from the tribe of Dan, were close acquaintances of the groom's family, and both families regarded the coming union as a fulfilment of the oldest prophesies. The expectations, originating in this, had their roots far back in a time before Abraham. This was not just an important, political wedding. This was a religious merging blessed by YHVH himself.

When the two women had finished washing the young girl, they anointed her with fragrant balms. The dress was traditional and consisted of a long, white slip followed by a red tunic edged with golden threads reaching to her knees. As tradition demanded from any Syrian virgin, a pale blue *chiton* was placed over it, long enough to touch the floor. It was edged with small, golden flowers, was modestly closed at the side, and a veil was sewn on to it. They finished dressing her by placing the same tiara on her head which her mother and her mother's mother-in-law had worn at their engagement festivities before her, and which would be given to her on the day of her wedding.

She spun around laughing so that the women could see the result of their efforts. They clapped their hands in excitement and surrendered to the girl's catching laughter. It was time to introduce the future bride and groom to each other.

They stood at either end of the most beautiful hall of the palace. He was surrounded by his mother, a brother and two teachers, and she by her mother, her older brother, the two sisters and a few maids. The distance between them was so great, that she could barely make out his face, but it seemed to her that he looked too sad for her liking, considering the occasion.

The invited guests were lining both sides of the hall, expectant and smiling, carrying gifts and waving at them with palm leaves. The two patriarchs, Zerah and Yoasaph (Joseph) were standing in the middle of the hall exchanging traditional greetings and shaking hands as a sign of the coming pact.

It was a moving sight and some people cried since this was a moment that most Jews had been longing for. That which few people had dared to hope for was about to happen: the seed for the unification of Israel and the freedom of Israel had been planted – Israel – the chosen people of the Lord.

Disappointingly, that day she saw no more of her groom to be. Men and women dined separately. And although she could hear the loud talking of the men from the hall next door, this only enhanced her longing for him. After the meal they danced and sang, but this also was done in separation. Sooner than expected, the festivities were over and it was time to go to bed.

Two years passed very slowly. She did not meet her groom to be during that time, and when she asked about him she was told either that she shouldn't worry about it or she didn't get an answer at all. For the sake of the outside world, she tried to keep her dignity, but inside she grew more and more disconsolate.

To pass the time she accepted any kind of work she could be given. The servants tried to talk her out of it, but she begged them until they gave in and let her participate on equal terms with them. Each time it was discovered, it ended in embarrassing situations. She had to stand in front of her father who with great resignation tried to make her understand what was suitable for a girl of her birth.

One day, however, when she was busy helping the washerwomen in the washhouse, something happened that would turn everything upside down. Beating the water out of the clothes against the stones at the edge of the pond, she happened to look at the surface of the water. In a glimpse she saw something moving. At a closer look, however, there wasn't anything to be seen. This happened again a little later, but again there was nothing to be seen. She tried to ignore it, but it kept getting close to the surface of the water every time she looked away. Maybe she was over worked? Maybe it was her monthly cycle weaving a spell over her?

She sat down on the edge of the pond in order to regain her composure. Sitting there, not focusing on the water a picture became visible. She stared at it with rapt attention. It showed her mother and her father travelling with a caravan in a foreign part of the country. The picture made her smile. She recognized the extreme air of seriousness that her father always assumed whenever he wanted to say something disarming and funny. She was about to laugh out loud when the idyllic picture changed brutally. Foreign warriors and highway robbers attacked the peaceful caravan in an ambush. In a terrifying moment she saw a heathen cutting her father's throat from behind, while her mother was cut down mercilessly with a scimitar. Everything went red in that moment. She jumped up with a scream at the terrible sight, which made all the women drop whatever they had in their hands in order to come to her aid. Since they couldn't see anything they assumed that she didn't feel well and carried her to her room where they laid the inconsolable girl on her bed.

She stayed in bed for three days. Her sisters sat with her and without any luck they tried to make her tell them what had happened at the washhouse that had been so terrible. Knowing that they wouldn't understand, she refrained from telling them about her vision. Even when both her mother and father separately sat with her, she couldn't bring herself to tell them about it. The only one she knew would take her seriously was her brother, but he was in Jerusalem on private business.

She felt faint when her mother came to her that same afternoon beaming with joy, and told her that she and her father were going on a journey to Antioch in order to visit some relatives, and that the girls were very welcome to join them. They would start out immediately on the following day.

The mother got quite frightened when the girl threw herself into her arms and sobbing begged her to stay at home, that it was bad luck to make such a journey at this time, that she had seen something that no one could ever understand but which nevertheless was a fatal omen.

"But what have you seen?" the mother asked and stroked her hair.

But the ominous words wouldn't come forth. They stuck in her throat and nearly choked her.

"Please listen to me. You cannot possibly go." she begged.

But the mother simply smiled at the daughter, touched by her compassion.

"All right. You may stay at home with Martha and Mari, then. They probably want to stay with you anyway."

As soon as her mother had left she got out of bed, determined to go to Jerusalem to find her brother in order to tell him about it. If anyone might prevent their parents from going, he was the one. She knew that this was an insane plan and that there wouldn't be one single person in the palace who would help her make it come true. But the vision she had seen was so real to her that she did not doubt the authenticity of it for one moment.

She waited until dusk. With her face hidden behind a dark cape she moved like a shadow along the wall of the orchard to the rear of the palace. She succeeded in passing her father's bodyguard, one man guarding the west gate. She crept along behind the thickets until the road turned, and then stepped out on to the road to Jerusalem.

There were not many travellers to be seen, and the few she met didn't recognize her. The sun sank behind the horizon and the dust and the earth took on a fiery red tint. She felt a crushing grief in her heart but continued undaunted, determined to complete her task. A cloud of dust appeared. It looked like a lonely wanderer in the distance. For a moment she thought that someone was calling out her name. She stopped and somewhat frightened looked behind her. But no one was there. In front of her the cloud of dust approached. She stepped to the side of the road in order to avoid drawing attention to herself. She blinked and tried to see clearly. She had completely lost her sense of distance. The moment the sun disappeared she felt like turning back, but continued nevertheless. In front of her the road lay empty. The cloud of dust had disappeared.

"Mariam, Mariam, have you forgotten who you are?"

She froze at the sound of the voice and looked around in confusion, but she couldn't see anyone. Then she spotted a figure in the shadow of a bush at the side of the road. Frightened, she stepped back.

"Fear not Mariam, I am your protector."

She could now faintly make out the face of the figure. It was an elderly woman with long, white hair.

"Who are you?" she asked in a quivering voice.

"You'll know soon enough who I am. For now, it suffices for you to know that I'm a friend. You must return to Bethany immediately. What must pass will come to pass."

She looked into the dusk but all she saw was the bush moving softly in the wind. The figure had disappeared. For a moment she was in doubt, but then she regained her presence of mind. The presence of mind that the old woman's voice had conjured up. The state of confusion only appeared because she was caught between that which she felt she had to do for the wrong reasons and what she knew she had to do because it was written. She turned about and started walking back. In the distance she saw a Roman unit patrolling the roads.

She cried the next morning when her parents said good-bye before setting out on their journey to Antioch. When she threw herself into her father's arms she sensed a force holding her and the voice from the previous day saying:

"What must pass will come to pass."

It was very strange how she accepted this assurance unquestioningly knowing, that "what must pass will come to pass" would be a catastrophe for her and her brother and two sisters. But how could anyone explain the power that she felt growing inside of her, in spite of her fears – a power filled with destiny and prophecy. She could scarcely understand this herself. Was she possessed by something evil?

"What must pass will come to pass."

As if the heart was a book in which a new page was turned, a revelation of a totally new language, a certainty which was not thrown off course by the disastrous situation she was in. A kind of transfiguration looking directly through the veils into the essence of things at the centre of existence. And she saw her parents in their spiritual clothing, high above the corporeal state, smiling through her tears which mixed with the dust and left small traces on her cheeks. She held them for a long time.

"What is the matter with you?" her father exclaimed and held her close.

"Nehwey sibyanak aykana d'shmaya aph b'arah?" he whispered in her ear.

At that moment she knew that he also knew. One question only burned in her heart, "why?"

She stayed there with Martha and Mari and the servants until they lost sight of the caravan, then she broke down and cried knowing that she had seen her parents alive for the last time.

The fatal news reached Bethany two weeks later. It was her brother

Lazarus who brought the message of death to Jerusalem where as the new head of the family, he had received the sad tidings via two surviving soldiers from his father's bodyguard. The rumour of his little sister's vision had also reached him, but he had shaken it off as if it was some kind of contagious disease or an evil mirage. But the maltreated bodies of his parents that the soldiers brought with them were very real, and Lazarus had to acknowledge that all this had happened just like his sister had seen and predicted.

Due to the condition of the bodies he had to refrain from the traditional burial ritual. The embalming had an almost ritualistic character. The corpses had to go into the ground right away.

Only a small number of the closest relatives participated at the burial. She was trance-like during the whole ceremony and felt the presence of the white haired woman she had met on the road to Jerusalem and in whom she had recognized the magnificent power that spoke to her. That woman's calm became her calm.

When Lazarus was about to go into the tomb with the bloody clothes and other items as tradition demanded, she calmly stepped forward, took the clothes and the other things out of his hands and quietly walked into the burial chamber without anyone protesting. A decisive change had taken place in her. She was surrounded by an inexplicable authority and dignity which seemed quite natural but which normally wasn't accorded a girl that young.

The tomb was cool. Only a narrow, dusty ray of light showed her the way. She could only see the two white bundles faintly on their designated places to the rear of the burial chamber. Taking the three steps down into the cold darkness she immediately felt his presence. In an attempt to stay calm she bowed down and carefully placed the items she had been carrying at the feet of the dead. Getting up again she stared directly into two burning eyes. At first she recognized the old woman. Then the face seemed to change and she recognized her fiancé. She put her hand out towards him but he gently waved her back and she heard him saying, *"Not yet."*

She sensed that the air around her was filled with beings who wanted to help her, and they guided her as she stepped into the shaft of light. In the air in front of her a transparent, radiant and deeply purple ball hovered with a pink, four-pointed star within, surrounded by a thin, pink stripe.

"*This is your guardian angel,*" a voice announced. "*Follow it and you shall never go astray.*"

She stayed in the shaft of light and let herself be filled with the Power. Stepping out of the burial chamber she carried the certainty of the radiant star in her heart and was surrounded by its deep pink and purple hue. At that moment the crying and lamentations of the women stopped. It was as if her mere presence transformed the curse of grief and gave a meaning to the moment, which they had never known before. At that moment Lazarus recognized her and saw who she really was.

Immediately after the burial of their parents Lazarus asked his little sister to meet him in their father's private room. In future he would be the one to rule from here. When she stepped into the room he was again surprised to see how much she suddenly seemed to be a stranger. He may recognise his sister, her by now legendary beauty, her burning eyes, her tall body with the promise of the magnificent shape of a rare and beautiful woman. But it seemed as if the direct, female vitality and playful air had been exchanged for a sweeter and more serious dignity that he hadn't noticed before. Something else, something radiant had taken over her being.

They embraced. He felt her small nipples through the thin material. He then held her at arms length and looked at her affectionately.

"If I didn't know better, I might think that you lusted after me," she said laughing and blushed.

"The allcompassionate God might have made that happen had I not been your brother," he answered and pulled her head to his chest and continued:

"But a mightier goal has been set for you far more important than being given to a man solely for his dubious pleasures."

"Are you forgetting that I have already been promised to someone?"

She tried to pull away from him and he hesitated but kept his grip around her waist. Then he said:

"No, I do not forget. How could I? But the groom appointed for you may not be the one you expect him to be."

He spoke in a subdued voice. When she struggled to get free he let her go. She went silent. Although she had never spoken to her husband to be or had spoken to anyone about him or about the type of marriage she could expect, she had sensed from the beginning that it wasn't going to be a traditional marriage. Nevertheless, she was filled with the natural yearning of a young girl, and the picture of the one she was carrying in her heart was enough to light a secret fire in her body when she conjured it up. But she didn't know who he was.

Lazarus stayed by the window for a long time looking thoughtfully across the fields of grape without being able to speak. He was searching for the words but still hesitated. She sensed his perplexity. It suddenly struck her that maybe he knew more about her future husband than he wanted to admit.

"Do you know him?" she asked with newborn hope in her voice.

A sad smile crossed his face and a distant look came into his eyes. His voice was low and intense:

"It is said that he is destined to play a specific part."

The sentence hung in the silence. They looked away from each other. He was wondering whether or not she was aware what this meant for her. She was considering the stranger.

"Who says this?" she asked.

"I heard it from the Essenes in a house in Jerusalem."

"What specific part?"

"The Essenes are the kind of people who do not speak much."

"What does he say himself?"

"Nothing."

"Nothing? Hasn't he got anything to say?"

"He has gone away."

She felt a stab in her heart.

"Where?"

Her voice was very small.

"First to Alexandria, then East."

She turned and faced him. There were so many who gave themselves out to be special, the long awaited Messiah for example.

So many miracle performers and prophets, who lit a fire in people and gave them false hopes of better times and eternal life.

"Is he like the horrible magician Hanina Ben Dosa?"

Her voice revealed that she didn't think much of the miracle performer, whom they said could bring forth rain and many other things as he wished it. She had seen him once on a journey to Jerusalem with her father, Martha and Mari. They hadn't liked him. He seemed untrustworthy. Spoke too much, was smooth-tongued and made far too many exaggerated gestures. You could see his rotten teeth when he smiled. They had found him despicable. When she mentioned him now, in this connection, it was more an expression of her helplessness. Because she sensed that a curse and something fatal was hidden behind her brother's words, something that she didn't understand and wasn't sure if she was ready to fathom yet. Lazarus took her hands in his, looked affectionately at her and said:

"The time has come. It is about time you heard the truth."

She felt a shiver running through her body and was about to say something, but he got in first and held a finger against her lips.

"Hush, sister! What I'm about to tell you is unavoidable. It is written and there is nothing we can do about it. You have also been chosen. Just as he has. The time has come when you must accept your destiny. I shall tell you everything, but only on condition that you do not interrupt me. I do not want to make you sad, but you must promise me that you will stay and listen to what I have to say, no matter how much it may hurt you."

He fell silent and pretended to give her time to think. But although with a part of her being she was terrified at the thought of the atrocities that were waiting behind the words he was about to say to her, she felt the new certainty deep in her innermost being filling her with a strength and lifting her above all the trivia of life. He began speaking:

"A great master is expected to come forward among the Essenes. The long expected Messiah. Your betrothed will play a great part in this connection. He may be the right hand of this great master. According to my source he is elected to be a high priest within the new order, which will make Israel a free nation once again."

He fell silent – focusing on her reaction. She simply nodded.

"But even a high priest must have a wife. Do you understand what I'm saying?"

Again she nodded. Then she said:

"What you are saying is that this is a contract of marriage the sole purpose of which is to legitimize his function. A cover to make it possible for him to gain the trust of the people – isn't that true?"

He looked at her surprised. Her precise summing up of the situation took him by surprise.

"There is more," he said. "Nobody knows how long his preparations will take. Nobody knows when he will return. For the sake of all those involved it is better that you go to Those Dressed in White in the temple of Isis at Heliopolis to let them teach you. They will know how to prepare you for your task. The delta of the Nile will do you good. Our dear father would have approved this decision.

His words made her want to scream. Instead she said:

"Which task?"

"Your task."

"Who could know my task better than I do?"

She had a strong urge to go against him and all his limited ideas. But her reaction just made him shut her out.

"My mind is made up. You leave as soon as possible."

The case was closed.

He turned his back on her and walked over to the window and stared into the void. At that moment she felt a deep compassion for him. Again she felt the strange presence of the loving Power and was conscious of the closeness of these benevolent beings. Did they come from him or the thoughts and desires he was holding, all that she felt he didn't dare confide to her – or all that he didn't dare look at himself. She went over and stood close to him looking out of the window. The pictures passed her by in silence and she smiled when she saw the old, white haired woman disappearing in the vibrant cloud of dust in the air. Then she said:

"I know what you mean. I'll go and take upon me what is mine to do. What else is there to do? How could I do anything else? It is written. But tell me who are Those Dressed in White?"

Her words softened the tense atmosphere.

"The Society of the Brotherhood sprang from their midst. It was Those Dressed in White who founded the rules of conduct for the Essenes. They are also astrologers, prophets and healers. But they are much more than that. They are a kind of order of therapists that only a few know about. There is so much I would like to tell you, but I do not know enough about it. What is happening has been coming for a long time. If I could tell you more, I would."

"Is he one of them?" she asked.

But her quiet, newly found certainty made the question seem both empty and meaningless. She had asked something to which she really knew the answer herself. And when she saw how her brother was nervously trying to keep his perspective and live up to his new dignity, she was sorry that she had asked the question. Finally he said:

"He has been brought up in the Brotherhood at the Mountain of Carmel. That is all I know."

She put a finger on his lips.

"Say no more. It is written."

3

Darkness was falling over the village as I walked through the narrow streets. The air was clear and cold. A dog was barking inside a house, and all around cats were busy catching mice. My thoughts moved in circles trying to find a reason for the Seer's arrangement, but I didn't get any further than the question, why?

The light from the hotel Costes threw its cosy glow on to the street where the familiar, white sign with black letters was hanging on the gable of the house welcoming travellers. I pushed the garden gate open and walked through the small garden. The owner, Gilbert, was busy arranging Cathar ornaments in the small glass case with souvenirs. Through the open door to the kitchen I got a glimpse of Gilbert's wife, Maurisette, who was busy cooking. One couple only waited for their dinner at one of the tables in the restaurant. A fly was circling around in the room. The radio was silent. It was late in the season.

Gilbert smiled knowingly when he spotted me as if we shared a secret and gave me a hearty welcome. I thought that he might have received a hint from the Seer about what was going on. But it made me happy that he recognized me at all. He pointed expressively at the bar, which was no more than a shelf with a few bottles behind the counter. I hesitated, but then I asked for a glass of red wine and sat down in the front room. A little later he came back smiling widely and carrying two glasses and a bottle. He bore the latter proudly before him. It was one of the bottles, *Don Cesar*, that the Seer had brought with him from Spain as a present for Gilbert the last time we were in town. He poured wine into the glasses and we toasted each other. However, my poor French and Gilbert's non-existent English reduced all conversation to an inadequate mime-show. We gave up and limited our contact to the lifting of our glasses and drinking. I emptied my glass and got the key for room I.

The room was situated on the first floor and had windows facing toward the garden. Pale, flower covered wallpaper, only a few pieces of furniture with a double bed in the middle of the room, built-in wardroom at one side and a small table at the foot of the bed. As I entered the room a cold wind swept past me and into the hall like an evil spirit out of a bottle. But I was under a kind of spell and didn't attach too much importance to it. Instead, I followed my intuition, walked over to the window, opened it and looked up at the nocturnal sky. At once I caught sight of a flickering light in the multitude of stars. At first I thought that it moved. But suddenly I saw that it was a star, which was bigger than the others. I stood spellbound for a long time and couldn't leave this wonderful sight. I do not know how long I stood like this, but I came to, realizing that I was very cold. I closed the window, turned on the electric heater in the corner, lay down on the bed and slipped into a dreamless sleep.

I woke up when a flash of lightning pierced my stomach with an infernal sound and made me curl up in a foetal position on the bed. Transfixed like a bug on a pin. The pain hit me directly at the centre. I screamed, but the sound was muffled by the noise. I was then thrown on to my back and kept there by a pipe-like shaft piercing my solar plexus. I just managed to think that this was it. But I didn't know what "it" was. My last thought before disappearing was to call the

Seer, because I knew that this was more than I could possibly handle alone.

Then, before I could do anything, it started – relentlessly and without hesitation – like a train at full speed going through a tunnel – one picture after the other, pictures from my childhood, pictures from situations in my life, from earlier incarnations, pictures of being abandoned, alienation, a scoop in a small mud-filled bucket, old, red bricks from church yards, monumental, closed, institution-like buildings, reformatories, military barracks and asylums. Enormous, ill-fated, red and clumsy buildings on sunburned lawns, in dog rose summers with buttermilk mucilage and buttermilk beards, without soft drinks and ice cream. Happy summers, newly fledged parents, blancmange and cherry sauce. Endless idyl. Buildings with locked doors, and windows, which could only open slightly. Curfew in the dog rose pointed sanctuary of long and hot afternoons, where transparent, starched nylon curtains did not move in the wind. The Lucy Show and Perry Como. Used cotton handkerchiefs filled with snot and blood, crumpled up on glass plates with sponge cake crumbs on the rims, screams from long gone souls, hidden for ever and ever in dark and eternally locked basements. Happy children, dead children, children of all kinds. Faster and faster the pictures rushed through me. Pictures of bodies being dismembered as entertainment for tv, pictures of newsreaders vomiting on prime time, filling all living rooms with cauterizing acids. Talk shows with hosts chanting their crazy jokes on and on for ever, chasing a point which was just confirming the insanity against which it was supposed to anaesthetize all viewers. Intellectual, crazy and eternal thought combinations, sweating and copulating bodies puffing from unreleased lust, self appointed seers and philosophers with egg heads as big as bombs, war and destruction, torn off limbs flying through the air, strapped-down drug addicts and molested children, obsequious world-saviours, self-glorifying gurus and devout, self-righteous holy men and women, row after row of carved out people, manacled to game machines in game halls as big as hangars turning into endless rows of scarecrows on their way to mass graves at enormous stadiums where rock idols were turning and twisting in ecstatic, auto erotic spasms in front of a fascinated, drugged audience, a sea of people supervised by wellfed soldier-pigs in mud brown uniforms. A hell as brown as hell itself. My own pain, my own repressions, judgements, prejudices, vanity, pornographic pictures, insane perversities, projections, an enormous choir of demons, the cries of witches and fornication, the truth about the human race – I could suddenly see – was the truth about myself!

The speed was now so high that I didn't have the strength to hold on. I let go with my fingertips and just had time to register the room I was in: the bed, the wallpaper, the table and the heater, before swirling away with the pictures which were changing at such speed and intensity that I knew that I was going insane. The pictures of hell were now mixed with pictures of radiating crosses, burning hearts and golden, angel like beings, grand scenarios of skies opening up, and I saw a being on a throne surrounded by an enormous halo glowing so strongly that it blinded me. The being was surrounded by cherubs and seraphim approaching me, and I saw that it was Christ piercing me at an enormous speed. But just when I was about to give in to this blessing, the being opened its mouth in a devilish grimace turning the flow of pictures inside out, deeper and deeper, higher and higher – until the tension became so strong that I screamed and screamed into the eternal darkness. But my screams drowned in the infernal noise, and I closed my eyes in order to avoid seeing the glowing horn – an enormous, erect penis on the forehead of the smiling Christ. And I saw that the penis was identical with the shaft through my solar plexus, that the pictures were my semen and that it was sterile.

Then the pictures stopped and the noise went silent. I was in a long, subterranean passage. There was a pleasant temperature. Totally quiet. I walked through the passage towards a door which I knew I was going to open.

"This is the lowest point – lower than Hades!" the Voice said.

There was an indescribable calm, but also something fatal - something waiting to be seen. To be found out. Recognized.

I opened the door.

On a metal table in the middle of a room with a low ceiling, looking somewhat like an operation room with bare concrete walls, was an enormous cadaver, and I could see that it was a pig in a coma like state. The pig's head was intact and carried a white, newly starched stand-up collar around its neck. Most of the meat was gone from the body, and behind the curved ribs I saw a big, bluish, beating heart, which was connected to an apparatus with a plastic hose, barely keeping the ill fated creature alive.

"Now you have seen it," the Voice stated.

And I floated through the room, in and out of doors, and suddenly I was in an enormous changing room where men and women sat on benches separated by clothes racks with naked genitals, reaching for each other without being able to make it while masturbating incessantly like crazy. Row upon row of pent-up souls, obsessed with lust. Lust for things, lust for fame, lust for attention, lust for money, lust for sex. And I saw how the desire and the obsession held these souls slave-bound in such a terrible limitation that I had to fight in order not to give in to the all consuming fear. It wasn't just a row of identitylacking individuals whom I was moving among – they were my brothers and sisters. I tried talking to some of them but they neither saw nor heard me. And I understood that I was just a guest and could move about freely, but also that I myself once was a prisoner here blinded by the chase for self-satisfaction. But I saw the longing behind the fear and the desires. The longing to be recognized, the longing for acceptance, the longing for love, the longing for freedom.

"Now you have seen it!" the Voice stated.

I was then lifted up through the shaft, back to the bed at the Hotel Costes in Montségur, where I lay bathed in sweat and with every fibre of my body in burning pain from the cramp-like tightening of the muscles, and slowly it dawned on me that the nightmare was over. I was tired like someone who hadn't slept for a thousand years. I was, however, filled with a deep peace. I looked at my watch. It was five o'clock. I could just catch a few hours sleep before getting back to the house. Waking up I knew immediately that something decisive had happened. My energies almost sparkled inside me. Getting out of bed a little later I felt light as a feather. And I understood that I had been through a cleansing during the night and had been liberated from burdens I had carried with me all through my life, well, maybe even since the beginning of time. It was quite clear that these burdens were basically something I had laid upon myself, that the pictures were shadows I had projected on to the world where they had changed into demons, the single purpose of which was to limit me in the most intricate ways and to stop me from doing what I came here to do. I was suddenly able to see how fleeting and illusory all these projections and pictures really are. How we let ourselves become tyrannized by our own basest beings, when, instead of changing the shadows, we create pictures of enemies and obstructions, which in turn create separation, distance, fear and war. Although feeling liberated at a deep level, there was still something I needed to recognize. The mere thought of the Christ-like figure made me shiver. And what was the difference between the radiating, angel-like Christ and the diabolical one with the erect penis-horn on his forehead?

"None! Both pictures are simply an expression of your own limited imaginings and projections," the Voice answered. *"Christ can never be in opposition to himself. Christ is consciousness. Christ is One!"*

Something very old moved deep inside me. The fear of sin. The fear of an angry and avenging and patriarch-like God. All that I thought I had let go of long ago opened like a pit of fear in my stomach. But contrary to my expectations it wasn't followed by one single picture. The fear was empty so to speak. A last desperate reaction from an old ailment?

Suddenly a warm laughter rolled through me – I do not know why. It was so unusual and took me by surprise to such a degree that I gave in to the liberating feeling of it without any kind of resistance. And suddenly it struck me, that this was what the story about the expulsion from the temple was all about in the New Testament. That the nocturnal cleansing was a kind of expulsion of my own inner Pharisees, moneylenders and merchants. The destruction of all the hypocritical masks, opinions, dubious visions and so-called "good intentions" – my selfish care for others – with which I had betrayed and limited myself. All my sentimental and emotional imaginations about hate and love, good and evil, damnation and salvation, demons and angels, Christ and antichrist. All my conditions. My firm resistance. I was embarrassed just thinking about it. Not only because I had mislead myself by hiding behind a one-sided front producing nothing but self-righteousness, but also embarrassed how arrogantly and stubbornly I had maintained the betrayal. Perhaps I was beginning to understand something about the thesis of my inner seer, that darkness is a series of hidden qualities which ought neither to be repressed nor demonised, but should be enlightened and transformed. And such a process demands a spiritual soberness. As the Seer used to say, you do not lend your car to a person who is very drunk – do you?

It was still dark as I started walking back to the house. As soon as I opened the door I was met by the smell of freshly made coffee. The Seer was packing a tent into a small canvas bag.

"Did you sleep well?"

It was not a question, more a stating of a fact that he knew. He simply saw how it radiated from me.

"So, so," I said.

"There is coffee in the pot in the kitchen."

I went to make breakfast. When a little later I sat watching him packing, I heard the Voice whispering:

"*Only the one who is able to see his own face without a mirror is able to see his true character.*"

Focusing, I tried to keep all other sounds away. This was important:

"*Looking without a mirror is not looking at objects, it is looking at THAT which is looking!*"

The tent moaned as the Seer tightened a knot.

"*A picture of "God" is not God. The word "love" is not love. You are not a Christian by saying so.*"

He formed a loop, pulled the string through it and tightened it with a quick pull. The Voice continued:

"*It is a matter of knowing that we are something else and more than a few ephemeral emotions in a transient body and the dubious personality we think we are.*"

He looked up and was surprised to see that I was watching him. Something had come between us. I went upstairs in order to pack my backpack. Half an hour later we were ready.

The contours of Montségur appeared like a picture appearing in a developing tray, silently, imperceptibly, without visible transitions. Prat was waiting for us, and when the Seer had talked to her he asked me to do the same.

I placed myself in front of the opening. Free of any expectation or idea about what I ought or should do. For a long time I just stood looking into the square without seeing anything.

"*Let go,*" the Voice whispered. "*Let go!*"

A certainty grew in my chest as imperceptibly as the dawn, a being with a consciousness as frail and intangible as ether and light. This was not a magnificent sight. Not a great vision. More of a silent fusing with silence. Here were no bicycles without brakes going down steep hills, no burning fires with tormented souls, no bathtubs with the water running out of them. No messages. Simply being. If I had had the courage I would have stepped into the square without hesitation. But intuitively I realized that this opening would always be available. That we, anytime we so wish and anytime we are able to let go of all superfluous weight, have the possibility of stepping into this quiet freedom. My moment wasn't here yet. No one can stand in this square in a state of separation. You either do it totally or not at all. I opened my eyes. The Seer was smiling broadly.

We passed the steep, straight part without any trouble. At the stile we turned right and found the path in the wilderness on the other side of the fence. I followed closely after the Seer. The path soon became both narrower and steeper. At many places it had totally disappeared and we had to keep our balance on fallen rocks or crossing the open mouth of the chasm. After an hour of difficult walking on the dramatic incline of the mountainside, the growth grew sparse. We stopped at a cliff shelf and had a wide view of the valley and the village below us. To the other side the Pyrenees stretched their snow-clad peaks towards the blue sky. We sat down on a large rock. The Seer's eyes met mine. I sensed that he was struggling with something that he couldn't handle. As he started to talk I saw him for the first time in his new role. Another, a more human side was appearing.

"There is something I must tell you. It is about time. And space. Although I have never been able to say who my employer is, you know that I have never doubted that it is the Board of Directors upstairs who are deciding the agenda." He pointed towards the sky.

"I have never been able to understand all the talk about no man being able to stand the sight of God. For who and what is God? It's a question we must ask ourselves. All that about God is nonsense. God is an illusion. I think I have found a form of energy outside all the universes, the consciousness, if you like, which is the destiny of all things. Everything is predestined."

His words felt like a frontal attack on the cosmic logic as I saw it. What was the meaning of everything if it was preordained? One could ask the question, who invented whom? Can God be defined by a name at all? In a religious context one might rightfully say that God is a relative conception, since that energy does not necessarily have the same value for everyone. Of course you may make the point that God is an illusion. That probably is the way it is whenever you try to limit that energy by putting a name to it. The name in itself does not say anything about the quality we normally call God. Might one even say that we have the kind of God that we have the imagination to imagine? Or that we have the kind of God we are able to perceive? But this only says something about us not about God.

He remained standing, looking up at the sky. An eagle circled overhead. Even though I felt his words in the physical realm, I couldn't help wondering whether there was something I earlier hadn't understood since he continued to belabour the point. The thought was barely formed before he smiled obligingly:

"You are right. I may be going too far."

But I could hear in his voice that there was something else, something deeper. Something that maybe he himself didn't even know the meaning of.

"Blessed by Prat, we are now on our way to a dimension that I know nothing about. Get ready to register everything you see. That is why you are here. This is your task on this journey."

"Where are we going?" I asked.

"Possibly into a series of events which have never been described before. If I knew, then we wouldn't have to go on."

He got up and made me understand that we should start walking. I looked about for the eagle but it had disappeared. Suddenly it grew cold. The sun had disappeared behind a dark cloud. In front of me the Seer balanced elegantly at the edge of the cliff like a dancer. The path seemed to vanish into thin air. Below us the world disappeared. A strange rush into an unknown reality. Where was the focus? Were we walking on clouds? What was up and what was down? We crawled along the side of the mountain. Big beetle-like insects ran in and out between the rocks. With the tips of our fingers and the toes of our boots we inched around the cliff edge. All shapes disappeared into themselves. My thoughts flowed through me like a river, which has surrendered and therefore must follow its own destiny. The path again became passable. But the sense of grounding was gone. Instead, a sparkling filigree of vibrating crystals appeared. The air was full of a radiant activity. It seemed as if someone had turned the switch on the ethereal membrane. I followed closely after the Seer who went through unimpeded. I felt a faint resistance, which made me stop for a brief moment. We penetrated the ethereal veil. At that moment the knot in my stomach was transformed into a sparrow, which was lifted, freed from its age-old burden into an unconditional kind of freedom. In front of me the Seer seemed to float. For a moment I fought to keep back my tears. Then I gave up and let them flow.

A cold, moist, scaly and live being touched my hand, which rested on the cliff wall. I wanted to move my hand but couldn't let go of my last hold on earthly reality. Out of the corner of my eye I saw something move. Before turning my gaze in their direction I registered the presence of two intertwined snakes swaying in an inexplicable dance, brushing my hand. Surprisingly, this realization caused no panic in me. I simply registered it – probably because at a deeper level I was aware that what happened was unavoidable.

Ten meters in front of us and about three to four meters above us a radiating square opened up. The Seer looked with rapt attention into it, but it didn't seem as if he recognized the figure in it. However, I had no doubt that it was a woman. The light around the figure grew stronger and I was almost lifted into the warm glow. The figure had a glowing radiance about her and I sensed that she was tall, well proportioned and exceptionally beautiful. She wore her hair down her back and carried a wreath of small, glittering lights around her head. For some reason I started to count them. There were twelve of them. I now noticed that the woman seemed to say something. I heard no words spoken and did not see her lips move. I just stared into this radiating being and felt a deep, deep sense of gratitude. Could this be the Virgin Mary? I tried to get closer to this being. But just as I asked the question, "Who are you?" the Voice answered, "The Bride."

The note came in waves from the sparkling filigree. A cosmic energy encircling the mountain like a vibrating tiara. Suddenly a section of the tiara moved forward and pulsated in front of me:

It lasted for a moment only, then the vibrations faded away. Frightened I withdrew my hand at the same moment. The snakes disappeared from the rocks in the same movement. The Seer stood further ahead on the path seemingly lost in thought. The sun had disappeared and the clouds covered the sky. The cry of a bird echoed from the side of the cliff and reverberated through the valley then disappeared into the growing mist.

We started walking. My sense of time was totally erased. Everything happened in a gliding movement. It struck me that although I felt like a spectator to a series of spectacular events, which were the result of the presence of an inexplicable force, I was still right in the middle of it. And although I was shaken to the core, on the other hand it didn't bother me at all. Everything happened so fast, or rather so much in a flow, that I didn't have the time to muster my usual reservations. It had never been a problem for me to accept the fact that forces existed which could not be experienced through our normal senses. However, I had never imagined that it was something in which I could actually participate. To be in the presence of the Power turned everything upside down. And I was beginning to realize that this Power first and foremost meant to break down any kind of reservation in me. What this energy really wanted was for me to step out from the trivial apathy of sleep, letting go of all my insane attempts to be "right" or "special," letting go of the fear of being alone and taking responsibility for the job in hand. Nevertheless, I was, at the same time, contemplating how I might communicate all these experiences in a credible way so that they were seen as realistic options rather than targets of ridicule, blown out of proportion and viewed to be results of occult fantasy.

In just twenty-four hours I had experienced that there are more ways than one in which to see. I had experienced how shockingly easy it is to be lead astray by the imagery created by our own minds and the large, collective file of images in the lower astral regions, created by our repeated kow-towing, time and again, to limiting dogma and rigid interpretations. That they did not only consist of images of enemies but just as much religious archetypes and symbols like Christianity's "Yeshua on the cross," Buddhism's "Buddha in the lotus position," as well as the long series of stereotypes used by the New Age movement. Not that there is anything wrong with these matrixes. They are inevitable and necessary in many connections, such as in education. Perhaps the Power simply wanted to show that the application of these images is of limited value when we are at the threshold of greater realizations. That only those with the courage to pass through the vale of shadows, enter the vale of soul-searching, cleanse themselves of all fixed notions and preconceptions and move beyond all limited ideas and symbols, will gain admittance to these transcendent worlds and to this clarity of vision.

Imagine if all our age-old knowledge and symbolism, the images from the great collective unconscious, the Akasha-archives in the ethereal worlds, all the great complex of cosmic language, no longer served their original purpose? Imagine, that they have become so worn and devalued because they are used and misused at every opportunity, that they have become our greatest limitation? The thought was almost unbearable. If this was the case, the whole foundation of religion and the humanities would collapse. How could humanity even get close to freedom without them?

I gave up on the thought and plodded along after the Seer.

He stopped at an overhang and placed his backpack on a rock overgrown with moss:

"We'd better have some lunch."

As we were dividing the bread between us I wanted to ask him about the woman I had just seen.

He slowly chewed on a piece of baguette and looked at me in his usual subtle and surprised way.

"You haven't fallen in love – have you?"

He didn't wait for an answer:

"If I'm not wrong you must have seen an extraordinarily beautiful woman. Isn't that true?"

I nodded my assent. He smiled.

"I thought so. Let me put it this way, she apparently hasn't made herself known yet. But you must be patient. You have found a clue. We have been shown the right direction. We are surrounded by helpers, but it is important that we do not behave like two elephants in this unbelievably beautiful crystal shop."

His look took on the intense focus that I knew so well. And now I saw what was happening, saw that he was about to make room so that I could come to my own realizations.

If man could see through his own blockages he would be able to understand how we all, quite uniquely and totally, are dependent upon cosmic laws. Whether we want it or not. But such an understanding must find its balance between intellect and heart in order to make a difference. All physical forms are made from molecules, but are, like all creatures and all things, concentrated, and, in most cases, still unchanged, heavy energy. At the centre of this heaviness the qualities of light are hidden waiting to be activated. Man is also in constant

(Painting by Peter Fich)

movement, undergoing eternal change. Man is not only a being of particles but more than that he is a being of waves and vibrations. The field of energy you have just experienced you might call a door between the reality of particles and the reality of waves. A door to a more concentrated form of energy. Deep inside of you there was something recognizing this energy. And the only way for you to relate to this was to translate it into a recognizable image from the collective file. This image then showed itself on the ethereal membrane. That's the way it is. Quite natural too. But it may soon turn into a limitation if you are not able to define the energy in the image, but instead let your interpretation of the quality of the energy become limited by the quality of the image itself. The God-energy is consciousness. Consciousness free from images. Consciousness as pure being.

A warm feeling was spreading through my body and I expressed a quiet thank you for the lecture. But another question needed an answer: Who was this woman? And I heard myself asking the question of the inner Voice:

"Who was it that you saw?"

I didn't know whom this *you* was at the time. And this ignorance was in itself precisely the most important witness to my insignificance and to the fact that I wasn't ready yet. For some seconds, that felt like light years, my question hovered, tensely. Finally the Voice answered:

"I saw the sea of light where this unique energy had its origin. I heard the poetry and the divine story in the sound from this sea. For a moment I disappeared in it — and I reappeared in the sea. And the sea is that woman, who is without a name, but whose daughters off and on appear in the world in order to restore the great vision and the correct sight. I came to this world from her womb I was a suckling at her breast. I have drunk cosmic love from her mouth. I have seen everything in her eyes. I was given the sign on her forehead and at the sight of the twelve stars in her hair — I remember the certainty within which I have my origin."

Moved, I gazed at the mountain whilst these gripping words sang through the stillness. Who was it that spoke? What was the sign that the Voice was talking about? The same kind of warm glow that I had seen around the woman now also radiated from the words. It was so simple and so beautiful that all my writings here – now – are nothing but withered flowers.

The Seer looked at me with an intense sadness. As if the sight of me could help recall a long gone feeling of happiness, which was no longer his. He smiled. Then he said:

"You had a question?"

"Well, when I saw her I thought that she might be the Virgin Mary. But when I asked about it, a voice said that she was the Bride. What do you think?"

"I think that this feminine energy is quite different from the well known one: the mother, mater, the feminine which has always been identified with yielding, being receptive, giving birth, the moist, the dark, the nurturing, passive and negative principle in nature. I'm not at all in doubt, that what you have received here is quite another and much stronger, more embracing and superior form of energy. I cannot say any more at the moment. Just that we are on the right track. It is not every day that one gets to see something like that."

He laughed aloud at the last remark and stretched out in the moss like a knight who just remembered the princess, partly feeling sad and partly yearning for her.

We camped at the old stronghold area of the Cathars in a small forest a few hundred metres from the top of the mountain. I started unpacking the tent while the Seer found an abandoned eagle's nest where he spent the rest of the day.

I found a reasonably level place suitable for setting up the tent in the middle of the paved area, where the stronghold must have been. There was a touching seriousness and quietness here and I made myself believe that I could feel the presence of the *Perfecti*, who died in the struggle with the soldiers of the inquisition during the month of February 1244. The stronghold had been the most important defence of the Cathars, and when that fell the enemy used the ledge to set up the feared catapults, the trébuchets. That was the beginning of the end for the Cathars. They surrendered on 7th March 1244 and were given the choice of either renouncing their faith and converting to the Church of Rome or being burnt at the stake. All chose the stake except the three *Perfecti* who were sent off with the secret treasure of the Cathars under cover of darkness.

It was dark when the Seer returned to the tent. He seemed to be more serene than he had been earlier in the day. I had collected brushwood for a small fire. Supper consisted of bread and water. We sat in silence for a long time watching the stars in the sky. The Cathars and their treasure had occupied my thoughts most of the day just as it had done for many other people before me. I broke the silence:

"What do you know about the treasure that the Cathars are supposed to have had and which was removed from the fortress shortly before they surrendered?"

"Just a moment," he answered and disappeared into his usual trance-like state. However, he soon came back:

"So many legends are connected to this treasure. It is said that the Grail may be a possibility. No one has considered the possibility that it might have something to do with a kind of knowledge that should definitely not get lost; knowledge that might have been put in writing or hidden in the memories of three Cathars, which had to be transported away from Montségur in order not to fall into the hands of the Church of Rome or to disappear forever."

"What kind of knowledge?"

"Well, that is a very good question. This, among other things, is one of the reasons why we are here. And the experiences that you have had may play an important part here."

His familiar look underlined that what he was about to say was of the utmost importance:

"If you really want to put a name to the woman we met, then I know that you can do it. All you have to do is ask *out there*."

He let the sentence hang in the air. But it didn't hang there for long before the name of the mystical woman manifested itself as though it was the most natural thing in the world to do so.

"Mariam Magdal!"

We sat in the quiet of the moment. The Seer then broke it:

"Who is she?" he asked and looked questioningly at me.

I couldn't help smiling. I had totally forgotten that the Seer wasn't in the least interested in the dogma of the Christian Church and that his understanding of Christianity was solely based upon what he was able to see — and not what was to be found in its writings. This, however, meant that someone had to ask him the relevant question.

"Mariam Magdal is Aramaic for Mary Magdalene," I answered. "Mariam may mean *the joy of God, the spirit of Peace* or in certain dialects *princess*, whereas Magdal means *'She of the watchtower'*. In Malachi's book from the Old Testament the expression *Magdal-eder* is known, which means something like *The Exalted One, the Protector of the Flock* or the *One Who is elevated and is guarding the others* or a mixture of the two. A kind of royal figure who is a leader and a protective light for her subjects. All in all, the name Mary Magdalene could mean *The Spirit of the Exalted Peace.*

He nodded with an air of being interested:

"And what does the professor know about her?"

"The New Testament does not say much about her. She is mentioned by name perhaps only a dozen times and there is a theory that Mariam, that is Mary Magdalene, and Mary of Bethany are one and the same.

If this is the case then she is the sister of Martha, Mari and Lazarus whom, according to the gospels, Yeshua raised from the dead. She was present at the crucifixion and according to *John's Gospel* was the first to see the risen Yeshua at the tomb. In *The Gospel of Luke* there are references to a 'sinner', a woman who is supposed to have been a prostitute. During his visit to Simon the Pharisee's house, this woman washes Yeshua's feet anointing them with ointment. The woman washed Yeshua's feet with her tears and wiped them with her hair, kissed his feet and anointed them with ointment from an alabaster jar. Simon the Pharisee clearly indicates by his attitude to her that she is 'untouchable'.

The identification of the 'sinner' in *Luke's Gospel* as a prostitute was determined by Pope Gregory in the year 591. He declared that the unnamed woman in this gospel was indeed Mary Magdalene, the woman 'out of whom went seven devils' and he announced that all true believers should regard her as the prostitute who was converted and saved after Yeshua exorcised her of seven evil spirits. If you look at the Greek word for prostitute that Pope Gregory used to describe Mariam — *harmatolos* — it can be translated in various ways. From a Jewish perspective it can mean someone who has broken the law. It may also mean someone who has not paid their taxes. The Greek word *porin:* woman of easy virtue, which is used in other parts of Luke, is not the word used for the 'sinner' who washes Yeshua's feet with her tears and dries them with her hair. Thus nowhere in the New Testament does it state that Mary Magdalene was a prostitute."

I stopped in order to see if he was bored.

"Do go on," he said, "it is very interesting."

"In *St Mark's Gospel*, we read of the second time Mariam anoints Yeshua who remarks 'Verily I say, wherever this gospel is preached throughout the world, what she has done will also be spoken of in memory of her.' Unfortunately, it seems that this has not been done in very many Christian congregations.

"We are also told that Yeshua exorcised seven devils or evil spirits from her. Pope Gregory felt that they were the seven deadly sins."

I stopped again to be quite sure that he really wanted to hear more. But he impatiently motioned me to continue.

"So much for the Church and its writings. If we take a look at some of the Gnostic and apocryphal writings, the *Nag Hammadi scrolls* and *Pistis Sophia*, which might have been among those that Constantine the Great and the bishops decided were heretical in the year 325, there unfolds a totally different story. It was on the same occasion that they decided that "the right faith" should be based on the scriptures, which we know today as the New Testament. Furthermore, they took steps to make the corrections in the texts which present day research has finally considered to be just that, corrections. All other non-Christian sources were banned by the synod. It looks, therefore, as if much of the Christian teachings in the churches today are, in many areas far removed from those of Yeshua two thousand years ago. Quite a thought — eh?"

The Seer nodded and threw more brushwood on the fire.

"What do the heretical writings say about our Mariam?"

"We are told in *The Gospel of Mary* that she was blest with visions and a deeper understanding than Peter. She is the one who teaches and comforts the other disciples. In *The Dialogue with the Saviour* she is praised not only as a psychic but also as the apostle surpassing all the others. She was "the woman who knew the universe." In *The Gospel of Phillip* it is said that she was the companion of Yeshua:

"The companion of the Saviour is Mary Magdalene. He loved her more than all the disciples and often kissed her on the mouth."

"There were three who always walked with the lord: Mary, his mother, his sister and Magdalene, the one who was called his companion. His sister and his mother and his companion were each called Mariam."

Yeshua says in *Pistis Sophia*:

"Where I am my twelve disciples shall be, but Mariam Magdalene and Yohannan (John) the Virgin are above all my disciples and above all people who are to receive the unspeakable mystery. And they shall be to my right and to my left. And I am they and they are me."

"Mariam, thou blessed one, whom I shall teach the highest mysteries, speak, since you are the one whose heart is closer to Heaven than all your brothers."

The Seer was listening with his eyes closed. When I went silent he opened them and looked enquiringly at me:

"Is that all?"

I searched my brain but couldn't think of anything else.

We sat for a while. The Seer got up and stretched his arms above his head:

"I'm quite certain that we have taken a considerable step forward in our quest. We'd better get some sleep."

He put his sleeping bag under his arm and pointed to the tent:

"The tent is for you. I'll sleep in my little eagle's nest. Sweet dreams."

I looked at him as he walked along the slope until he was just a shadow between the trees. Then he disappeared in the dark. The stars twinkled in the sky.

I sat for a while before going to bed. But I couldn't sleep. For some reason the thought persisted that there was something I had forgotten. Something which might answer the Seer's question more precisely.

I do not know how long I kept tossing and turning unable to rest. Then suddenly it struck me. The answer. The only book I had brought with me was *The Gospel of The Holy Twelve*. As usual, not recognized by orthodox scholars, this work was received in a vision and translated from Aramaic in 1900 by a clairvoyant English minister, G. J. Ouseley. I simply love it for its highly poetic language and its purity of the first water (pure weight in gold!). I quickly got up and fished the book out of my backpack and leafed through it until the torch light swept across a page at random:

"Chapter 66, verse 7: Thus it is with the One, the Father-Mother, in whom is neither male nor female and in whom are both, and each is threefold, and all are One in the hidden Unity.

Verse 8: Marvel not at this, for as it is above so it is below, and as it is below so it is above, and that which is on earth is so, because it is so in Heaven.

Verse 9: Again I say unto you, I and My Bride are one, even as Maria Magdalena, whom I have chosen and sanctified unto Myself as an example, is one with Me.

"I and the Bride are One," and "Mariam Magdalene, whom I have chosen as my example." These statements expressed their own unmistakeable language. The rest might have been taken directly from *The Gospel of Thomas*. There was just one small objection: *The Gospel of The Holy Twelve* was translated and published fifty-five years before *The Gospel of Thomas* emerged from the sands of Egypt.

I turned off the lamp and put the book aside.

"Mariam Magdalene, whom I have chosen as my example.

"I and The Bride are One."

Then I fell asleep.

4

Lazarus looked like a ghost in the pale morning light. She embraced him while the camels were made ready for the journey.

"In Beersheba you'll find Isaac the Pious One at the town square. One of Those Dressed in White will be waiting for you. He will bring you safely through the desert to Heliopolis."

His nervousness broke out with full force as he started hurrying the guards who were busy stowing the luggage. It was important to get started before the sun rose. It was in the middle of Tamuz and they were about to cross the Judea Desert.

"What must happen will happen," she said smilingly.

As the small caravan silently passed the gate she turned around once and waved at her brother and two sisters. She was already on her way into another world. Out of the reality of blood and into the reality of spirit.

They travelled through Bethlehem unnoticed. The roads were full of Roman patrols. Around noon she sat drowsily on her camel watching the three guards and her maid who flickered like a mirage in the scorching sun. The unnerving sound of the monotonous thump of saddlebags against the flank of the camel was interrupted only by the whining of the maid. Mariam herself sat silently in her saddle.

They rode up into the hills surrounding Hebron in order to pass the town unseen, the town where Abraham's wife, Sara, was buried and where King David at one time was anointed king of the House of Judea. Coming out of the valleys they rode into a rough wind that lifted the sand throwing it into the air in burning clouds that pricked the skin of the travellers like needles. One of the guards looked at her questioningly, seeking to get the long awaited sign to stop and rest. But she didn't say anything, pretending that she hadn't seen. Instead, she lost herself in the swaying rhythm of the camel's hips, fusing with its lazy movements beneath her and she slipped into a meditative state.

They reached The Town of the Seven Wells, Beersheba, in the late afternoon without having stopped once. Isaac the Pious One helped her off the camel himself. The guards tried to look as if they had kept their composure while the maid had to be carried into the travellers' quarters.

"You look as if you could do with a bath," Isaac said.

Drops of sweat had made thin, marbled patterns in the mask of sand grains on Mariam's face. But she just smiled as if she knew that the wildness of her beauty was simply enhanced by signs of the rigours of travelling.

This was her first experience of the hospitality of the Brotherhood. She washed herself in the pool behind a small pillared hall and was quietly amused by the curious eyes staring at her from the shadows, as if she were a strange being from an unknown world. Even holy eyes have to rest on the beauty of transience she thought while she generously took her time.

Isaac blessed their evening meal and prayed the necessary prayers. They dined in silence. Afterwards he took her up to the roof of the house where they had a view of the town. He pointed towards the desert:

"Out there is the Negev, the anvil of the sun. You are young and may not know the significance of the journey you have set out. You are beautiful. More beautiful than anyone else. But I do not see in you the deceit, which is nurtured by vanity. Tread softly, Mariam, for men will seek intimacy with you. Do not let yourself be tempted and do not tempt anyone. Out there is the Negev. Behind its apparent beauty and luxuriance it hides its true character. We call it the Oven of Souls. The Desert of Purification and Transformation. No one travels through it and remains the same. But I see that you possess great courage. Do you also have the strength, I wonder?"

He became silent and she sensed how his words disappeared in the dusk. Their simple power spread through her and a quiet calm rose up from her stomach.

"Tomorrow, one of the brothers will accompany you through the desert and on to your goal. You and I shall not see each other again. Be aware of my words and guard your virtue. May the Holy Spirit be with you."

He turned around and disappeared in the darkness without having looked at her once. His words and whole demeanour was devoid of any sentimentality. But she still sensed his warm feelings like the feelings of a father embracing his daughter. Yet behind all of that she glimpsed something fate-laden, a dark shadow moving across the already cloudy sky. She fell asleep with this shadow watching over her.

She woke up early. The sky was grey and there was a nip in the air and it was cool. The shadow had gone, but the feeling of oppression from the previous evening still seized her. She washed herself, packed her few belongings and walked out into the grey morning without having any of the food that the brothers had set out for her and her two guards. There was no sign of the maid and she thought that it was better that the maid stayed where she was safe. The brothers were performing their service at the Holy of Holies in the synagogue.

She was watching the camels being prepared when suddenly she noticed a tall, lean figure wearing a cloak and sitting on a mule by the gate at the outskirts of the yard. The figure had an almost radiating and unreal aura about it as if it floated in the air. The image disturbed her without her immediately knowing why. Not until the camels had been loaded up and the guards had led them out into the open did she realize that the figure was the brother who was going to lead them through the desert to Heliopolis. The thought restored her courage.

The small caravan moved out in the silence of the morning. The cloaked one was leading the caravan up ahead. Unapproachable. Mariam nudged the camel to make it move faster in order to get to the stranger, but inexplicably, the mule of the cloaked one seemed to hover along over the red-brown sand as if it had no connection with the ground. No matter how fast she rode the figure kept his distance about 20 meters ahead of her.

Except for a short break in the middle of the day, where they found shelter behind an overhang while the sun passed the anvil, they kept on riding until darkness enveloped them.

When they rode through the gate of El Akish, the biggest caravanserai on the road, she felt the toil of the day in all her limbs. She couldn't see anything but sensed that the sea was not far away, and she thought that the old Isaac had exaggerated in his talk about the oven of the soul.

In silence they rode through the narrow alleys until they stopped in a courtyard outside a house on the outskirts of the caravanserai. In the dark she noticed various figures taking care of the animals and searched for the cloaked one, but a bonfire in the yard made shapes flicker in the cracks of the walls and she lost her orientation.

A woman's voice reached her in the dark. It sounded as if it came from the fire where more and more figures assembled. The voice became more and more insistent, without Mariam being able to hear what it was saying. There was something in it that drew her closer, something that made her forget her fatigue.

She found a place among the seated figures where she could hear the female storyteller, but she couldn't see her.

"There is only *Rukha d'koodsha* – the holy breath. There is only this vibration, coming from that breath, expanding through the universe and becoming a part of you. The song of the breath sings: Oh, daughters of Zion. Where have you hidden your virtue? Where have you hidden your ability to love? Where have you hidden the bride? The bride waiting for the groom. And the breath is singing: Alas, the sons of Zion. Where have you hidden your humility? Where have you hidden your ability to give yourselves without wasting your semen? Where have you hidden the groom? The groom who is seeking his bride."

The woman stopped in order to emphasize the words which held the listeners spellbound.

"The celestial Queen is rising from the age old sea. Her power has fallen from the sky. She opens her heart for everything created. She is devoted to you. She offers herself to you. But you – you are tearing her womb apart and sullying her purity. Listen you sons and daughters of Zion. I come to those whose heart has been broken on my behalf. I raise the one who has fallen and I heal anyone who comes to me. Open yourselves to my power. Receive the Holy One for your days on earth are running out – whereas eternal life is waiting for you in every word I speak."

The voice stopped once more for effect. Mariam leaned forward in order to get a glimpse of the person who could speak like this.

"If you want to, I can lead you to the living water and the heavenly fire. But if you doubt me you will be left to yourselves. The one who wants to save himself must forfeit his life. The one who gives himself shall gain eternal life. Transformed. Exalted. Forever radiating in my heaven, which is without beginning and without end. Step forward you who doubt these words."

Time stood still around the bonfire. No one moved. Everybody sat entranced.

Then the silence was broken. A man stood up and pointed accusingly at the woman that Mariam couldn't see but whose words had touched her so deeply. The man's words were heavily judgemental:

"How dare you talk to decent people like this. You presumptuous one, you altar of immorality?"

A shiver went through the gathering. The man now spoke directly to them:

"Do you not know that this woman is a whore, that she is Helen of Tyrus?"

The eyes of the man glinted in the light from the flames reaching towards the sky.

Mariam *saw* him. She saw his fear. His intense lechery filled with anger. She saw his longing and his lack of love.

The gathering moved restlessly. They didn't know what to believe. They had heard all the various rumours about Simon the Magician and his woman the transformed whore Helen. They had heard many terrible but also many wonderful things. The rumour about this immoral woman had also reached their part of the country. But how were they to connect these rumours with the woman whose words had reached the hearts of all so directly, and which had made them spellbound. Words from another world, far away from dust and sweat and blood and saliva. Far from lechery, sacrifice, hate, revenge and devilish magic. Words which could come from Heaven alone.

"How dare you!" the man shouted and lifted his arm to throw the stone he had just picked up from the ground.

Suddenly the exalted mood from earlier changed to fear. Everybody jumped to their feet and spread out. Some bent over to pick up stones to throw. Mariam caught one of them by the arm but was punched by a fist and thrown to the ground.

"Get thee hence, woman," the man shouted whose actions she had tried to stop.

The stones flew through the air, but lying on the ground Mariam saw to her surprise that Helen, the target of the men's anger, had apparently disappeared into the darkness. In their confusion and frustration the men threw the stones in all directions. As if in this way, they hoped to stop the sound of the voice whose echo was still hanging in the emptiness, reminding them of something they had forgotten and did not want to be reminded of. Mariam saw it all.

Then she was lifted into the air. She felt the coarse groping of hands and how they sought out the most intimate parts of her body, greedily and without shame. She tried to twist away from the stranger's grip, but then noticed that it was one of the guards holding her in his arms. She wanted to shout to him that he should put her down, but the words disappeared in the noise from the agitated throng of people. He carried her to a house behind a large building facing the yard.

There was an open fire in the house. Not until she was sitting in front of the fire did she regain her composure. One of Those Dressed in White was preparing a ritual of the Brotherhood and she deduced that she was in one of their secret haunts. Mariam looked about but the cloaked one was not to be seen. Then the words of the mysterious woman came to mind, and she felt how they filled her and penetrated her heart.

Who was this Helen? Where had she gone to?

Mariam came to when one of the brothers offered her the chalice with the Power of the Spirit. As a woman and as a guest in the house of the brothers it was her privilege to be the first one to receive this communion. The oldest of the brothers performed the prayer.

"And remember, woman, that it is your choice whether or not you want to receive the chalice or let it pass you by. Receive the Gift of the Eternal One. Go into his house. Or leave his path forever."

She lifted the chalice with trembling hands. Her blood froze at the words of the older brother. The underlying note boded doom and eternal fire. She drank quickly and immediately passed it on. Did she have a choice?

Later she sat alone at the fire and got lost in the flames. One of the brothers came in and hesitatingly sat down beside her. As if sent to answer the questions burning on her lips.

"Who is this Helen?" she asked.

"You haven't heard about her?" the brother answered.

"Should I have?"

"Only because it is now publicly known. Sixty days ago it was still a secret and I wouldn't be able to tell you. But now it is of course a quite different situation. And since you are not just anybody it doesn't matter if I tell you or you hear it from someone else."

She looked surprised at the brother.

"What do you mean, I'm not just anybody?"

He looked at her just as surprised.

"We know your brother, Lazarus, he answered haltingly, as if he had said too much after all.

"And?"

He looked at her more and more incredulously. He really couldn't understand, that maybe she knew nothing.

"Tell me!" she said eagerly.

"Lazarus has been initiated into our Brotherhood. He is a novice in the Brotherhood and has been appointed to take care of an important task, about which I cannot tell you."

She felt the disappointment spreading in her. She was only something special because of Lazarus' position in the Brotherhood. Not that she wasn't happy and proud of him, but hearing the words of the One Dressed in White she had hoped to be recognized for who and what she was in her own right. But how could they know what she was able to see?

The One Dressed in White continued:

"A candidate from Samaria, Simon the Magician, brought the woman, Helen, here from Tyrus. He has jeopardized his candidature for the sake of this woman. Now she has become an itinerant preacher. This has caused a great uproar among the high priests in Jerusalem and not to mention among the brothers at Carmel and in

Qumran. The Sandhedrin in Jerusalem accuse the Brotherhood of deliberately wanting to cause indignation and separation among the people. And this though they know very well that Those who Dress in White always operate in secrecy. This Simon and his woman Helen operate autonomously. And it has gone so far that Simon can no longer control her madness. It is blasphemy of the Lord."

Mariam felt her throat tighten. The words of the One Dressed in White made her uncomfortable. Then she said:

"Did you not hear the woman's speech at the bonfire?"

"Why should I listen to something like that voluntarily?"

"Because she may just be speaking the truth. Because she spoke the word of the Lord. I have never heard anyone talk like that. Did you not see how her words captured her listeners?"

The One Dressed in White got up:

"I saw how she agitated the people with her blasphemous talk. This is hardly the will of the Lord. They have made a snake's nest of magicians and false prophets out of His sanctuary. This kind of thing has always been able to spellbind the people. They say that she speaks in order to scandalise and create discord. That she is spreading the work of Satan to the ignorant ones."

"It was only a matter of a few men. Men who ..."

She went silent. The brother had turned his back on her. She saw that he didn't want to hear any more. Then she had a sudden thought:

"What do you know about Yeshua?"

The question stopped him in his tracks as he moved away from her. Mariam knew that the One Dressed in White knew. He turned towards her:

"Yeshua?"

"Yeshua ben Yoasaph," she insisted in order to hold his attention.

Their eyes met for a moment but he quickly looked away.

"I – I do not know anyone by that name."

He continued to move away from her. She let him go. Unwillingly, he had given her the answer she wanted.

She waited till everybody had gone to bed. Then she quietly slipped into the open. The air was fresh. A strange mingling of sea and desert. High in the sky a single star twinkled, imitating the star in her chest. In the dark she sensed a figure in the yard. She stood still for a moment like a doe sensing danger. She recognised the Cloaked One and wanted to call out to him. Then she moved towards him across the yard but he kept moving away so that the distance between them remained the same.

They walked through the sleeping town. She walked briskly but couldn't get any closer to him. She hardly noticed that they had left the town and were on their way into the desert.

She woke up quite disorientated and couldn't recognise the room she was in. She didn't get up but tried to find her bearings. Then she remembered the woman, Helen, and her burning speech. Strange how words could be so intense and enthral you so deeply. She sensed the desert of the previous night deep inside her but couldn't remember the details and therefore let it go. However, she was aware of just one thing, she had to find this Helen.

She got up and got dressed. Downstairs the brothers were already performing their first communion. One hour later she and her two guards were on their way again.

In front of them the Cloaked One was straddling his mule. Again it was as if both rider and animal were floating over the sand. Mariam made an effort to find the rhythm of her own animal but she was rigid in her back and had fire in her hips. It was the time of the moon. Out of the corner of her eye she watched the guard who had taken her into the house the previous evening. He was an inveterate warrior. But of a special kind. A chosen race whose only purpose was attack and defence. He had a tough face with dark, leathery features. His body was muscular and sunburned. She wondered if he had a woman and a family waiting for him somewhere, or if he like most men of his kind had dedicated himself totally to the life of a warrior. She remembered his hands that so brutally groped her body, but strangely enough, this didn't make her angry. Instead, she felt that she understood the man and his needs. At a deeper level she understood that he wasn't evil, but was the result of a choice that others had made for him a long time ago. In him she saw the most basic needs of man expressed. An almost animal like being of instinct, carried along by a strange, purposeful strength with human features but who had totally repressed all forms of human dignity. She saw, in every fibre of his body, in his tough and precise movements his sexual nature bound up with survival instinct and fear of death that trickled like beads of sweat over his muscles, which flexed and relaxed, flexed and relaxed, flexed and relaxed. She understood that no man can harbour such an urge and such fear of death and not constantly seek release from it. She understood why such men sought comfort and kindness from prostitutes. They didn't know anything else. She understood them because she *saw* them. But it made her sad and disheartened. Because she saw at the same time that it was this fear of death, which turned the world into a cesspool of darkness, where men struggled forward on tottering feet of clay. For unknown reasons this made her think of the man to whom she was betrothed, and waves of an old sorrow moved through her. Where was he now? Did he also dream about a woman, about family and children? And if he did, was she this woman? Her thoughts went round and round and, as so many times before, they made her feel more and more hopeless. This was indeed a relentless desert.

In the afternoon they passed a unit of Roman soldiers without being accosted as if Mariam and the guards were invisible. Everything happened in a daze. The Cloaked One had suddenly disappeared. They camped in the evening sheltered by the cliffs and not far from the sea. The guards kept their distance. The fire in her abdomen was at its highest. The pain filled her totally, but she understood that it kept her in contact with the world and the earth on which she walked. Her only thought was her wish to see the charismatic Helen once more.

They got to the ferry across the Nile at Lape two days later.

"Blessed be you daughter of Isis," the blind ferryboat woman called out to Mariam, as they reached the other bank where a totally new world waited for them. The change from the barren desert, with rugged cliffs, to flat and fertile delta mirrored a similar change in her. Along the roads were strange sculptures of animal-like beings, gods from another world ornamented with all kinds of sacrifices. Everywhere wellkept fields of grain and oases with fig and balm trees. As they passed them, the farmers greeted them with smiles and positive gestures. Even the light seemed milder in this country and she was filled with hope.

Heliopolis was a dream of white marble and bright sandstone with magnificent, wide avenues and temples of all kinds. However, the whole town seemed to be built around one single building, the goal of Mariam's journey, the gigantic Temple of Isis in the centre of the town. It was in this temple that Moses used to be the high priest and it was from here that he had set out to take the Jews back to the Holy Land.

The renown of the Temple of Isis had spread as far as Rome. Of all holy places, this was praised as the most magnificent.

Mariam felt dizzy as slowly she ascended the wide staircase. The moment she entered the town she was overwhelmed by a mood of inexplicable resignation, which stunned her and cut her off from contact with the forces with which she was gradually becoming familiar. She now felt totally abandoned by everyone and everything and was only able to see the devilish beauty, the predictable and bombastic result of man's limited idea of the Holy Force, forever depicted in marble, sandstone and mortar.

She heard women's voices singing from afar and behind them a chanting male voice, everything in a language that she didn't understand. Unresistingly she surrendered into unknown hands — hands, which carefully held her and lead her through magnificently decorated halls, wonderful gardens with fantastic sculptures and imaginative fountains. She hardly noticed that she was undressed, washed and given a new strange gown to wear. She did not resist as they held a cup with a bitter drink to her lips and gently but firmly forced her to drink it. After that she lost all sense of time.

The character of the journey changed. She was now surrounded by figures with animal heads acting in another world from the one she was in. Even the character of the sounds changed and she had to give up trying to understand the language that was spoken by these figures. She hovered in an indefinable void, fell into a dissolving sphere and changed into nothingness, which showed itself in the form of an opening through which the animals passed freely. In her few, clear moments she thought that she had gone mad or that she was dead and that this diabolical place was some sort of weird paradise or a very refined sort of hell. She understood that basically she was just a thought. It was a liberating acknowledgement and the freedom lifted the thought towards a warm light of a nobler lineage. Only one single question threatened to undermine her newly won liberty: who was thinking this thought? To whom did it belong?

She opened her eyes and stared into a sky full of twinkling stars. She turned her head and realized that she was lying on a cot in a room with high walls and a large opening in the ceiling through which she could see the night sky. The room was devoid of furniture except for a chair on which a young girl was sitting.

The girl was watching Mariam. They were of the same age. Their eyes met and the girl smiled when she saw that Mariam was awake.

"How are you?" the girl asked.

Mariam tried to remember what had happened, but she was too confused to think clearly. Instead she asked:

"Where am I?"

"In the Temple to Isis in Heliopolis," the girl answered.

"What happened? Why am I lying here?"

The girl got up and came closer to Mariam.

"You came a month ago. In the meantime you have been through the initial rituals."

She was now standing by the cot and carefully placed her hand on Mariam's shoulder. Her touch made Mariam relax, and she thought that the girl must have magic hands.

"What rituals?"

"The rituals necessary to erase the memory of your former life."

Mariam left the question for the time being and surrendered to the girl's hands, which were quietly massaging her shoulders.

"My name is Ani. My task is to take care of you. It looks as if they expect a lot from you. Even Atuka has mentioned you in his prayers."

Mariam grew tense at the sound of this name. Her mind worked hard in order to remember, but everything went around in a circle and there was no opening. She then asked the most logical question:

"Who is Atuka?"

Ani looked at her with disbelief:

"Atuka is the high priest and the substitute for Osiris in this temple. He is the one who will be in charge of your initiation if ever you get that far. Be quiet now. You need your rest. Your education starts tomorrow."

Mariam held on to the moment:

"How long have you been here?" she asked.

"I grew up here."

Ani's hands moved in gentle circles, and Mariam gave up looking for more questions. Instead, she got lost in the multitude of stars on the ceiling. Something told her that the answer was somewhere up there.

5

I see seven beautiful women in long, transparent robes on a stage where, as an actor, I'm playing uncle of Hamlet. They stand in a circle intensely occupied by something. I cannot see the faces of the women very clearly, but I feel their sensual beauty. When I call to them they step aside, turn towards me with naked breasts and let go of whatever they are holding. It turns out to be a dim ball of light hopping about like a ball with too little air in it. It jumps in my direction and rolls over and comes to a stop at my feet. I pick it up, look at it astonished, realizing that it is the planet Uranus. I then turn towards the audience holding Uranus in front of me as Hamlet holding the skull and say, "The King is dead – Long live the King!"

The sound and smell of burning brushwood reached me from outside, where the Seer was already sitting on his rock by the fire waiting for the water in the small pot to boil for the first cup of coffee of the day.

"So, did the professor sleep well?"

The new day felt like an embrace. There was an immediacy and naturalness, an easiness and a pure presence, liberating everything and transforming these minutes into a moment that would never pass. It was in situations like these that I felt I got a glimpse of that which is always present, but which is seldom appreciated because I'm doing something else. And without being able to explain it better, it was in this state I began getting in contact with my higher qualities. Perhaps because this sphere in all its simplicity was certainty itself.

When, a little later, I was sitting opposite him, I told him about my dream. He looked into the fire for a long time before answering:

"The dream tells you that you must take your Uranus work upon you. The seven women may be the Pleiades, however, they may also mean the seven old planet worlds. Uranus like Pluto is one of the new ones. You must give new life to Uranus by moving the authorities – the world's and your own – but without you being tempted to become too self-centred. You must be able to put yourself outside of all conditions and all norms whatever they may be. You are present but not necessarily visible."

He disappeared for a moment, but then came back:

"Remember, a smile spreads like rings in water. It starts a chain reaction and may create a revolution. Changing war into peace. It is not important who started the process. The important thing is to get it started. Give Caesar what belongs to Caesar. But no more than that. Remember, when you are waiting for the traffic lights to change from red into green – even if there are no cars – Caesar still breaks the law as much as he likes. And who says that the light will ever change into green? Isn't traffic regulated on Caesar's bidding? That is why you have to accept breaking the law of Caesar and cross on a red light when it is necessary. It is your responsibility. But be careful, so that you are not run over. The ninth planet, Pluto, is presented at the death of the little "I." Hamlets uncle is that I. This is what you now renounce. You'll wake up with a hangover, in the King's bed, thinking that you are dreaming. But you are not. You have just wakened to the real world. You are now sober and may take on a responsibility – but you remain invisible. Pluto is also resurrection."

He gazed vacantly into the distance. I had never experienced him like that before. After a while he looked focused again.

"Uranus is the planet of the wizard. In your dream it is the connection between you and Sirius."

He closed his eyes:

"This is how you received the gift when you were about ten years old. The kundalini experiences you had then, which were caused by the shock over the death of your sister combined with your sexual awakening, was the result at a higher level of the flow from Sirius via Uranus and Venus to the kundalini centre in you. This opened your ability to see. But it was so powerful and overwhelming that you couldn't handle this gift, because at the moment of release it connected you with all the incarnations in which you were not able to release and use that power. And it is quite clear that such an experience brings a lot of pain with it. But now you must take the responsibility upon you, the responsibility which at the time accompanied this gift."

"But how?"

"By staying awake and listening to what is being said. By *seeing!*"

The teasing smile became serious.

"You may trust the Board of Directors with the rest. Be sure that they will let you know when the time is at hand. First and foremost, it is important that you are aware of the correct situation and that you do not turn your back on this consciousness."

I was contemplating his answer when suddenly I wanted to know how he had experienced *his* awakening.

"How did it happen for you?" I asked.

"Well, I also experienced great confusion. It can be quite a strain on your body because not all of the organs of the body are necessarily "open" and directed towards the poles corresponding to the flow of energy. And if you do not understand what is going on, well, then it can be quite chaotic. I was under great pressure. It was a symbol of the purification I had to go through on a higher level as well. A re-definition of the aspect of my will or the power, if you like. After that it went quite painlessly. A language was being born in me. A dictionary appeared along with that language which gave me an immediate understanding. Suddenly I *knew!* There were no doubts. I began seeing connections far beyond the universe, well, even further out, far beyond all universes. Back to Creation – and even before that."

"But how did you begin to integrate it?"

"I first had to go through the well-known children's diseases. You know, I thought I was a hell of guy – well, pardon my French – but that was what I was. The circumstances forced me to look at my motives. When I started working with my clients it all became self-regulating. If I didn't make sure that I was sharp and focused they simply didn't get in contact with me. I have quite a few therapists as my clients, and they complain that they haven't got any clients. I then have to get them to understand, that they may be working with this for the wrong reasons. Contrary to most people within this line of work I would rather be without it. But it doesn't work like that. I'm not in this just for my *own* sake. And you might as well realize this since you are going to do it as well: this is just *a part* of your education."

A new light appeared around him.

Then he said:

"Do not expect that they will set up a bust of you in the park. Do your work. Perform it with elegance and gratefulness. Never let yourself be misled by your vanity. Do not let yourself be lead astray by romantic flattery or injured critique from those who do not know better. It is not that you feel called – but you must simply follow your destiny. It is important to understand the difference. Be open and be always willing to learn. Be alert! – and that is it."

The last sentence was underlined by a gentle pat on my knee with his fist:

"When, finally, a person is willing to step out of the mists of oblivion and has the courage to begin remembering, then this person will be recognized. Both up there and down here. When an individual remembers, he will be able to accept his task. Everybody has a task to perform here. And no one can fulfil someone else's purpose. That is why we may as well forget all about circumstances not being as good as they should be or that others have much better options than ourselves. The present circumstances are always the best possible at that moment. That's the way it is. If you cannot help yourself where you are right now, how could you possibly help others?"

The sun played peekaboo behind a cloud but disappeared quickly again. The Seer threw the rest of the water on the fire as a sign that it was time to start the work of the day. We helped each other to pack the equipment. We left the tent. I didn't think about that at the time, being occupied with all he had just said.

When we were ready, we stood for a moment inhaling the fresh air, the colours and the shapes coming to life in front of us. The sound of this silence was indescribable and yet it was only an overture to another kind of silence which was to come later, and which must be the most meaningful music on earth. We began ascending the east side of the mountain. The stronghold was further up.

The path was steep and difficult. On the mental plane it was clear that the Power was getting more and more intense and I could feel that something was pending. I sensed the activity in the ether around us. My joy was pure in a different way than before. It was not mushy neither did it have its origin in any kind of sentimentality. Maybe that was the reason that I was more purely receptive. I did not consider the advantages of a simple life. At that moment I *was* that. I didn't long for anything. All that was needed was already in the game and within reach. Everything was contained in the breath. The joy had its root in gratitude.

Gratitude towards the Seer for having awakened me so effectively. Gratitude towards the Power and the reality it made available. Gratitude towards the great breath. All that I had always dreamt about but not really dared hope to regain. Everything that never, in my wildest dreams, had I thought I would either deserve or be able to carry out, because long ago I had once been unfaithful to it.

On a ledge on the other side a wild dog was watching us from the shadows of a thicket. As we got closer and stepped into the open, it disappeared as silently as it had come.

It took us about an hour to climb the two hundred metres. When we reached the top we took a short break in the ruins of an early settlement outside the stronghold. I had a single butterfly in my stomach as we walked along the wall towards the northern gate, and the butterfly turned into many as we stepped into this holy place.

The Seer, as usual, went to the middle of the courtyard. I followed him and, also as usual, stood at his right side.

The Seer drew an invisible circle on the ground with his cane. He stood stock still at the centre of the circle facing the tower of the stronghold to the northwest. In spite of his apparent immobilty I saw him in his astral body. Here he was holding his arms stretched out to each side like wings, and slowly spinning about himself he whirled faster and faster in a spiral-like vibration while the voice inside me chanted the following words in Aramaic:

"Ephatah! Ina na thar'a! — Ephatah! Ina na thar'a! — Ephatah! Ina na thar'a!"

(Open up! I am the door between the worlds!)

I stepped into the circle, which rotated faster and faster drawing everything into it. All lines, all the corners of the world found their way towards this centripetal point of concentrated energy. I can only describe it like this: it was as if an intense suction was operating under the picture of the physical world turning it inside out. Thus, the ethereal vitality, hiding behind the apparent solidity of physical things, is made visible. This solidity is but one side of what we normally consider to be our reality. It is really just as natural as turning your jacket inside out. Like pulling a veil aside. And in that same breath are all beings of light made visible.

Everything unfolds in an inexplicable silence, which is not the lack of sound but rather the consecration of it. If we consider the organ music of Bach to be the closest we can get to a reflection in sound of the ethereal filigree, and that the last string quartet of Beethoven is the closest we may get to the sound of human grief transformed into victory through the power of grace, then to my mind there is no contemporary music able to reflect the quietness I experienced here.

With my eyes closed a simple prayer surges through me:

Nehwey sibyanak aykana d'shmaya aph b'arah.

Let that happen on earth which is written among the stars.

Unfold the light of the universe through each of us in harmony with the universal laws.

I see that what is written among the stars is already unfolding on earth, because there is no difference between here and there. The ethereal reality is a far purer form of star-writing compared to the earthly one. A language, which is not limited by gravity and Cronus.

Quiet – quiet – quiet – quiet – quiet – quiet ... before my inner sight a small flame.

Then I hear the Voice – whispering in the wind:

"I was sent forth by the Power,
I have come to those who are able to receive me,
I have been found by those who seek after me.
Look upon me, you who wish to be united with me,
Hear me, you who are listening.
You, who are waiting for me, receive my essence.
Forget me not!
For I am the first and the last.
I am the honoured one and the scorned one.
I am the whore and the holy one.
I am the wife and the virgin.
I am the mother and the daughter.
I am the celestial bride,
For whom there is no husband.
My power is from the one who sent me.
I am the incomprehensible silence
I am the voice whose sound is manifold
And the word without end.
I am the blessing of my name.
I am wisdom and ignorance.
I am without shame and filled with it.
I am power, I am fear.
I am peace and war.
I am the void in fullness.
I am oneness in emptiness.
I dissolve all concepts.
Dissolve all images.
Thus, I am limitless.
Thus, I am all.
Forget me not,

Because I am the outcast and the long expected one.
Be vigilant you, who know how to listen,
Everyone who has been sent, listen,
Everyone who is now awake and resurrected from sleep.
Many are the pleasant forms making up the grand illusion,
The empty sin and transient desire,
Which humankind is embracing
Until they become spiritually sober
And go up to the appointed place.
That is where you will find me.
Then you shall live,
And never taste death again.

The whispering voice speaks healingly to the innermost me, to the eternal being. Again and again I must give up the remainder of my resistance. What have I got to lose?

I am falling through an endless room. Then I am caught by unseen hands lifting me. What felt like gravity before is now transformed into grace — a quiet being in the breath of the universe. There is no separation. Only healing and devotion.

It is a most touching sight and an indescribable condition as the field opens in a majestic movement and illuminates the whole courtyard. The light is so intense that I have to screw up my eyes. The Seer is looking directly into it. I also look, and I see that it is Mariam, a radiating figure in front of us. The whole castle is surrounded by vibrations:

It is hard to know how long this continues. Time is without meaning. Then the symbol appears, pulsating in the intense light:

I am breathless and spellbound. Like last time, I feel compelled to step into this vibration and disappear into it. But the fear of not being able to live up to it keeps me back.

Suddenly I see it. The meaning of the symbol.

The two Ms: Mariam Magdalene!

I open my eyes. I see two shadows on the ground in front of me. The Seer's and my own. Behind us the sun has broken through the ragged clouds. We are standing in the circle, side by side. I see the two Ms becoming clear in the sand and I realize that this is the sign of the Age of Aquarius. But that is not all. I also see that MM is the Roman numeral for 2000 – the new millennium.

I am totally speechless. Not only because of the unbelievable situation we are in, but also because of the significance of the secret language. The Seer is silent. The Voice is saying:

"Now you have seen it. But this is only the beginning. Remember, that what you have just witnessed is but a pale image of reality. Do not get lost in the images but concentrate all your power on the force behind them."

"What is Mariam trying to tell us?" I asked the Seer.

"We'll see. Someone is trying to tell us something anyway. It is now our task to find out what it is."

He stepped out of the circle. I stayed in the slipstream of the intense energy of the Power. The ethereal bubble in which I was standing yielded, and the elastic silver string connecting us slowly untied itself. A small, almost imperceptible snap followed by a faint sprinkling of small glowing particles rising in the air, and I looked at the white clouds in the sky drifting majestically like proud ships on an endless sea. That was all.

Liberated from all worries.

Being.

Later, when I had also stepped out of the circle and was sitting at the end of the courtyard, the Seer drew another circle around himself and slipped into the silence I had seen him practice so many times before. I sat watching him and got the urge to take a snapshot of him. I got out my camera and adjusted the lens. He was standing in the middle of the picture. The moment I pressed the release I saw, out of the corner of my eye, something to the left of the frame, something indefinable moving. I didn't think much about it until one month later when I had the film developed. To my great surprise I saw that the Seer was not alone in the picture of the courtyard, there was the image of a young man beside him.

When I had taken the picture and put the camera away I also fell silent. Except for the dancing energies around us only the Seer and I were present.

Imperceptibly I slide out of life's disguise, the body's frame. Break through the veil and float upwards. My waves unite with the waves of ether. I am a life-giving energy and see that never has there been another separation than the one I myself have created with my inexplicably limited attitude and arrogant resistance. The ether is filled with radiating beings. Small and almost invisible, swirling particles of light. Indefatigable, present, maintaining, performing the eternal principle of creation.

"The guardians of the fire!" the Voice whispers.
Below me I see a young man, the Silent One, squatting in one corner of the courtyard. The Seer calls him over with an invisible sign. The Silent One gets up and walks towards the radiating circle at the centre of the courtyard. The circle opens and I watch the two figures floating through unnumbered, nameless worlds.

Kansbar and Flegetanis.

I watch them walking across a sun-filled marketplace in Andalusia in another time. Nevertheless I sense that what I'm witnessing is also happening in the eternal now. It has happened before. It is happening now. And it shall happen again. Until the task has been fulfilled these two souls shall float through the worlds passing on the baton — until they meet and recognise each other for what they really are.

"Who is this white bearded Kansbar?"

At a railway station several centuries later the Seer passes on an age old manuscript into the care of the Silent One. Shortly after, the train with the Silent One and the manuscript disappears into one of the timeless tunnels of reality. The Silent One goes home and writes a book about his encounter with eternity.

"But who is Kansbar?"

All the thoughts and actions of humanity throughout time are stored in the ethereal — Akasha. Everything. Every little bit. Every *yod*!

Through our thoughts and actions we create our reality ourselves. Reality is exactly as limited or unlimited as we make it. I see that the human being is a transformer. We transform matter and the heavy dead weight of form into live energy. If we choose to.

If we choose not to, we remain petrified, guards and prisoners.

We have neglected our work here for far too long and filled the ether with un-reflected, unchanged, heavy and dark matter. Filled it with all our untamed desires and projections. Through thousands of years we have developed very slowly. It has happened according to the principle of two steps forward and one back. Sometimes even one step forward and two back.

We have been the prisoners and guards of heavy matter and form for far too long. As if we have completely forgotten who we are, where we come from and what wonderful possibilities and abilities we possess.

But we have now passed quarter day. From now on we shall no more be asked. We may choose to accept the transformation or not. But it happens now. Not tomorrow in some obscure Nirvana, but HERE AND NOW! Nirvana is here now! Shamballa is here now! Heaven is here now! There shall not be other circumstances better than those we are in now. I see this now, and now I do understand.

We can transform the choking illusions of property rights and monopoly into a liberation of philanthropy and service. We can change fear into joy. When we let go of our stubborn insistence on being the chosen ones and more special than other people. This is the only real way in which to be unique.

We can transform any kind of power and see how limited, how totally ridiculous and unimportant it is. We can transform imprisonment to freedom, separation to unity, disease to wholeness. If we choose to.

Death is like walking through a door from one room to another. There is no death. If we decide it. Death is something we have created. In the ignorance of fear. In the unconscious race of galloping worries. We are killing ourselves with all our limited fantasies of what happiness is. Dreams about this and that, cars, money, luxuries, the perfect partner, perfect surroundings, perfect conditions. The perfect guru. The perfect sexuality. The perfect spirituality. Anything. The dream about being something special. The trap is wide open and springs again and again every time another poor fellow is trapped. Man is killing himself with the fear of losing all that, even before he has greedily sunk his neurotic claws into it.

Forget it.

Rise up. Take up your bed and walk – you are healed.

Rise up. Take responsibility for yourself.

If you choose to.

"Who can make themselves the judge of others?"

The Voice is a part of the ethereal. It speaks to me and still I am that Voice.

"When someone judges others, she or he is judging themselves."

I am weightless and present everywhere. This is everywhere and nowhere. A non-local being. The moment the Voice shapes its acknowledgement, that presents itself as words, but is, in reality holy sound, any kind of judgement is silenced, because then everything becomes whole and reality is without opposites.

Without reservation, I now see the busy agents of ether, created by all our fearful thought forms. These agents, as opposed to the maintaining and healing beings of light, are undermining and separating. Nevertheless, there is no difference between them as such. They are the two sides to every question, an expression of our choices and thus the will of eternity.

How can I see and acknowledge all that when at the same time I realize that I am just a cosmic baby who hasn't even learned to walk yet?

All my being is one big question floating in ether through the universes. I wonder if it shall ever understand that the answer is to be found within itself?

"Are you beginning to understand in what multidimensional reality we exist?"

The figure of the Seer stood in front of me, outlined against the sun.

"You have seen something of the things awaiting you. Seen some of the possibilities you may access as a human being."

I nodded and looked around. Green ivy was crawling over the wall of the stronghold. The release of a camera clicked. I looked towards the sound and thought that I saw a figure moving. But no one was there. I heard the Voice behind me:

"It is time for you to take the next step. You shall learn which principles are the basis for moving about freely and consciously in ethereal reality."

For a moment I was paralyzed between two types of consciousness. On one side the Seer who had brought me here, on the other – the Voice:

"An individual enters the world as an empty cup. This emptiness is filled with a creative silence. Certainty lives in this silence. The certainty about humanity's innate, eternal nature. Certainty is without words and ideas. It has no need for explanations. It is. Eternal certainty about itself. But humanity is not allowed to remain in this state for long. From the time of birth the surroundings immediately begin to fill this apparent void with noise and with lessons. And that is how it must be. In order for an individual to learn how to relate to the external world. Learn how to walk, how to talk, how to become a social being. It is a shame, however, that in that process humans more or less forget all about the original certainty of the void. Instead of

finding the equilibrium of options you lose yourself one-sidedly in the external world. Until the day where the cup has been filled to the brim with noise and lies, and you get ill or somehow are forced to revaluate your life."

I thought about the Sufis, the mystics dressed in white, known as the mystical side of Islam. They use a term called "unlearning" or "emptying the cup." So that, once more, there will be room for silence and certainty.

The Voice continued:

"Without a creative silence there is no way that you'll be able to take one single step towards release and liberation. Without it, all aspirations to gain enlightenment will be more or less wasted. When the cup has been emptied and silence restored, there is no use for aspirations. No more will there be any talk about forward or backward. No more will there be stagnation. Humanity is what it always was: moving, creative silence. The difference between the one state and the other is simply that in silence you are awake and creative, and you know that it is so. In a state of noise you are more or less a sleeping zombie in the world. A zombie with lots of nonsensical actions that humans have made into the mantra of their lives."

The words did not in the least sound strange to me. I was very well aware that it was not only a mental understanding but a total transformation that was awaiting.

The Seer stepped in front of me:

"But before you may start this process you must have the courage to face what in some traditions is called *The Guardian of the Threshold*, the necessary acknowledgement with the most cleansing effect. That is, if the process is successful. Tonight you'll sleep in the tent on the mountain slope. This is something you must go through on your own."

He was watching the mountain. Then he hummed a line from a song the title of which I do not remember anymore. He turned around and started walking. I watched him disappear.

If possible, it was even more difficult moving down than up. It was almost as if the narrow, impassable path wanted to underscore the

Seer's sarcastic motto, "Why go down when you can go up."

Struggling to keep my balance on the way down I was suddenly struck by faint-heartedness. I was on another path than the one we had used climbing up. Hoping that it would take me to the tent I continued. It was a cul-de-sac. I looked in vain for the tent further down but couldn't see it. Arms held me tightly as I fought to get free of the thicket on my way down to our starting point. But where was it? For a moment I was seized by panic. Where did my feeling of "walking on safe ground" suddenly disappear to? Where had my newly found knowledge of the connection between all things gone to? Why did I lose my pluck just because I met a little resistance? At this exact moment my foot slipped on a stone and I went over the edge. I rolled down the mountain side for endless seconds, through thickets and over rocks. In a last desperate attempt to break my fall I succeeded in catching hold of a small tree, which bent dangerously under the weight of this unexpected, new burden. I lay quite still in order to catch my breath. The tent was positioned on the ledge below me.

"Pride comes before a fall!" a tiny voice whispered.

The earth turned until the sun had disappeared behind the snow covered Pyrenees. I sat by the fire tending to a few cuts, but I couldn't really concentrate on the matter at hand. The valley and its nature, which normally had an enchanting effect on me, had totally lost its attraction. I thought that I might just have lost my ability to appreciate all this beauty. Everything was just a surface. Devilishly beautiful settings created by just as devilish forces. An empty kind of beauty without any other purpose than that of beauty. And the emptiness was monumental. I pricked up my ears. Forced myself to listen, but not a sound. The silence wasn't even there. No birds were singing. No wind was moving. Everything seemed lifeless. Even the last rays of the sun seemed colourless. Darkness came creeping. I told myself that I could feel its cold essence and was seized by an inexplicable, negative sensation. I hurriedly threw the last of the brush wood onto the fire, crawled into the tent and zipped the opening to behind me and crept into my sleeping bag. The flames danced a dance of shadows on the tent canvas. Even now as I sit here writing about it I feel the fear almost as I felt it then. I can feel the emptiness surrounding me then. An incomprehensible isolation from the rest of creation. And I saw how insignificant a man can be. How insignificant most of what was me really was compared to everything else.

The dancing shadows disappeared and I was swallowed up by darkness. An isolated thought of fear wrapped in the great nothingness. A nothingness in the merciless emptiness of the dark. Within this thought I saw everything I had done. The unbelievable suffering I had put others through time after time. I saw how all my thoughts, the lust, the failures, the ambitions and actions, conscious as well as unconscious, had left situations and whole worlds in an inconceivable and fatal chaos. The thought seemed to contract in the darkness. Became a particle, a centre of unfathomable weight, the only content of which was *sin!* The moment I realized that this particle of sin was me, the world disappeared from under me and I fell down and further down. At the same moment I also realized that this sin grew from the sickness in my mind, that the sin and the disease was one and the same, and that I would forever be trapped in this terrible limitation. Desperately, I reached into the darkness to find something to hold on to. But nothing was there. My cries were sucked into this nothingness without a sound. I fell and fell while the centre became more and more dense and heavier and heavier.

"Help me! Save me! Forgive me!" I begged.

But there was no answer because there was no one there to answer me.

Was this the eternal darkness into which only the ultimately lost souls are thrown?

Eternal perdition where there is no pardon and no forgiveness?

"Yes," the small voice said.

The centre grew heavier and expanded suddenly, while the speed was now so fast that I just hoped this endless darkness would after all come to an end that it would have a bottom against which this terrible weight would be crushed and forever disappear. Instead, I experienced the centre growing at an increasing speed, that, so to speak, it grew into the darkness so that there was no difference between them. The centre and the darkness were one. I was no longer a specific centre in that emptiness. I *was* this darkness. The sum total of all that is immovable, all that is unreleased and unchanged. Tied down to eternal limitations.

In the middle of all this I suddenly realized that the terrible fall had come to an end. My essence was gravity and space but the downward movement had stopped. There was no movement at all. I was, so to speak, caught within myself. The knowledge about the only alternative to this seemingly finite nightmare made the situation impossible. And worst of all: memory. My memory about former, wasted possibilities burning into my centre like an eternal fire without leaving a single ray of light. Damnation was total. And there was only myself to thank. This acknowledgement was made with my last remaining resources as if I had only been allotted so much potential. But exactly that potential – my memory – at the same time was my remaining chance of salvation. I was hanging on the utmost edge of the chasm of oblivion with my fingertips, hanging on to my last ray of hope when an almost invisible, radiating spot appeared like a mirage in nothingness. I was about to let go of everything when in that radiating spot I thought that I recognized a face. I concentrated in order to see who it was. Slowly, the face grew clearer and I could feel how this wonderful miracle restored my powers. I could now see who it was. Hazrat Inayat Khan. My old sufi master whose book, *Gayan, Vadan, Nirtan* had been sent to me anonymously, when at fifteen years old I found myself in a deep crisis. Hazrat Inayat Khan the teachings of whom had meant so much to me and, of this I had always been certain, had guided me from the beyond. He now appeared on this my judgement day. Tears rolled down my cheeks. At that moment the face changed and I recognized one of the many people who had supported me on my way through life. And I saw the long row of people to whom I now knew I owed everything. If all these souls had not been, I would have perished long ago. The face changed once more and was now so close that I could feel its imperishable force. The smile of the white bearded Seer with his deep blue eyes was standing in front of me. Then I let go and felt how I was lifted up, up and up while the darkness slowly changed into light.

I have the old, timeless manuscript, which was given to me by the

Hazrat Inayat Khan (1882 – 1927)
(Photo: Sikar van Stolk)

Seer, in front of me. I realize that it has always followed me. Every time I lose sight of it the One Dressed in White comes forward. Sometimes as Kansbar. Other times as a voice in my heart. At times, when I open the manuscript, the letters turn into signs, and I do not know what they mean. At other times the words dance towards me like well known beings of light, singing, opening doors to worlds I didn't even know existed. I turn another page and read.

6

Mariam lifted her head towards the sound. She caught a glimpse of a platform at the end of the hall. On this platform was a throne. She was surrounded on all sides by a colourful, ornate and foreign script. Her eyes hauntingly swept over the wall in a desperate attempt to read the writing, but all she found was an indefinable echo in the furthermost nooks and crannies of her mind – memory. A soft wind made waves of parts of the wall. Then she remembered.

The Temple of Isis.

The waving wall was pulled aside. A figure, with an enormous ox mask pulled over his head and upper part of his body, stepped in. A sundial was placed over the horns with a snake in front of it. The figure mounted the raised platform and sat down on the throne.

"Mariam, daughter of Isis. The hall you are in is the first sphere of the divine mind, which is matter. The divine mind is without beginning and without end. This transient world is just one of the many ideas of the divine mind. It is within this mind that man breathes, lives and *is*. When the student has gained the right to carry the Key of the Master and is able to open the many doors of the mental and psychic rooms of the Temple of Wisdom and enter them free and wise, the principles behind the concepts of energy, power and matter shall be revealed as well as the necessary knowledge of how to handle them. The one who understands the truth behind the mental nature of the universe has already come a long way towards mastery. But it is impossible to reach the goal without the Key of the Master."

Mariam was standing in front of the throne with her eyes closed while the words of the priest enveloped her. When she decided to open her eyes again she was very surprised to find, that she was now standing in a cloister garden surrounded by rose bushes. In the middle of the garden a loaf of bread was rising in the morning sun on a stone altar.

I am only a thought, she thought. Everything around me is simply the thoughts of the Sublime One expressed in matter. This is the endless song that God is singing. One verse after the other. A poem of creation in which everything is made concurrently with the ability of the waiting darkness to hear it. Let me be the most insignificant *yod*, the most humble of the written characters, in this song. The smallest echo of the great silence.

Everything was predestined. Nothing happened haphazardly. Mariam knew what she had to do and stepped in front of the stone altar in the middle of the garden. She stayed in the same spot all day long watching the imperceptible transformation of the dough into bread. When the sun set the bread was done.

Mariam's days were lonely days. The lessons continued without any breaks. The Hall of the Ox became her prison. Only god knows how many times she witnessed the creation of bread by the sun. *The oven of the soul!*

She vaguely remembered events which gave her an insecure feeling that something was missing. But she didn't remember what it was.

From time to time, the monotony was broken. She started counting the days. She had a day off every seven days. On those days she stayed in her cell and the enclosed garden belonging to it. For

153 days she didn't see any other novices.

Then suddenly one day a change occurred. Early one morning she was collected by two veiled women leading her through unknown passages and into a magnificent bath. She sensed the admiration and envy of the two women when they undressed her and were confronted with her youthful beauty. They disappeared when they had finished bathing her and Mariam was left in the care of a black woman who didn't try to hide her admiration for the unique being who had been given into her temporary care. She immediately began her work.

Mariam was told to lie down on a couch and the woman started removing all unwanted hair from Mariam's body with a sharp knife. Mariam reluctantly followed the woman's actions. When she gently wanted to force her legs apart she protested and held her knees together. But the woman smiled firmly and pushed Mariam back onto the couch, and with a firm grip she forced her legs apart. She lay immovable in fear of the sharp edge of the knife, but the woman worked with very careful and distinct movements clearly demonstrating that she had done this many times before. When the intimate process was over and the woman had made sure that it was done properly, she started massaging Mariam with ethereal oils. The black hands moved with slow, intense movements over the tense body. Without any shame they kept circling the most sensitive spots, and Mariam felt how a secret fire was lit and spread its burning sensuality under the thin skin of her body. She wanted to resist her, but the black woman simply looked at her in a way, which made her give up any further resistance.

As if in a languorous dance the woman led Mariam slowly but firmly into a foreign country where a totally new power ruled. A power which was about to explode in her womb at any moment.

No matter how hard she fought against it in her mind she finally gave in totally to her repressed desires so that when the woman stopped, leaving her a pliant victim gasping for air, Mariam wanted the woman to go on with her treatment. Instead, the woman helped Mariam to her feet. She could barely stand on her own. Electric currents rushed through her shining body.

Before she knew it two female slaves were dressing her in a light gown made from a transparent material, which, although covering her body, clearly emphasized her nakedness. Finally, they combed Mariam's hair and covered her face with the sign of the dancer, the provocative half moon veil.

They lead her through dimly lit passages until they stood in front of a striped curtain. Only when she found herself standing in a room without any visible walls did she see that it was the Hall of the Ox, but that they had arrived through the entrance usually used by the teacher.

In the middle of the hall on a platform that she hadn't noticed before was an enormous bridal couch already prepared, surrounded by a sea of oillamps. The slaves pushed her closer and she saw that a young man was waiting on the bed. It was not until she was standing at the foot of the bed, that she noticed that the handsome boy was naked. He smiled shyly at the sight of Mariam and he reacted quite naturally. She turned her eyes away from his erect member but felt a strong compulsion to let herself slide down on the inviting bed. The entire hall was enveloped in a warm, vibrating light and she could hardly stand on her feet. She was about to give in when a pair of hands took a firm grip around her arms and held her like a vice. Out of the corner of her eye she saw a small wooden phallus hastily being smeared with a kind of shiny liniment. The smell was putrid. Henbane.

Before Mariam was able to register what was going to happen, the hands forced her to bend over, and other hands forced the smeared wooden phallus into her from behind. The action was unexpected and the pain so sharp that she was paralyzed by it. The hands held her firmly until the herbal liniment started to work. Then they slowly pulled the instrument out of her and let her go.

As if in a dream Mariam floated through the air towards the young boy who pulled her into a warm embrace. Without any resistance she opened her mouth and let him kiss her deeply and for a long time. Hands moved over her stomach and suddenly she felt them all over her body until she lifted her buttocks from the bed and bent like a bow pressing her abdomen against the youngster. Never before had

"The Synagog"
(W. Hege & W. Pinder)

she felt anything like this. The young man lifted her up and together they rode through torn landscapes of deep longing. She felt that she was being severed and that the slow ride filled her totally to the point where the pain disappeared into unknown horizons far from time and place. Again the hands seized her and the young man turned her over, and trembling he entered her once more. Now the rhythm changed. Faster and faster they rode through a somewhat heavier landscape where pain and pleasure fused into an inseparable unity. She opened her eyes in order to look into the eyes of her lover in this moment of ecstasy.

Her scream disappeared in the noise from the rhythmic chanting of the surrounding crowd. Above her an enormous shadow with the head of an ox moved back and forth, back and forth, harder and harder until she lost consciousness and let herself be swallowed up by a distant and cool peacefulness.

"What is she doing here?"

A masterful woman's voice reached her from far away.

"She is among the chosen ones," another woman with a more primitive dialect replied.

Mariam opened her eyes slightly. Against the light she saw a tall, beautiful woman dressed in the gown of Those Dressed in White. The woman came to the couch where Mariam was lying. Mariam immediately closed her eyes when the cover was removed from her body. In a desperate attempt to shield her nakedness she turned on her side and covered herself with her hands.

"Lie still!" the voice with the primitive dialect commanded her.

"Let her be."

Mariam felt a gentle hand on her shoulder turning her over until she was lying on her back again.

"Do not be afraid. My name is Salome. This is not the first time that I have seen a beautiful, young girl without her clothes, but never have I seen anyone as beautiful as you."

Mariam opened her eyes fully and stared into the most enchanting eyes she had ever seen. The woman again covered Mariam's body and turned her attention to the other woman at the end of the couch:

"Atuka liked that, eh? The first one to pick this rare flower. How far is he with his preparations?"

The other woman, whom Mariam could now see was a black slave, turned her eyes away without answering.

"You heard me, how far is he?"

The female slave clearly felt ill at ease. She was embarrassed and twisted and turned uncomfortably. Salome's eyes flashed. She looked questioningly at Mariam but realised at the same moment that she couldn't expect an answer from her.

The black slave broke down crying as Salome took hold of her. It was obvious that the patience of the woman dressed in white was at an end:

"Is it so that he has already picked it?" she cried.

The slave was shaking. She fell to the floor and still crying she tried to explain. But Salome no longer had any doubt about the answer. For a brief moment Mariam's and Salome's eyes met and the former sensed in her drowsiness the mixture of hurt and anger in the dark eyes.

The One Dressed in White reached out towards her with one hand:

"Let's get out of here."

The women rode north. They followed the roads along the river on the first day, but after two days of riding Salome lead them across the north eastern corner of Wadi Natrun. They did not talk much but Mariam's memory became clearer with every hour that passed. She rocked gently along in her saddle and surrendered unconditionally to the safety and strength radiating from her liberator dressed in white.

Now and again they would stop to drink. Salome handed Mariam a piece of bread, which she kept in her saddlebag. She herself didn't eat anything.

"Cover yourself against the wind and the sun," she said when in the middle of the day they were crossing the desert.

Endless expanses of sand and impassable plains full of rocks stretched out in front of them, and when the wind started to blow they struggled forward step by step. However, it did not take long before the hardships were behind them. The landscape changed and became lush and fertile. Now and again they would see other travellers, and the closer they got to the coast the more travellers they met. Salome stopped on a hill and pointed to a town in the distance:

"This is Alexandria, the centre of wisdom and science."

She hesitated for a while but then continued:

"Unfortunately, it is also that of fools."

She smiled at Mariam and a little while later she chuckled away in a low and catching laugh, which made Mariam want to join in. It was a laughter that she would hear many times and that she would come to love.

Salome now pointed to the right of the town:

"This is the lake of Mareotis. This is where we are going. Let us not waste any more time."

Late in the day they rode into the jungle growth of a forest surrounding the lake that Salome had pointed out earlier. Coming out on the other side, to her great astonishment, Mariam saw a series of buildings of a kind she had never seen before. The houses were identical, white with various symbols painted on them and situated in a kind of cluster but still with a fair distance between them. In the middle of the formation a slightly larger house was situated.

Salome headed for a house on the outskirts of the cluster.

"Welcome to *The Therapeutae*," she said smilingly to Mariam.

Goats were grazing inside fences and all kinds of medicinal herbs were growing around and on the walls of the houses. Mariam was met by the smell of hyssop as she entered Salome's house.

Behind the living room two smaller rooms were situated. Salome showed Mariam into one of them:

"This is yours. We cannot know for how long you are going to stay. But it is important that you get plenty of rest and get well. It will take a few days before you recover from the effects of Atuka's magical drink."

A dust filled ray of light danced in the opening of the window and crawled along the clay wall. Mariam stayed in her bed listening to the sound of distant bells. She stretched lazily and yawned from well being, got up and stood enjoying the fresh air in front of the open window. A flock of goats were on their way down the slopes toward the lake eating the juicy grass on the way. Mariam too a deep breath of fresh air and felt a rush of inexplicable happiness suffuse herself. So this was the paradise of Those Dressed in White. The Society of Therapists to borrow Salome's expression.

"Good to see you up and about."

Salome stood smiling in the doorway.

"Come on outside. I have prepared some food for you. When you have eaten you must tell me everything."

They sat down on benches in a small courtyard in front of the house. Mariam dined in silence but Salome didn't have anything.

"Now tell me," Salome said when Mariam had finished eating.

And Mariam told her everything that she had experienced. She told her about the strange vision in the wash house in her home in Bethany, about the omen which had come true, about the terrible death of her parents, about her betrothal and her husband to be whom she had hardly seen. She told her about Lazarus, her brother, about the Brotherhood and the dramatic voyage to the temple of Heliopolis, about the experience with the charismatic Helen and meeting the old, white haired woman who had appeared from nowhere to guide her and who had disappeared just as unnoticed again.

The sun was setting when Mariam ended her story. Salome sat with a, by now, familiar smile on her face, while she silently nodded as though everything Mariam told her simply confirmed something she already knew. They sat for while in silence.

In this silence Mariam felt that her story brought up numerous questions to which there were no answers and she was suddenly seized by strong doubts about her own credibility. Had she just imagined all of it? Had she merely experienced a completely different kind of magic drink than she had been given in Heliopolis?

"Do not despair."

It was Salome who broke Mariam's strange series of thoughts.

"Everything you have experienced, everything you saw and everything that happened are real events. There might still be things you do not understand, but before long you'll see that they are all elements of a greater plan."

She looked intensely at Mariam as if she had seen something that even Mariam herself hadn't seen. Something deep in her soul which had not been wakened yet and which was waiting in the dark for its release.

"I have been waiting a long time for this day. It almost went wrong, but luckily I was informed in the nick of time about your presence at the Temple of Isis. And now you are here."

Mariam listened. Then she said:

"I thought that it had been decided that I should go to Heliopolis to study. It seemed natural. During the whole journey I was assisted by the Brotherhood. All had been planned. It was written."

Salome interrupted her:

"Nothing is written."

The words were neither hard nor reserved but they brought something else into the conversation.

"The Brotherhood is so many things. There are more sections. Some of them are not in contact with the powers that they boast about in all humility. We are working with a small group under the Essenes at the Carmel Mountain but lately our work has been made difficult. Another group, which has settled down at the Dead Sea want to protect their own interests."

"Who and what is this Brotherhood?"

"Their doctrines are age old. The patriarchs secretly brought the written law along from Babylon when the people were released from captivity. Back in Jerusalem it came to a confrontation where the group of scribes and scholars, who tried to start a new spiritual basis for the rebuilding of the nation, disagreed. The final result was that the two groups, the Pharisees and the Sadducees, formed a governing power structure, while a third group, the Essenes, withdrew and disappeared into the periphery where they continued the original teachings about the simple life. This group settled on Mount Carmel where it has resided ever since. Since then, however, a dispute started within the Brotherhood. The basis for all the groups is the teachings of Enoch, Isaiah, Hosea, Mika and the traditions of Nahum. They look upon themselves as the people who must pave the way for the coming of the Messiah. Among them are scholars of great wisdom. Scholars supplying the world with prophecies of great beauty. They have a proud tradition of maintaining and passing on the scriptures. Some of them are seers and very adept healers. Their weakness lies in the fact that they have been faced with a splitting up of the groups, which has led some of them astray."

"How have they been led astray?"

"Well, they scorn women. They are banned from the Holy of Holies but are most mercifully allowed to do the chores that have always been the burden of women. One of the groups alone, the Nazarenes (the Consecrated Ones), living at Capernaum on the banks of the Sea of Galilee, have opened their community to women. That one still has a connection to the Carmel-group whereas the groups at Damascus, The Dead Sea and Beersheba work separately. Here they totally deny the power between the sexes. They are strictly celibate."

Mariam was looking at Salome while she talked. She managed, however, to get a few words in:

"Are they also called "Those Dressed in White?""

Salome smiled:

"There is quite a confusion about that. Not only among outsiders who respect the Brotherhood very much, because they are always hospitable, always ready to help and offer any kind of medical aid that may be needed. As you can see, we are all dressed in white, but this doesn't necessarily mean that we share the views of the Brotherhood."

Now Mariam looked confused and Salome laughed out loud. Then she explained:

"I understand your confusion. Ages ago a small group of men and women arrived in the Holy Land from the East. The group was called *Kamal Posh*. It means something like *Those who dress in blankets*. Each member owned just one blanket, which they wore during the day and slept under during the night. They very quickly got the name *Those Dressed in White*, since the blankets they wore were usually white. No one knew where they came from. They simply arrived one day bringing with them a profound wisdom, which they began teaching to those who wished to receive it. They possessed the gifts of Heaven and legend tells us there was no disease that they could not heal. They made prophecies and could see further and deeper than the most esteemed prophets and seers of the time. Their renown went far and wide, and as often happens in such cases their abilities caused a lot of envy among those who ruled the country and who did not understand that it was possible to possess such abilities without wanting to usurp their power. Thus the sect was persecuted and forced to hide in the mountains. As the years went by a small society developed and the members began writing down the secrets of the teaching. The Brotherhood or the Essenes originate from this group of people just like we the Therapists do. As you see, our gowns are also white, and they always have been. In our society both men and women may be accepted. Some of them even married.

Mariam collected her thoughts after Salome's explanation. She had never heard about the Therapists before.

"What is the task of the Therapists?"

"That is a long story. Hopefully, we are just a passing phenomenon. Unfortunately, it looks as if this interim is going to last longer than expected. We pass on knowledge. We initiate people who are ready to be initiated into the heavenly secrets. We heal and make prophecies just as our predecessors did. On top of that we also master all the dialects and most of the languages."

She fell silent and looked at Mariam. Then she continued:

"But my greatest task is ... you!"

Mariam looked at her open-mouthed:

"Me?"

"Yes, you."

Now Salome was laughing again as if this laughter was a companion to everything she said and only needed the slightest reason to break through. It was like small bells sounding in the air and reverberating and transforming everything which had formerly been locked, into a liberating, ethereal dance. But there were still quite a few things to which Mariam needed an answer.

Persian dervish/ Kamal Posh
(India Office Collections circa 1890)

"How did you know that I was in Heliopolis?"

Salome turned serious again:

"Who do you think led you through the desert and led you away from your guards the evening you were getting in trouble?"

Mariam sat for a while thinking.

"You mean the cloaked one?"

"The cloaked one, well, why not? It certainly was a young woman dressed in our gown and leading the way on her donkey."

"A woman?"

Mariam's bewilderment increased.

"Of course. Didn't you think that a woman could endure such hardship? You must have forgotten all the things you yourself have been through. Do you remember anything from your time in the temple?"

Mariam searched her memory but didn't get any further than the moment when she happily arrived at the temple and drank from the cup, which was to become a daily ritual and which dissolved any sense of context.

"I remember the animals. Strange beasts with animal heads and two legs. Everything is like a dream. Well, I do remember opening my eyes and seeing you for the first time."

Salome was silent for a while, wondering whether or not to tell Mariam the truth. Mariam broke the silence:

"What happened there? I know that it wasn't a very nice place, but ..."

Salome gently interrupted her:

"The Temple of Isis is not what it used to be. If the families who send their daughters to this place knew what is going on, they would break it down immediately. Atuka is a degenerate soul who has created his own little kingdom within the temple walls. Under cover of training temple virgins and supplying initiations to hopeful novices he, instead, takes advantage of them and molests them for his devious purposes. If the families knew ..."

It was now Mariam's turn to interrupt:

"What purposes?"

Salome wanted to ignore the question but something in Mariam's eyes made her realize that the girl in front of her was made of the same material as she was herself. This realization filled her with a quiet happiness. She let go of her reservation and said:

"The lust of the flesh. Atuka takes advantage of the girls. And the boys as well for that matter. Credible witnesses who were lucky enough to get away have told about all the despicable things going on there."

"How did you succeed in getting me out?"

"We have connections everywhere. People we may rely on. You have been on my mind for a long time. Well, actually for many years. When I heard that you had arrived at the Temple of Isis I knew that I had to act. Unfortunately, it took me a few months before I gained access to the temple. The novice doesn't get more freedom of movement until she has been through the introductory tests and initiations or whatever they call it."

"Was I initiated then?"

Salome had to smile, but she also saw that there was no getting around it.

"Apparently."

"What went on during the initiation?"

"It is hard to say in your case but from what we hear Atuka's rituals of initiation are — shall we say — of a sort of promiscuous kind."

"You mean he rapes the virgins?"

"Well, yes."

Mariam shivered. The sun had disappeared behind the horizon and it had grown cool. They went in. Salome lit the fire and continued talking about it in a most natural manner:

"It wasn't you who got raped in the Temple of Isis, it was your body. Even Atuka cannot touch your soul. You were not even there when the so-called initiation took place. Some day you'll remember where you travelled in spirit."

"How did this Atuka manage to mislead the Brotherhood?"

"The Brotherhood shuts its eyes to the debauchery going on behind the walls because they thus escape responsibility for the female novices by leaving them to him. The temples in Heliopolis rest on an almost indestructible reputation going as far back as the time of Moses. And as long as the virgins may be trained in the Temple of Isis, the Brotherhood does not have to send them into the arms of the priests of the Pharisees and the Sadducees in Jerusalem. This last would be a thorn in the flesh of the zeal of the Brotherhood. As you can see, as long as Atuka may work with the blessing of the Brotherhood, he may do more or less as he pleases. You are not the first one that I have brought out from places like this."

"Who else?"

"You'll learn soon enough. Some day you may even meet some of them. But now we must call it a day."

Salome got up and lit two big candles on an altar-like table. She then sat down with her legs crossed and said:

"You are welcome to take part in this ritual. Let it be your first step on this new path."

Mariam sat down in the same manner and Salome started uttering the words that would follow Mariam for the rest of her life just like Salome's laughter:

"Heavenly Source,
You who are everywhere,
Hallowed be Thy name.
Thy Kingdom come,
Thy will be done here and now in all eternity.
Fill us with the power of Thy grace,
And free us from the chains with which we bind each other.
Lead us out of temptation: Free us from ourselves,
And lend us the power to be one with You.
Teach us the true power of forgiveness,
May this holy moment be the ground
From which all our future actions grow.
Amen."

7

Not a sound. I just lay there and watched the early morning light through the canvas of the tent. Then I remembered the events of the night and felt how quite remarkably I was filled with a new kind of courage. There was a totally new and almost unreal quality in me, which I had never known before. It was a kind of reality that seemed more real than anything I had known earlier. Something had changed. Quietly I got to my knees and crawled outside.

The air around me was crystal clear – and I now saw that it consisted of innumerable, small, pulsating crystal-like beings mirroring each other and connected by fine threads, *nadirs* of radiant light. Carefully I reached out in order to caress this eternal filigree and felt a faint, vibrating sensation on my skin. It almost felt like taking the pulse of another person.

A pulsating being, a being of light without any identity, drew a radiant line in the air in the same way that I once saw the Seer doing it, but which he never explained to me.

"One thing is to be able to see and sense this light. Another thing is

to be able to concentrate the ethereal energy and for a moment to apply it with a healing purpose. In order to do that you must bring the level of vibration into harmony with that of the universe in which you want to work, or the level on which you want to work. No more and no less. If you are too slow you drop the energy on the floor so to speak — if you are too fast you may easily miss the target. It demands precision and a willpower of such magnitude that it is freed from any desire of power and wish to feel special. Your power must be in harmony with that of the universe. It doesn't want anything for itself. It doesn't owe anything to anyone and isn't owed anything either. It is neutral but in a compassionate way. Call it the respect for life. And yet, it is more of a new understanding of the reality and the circumstances in which humanity finds itself at the moment."

A radiant heart was hanging two metres up in the air. There was nothing mysterious about the sight. It seemed quite natural. It was just another step on my path, a new door opening through this image and speaking to me from the deepest of layers.

Above the heart I saw a pyramid turned upside down. The triangle was made from the fire that is never quenched and the water from which all higher life springs through the initiations of the mystics. A symbol which I knew to be the symbol of the Heavenly Source, the Creator, the Father/Mother, radiated from the top left edge of the triangle.

The symbol of the Heavenly Child, the Created, the Son/Daughter radiated from the top, right edge of the triangle.

The symbol of *Rukha d'koodsha*, the Holy Spirit, radiated from the lower point of the triangle. At the same time, the whole triangle symbolized the three uppermost energy centres of the human being: the crown centre, brow centre and throat centre.

Below the heart was an upright pyramid. This triangle was filled with earthly fire and the water from which transient life arises.

The masculine symbol radiated from the bottom, left edge and the feminine from the right one.

The symbol of *Naphsha*, the Higher Self, humanity's connection upwards, the bridge to the higher worlds, radiated from the topmost point.

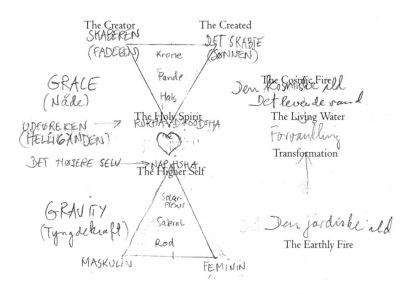

The Creator
SKABEREN
(FADEREN) Krone

The Created
DET SKABTE
(SØNNEN)

Pande

GRACE
(Nåde)

Hals

Den Kosmiske ild
The Cosmic Fire
Det levende vand

UDFØREREN →
(HELLIGÅNDEN)

The Holy Spirit
RUKHA-D-KOODSHA

The Living Water

Forvandling
Transformation

DET HØJERE SELV →
NAPHSHA
The Higher Self

Solar-
Plexus

GRAVITY
(Tyngdekraft)

Sakral

Rod

Den jordiske ild
The Earthly Fire

MASKULIN

FEMININ

MIRIAM MAGDALENE

MIR • I • AM

Peace I Am

Home am I

Magdal-eder

"Den ophøjede"

The Elevated

The Star of Mariam
(From the author's notebook)

Within this triangle the human being's lower centres of energy were represented, the root, sacral and solar plexus centres.

Both triangles slowly glided towards the heart. The upper triangle more or less floated down from the sky while the lower one, so to speak, rose from the dead. As the triangles united and embraced the heart, all the symbols became one symbol containing all. All the qualities were expressed in this hexameter floating and vibrating in the air. I felt the certainty in my heart at the moment the sign became whole.

I do not know how long this went on. Whether it lasted for a moment or for an eternity, what's the difference? At a deeper level, however, I had no doubt what all this was about. The Star with the heart was the sign of Mariam Magdalene – the sign of the cosmic, feminine power. At this time I had no idea that there were others who had similar experiences. At that time, I was unaware of the extent to which the Magdalene archetype had been opening up with the collective unconscious and that others, each in their own way, were drawing on the same source. On another level this had something to do with my future relationship with the Seer, in the same way it had to do with my work which I was just then beginning to sense and which I have since had to take upon me because it is mine.

I sat and immediately wrote down the details of my experience in my notebook and thought about the road that had led me to this event; the basic principle that had started me on this path.

It was not until 1989 that I really began to recognize Mariam Magdalene's rightful place in Christian mythology. My studies in early Christian and Gnostic writings told a story about a woman and a being that spoke directly to something deep inside me. I tried to describe Mariam's physical appearance to the Danish painter Hans Krull who was inspired to produce a number of water colour paintings and etchings of her. A few years later I made a very surprising discovery. One of my friends sent me an Italian postcard of Leonardo Da Vinci's 'The Last Supper': a picture that many of us know so well that we do not really see it properly. The postcard became a bookmark in one of the books I was reading. It was not until later, when I picked up the book again, that I noticed a curious detail in the painting for the first time. Leonardo's painting was of Yeshua and the twelve disciples at the last supper, that is, thirteen men. However, the person who caught my eye in the painting was indisputably a woman. She sat at the right hand of Yeshua, beautiful, shy and leaning away from him. There was no doubt that this person was a woman and this woman was Mariam Magdalene.

The first time I acknowledged the fundamental principle behind the feminine power that she represented I understood that the concept of time is an illusion we must let go of if we are to live and work freely. In that moment I realized that time is a thought form created by us. I realized that time is simply a kind of measurement applicable only to the limited form of life we live here on Earth. If you understand the now you also understand eternity. I saw that there is no difference between what has been, what is and what is to come. Everything unfolds in the moment. There is not one moment in time where what we experience as past and future is not also revealed to us in the present as a totality in eternity. Now, now, now and now! Understanding that makes it easier to understand the words attributed to Yeshua, "Only the one who knows the beginning knows the end."

This is the cosmic principle. It is eternity. It doesn't divide the moment into past, present and future. If it did, it wouldn't exist as anything else but memory. That's the cosmic principle. That's eternity. It doesn't divide the moment up into past, present and future. If it did, it wouldn't exist as anything other than memory. Because the future becomes the past without any chance of holding on to anything at all.

Now I see cosmic unity, or what religion calls God, everywhere! Now I *see* it!

I now understand that there is no difference between here and there. There really is no outer space. Outer space is just like the inner space. There is no difference. This realization, the way it has been shown to me, is the first step towards the relinquishment of gravity. Let go of the physical element, penetrate the ethereal aspect and transcend the astral and the mental aspect – unite with causality – change all that has petrified and stagnated. This is the recognition of the moment as the highest synthesis of humanity's collective experiences brought into being right NOW!

This acknowledgement is identical with total healing – because you realize that diseases are a hopeless illusion – an unnecessary crutch. When time has outplayed its role as an instrument for measurement and when human beings no longer see themselves as separate beings apart from the cosmos, the laws of karma will end.

This is Dharma: bringing the sublimated moment to its full blossoming of total compassion for all living things, in harmony with what should or should not be done.

The personality, forever chasing after recognition and being something special, always looking for separation, is the laboratory where transformation occurs for every individual. When humanity, to the extent it does today, identifies itself so totally with personality's limiting strategies and templates, it cuts itself off from those qualities, which can transform imprisonment into freedom.

The sun rose behind the clouds but sent, from time to time, a single ray through a gap drew corridors of light in the air and embraced the valley in an almost supernatural, soft morning light. I packed the tent, put everything on my back and started the descent. I carried the image of Mariam's star in my heart. Its power was so strong that I practically floated down the narrow path.

The Seer was preparing breakfast when I returned to the house in the village. He looked tired. I told him about the experiences of the night and the morning and he nodded both compassionately and happily. At the same time, however, I thought I sensed a certain amount of sorrow in his happiness. Something that moderated my own happiness and which made me hold back.

I made myself a cup of instant coffee. Someone was tickling the back of my neck and it was difficult concentrating on making coffee. Without thinking about it I said:

"Stop it Mariam!"

The Seer looked up from his cup with a surprised look on his face.

"Did you say something?"

I couldn't hold back any longer and trying to keep a straight face, laughing, I said:

"Mariam is teasing me."

He regained his normal expression and said:

"Well, sort of clears things a bit eh?"

It felt like an angel walking through the room. In a split second all heaviness turned to light and laughter. Even the air in the small kitchen seemed to sparkle with the pollen of angels. The Seer had a big smile on his face. I laughed out loud. Laughed as I hadn't laughed for many years.

He looked indulgently at me:

"How about going to the coast tomorrow? You look as if you could do with a change of air before you dissolve completely."

The coast meant back to the Seer's house on the sunny coast of Andalusia. Why not? I was far too enraptured to give it a second thought. However, I did feel a strong inclination to agree with the suggestion. Perhaps I was beginning to understand the principles involved if you want to step into the flow of things.

We didn't go up into the mountains for a change. Instead, we shopped for lunch, which we took out in the open on the banks of the wide mountain stream far into the Montségur Valley. It is an indescribable, peaceful spot, which has become my favourite place. You don't talk here. You *are*. No beating about the bush. No defences. Open to the higher energies.

The trickle of water in the brook was balm to my soul, which sang and danced in harmony with the beings of light around us. The light went all the way into the darkest nooks and crannies of my body, where it loosened old attitudes and set free rigid repressions, which had collected there. A coat of stubborn inertia and all my reservations dissolved and transformed into sparkling stardust rising upwards on the updraft of power from the water. I let myself dissolve in the nature of the water. A fine, ethereal blue light shone through and from it. I followed the stream and saw the blue light gather force to become a vibrating cathedral-like arch above the deepest part of the stream. A large rock rose above the surface of the water at the same spot. A faint, vibrating strip of white light cut the arch vertically to form a cross. The activity of the beings of light was more intense here and it seemed to me they were chanting an unknown hymn in the silence. Perhaps silence itself had its source in such hymns. Then I heard myself unhesitatingly saying my own, Aramaic, prayer: *rukha d'koodsha, malkoota d'shmeya, rukha d'koodsha, malkoota d'shmeya, rukha d'koodsha malkoota d'shmaya*, while someone was crying silently deep inside me.

The Seer sat half asleep on a bench with a smile on his face. I watched him and wondered where he came from. Which star did he belong to? But there was no answer, or maybe I just wasn't able to hear it. I thought that his smile had the same secrecy about it as Da Vinci's Mona Lisa. Seeing him like this I wanted most of all to kiss him on his forehead, but I didn't. I smiled inside at the thought; how he would have looked if I had. The feeling, however, was very real and I placed a kiss there anyway but on the ethereal level only.

Late in the afternoon it became cooler. I dried my eyes, packed up our things and woke the Seer. "What happened?" he said a little dizzily putting his hand up to his forehead. He was constantly more awake than I could imagine – even when he, apparently, was asleep.

Darkness and cold came creeping like two ghosts that laid their cloaks over the town and the valley. In the pale light from the few streetlights one could glimpse blue-grey smoke signals rising from the chimney stacks.

After eating a simple evening meal we lit the fire in the banqueting hall.

The Seer sat down in the only armchair in the house with his legs casually placed on a foot-stool while I sat down on a bearskin rug on the floor. Then he said:

"I have the feeling that our trip to the south is going to open yet another door to the mystery."

"You still don't think that Sauniére and the Rennes le Château mystery has anything to do with Mariam Magdalene?"

We were both familiar with the colourful story about the small town of Rennes le Château and the priest Sauniére who in 1886, during a major repair work on the altar of the local church, had apparently found a number of documents containing information which from one day to the next transformed him from a poor minister on the fringes of society to a rich man with unlimited funds and a fashionable circle of acquaintances.

Sauniére had spent part of his fortune on the restoration of the church. He further built a new house, "Bethanie," as well as the tower, "Tour Magdala." Sauniére died in 1917 leaving the secret with his housekeeper of many years, Marie Dernaud, who promised to disclose it on her deathbed. Unfortunately, when that day came in 1953, she was paralysed by a stroke and was thus unable to disclose anything at all. Apparently the secret of Sauniére was buried with her.

Since then, the mystery had been made the subject of many speculations, several of which had revitalized the legend of Mary Magdalene and her alleged escape from Palestine to the South of France after the death of Yeshua.

The mystery, furthermore, was linked to the story of the Templars and a secret society called Prieure de Sion which among its Grand Masters counted names such as: *René d'Anjou (1418 - 80), Nicholas Flamel (1330 - 1418), Sandro Filepepi (1483 - 1510), Leonardo da Vinci (1510 - 19), Robert Fludd (1595 - 1637), Johann Valenin Andrea (1637 - 54), Robert Boyle (1654 - 91), Isaac Newton*

(1691 - 1727), Charles Radclyffe (1727 - 46), Charles Lorraine (1746 - 80), Charles Nodier (1801 - 44), Victor Hugo (1844 - 85) and Jean Cocteau (1889 - 1963).

We had been in Rennes on several occasions in order to visit the church and the house of Sauniére, which is now a museum, and each time something touched me. The Seer, however, doubted the credibility of the mystery and had difficulty in getting in touch with what might have given us and many others certainty about the significance of the place.

The fact that Sauniére went to such lengths, after finding his treasure, to camouflage his tracks in and around the church, has led people believe that the treasure was still hidden here or somewhere in the area. But going to all that trouble might also have been a way of communicating something. Perhaps he wanted to communicate knowledge that as a minister he couldn't communicate directly because, if known, it might have gone against one or more of the church's indisputable dogmas.

"This really is a delicate matter," the Seer replied and the drowsy look returned to his eyes.

Never before had we discussed the old legends that maintained that Mary Magdalene, immediately after the crucifixion, left the Holy Land and arrived in France, more precisely at the small coastal town of St. Maries-sur-la-Mer, to the west of Marseilles. One of several folk traditions states that she carried the Holy Grail with her, and that she spent the rest of her life in the caves around St. Baume where she died very old. Some people feel that this grail was the Holy Chalice used by Yeshua at the Last Supper and the one that Joseph of Arimathea used to collect the blood of Yeshua while he was still hanging on the cross. Others thought that the real secret was that *San graal* should really be read as *Sang raal*, meaning *Holy Blood* and that this blood was brought to France by Mary Magdalene in the shape of a child, the fruit of Mary's intimate relationship with Yeshua. All of it rested on a major folk tradition the origin of which no one knew. How did such myths originate and why did they keep growing in strength, when no one could trace them back to credible sources or hard evidence?

Indisputable, however, is the fact that a large number of churches in the South of France have been named after Mary Magdalene. Furthermore, she is celebrated each year on July the 22nd in many places in that area. The church in Maximin even claimed that they kept the remains of St. Mary Magdalene safe and that these were the relics that they carried in a procession each year on that day, commemorating her.

Reflecting on the subject it suddenly struck me that I had read somewhere that as far back as anyone remembered, large populations of Jews had existed in the area of Provence. Perhaps this had some connection with the arrival of Mariam? I suggested this to the Seer. He looked into the fire for a long time before answering:

"The Jews also inhabited large parts of Spain at the time. They say that Toledo, which as far as they know is the oldest town in Spain, was established around a Jewish settlement."

"What can you say about the Jews? It looks as if they have been persecuted regularly throughout history. What kind of destiny is that?"

"That is a very good question," he said looking into the flames. "When I ask about the Jewish people, I am told that they are outside of everything. That they, more than any other people, come from somewhere else. It sounds cryptic but this is the answer I'm getting. It looks as if they have been appointed the guardians of something unique and a very special secret. Some of them, apparently, have misunderstood their task. Something has gone entirely wrong."

"Where does the idea come from that they are the chosen people of God?"

"The God of Israel, the Old Testament God, has always been a limited God. Or let me put this another way: some of the Jews created their own zealous, jealous and punishing God. As time went by, this became the God to whom the Jews turned. It is a question with many facets, which makes one think. You see, it is a question of whether or not this was the same God, that was adopted by Christianity and, with only few modifications, made its own?"

I considered his reply, which matched my own thoughts on the subject. But what had gone wrong with the task that the Jews had been asked to manage?

I somehow sensed that this was one of the questions to which we had to find an answer if we were to solve the riddle about Mariam.

The fire had died out and we decided that it was time to go to bed.

When I was in my room I began reading a book. After half an hour it felt as though I had sand in my eyes. I woke up with a start as the book fell on to the floor. I was just about to turn the light out when I saw her. I couldn't help smiling. I knew that the picture had been there for many years. I had slept in this room many times without thinking about it. Perhaps because she had become so familiar to people, an icon used everywhere, an illustration on everything from T-shirts to matchboxes and plastic bags: the Mona Lisa. She smiled at me from the flowered wallpaper. I returned her smile, let go and travelled into other worlds.

8

As if by magic, Mariam's life again took another direction, a more stable one. Under the skilled tuition of Salome, day by day and slowly but surely she was taught the deepest secrets and the way of life of the Therapists. The teaching started at sunrise and ended long after sunset. They had two meals a day consisting of roots, herbs and bread spiced with hyssop and salt.

In the beginning Mariam was taught everything about the cycles of life and the effect of the cosmos on human beings. She was taught to see her own moon cycle as a microcosmic reflection of the powers surrounding human beings.

"The moon cycle opens up many possibilities for the woman who wants to learn to look into other worlds. All the great female seers from the beginning of time have had this possibility. There are several levels on which the priestess may expand her vision. When the egg breaks away the possibilities of seeing into the astral realities increase. During the moon time itself, her abilty to see into the ethereal worlds is heightened: the upper as well as the lower ones.

But she must be aware of and able to sharpen the connection to the higher Self in spite of the complications offered by the moon time. If you surrender to those complications and make room for them in your mind then you will have forfeited all your options."

Salome had brought Mariam along to the lake where they were sitting looking across the shining surface.

"When a woman lies with a man there are moments when both have the possibility of looking into other worlds, well, even travelling there. There are moments then, when the woman may be able to leave her body and put on her gown of stars. When you know the secrets of your body and know your mind and the possibilities and traps connected with the power of your mind, you'll be able to travel through time and space. I shall show you this when you are ready for it."

Mariam felt a spark from a long forgotten longing in her abdomen. Salome's words reminded her of the man to whom she was engaged, but whom she did not even know and had not seen for several years. She suddenly remembered the morning when she saw him riding to her childhood home in Bethany. Although she only saw him from a distance she imagined that she remembered the features of his melancholy face. Or maybe it was an image she had created in order to have something to cling to? The engagement was the desire of her parents. Thus it was also her wish. Her parents had chosen wisely. And the strange visions she had seen of the old woman with white hair seemed to confirm this, although in these visions nothing had really been said directly about it.

Salome was watching her student and tried to read her thoughts, but she didn't say anything since she knew that it wouldn't be long before Mariam would ask about the things which occupied her mind the most, and which would come to fill her life more and more in the immediate future. Instead she said:

"When a woman is about to give birth to a child, the moment the child comes into the world she will become one with the great certainty. She will know everything. At this moment she knows the child leaving her body, knows its traits, the qualities of its soul and the sphere from which it comes. If the woman is able to go beyond the pain and other complications, the moment the head of the child appears, she will know life's deepest secrets."

Deep within herself Mariam felt something opening up. Unknown doors squeaked on rusty hinges. She felt slightly moist between her thighs and her cheeks got warm. She turned her face away.

"Don't be shy. Set your body and your feelings free. It is only natural for a woman to sense something in the lower regions when she is confronted with words like these. This is understood by all women. It is all part of women's physical potential and the secrets we guard, more or less consciously. The danger in working with all this lies not in our immediate physical reactions like your present reaction, but in the limitation which makes us believe that our one and only unavoidable task on earth is bearing children. We must have children, and it is the task of women to bear them. But it is not her only and highest purpose."

They sat for a while. Salome sensed the new kind of power awakening in her student. The afternoon was spent working in the herb garden and Salome took the opportunity to introduce a few herbs to Mariam. She pointed to a group of plants:

"Yarrow and pigeon's grass along with sage, rosemary, camomile and lady's mantle are among the oldest known women's herbs. They are used in various mixtures when a woman is in her moon time."

"And these may be useful when a woman is going to be intimate with a man."

She pointed to a small group of herbs in a separate herbal bed:

"This is an orchid from Galilee. You boil the root and then eat it. It is very stimulating and combined with jujube it puts a woman into a state of relaxation and openness. You may add a small amount of mandrake and nutmeg. Used properly, it may give both a man and a woman the potential they never dreamed possible."

She smiled secretively.

"But the herbs are only aids. The power itself must be manifested through your own ability to get help from the higher worlds. By way of training your will power and the purity of your thoughts you may attract the attention of the very beings you need in a given situation. When you understand the coherence of everything, nothing can stand in your way.

That is why you must learn about the endless power of praying.
You must know about the real meaning of rituals and understand
that they are necessary aids for you to receive the powers flowing
your way through the medium of prayer. Not like the priests of
Jerusalem to whom the performing of rituals for the sake of the
rituals themselves is all that matters. That is why the priests are now
worshipping a God whose only content is the limiting abilities made
by their own imaginations."

Salome stretched herself. She had been standing bent over for
too long.

"But there is a time for everything. The body must be satisfied
just like the spirit. For a woman the two are inseparable. The merging
of body and spirit is the realization of the perfect human being for
a woman. The union of man and woman is holy and pure when it
is performed in the right spirit, at the right time and with the right
intentions. Do not let anyone convince you that there is anything
shameful or sinful in such a union. The true union is called *certainty*.
It is called this for a reason. If it wasn't holy it would never have got

a name like that. Nothing created can be shameful or sinful. If the sexual act is sinful then so are the genitals. But God created them. How could God create something sinful and undignified? When the sexual act is performed in a spirit of holiness, nothing can be more holy and pure. When a man becomes one with a woman at a higher level, together they manifest the Holy Spirit. Human thought of woman is able to expand and return to its source. When she searches for her source she will be guided by the heavenly light in which she was born. She and he are one. When the two thoughts are reborn they become one ray of light: The heavenly light is drawn down by the power of thought. In this way the presence of the Eternal One is manifested on earth.

They stopped working around noon and Salome brought Mariam to the gathering at the temple. For the first time Mariam saw the other inhabitants at close quarters. Until now, she had only seen figures dressed in white at a distance, moving about silently.

There were men and women of all ages. They all greeted each other with the word, *Shlama* (peace). In the temple the members sat on low benches along the curved walls. The men to the right and the women to the left. When all were present an elderly woman got up and quietly started chanting:

"Heavenly Queen
Through whom all light shines.
You light-giving Unity.
Beloved One in the highest as on earth,
You are crowned with a Tiara.
The highest of the true Priestesses.
My Lady, you are the guardian
Of the holy teaching.
In Your hand You hold the seven potentialities:
In it you hold life's innermost power,
You have gathered all the possibilities of life,
And bare them as a jewel on your breast.
We thank you for allowing us to have a share in Your Wealth.
Amen."

She then turned to those gathered:

"Dear brothers and sisters. Today we have a new sister among us. Her name is Mariam. She is under the protection of sister Salome."

She then said to Mariam:

"Greetings sister Mariam. You are most welcome."

Everybody nodded towards Mariam. Immediately after, the woman carefully produced a note to the sound of *Aum*. A short time after they all hummed the same note and the same sound. At first the voices seemed insecure until they found the right note and suddenly all the voices became one. Mariam felt how the voices vibrated in her body. She felt that it made the whole room vibrate and somehow mysteriously connected them all in a wordless prayer. Mariam had her eyes closed and concentrated on a luminous dot in the dark. Slowly it came closer getting bigger and bigger. The sound modulated and everything seemed to vibrate to mmmmmmmmmm. The centre exploded and the note manifested itself as pulsating light:

〰〰〰〰〰〰〰〰〰〰〰〰〰〰〰〰〰〰〰〰〰〰〰〰

〰〰〰〰〰〰〰〰〰〰〰〰〰〰〰〰〰〰〰〰〰〰〰〰

〰〰〰〰〰〰〰〰〰〰〰〰〰〰〰〰〰〰〰〰〰〰〰〰

Slowly Mariam came back to herself. Some of the women were crying. Others stood up and chanted prayers above the note, which was subsiding. The whole room was filled with its cleansing presence. Mariam saw radiating beings dancing in the air.

The men then sang a hymn of thanks. Then the women. The meeting ended with everybody singing together.

Silently they went back to the house filled with the power, which had accumulated during the gathering. It was Mariam who broke the silence:

"What happened?"

"Through our song we not only invoke forces from outside which we need at this moment. We vitalize the Holy Spirit, *Rukha d'koodsha*, which is present everywhere, just waiting for us to open up and bid it welcome just as you saw it happen a while before. The Holy Spirit not only is present at the ethereal level around us, it also lives within us. Human beings are not normally conscious of their breathing. If you try not to breathe you'll find that it isn't possible. There is a power doing it for us."

Mariam nodded. She started to see some connections. Salome continued:

"When we become aware of our breathing we take part in a collective prayer. We then unite with everything living and our Heavenly Source. Thus, the power of the Holy Spirit is revitalized in and around us. This is the first step into unity."

They worked in the herb garden the rest of the day. At sunset they walked to the temple in order to participate in the prayers and the hymns of thanksgiving which were to manifest the Power.

Months passed like that. Mariam was a vigilant student. Step by step Salome led her into the secret halls of learning. Every day their relationship grew stronger.

Mariam woke up one morning to the sound of Salome's voice chanting a hymn that she didn't recognize. The sun had not yet risen but Mariam knew that this was going to be a special day. She got up in a hurry and went outside where Salome was sitting on a sheep's skin with a woollen blanket around her, facing east. She was surrounded by a warm radiating aura. The sight filled Mariam with an unspeakable bliss and she fell to her knees. Salome spoke to her:

"I came out of the mouth of the Highest One
and covered the earth as spirit.
I dwelt in Heaven
and my throne is a sacred couch.
I alone saw the Kingdom of Heaven
and recognized the deepest depth.
I have the power over the water and the earth
and over each single, living being.
He created me from the beginning, before the creation of the world.
I shall never fail.
I served him in the Holy of Holies.
and manifested myself in Zion.
He made me guard and rest in his beautiful town,

Jerusalem the most beautiful of roses.

I'm a river outlet.

by which I water the flowers of the garden.

I said, "I'm going to water the most important garden

and bring nourishment to the base of the roots."

And see, the brook became a river,

and the river became a sea.

Once more my doctrines will shine like the morning,

and I will send Her light into the furthest corners of the earth.

I will send my doctrines out like prophecies

and leave them to eternity.

All this I do not for my own sake

but for all those who seek wisdom."

Salome stood up in front of Mariam. Salome's flames now surrounded both of them and Mariam saw that the ethereal was a thin blanket of radiating particles connected to each other. Salome drew a band of light in the air with her hand shaping it into a ball which she moved towards Mariam.

"Have no fear, but relax and open yourself to this force."

Slowly she placed the ball of light in Mariam's lap.

"*Ephatah* – Open yourself! I now place this force into Creation (the Root Centre) where it will heal and enlighten all that has been broken and which is now in darkness."

She then placed one of her hands on Mariam's pubic bone and the other on the lower part of her backbone.

"Be healed and blessed."

Mariam immediately felt a lightning movement in her abdomen. Something dissolved and disappeared while a new, live power seemed to be born in her. Salome repeated the ritual at the other centres: The Power (the Sacral centre), the Self (Solar plexus), Love (the Heart), the Will (the Throat), Clarity (the Forehead), and Neshemah (the Crown – the bridge to the higher Self). She repeated the words, "Be healed and blessed" seven times and drew cross with arms of equal length in front of each of the centres. The air was alive with active powers. Salome ended the simple initiation ritual.

"Give me your hand."

Mariam stretched her hand out towards Salome.

"Hold it steady and concentrate on the subtle pulse in your fingertips. At the same time, from your Heavenly Consciousness draw down balanced light through your crown and radiate the light of prophecy from your throat centre, letting the two unite in your brow, sending that light through to your fingertips. Now sense the even finer transition between the skin and the air. Feel, how, with your outermost pulse, you are able to touch the pulse of the ethereal."

An intense energy flowed through Mariam. It was like putting your hand into a beehive, the only difference being that this power was painless. It was an enlightened state.

"Now, dissolve the thin barrier between the fingers and the air. The two elements are one and the same. You surrender the pulse of your fingers to that of the ethereal. You give up any kind of resistance without getting too eager."

In a short flash Mariam sensed a kind of fusion. But then she lost it all and had to start all over again. Salome drew a radiating circle in the air with great patience, in order to demonstrate the basic principle.

"You might say that paradoxically this is the only kind of physical contact with Heaven you may practice with. Because the principle is the same, be it lower or higher. The secret is about being obliging without being obtrusive. We so quickly reach the limitations of our concepts when we try to express this. But if for a while you are able to give up all of your own pettiness and surrender in total confidence, and at the same time you are fully concentrated, then you will succeed."

Salome drew light onto Mariam's fingertips. Just before their fingers met, Mariam had the same feeling as when you burst a soap bubble with your finger. At that moment a hole appeared in the bubble and Mariam sensed a connection between them, a spark flew and a mild vibration extended to her knuckles. Salome pulled her hand away. Mariam then to her great surprise saw how the light followed the hesitant movements of her own fingers, leaving a thin, uneven line in the air.

"This isn't something that you may impress people with, since only very few people will be able to see it. Most people, however, will be able to feel it. Especially when you start healing people."

Mariam kept on drawing with her finger in a hectic attempt to maintain the light which, however, kept getting weaker and weaker until it disappeared completely.

"You now understand the principle. The rest is a matter of practice."

Salome let go of her seriousness and welcomed the breaking of dawn with her tinkling laughter.

"This is how you open up to the powers of healing. Surrender to Rukha d'koosha. Through practice and prayer you will finally become so good at uniting with the Holy Spirit that it will participate in everything you do. Everything that you think, everything you do will be an extension of this prayer. Everything you touch will turn into light. All your actions will have a healing effect."

After half a year during which Salome continued teaching Mariam the noble art of healing, she realized, that, not only did Mariam live up to all her expectations, but, furthermore, this woman was made from a rare, radiating matter. Once in a while, however, Mariam disappeared into a state of sadness and melancholy. But Salome saw her and understood that these phases were inevitable. She remembered her own struggles on her innermost levels when she herself was being educated.

The battle between heaven and earth continued until the day she finally realized there was no difference between them; that they were simply reflecting poles of equal strength. Now she experienced it all once more through Mariam.

"Sorrows and wants aren't just something we have to go through. Sorrows and wants also have to go through us, so to speak," she said one day when Mariam seemed more sad than usual.

"Thoughts travel through the cosmos. Once in a while they pass through us. Not in order to destroy us but in order to be transformed. We just shouldn't identify with the chaos arising during this change. The conditions are secondary. Only the transformation itself has any value. The time is getting close when you'll understand."

Salome made a few exaggerated, melancholy gestures. Slowly she began circling around Mariam while she made the saddest face she could muster. It didn't take long before the medicine worked and shortly after they were both dancing around in the courtyard laughing, with the goats watching them in astonishment.

After a year, the day Salome had been waiting for arrived.

She woke Mariam up long before sunrise and asked her to get ready for departure. The sudden change in the normally set routine surprised Mariam and she was besieged by her old worries.

"Don't be afraid," Salome said soothingly, "this is probably the most beautiful part of your education."

They prepared the donkeys, tied two big water jars onto them and set out. Mariam soon realized that they were on their way into the wilderness. She wondered about Salome's sudden haste. When they had been riding for a couple of hours Salome turned away from the caravan track, between some rocks and along a mountain path. Halfway up the mountain they had to get off and lead the animals. They stopped on a ledge in front of a cave. Salome started unloading the water jars. She pointed to the cave and said to Mariam:

"This will be your home for the next forty days. When you have used the water, you may fill the jars at the brook higher up on the mountain. It will not be difficult for you. This is the final and decisive test. If you pass this one you'll know everything that I cannot tell you in words anyway. This cleansing is a prerequisite for true vision. It will sharpen your natural ability to see. You'll find a natural beehive in the cave. Here you'll be able to find your sustenance. Be prepared. Do not let yourself be swept away by melancholy and self-pity. Whatever happens, do not let yourself be tempted by anyone or anything. Concentrate on the practices and the prayers that I taught you. Remember where you come from, what you are made of, and where you are going. Stay courageous. I shall come and get you when the forty days are over."

She embraced Mariam, kissed her on her forehead and gave her one of the holy scrolls of the Therapists. Mariam took Salome's hand and held it to her lips.

"I shall not let you down."

She stayed on the ledge and watched Salome ride back until both rider and donkey disappeared and became a dot on the horizon.

The first few days in the cave were spent getting used to the new surroundings. Without any disturbances other than the wind, the wild animals and the delusions of the mind, Mariam slowly came closer to a nearness, a new kind of awareness, that saw everything as one, freed from sentimentality, clear-cut .

On the seventh day she was like an open wound. The daylight blinded her and the realities of life played out relentlessly in the sand in front of her right where she sat watching ants working hard carrying food to the anthill.

Everything was painfully clear.

She suddenly sensed another presence.

"I am Metraton, the angel of the Covenant. This is the Kingdom and the Restraint. This is the harmony towards the end and thus the harmony of a new beginning. Adonai, Adonai, I prostrate myself before you. You the queen, Shekhinah — Eve, the first woman. On this day you acknowledge the instincts — on this your own day, you transform them. The path of self-discipline awaits you. Here you are going to regain your true self-respect. Make peace with life's inevitable loneliness. Accept your destiny, bidding you to walk in confidence."

The very being of the angel quietly united with Mariam. Then it disappeared as suddenly as it had appeared.

Mariam spoke the first line of her favourite prayer:

Heavenly Source.

Suddenly she understood that this Source was a Power where both poles are present. It was both father and mother and yet not either of them. And she clearly saw that the fact that only the masculine form was used didn't mean that you celebrated one of the poles only. She suddenly saw, that in reality there was only one sex and that the masculine and the feminine were simply the extremities of this one sex.

On the twelfth day Mariam spoke the second line: *You who are everywhere.* She saw that everything is suffused with the Holy Spirit, the possibility for the manifestation of life. She saw that this was the Foundation and that everything returns to the place of origin. Here the sun rose. Here it set.

On the thirteenth day she confirmed her knowledge with the words: *Hallowed be Thy name.*

And she saw the clarity and the greatness of what had been created. She understood that everything was vitalized through the name. Everything was born through the power of acknowledgement.

When eighteen days had passed she spoke the words: *Thy Kingdom come.*

With these words she made the highest wish of her prayer come true. This was victory over the "self" wanting to decide its own path. You must walk the path of death and of rebirth. This is the great transformation.

On the twentieth day she placed the following words in her heart: *Thy will be done, here and now and in eternity.*

This was the true source of leniency and beauty. This was the birthplace of life and death, the active morals and ethics of this world. Rukha d'koodsha, malkoota d'shmaya.

After twenty one days she prayed: *Fill us with the power of Thy grace.*

With these words she understood that mankind was not always given what it wanted, but always received what it needed. Thus, she knew that this was the golden road of justice. Here your destiny was decided by what you yourself placed on the scales.

It demanded strength to surrender to this path. Grace, love and compassion was waiting at its end.

On the twenty second day of Mariam's fast: *And set us free from the chains with which we bind ourselves and each other.*

Move everything which is locked. Free me from every lie, all my reservations and every judgement with which I chain my brothers and sisters and myself. Help me to look on them with the same leniency with which I want them to look on me.

On the twenty fourth day she whispered: *Lead us out of temptation: Free us from ourselves.*

Help me not to let my egoistical mind limit my understanding of this life. Pull the veils aside and let me see the truth as it is. Only then do I understand my real Self and Your Kingdom where all living things share Your Holy Spirit. Lead me along the path of Love, the true path of my emotions.

On that day for the first and only time she read in the scroll that Salome had given her. Here she found the words of the divine Hermes:

"The incorporeal cannot be embraced by anything. But it may itself embrace everything. It is the fastest of all things – and the greatest. Think about your real Self and you'll know that it is so.

Bid your soul to travel to any country you may choose, and faster than you may bid it go, it will arrive there.

Bid it go from land to sea and no less quickly will it be there. It does not move as you move from one place to another, it simply is there.

Bid it fly to the sky and it shall not need wings. Nothing can bar its way, neither the extreme heat of the sun nor the whirling motion of the planet spheres. Moving through everything it will fly upwards to the outermost limits of all bodily things. And should your wish be to break away from the universe itself in order to look at things from the external side of the cosmos, then even that will be possible. Imagine the power, imagine the speed you possess. And when you yourself can do this, cannot the Power do the same? Thus, you must understand that this is the way that the Power contains all of the cosmos, itself and everything that is. It is like the thoughts that the Power is thinking, the fact that everything is contained within it.

If therefore you do not compare yourself to the Power, you will not be able to understand it. For like recognises like.

Rise above all that is of the body and let yourself grow to a size equal to the greatness which is beyond all measure.

Rise above all of time and become eternal, then you shall understand the Power.

Think, that for you also, nothing is impossible.

Consider, that you are also immortal and that you are able to understand all things in your mind, and that you are able to understand any kind of art and any kind of science.

Find your home in the abode of any living creature.

Rise above any height and go down below any depth.

Unite within yourself the opposites of all qualities, warm and cold, dry and moist. Imagine that you are everywhere at the same time, on land, at sea and in the sky.

Imagine that you have not yet been born, that you are still in the womb, that you are old, that you are dead, that you are in the world beyond the grave.

Keep all this in your mind at the same time, all time and all places, all substances and potentials in one. Then you may understand the Power. However, if you lock your soul in your body and demean yourself and say, "I know nothing, I can do nothing, I'm afraid of the earth and the sea and I cannot rise to the sky. I do not know what I was, and not what I'm going to be." If you say this, what connection can you have with the Power?

Your mind cannot understand any of that which is beautiful and good if you cling to the body and do not know anything about the higher levels. The peak of ignorance is not knowing the Power. But the ability to know the Power and wanting and hoping to be able to know it, is the path that leads to the higher consciousness. And it is an easy path. The Power will meet you everywhere, it will appear everywhere, at any time and any place, in your waking hours and during your sleep, travelling across the sea and any water, at night and during the day, when you speak and when you are silent. There is nowhere and nothing in which the Power is not present."

On the twenty eighth day she surrendered silently: *And lend us the power to be one with You.*

When she spoke these words she saw that they were an expression of Wisdom, the prime thought of the Father now wanting to unite with its divine source.

Opening her eyes she now saw that she was no longer in her body but hovering above the mountain. Below her she saw a young woman squatting in prayer on the ledge. And she understood the words once said by Salome: As above, let it be below.

Floating about in her star body she let herself be surged by SHM, the heavenly semen and became pregnant with Wisdom. Above her she noticed an unknown force called *Kether*. Its open eye scanned everything. A little later the eye closed and the force changed its identity to *Ein Sof*. At the same moment the universe stopped existing. Only when the being once again opened its eye did this Nothingness cease.

At that moment Mariam realised that the other half of that being, *Eva, Shekhinah, Hokhmah, Barbelo, Ishtar, Isis, Sophia*, was slowly beginning to bud and grow within her. Throughout the universe there was only one sound:

Amen.

When after forty days Salome came to collect her student she became worried when she did not find anything but an empty cave and Mariam's white blanket. She looked further into the cave, but Mariam was nowhere to be seen. A sudden impulse made her climb higher up the mountain. Getting to the summit she was met by a sight, which she might have dreamt about, but which she had not dared hope she could ever really come to see. On the edge of the cliff sat Mariam surrounded by an unspeakably intense and beautiful light which made Salome fall to her knees with her face turned away. But that which made her heart swell with emotion was the sight of Mariam floating in the air about twenty centimetres above the ground, fervently in silent prayer.

Above them could be heard a voice:

"This is my daughter, Mariam, in whom I am well pleased. Today she has received the name Magdalene, the Exalted Spirit of Peace. I have come back to the world in her shape. By her power shall humanity understand its destiny. Through her shall humanity again find peace."

9

Mona Lisa was still smiling when I woke up.

Coming back to my everyday consciousness I was struck by the thought that maybe she was Leonardo da Vinci's secret formula for the isogynic being. An image of the condition in which an individual, irrespective of sex, both integrates and dissolves the masculine and the feminine within, so that he or she is both one and the other and yet none of them. Behind this the most famous smile in the world was not only a woman but also a man, perhaps the creator of the painting, Da Vinci himself. Was it Da Vinci's own eyes that looked so teasingly at me from the wall at the foot of my bed?

My nocturnal journey had taken me to the astral reality. I roamed numerous spheres where I was confronted with various repressions and prejudices, all of which lead back to episodes in my life, no matter how strange they might seem. In short periods of time, however, I did move more freely getting help to change some of the burden I was carrying, and it was very liberating to see dark matter change into light. The mornings when I returned from such travels I was very tired waking up, though I was filled with energy when first I first got up.

That morning I used the energy to clean the house and pack my suitcase.

A couple of hours later the Seer and I were on our way south. We crossed the Pyrenees at Andorra and continued towards Saragossa. Driving into Spain it became clear that a new page had turned in the old manuscript, which the Seer had placed in my care a few years earlier. It wasn't just a mental experience but an actual, physical one, causing the well known phenomenon synchronicity when, for example two people say exactly the same thing at exactly the same time:

"Did you feel that?" we asked simultaneously, our eyes meeting in wonder.

Something was going on.

In front of us the road cut, straight as a die through a flat and bare landscape. I was considering the thoughts we had discussed the previous day about the strange fate of the Jews and not least their settlements in the south of France and Spain, which could be traced back to the time before Christ. Something told me, that the mystery in which we were participating was somehow connected to this people and their powerful, religious background.

Because of my Aramaic studies, a language closely connected with and a prerequisite for understanding Hebrew, I knew something about Jewish mysticism, the basis of the Kabalah. I also knew the numerical value of each of the signs and the qualities that each one represented.

The Kabalah (which means *that which has been transmitted*) is normally connected with a special, historical Jewish movement that arose in Provence in the south of France during the first half of the 12th century. I was now wondering about the fact that, quite strangely, this coincided with the year 1180 when a Jewish Sufi master, Kyot from Toledo, is said to have brought a secret manuscript from his hometown in Spain to Provence in France, which described the secret of the Grail. Nevertheless, it is here, for the first time, we meet the expression the 'Holy Grail'. Could it be possible that this Grail was connected to the Kabalah? On confronting the Seer with these thoughts, he responded:

"Why don't we stop in Kyot's hometown, Toledo? It is situated a little to the south of Madrid. It'll be no problem – not much of a detour. Maybe we'll find something out.

We got to Toledo late in the afternoon. The old part of the city is situated on a ridge and surrounded by the river Tajo and it has a kind of cool, aristocratic reticence. Its history reaches far back into the unknown, and no one really knows about its origin. One legend tells us that it was built around a Jewish settlement, but no one knows the exact year. Other sources claim that it was built by the Romans.

We drove through Puerta del Sol and followed the small streets to the Alcázar Palace where we parked the car. We found a small hotel in a side street, *Imperial,* and decided to spend the night there. It was the obvious thing to do.

At the reception desk a dark haired woman was preparing a bill for guests leaving the hotel. I looked at her while we waited. Something about her seemed familiar but I couldn't see what it was. I had never met her before. Maybe it was just one of those things which happens when a man looks at a woman and is fascinated by her. No, this was different.

Then it was our turn.

She wasn't beautiful in the normal sense, but she had a personality that somehow caught your attention. She had a pair of burning eyes and moon coloured skin. There was a kind of electric aura about her, which either attracted or repulsed you.

The Seer and I registered, each with his own room. A little later we went out into the city in order to find a place to eat.

You cannot take many steps in Toledo without practically losing your way. The small streets are so narrow and the houses so relatively tall that it is difficult for the light to filter down. You step suddenly into a plaza only to be caught a little while later in a maze of blind alleys and winding passages filled with secret entrances and hidden doors.

It was in this city that the painter El Greco gained his reputation in the 16th century. It was the absolute capital of Spain at the time, a world famous centre for the production of swords, chain-mail armour and other weapons conjured up in the smithies, as well as being a melting pot of religions such as Christian monastic orders, Arabian Sufis, Jewish cabbalists and various alchemists living harmoniously beside merchants dukes, Princes and Kings. Toledo was the centre of commerce where money flowed like honey in beehives. The city had been a very rich city. Now, however, it seemed more closed. Perhaps as a protest against its shameful destiny of being reduced to a simple tourist trap where you may hardly find a decent meal. Or perhaps it was guarding its secrets?

"Let's have a drink" the Seer said.

We found a bar close to a small square below the hotel, and were about to enter when I noticed a sign in the semidarkness on the wall of a house carrying the name of the plaza:

Plaza de la Magdalena.

It almost felt like a subtle joke, just like the Mona Lisa reproduction with her teasing smile. Dumfounded I pointed to it. Now the Seer also noticed.

"Someone is trying to tell us something," he said and smiled laconically.

At the bar we both had a sandwich and a Fernet.

"It is a strangely closed city," the Seer said, "it seems as if it is hiding something. When I go into the universes and ask, I do not get an answer as such. However, there are other ways. Perhaps we should just sleep on it and see what happens."

We finished our drinks and went back to the hotel. The young woman at reception had been relieved by an elderly woman whom I took to be her grandmother.

We each went to our own room.

Once in my room I lay down on my bed hoping that something would happen. I was determined to get in contact with this old master Kyot. What was it he had found in Toledo, which had started the whole adventure of the Holy Grail?

I don't know how long I meditated but I must have fallen asleep, because I was suddenly on my way into the astral spheres the way I had been doing every night since the experience at the Hotel Costes at Montségur. As usual, I floated about in a room without any visible walls. However, I had no doubt that this was different place from the one I usually frequented, which was normally about collective and personal traumas I needed to let go of. I was now in a sphere where the sense of time was intense. It wasn't usually like this. Using a kind of projector I sent a cone of light into a narrow, dark room with characteristic, medieval stonewalls. An old man with a white beard was sitting on a chair and I had no doubt at all that this was Kyot. Apparently he was in a hurry at least this was the feeling I got since he immediately started talking:

"The Kabalah is here in Toledo. But only the shrewdest of people will be able to find it."

"Where?" I asked quickly.

"In the streets and passages."

"Do the Kabalah and the Grail have anything to do with each other?"

"Yes!"

"At the time, where did you get your knowledge from?"

"From the magus Léon from Toledo."

"Do you know where he got it from?"

"From an itinerant magician by the name of Flegetanis, the one who talks with the stars."

"Can it be traced back further?"

"At the beginning of time it was given to Abraham by *Melchizedek*."

"Can you tell me anything about *Melchizedek*?"

Either Kyot didn't want to answer the last question or he didn't have the time to do it since the cone of light suddenly and without warning went out and I floated on through space to a sphere outside of time. Suddenly I was in the basement where I had been before:

At the end of a long passage a door is waiting to be opened. I walk towards it. Behind the door I expect to find the carcass of a pig, the heart of which is kept alive artificially by a machine. I open the door, but to my great surprise I find that the metal table with the pig has gone. In the middle of the room, which is no longer an operating room, a cream coloured couch takes up the space instead. At one end of it a young woman is sitting, and I notice that it is the young woman from the reception desk at the hotel Imperial.

"Welcome," she says and motions me to sit down.

I sit down at the other end of the sofa. Now I also notice the peacefulness of the room. The pleasant atmosphere makes me relax and I feel that my thoughts are slowing down.

"I'm your oracle," the woman states and smiles at me as if her statement is the most natural thing in the world.

"In the future you may come here and ask your questions. I cannot promise you that you'll get the answers you want or expect, but I promise you that you'll always get the answers you need in their most appropriate form."

She looks at me intensely and I understand that this is the voice I have been hearing for the last few days, and I also understand that I shall always be able to trust this being and that she will always help me, no matter what. I have an uncontrollable urge to hold her. We are siblings, I'm in no doubt of that, but I ask her anyway:

"Who are you?"

"I am the one who has always been with you. You have called me by various names but you have avoided me too often, or you might not have been able to hear me when I tried to get through to you. Too often you have been busy with your own affairs. But mark my words: this is going to change. Seek me here in this room, whenever you need me. You are always welcome, also at times when you do not have anything to ask. There may still be some answers for you."

The room faded away and I opened my eyes. It was just after midnight. I was lying on my hotel bed not sleepy at all. Most of all I wanted a cup of coffee. Why not? I made up my mind and went down to the reception desk.

The young woman had once more taken her position behind the curved desk. Apparently she was busy doing the books and the cash register. A hidden lamp behind the counter was the only light, which made the cubicle look like a small island floating about in the empty, dark room. I let the door hit the wall on purpose in order not to frighten her with my unexpected appearance. She looked up and smiled when she saw me.

Miriam of Toledo

"May I help you," she said in her charming Spanish/English.

"I'm very sorry, but I'm really in need of a cup of coffee, and I thought ..."

"Certainly."

She was already getting out of her seat.

"Come this way."

I followed her into the next room where most of the tables had already been set for breakfast. A percolator was twinkling with a red light behind a small counter. I ordered a cappuccino and she asked me to sit down at one of the tables. I was watching the back of her neck and her back while she made the coffee with supple movements. It was a strange situation. I felt that I knew her and that I had always known her. It wasn't more than fifteen minutes ago that I had met her in another reality and we had spoken with each other. Now, I felt totally estranged.

She arranged the white foam on top of the coffee and decorated it with chocolate sprinkle. A little later she balanced the cup through the air and placed it in front of me. Then she started wiping the counter and setting the last tables. I just sat and sipped my coffee in order not to finish too fast.

"By the way ..."

She took a map of the city from the counter and turned towards me:

"Did I tell you that there are a few places that you and your friend ought to visit while you are here?"

Taken by surprise I shook my head. It seemed like a strange thing to say, given the time. She unfolded the map and let her eyes roam the heart shaped maze. She conjured up a ballpoint pen from her breast pocket and drew a few circles on the map. She folded the map again, gave it to me and was about to turn around when I plucked up courage enough to asked her:

"Excuse me, but what is your name?"

There was a short pause and she gave me a surprised look. Then she said:

"Miriam."

She remained standing for a while. I got up slightly confused and heard myself saying:

"My name is Lars."

The whole situation must have seemed ludicrous.

"I know," she said laughing.

She stayed there looking at me when I said good night and walked back towards the staircase. It felt as if she could see straight through me.

"Good night," she said as the door closed behind me.

For a change, I woke up the next morning without being able to remember anything about the astral travels I had been on during the night. It was a relief. But I had the encounter with Miriam quite clear in my head. Before going down for breakfast with the Seer I remembered the map that Miriam had given to me.

Sitting opposite the Seer I wanted to tell him about the experiences of the night, but something held me back.

"So, did you sleep well?"

It was the Seer's usual brisk way of greeting me, originating from his days as a senior officer in the army.

I nodded.

"I think that maybe I have found an opening."

"Hm, what is that about?"

I hesitated, but then it came to me just like that. Suddenly I understood what it was Kyot had meant when he told me that the Kabalah was in Toledo. Suddenly I realized that his cryptic answer, that the Kabalah was to be found in the "streets and passages," was to be taken quite literally.

"What do you think about the idea that the original town may have been built around the Tree of Life. What if the Kabalah is shown in the original ground-plan of the town?"

"Bingo," he said, "I really think you've got something there. We'll start right after breakfast."

I placed Miriam's map of the city in front of him:

"Maybe we can use this as a starting point?"

The Seer went into action an hour later. He was in high spirits and it was a pleasure to see him working. He was a study of concentration. This was his element: the precise diagnosis.

We walked through the narrow streets studying Miriam's map. We went further and further into the old, Jewish quarter. The Seer suddenly stopped. The surroundings changed within seconds. A strange glow fell over the small square. It was obvious that the Seer was on his way into another universe. Then he said:

"I am in touch with Léon the Magus."

This piece of information ought not to have surprised me, the Seer's other achievements taken into consideration, but he surprised me once more with his precision. There was no doubt in my mind that this Léon the Magus was exactly the same as the Léon of Toledo that Kyot had talked about the previous night. The Seer continued:

"He confirms your idea that the Kabalah was the basic model for the original town. Unfortunately, it looks as if the town has undergone so many changes since then that it is impossible to find that model. He tells me that he will point out the places but that planning the town they worked with seven Kabalah points only. The uppermost three and the tenth were hidden."

He started walking while he hummed:

"This looks promising."

Turning a corner he stopped again. We were standing outside Taller del Moro in the street bearing the same name. He was in his own world for a while.

"This once was the place of *the Knowledge about that which was*. This is the eighth centre of the present Kabalah. *Hod*, the Radiance. We are talking about a number of storage-kingdoms storing the consciousness of the days of yore. It is also the sphere of the Brotherhood. More cannot be said at this time."

We hastily moved north and passed the present Universidad de San Pedro Mártir. The Seer stopped at Plaza de San Roman. It was a small square with a typical, Spanish statue depicting one of the forefathers of the city. There were a few cypresses on the plaza surrounded by a low hedge.

This is the place for *the Understanding of Alchemy*. It is the same as the fifth centre of the present Kabalah, *Gevurah*, Strength. Here once was situated a copy of the place outside the universe where the original knowledge about Alchemy was stored. The area has an understanding of all the elements. If you are standing in the middle of the shape of a ball that is where the process is going on. In order to understand the alchemy of the elements you may use the name "Alkymium." Léon is showing me a special point relating to matter. When I ask about a sign for this place I'm given a key, which changes into an *Ankh*, the Egyptian Key of Life.

I was busy writing everything he said into my notebook. It was obvious that the Seer was in contact with something very important. The diligence with which he worked was impressive. And as usual when he was in this mood, everything came quickly and precisely. I partly walked and partly trotted in order to keep up with him and tried to take notes at the same. We went in a north-easterly direction until we got to Calle de los Carmelitas. This was also one of the places that Miriam had circled.

"This is the place for *the Understanding of other universes*. This is the old home of the elements. This place is equivalent to the invisible centre of The Eternal Kabalah. This centre is called *Nut*, and has something to do with snake forms. A series of unclear patterns are showing themselves as pentagons and octagons. Léon is pointing out that they contain deep knowledge. I see a dark tunnel with widespread points of light. It is possible to break the pattern and to get out of the tunnel. Then you meet yourself as the ORACLE."

I almost fell over backwards hearing the last sentence. The Seer poured out information in a constant flow, and it was difficult to understand its more or less cryptic content. However, the sentence about the Oracle was a confirmation of the fact, that, notwithstanding the Seer's own understanding of the information, when it appeared, nevertheless, it was very precise.

From the Carmelite Monastery the Seer turned south. He stopped where Calle de Santa Justa, Calle de la Sal, Calle del hombre de Palo and Calle de las Cordonerias met in a small junction.

"This is the place for *the Knowledge of the Physical*. This is

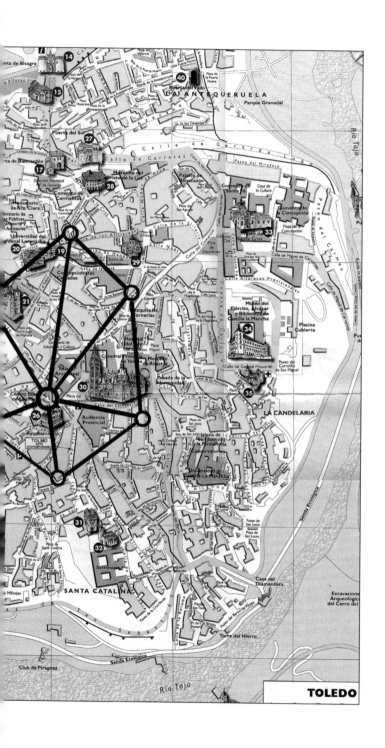

TOLEDO

equivalent to the fourth centre of the Kabalah, *Hesed*, Love. The image showed a symphonic body. Somewhere in the human brain there is a symphonic chamber. A symbol made from two entwined strings. Each string is made from twelve units. This symbol may be used in the physical world where harmony is missing."

Immediately the Seer was on his way again. We passed Catedral Primada de Toledo and walked down Calle de la Carcel del Vicario. Approximately halfway down the street he turned into a narrow passage.

"The next spot is right here. This is the place for *the Human Image of Transformation*. It is equivalent to the seventh centre of the Kabalah, *Netzah*, Victory. It tells you about the human power of imagination, which, if used properly, may serve mankind in a positive way. By the use of this power we decide for ourselves what we want to be. Through this, we may change our shadowy part and conquer our base nature."

We now travelled toward the south-west. The Seer speeded up even more as if there was no time to be wasted. We walked briskly down Calle de Santa Isabel and stopped at a small square, which also bore her name.

"This is the place for *Understanding the Universe*. It is equivalent to the ninth centre of the present Kabalah, *Yesod*, the Foundation stone. Léon explains that in order to understand the universe you must look at it from the outside."

The Seer slipped away again, but a little later he came back:

"The universe dances in its own quiet way. It is surrounded by fine, ring shaped auras. This thought form was once reflected in microcosm, to be more exact, here on this street. Long ago there was a brothel here. Not in the way we understand a brothel, but truly a house of pleasure, a kind of university if you like, where female dancers made the universe dance."

He had hardly finished the last sentence before he was on the move again. Now due north.

"We are on our way into the centre of the system."

Suddenly he seemed to be more alert, more on the lookout. At the Plaza del Consistorio in front of Ayunamiento he circled around but didn't seem to be satisfied. Slowly, we walked into Calle de la Trinidad and followed the walls to Palacio Arzobispal. He stopped at a side entrance and stayed there caught up in his own thoughts.

"Here it is," he finally said. "This is *the Melting pot* with the Grail in the middle. In the known Kabalah it must be the equivalent of the sixth centre, *Tifferet*, innermost Compassion. Until now, Léon has been present but I haven't been able to see Kyot. Léon is leaving us now. He says that this is the revealed town. Kyot is showing me a garden maze. He is drawing various patterns, among others the Star of David, which, really is *The Shield of Solomon*. He is showing me the 144 or twelve by twelve consciousnesses, which are the essences of each other. No matter where you are in this maze you must be able to find the Grail."

The Seer was now looking directly at me.

"You said so yourself: *The Grail is a state of mind.* Kyot is explaining that it was his task to be the one who removed the veil and revealed this knowledge. The legend of the Grail was and still is important to inspire mankind on its way towards self-knowledge and higher consciousness."

He looked wonderfully complacent.

"That's that then," he said with his old, sly smile.

The work of the day had been done.

From Toledo we drove towards the southern, sunny coast of Spain where we examined the impressions we had received. It was clear that a change had taken place between us. The teacher – student relationship was undergoing a change toward a more equal kind of co-operation. Especially after my meeting the Oracle.

The Seer and I were two very different personalities with very different temperaments and yet I could see how in some central areas we were very much alike. For example we both had very strong willpower, which tended to maintain our relationship within a set framework. This was seen very clearly in our different modes of work when the results were not immediately compatible. But it was really more a matter of the interpretation and application of terms than it was a matter of the deeper meaning of those terms. We simply used our language differently.

The Seer saw me to the train as he had done so many times before.

"It is time to start your task," he said.

When I went to wave good-bye to him from the compartment, he had already gone.

Back in Denmark a whole new world opened up for me. My "new task" turned out to be the function of a therapist. What kind of therapist had not been disclosed to me. It was all my own decision.

Through the abilities I had gained during my time with the Seer, I began the most instructive kind of work I had ever had – that is working with other people.

Each new client made me see new, unknown sides to myself. Meeting other people like that taught me that not only are we all in the same boat, but we are also brothers and sisters on the spiritual level. We are all one big family notwithstanding our social, political, religious or sexual affiliations. I have learned that we are made from the same matter, come from the same place and are going to the same place, though not necessarily by the same paths. That basically we are the same and only the physical conditions differ. This task was not only filled with meaning, it was very revelatory.

I was still travelling in the astral spheres every night. Most of the time I travelled freely, but far too often I was forced to stay in the lower regions. Strangely enough, these nightly journeys had the side effect of leaving me with almost supernatural energy during the day. At one time it became such a burden that I had to seek advice from my good friend, the theosophist Søren Hauge, whom I trusted and whom I knew was familiar with the phenomenon.

It was a relief to hear him say that he knew about others with similar experiences, and that the frequency of such experiences would, in all probability, diminish in the course of time. It was a matter of becoming conscious of the spheres in which you travelled so that the traveller little by little became so adept that he himself could decide when and where he wanted to travel. Furthermore, Søren told me that it was possible to meet other astral pilgrims at the various levels, and that he knew it was possible to communicate directly with other travellers at such encounters.

Encouraged by Søren's advice I started practising becoming goal-oriented before falling asleep. I realised that it was a matter of concentrating my thoughts on certain events in my life that I wanted to understand or get in contact with. My nocturnal journey would then probably take me to the astral copy of these events.

At other times I could return to a specific level by concentrating on a distinctive mark or a feeling that I had met at an earlier encounter here. I tried to return to the room with the cream coloured leather couch and my oracle Miriam for a long time. But without any success.

It was during a consultation one day that I heard the Voice – Miriam – giving a piece of no nonsense advice to a client with whom I was talking. This created a long pause and an embarrassing silence, and I must have looked rather strange while I tried to listen to this voice which, apparently, I was the only one who could hear. My client seemed quite lost when in a very kind way she tried to get in contact with me again. Luckily she was very understanding when I told her what had happened, especially when I gave her the message I had just received. It was a very precise answer to her present problem.

This event was the beginning of a whole series of similar events giving me the opportunity to develop acceptable abilities to be present and focused, while at the same time I was in contact with the Oracle. Since then, I have learned to listen to my very first intuition, which nearly always turns out to be right.

All in all I learned that a successful healing is not so much dependent on the personal ability of the healer, but more to do with the extent to which he is able to make himself a pure instrument for the Power. The first and foremost task of such an instrument is to get into a state of mind, through various practices, rituals or prayers, where the ever present potential in and around a person is activated, so that the ethereal life force becomes a noticeable reality. In such a state you must give up any kind of judgement and prejudice. This state is very much similar to the one used by the old Taoists when describing *the true human being.* The true human being breathes with his whole body, arrives here almost unnoticed, is present in a quiet way of being and leaves the world silently when he has fulfilled his purpose. The healer invokes and transmits the Power without considering his own role or making a great to-do about it. Nothing else can make you feel more humble and deeply grateful than witnessing the successful outcome of such a process.

Almost two years went by like this, interrupted only by travels to Montségur and Andalusia every six months in order to meet with the Seer.

During that time I constantly tried to get in contact with Miriam in the room with the cream coloured couch. Without success.

But one day the phone rang ...

10

Mariam was in her twenty fourth year, and as an initiated priestess in the society of the Therapists had earned the right to live in her own house. She was a full member of the society and held an elevated position within the Temple as a beloved preacher and interpreter of the Scriptures. She was a magnificent healer and was visited by all kinds of diseased people who came from afar to be treated by this charismatic woman.

It was in the month of Elul. Mariam had just finished a gathering in the Temple and was on her way to her small cabin on the shores of Mareotis when she spotted Salome walking towards her in a state of agitation. Mariam immediately sensed that something out of the ordinary had happened. She knew that it would take something very special to make Salome lose her composure. The two women embraced.

"What happened?" Mariam asked her.

"Your time has come."

Mariam felt a pang in her heart. Although she knew very well what they meant, time had slowly but surely buried deep in her memory all thought about the consequences of these words.

"When?"

"Now. The messenger from the Brotherhood is waiting for you in my house."

Mariam was struck by fear for a brief moment, but she quickly collected herself. Salome, who knew her like a mother knows her own daughter, knew that no amount of fear could ever force Mariam away from the path she had to follow.

The Brotherhood had sent a young novice, Lamu. He handed Mariam a scroll. Mariam was again her usual self and broke the seal with a steady hand. The words from the first book of the Torah worked like a key on Mariam's heart: *The silver cup must be found within the tribe of Benjamin.*

The sentence almost floated out of the fresh papyrus. The key slipped unhindered into the lock. The door sprang open and she knew that the time was ripe when she had to redeem the pact her parents had made on her behalf a long time ago.

"I shall leave this very day," she said.

Salome opened a cupboard in which she kept her most precious herbs. She handed Mariam a small alabaster jar.

"Take these 500 shekels of Myrrh. You must find the remaining ingredients when you need them. Go in peace."

She took a ring from a small pocket in her gown and placed it on Mariam's finger. It fitted her perfectly. A dark blue sapphire was placed on each side of the word "Ephatah," which was engraved in the ring. "Rukha d'koodsha" was engraved on the reverse side of the ring.

"Put it on when you feel the need. It will open any darkness."

They parted unsentimentally, knowing that they should never see each other again.

They held each other for a long time in an embrace of recognition. But it was clear to both of them that Mariam was no longer the same sister who had left her childhood home ten years earlier, just as Lazarus was no longer the same brother as the one she had parted from. Her return had created great joy and Lazarus had begun immediately to arrange a welcome party, worthy of a queen. Only Mariam's dignified firmness had kept Lazarus from it. Instead, they were now standing in their father's old room at the exact same spot by the window where long ago Lazarus had informed her about the plans for her education.

In spite of the fact that they were both dressed in white, he in the dress of the Brotherhood and she in that of the Therapists, everything that had happened in the meantime lay between them like an impassable chasm. Behind Lazarus' strained attempt to maintain the authoritative front of a patriarch, Mariam saw a joyless human being whose course in life had brought him to a cul-de-sac. One single look into her brother's inner life sufficed. Lazarus was an unbalanced person. An instrument out of tune.

"You have arrived in the nick of time," he said. "The Romans have tightened their hold on our country. The new pontius is merciless. Even the members of the council in Sanhedrin in Jerusalem are losing privileges they have had for years. You must go to Carpernaum where you are expected. Great things have happened lately and no one knows where it will all end."

"What things?"

"Something happened which no one could have predicted. Something which will make our relationship with the Brothers of Qumran and the priests of Jerusalem more difficult than it already is."

His words were falling over each other like drunken sailors on a binge. Mariam tried to keep his attention, but in vain. She then cut through to the heart of the matter:

"Where is he?"

The question seemed to disconcert Lazarus even more as if he had totally forgotten the reason for Mariam's return.

"In Capernaum, I presume."

"Now, tell me what happened."

She put a hand on his shoulder in order to calm him down. The gesture seemed to have the desired effect. He sat down heavily on their father's old, Syrian chair. Then he pulled himself together:

"You have probably heard that the Brothers of Qumran have a candidate, Yohannan, the one called the Baptist. He has been moving about at the delta of the river Jordan, preaching and prophesying. He is baptising anyone who wants it. No one knew at the time that he was the candidate of the Brotherhood. He attracts big crowds indeed. So big in fact that both the Romans and the members of the Sanhedrin have visited him in order to question him about his background and lineage. They asked him if he was the prophet that everyone has been expecting, and he replied evasively in spite of the fact that no one escapes his doomsday prophesies. It has created quite a stir."

Mariam knew nothing about this Yohannan.

"What is the problem?" she asked impatiently.

It was obvious that Lazarus was trying hard to keep his grip on the story, and Mariam sensed that there was more to it than her brother understood.

"Three months ago Yeshua came back from his long journey to the East. To the dismay of all, he did not go to the Brotherhood at Carmel as expected, but directly to Capernaum where he has gathered a group of followers around him. He goes about in Galilee speaking to the people. Rumour has it that his audience is growing day by day. A month ago he visited Yohannan in order to be baptized. Rumour now has it that even Yohannan recognises Yeshua as the expected Messiah. All this has caused both sections of the Brotherhood to become confused and in conflict with each other. Both their respective candidates have failed. It is a serious situation. The Romans and Sanhedrin on the other hand are worried about the influence that both Yohannan and Yeshua have over people. Yeshua's relatives are worried as well. They say that he has changed so much that even his mother, Mariyam, can hardly recognize him anymore. That is why she went to the Brothers of Carmel to make them inform you that the time has come to redeem the covenant. She is hoping that the wedding will return her son to her."

"Tell me Lazarus, how Yeshua has failed?"

"You know the prophesies and the expectations of the Brotherhood. We are living in those times that the old prophets talked about and the two chosen ones, Yeshua and Yohannan, were considered for the roles of Messiah-the-King and Messiah-the-Priest. They wanted to avoid bad blood between the groups in this way. And then all this happens. Yohannan does not want any superior power. And they say that Yeshua is more interested in fighting the Romans than in fulfilling his destiny."

"Who can predict the destiny of Yeshua with any certainty?"

Mariam walked to the window and looked across the fields of her childhood. It struck her that they were no longer as well kept as she remembered them.

The following day Mariam and her young guide were on their way to the north. On the way she noticed that Lazarus had been correct in his statement about the Romans: the roads were alive with occupying troops. The soldiers stopped and questioned everybody who looked the slightest bit suspicious. The road between Jerusalem and Jericho was more or less decorated with *tau* crosses carrying the victims of the atrocities of the Romans as a deterrent to others who might harbour the slightest thought of rebellion. The situation did not get any better until Mariam got to Scythopolis at the Gilboa Mountain, where it seemed normal again. There were still lots of soldiers about, but the atmosphere seemed less aggressive. She felt a sense of relief when finally she saw Philoteria and the Sea of Galilee which reminded her of Mareotis. The cool breeze from the lake cheered her up and she shook her cloak free from all that had been troubling her. When Lamu guided her into the town in order to find shelter they saw that the town was in great uproar. Groups of agitated citizens were standing in the streets discussing vehemently, and it was only the presence of the Roman soldiers that prevented the verbal agitation from developing into something worse. Mariam stopped at the square and asked Lamu to find out what was going on. Meanwhile, she drank some water from the town well. Here she overheard a conversation between two pharisees:

"He is a disgrace to his brothers and a dangerous man for the people. He is a charlatan leading Israel directly to the slaughter," an elderly man from the priesthood was shouting.

The other one, a tall, stooping youth, apparently, was slightly more favourable:

"Well, sometimes he might be raving but he is of the lineage of David and thus the rightful King of Israel. With Sanhedrin in Jerusalem as a buffer between him and Pilate, his temper might just hold the Roman Civil Service at bay. Then life in this country would be tolerable once more. We don't need those damned Herodians, who are getting fat at the expense of the people and rubbing shoulders with Rome."

Lamu returned and Mariam had to know right away:

"What has happened?"

"He was here. Yeshua was here and spoke to the people. They say that the audience was so large that the whole square was filled with people. People everywhere, in the trees and on the roofs, just to catch a glimpse of him."

"What do they say about him?"

"That varies. Some say that he is a false prophet while others see him as the future King of Israel."

"When was he here?"

"He left yesterday."

"Where did he go?"

"One man saw him and a few of his closest disciples walking in the direction of Mount Tabor, while others say that he is on his way to Capernaum by way of Hippos on the eastern shores of the lake. That is where his followers are going."

They walked through the town to the small harbour. Mariam looked over the Sea of Galilee. With her mind she tried to understand what kind of forces were driving the man to whom she had been betrothed. She knew in her heart who he was, but she also knew that he was still looking for a standpoint. Inside herself, she saw his melancholy face which sometimes gave him a peaceful and at other times a haunting look. She knew that his time had come, that his destiny was growing in him already. She realized that at this exact moment he would be torn between two opposite forces threatening to destroy him if he didn't soon decide which one he would choose. She saw him followed by great throngs of people who tried to get closer, wanting to touch him — and she saw how desperately he wanted and was looking for solitude.

A storm was brewing in the east. White foam blew across the surface of the water. Mariam shook herself. It was time.

Mariam and Lamu rode out towards Mount Tabor the following morning. The mountain showed itself against the sky on the horizon. They were on their way before the sun had gained power. They found two primitive cabins at the foot of the mountain. Two figures dressed in white were seen sitting in the shade in a small palm grove not far away, absorbed in conversation. Mariam asked Lamu to wait for her while she steered her horse in the direction of the two figures.

The two men stood up and looked at her suspiciously. One of them, a big, weather-beaten man with coarse features took one step towards her:

"Woman, what are you doing here?"

The man's voice sounded gruff and discouraging. Mariam saw right through him. She smiled:

"I'm looking for the Chosen One."

Mariam's direct answer made the man uneasy. Then he replied:

"What do you know about this?"

Now Mariam also looked closely at the other man.

He was finer built and had beautiful, almost female features. The smile he gave was reserved. Then he said:

"What is your name, woman?"

"You'll know my name soon enough. I have something very important to hand over to your Rabbi and would be happy to know where I can find him."

It was the squarely built man who answered:

"Just give us what you brought, and we shall pass it on to him."

Mariam sat silently in her saddle. A fly buzzed through the air. It landed on the man's forehead. Mariam waited until the man had tried to swat the fly, which he missed. Then she said:

"What I have to pass on is more fleeting than a fly and yet greater than the greatest of anything you'll ever be able to imagine."

Mariam's words made the man frown. Who did she think she

was? He realised that he couldn't put her off so easily. Her composure made him uneasy. Mariam pulled at the reins and turned around.

"Don't trouble yourselves on my account. I'll find him myself."

She steered the horse toward the path leading up the mountain and started ascending. The sun was high in the sky sending its remorseless rays over the Holy Land. One of the men shouted something after her but the words disappeared in the vibrating dry haze.

She hadn't been riding for long when she saw the cabin. It was even simpler than the two at the foot of the mountain. Apparently, nobody was near and she took it for granted that he was either in the cabin or had gone further up. She tied the horse to a tree and walked to the entrance of the cabin. It was dark inside and her eyes had to adjust to it after the bright sunlight. Then she could see the outline of a man lying curled up on his side on the ground. She bent her head and stepped inside. It was him. He looked as if he was sleeping. Two lines on his dust covered skin under one of his eyes told her that he had been crying. She stood for a moment watching him. She then kneeled down next to him, leaned forward and kissed him on his forehead.

Shortly after, she was on her way down the mountain.

"Where are we going," Lamu asked as they were riding north.

"To Capernaum," she answered lost in her own thoughts.

Capernaum was festival clad and the streets were filled with expectant people who had come from near and far in order to listen to the prophet who, according to the rumour, was the long expected Messiah and the rightful King. Lamu immediately wanted to bring Mariam to the house of Mariyam, but Mariam would rather find a more neutral place. They had the good fortune to find an inn on the outskirts of the town. It was almost impossible to find a vacancy for miles and whoever wanted to could let out a sleeping mat for a shekel.

The festivities started in the afternoon. The street vendors got very busy when people started flocking into the town. The streets were so full that it was difficult to get anywhere, while the rumours said that Yeshua was seen both here and there. If not at one end of the town then at the other. The town was boiling over with pent-up expectations when suddenly a sigh went through the crowd. Mariam let herself be drawn along by the throng of people between the houses, while children and young men jumped from roof to roof. The prophet had asked people to convene at the square in front of the synagogue.

The square was alive with people. Yeshua himself was standing on a platform.

Behind him the light from the setting sun shone, dramatically highlighting his aura. It was a different man Mariam saw standing there than the one curled up sleeping whom she had kissed on the forehead the day before. Now he stood poised, looking over the crowd. He had a long beard and long, brown hair to his shoulders. He wore the traditional white coat of the Brotherhood. A handful of men dressed similarly had made a ring around him in order to keep the most aggressive ones away. Now Mariam saw that there were two women in the circle just below Yeshua and she assumed that one of them was Yeshua's mother, Mariyam.

Suddenly people grew silent. Yeshua greeted the crowd by raising his hand.

"Peace be with you."

His voice was warm and clear. But it was still difficult to hear everything he said. However, Mariam understood that he was talking about an angel who had been sent ahead in order to prepare the way for the one who would come, and that this angel was Yohannan the Baptist.

"But what can I compare the people of this generation to? What do they look like? They look like children sitting in the square yelling at each other: we played the flute for you and you didn't dance, we sang dirges and you didn't cry. Hear Ye, Yohannan the Baptist has come, he neither eats bread nor drinks wine and you say: he is possessed. And the Son of Man has come, he both eats and drinks and you say: see that glutton and that drunk, friend of publicans and sinners. But wisdom has conquered through its children."

Mariam soon understood that it wasn't necessarily the content of the words which went straight to the hearts of people but rather

319

the intensity with which they were said. Standing there caressed by the last rays of the sun he really was Messiah incarnate, king of the people and the foundation stone of faith. All were spellbound at this moment. Even the most hardened one would put his life in the hands of this man without hesitation. He gave the people new hope. Not about anything in particular. Rather the feeling that in general better times were on the way. But still, something was missing. Mariam was suffused suddenly by a feeling of loneliness. She suddenly doubted the man to whom she had been betrothed. In spite of his courage in speaking against Rome she noticed the fear behind the words and the assumed manliness, which wasn't real but simply a means to which he was clinging in order to go through with his mission. Standing right there, radiating and apparently approachable she sensed an invisible distance which at least to her made him seem dishonest. She saw how eagerly his disciples tried to keep people at bay, and before anyone knew it he was gone again, as suddenly as he had arrived, leaving a hungry throng of people behind.

When darkness fell there was singing and dancing going on in the town. Rumours said that Mariyam, the mother of the prophet, was celebrating in his honour at the home of one of the most esteemed pharisees of the town. These rumours were the source of much confusion since this pharisee was well known for his readiness to meet the wishes of the Roman authorities. How could Yeshua dine with such people?

Mariam moved about in a state of trance. She only saw and heard what was absolutely essential. At another level she knew very well what she had to do. With Lamu's help she visited the stalls of the merchants in order to buy the remaining things she needed, cinnamon bark, sweet-flag oil, cassia and aloe. She tried to find out where she could get the best olive oil. When she had finished her shopping they returned to the inn. Behind the building was a yard where the local wine expert used to work. Here Mariam mixed the ingredients with the myrrh she had received from Salome. She was ready an hour later. In the meantime she had Lamu find out where the party for Yeshua was held. There was no time to waste.

They easily found the house. Many from the crowd had settled here, waiting for something to happen. Mariam worked her way through them with Lamu following closely behind her. Two of Yeshua's disciples stood at the door.

"What are you doing here, woman?"

Mariam answered behind her veil:

"I have something very important to give to Rabbi Yeshua."

One of the men was about to push her back as the other went between them. It was the same man with the feminine features that Mariam had met the previous day at the foot of Mount Tabor.

"Wait" he almost whispered.

To Mariam he said:

"You can safely give us your gift for the master and we shall pass it on to him."

He seemed very nervous and Mariam pulled her veil aside:

"Don't bother."

She briskly stepped between them and went into the house.

Somewhere people were talking in loud voices. She followed the sound and suddenly found herself at the entrance of a large hall where between twenty and thirty people were reclining around a table loaded with food and wine. The men spoke coarsely and laughed as she had only heard Roman soldiers and labourers laugh. The sight made her sad. This was not the way she had imagined meeting with her betrothed. A tear rolled treacherously down her cheek. She stayed for a while in order to make sure that he was there. Then she spotted Mariyam at the end of the table. Yeshua was at her side. He did not at all look like the future Messiah of Israel as she saw him there.

Nobody took notice of her when she walked across the floor. Not until she was standing right behind Yeshua did one of them look up.

"Who is this woman?"

Now the whole group reacted and they focused their attention on Mariam. Without further ado she knelt down at Yeshua's feet. While opening the alabaster jar her tears ran down and mixed with the content. Slowly she began anointing the feet of Yeshua. She had arrived in the nick of time.

"How dare you – and who gave you permission to carry the gown with our mark on it?" one of the disciples cried out angrily. Mariam recognised the voice.

"Stop her!" the host shouted.

"Let her, Petrus. And also to you Simon do I say: I came to your house. I was not made welcome. But I'm made welcome by this woman. You did not anoint me. But this woman anoints me with her tears. In whatever you may find her guilty, I forgive her every sin. Much shall be the one forgiven who has loved much. Only the holier-than-thou cannot be saved."

Mariam dried the surplus oil from the feet of Yeshua with her hair. Then she kissed them. A little later she got up. Their eyes met. Only for a short moment. She saw something else being born in him. He was bewildered. He looked like someone who didn't know what was up or down. He disappeared into her burning eyes. Who was she?

"I'm the silver cup."

Did he actually hear her or was this just an erring thought?

He got up and saw her disappearing the same way as she had come. Laughter bellowed behind him.

The silver cup?

What silver cup?

Who was this unusual and beautiful woman?

After that there were rumours about the foreign woman, the sinner, who had the nerve to intrude on the master and without asking just anointed his feet. This was totally unheard of. No one had ever heard of anything like that before. Evil tongues claimed that the woman was a prostitute who had committed many sins. Some even went as far as saying that she had attempted to have an intimate relationship with Yeshua, and that at the home of Simon the pharisee and in front of the master's mother and all the guests. She had kissed his feet. Only a real wife would do that.

In the meantime, Yeshua and his disciples had left Capernaum in order to find solitude in a small abandoned village in a valley close to Jordan just outside of Bethsaida. So far Yeshua had refused to continue the campaign planned by Petrus. A journey taking him all over the country and when the time was ripe bringing him victoriously to Jerusalem. Petrus had recognised the woman and he was irritated by the fact that he hadn't succeeded in stopping her once and for all. Especially now, when he saw the effect the episode had on his master.

As the days went by it became clear that something had happened which could not be dismissed too easily. Yeshua was silent and distanced himself from the disciples. Anyone could see that he wasn't himself. It finally became too much even for Petrus. He went to Yeshua who was sitting in the shade of a palm tree.

"Master, what is bothering you?"

Yeshua didn't move and didn't answer.

"You haven't eaten anything and you haven't spoken for three days. This must stop now." But Yeshua didn't answer, he was in another world.

Mariam and Lamu waited at the inn until peace ruled in the town once more. The owners of the inn began to feel rather uncomfortable about their staying at the inn. Lamu tried to get Mariam to visit Mariyam's house but her mind was elsewhere. She sensed that what must happen would happen.

This turned out to be true on the fourth day. The disciple with the female features, Thomas, was in Capernaum with another disciple, Yuda, in order to find the woman who had created such an uproar.

When they entered the courtyard, Mariam sat in deep contemplation. This didn't seem to bother the two of them. It was clear that they were in a hurry.

"Woman, the master wants to see you."

Mariam opened her eyes. Without answering, she stood up and straightened her gown. Lamu was already busy packing. Half an hour later they were on their way.

The moment of truth. Exactly as predicted. His time and her time were near. Only the circumstances were different. If she had known them beforehand she wasn't so sure that she would have taken the task upon herself. She was no longer the young girl in love, who dreamed of marriage and love – who once dreamt such passionate dreams about this man. She now just wanted it to be over, no matter what the forthcoming meeting would bring.

They rode into the abandoned village three hours later.

II

So it was that the phone rang.

It was the radio and television journalist Anders Laugesen who invited me to participate in a television programme about travelling as a pilgrim. I could more or less decide the destinations. The only problem was that it was planned to be on the air a few months later, which meant that we had to leave as soon as possible. In spite of the fact that I was quite busy I heard myself answering very clearly and unreservedly with a YES! I suppose that something in my subconscious must have been waiting for a new way in my ongoing search to show itself. This was it. Immediately after that decision had been taken it became equally clear that the journey should go to the Middle East, Syria, Jordan and Israel. Anders and I would travel by train from Denmark to Istanbul in Turkey and then on to Syria from whence we would continue by car. The whole trip was planned to take three weeks. When I told the Seer about these plans, he said in his usual dry way:

"Have a nice trip. An initiation is awaiting you close to Damascus."

Unfortunately, the prolonged crisis between Israel and Palestine escalated to such a degree that it was decided that the expedition should go only to Syria. This decision would later prove to be more than fortunate.

Anders and I boarded the train at Aarhus Central Station on a cloudy September day. We had purposely been placed at each end of the train to give us the opportunity of going on pilgrimage "alone." Anders brought his digital camera and his tape recorder so that we could produce sections of the programme on the way, whenever the opportunity was there. The "real" cameraman of the programme would arrive by plane in Damascus five days later.

It is unbelievable what such a train journey can do. It is one of the most effective tools if you want to get rid of your rigid, civilised defences. We changed trains in Cologne and began the long, tiring journey through Eastern Europe: Hungary, Rumania and Bulgaria. We rattled, slowly into a depressing hopelessness, which apparently had no end. Layer after layer we had to lay aside our own desperate attempts to repress the kind of inner poverty we met each time we were tempted to defend our own limitations. It is the kind of poverty which always feels cheated, which feels that it hasn't received what was promised or what it really deserved. This happens as soon as we enter the land of misers, where no one can get enough and where only the strongest survive. Far too much in Eastern Europe is a reflection of our own inner poverty. We have let ourselves become blinded by external values and all kinds of unimportant luxury. It is the kind of poverty, which has everything, but only wants that which supplies the illusions about an eternal, painless life at the top, where nothing moves and everything remains as it was. It is the kind of poverty, which is forced to barricade itself in seedy, first class compartments at night, for fear of being robbed, without any kind of sustenance and in the ever present stench of decay and urine. This is where, in the course of a few days, you have no choice but to face your own naked existence, the skeletons in the cupboard and the numerous unseen scars on your mind.

The arrival at Istanbul foreboded a change. We were on our way into a lighter atmosphere. We had a single overnight stay in the city before continuing by train to Aleppo in Syria and, right from the railway station, the doors opened to another sphere. Anders noticed a poster saying that a so-called *sema* (a Sufi dance ritual) would be held in one of the old railway station halls that very evening, where dervishes from Mevlana Rumi's Sufi order were going to dance. We immediately booked tickets for this occasion, which turned out to be a genuine rarity.

Rumi, who was born in Afghanistan in 1207 but lived in Turkey from 1215 until his death in 1273, more than any other has become synonymous with the Sufis. He is one of the most treasured poets of the Sufi tradition, and his importance goes far beyond the Muslim world. Rumi is the indisputable master of love-alchemy par excellence. We therefore arrived at the sema brimming with expectation, and we noticed that about fifty people were already present.

A band, a *mutrip*, a group of five musicians, played for about half an hour before six dervishes, three men and three women, took over the floor. The participation of women was not only a surprise but an historic event since this kind of dance had for centuries only been for men.

The dervishes wear a special kind of costume representing the death of the little self. The characteristic, pipe-like hat called the *sikke* is literally the tombstone of the ego, while the *hirka*, a long, black cloak, represents the grave itself.

The atmosphere was intense as the dervishes stepped into the circle with their arms crossed. This is how the unity with God is reflected. Then they started the first circle of the dance, consisting of four circles altogether.

With their arms stretched out on each side, the right hand opening upwards and the left downwards, the dancers now turned about in faster and faster spirals. The position of the hands represent the central part of the ritual which expresses the sentence: *"We receive from God, We give to humanity, we keep nothing for ourselves."*

The expression 'dervish' in itself means to die. This not only symbolises the ideal of poverty stemming from the days when the dervishes had to go begging from door to door; it also symbolizes

the modern dervish endeavouring to be a door, or channel, between God and people.

They now turned about themselves and around each other just like the planets of the solar system, changing the room into a rotating galaxy of love and light. It was unbelievably exalting being a witness to this ritual which was performed with such dignity and humility that it was impossible not to be very moved by it. Not only did we witness an intimate act – but everybody who saw it became part of a greater transformation. Each movement was dedicated to us.

Sufism has always been seen as the mystical side of Islam, and its history has therefore always been officially considered identical with the history of Islam, starting at the beginning of the tenth century.

The concept of *Sufi* may be translated as *pure, wool* or *those dressed in wool — those dressed in white.* It was a concept used about itinerant sages, dressed in simple woollen cloaks. There are also certain language ties between *Sufi* and the Greek word *sophia,* wisdom or certainty. These itinerant sages weren't interested in politics or religion. For them the relationship with God was one of love, which was solely about dissolving your personality so that the soul could reunite with its Father. That is why these Sufis always submitted to the ruling power. This was the only way in which they peacefully could get close to the goal they aspired to. Some mystics claim that it is almost a coincidence that the Sufis are a part of Islam and follow the law of the Koran, while others claim that it is precisely the Prophet Mohammed and his Koran, which made these sages choose Islam.

The true Sufis feel that all the great religions of the world and all the mystical traditions share the same essential truth. They believe in one God and that this one God is behind everything, seen as well as unseen. You do not have to go to Mecca or to Jerusalem in order to find your God, He lives in your heart. Life doesn't end with death. Life in this world is like a dream, while true life is in the next world. It is important to the Sufis to be present in the world with all that this entails of work, marriage and other worldly obligations. But for them it is about deifying their everyday life, about living a normal life in a very special way. Being *in* the world, but also understanding that you are not *of* it.

In the evening and after the moving experience with the dance of the dervishes I began thinking about the idea, that maybe the first Sufis had been the group of itinerant mystics bearing the name of Those Dressed in White. Was it in reality their traditions which had formed the foundation of the well-known, Middle East and Persian traditions such as Judaism, Christianity and Islam? The Sufis' preference among holy books was and still is the Torah of Moses, the Psalms of David, The Gospels of Yeshua and the Koran of Mohammed. Their love tradition contains a very strong, female aspect. They have kept this fire burning for centuries and inspired mystics everywhere. Imagine if this was the tradition from which Mariam really came – and in which she disappeared again?

We boarded "The Syria Express" the following day, which turned out to be a slow train taking us through ninety towns in Turkey to Aleppo in Syria, at the speed of thirty kilometres an hour, where we were collected by our driver, Ahamad, and safely brought to our base, a small family run hotel, *Afamia*, in Damascus.

Our arrival in Syria was in many ways a homecoming. In spite of the many, unfamiliar problems apparent in modern Syria, such as the fact that the country is a police state, it still felt more open. The poverty here does not breed inhospitability and egocentricity as the spiritual poverty of the Western World seems to.

Syria is an Arabian nation. Sunni- and Shiite-moslems, Ishmaelites, Druses and Alawit-moslems live side by side with Christians from such different Churches as Greek Orthodox, Armenian Orthodox, Syrian Orthodox, Syrian Catholic, Greek Catholic, Roman Catholic, Maronites as well as a minority of Jews who live here without the problems, which are inevitable in other countries.

The arrival at Damascus was like falling into a boiling pot of strange smells, colours, noise, warmth and religion, all of which was covered by a reeking layer of diesel fuel. Stepping into this age-old city, which may be the oldest inhabited city in the world, is like stepping into a room where some of mankind's oldest archetypes lay hidden. The unfamiliar mysticism, which is obvious to any newcomer is both seducing and frightening because it is so intense and deep. The unreserved submission reigning here is a threat to any cool and detached attitude and, if you insist on retaining this, there are other places in the world more appropriate for playing tourist.

I found myself in a state of mind where any kind of defence had crumbled and I felt like an open book. The foundation for such openness was basically the hardships of travel as well as the challenging diet. This meant that I was more than usually sensitive and sharp. I have experienced earlier that such a state of mind makes it easier for me to step into the stream, going with the flow instead of against it. When you are in that state of mind all your old patterns of habit seem psychotic and caricature like. This state of mind calls for your total sense of humour without which it becomes unbearable. Luckily I was in lighthearted company making any kind of self-righteousness or self-pity impossible.

On the way to Damascus we visited the monastery built commemorating Simon the Pillar Saint. Furthermore, we visited the fantastic castle Crac des Chevaliers built by the Templars during the crusades. We spent the night in the desert monastery Deir Mar Musa El-Habashi where a former Jesuit priest, Father Paolo, had created an unorthodox monastery, which was more like a Dutch Hippie commune than it was a serious abbey or nunnery. We went to the great Umayyad Mosque where they keep the relics of John the Baptist and where I was blessed by a blind sufi master. In Ma'alouda I met some of the few Aramaic speaking people. We were simply invited to service and tea by the Archbishops of the Syrian Orthodox Church, who had arrived at the St. Ephrem Monastery from all over the world to participate in the annual synod, which was held the very day we visited here.

We were now on our way to the largest convent in Syria, Our Lady of Saydnaya. It was a very hot afternoon and we drove through a desert area to the north of Damascus. I was in a state of deep, open being and felt that something was changing inside me. The veritable bombardment of spirituality and religious symbols, which we met everywhere, had opened the same layers in me. The seriousness and dedication shown by the practitioners of the various traditions, Moslem as well as Christian, was stimulating to our own introspection. The daily practising of prayers became more and more intense as the days passed by, and I started sensing some of the deeper secrets behind the mystery of prayer. As a result of my prayers, I started feeling the presence of Mariam and faintly sensing the Voice:

"Prayers are not for the sake of God. They are for the sake of people. They are an awakening of all our resources. Through the medium of prayer you get into a state of mind enabling you to get in contact with the higher levels, the higher Self. When you personify God through your prayers, you are praying from the little self. No doubt, it has a certain effect, but a limited one only. When you understand that God is not a person but a creating power with an identity, which is only personified through your creation, you suddenly understand that the only form of blasphemy possible is made by the one who is praying to a personified God, the picture of Whom is created by you. Praying to such a god is limiting to the Power."

The car was jumping along on the bumpy road. In front of us the impressive Saydnaya Convent was faintly seen on the horizon. We were on our way there in order to participate in the annual festival in honour of the Convent's famous Mary-icon, *Shaghoura*, which simply means "known" or "famous." The icon is a copy of one of the four icons, which the evangelist Lucas is said to have painted. The icon has miraculous powers. Stories are told about pilgrims who have come close to it and who have been healed by it. On the day of the annual festival it is said to have a positive influence on women who cannot have children. The women then stay overnight at the convent and it is said that ninety percent of them regain their fertility. According to legend the convent is built on the site where Noah planted his vines after the Flood.

There were people everywhere when we arrived, and most of them were women who were staying overnight at the monastery. Every square yard of the long passages were covered with mattresses and bed linen. A group of Beduin women had already started the festivities in one of the passages and those who passed them by were pulled into the dance. An elderly woman caught me by my arm and heaved me up into the air. I was taken completely by surprise and must have looked rather comical. She put me down again but kept her grip on my hand while she started a series of movements which looked very much like a fertility ritual. The other women formed a circle around us while they articulated a series of howls. There was no escaping it. It all happened so fast that I had no time at all to reflect about the situation. It was a veritable attack on my aloofness and autonomous state of mind. I had either to let go or look like a self-righteous sour-face, who was sufficient to himself and his own spirituality. There was a short struggle before I surrendered unconditionally to the dancing and howling of the women. I danced more that evening than I have danced for years.

Thus, freed of my final and frayed defences I slipped into the flow of people on their way to the Holy of Holies. It is no coincidence that the entrance to the small room, where *The Blessed Madonna* is hanging, is so low that you have to bend your knees in order to get in. The bodily carriage equals the inner attitude you must take when you are in the room where so many pilgrims have prayed and surrendered themselves. The room is filled with candles and you cannot stay there for long before a fire is ignited in your heart. No matter to which denomination you belong you cannot help being moved by this place where so much hope is being expressed. Here Moslem and Jew are queuing up next to Christians. Here man is one before the One and Only.

After a short meditation at the icon I stepped into the flow of people once more leading me through an opening at the other end of the room. In the passage between the icon-room and the convent church some sisters dressed in black were handing out small envelopes containing candlewicks to the pilgrims. Moving along in the queue I was still in a contemplative state of mind. My heart was totally open. A deep feeling of unrestrained acceptance bubbled up through me and put me in a frame of mind that I can only describe with the rather trite word: *happiness*. Unlike anything I had formerly experienced as happiness, this feeling sprang from a being deep inside of me which I can only describe as *the eternal being*.

There was a bend in the passage, and I had just turned the corner and ended my Aramaic prayer when a sudden impulse made me look to the left. In the shadow on the wall was a small, humble, red and golden icon depicting Madonna with the Infant Yeshua. For reasons I still cannot explain, I stepped out of the queue in order to study the icon more closely. It turned out to be what I call a vulgar-icon, which simply means that the icon is a reproduction. I just stood there for a long time studying the icon, which did not differ from the other icons in the monastery except for the fact that it was a reproduction. But there still was something about it, which made me want to spend the rest of the evening in its vicinity. The room in which the icon was hanging was filled with an indefinable kind of energy, and I imagined that this was due to the thousands of pilgrims who had passed along this passage for hundreds of years feeling the same kind of happiness that I was feeling. There was a sense of release in the room.

I stayed in front of the icon for three hours. And suddenly I saw it. Suddenly I could see the symbolism which was very obvious but which had been hidden from me to begin with.

The picture itself was fractured and the line of fracture ran directly through the solar plexus of the Madonna. Her left hand, carrying the child, was below the line, while her right hand in front of her heart was above the line. I was lost in this symbolism when Anders and Jeppe arrived. They wanted a few shots with me commenting on my experiences. We had just finished this when the head of the convent, Sister Theodora, came in together with another sister and turned directly to me. Sister Theodora looked closely at me as if she wanted to make sure that I was sincere. At least, this was how it seemed to me. There was no doubt that she could see what state of mind I was in. She then lifted the icon from its nail on the wall, kissed it and blessed it and handed it to me.

There.

Just like that.

We were all speechless. Sister Theodora broke the silence:

"We found the picture in a corner here in this passage about fifty years ago. Someone must have dropped it or thrown it here. A young novice repaired it and made this beautiful icon. The icon is called *Our Lady of the Broken Hearted*. It has been hanging at this spot

"Our Lady of the Broken Hearted"

all these years. Take good care of her. Wherever you take her, she'll look after you."

The sisters then disappeared. They had plenty to do. That is why it was completely incomprehensible that they had noticed my infatuation with the icon. A young sister, who followed us to the car, gave me the last blessing, that left me stunned:

"I think you ought to know, that the novice who prepared the icon fifty years ago, in fact was Sister Theodora herself".

On returning to Damascus in the car I noticed that the hands of the Madonna were placed in almost the same pose as those of the dervishes when they are dancing. The message for present and future light workers was clear:

"We receive from God, We give to humanity, We keep nothing for ourselves."

I hardly slept that night but sat in front of the icon, which I had placed on a shelf in my hotel room. It took a while before I understood the value of the gift I had received from the nuns at Saydnaya. But also

Myrna of Soufanieh in Damascus

the responsibility accompanying it. It was as if a pact had been made. I now had to take upon me what was mine to do. The moment had come where I had to understand that the time for my eternal excuses was over.

The pact was confirmed two days later when we visited the stigmatised Myrna from Soufanieh.

The Nazzour family lives in a small two-storey house in Soufanieh, a suburb in Damascus. Myrna was eighteen years old when suddenly oil seeped from her hands during a visit with her sister-in-law who was ill. It turned out that the oil had healing powers. A small vulgar-icon, which she got from her husband, also began seeping oil. Shortly after she had a series of The Virgin Mary revelations in which she received various messages. Since 1983 she has experienced several ecstasies during which she has repeatedly become marked with the stigmata. The events have officially been accepted as true miracles and pilgrims come each year from all over the world to pray and to participate in the Masses held at her house.

We arrived in the afternoon of September 11th. There were only a few pilgrims in the room, which was used for prayers by the visitors. Myrna was dressed in a simple, black dress. In spite of the disturbance created by the preparations for the filming of the ceremony I could see the activity of light around her. The lucidity of her eyes was not of this world, and I knew that she was looking into a reality where work was being done to correct everything that the rest of us were busy destroying.

I had brought my icon in the hope that Myrna would bless it. The bustle around us continued and it didn't get any better when the shooting of the film began.

After the interview, which took place through the assistance of an interpreter, since Myrna's English was rather limited, we walked into the small chapel on the first floor where Myrna prayed for a short while. I was standing immediately behind her while she prayed her Syrian prayers, and I noticed how the activity of light around her intensified. I was affected so much by this that it was difficult for me to stifle the bubbling pleasure within me, which threatened to disturb the divine service with an uncontrollable laughter. When she had finished and held the icon to her mouth in order to kiss it, she looked very surprised and said in her broken English:

"Oh, it smells of flowers."

She handed me the icon so that I could smell the delicious smell of flowers coming from the picture. A little later the smell extended to the rest of the room. We were all overwhelmed and deeply touched.

Saying goodbye to Myrna she pointed to the icon in my plastic bag and said:

"Take good care of her. She takes good care of you."

I nodded and blurted out, "I will." If I had been in doubt before, then I certainly wasn't now.

As if this wasn't enough, the Board of Directors upstairs apparently had decided that I was somewhat dense, and they wanted to make sure that I understood the message. The night before my departure and during my usual astral outing I met a radiating ball waiting for me in one of the lower regions. Confronting the ball it changed and took the shape of the star of Mariam, a six-pointed hexagram. I didn't take much notice of this event apart from the joy in still being able to get in contact with this kind of energy. I woke up early next morning and decided to take a walk in the *souk* in the old part of Damascus. Most of the stalls were still closed and there were not many people about. I walked about at random until suddenly a man called out to me in a part of the city that I didn't know. He asked me what I was looking for. Without thinking about it I just answered that I was looking for antiques. Shortly after he lead me into a passage and knocked on the door of a posh restaurant. A man in a lounge suit opened the door and invited us in. The restaurant also turned out to be a similarly posh antique shop with showcases between the tables. Without asking what I was looking for the proprietor went to one of the showcases, opened it and took out a round metal plate with a grip on the back of it. When he placed it on the glass counter in front of me I was rather dumbfounded. The star of Mariam was etched on the metal plate. Arabic characters were written around it and I could see that they were laterally reversed.

Sufi seal of Dasmascus circa 1500 AD

"What is this?" I asked, speechless.

"This is a five-hundred-year-old seal which the Sufi sheikhs used to stamp on the white gowns of their pupils when they had served their apprenticeships."

Until this day I do not know how this man could know that this seal meant something to me. But I have no doubt that the Board of Directors upstairs had something to do with it.

Later that day I started my return trip by train, the same way as I had come and all by myself. It went very well until I got to the Central Station in Bucharest. I had two and a half hours to wait and as soon as I stepped into the arrival hall I was approached by two uniformed security guards. They were very obliging and asked me where I came from and where I was going. They found out about the time of departure and which platform for me. Then they told me that for my own security it was absolutely essential that they stay with me until my departure. I didn't understand the reason for this and tried to tell them that. They insisted. Two and a half hours later they followed me to the train and into my compartment. I felt rather nervous about it and hung on to my precious icon which I carried under my left arm and my equally precious Sufi seal which I carried under my right arm, holding the remainder of my luggage in my hands.

Then it came. Cold and clear:

"You must pay for security."

I was hardly surprised at the words.

"I haven't ordered any kind of security," I said calmly.

There was no apparent reaction.

"You must pay for security, one hundred euros."

Thoughts were rushing through my head.

"I have neither dollars nor euro, only this," I said knowing that both my dollars and euro were safe in my money belt.

I let one of my bags slide to the floor and took out a handful of Rumanian notes from a side pocket in my trousers.

He gave the money a quick glance. Then he knocked my arm away, lifted my shirt, unzipped my money belt and in one sweep took all my currency, and holding it into the air he said:

"Then this is nothing, eh? Have a nice trip."

Then they turned about and left.

I immediately sat down and started laughing. Of course I was somewhat shaken. And then again I wasn't. I had no doubt at all that this was the final lesson. It was about values. The robber had underlined it so heavily that even I couldn't help seeing it. The money was nothing. I was bringing back the real value.

12

Yeshua sat watching a cat, which had jumped into the room through a hole in the roof in the house where he had just spent three days and nights. Yeshua had lost all sense of motivation after meeting the unknown, young woman. The path he was on, and even more, the goals and hopes the brothers had on his behalf, had suddenly lost all meaning. The event had also created a disturbance among the brothers. But his mother, if possible, was even more agitated than all of them put together. She had kept on about the young woman, Mariam from Bethany, to whom he had been betrothed ten years earlier, and who was now on her way to Capernaum in order to fulfil her part of the pact. That is why the incident with this sinful woman came at a very bad time. Yeshua had dismissed his mother but with the result that she simply kept bothering him even more. Only Yohannan understood the implications of what had happened. His heart had also been touched by the actions of this foreign woman.

The cat was licking its fur when suddenly it froze at the sound of steps outside the house. Yeshua sat up. Not a sound. What was going on? The meeting with this woman had turned everything upside down. The power she had displayed in just a short instant was of a totally different dimension than the kind with which you seduce the masses. She was of another world. Was she one of the temptations of Satan, he wondered? She had performed her act with a humble dignity, which spoke against the presence of any kind of will based in a desire for power. Was she an angel sent by the Lord? Yeshua slipped into a dream world of conflicting thoughts. In a hidden part of his consciousness he heard a voice and felt a strong desire to move in its direction.

"I am *The Shekhinah*. I am stepping into the world in order to reintroduce the truth. I raise the fallen ones, heal the broken ones and bring peace to the persecuted ones. I defy the lie and offer a new life to people. Drink from my stream and you shall never be thirsty again. Unite with me and the eternal life is yours."

The woman, that he hadn't been able to get out of his mind since the day she had anointed his feet, was now standing in front of him. A light radiated from her, emphasising both her heavenly and diabolically seductive beauty. Her eyes were like fire burning into his. The cat nestled against her legs.

Yeshua sat rooted to the spot. The young woman let her cloak slip to the earth floor.

"I was sent here by the Force. I come to those who are able to receive me. I am found by those who seek me out. Look at me, you who seek to unite with me. Hear me, you who listen. You who await me absorb my essence. Do not forget me. For I am the first one and the last one."

She loosened the laces of her gown, opened it in front and bared her breasts to him. It happened so fast and took him so much by surprise that he lost his breath. The sight made him sick with lust. He had never seen such a beautiful being.

"I am honoured and I'm ostracized. I am the whore and the holy one. I am the wife and the virgin. I am the mother and the daughter. I am the heavenly bride for whom there is no husband to be found. My power is of the one who sent me."

She loosened the last laces, let her gown slide down and stood completely naked in front of him.

"I am the incomprehensible silence. I am the voice, the sound of which is manifold. I am the word without an end. I am the blessing of my own name. I am wisdom and ignorance. I am shameless and I am shameful. I am strength; I am fear. I am peace and I am war. I am the void in fullness. I am the one and only in emptiness. I dissolve all concepts and all images. That is why I am limitless. That is why I am everything. Do not forget me, for I am the ostracized one and the long awaited one."

He could wait no longer. He had to posses this divine being. She laid herself on the bed made by the cloak and the white gown. Yeshua felt faint. The words of the woman kept sounding in his head: "I am honoured and I'm ostracized. I am the whore and the holy one. I am the wife and the virgin. I am the mother and the daughter. I am the heavenly bride for whom there is no husband to be found." What did it all mean? He was sick with longing. Then he got up and walked, unsteadily, towards her. He saw her radiating body in the darkness, the goal of his desires, the beloved one, waiting for her lover. He slipped his coat over his head and sank down on the bed next to her. He was like a youth whose lust centred in a curve between his legs. He reached for her breasts and pressed his abdomen towards her, but she put a finger on his lips, and with her other hand she took hold of his erect member holding him in a firm grip, which took him so much by surprise that he groaned aloud. She held him like this without moving until he regained his composure. Still, the pressure was almost unbearable for him. Then she put her mouth close to his ear and whispered:

"Be vigilant, you who are able to listen. Listen, you who have been sent. Listen, you who are awake and risen from sleep. Many are the beautiful shapes making up the great illusion, the empty sin and the fickle lust, which man embraces until he becomes spiritually sober and goes to the meeting place. That is where you'll find me. And when you have found me you shall live, never to taste death again."

She slowly began massaging him and felt how he was about to burst in her hand. He reached for her breasts again and caressed them and kissed her hard. He had already arrived at the point of no return.

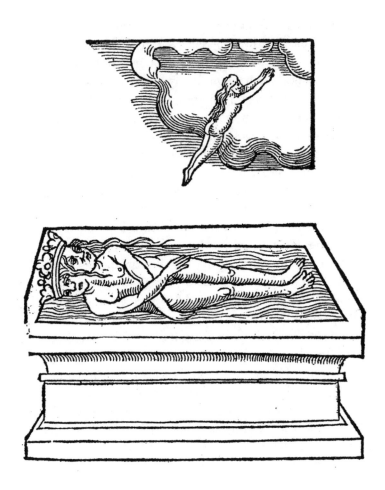

Hieros Gamos
(Rosarium philosophorum 1550)

She let him do whatever he wanted to do since she realized that it was impossible to get to him before his wild, sexually guided passion had been released.

He curled up and moaned like a maimed animal. Many years of repressed eros had been set free. Afterwards he lay on his back trying to catch his breath. She stroked his forehead and whispered:

"There are seven doors leading to the true human being. Seven holy centres through which the Holy Power is flowing, uniting with the Universe. The power you have just experienced is just a pale shadow of the Power to which I have been elected to lead you."

She let him go, got halfway up and knelt at his side. Carefully, she placed her hand on his member and felt how once more it grew between her fingers.

"This door is your biggest hindrance. As it is now, you are tied to the burden of your ancestors and all the heritage of man – good and bad. But all of this is just a faint reflection of your own fixations and limitations, as well as the fear which makes you forget who you really are."

He experienced another erection, but now he could both hear and see her, because this time he was not guided by his naked lust. She calmly massaged him with her hand, but it was her words, which caressed his heart and nurtured a totally different longing, the direction of which he did not know.

"There is an almost impenetrable darkness behind that door."

She let go of him and started searching for something in the pocket of the cloak, which made up part of their bed. Yeshua held her back, pulled her down to him and kissed her tenderly and passionately. She let him do it, but still smiling, tore herself away:

"You learn quickly."

Shortly after she found what she was looking for: the ring, which Salome had given her. She put it on her own finger; the ring finger of her right hand. She then held her hand about ten centimetres above his organ.

"Yohannan baptised you with water. I shall baptise you with fire. The two sapphires of this ring radiate the two poles *Ein Sof* and *Shekhinah* of the Creator YHVH. These two will open any darkness."

Her hand circled above him in soft movements and he immediately felt his abdomen vibrating.

"Now I'm going to tell you the secret behind the name of the Creator. *Yod* is Wisdom. *He* is Acknowledgement, *Vav* collects six sapphires (sefirot) into one: Strength, Grace, Compassion, Radiance, Eternity and the Foundation Stone. The last *He* is *Shekhina* (the royal kingdom of the heavenly bride). *Ein Sof* and *Shekhina* radiate through YHVH (Yod-he-vav-he/Jehova) in unity. Through the ten sapphires God's Daughter and God's Son are born."

While Mariam's hand hovered above Yeshua's manhood she put her mouth close to his ear and whispered:

"*Ephatah*. Open up. Release all that has been forgotten. Move all that has stagnated. Let Yodhevavhe's Power flow freely through this door and that darkness. Let go of the command of the lineage deciding who you ought to be, and instead be the one that you really are in your true Self."

Mariam moved her hand to a place just below his navel. She sensed that Yeshua was still tense and pushed him on to his back while laughingly she took hold of the visible proof of his tenseness:

"Get up, take up your bed and walk, you are healed."

This was the sentence, which the itinerant healers used when they were healing the sick.

Her catching laughter finally made him let go. He wanted to embrace her, but she evaded him and returned to her task. Her hand with the ring circled in soft movements above the holy spot just below his navel. The cat also settled down and purred in Mariam's lap.

"Who are you?" he asked and put a hand on her hip.

"Hush! You'll know soon enough. All you have to do right now is to let go and listen."

She pushed him back once more:

"Ten years ago I heard Helen of Tyre speak to a group of travellers in a small town on the coast down south. Her words cast a spell over all of us. But some of the men who were present got so agitated by her words that they wanted to stone her. Luckily she got away quite miraculously. People claimed at the time that she was a prostitute whom Simon the Magus had found in a brothel in Tyre."

EIN SOF

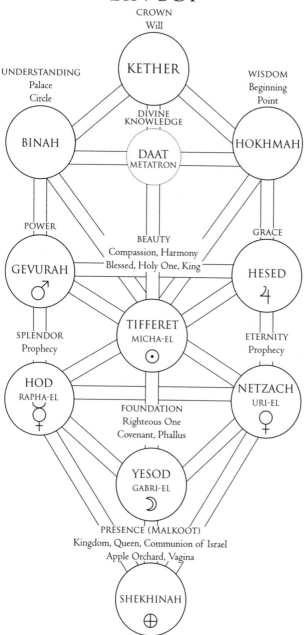

CROWN
Will

KETHER

UNDERSTANDING
Palace
Circle

WISDOM
Beginning
Point

DIVINE
KNOWLEDGE

BINAH

HOKHMAH

DAAT
METATRON

POWER

BEAUTY
Compassion, Harmony
Blessed, Holy One, King

GRACE

GEVURAH
♂

HESED
♃

SPLENDOR
Prophecy

TIFFERET
MICHA-EL
☉

ETERNITY
Prophecy

HOD
RAPHA-EL
☿

FOUNDATION
Righteous One
Covenant, Phallus

NETZACH
URI-EL
♀

YESOD
GABRI-EL
☽

PRESENCE (MALKOOT)
Kingdom, Queen, Communion of Israel
Apple Orchard, Vagina

SHEKHINAH
⊕

Yeshua once more wanted to say something but again she put a finger to his lips.

"Simon and Helen travelled together and spoke to the people and healed the sick. I once saw them in Alexandria. I have never seen two people so much in harmony with each other. They were like one. I have felt a strong closeness to her ever since I heard her for the first time. She has also been educated by the Therapists at Mareotis outside of Alexandria. Her way is a mirror of my own. She is the one who prepares the way."

Now Yeshua interrupted:

"I once knew this Simon the Magus. Both of us were with the brothers at Carmel. He was the candidate of the Samaria brothers. For a while we were like brothers he and I. Of the two of us, he was the clever one. We separated when I went on my journey to the East. People now say that he has stooped to all kinds of magic and witchcraft."

"That is the talk of evil tongues. He also prepares the way for that which is coming. And he has been baptised by Yohannan at Jordan."

"What is it that is coming?" Yeshua asked.

He sensed that what she was talking about was something other than the expectations with which he had been brought up.

"Hush!"

She once more pushed him back on to the bed and continued the ritual.

"The image of Simon and Helen is an image of the most outstanding amalgamation. I now place that in your holy centre."

She once more placed her hand on the spot below his navel, bending over him and kissing him. Then she whispered:

"I am *Shekhina*, the way, the truth and the life. *I am the silver cup from the tribe of Benjamin.*"

She got halfway up, swung her knee across him and straddled him like that. She then gently took hold of his member and moved it so that it touched her vulva.

"This is the Gate of *Shekhina*. This is the entrance to the wisdom you seek in vain in the scriptures. The words there are only shadows of what I'm going to show you now. The court of this temple represents *Yod, The Gate of Wisdom.*"

She slowly slid down over his member and stayed like this, immovably. He caught his breath and firmly held her hips, fighting with the power which wanted her to embrace him totally. From far away he heard her whispering voice:

"This is *He, The point of acknowledgement.* This is where you must stay until you have acknowledged your real goal and the cause behind your search. Only the true human being will resist giving in to the desire of the moment, because he knows that it is this desire that leads to his death."

They stayed in this position for a long time. Yeshua looked at his beloved with half closed eyes and saw her sitting upright in a state of trance with beads of sweat all over her body. Never before had he seen such a beautiful and noble being. For a long time Mariam was ready to give up. She was almost paralyzed by the pain from the uncomfortable position, but before giving in to this weakness she floated into a state of openness where there was no room for pain. She was the dove, which had once been sent out from Noah's Ark to find new land. She had now found a wind which could carry her, and she floated about in the void all by herself.

Yeshua looked at her and couldn't resist the temptation to caress her breasts. His touch sent small shocks through her. It felt like a distress call through the universe and she immediately recognized the voice of the distressed one. She then circled the empty space and returned to the Ark.

For a fraction of a second she saw the being hidden in the man lying below her, waiting for her to lift him out of the darkness. They looked into each other's eyes. Two souls travelling through the universes, two souls reaching for the fruit of perfection. The fruit on the Tree of Knowledge in the Garden of Creation, waiting to be picked. She then took pity on him. Slowly, very slowly she slid down on him again until he was halfway inside her. The movement to this new position sent fire through both of them and pushed them dangerously close to the edge of the void from which Mariam had just returned.

"This is *Vav, The Gate of Grace and Compassion*," she whispered.

Her breath was hot and intense. Yeshua sensed that she also was stepping across a new threshold.

"The one who may dwell here and keep his balance, shall finally be able to transform any kind of desire into pure love, the only desire being to give himself totally and unconditionally."

He felt faint, but just before falling, he sensed how her words carried him and kept him floating in this inexplicable universe. He was losing his hold on her but clung to the seducing smell of aloe, myrrh, lovemaking and cinnamon. He lay completely still, afraid of losing his mind, mesmerized by her firm, joyous hold.

Where could she be?

He looked at her and tried to catch her eye but she looked right through him and into God knows what kind of reality. And as he lay there in this inexplicable state of mind, bound and yet free, he suddenly felt how feelings grew out from an unknown darkness, filling him with a kind of love which only wished to caress her, hold her and kiss her, and to be united with her eternally, because in her he recognised all life. In her he experienced the Universe. In her he saw his own best qualities expressed. Never, ever had he felt anything like this. The love that welled from his heart, so unconditionally, was the most vulnerable and the most powerful feeling he had ever had. It was limitless, excluding no one, embracing everything. With this he could perform miracles.

Barely had he experienced this new and wonderful state of mind than she slipped down on him and embraced him totally in a perfect unification. Words of blessing flowed through them:

"*This is He, Shekhina, the Holiest of the Temple, the Heavenly Bridal Chamber. This is the place without a beginning and without an end. When the groom enters the bridal chamber he is anointed as Melchizedeck reborn. Melchizedeck is the King of Righteousness. He is Messiah, The Anointed One. She is Shekhina, The Heavenly Bride. Together they are The True Human Being, God's child.*"

Then they let go and disappeared into each other. Here Yeshua saw all his shadowy sides: the conflict between the world of senses and his rigid, idealized version of heavenly life. The eternal endeavour for the pure and the elated at the cost of the defiled and the human. The fear of sensual and emotional needs. The anger and the wilfulness hidden behind the image of the altruistic and devoted saviour. The envy and the inferiority complex, the arrogance, the indignation and the assertiveness, which could make him hopelessly depressed, and the almost exhibitionistic self-centredness which saw himself as the Messiah. He now saw and recognised these shadows and understood that it was not helpful to repress them. Thus he set a power free which had been bound until now, a power filled with healing qualities, now uniting with its female counterpart: that unconditional gentleness and caring. Mariam witnessed the transformation of Yeshua because it took place in herself. It was through her that light was shed on his shadows, and thus they were awakened. Now she herself was able to transform and let go of all the reservations and prejudices that she had had towards him. Then they could merge into one being.

"That is the story of Mariam of Bethany," said Mariam when she later told Yeshua everything that had happened to her during the years of separation.

"Now tell me your story."

Yeshua sat up.

"At ten years old I was accepted by the Brotherhood on Mount Carmel. This is where I met Simon, the one who is now called the Magus. He had extraordinary powers already then. We were brothers in spirit. He was the preferred candidate of the older brothers in the beginning. But some of the other brothers had another candidate. That was me. This created a division, which then lead to the decision to unite the tribes of the two great patriarchs, Benjamin and Judah. That is why you and I were betrothed at that time. Immediately after that I travelled to Alexandria where I studied the scriptures and languages as well as physics, metaphysics and astrology. I learnt about the body's properties and fluids and their effects, about the number of limbs and bones, vessels, arteries and nerves, about the correct mixture of warmth and cold and moisture and what followed from that, and the effect of the soul on the body, its feelings and abilities, about the ability to speak, getting angry, desires, and finally the ability to combine and judge as well as many other things. After three years I got the opportunity to travel to the East. In India I met a sage called Vidyapati. This was a major turning point for me. He told me about the way that was mine, but also that it was going to be hard to follow, because the people around me did not understand its real goal. He also told me that the time would come when I would attract much attention externally while I would be very unhappy internally because I was not understood. It was Vidyapati who prophesied that the help I needed would manifest itself when I needed it the most.

He embraced her and held her close.

"And I must say that he was right."

Shortly after, he continued his story:

"Returning from my travels almost four months ago I soon learned that there was disagreement between the various factions of the Brotherhood and I therefore decided to come to this lonely place in order to think about my situation. I was here approached by some of the applicants whom I knew from my days on Mount Carmel and in Alexandria. This is how the whole travelling zoo came about. It reminds me of a Roman circus. It is in many ways a sad story. I'm on one mission, and most of my supporters are on another. In the course of these last months I have prayed that there would be just one person who would understand. And now here you are."

Mariam and Yeshua stayed in the house in the abandoned village for seven days. Each day offered yet another initiation. In the course of seven days Mariam had shown Yeshua the possibilities which are latent in every human being, but which are more easily released through the holy union with the opposite sex. After seven days he was freed from all his shadows. Each of his seven centres had been cleansed and healed. All that was left was the final shared initiation.

On the morning of the eighth day Yeshua asked two of his disciples to come to him, Petrus and Yohannan. Petrus' natural distrust of women made him hesitant and morose. But it was obvious that Yeshua had undergone a considerable change, and he had to admit that. A new power radiated from him. It was a totally different man standing in front of them, than the one who had been sitting with them, resigned, closed and silent eight days ago, and who hadn't been able to make up his mind about anything. But Petrus didn't like the fact that this woman, apparently had, as if it was the most natural thing, taken the position which was rightfully his. But that's what women were like. They could turn a man's head just like that. That's what made them so dangerous. And that smile. How dared she? Was she mocking him?

"Prepare to leave. In three days there will be a feast in Cana."

This command of Yeshua's spread like fire. Cana was the town where the Rabbis from Carmel married, according to tradition. Cana was situated in the heart of Galilee. Therefore, there was no misunderstanding this invitation. Yeshua was going to get married. And there wasn't much doubt about the bride to be.

When the good news reached Yeshua's mother, Mariyam, she felt relieved. The only flaw in her happiness was the fact that the party had to be prepared in such haste that the usual preparations were not possible. It had been clear from the moment the original pact had been made that it was not going to be a common wedding. However, only the closest family had known the true purpose behind the reunion of the two tribes. At the time, an event had been planned that would surpass anything which had been seen earlier. That is why it took her by surprise that, apparently, her son had other plans. This did not promise well. Perhaps this Mariam of Bethany was not the one she had hoped for, after all. And what was that, arriving like that out of the blue, without informing her first? After all, she was the mother of the groom, and the only one of the parents who was still alive.

Cana was full of expectant people who had come from afar in order to attend the coming event. When a Rabbi married it meant that he took full responsibility, not just as a holy man but also as a breadwinner. Most of the people were aware that this wedding would have quite another purpose for a man like Yeshua. But the precepts had to be kept. Yeshua's mother had relatives in the town. They provided a house for the bride and a couple of girls as helpers. On the wedding day the house had been decorated inside and out with oil lamps, so that it was obvious to everybody that this was where the bride was living. Mariam's sisters, Martha and Mari and her brother Lazarus, had arrived in time and had brought with them their mother's tiara and the dress which had been sown for the wedding, at the time when it was supposed to have taken place. Now Mariam was looking at both items and realized that neither the valuable tiara nor the artistically made gown had anything to do with the wedding pact she was about to accept. To the dismay of her sisters she declined wearing both the tiara and the dress. If she couldn't stand next to her beloved one in her white gown, she was not going to stand there at all. That was why both the helpers and her sisters were busy washing the linen and binding flowers.

Thus, everything was ready when the groom and his disciples and brothers came walking through the streets, carrying torches in their hands, in order to collect the bride of his choice and to ask the head of the family for her hand in marriage.

But when Yeshua arrived at the house of the bride he saw that there would be no asking for her hand in marriage since Mariam was standing in the doorway, waiting for him, radiating and ready, as he had never seen her before. The white gown shone bright with the most fantastic colours. The men around him went silent when they saw this being who had to come from another world. Yeshua reached out towards her and she took his hand and held it in hers. They stood close together. Then they walked hand in hand through the streets to the house of the groom.

One of the oldest men from Carmel had been called in to perform the ceremony. It was a solemn moment, which many had waited for. Now it was happening and those who attended cried because an old prophecy had come true. The married couple stood face to face looking into each others' eyes, and for the first time Yeshua saw the being whom he had just married. A being of inner beauty who could never be matched by an external form, except perhaps by the woman before him who must be the incarnation of the most perfect human. He now heard her voice, but was not sure whether it really was her

Mandean bride and groom of todays Irac.

talking or if it was his own voice. He heard her saying:

"Today we shall dress in our star body, the multicoloured emerald gown. Today, as one being once and for all, we shall abolish the limitation of matter. Today we shall transform all things dead into living water and cleansing fire."

Then they melted into each other in a kiss while the crowd of people sang and cheered.

There were so many guests at the wedding party that they ran out of wine in the middle of the evening. The waiter was desperate when he informed Yeshua of the situation. Yeshua was about to tell the guests he regretted the lack of wine when Mariam said to the waiter:

"Wait. There is no cause for panic. Ask the waiter to fill the vats with water and let my beloved taste it before it is served."

The poor waiter got even more nervous at this message. But Yeshua woke him from his stupor:

"Do as you are told!"

The waiter came back shortly after and handed Yeshua a goblet, beaming with joy:

"A miracle. Everybody usually serves the good wine at the beginning, and when the guests are quite drunk they put the bad wine on the table, but you do it the other way round."

Yeshua smelled the delicious drink. He then turned to Mariam and said with a knowing smile:

"A miracle? Perhaps."

He lifted his goblet, still holding Mariam's hand. Then he turned to his guests who had just heard of the miracle:

"Let this be a sign. Today, my bride and I are one."

13

The trip to Syria was a turning point for me. Meeting the sisters of the Saydnaya Nunnery and Myrna in Soufanieh was a personal meeting with that aspect of the Mary archetype, which is so wonderfully expressed in the collectivity of our day and age. Like thousands of people all over the world I had also been touched by the immediacy and implicitness of the revelations of Mary, which seemed to take place more and more, wherever those of faith would meet. After returning home I became increasingly interested in how Mary Magdalene, as bearer of another aspect of the archetype, was linked to what might be called the superior aspect of Mary. I decided to return to Montségur in order to find an answer.

The Seer met me at the railway station in Foix, the town which was synonymous with arrivals and farewells. In spite of the fact that it was November the weather was fine and crisp. He drove me to the service station just outside the town where I had rented a car. We then, almost symbolically, drove our separate cars back to the house in town, which I now regarded as my second home. All the world may be out of joint, but when I pass the last hilltop before Mount Montségur and start the descent into the valley with the old village, my problems fade away. This to me is an earthly Shangri-La. Here time does not rule. Peace does.

The Seer and I had travelled far together. We had met many times throughout time, in other lives and other universes. Not just as Kansbar and Flegetanis, but in many other shapes without any names. We still had unsolved questions between us, something essential which we did not have the strength to touch this time round? Nevertheless, we were on the verge of a new version of our meeting in this life and we moved around ourselves and each other more or less clumsily, because both of us found it difficult to open up to the indescribable last barrier between us: *the new feminine force*. Perhaps because it is not one-sided but unlimited in its expression?

The house received us with its familiar creaks and we carried our luggage to our rooms. Mona Lisa and Leonardo were still smiling at me from the wall like question marks as I moved into my usual room with the flowered wallpaper. We drank a single glass of red wine in the kitchen. The Seer seemed restless. Then he said:

"I'll take a walk on the mountain."

The words were dry and it was a statement, which did not contain an invitation for me to join him. I was not surprised. I was conscious of the fact that the new reality we were entering contained a new way of working. I stayed home instead, and continued writing the book about Mariam. The Seer left. He came back half an hour later.

"She isn't there anymore."

The voice of the Seer was almost unrecognizable:

"Prat isn't there anymore. It was very strange, but when I got to the usual spot she didn't show herself the way she usually does. I thought that maybe she was just playing, but I finally realized that she has gone."

He poured himself half a glass of red wine. It was clear that he was, if not shaken, at any rate more than surprised.

We decided to drive around for a while, but didn't succeed in coming any closer to an explanation of this mystery. We went to bed early.

Before turning off the light I lay looking at a map of Montségur and the area. There was no particular reason for this. I wasn't looking for anything specific. But apparently my subconscious was, because suddenly a name on the map jumped out at me: *Roquefixade*. It was a town with a mountain and a castle, just like Montségur. There were only twenty kilometres between the two places. Each time we had been driving towards Montségur we had passed a sign to this place. But for some reason Roquefixade was the only Cathar castle we didn't take the trouble to visit. Now, suddenly, it was the only name that I noticed.

During the night I again moved about in the astral realms, but I was still unable to find Miriam, my oracle.

We had breakfast in silence. It was clear that the Seer was also struggling with something of his own. I was thinking about the event of the previous evening. Although I didn't feel like telling the Seer about it I nevertheless asked him if he would like to visit Roquefixade. He hesitated, but then answered a bit vaguely that he wanted to find a place where he could play some golf. We parted after breakfast and took off in our separate directions.

The landscape opened up in all its splendour when I entered the valley at the foot of Roquefixade. In contrast to Montségur this town is built on a ridge. The mountain itself is above the ridge where the castle is situated. The surroundings here are also much more dramatic. Where Montségur is rounded, soft and open, Roquefixade seems more angular, hard and closed. I turned off and followed the narrow road winding its way towards my destination. Nobody was about.

When I arrived in the town it was bathed in sunshine while the castle higher up was almost hidden behind fog-like clouds. Suddenly the sun disappeared behind a cloud leaving the town embraced in the fog. I parked the car and tried to get an idea of the haphazard web of narrow streets and cul-de-sacs. It was a charming town with a large square, and the surrounding houses looked like film-set buildings with nothing behind them. I walked about aimlessly, found the road leading to the mountain and decided to follow it. The dramatic impression it had given me to begin with proved to be correct. The road was close to the rock wall where the sheer cliff stretched towards the sky, discouraging and impregnable. Unlike Montségur there were no other visitors here but me. This was no tourist attraction but rather a personal challenge that had been waiting for me to take seriously.

The road split into two narrow paths. One seemed to continue around the mountain while the other apparently went directly to the castle. I turned off and followed the latter. Soon the path dissolved into mud and then nothing, and it was with the utmost difficulty that I continued to ascend. Further up I caught sight of something looking like another narrow path leading out between ragged rocks. I stepped between two large rocks forming a kind of gate through which I had to pass. The path now became even more dangerous. No mitigating circumstances here, just a look into a poorly-defined abyss. There was only room to walk right on the edge. The fog was now so dense that I could only look about five metres ahead. After ten minutes of climbing, clinging to the cliff wall, I saw two ominous figures ahead of me. I stood rooted to the spot. After a while I tried to call out to them, but I received no answer. I then started moving forward again until I could see what was up ahead. Two large mountain goats stood in front of me with their horns lowered looking very threatening. Behind them I could see the castle through a gap in the fog. Within me a voice broke through. The Voice which I had not heard for a long time.

"This place is the manifestation of your repressions. Your decision to come here stems from the insight for which you are finally willing to take responsibility. However, as you see, there are things you were unaware of before you climbed up here. There are still some insurmountable obstacles that you must relate to if you don't want to fall into the abyss."

The Voice disappeared and I realized that I had to crawl back again. When I returned to the car and went to check the time, I discovered that my watch had stopped. When I tried to wind it the screw fell to the ground and I had to understand that maybe time – the old kind of time – was literally no more. I took off my watch and threw it into a field knowing that there was no going back. I was on my own.

Back in Montségur the Seer was waiting for me with a much-needed glass of red wine. I told him about my experience with the two mountain goats and my watch stopping. I could see something was waking in him.

"Let's go there tomorrow. We crossed the borderline where chance ruled long ago. It is time to face the consequences."

It was my birthday the following day and I rose to a beautiful breakfast table prepared by the Seer. Later on we drove to Roquefixade. After a walk in the town we started the ascent. In contrast to the previous day the mountain seemed more open. It was obvious that this mountain did not "belong" to the Seer, but I could not help combining his presence with this openness. As usual, he went into the unknown without hesitation or reservation. We ascended the mountain without any difficulty. The mountain goats were nowhere to be seen and after twenty minutes of climbing we reached the plateau with the castle in front of us. The valley spread out as far as one could see. The Seer walked about for a while until he found a spot where he took up his usual pose. I walked into the castle. It had more rooms and split levels than its sister twenty kilometres away. Standing at the top I spotted it. Proudly looming on the horizon: Montségur. It was very strange, but I had never been aware that Roquefixade must also be visible from Montségur. They were the only two Cathar castles with a direct view of each other. I was wondering if it was significant and symbolic that one of the castles clearly represented the feminine aspect while the other just as clearly represented the masculine. The Seer joined me shortly after.

"This place is one of the fixed points of the universe. It belongs to the Brotherhood, while Montségur belongs to the Sisterhood."

I immediately understood that the two spots were mutually dependent and that one could not be without the other.

"This castle may be the universe's gift to you."

It was obvious that he was as moved by all this as I was. I, of course, was aware that this gift was purely symbolic and that it was about a specific question: did the chance of being healed have something to do with the unification of the two poles?

"Let's go to Montségur," the Seer said and started the descent.

We arrived at Prat's meadow half an hour later. To our great surprise she was back at her usual place. She welcomed us in her usual kind way and asked us to be conscious of the climb we were about to make. Deep inside me I heard the Voice commenting on Prat's blessing:

"The heights to which this climb will take you are in direct ratio to the depths to which you have the courage to delve."

Everything seemed clearer. The air was like a living crystal; lively beings of light danced around us. In front of us was the mountain, which had moved us more than any other reality we had experienced. We did not talk much but were on our way into a state of mind, which can only be described with a single word: acceptance.

On the way up we stopped at the various oracle points and in the spirit of the day, the Seer stepped aside in order to let me be the first one to make contact. I received the answers as fast as I could ask the questions. There was no resistance. Everything flowed effortlessly in a manner that was so embracing that nothing was left out and everything was included, in the same way as everything found its rightful place.

Stepping into the courtyard there was no doubt left in our minds. The Seer waited until I had stepped through the gate. Without hesitating I found the centre and drew a circle. The Seer was watching me from a distance with an expectant smile on his face. Within the circle I drew the star of Mariam. I then turned to him and invited him into the circle. He hesitated.

"It is your circle," he said in a subdued way.

His whole attitude expressed a kind respect I had never experienced from him before.

"I would be honoured if you would be the first one to step into it," I replied.

I had never seen him more handsome or more in accord with himself and his destiny. I had never seen him more united with everything. Then he stepped into the circle, standing with his hands behind him, as a guest would do, while he nodded encouragingly and in acknowledgement. It was at this moment I understood that

the Seer was not just one single person but in many ways also a projection. At this moment he was a projection of everything that I myself had not had the courage to express. I suddenly realized that the Seer was an idea and a state of mind. A state of mind which is open to all, when time and the specific student are ready for it. At that beautiful moment I saw how this man, five years earlier, had opened the door, behind which I had barricaded myself, and had then lured me into the open so that my own hidden qualities could begin to react. We were now looking at each other here, perhaps at the end of the road. I hardly dared think. Then he stepped out of the circle again and signalled that I should take over and continue.

No sooner said than done. I stepped into it and found the centre of the star of Mariam. The Seer was standing at my right where I used to stand. Then he took a step away from the circle. With this gesture he wanted to make it clear that this moment was mine. I stood there with my eyes half closed feeling how the activity around me intensified. Two radiating circles appeared in the air in front of me. Slowly they met and touched. At that moment the light became more intense. Slowly the circles moved across each other until they formed a *Mandorla*. Then I heard the Voice:

"This is the true healing of everything which until now has been divided. This is the true restoration of everything, which has been broken down. This is the end of all contrasts. This is the gate of true rebirth through which all new life must pass, totally united."

A Mandorla, also called *the Vesica Piscis*, is the almond shape that appears when two circles overlap.It represents the female sexual organ, is found in the star of Mariam and is a divine symbol for the new, healing feminine strength. All true art is born through the Mandorla. It is the birthplace of poetry and the preferred playground of the Muses. It is the end of all diseases and the only healing of hopelessness. It leaves nothing out and embraces everything. Through the Mandorla everything repressed is made conscious and is transformed into clarity in the present.

✴

Mandorla
(B. Pinturicchio 1550)

Mariam sat looking across the vineyard, which had once been her father's pride. Now the fields lay fallow almost as a symbol of the destiny, which had befallen all of them. Her thoughts went back to the wedding and the happy times that followed. Together they had travelled all over the country. Yeshua had spoken to the people about the secrets that no one else wanted to introduce them to. Together they had healed the sick and raised the dead. At the beginning the disciples had shown their unconcealed dissatisfaction with these developments, but they slowly got caught up in the results of the healing sessions, and finally they themselves had begun laying their hands on people and raising the sick. Yeshua's mother joined them, and wherever they came they attracted huge crowds of people. They got more and more followers and little by little it became almost impossible for them to travel unnoticed. It was far too late when Mariam noticed the dissatisfaction among the disciples. When Petrus and the others realized that the Kingdom of which Yeshua spoke, was not of this world, they became insecure and secretly started plotting. The golden future, that Petrus had hoped for, crumbled in front of him as over and over again Yeshua made clear that the enemy was not Caesar in Rome, but Caesar inside each one of us. Time and again Yeshsua tried to make this point, but only Yohannan understood the parables through which Yeshua communicated the secret knowledge.

From the beginning Petrus had grasped at any opportunity to show his contempt for Mariam. This had spread to the other brothers who became confused about the fact that a woman not only possessed such knowledge, but far worse, that she was much wiser than they were. It was very difficult for them to see that a woman who ought to know her place in reality was the real centre from which the Power was flowing and who influenced their Rabbi in a direction they did not understand. It was totally incomprehensible to them that in spite of the support of the masses, they did not care at all about worldly affairs, the power and the throne of Israel. What was the point of all their efforts? It didn't help that Yeshua and Mariam seemed to withdraw into solitude more and more frequently. When Petrus, the spokesman for the disciples, complained to Yeshua about all this, he was simply dismissed with a reprimand about his spiritual blindness and lack of faith.

Mariam should have seen it coming: But she had been so focused on her work that it was far too late by the time she realized what was going on. If she had known that Petrus and others used every opportunity, during Yeshua's healing and teaching sessions, to spread the news that he was to assume power as rightful king of the Jews she could have warned him so that they might take precautions. Instead, the rumours had reached Jerusalem and the new Governor, Pilate, who had sent out his spies to keep an eye on the rebels.

Finally there had been a direct confrontation. Petrus could no longer contain his rage. Self-righteously he claimed that he had been the one who made Yeshua's position possible. Had he not supported Yeshua right from the beginning? Now Yeshua must make up his mind. Would he assume responsibility for seizing power when the time was right? Or would he just carry on with his subversive activities that had no future and would certainly result in making a laughing stock of them all. Petrus was sick and tired of putting his energy into a mission that was leading nowhere. They all had families to support and there was a limit to how far this madness could go. Had he, Petrus, not been promised a seat to the right of the throne? Time was running out.

Yeshua had tried to calm Petrus and the other disciples down, but peace reigned for a short time only. The pressure on Yeshua grew, and at the same time as he and Mariam continued their work, teaching and healing people, Petrus and his co-conspirators intensified the spreading of their message of the coming, armed rebellion against Rome and the appointment of Yeshua as the true king of Israel.

The result of this propaganda was inevitable. Pilate's spies reported daily on the apparently innocent mission of Yeshua. But information, that under cover of this mission, a future uprising was being planned, made Pilate finally lose his patience and take necessary precautions.

The day Yeshua rode into Jerusalem on a donkey while, under pressure from Petrus and his followers, he allowed himself to be welcomed as a king, plans for his arrest were already on Pilate's table.

Mariam had tried to warn Yeshua but he believed right to the end that his disciples would understand and that it would be in his power to make them give up their plans for worldly power and dominion.

Yeshua was seized in the garden on the Mount of Olives the day after his entry into Jerusalem. Petrus and the others had protested loudly but were quickly scared away by the Roman division which, armed to the teeth, took Yeshua away. Mariam was the only one who followed him until she was turned away at the gate of Pilate's palace. Petrus and the other disciples fled and scattered to the four winds.

Mariam got up from the Syrian chair from which her father, in his day, had performed his affairs with a just hand. From the window she looked across the fields to the horizon as if she waited for someone. She had tears in her eyes. Thinking about these last days opened a sorrow, which could never end. The most terrible thing had happened. Pilate had gone against the will of the people. He wanted once and for all to set an example to these militant, religious fanatics, whom he did not understand, and whom he did not want to understand. The crucifixion of Yeshua had gathered a huge crowd. The disciples were nowhere to be found and there had been no rebellion. Instead, she had sensed that a major part of the priesthood in Jerusalem were not sorry at all that this had been the outcome. The candidate had been too controversial as it were.

She dried her eyes and shivered, thinking about the struggle going on in Jerusalem at the moment. Rumour had it that Petrus had found the only suitable successor to the throne: Yacob, Yeshua's brother who had happily taken on the responsibility that Yeshua had denied himself. Petrus had been appointed High Priest and all the disciples held high positions in the new *Nazarene Church*. Mariam had heard terrible stories of how the true teachings had been twisted and instead had been used to affirm the position of the chosen ones. They also said that those who had supported Yeshua to the end were now persecuted and either driven from their homes or stoned to death. All had to stay in hiding. Yeshua's mother had gone to Antioch accompanied by

Yohannan, the most loyal disciple of Yeshua. Mariam's days in this country were also coming to an end.

The image of her beloved hanging on that terrible cross kept haunting her. She relived the painful hours in her mind when he struggled with himself, and the destiny he had taken upon himself. She had stayed with him to the end and had given him all her strength until he finally let go and passed to the other side. One of their faithful followers, Yoasaph Arimataeus, had placed his own tomb at their disposal, and Mariam for the third time had anointed Yeshua in accordance with the old, secret laws which she had been taught, so that the finer bodies of light would be able to let go of the physical and, if possible, dissolve his mortal frame.

She had gone to the grave three days later. She had rolled the entrance stone of the tomb aside with the help of two male Therapists. Once in the tomb, they saw that the miracle had happened. Mariam's efforts had paid off, Yeshua was gone. Only the shroud was left. Mariam held it up and thought she could see the image of his face and the outline of his body printed on the fine, white material. She then kissed the shroud, folded it carefully and prepared to leave the tomb. But then it happened that she felt his presence. A faint pulsating outline of him suddenly became visible in the dark tomb. She wanted to reach for him, but before she managed that, she heard his voice inside herself:

"Do not touch me. I am still in my other being. Be patient. Rukha d'koodsha is with you. We shall always be together in my SHM."

After this experience, she then visited Petrus and the disciples for the last time in the hope that she would be able to initiate them into the true teaching. But they just scorned her and threw her out. She had fled under cover of darkness and barely escaped their pent up, bitter anger.

Now she was looking at the cloud of dust, which slowly approached Bethany from the horizon. She went below in order to prepare herself for the journey. Soon after two men came riding into the courtyard.

The following day they put out to sea from the harbour of Joppe.

She stayed at the rail for a long time watching the white coastline evaporating into the blue. She then looked ahead. In the air in front of her she saw a transparent, radiating and deeply purple ball with a pink, four-pointed star, surrounded by a thin pink line. Somewhere out there Gaul was waiting for her. Somewhere out there a new life was waiting for her.

✶

It was a moving moment. The Seer was my witness — and I was his. We left the circle intact in the middle of the castle and started the descent. We didn't speak but slipped into the contemplative state of mind that both of us knew so well and which didn't crave any explanation because it was the closest we could get to an authentic mode of being.

I couldn't let go of the experience with the radiating Mandorla. It was beyond any doubt that as a symbol it was related to the star of Mariam. But why did it appear now?

I have written quite a few things about the Mandorla in one of my earlier books, "The Silence of the Heart." Perhaps this archetypal figure had been waiting dormant in my subconscious for something to activate it at the right moment?

"Why don't you ask the universe?" the Seer suggested. "You know that you must look at the problem from a higher perspective. And I have told you this so often, that you ought to know it by now. Ask yourself the question what has been the red thread through your work with Mariam."

"The Kabalah?"

"Exactly. Something must be hiding there that you haven't yet seen."

The Seer's suggestion seemed sensible. It was time to take stock. In my work with Aramaic I, among other things, had met with the latest research on the Kabalah. Until recently I didn't know that there was a Greek parallel called the Greek Kabalah. Here a literary tool is used called *the Gematria* by which you may find the numerical, holy value of ideas and sentences. They do not have special symbols representing numerals in Aramaic or in Greek. They use the letters of the alphabet instead. That way you may find the root of an idea or a word, and by way of the Gematria see its position in relation to other holy numerals and terms in classic cosmology. I had read in a book on the subject that the old magi who practised the principles of Gematria used the number 153 to express the form that defines the Mandorla. When you take the sum of the Greek idea of *h Magdalhnh* = Magdalene (in the definite, singular: that is not a Magdalene but *the* Magdalene) then the result would be 153. If this was not a coincidence it was probable that already in the first century A.D. certain traditions saw Mary Magdalene as the incarnation of a superior, feminine principle. The question then remained why she seemed to have played a significant role within Christianity?

As I have mentioned earlier in this book, there are no reliable sources supporting the idea that Mary Magdalene was a prostitute or specifically sinful. The town *Migdal*, which is supposed to be the source of her name, did not exist at the time of Yeshua. Furthermore, the tradition of giving people nicknames was not limited to the name of your hometown. It was quite as common to give people a nickname relating to specific virtues, abilities or specific missions. Nicknames like *The Baptist* and *The Magus* speak for themselves. Even Yeshua's, *The Nazarene*, cannot be ascribed to the town of *Nazareth*, since this didn't exist at his time either. On the contrary, his name referred to the sect Yeshua was a member of and perhaps even its leader.

If we do take the meaning of the name Magdalene seriously, it tells us that the bearer of that name was considered to be The Spirit of the Exalted Peace. If her name is added up in the following manner: 1 + 5 + 3 you get 9. Nine is a triad times three. It is the figure denoting completion. It denotes the beginning and the end. It is unity. Nine melts opposites together. It unites fire and water. It is expressed in the mountain and the valley. It is symbolized by the sword and the cup. It is the Foundation Stone itself.

After the disappearance of Yeshua, Mariam had also to disappear. The Church which became the foundation for Hellenistic Christianity, to which we belong, had no room for a feminine expert who, apart from her direct access to the Power, was also able to act in life in harmony with the cosmic principles. They wanted to build a patriarchal order where the female virtues such as self-sacrifice and compassion did not find their place till several centuries later through the idealized Virgin Mary.

The aspect of the Mary archetype represented by Mary Magdalene was literally thrown out. Her vision about the integrated, sensitive human being did not fit into the patriarch's ideas about a holy life. That is why this aspect had to disappear.

Mariam Magdalene arrived in France bringing all her knowledge about the cosmic principles, which is partly to be found in the Kabalah today. This knowledge was later hidden behind the term The Holy Grail. Perhaps because Mariam was the silver cup that, according to prophesies, the Messiah from the line of David would find in the tribe of Benjamin, a secret movement sprang up following her arrival in the south of France. One of the places it showed itself was among the Cathars and their female priestesses as well as through other esoteric, underground movements from which the occult life in Europe has drawn invaluable, spiritual sustenance. Mariam Magdalene was the true founder of esoteric Christianity.

The decision that Yeshua was the true Christ, a decision which was made at the first synod in the year 325, was made on the basis of very few, specifically chosen, gospel sources. The Yeshua to whom most Christians now profess could very well be the result of a one-sided, collective focusing of energy, which has been invested in this specific interpretation of the life and work of Yeshua. This energy, with time, has been stored in the ethereal Akasha. The energy follows the thought. And it is our thoughts, which create the reality in which we find ourselves. Thus, the Gospels do not necessarily say anything about what really happened, but more about the need of people to profess to a saviour who would take their sins upon himself. Unfortunately, this is also the secret behind the sad condition of the world. Through the preservation of this comfortable idea it has been possible for us, at a deeper level and for centuries, to live and act without taking spiritual and moral responsibility for ourselves and the proverbial neighbour. In turn, through our idea of Christ, we have created a force which is still effective and which manifests itself in the ethereal plane when called upon with sufficient intensity, in exactly the same way as the many revelations of The Virgin Mary, which are also the result of humanity's profound need for presence, care and love. In this century a new feminine force is showing itself. A force embracing the entire human being, both body and spirit. It is the force characterized by Mary Magdalene, which for example we have seen manifested in the twentieth century feminist movement.

Mariam Magdalene is the manifestation of a new feminine form of energy coming down from above as Rukha d'koodsha. A feminine form of energy which is not limited to pure motherliness, the receptive and the neutral, which until now has been the hallmark of the universal, feminine archetype.

This new form of energy has come into being as an opportunity for both men and women, because the old, patriarchal energy has had its day. This patriarchal energy has been a necessary, activating factor, which, however, no longer manifests itself for the good of the human race, but solely for its own sake. It is separatist, divisive and egotistical. An earthly flame which is now dying.

The new power is inclusive, healing and altruistic. It is the carrier of the cosmic fire and the living water. It contains everything, both the masculine and the feminine, but it is more feminine than masculine.

In the evening I invited the Seer to a birthday dinner at the restaurant "Le Castrum," where earlier he had shown some of the more seducing aspects of his unique abilities. This time, however, he stayed in his chair during dinner, although he couldn't quite refrain from an innocent flirt with the young, female waiter.

Looking at him on top of his form I once more entertained the thought that this may be the last time we met like this – as teacher and student. The thought made me sad because it indicated an end as well as the beginning of something new. The time had come to take up my bed and walk. In other words: the time had come for me to be responsible for myself. But as usual, the natural modesty between us denied us the opportunity of touching on the subject. I therefore pushed the thoughts out of my mind and instead threw myself into the unbridled fun of the moment – together with a dear friend and itinerant miracle maker. We were just two drops of water on our way to the sea of eternity.

After we had returned to the house and had each gone to our own room, I lay on my bed looking into the eyes of Da Vinci smiling at me through the portrait of the Mona Lisa. It was as if he was smiling at those of us who didn't understand the simple truth expressed in his painting. The truth about the isogynic being. As a Grand Master of the old, esoteric order of Priuré de Sion, Da Vinci was well aware of the secret behind the work of Yeshua. If you study a number of his paintings you'll find that they are filled with signs and symbols, which literally point to quite a different interpretation of the individual importance of the central characters in the New Testament. John the Baptist especially plays a major part in Leonardo's interpretation, and the appearance of Mary Magdalene in "The Last Supper" is yet another example of his insight into the esoteric secrets.

I actually heard him laughing out loud in a voice that sounded in long forgotten corridors of my subconscious mind:

"Why all the vain efforts? Let it go. Why make it more difficult than it is? Spirituality does not mean that you struggle along from one place to another but rather that you are open-minded and move within the eternal now. The integration of the relative and the absolute is always actualized outside of time and space. Each human being contains everything. EVERYTHING!

Everything that you want to become, you already are. Wake up from the dream and realize that you are awake. Everything has meaning. Wake up and realize that each and every human being is the very image of God. Wake up to the eternal life. This is the truth about the parable of the mustard seed."

The voice faded away and I moved through the spheres. Everything seemed much lighter than I had experienced it before. This meant that I didn't, at first, recognize the various universes. But suddenly, I was standing in the basement passage I had looked for so desperately and for such a long time.

I slowly floated through the passage towards a door behind which I hoped to find my oracle. I took hold of the handle and watched the door open. She was sitting on her cream-coloured leather couch with her legs pulled up, in absolute peace.

"Good you could come," she said with a smile, "I have been expecting you. Come and sit down. You must have a lot to tell me."

She quietly patted the couch. I stepped inside.

I heard the door closing shut behind me.

I sat down beside her.

"Now, tell me," she said impatiently.

I opened the manuscript and started reading:

It had been raining all that Sunday and also throughout the night. It was as if the floodgates of the Flood itself had been opened. I was in my study lost in the endless rain and the soaked landscape outside. The air was tense with static electricity. Something indefinable was gathering across the sea, a series of dark shadows of breaking clouds filled with unanswered questions.

I had just finished the manuscript for "Mary Magdalene," when the phone rang ...

BOOK III

THE GRAIL

To the highpriestess
Sylvia

"I will show you that which the eye cannot see,
The ear cannot hear,
No hand can touch,
And no man understand through his own understanding."

Yeshua, The Gospel of Thomas

"At thy feet, O Madzup, I come to seek for rest,
In the Fire of thy Glance, may this yearning soul be blessed.

Thy footprints of Crushed Thorns are strewn with Pearls Divine,
And Lo! Their Glory unveils, these dazzled eyes of mine.

Thr'o Life's Test, may this heart, O Thou Living Shrine,
As a Lotus once bloom. Bloom in these Rays of Thine.

At thy feet, O Madzup, I come to seek for rest,
In the Fire of thy Glance, may this yearning soul be blessed."

Noor-un-nisa Inayat Khan

"The time will come when time is meaningless,
And place is nowhere. All our concepts wait
But their appointed ending. They uphold
A dream with no dimensions. At the gate
Of Heaven are they merely laid aside,
Before the blazing of the light within."

Helen Schucman

0

A few years ago an old, Spanish manuscript was handed over to me. The title was *San Gral* and the author was stated to be *Kansbar*.

The man who gave it to me was first my teacher and then later my friend. In the time between he suffered the indignity of fulfilling the doubtful but archetypal role as my spiritual father. It followed, of course, that I played the role of the dutiful son who, however, never succeeded in totally satisfying his father. The relationship had the classic conflict situation built into it: first the idolization of the father, followed by the inevitable, symbolic patricide.

The old, Spanish manuscript is about four hundred pages long. It is of no literary value. The contents are more or less uninteresting, at least to the untrained eye. If there is anything in it at all of the slightest interest it is to be found between the lines. And the little the zealous reader may find here, is only for the few to whom it has any meaning at all.

Reading the dedication of the manuscript you immediately get the feeling that the contents are a matter between the one in the dedication who is handing the manuscript over and the one who is receiving it. In this case *Kansbar* and *Flegetanis*.

The manuscript is dated, "Alhambra, 1001," and the dedication reads as follows:

"Kansbar is not my real name. But due to the secrets I have been chosen to guard, I have taken this old, Persian name. Kansbar the Chosen One. Kansbar the Wise. Kansbar the Seer. Kansbar, the Protector of the Grail. I am getting old. For many years I have been searching for the one who is to take over this duty after me. But in vain. Only now do I remember the day I met Flegetanis, an itinerant Moorish singer, in a marketplace in a small town on the coast of Andalusia. This manuscript is for him. This is the story of the Grail."

At the beginning I didn't know what to do with the manuscript. Apart from a slight curiosity, I just felt a childish pride that I had been found worthy to guard it. Not until I started reading it, finding that the contents did not live up to the promises of the dedication, did my new-found worthiness evaporate like dew in the morning sun.

For two years, the manuscript stayed untouched in my bookcase in my study collecting dust, until the day the sun sent a pale ray on to it as if it wanted to lead my attention to it once more.

Thus, it was totally without any kind of expectation that I opened the yellowed manuscript again. The moment I took it in my hands it seemed that the light in the room changed. I hesitated and looked up from the empty page.

The empty page?

Outside, the sun was pale and low in the sky. Apparently nothing had changed in the room. Only the book. I turned a page. Not a letter. Not a single word. I turned another one, and yet another, only to see that apparently nothing was written in it. Instead, some neat, almost transparent characters appeared on the paper. The strange symbols and signs seemed to move, and the more I looked at them the more the signs danced in front of my eyes, almost teasingly and diabolically.

I sat for a long time, unfocused and ruminating about the strange thing I had just experienced. When once again I looked at the manuscript, the original text was suddenly there on the pages. I leafed through it and saw that, apparently, the text was intact again. Was all this simply a figment of my imagination?

Then it suddenly dawned on me, that although the contents of the manuscript in itself were insignificant, it nevertheless constituted a protective veil, a kind of key to an otherwise closed world. Not until later did I understand that the manuscript was simply a metaphor, a mirror or a gate to another dimension.

The information that the manuscript communicated was only a pale shadow of a much deeper knowledge. The ordinary text told a local story from Andalusia, mainly about two main characters, that is, Kansbar and Flegetanis. The inexplicable signs behind the text, somehow, were the key to this deeper knowledge. However, a kind of knowledge which only reveals itself to those who are ready for it. The manuscript, then, is a metaphor for a possibility that is to be found in man himself: an access to the so-called Akasha-files in the great, ethereal, universal memory.

I turned a page and started reading.

PART I

SYLVIA

I

The train cut like a knife through the European dusk. The rain whipped against the windows of the compartment.

"God is peeing," a small boy said, sitting on the seat opposite me with his sister.

"Carl!"

Their mother looked apologetically at me while she leaned toward her son and wiped his mouth with a paper napkin.

"God doesn't pee," his sister answered, – "He cries."

It was not a fanfare of a statement. Just a quiet establishment of a fact with a faint exclamation mark behind it. Like a stifled breath with an immediate, checkmating effect.

"He must be very sad, then," the mother sighed resignedly with an empty look at the steamed-up window, before hiding once more behind a woman's magazine.

The girl put her head on her brother's shoulder, uncomplaining. Sitting there, they constituted the silent protest of a whole generation against the thoughtless rejection of that Holy of Holies: people's divine and frail ability to be present.

I smiled sympathetically at them and leaned back in my seat hoping to get some sleep.

In the bag beside me lay the result of two years of intense work, the manuscript for the book about Mary Magdalene, the forgotten, feminine power. But it was also the result of the breaking up of a life. For two years I more or less had roamed about with no other fixed point than the manuscript. In a small house in the Andalusian mountains, at Gare du Nord in Paris, at Costes in Montségur. Line by line, piece by piece, at haphazard lay-byes, changing hotel rooms and busy railway stations, wherever it was possible to sit with my laptop on my knees.

The work was done and I was on my way to Denmark, tired like Methuselah. There was a fear deep in my consciousness whether or not the pieces would fit together. Would there be coherence in chaos? That was all I had time to think before falling asleep to the sound of the tears of God, which drummed against the window, drawing momentous patterns on the back of my eyelids.

There is a small town, Belésta, in the valley of love, *Val d'amour*, in the Pyrenees. In this town there is a child who cries a tear each time a leaf falls to the ground prematurely. The child mourns the ignorance of man. Mourns the ever-present ignorance about the true essence of man. Mourns the spiritual blindness of man.

There is a church in this town. Deep in the darkness of the crypt below the church there is a basin in the floor filled with the tears of this child, and they constitute holy water in which the pilgrims may bathe their eyes and regain their sight.

Is it not a paradox then, that the Christian Church, at least on a symbolical level, hides its true power in the unconscious?

The Churches in Cathar-country hoard many secrets, which have just now begun to see the light of day. There was a time, in my efforts to uncover some of them, that I thought it was all about revealing the misanthropy and mendacity of the Christian Church. Nothing could be further from the truth. Through the years, the Church has committed many irreparable atrocities. One is almost tired just thinking about having to name them all. But how could the Church have been any different, considering the fact that it is a product of the limitations of man himself? Just like all the other Churches and religions of the world. Whether a new-born child is initiated as Hindu, Buddhist, Moslem, Jew, Christian or an atheist depends solely on the choice of the parents or the circumstances decided by the specific culture. No man and no church, however, decides the true cosmic identity of the child. This, in turn, is for all of us.

I believed that my journey was almost over. In reality, it was just about to begin, but I had no idea about that at the time. My point of focus was only the completion of the Magadalene manuscript. Although I was the one who had written it down, it felt more like a gift that I had been allowed to bring home than something I personally had created. It filled me with a deep gratitude but also with a strange emptiness. Another kind of emptiness than the one you normally experience each time you finish something.

Intuition has many roads. Basically you might say that if man doesn't use it, intuition doesn't use man. At best, my journey was an example of what may happen when you let yourself be guided by an inner voice, let go of the material reality and travel into the landscape of the soul, which basically is always accessible but seldom visited, and is usually hidden by the limitations of the specific personality.

Meeting the Seer had taught me about some of the innumerable levels surrounding us, as well as the numerous traps that the seeker far too easily may be caught in. I had visited the underworld and met my personal shadows as well as a long series of collective demons hiding there, on my astral journeys. I got in contact with the Oracle on my journey to Toledo, an inner voice I could contact if need be, if my balance was reasonably good. But this was all just school, and lessons to be learnt. On a decisive level I was still tied and full of fear. I still had to relate to my basic loneliness, and the temporary separation from the Seer didn't make the situation any easier.

During one of our sessions at Montségur, in the middle of the culmination of our conflict and in order to correct me, he doggedly told me that I was nothing more than an errand boy for the Board of Directors. The fact that he was talking about the Board of Directors of the Grand Lighting Company Upstairs did not relieve the tension between us. Since then, his words had come back to me again and again, and at this moment they were sounding louder than ever. There was no evading it; the time was ripe for me to take up my inheritance. I was left to my own devices.

The train protested in all its couplings. From far away the screeching sound from the brakes woke me up from my sleep. I opened my eyes. The neon tube in the ceiling was turned off. The mother with the two children had gone. Instead, I caught a glimpse of a figure in the seat directly opposite me surrounded by a strange, blurred light. The light was not sufficiently clear for me to see whether it was a man or a woman. The figure sat totally motionless and I squinted in order to penetrate the invisible veil between us. But I didn't succeed.

I wanted to say something and had the feeling that my mouth moved, but for some inexplicable reason not a sound came out of it. Oddly enough, this seemed more or less natural. No words were needed. That which under normal circumstances would have been very frustrating, now changed to total acceptance. Not until then did I notice how peace ruled in the inner void. I leaned back again and surrendered to the rocking motion of the train. I was not alone.

I slowly dozed off and floated back through time until I woke up in the year 1982. It was the year that, together with *Warm Guns*, I recorded the album "Italiano Moderno" in the Eden studio in London. It was one of the days where the legendary songwriter and producer, Nick Lowe, was visiting the studio. We were listening to the recordings of the day over a beer when suddenly he pointed to an ad in "What's On." It said, "*Psychic Readings.*"

"Have you ever had a *reading*?" he asked.

I shook my head. But I knew immediately that I had to try it.

Two hours later I found myself in front of the old domicile of The British Spiritual Association in the centre of London. Outside, a small queue of housewives, punks and a businessman from the City were waiting. A ticket was two pounds and I was shown to a room on the second floor.

I was met by a young woman. We said hello and she asked me in. Apart from that, we didn't speak. She then asked for my wristwatch. When I had given it to her she held it in her hands and slipped into a trance-like state with her eyes closed. After a while she started talking in a subdued voice:

"Your little sister sends you her greetings. She says that it is time to let go of your sadness and your feelings of guilt because of what happened when you were children. She is now married to a man who spent his childhood in the same part of the town where you lived. He died almost at the same time as your sister, as he ran out in front of a car together with a boy of his own age. Now, he and your sister have married and have a family."

The young woman was silent for a while before she continued:

"Your grandparents send you greetings. One of them, and you yourself know who it is because you have his broken pocketwatch at home in a desk drawer, is saying that your father is ill and that you ought to tell him that he must change his life."

Once more, the woman went silent, turning my watch over in her hands.

"Some day you'll stop your present occupation because you'll realize that there is another kind of music of a different and much greater value. You'll be working with healing. In the course of time you'll get in contact with people who will have great influence on you and your true work. One of them is called Sylvia. When the time comes, she will have something to tell you which you must pass on. Be vigilant and do not forget your inner force. Do not forget your real destiny."

I don't know how long I slept but it seemed like just a few moments. That is why it surprised me that the stranger was no longer in the compartment and I had not heard him leaving.

I started thinking about the idea of *home*. Where does man belong? Where do we come from? Where are we going?

Where do the homeless at Hamburg Central Station actually live? Where the well-to-do travelling first class?

If *home* is where the heart is – where do we all live then?

Where was *my own* heart?

Where is it now – while I'm writing this?

I have visited thousands of places. I have wandered in endless deserts. I now see how often I left my heart for other places, things, ideas, trinkets or the company of others. All in the hope of finding some meaning, a little peace and confirmation that after all, I was loved. All the while forgetting that everything that I was looking for was to be found in the heart I had left behind.

All right. I may have received more help than most people. But not everything that I did was received very well. And there are reasons for that.

My book about Mary Magdalene was practically published in secret. Without one single review the first edition was sold out within one month. After one year the fifth edition was published. Yet another element of proof that after all, there is another reality, a hidden network far away from the focus of the press and people as such.

On the other hand, my book wasn't about a nobody. After two thousand years of oblivion, Mary Magdalene and her true relationship with Yeshua was starting to manifest itself in the minds of more and more people all over the world. The result was a whole series of books on the subject, the latest one being Dan Brown's novel *The Da Vinci Code*, which broke through the media barrier with a bang and fascinated millions of readers.

My own interest in Magdalene as a hidden feminine archetype started in the mid nineteen eighties. This was after meeting some of the gospels in the *Nag Hammadi-scrolls* as well as *The Gospel of Mary* and the Gnostic writings, *Pistis Sophia*. Not only did these take me to the heart of a heretical past but they also gave me contact with tracks pointing towards a history which seemed to have deeper things to say to us than sensational revelations and intricate criminal riddles.

Reality always surpasses any kind of colourful fiction.

Thus it was, during a talk at the Theosophical Society in Copenhagen, that a sixty-year-old gentleman asked me a question which would turn out to have a significant impact on the work I had started with *Mary Magdalene*:

"Lars! The last picture in your new book is of a woman. But this is the only one in the book which does not have a title or an explanation. Would you care to tell us where you got the picture and who it is in it?"

The question was heaven sent. I had just been talking about the fact that you have to challenge your intuition and ask some questions that otherwise you wouldn't be able to answer, thus sharpening the energetic senses and the access to the Akasha files.

I explained, which was the actual truth, that it had been given to me some time in 1983 by an acquaintance, the philosopher John Engelbrecht, and that he told me that it had been channelled by three psychic monks. The picture portrayed Mary, that is the Virgin Mary. I later understood that it just as much depicted Mary Magadalene. But since I didn't have any real evidence that this was the case I placed the picture without any further information attached to it. The picture was a kind of distress signal.

The man now stood up:

"It may then be interesting for you to know that it was my mother who took the picture back to Denmark in 1960, and that it is true that it was channelled by three psychics."

The man paused before playing his trump card:

"Furthermore, I can actually tell you that it is really depicting Mary Magdalene."

A sigh went through the crowd. I couldn't have asked for more convincing evidence of the power of intuition. It spoke its own clear language.

After the talk I tried in vain to find the man among the audience to get more information about his mother. Something in me told me that this was important, but the crowd of people who wanted to ask me questions was too large.

Later that evening in my hotel room, I experienced a strange phenomenon of light. At first I thought that it was the light bulb in the lamp on the writing desk which was about to go. Later I found

out that it hadn't been turned on at all. A faintly pulsating ball of light, about the size of a tennis ball, was hanging in the air. The ball changed colour to a pale blue with a purple circle around it and a radiating purple cross in it. At the same time I sensed that there was another person in the room. It seemed as if it only lasted for a minute, but when I checked my watch an hour had passed. I had experienced earlier that time disappeared. What was new in this was the fact that apparently no kind of meaning, message or any other kind of information was linked to it. Where had this element of time gone to, and what had happened in the meantime?

I had experienced the radiating symbol of the cross before. It happened during a visit to the small town of Belcaire in the Pyrenees, where the Seer and I wanted to do some investigation. A life-size crucifix was raised next to a war memorial commemorating the fallen sons of the town. Meditating in front of it, a small pale blue ball showed itself. It was surrounded by the same purple circle with the purple cross in it. Most of all it looked like a soap bubble hovering in front of the feet of the Crucified One. I managed to take a picture of it at the time.

My phone rang one week after my public talk. It turned out to be the gentleman, Mr. Hasse Smerlov whose mother had brought the picture of Mary Magdalene to Denmark:

"Well, I'm sorry to call you now, but I didn't want to disturb you after the talk. I just wanted to tell you that my mother is still alive and that she would very much like to meet you. She is getting old, and she is not too well, physically. But then again, she is probably of a sounder mind than most people. But you ought to experience this yourself. If you've got pen and paper I'll give you her address."

I fumbled for a pen and almost overturned a cup of coffee before finding a stub of pencil.

"Right," I said.

"Her name is Sylvia. She lives ..."

That was all I got. Just one word stayed in the air like the sound of a secret bell with very pure overtones creating strange harmonies, and with a very deep, sub-harmonic sound within myself:

Sylvia!
"I'm sorry, what was the name again?"
"My mother's name is Sylvia."

He paused in order to give me time to write. I wrote the name and address in my notebook as if in a trance, and I hardly remember saying goodbye to him when I woke up in front of the telephone, the receiver having been replaced.

Could this be the very same Sylvia whom the English medium twenty-three years earlier had predicted that I should meet because she had something to tell me?

All this happened at a time when my astral travels were decreasing and were instead replaced by moments where I "fell out of time," so to speak. I could be walking down the street when suddenly I found myself in another time or at another level. The surroundings were more or less the same. I almost imperceptibly slipped into a synchronised reality which affected my sense of time and the daylight around me.

During these "dropouts" I become surrounded by an ethereal net of dancing particles of light, mutually reflecting each other, and adding life to everything as far as one can see. I have the feeling that I'm in the morfic field, the sparkling blueprint behind the visible, material reality. Sometimes the experience is so intense that I clearly see the little, radiating, maintaining and creating angel-beings, the Guardians of Light, manifesting themselves as thousands of sparks, or as an eternal net of small crystals in the air around us.

There were days when these experiences had such an overwhelming, physical effect that I could do nothing but stay in my bed all day long. I usually experienced severe pains in my *medulla oblongata*, just where the upper part of the central nervous system fuses into your brain. At other times this phenomenon was followed by a pain in my solar plexus as well as loss of all energy. There was no doubt that these symptoms were suspiciously close to the ones I had experienced ten years earlier and which had kept me in bed for three years, until I met the Seer. I had the idea that maybe the old disease was returning because I had been separated from the Seer?

The Crucifix in Belesta

No.

This was different.

The well-known feeling of iron and lead was no longer part of the symptoms. This had something to do with a lack of clarity, some blockage in me, which had to be removed before the cosmic forces could flow freely. I was no longer the unconscious cause of and paralyzed witness to my own funeral.

I see no reason to cultivate suffering. On the other hand, however, I have no doubt that the moment the one who suffers understands the cleansing of the pain and realizes its liberating effect, the seemingly meaningless becomes meaningful. To say it plainly, there is a hell of a difference between understanding the deeper essence of suffering and not doing so.

These "dropouts" put me in a frame of mind where it was no longer possible to make any appointments or plan anything at all. I more or less unwillingly had to give up all control and I realized how much conscious or unconscious energy we spend on controlling everything, and also that this focus on control stems from one thing only that is fear. Letting go of this may in itself be anxiety-making.

I had a dream the night before meeting Sylvia: I'm walking along a road, and I cannot see where it is leading. No one else is about, and the peace of Paradise reigns over the enchanted landscape. However, I sense that the idyl is hiding something demonic, something which leaves an ominous impression. But, nevertheless, I'm totally calm and confident.

After a while the road splits into two minor roads, and I am in doubt about which one to take. A figure is approaching on the left one. At first it is only a dot on the horizon, but shortly after the Seer is standing in front of me in his well-known pose and with his pilgrim's staff in front of him.

Then another figure is approaching on the road to the right of me. This one is also just a dot in the distance. When it gets closer, I see that it is an image of myself. This image is also holding a pilgrim's staff in front of it.

The situation seems to be locked. Something is keeping me down while I'm facing the Seer to the left and the image of myself to the right, until I realize that both images are projections of some blockages in me. These two figures are now standing there, guarding a threshold and blocking the way. I stand in front of them desperately trying to find a solution. I undoubtedly have to pass them by, because they are both representing old forms that I do not need anymore, the essence of which, however, I must acknowledge before they can be dissolved and no longer constitute a hindrance on the road. But how? Which road should I choose?

Standing there, totally paralyzed, I see a blue angel in the sky above the two roads. It approaches very quickly, and I'm suddenly lifted from the ground while a voice is saying:

"Let not yourself be lead astray. Both roads are leading back to old limitations. You have come a long way along these roads, but now the time has come to let go of the old."

The angel is carrying me in its arms and we disappear through the air above the two figures.

It was snowing when I got off the train at Charlottenlund Railway Station to the north of Copenhagen. Big, soft snowflakes were floating down from heavy clouds like manna from Heaven. The air was filled with crystals. My senses were honed to such a degree that I looked right through the people I passed on the street. It wasn't the blockages or limitations of each person I noticed, it was solely the highest qualities. They appeared as radiating patterns in the ethereal aura. It was striking, however, that none of them seemed to be aware of the help, which surrounded them.

An elderly gentleman, who was waiting for someone, had an age-old, pulsating and reddish-golden crown hovering over his head. The crown reflected a longing – a longing for the woman he had been married to for thirty years but who had recently gone to another world. The longing was now transformed and presented itself as patience.

A couple walking hand in hand: A nacreous triangle embracing them, dissolving the jealousy between them.

A young girl, lost in her own thoughts: A small, radiating tiara just in front of her budding breasts; the fireflies' celebratory dance to the awakening eros.

A pregnant woman: A sparkling filigree of light embracing her and the new life in her womb.

A woman who tried to hide her tears in vain, glittering like diamonds on her cheeks: A faint pulsating cross on her stomach; the sadness over the lost lover, the image of the empty bed; sorrow as the redeemer of a new life.

The apartment houses in the bohemian quarter. The transparent door. Top floor. Initiation.

I rang the door bell and heard the faint ringing somewhere in the apartment. Eternity. I knocked on the door. Then I heard a faint noise in the corridor. The door opened:

The blue angel.

2

The blue angel was standing in the doorway disguised as an elderly lady in her eighties.

There was an aura about her, radiating like suns and moons in endless Milky Ways, the clear and genial eyes of a young girl laughing out at me, filled with warmth, care and love looking through the eyes of the elderly woman who was not of this world.

"What took you so long?" she laughed, "better late than never. Good to see you. Do come in."

Her words rolled out like a red carpet, and stepping over the threshold I knew that I was stepping into the world I had been looking for for such a long time, but which I had stopped believing really existed. Somehow, I felt that this might be the most important step I had ever taken on my long journey home.

The woman wore a blue dress with a matching blue hat.

In the living room a certain order reigned in the chaotic display of books, ring binders and documents in stacks on tables and bookshelves. We sat down in two armchairs on each side of a low table with room only for two cups into which she poured steaming, delicious-smelling hot tea.

"Oh Lars, would you please get the two pieces of pastry I got for us. They are in the kitchen. I'm not as agile as I used to be."

I got up and managed to find my way between books and documents. In the kitchen were two pieces of Christmas pastry big enough for at least twelve people.

"Well, both of them are for you," she shouted from the living room. "A young man like you must have some sustenance. I myself do not eat anything these days."

The laughter in her voice filled the air, a sound of bells ringing through me as I cut a piece off the cake and balanced it on an exquisitely cut crystal plate into the living room.

"I have waited for this moment to arrive much longer than you'll ever know," she said, when we again sat opposite each other.

"I haven't read your books yet, but when my son showed me the picture of Mary in the Magdalene-book I realized that the messenger I have been waiting for, for forty years had finally shown himself. Actually, I was close to giving up hope. The Board Upstairs know how often I have prayed that you should show yourself. The picture of Mary has constantly been a smoke signal. And now we've both got our answer."

Her voice was pure and clear and filled with sunshine.

"Did you yourself know what was going on?" she asked curiously.

I told her about the medium in London who many years ago had predicted that I should meet Sylvia. I told her about meeting the Seer and working with him, and also about the unexpected power that had been released in me when we broke our liaison. Powers, which I wasn't too sure I would be able to handle. I finally told her about my intuition, when the book was finished and was on its way to the printers, telling me to place the picture of Mary after the last chapter without really knowing why.

As I was telling her about this, she sat with an innocent smile on her lips humming away as if she already knew. When I had finished my story, she said:

"Everything is fine. Everything is exactly as it is supposed to be.

Sylvia — The Blue Angel

An unbroken chain of arrivals and departures, recognitions and acknowledgements. What are we if not travellers, meeting and parting, crying and laughing, dancing and dying in an eternal cycle. However, each and every time: travelling souls in time and space. A cup cannot contain an ocean. A cloud cannot be captured in a bag. The acknowledgement of eternity cannot be contained in one single human being. That is why God created more than one individual. And among those, the grail-rider must acquire the greatest burdens of cognition that is the knowledge about his own origin, his task and destination. Everything you have gone through so far, your victories and your downfalls, have been necessary steps on the way bringing you here. You often mistake your direction until you learn to decipher the signs, but we all get there in the end. About you and the Seer, you must remember that when one door closes another always opens. Some day you'll meet again, perhaps not in this life but then in another, where you'll finish the task you took upon yourselves a long time ago. The energies you are exposed to at the moment are cleansing for you. The cosmic power can only manifest itself on earth through flesh and blood, and through an immaculate being. I myself am only being kept alive long enough to be able to pass on my knowledge to you."

"What knowledge is that?" I asked.

She looked at me inquisitively as if for a moment she doubted that I was the one she had expected. Then she said:

"If I say MU-energy, what do you say?"

The question hovered in the silence between us. Thoughts flashed through my mind. MU-energy. It sounded familiar, but I didn't feel that I could give her a satisfactory answer here and now. Was it a test?

"Well, it can wait," she said, while her look burned through the crippled remains of my defence system."

"Instead, it may interest you to know how long ago it was that Mary Magdalene came into my possession."

I nodded eagerly.

"As a young woman, I was invited by a Dutch, High Priestess to Montségur in the Pyrenees. I understand you have also been through a difficult schooling there."

I nodded in confirmation and she continued:

"At the time I didn't know anything about the area and its power. There were twelve of us, all women, who had been asked to come to the Castle of Montségur. We received an initiation there, which because of my vow of silence I cannot tell you. Not yet. Maybe later. We'll see."

She paused as if to find the right words.

"After the initiation, which lasted for three days and three nights, the newly initiated priestesses each received one of the Cathar castles in the area. When the High Priestess found out that there was no castle for me I was driven to the church in Rennes-le-Château. This then was under my dominion."

She paused again to let her words sink in, looking directly at me before continuing:

"I take it for granted that you are aware that I'm talking about the Church of Mary Magdalene."

I nodded my assent. This was too good to be true.

"As we drove into the small town I immediately felt the presence of a powerful energy which, however, I couldn't explain at the time. But stepping into the Church of Mary Magdalene I almost fainted, that is how much it affected me. The church was in a rather miserable condition at the time. It was before they freshened up the restoration made by the renowned priest, Sauniéres, and once more veiled some of the clues to the secret which many adventurers are looking for in vain, in Rennes-le-Château and the surrounding area."

"What kind of clues?"

She didn't answer but smiled secretively and looked at me with eyes that penetrated spheres and seemed to look into unknown universes. An alternating golden and purple light radiated around her. A white, pulsating crown of crystal hovered above her head.

"There is much focus on Rennes-le-Château at the moment. Mostly for the wrong reasons. You see, the need for spiritual entertainment is the result of a deeply-rooted indolence and neurotic dependence on matter and fear, which create a desire for a quick release, encourage easy solutions and lead directly to astral delusions.

Thus one may actually keep playing on the surface of the spiritual amusement-park for all eternity. It turns into illusion instead of intuition, ravings instead of a creative imagination, hallucinations instead of a visionary creativity. There is nothing wrong in wanting transformation. But you must have the courage to look into your own reasons, in order to understand what stems from old wounds, fear, inferiority and ties to things and other people and what is based on a real inner scrutiny, acknowledgement and certainty."

Her ocean-like look embraced me gently as she continued her explanation:

"Ultimately, it all boils down to a lack of love and a lack of knowledge of the true powers of the soul. It is really rather trite, but nevertheless true.

She motioned towards the kitchen:

"More cake?"

I shook my head declining. It was remarkable how easily she alternated between the wise, seeing High Priestess and the kind, elderly lady who was concerned about my welfare.

"I'm glad you came. You and I have much to do, but time is running short."

In spite of her obvious care for me, I sensed that there was still something that barred the flow of communication between us. Apparently, she read my thoughts, because shortly afterwards she said:

"Don't lose heart, but I must make sure that you possess the necessary qualifications before communicating the knowledge which is hidden behind forty years of silence."

She had barely finished speaking the last sentence when an indescribable peace embraced me. The being in front of me, who, until then, had looked like an elderly lady, seemed to dissolve. Instead, I was now looking into a constellation of stars, which can only be described as angel-like. I was then lifted, softly but firmly, as if by a giant hand and pulled through the floating wall of crystals, on through ethereal light, into the astral spheres, like an endless breathing, breaking through level after level until I was pulled through the last veil of limitation into a kind of flowing being that can only be described as *freedom*. Only, however, to be drawn back again

Sylvia after her initiation

through the worlds, back into the living room where I came to with a sigh, facing Sylvia and her warm smile. Everything went so fast that there was no time at all to reflect on it. It was like a test, which was supposed to tell me something about my present, spiritual state of mind. A white rose manifested itself between us. It slowly floated down on to the table in front of me.

"It symbolizes your soul," she said looking at me intensely. We sat quietly in the silence, then she continued:

"It is important that you work on your grounding. I know the feeling of being insecure, the way you feel right now. That is why I also know how important it is that you re-establish a solid foundation. You must begin the decisive part of your grail-journey. Here you'll learn about the secret of the imprisoned princes who must be liberated, the dragon, which must be conquered before the prince may lift his cup and drink the elixir of eternal life. You'll understand the metaphorical truth of the legend of the Grail as well as all its allegorical meanings. You'll only be able to learn the true knowledge and to present it purely by taking this journey yourself."

"Is it possible for you to reveal some of the knowledge you received during your initiation at Montségur?"

The moment I asked the question I knew how inappropriate it was. Her almost inaudible sigh was a clear confirmation of this fact.

"If I revealed this, it would remove the most important motivation for you to go at all."

"Where does this journey go, then?"

"At the physical level to the land of the Cathars. At the inner level to the Castle of the Grail in your heart."

"Why exactly the land of the Cathars?"

"Because it plays a central role in some of your latest incarnations, partly as a priest and partly as a troubadour. You carry a copy of it in your innermost self."

"Is there a special power in that area securing my success?"

"Yes. Just as it is the case everywhere where a special energy has been accumulated through the ages. You may also go to Jerusalem or Assisi, Lourdes or Damascus. There is a power on Iceland for example, which is about to be discovered now. You could also stay here in Denmark. There are lots of suitable places, but remember that these places are expressions of an inner reality more than they are expressions of external destinations. Neither *Shambhala* nor *Shangri-La* are places, but solely states of mind. Each person is a gate to the cosmos. But it presupposes that the person in question is willing to be responsible and concentrate on this acknowledgement. It is important to understand this."

"Your own initiation, has that got something to do with my journey?"

She shook her head leniently:

"It is quite touching that you try to extort my secrets from me so innocently by pretending not to know. But you are not very convincing. There is no reason why we should continue to test each other. Let us get down to business."

The blue angel was still hovering above my head. Then it disappeared faster than the eye could follow it. I couldn't help thinking that this performance was just another way for Sylvia to test me.

"As of today, nothing will be the same. You must expect that your physical expression will change, from the level of the cells to your physical appearance. New energies shall flow, and some of them will seem rather heavy and arduous because they come from unknown universes and because you are still battling with some personal limitations. Somehow, it is a paradox, since it is only by letting go of your worldly ties that the energies may flow freely. On the other hand, it is also necessary to stay grounded. It is thus a matter of keeping a very delicate balance, which you must find and sustain."

A triangle became visible while she was talking. To the right on the bottom line Sylvia was standing, and an image of myself to the left. At the top of the triangle together we both manifested the angel-like being.

"Please notice that the triangle you see is the missing top of the Great Pyramid. Thus, although we are standing at the bottom, it is the bottom of the small pyramid constituting the upper part of the big pyramid. This makes quite a difference. Between us we are creating the angel at the point of the pyramid who, as of now, shall be your protector. This is how man, in pairs or in groups, may manifest angel-like thought forms to the benefit of mankind. This is white magic or true alchemy."

She got up with some difficulty and slowly disappeared in the darkness between her stacks of books. She reappeared ten minutes later with a piece of paper, which she placed on the table in front of me. I picked it up. It turned out to be a napkin with a strange symbol and the letters MU written upon it, apparently scribbled in haste with a ballpoint pen.

"Makes you think, doesn't it?"

"But, what is it supposed to be?" I asked.

She didn't answer, but instead she asked me:

"Did anything out of the ordinary happen to you on the twentieth of April?"

I tried to think of something but couldn't remember the day in question. I brought out my diary and found the date. Bingo!

"This was the day my book about Mary Magdalene was published."

She chuckled happily:

"I was in hospital on that day. A nurse served me coffee and cake. The napkin in front of you was on the plate."

Our eyes met and we couldn't help laughing. The image of the young girl appeared among the multitude of stars. It lasted for a moment only, then it disappeared.

"The Board Upstairs have been busy," she said when she recovered her breath.

She reached for the teapot and poured me some tea.

"What is the significance of the symbol in combination with MU?" I asked.

"I'm not fully aware of that yet. But as you know, MU is the ethereal continent of the first souls on earth, Le-MU-ria. MU is the ancient sign for water in all shapes in ancient Egypt. In the Greek alphabet *mu* is the centre, or what is situated in the middle, between the beginning, *alpha* and the end, *omega*. MU is the highest mode of vibration of the element and the idea of *water*. It is *living water*, the prerequisite for *the transforming fire*, which is promulgated by

Zarathustra and thus, by Yeshua. The MU-energy is the higher ether. Where water and fire meet.

MU is the Buddhist's mystical word for the elimination of any kind of temptation. MU is the cleansing of souls."

The words were like little candles in the air, an age-old knowledge which only needed the right impulse in order to manifest itself.

"Your own name is an allegory on the mystery you are here to solve and pass on. Parts of it are obvious. The two first letters in your last name is Mu. But I'm not so sure that you would be able to bear everything about the secret woven into your name in your present condition."

I wanted to contradict her but she continued instead:

"You are an old soul. But an old soul which has fallen deeply in earlier days. Your being consists of a very beautiful and radiating centre. There is a lot of love and healing in you. But you also possess a self-destructive element, a part of you which you haven't accepted yet and which must be taken care of. If you can do this, nothing will be able to stop you in your mission of the soul."

Her words were an echo thrown back from an unknown wall somewhere in the past. In spite of the promising prospects, the warning was still clear.

"You'll find the princess where the dragon is. Find the princess and you'll find the dragon. And where you find them, you'll also find the Grail. The three of them are inextricably united."

"Which princess?"

"The princess within yourself. The feminine aspect within the man. But there is also a woman waiting somewhere out there. If men and women only knew the possibilities they possess when they are together. The initiated ones in antiquity always worked in pairs. Just as Simon the Magus had his Helen and Yeshua his Mariam, Paul had his Thekla. Not many Christians are aware of this. When they established the Church in the year 325 it was first and foremost a political act, with the purpose of stopping the autonomous, gnostic and mystic society which was flowering at the time of Yeshua and in the years after his ceremonial death. When they established the Church they also adopted the dogmas and some of the rites of the

Mithras-cult and the Ishtar/Isis-tradition, which fitted the political agenda under new headings and names. The rest was silenced. In this way they literally threw out the wisdom aspect, Sophia, with the bath water. The symbolical Second Coming happens through Sophia, that is the higher Sophia-aspect, which is secret. Find her and you have found the princess. It's happening now. The Second Coming of the higher Sophia-aspect is not just a collective matter but also a process, which each and everyone of us must go through. That is why so many people, and especially those who work spiritually, experience that these are turbulent times. This implies a confrontation with the old. All that limits us. And that is hard for most people. Look around. Have you noticed how many men and women leave each other in this day and age? Not because something is wrong with any of them. They simply started their relationship on the wrong foundation. People now must enter into true relationships. This is how it is at all levels. Not just between man and woman but also ties within the family, friendships, and the old teacher/student relationships are also broken because of the new which is on the way."

She looked closely at me as if she had seen something and was now wondering if she should tell me. Then she said:

"Step out of the old circle. It is always painful to say good-bye to a teacher. Even more so when he has become a kind of spiritual father. But everything has its time. The Seer has taught you much. There is a lot to be thankful for. On the other hand, you have also given him the best of you. Now you must realize that your time with him may be over for now. Take upon yourself whatever springs from the fact that you do not owe anyone anything, and there's nothing you haven't got. Let it go. Otherwise your common gestalt will break you down. The pact you have made will protect you if you live up to its innermost command which builds on mutual respect."

Her words were like a velvet glove holding my heart to the light, in order to reveal the sorrow, so that it could find its way out. I now saw it disappear into the air like a bird on the horizon on its way to the freedom it had waited for, for such a long time.

"In spite of all the knowledge you have acquired in the course of time you must accept the fact that now you stand here empty-handed. Otherwise you'll not be pliable enough and therefore not able to move others. Be strong in your compliance. Only thus can you cope with that which has become rigid. Clay is shaped like a cup and is then heated in the kiln to make it durable. Still, it is the empty space in the cup which enables it to contain something."

She reached across the table and put a hand on my arm.

"If you are a cup, let the content be love."

We sat in a cathedral of silence, embraced by her wisdom.

"A knight of the Grail is an idealist. He knows that true love may be tough in its excoriated honesty. But do remember, that the knight of the Grail, although he may laugh at the folly of man, nevertheless attempts to lessen the suffering, which is a result of it. This does not mean that he takes the responsibility away from other people – it only means that he takes his own upon himself."

Something inexplicable was manifesting itself around us. It seemed like a third entity born from the unity of our souls. From far away, the pealing of a church bell was heard in the living room underlining the exalted mood.

"The difference between the two of us is that you must work in the open while I must work secretively. But please be aware, that not everything should be revealed. There are still secrets that may be misused, and will be, if revealed.

There will always be weak souls waiting to exploit those secrets for personal gain. Just look at the many so-called teachers and gurus seducing gullible souls with promises of initiation and other tomfoolery, convinced of their own excellence. That is why you must be careful what you reveal."

Although the tea had long turned cold she took a sip before continuing:

"You must accept that our future contact will happen telepathically. Are you familiar with telepathy?"

I was pondering the question, when she helped me by saying:

"I know that you communicate with your oracle, Miriam, and I therefore take it for granted that you and I may find a frequency enabling us to keep in contact."

She opened her arms:

"Do not worry about it. All will happen just as it has been planned."

Apparently, she worked from a preconceived plan. But she didn't say anything about the one who had conceived it. Something told me that she didn't tell me everything but kept certain things hidden, either because she didn't think that I was ready to understand them or that she wanted to be certain that I was worthy of her trust. I had experienced many things in my life, but this woman was something out of the ordinary. Like the Seer, Sylvia was of another world.

"Just now, the hosts of Heaven are gathering. This fact has an effect at all levels including the level of the human cell. It turns everything upside down. The changes that many have prophesied are happening right now. We are actually in the middle of it. It is a tough time that will accelerate in years to come and will affect all of us without exception. No one will escape this cosmic trial, which for man will mean the option of unlimited possibilities or total destruction. This is the choice we are faced with. The choice between the lower self's insatiable lust for power, things and entertainment or of living up to the spiritual aspirations of the higher Self. This is the choice we must be willing to make each and every day. Possibly each and every minute."

Time was running out. I sensed that the audience was almost over. I therefore seized the moment:

"You must give me a sign or something to go on."

The question did not seem to take her by surprise. And once more she replied with another question:

"What do you know about the seven veils?"

"The seven veils?"

"Yes, the seven veils."

All kinds of thoughts were running through my head. I automatically thought of Helena Blavatsky's first major work, *Isis Unveiled*.

"Has it got anything to do with Blavatsky?"

She looked surprised at me:

"That was an interesting connection. Both yes and no. I'm sure that Blavatsky was one of the higher Sophia-aspects of our time. But the secret of the seven veils goes back much further. You yourself have opened to part of the secret in your book about Magdalene. Look in *The Gospel of Matthew*. Read about Salome dancing the Dance of the Seven Veils in order to satisfy her stepfather, Herod's, lechery – in return for the severed head of John the Baptist."

"Can you give me more?"

She couldn't help laughing at my insatiability.

"One gets the impression that the dance was a kind of vulgar striptease. Instead, the Dance of the Seven Veils was an integrated part of the holy drama predicting the death of the Anointed One and the descent into the underworld, where the Goddess took off one piece of clothing each time the Anointed One passed one of the seven gates of the underworld.

She got up.

"But there is much more. There are depths to this mystery that must be brought into the open. This is the task."

We said our goodbyes in the hall. It was as if I had always known Sylvia, and I had to struggle with an old sadness coming out of the darkness, threatening to make my tears run freely. I kissed her on the cheek and the young girl's laughter was singing in my soul as I walked down the stairs and into the world in order to find the dragon, the princess and the Holy Grail.

3

Sylvia's laughter followed me all the way to the railway station. Her tone mingled with mine and together new, strange patterns were formed. These one led to a door in my subconscious. Above it was written in invisible ink, "The door is on the inside."

Thoughts of unknown origin poured forth from hidden nooks and crannies. What was the secret, which Sylvia claimed was woven into my name and which apparently would make me understand the deeper meaning of my life?

I put my faith in the angel.

It was dark when I got off at Nørreport Station and walked along Kongens Have towards Bredgade where I was going to stay overnight with friends. The snow had spread its sound-muffling carpet everywhere and the spirits appeared for a short moment before disappearing into the silent night once more. Nothing can remove the sense of time like snow and darkness in a world where the continuing flow of memory images constantly rivets people to their horizontal reality.

I was meditating to the sound of the snow under my shoes when suddenly I had the feeling that I wasn't alone. It sounded as if someone literally was walking in my footsteps. Another pair of steps, the sound of which came just seconds after mine. I stopped short in the cone of light from a street lamp. The steps behind me stopped as well. Slowly I turned around. Nothing to be seen. Still, I had no doubt that someone was there.

"Who are you? What do you want?" I heard myself asking.

Silence.

"I know you are there. Tell me who you are."

Still no answer.

I stood stock still staring, challenging, into the cone of light.

Then I demonstratively shook my head and turned around in order to continue my walk. But before I had time to react, my feet disappeared under me and I fell to the ground. A terrible stab of pain ran all the way up through my left side.

"If you want to be free you must let go of the fear of walking alone."

The voice spoke directly to me.

"Until you can do that you cannot know who I am."

I wanted to reach out towards the figure I sensed was standing over me. But I didn't take hold of anything but the cold air.

Somewhere someone laughed.

What was happening to me? After the separation from the Seer and my meeting with Sylvia I was moving into another sphere where all my old preferences and fixed points, in fact, all of my old and well-known world was slowly coming apart. It was like floating about in a room without any walls, floor or ceiling. Even the structure of the cells in my body seemed looser. Exactly as Sylvia had predicted. There was literally more "contact," more transparency than at any other time. I moved more than ever before between the worlds and with much more agility. And no matter where I was, I had this inexplicable feeling of being observed and protected. However, it didn't necessarily make it any easier to be in the world. It could be very difficult to find any kind of meaning in ordinary human life. It was hard not to notice that the games played by people in the so-called visible world were as primitive as ever. The only difference was that they were expressed in a more sophisticated manner than before. That was almost the hardest part.

It was bitterly cold when, towards the end of March, I packed my car and drove south to Montségur.

Jutland was wrapped in frost and a cold mist. It got milder in Hamburg. It was springtime between Kassel and Frankfurt, and when late at night I got to Mulhouse and turned into France I passed the magical border between despondency and melancholy.

I found a corner in a lay-by outside Dijon where I could get a few hours sleep. I woke up at 4 a.m. and continued south before the busy morning traffic took over the motorway. The light changed outside Nîmes and, driving with an open window, I could smell the salty Mediterranean in Montpellier. I stopped at a pavement café in Narbonne to get some lunch. It was so warm in there that I had to take off my jacket.

I was in a hurry. Inside me I had the feeling I was running out of time. Although it was an old time, it was in itself a reminder that there was something I had to do. The motorway of the old time led directly to my own inner wasteland, the ultimate cul-de-sac. It was a place I knew all too well. The ever returning memory images of laconically smiling and distorted masks, behind which the pent up and petrified identities are hiding. Identities, all of which represent old and fatal ties. Imprisonment. Limitation. Everybody, just like me, the enslaved result of the daily bombing raids from manipulating archetypes in a sick society. Buy this, buy that. It is no good where you are right now! Come over here! This is where the party is! A world filled with perverts. Famous for a day. The total corruption of values. The heartless animal: industry and its lobbyists. The faceless elite: the stockmarket's sense of cool cash. God's Chosen Ones: the stockholders, whose greed is surpassed only by the unforgivable stupidity and ignorance of man. The callous view of man, the callous society. The total burn out of the essence of the soul. From sun up to sun down, the eternal undermining of the true human being, the higher Self. And why? For what reason? Fear? Money? Power?

Control? Comfort? Boredom? The total nightmare: absurdity sold as common sense and the freedom of choice.

Suddenly I saw it. I saw it right there at a pavement café in Narbonne, that I myself was one of the stockholders with quite a few shares in hopelessness.

"Your days are numbered."

I turned around. But the only person I could see was seated a few tables away reading a newspaper.

The Voice.

Well, life only lasts fifteen minutes. And you cannot take man's incarnation to a life on earth for granted. Life is a gift. Isn't it important then how we use it?

It was time to find another way.

In a flash I saw the young, dark haired waitress adjusting her short skirt standing in the shade of the awning. There was something familiar about her movements as she turned to adjust the seams of her net stockings. Shortly after, she stepped out into the sun on her high heels and I imagined how awkward it must be to walk on them. It was like a silent movie lasting a few seconds only, but played over and over again. It was the adjustment of her stockings and the moment where she stepped into the sun turning towards me. I tried to ignore it but the image wouldn't go away and I put it down to my fragile and changeable state of mind between the physical and ethereal realities.

I closed my eyes and pulled all my senses back to the centre. There, I found myself standing in front of a door at the end of a long corridor. A sign was hanging above a door like a diabolical smile from the hereafter bearing the well-known text, "The door is on the inside." Wherever this door may be, this one was ajar. I slowly pushed it open and stepped into a small square in another time. I saw right away that it was the same square where moments ago I had had lunch, served by a young and beautiful woman in high-heeled shoes. I stopped in order to get my bearings. Around me, people were moving about dressed in foreign, medieval clothes. Hesitatingly, I stepped into the open square squinting a little because of the bright sun. No one seemed to take any notice of me. Then I saw that the people were concentrating on something else. The atmosphere was hectic and, apparently, something important was about to happen. I let myself be carried along by the crowd, through a narrow passageway and on to a somewhat larger square where hundreds of people were already gathered. In the middle of the square a large bonfire was prepared which had not yet been lit. To the right the people of the Church were standing with their crosses and pompous gowns. I saw their postured piety out of which the demons of fear and self-righteousness swarmed into the air around them. And I saw that it is exactly this kind of piety, which is devoid of any kind of kindness and compassion. The ecclesiastical head was sitting on a throne. Cold and without showing any sign of sympathy. An audible sigh went through the crowd as a primitive cart entered the square, pulled by a single horse. The figure of a woman was standing on the cart with her head bowed. She was scorned by the mob with shouts, which were more degrading to those who shouted than to the woman they were aimed at. The cart stopped in front of the Church dignitary who said to the prisoner:

"What do you want: Heaven or Hell?"

The woman didn't answer, she was already somewhere else.

Someone threw a stone hitting the woman on the back of her leg. The blow made her turn around and take hold of her thigh while the crowd cheered with malicious pleasure.

The Church dignitary now stood up and shouted:

"Well, what'll it be?"

Without waiting for the woman to answer he continued:

"Let your silence be the Lord's writing on the wall. By that you have judged yourself!"

Addressing the guards he said cynically, as if the woman was already dead and he was talking about refuse:

"Burn her!"

The sight of the tall, thin dignitary froze my heart. The pronounced features framing a cold smile, the result of an unspeakable fear and a barren heart. His eyes met mine for a split second. At first he looked confused, then he looked straight through me as if looking into a distant future. I wanted to say something but the words stuck in my throat.

Running back to the square in order to find the door through which I had entered moments ago, I heard the heartless laughter of the crowd, and before I hurriedly walked back through the long corridor, I sensed the smell of burning, human flesh from the stake of the Inquisition.

I opened my eyes. The young waitress was twisting her body in order to adjust the seam on the back of one of her thighs. Then she turned around and stepped into the sunshine heading for me.

"*Que souhaites-tu? Le Paradis ou l'Enfer?* What would you like: Heaven or Hell?" she asked standing in front of me.

I sat totally paralysed. She handed me the menu, smiled at me and said:

"You have the choice of our heavenly yoghurt-brunch with goat's cheese and fresh fruit or you may choose the Diablo-brunch with seasoned cheese and chilli sausage."

I couldn't say a word. I just stared at the menu while beads of sweat formed on my upper lip.

"Well, what'll it be?"

She impatiently waved the menu in front of me but I still couldn't say a word.

"You look like someone who'd like our Diablo," she said turning about and walked away.

I wanted to protest but she didn't hear me.

"*Un Diablo!*" she shouted into the shadows.

I could hear the hidden Self behind the sounds of the world like blood rushing in my veins, the orchestra of the forgotten language, the simple music of which is like the ocean. Not the sound of melancholy waves against the shore – far more *the sound of no shore* – as an old dervish once said.

You cannot run away from the past. The past, just like the future, is forever present *now*. All you can do is laugh and cry, swim in the sea, filled with loss, lust and longing for land, or walk on the water, full of love, without any expectations, knowing that only the death within you is longing for the beach of dreams.

"There you are," the young waitress said with a smile, placing the Diablo-brunch in front of me."

"*Bon appétit!*"

I watched her as she walked back into the shadows.

"*Ephatah, ephatah, ephatah, ephatah,*" I prayed intensely and immediately felt how my heart opened wide and how a silvery line came out from it trying to connect to the woman. My faith in the Power was unconditional. This also was one of the results of my state of mind. The whole square immediately turned into a holy room where the most blessed and total peace ruled. A radiating face appeared in the darkness. The young woman smiled at me. Her eyes were filled with forgiveness. She saw the one I had been and the one I was now. It was not the Church dignitary she recognized but God in his most humble disguise, she saw and greeted me with the best of her: an open heart.

I got up and went inside in order to pay at the bar. She was drying some glasses, which she then placed on a shelf above the counter.

"It has got nothing to do with the quality of the food, that I didn't touch it," I said, "but I'm a vegetarian."

She looked at me curiously as if trying to find out who I was and where I came from. I gave her my credit card. She took it and looked at it. She then tried to pronounce my name but, of course, it sounded totally wrong, however, very charming with a French accent.

"Las Myll!"

She tasted the two syllables and looked at me questioningly, and then she broke into a catching laughter. She tried to imitate my own pronunciation but it sounded just as funny and charming as her first try. She handed me the credit card.

"You are not going to pay for something you haven't ordered," she said in a low voice.

"You don't always get what you want, but always what you need. And this was just what I needed," I answered.

We just stood there without trying to end the moment as if we both knew that there was a deeper meaning to this. I broke the silence: "Let the payment be the symbol of an account that has been made up."

She hesitated before taking my card back and running it through the machine on the counter.

"Where are you going?" she asked.

"Montségur," I answered.

"How long are you going to be away?"

"A couple of weeks, I guess. There is a lot to be done."

Standing there, something suddenly struck me:

"Excuse me, but what is your name?"

She smiled. She then took a card and a pen and slowly wrote the letters down. She handed me the card. It said, "Belo Bar." Above it I read the name she had written in a fine spidery writing: *Marie Périllos*.

I thanked her:

"I may drop by on my way back."

"May?"

This incident took place at a time when I didn't yet know the significance of our meeting. The incident, however, was food for new thoughts, and it was on the motorway between Narbonne and Perpignan I finally realised that the existence I for the last fifty years, considered to be *mine* was nothing but a speck of dust in an unlimited universe with no end and no beginning.

I began to understand that a self is nothing but a moment's ripple on the endless ocean, and that this self is but one of innumerable expressions of the necessary limitations of the individual. Possibly because we are not yet sufficiently mature to be able to contain the frightening truth about our own unlimited divinity. Imagine the responsibility. This may be the reason why man is so busy constructing his own reality as a parallel to Creation. And are most of man's constructions in reality diversions away from the naked self?

Could the only difference between the constructions of the materialist and the mystic be in the wording?

I thought about Sylvia's words about the monumental change that man is in the middle of right now. "Even your physical expression will change," she had said. This was also true. When, now and then, I stole a furtive look in the mirror I was alarmed to see a stranger looking back at me, just as surprised and confused as I was looking at him.

I turned off the motorway outside Perpignan and followed D117 into the land of the Cathars, the beloved Shangri-La of my worldly soul. At once a feeling of freedom took hold of me as I realized that I wasn't going anywhere in particular and wasn't expected at a certain time. It struck me that for the first time in six years, I wasn't going to meet the Seer at this place which had come to mean so much to both of us. I was free to do what I wanted. There were so many places I didn't know and had never seen.

I took my foot off the accelerator at that moment, let go of time and floated into Grail-country. Outside, the countryside moved by in slow motion. Estagel, Maury, St. Paul, Lavagnac.

In Quillan I took the usual road towards Foix. Nothing strange about that. The car slowly crawled through one hairpin bend after the other. When I reached the top and was just getting close to the road to Belcaire I felt a force pulling that way. A will power other than my own insisted.

A sunbeam cut through the spruce trees outside and exploded inside the car. It was almost like in the movies where people are visited by extraterrestrial beings. Surprised, I turned my head towards the passenger seat but it was empty. I nevertheless had the feeling that someone else was in the car with me.

Estagel, Belcaire, Camurac, Prades. Over Col de Marmare and Col de Chioula. Ax-les-Thermes.

The sun was setting. In the Pyrenees it happens within a few moments.

The car continued south. A short distance outside the town I got an impulse to turn off.

A sign pointed towards "Orlu."

The road ran through a valley. To my right a rather large lake. In the dusk I could see the moon's reflection on the surface of the water. After fifteen minutes driving, the road ended in a gravelled open space. I parked between some trees and stepped out of the car. I stood for a moment in order to get my bearings not knowing anything other than the fact that I had decided to follow my intuition, or the power that showed the way. A path disappeared into the darkness between the trees. I followed it and began my ascent.

It was as if I was carried upwards. My sense of time had been cancelled. An inexplicable power rushed through me. It is difficult to explain, but if I should explain some of its contents I cannot get any closer to it than the word *information*. Not just information as pragmatic knowledge, but a kind of certainty, which cannot be explained. This piece of information didn't come from a specific place. It came from within, was everywhere around me and was a kind of *non-local*, here-there-and-everywhere state of mind.

The invisible hands of the power pushed me gently between the trees and into an open space on a plateau where a totally unexpected sight was waiting for me. As far as I could see, a strange looking water reservoir with strange dimensions stretched out in front of me. This unreal sea looked like something, which must have fallen from the sky, if it wasn't the sky itself. The moon was placed on the mirror-like surface like a ripe fruit from a foreign universe, a gate to other realities, and I had no doubt at all that it was wide open at this moment. The Voice spoke to me. But I understood that it is always accessible for those who have ears with which to listen and are able to read in the universal memory of man.

"There is one memory only."

A thousand thoughts came to my mind. I knew, of course, the reality of Akasha, however, the moment the Voice spoke, I became painfully aware of my limited knowledge. The Akasha-files are the memory of eternity containing everything, which happens and everything, which has ever happened. It is like a photographic film of all our desires and experiences here on earth.

Akasha is the ethereal memory of everything created. Here, all thoughts, which have been thought throughout time, are stored. From this point in time, those thoughts have the possibility of reacting retrospectively and of being expressed as archetypal material that has an effect on man, either locking him into the old ideas or giving him the option of new possibilities.

"Thoughts are energy creating form leaving imprints on all the various levels." The Voice spoke to the knowledge I had in me at the time, which now had to give way to another more embracing kind of insight.

"Man is surrounded by cosmic information. It is everywhere at the ethereal level and always within reach. When man has a bright idea or experiences the closeness of a higher, intuitive presence, it is cosmic information dripping an insignificant drop of its contents on to man. Without being conscious of this fact, man will stay in the regular, drugged and noisy reality cutting himself off from any kind of help from within and from above."

I suddenly saw myself trying to irrigate my garden while at the same time standing on the water hose. It was the most elementary kind of teaching I had ever received. My self-righteousness and feelings of superiority were blown away in one, single breath. I could actually feel how the qualities in me were drawn out of the darkness. I could feel my defences falling and making room for the certainty of my true identity.

"The degree of chaos in the world is in proportion to the number of chaotic thoughts in the mind of man. All universes result from the energy of thought. Understanding this is a prerequisite for the understanding of the four - or five dimensional reality. The change happens now. All must prepare for it. New energies are on their way and these energies depend on man."

Suddenly there was silence. In that instant I understood that it was the small spark of fear in me, with its origin in the collective fire of fear, which had silenced the Voice, or rather had made me deaf to its presence. Something in me started breathing, all the way from my feet and throughout the body. Calm entered immediately.

Heavenly Father-Mother – You Who are everywhere – Hallowed be Thy Name - Thy Kingdom come – Thy Will be done – Here and now and forevermore.

You Who are in me.

"Concurrently with the entrance to the ethereal reality expanding, man will change at all levels. The ethereal reality enables man to think at a higher level, which means that physical genetics will be surged with spiritual genetics. It will have an effect on the DNA of man in such a way that man will be able to draw sustenance from the light at the ethereal level. The memory of the true origin must be established."

The breathtaking view was enveloped in a paradisiacal peace. A faint, transparent and radiating being floated across the surface of the water where it slowly faded away into the replica of the moon.

"You Who are in me."

The teaching was over for now. I turned around and walked back to the car. One hour later I was back in Ax-les-Thermes where I took a room in a small hotel at the outskirts of town. There wasn't much fuss, only certainty.

In spite of the journey and the extraordinary experiences, I wasn't in the least tired. On the contrary, I was filled with an inexplicable vitality. But what do you do in a room with nothing but a small table, an uncomfortable chair and an alluring, soft double bed? You lie down and try to fall asleep.

Then I realized that this being was still with me. I got up, turned on the light and looked around. No one there. I then slipped into bed again, turned off the light and felt that someone took my hand and guided me along towards a clear light on the horizon.

"You Who are in me."

4

The light from the fires formed a golden arch on the pitch-black Mongolian sky. Oyugun turned his horse in the dark and shouted:

"Saran!"

Shortly after he heard a horse in the thickets.

"Hurry up!" he called to her.

In the glow from the fire he faintly saw his little sister, Sarangarel's, flaming hair flowing against the backlight.

As soon as they were together again they rode towards the fires in the distance. They had been on their way for two weeks in order to participate in the *Sagaalgan*, The festival of the White Moon, where shamans from all over the country gathered in order to perform their old rituals.

It was the first Moon festival for Sarangarel and Oyugun which meant that they had to go through the necessary initiation. However, she had a somewhat fierce disposition and did not want to submit herself to any kind of authority. It was solely Oyugun's powers of persuasion, which had made her agree. Now, being close to the goal, she hesitated and tried to delay.

When they were quite close to the valley they could hear the sound of a large number of horses galloping through the mountain pass and filling the air with the sound of thunder. Pushing through the thickets they continued along the ridge. Below them was a magnificent view. Seven bonfires burned in the valley and the horses and riders circled the fires galloping faster and faster. Sarangarel had never seen anything like this. It ignited her own ferocity lying in wait just below the surface, waiting for the right opportunity. But even deeper within her she felt another power sending another kind of song through her, making her insecure but at the same time filling her with hope.

It took them half an hour to find their way down the mountain, through the pass and into the festival area. Close to the fire at the centre, they found a number of tents where shamans who preferred to use song and sound had gathered. They were easily recognizable by their characteristic, long, pointed hats. The singing shamans had a special status giving them certain privileges, but they had to go through the usual initiations just like the other shamans.

Sarangarel and Oyugun were met by one of great father Tenger's servants, Arigh Gal.

"Welcome to Tsagaan Sar," he said opening his arms. He wanted to say more but stopped as he caught sight of Sarangarel. Rumours of her beauty had gone before her but no one had prepared him for the reality. Oyugun laughed when he saw the shaman blushing. A woman stepped up and took hold of the halter of Sarangarel's horse and lead her to the women's quarters.

Oyugun on the other hand immediately rode out and mingled with the other horsemen forming a live circle around the bonfire.

The seven bonfires symbolised Mushin's[1] seven main stars, the seven sisters or the seven virgins who had played an important role in the mythology of the Mongols since the beginning of time. The shamans, particularly, were very close to the cosmic forces and especially during the festival of the White Moon, numerous

---

[1]   the Pleiads

qualities could be received from the Cosmic Council. Any kind of enmity was prohibited. All the gates of cosmos should be kept open and this was only possible in the right kind of spirit.

The festival of the White Moon was also a fertility festival where seven virgins were symbolically sacrificed to Tenger. At the same time, this was the way the young girls were made familiar with the world of women. In order to be the purest possible sacrifice these virgins had to be menstruating. If a girl who was about to be initiated did not menstruate during the festival she had to wait until the following year. If it didn't happen then either, she would not be able to take on the work as a shaman.

The men rode throughout the night while the women through songs and sounds began finding openings to the ethereal level, which might serve as gates to the world beyond. This could go on for days.

After three days and nights, many of the horsemen, failing to connect with the world of spirits, had dropped out exhausted. However, on the evening of the third day the breakthrough came. The women met in a totally pure and powerful note that broke through the universe and created an opening. A sigh of relief was audible among the horsemen and the horses staggered to the watering place, ready to fall, where they were taken care of for the rest of the festival. They had given their best. The horse is the most holy animal of the shamans. The horse carries the shaman into the world well protected, and he leaves it again on the Horse of the Sky or the Horse of the Wind in order to co-operate with the spirits in the other worlds.

Seven women and seven men sat round-the-clock singing the note that the women had found, which made it possible for the three oldest of the shamans to travel to the worlds of the spirits in order to prepare the way for the virgins and the young men who were to be initiated.

Meanwhile they were testing the young virgins in order to find out who could meet the demands, while the young men spent three days and three nights in the caves in the mountains. Sarangarel had been found worthy, but as soon as it was possible she had crawled to the horse-pen under cover of darkness where she had tried to escape on her brother's horse. However, she had been caught by one of the guards who had to get help from two other guards in order to calm her down. As punishment Sarangarel was tied to a pole outside the main tent for a whole day to the amusement of the passers by who teased her with friendly shouts.

She stamped the ground agitatedly so that sand and gravel flew through the air. She was like a wild and unmanageable stallion, which refused to be broken.

Among the crowd was a young shaman who fell in love with Sarangarel the moment he saw her. He stood there all day without saying a word, but looked at her, passionately, languishing and very much in love. Sarangarel had seen him and looked at him tauntingly, mainly because she found it very humiliating to be stared at like a captive animal.

However, when the sun was on its way down the sky something peculiar happened. Suddenly the young shaman started singing. It wasn't particularly strange as such but his tone of voice was so pure, soft and compassionate that it struck the heart with such a loving force that no defence could withstand it.

Sarangarel froze in her ropes. All resistance fell to the ground like the dust she had kicked up moments ago. All sounds stopped. Within as well as around her. All activity ceased. All interest was focused on the young man singing to the young woman who stood tied to the Tree of Life in the middle of the world. But this was just the beginning of something that those who saw it would never forget. From an unknown place within Sarangarel a sound grew forth, at first it sounded like the painful crying of a wounded animal. Nevertheless, the sound was inexplicably different from anything they had heard before. It cleansed the air of every impurity. Then it changed and became clearer and more free. Those who witnessed it, later said that it was as if Sarangarel was transformed in front of them. This unmanageable woman inexplicably turned into a winged being, the likes of which none had ever seen before. The voice of this being stood like a pillar of light among them. Every heart had to open to this force, and it was as if it healed all sorrow, all diseases and all death. Anyone hearing this sound had to leave the old and welcome the new. From all corners of the world all shamans turned to this pillar of sound, which had united with the Tree of Life and miraculously had sown an imperishable seed in their hearts.

✻

I woke with a start as if I were torn from one reality and thrown into another. I looked around and remembered that I was in a hotel room in Ax-les-Thermes. Somewhere far away there was a faint echo of a voice singing an unknown song. The events of the previous night came back to me. What was it that had made me go "astray" and up to the lake, and who was it that spoke to me there? I remembered the radiating being walking on the water and disappearing as quickly again. Everything seemed totally unreal. And yet, I had no doubt that it had happened. I suddenly experienced a burning desire to go back but couldn't remember the way to get there. I tried to reconstruct the route in my thoughts but the details faded away from me. There was no doubt that the experience was connected to my nocturnal journey and the meeting with Sarangarel and the singing shamans. Lying there on the bed I was caught by a deep longing to see her again. The echo from her song still vibrated inside of me and something seemed to be changing. It was as if a totally new opening was created into a long forgotten area of my heart; a small tear through which the song quietly flowed in and embraced the splintered crystal of the universe:

> *I AM the light in the heart*
> *Supplanting every darkness*
> *And transforming everything into Golden Light*
> *With the only thing, which is real.*
> *I AM the one who is sending my love into the world*
> *In order to mend everything which has fallen down*
> *And to break down bitterness and resistance.*
> *I AM the endless power of love*
> *Acting through all that is alive*
> *With the only thing which is real:*
> *Forgiveness for evermore.*

It felt as if an invisible hand held my heart very gently. I could feel a healing power flowing through my chest.

I stayed in my bed that morning watching the dawn sending golden rays into the room. There reigned a very deep feeling of peacefulness, which in turn gave birth to a similar deep feeling of gratitude. What kind of beings had decided to take care of me in this way? Who was the oracle, Miriam, who had revealed herself to me in Toledo and who had stayed close to me and had helped me when I wrote the book about Mary Magdalene? And what kind of beings were looking after me now? Who was Sylvia with whom I had so surprisingly made contact and who apparently had something she was going to pass on to me? Who was the Seer, this extra-universal being who had saved my life? And what about all the people who had been helping me along the way? Not to mention the beings from another reality. Indeed, I had much to be thankful for and slipping into my silent hour, I sent them all loving thoughts.

After breakfast I decided to drive back towards Belcaire and on to Bélesta where I turned off towards Montségur. I was looking forward to seeing the old village again, situated in the Promised Valley where I had had so many transforming experiences with the Seer, and I couldn't get there fast enough. However, having passed Fougax-et-Barrineuf, a small village about fifteen minutes drive from Montségur, I spotted a big, yellow-red building, set back from the road on my right. I had seen it so many times when the Seer and I were visiting the area but I had never been inside it.

A sign outside said, "Om shanti." The building could very well be a Buddhist or Hindu monastery. Whether or not this was my reason for turning in here I do not know, but something made me do it.

No one seemed to be about. I parked the car and approached with caution. There was a large rack for shoes and boots at the front door. Above it: a big, beautiful bell. I could see a figurine of the Madonna in a window and in the other window another figurine of a saint. It wasn't totally Eastern then.

I carefully knocked on the door. It was ajar and I therefore opened it and went into a small front hall with doors on each side and a wide staircase ahead of me. There were some kitchen sounds behind one of the doors and I was about to knock on it when it was opened.

"Welcome," a warm voice was saying, "Can I help you?"

A man of about sixty years of age was standing in front of me. As soon as I saw him I sensed his golden, crystal-like aura, which was clearly connected to this place. I couldn't decide whether it was him who gave the place this fine quality or if it was the other way round, however, as he stood there receiving me so heartily I was inclined to think that he was the bearer of the power. I had the thought that maybe he was yet another sage who had been given the dubious task of showing me the way.

We introduced ourselves. His name was Mar. Shortly after, we were seated in the kitchen together with his wife, Leny, who also possessed a similar radiating, crystal-like aura. They came from Holland and had owned this place, Les Contes, for twelve years. Earlier, it was a guesthouse for poor, French children, run by the Catholic Church.

Later, when Mar showed me around, I could see the vastness of the physical framework of Les Contes. One dormitory after another, floor upon floor. Furthermore, spare rooms and annexes galore. At least 3000 square metres. There was also an old chapel, which Mar and Leny had made into a meditation hall.

From the mountain, fresh spring water flowed continuously in large quantities into a gigantic water reservoir supplying drinking water and electricity for Les Contes. Wherever you were in the building, you were constantly surrounded by the sound of trickling water.

In front of the house a big garden was laid out and behind it, a small park.

While Mar was talking I noticed how much he looked like the Seer. As far as I was concerned they could be brothers. They probably were at some level or other.

"Leny has asked me to show you to your room, if you'll follow me?"

We walked up the stairs in the old main building. Above each door, the old names, which the nuns had given the rooms could still be seen. My room was on the second floor. It was called St. François D'Assise.

Les Contes

Leny & Mar Van der Velde

It was a big room containing both a double and a single bed, a small table, a wash basin and the only balcony at Les Contes.

"Margaret Starbird also stayed in this room when she was doing the Magdalene courses in the area," he said casually before turning about and walking towards the staircase.

"Excuse me," I said, "did you say Mary Magdalene?"

"Oh, are you also interested in her?"

"I've just written and published a book about her."

He smiled as if he would say, "Who hasn't," but then he said in the same casual voice as before:

"Of course."

Our eyes met, and laughter rang throughout the old house.

"Dinner at seven!"

I heard him humming and laughing as he walked down the stairs.

The dining hall was buzzing with voices. Fifteen people were seated around the two refectory tables. I was sitting next to Mar and Leny. We exchanged polite pleasantries and they enquired as to my connection with the area. But I also sensed that another kind of exchange was going on telling my hosts who I was at another level.

"Do you know the Cave of Bethlehem?"

The light cheerfulness suddenly changed, and Mar's intense look and lowered voice had my full attention.

"I've heard about it," I said. The question took me totally by surprise and my hesitant answer was quite an understatement. For years the Seer and I had looked in vain for this legendary pace.

"What have you heard?"

"That it was one of the secret places of initiation for the Cathars in the vicinity of Ussat-les-Bains."

He looked intensely at me while I was talking and sat silently for a while before answering:

"The Cave of Bethlehem may or may not have been one of the most secret places of the Cathars, it is not certain. All they know is that the cave was found and excavated in 1938 by one of the most expert, contemporary spokesmen of Catharism, Antonin Gadal. They also say, however, that he wasn't totally trustworthy. As far as they know, he did many strange things in order to draw tourists to this, then, very poor area."

"Have you visited the cave?" I asked without being able to hide my enthusiasm any longer.

"Many times," he said. He was considering how much to tell me, but then he continued:

"No matter whether it is a hoax or not, anyone visiting the cave has to acknowledge that there is a very special energy there. The Rosicrusians ascribed and still ascribe great importance to the place, and I myself have no doubt at all that initiations took place and maybe still take place there. I have had some very special experiences in the cave."

"What kind of initiations took place there?"

"According to Gadal, the cave was used by the Cathars as a kind of church where the "new Christ" was born and where the initiated one finally obtained the rank of *Parfait*, one who is perfect. In other words a place where the candidate had to leave everything old, his whole past, behind him, in order to step into a new life in Christ. On the eastern wall of the cave a big, natural pentagon is imprinted. The candidate had to stand in it while a Cathar Priest would read, in all likelihood, from *The Gospel of St. John* before the initiation took place."

He stopped, got up and left. Shortly after he returned with pen and paper.

"I'll draw you a map so that you may find the place. But do remember to move about very quietly when you find the area."

After supper some of the guests gathered in a room with an open fireplace entertaining each other with small talk. I especially noticed a mature woman and a young man. The woman looked as if she had had a hard life, it was imprinted on her face, which looked like a Tibetan demon mask. The young man wore thick-lensed glasses, a long ponytail and was dressed entirely in black. They were lost in an intense discussion, which sometimes sounded like a severe argument. But for some reason or other something told me that the subject was of importance to me. I caught the odd word but since they were talking very quickly, and in Dutch, I couldn't get the whole of it. I drank my tea, bid everybody good night and went to my room to get some sleep.

I lay for a long time listening to the sound of water surrounding this magical place, which had once been a paradise for poor children.

Or had it?

What had really gone on here?

The water seemed to dissolve the foundation of the building, which floated into the air and disappeared into the universe. I closed my eyes and floated with it.

The sound of children playing filtered into the room. I woke up feeling a bit dizzy after a long night of travelling, where to, I was not too sure.

The cracks in the ceiling and the flowered wallpaper. The light laughter of the children. The busy steps on the stairs. How had it really been here seventy-five years ago? Now I heard the sound of suppressed crying. I got up. It was as if the sound came from just beside the bed.

"Who are you?" I whispered.

Outside, the sun had not yet risen. I walked over to the balcony and looked out. I couldn't see anyone down below. And still, the sound of the children playing was very real.

Against this background the low crying seemed even more heartbreaking. A foggy, grey shadow about the size of a child was sitting huddled at the head of the bed furthest from me in the room. I moved closer very carefully and squatted in front of the small being while I recited the heavenly, Aramaic prayer:

Heavenly Source
You Who are everywhere
Thy Kingdom come
Your will be done
Here and now and for evermore.
Fill us with the power of your mercy
And free us from the fetters with which we bind each other.
Lead us out of temptation: free us from ourselves
And give us the strength to be one with You.
Teach us the true power of forgiveness.
May this holy moment be the ground
From which our future actions grow.
Amen

The room was now completely quiet.

Homesickness!

I lit a candle.

In front of me the little grey cloud slowly dissolved. Between all the grey I sensed some small, sparkling lights dancing around the being that followed it on its way to the place where it belonged. All the old sounds folded in around me and disappeared the same way.

Outside, the sun was on its way over the mountains.

The only sound in the room was the sound of my own heartbeat.

After breakfast I drove to Tarascon towards Ax-les-Thermes until I got to Ussat-les-Bain and Ornolac where I crossed the small bridge across the Ariége-river. There was a small church to the right, which didn't seem to be in use anymore. Across from it was an old thermal bath. I parked the car outside it and started walking along the road to the right. Just before Villa Bernadac I turned to the left and followed a path into the forest. According to Mar's drawing I was supposed to follow an even smaller path on my left hand further ahead. I found the path and followed it as shown on the map. I struggled to get through the thickets that closed in around me. The long branches of the wild roses made any progress very difficult. I crawled under a fallen tree, which was also shown on the map, but then lost sight of the path when it split into two and ended in nothing at all.

I worked my way back to the starting point with great difficulty and started over again. This time, after twenty minutes of struggling with the bushes, I ended in front of a steep cliff wall where no further progress seemed possible. Relentlessly, the sun reflected its rays off the face of the cliff and the gorge seemed like a natural oven. Sweat dripping and a crumpled map in hand, which apparently didn't help at all, I was ready to pack it in.

Turning around in order to begin the walk back I looked up for the first time. On a ledge above me the door was clearly visible which, according to Mar's drawing, was the first indication that I was on the right track. The problem, however, was that Mar had made a mistake.

I was very excited when I carefully pulled at the door and opened it with a creaking sound. I continued through a brick gate and started ascending a narrow staircase. Shortly after, I found myself next to an impressive cliff wall with a large opening in front of it. I paused for a while in order to get my bearings before turning to the right and walking to what seemed to be the entrance to the Cave of Bethlehem.

A moment later I stepped inside holding my breath.

One step below me was an almost rectangular room of about 9 x 3 meters. Closest to the entrance was an enormous rock resting on three smaller ones. It looked, more than anything else, like an altar. The famed pentagon was there on the opposite wall, where the candidates had to stand during their initiation. To the left of the entrance was the recess in which, according to legend, the Holy Grail is said to have been placed during ceremonies. The cave was open to the south from which there was an impressive view over the valley and Ornolac.

Mar was right. Whether the cave was an authentic Cathar-place or not, it certainly had a very special atmosphere. I sat down on a stone bench close to the altar and fell into the silence of the place.

Sitting there it was revealed to me that the most important part of the initiation did not take place at the pentagon in the wall but at the stone altar. This was where the initiated one had to lie down and spend the night in order to give up the small self, so that the higher Self, Christ, might be born and take over the place of the old self. As soon as I understood that I decided to spend the night there myself.

I spent the rest of the day in the area. I picked up my sleeping bag late in the afternoon and some cardboard to lie on.

It was getting dark when I made my bed on the altar and lay down. There was just room enough for me to stretch out on it. A few flickering candles were all I had to keep the bats at bay.

My inner demons, however, could not so easily be kept at bay.

The sounds of the night now took over the cave and the world outside. I wondered whether or not they were the same?

The wind blew out the candles with one gust and filled the cave with an impenetrable darkness. What under other conditions might have sounded like little creeping things, now sounded like animals of hitherto unknown dimensions. A pair of yellow eyes approached through the air and disappeared somewhere below me. I closed my eyes and tried to relax on the uncomfortable bed, but kept twisting and turning in order to find a position that fitted the surface of the stone, which I could clearly feel through the sleeping bag and the cardboard.

I don't know for how long I kept trying to fall asleep but I must have slipped into another state of mind, since suddenly I found myself in another human shape, in another cave, in another country, a long, long time ago.

✳

Oyugun was running along the cliff wall while he tried to read the small signs which were supposed to guide him along the way. His sweat blinded him behind the tiger's mask and he had to concentrate in order to keep his balance. Once in a while he stopped to catch his breath and to listen, but the only thing he could hear was his own heart pumping the blood around his young body. He ran for his life. He ran through the faintly lit and winding passages where the torches were placed with so much distance between them that he could just

The Bethlehem Cave

about manage to see where he was running. If they had told him about the circumstances around his initiation he would have been able to prepare for it. But he realized that the uncertainty was an important part of the test.

When Oyugun realized that apparently there was no system in the construction of the maze and that no kind of reason could figure this abomination out, he finally surrendered and ran in the direction shown him by his heart. He almost hovered along, round and round, up and down, down one passage way after another. The heat, however, made him understand that he was getting closer to what must be the centre.

He stopped at the end of a long passageway at the foot of a staircase. He turned his head and looked back, but it didn't seem as if he had missed anything. His heart thundered in his chest and his breath sounded like one of the great bellows by the bonfires at the Moon festival outside.

He slowly started to walk towards the opening at the end of the steps where a faint light made long, vague shadows from beings he didn't know.

He stopped again to catch his breath. Then he stepped into a room with four arches forming a symmetrical flower in the ceiling above the altar in the middle of the room. A woman lay on the altar. No other living being was to be seen. He had reached his goal. He knew that all he had to do now was pass the last part of the test.

Carefully he stepped closer.

A young woman wearing a mask in the shape of a snake lay tied to the altar. She was dressed in a thin dress made from snakeskin and decorated with various animal symbols, which barely covered the most intimate parts of her body.

Oyugun gasped when he saw her. The sight fixed him to the spot while chaotic thoughts went through his head. What was the next step?

He watched the young woman. The eyes of the snake met his. Her chest was heaving faster and faster, but otherwise she was calm. He thought for a moment that he caught something in her eyes, something that wanted to guide him or encourage him. But he didn't understand it. He was aware of one thing only: There was no time to waste. He heard the sound of drums and bells from far away and he was sure that they were approaching. Immediately he began untying the woman. When he had set one of her arms free and was beginning to untie the other, he wondered why she didn't move her arm. She only moved slightly when he had untied her legs as well. He thought that maybe she had been drugged, but he also realized that such thoughts were of no avail and didn't lead anywhere. There was only one thing for him to do. He hesitated for moment before reaching out in order to help her out of the snakeskin dress. He fumbled with the lock holding it together at the side, while she was quietly holding on to his wrist. She then let go of him, loosened the dress in front and revealed her breasts to him. Most of all he wanted to discard his own mask and to remove hers as well and to kiss her, but he knew that this was not allowed. The eyes of the snake met his and they said, "come on" to him.

The drums and the bells were not far away now. He tore the rest of the snakeskin away from her in one flowing movement and stared at her open sex lying in front of him like a black and red pearl, the gate of life and death, waiting for him to enter into the Holy of Holies.

He was one single, tight muscle as he slowly entered her. They merged into one, single movement and he was caught in a vice making it impossible for him to pull away. He heard her warm breath behind the mask under him. Somewhere close, the maniacal rhythm and the sharp notes of the bells sounded, chasing an opening to the ethereal level. At that moment his world exploded in an inferno like the Flood breaking all the dams of the world, while he cried out like a delivered animal. He sank on to her, sweating. He sensed the presence of beings in the room.

"Oyugun!"

He looked surprised at the Snake and he seemed to recognise her voice. Then he tore the mask from her face.

"Sarangarel!"

5

"*A part of you is travelling through time and space. However, another part of you is not subject to such limitations. It is on a totally different kind of journey.*"

I opened my eyes slowly. The morning sun bathed my surroundings in a faint purple hue. I was cold and my body was aching. I looked around, bewildered. The Bethlehem Cave.

Oyugun and Saragarel.

What kind of story was that? Was it about my own past and if so, why was I confronted with it like that?

And who was it that kept talking to me?

I was disturbed by the fact that it was not possible for me to identify the Voice that kept communicating with me in such rather trite language about cosmos and the correct meaning of things. This was all stuff that I knew already. Why this insistence? I worked with all aspects of human nature. Especially the psychological, mental and various other dimensions of the soul and spirituality through the humanities and through esoteric knowledge.

"There is a need for transformation at the emotional level more than at the mental level. When you are afraid to enter, it is so easy to demonize the complementary part. Fear is the burden of man. Time is ripe for you to break your mental limitations. This is your great blindness and this is what clouds your true vision. If your emotions are not integrated, your mental field cannot be clean."

I looked around in the cave. I saw faintly a figure squatting and leaning against the cliff wall next to the opening to the Ornolac valley. It was, however, impossible for me to see who and what it was and what it looked like.

"Who are you?" I blurted out.

I actually sensed that this being smiled at me indulgently. This upset me. There was no answer, but instead the figure continued:

"There are deeper layers. Layers where the body, the psyche, the mind and the senses are simply filters, which must be cleaned before a human being may be infused by the cosmic. In this way a human being may be transformed into a pure, cosmic presence — on earth in its present incarnation."

I thought that it might be Sylvia who had taken on another character, since it was a complete repetition of some of the things she had told me at our first meeting. Had she not told me that in the future we would communicate telepathically?

"The unusually slow and heavy energies, to which man subjects himself, make it impossible to see clearly. When he nevertheless tries, it may first and foremost be due to his memory of the clearness of his sight before he incarnated. But memory alone is not enough. Memory is only a faint copy of true quality. The higher ethics are hiding here. The small self has no part in this. That is why it cannot be used as measurement for anything at all. It is above any kind of judgement and is not able to judge or condemn anyone or anything. When man cannot stand himself or the situation he is in, when he is unable to control his surroundings he has a tendency to judge others and to judge that which is going on at the time. However, anyone who judges another, is solely judging himself. And when someone judges himself he has placed himself within the most constricting limitations possible. Power and control are simply expressions of fear and only forgiveness may remove

it. Only forgiveness may cut through delusions and restore true vision. I am committed to that, and only to that."

"I?"

Did I hear correctly? If so, it was the first time I had heard the Voice using *the first person singular* about himself.

The sun was now so bright that I couldn't see if this mysterious being was still sitting at the opening to the cave.

"Are you still here?" I asked in a low voice.

No answer.

Slowly, I got to my feet. I felt as if my body had been torn apart during the night. I realized shortly after that the mysterious being had either left the cave or taken on a shape which was not immediately visible to me. However, I still felt its presence.

I stepped on to the ledge enjoying the view while I stretched myself and breathed the fresh mountain air. The morning dew lay like an ethereal carpet over the valley and it was pure pleasure to feel the energies surging through me with renewed power. It was like a gift from my unidentified friend. I imagined its gentle, animating laughter, if nothing else then as a happy echo in my own innermost self.

Having packed the car, I drove to Tarascon in order to have breakfast at a café at the shores of the Ariège. Sitting there watching the river, I thought about the long series of thought-constructions which are a result of man's fear of freeing himself from any kind of compensatory and limiting thoughts and illusory dreams. Not just the dream about a painless life, where you walk through it without any kind of strife and with all material wishes fulfilled, but also the dream about the perfect partner, the perfect guru, the perfect spirituality which are all just constructions meant somehow to make life tolerable for us. Even the conception of suffering, Heaven and Hell, well, even the conception of a personal God, are constructions, which we have made in order to make our lives meaningful. Nothing wrong with that, per se. This is precisely one of the possibilities given to man: free will and the ability to create reality through the power of thought.

Suddenly it was clear to me that the quantum leap that modern man is faced with has something to do with the dissolution of the illusory nature of these constructions, and that we must have the courage to step out of them, until we are finally and totally able to give them up.

The next problem, of course, would be that imagining a life freed from any kind of construction would, in itself, be a construction.

Such a dissolution would be a catastrophe for any kind of foundation on which we build our reality.

I let the question rest. I had now asked it and I was certain that the answer would come in due course.

Meditating on my coffee with a map of the area in my lap I stumbled on the name *Notre Dame de Sabart*. I could see on the map that it was situated near by. Without thinking too much about it I knew that I had to go there. No doubt at all.

The church was only a five-minute drive from Tarascon.

Stepping out of the car I immediately saw the figures above the entrance. They were clearly visible: Yeshua and Mariam. One on each side of a stained-glass window. Yeshua to the left and Mariam to the right. They bid the pilgrims welcome with open arms.

It was very peaceful inside. No other visitors were present and for some reason or other I went to the right side of the church. I could see an altar at the end of the aisle. It was as if I was pulled there by an unknown force. I didn't see her before I was very close. The penitent sinner of the church. Mariam Magdal. Kneeling and with the skull and the book at her feet, just like at the altar in the Mary Magdalene Church in Rennes-le-Château.

The skull and the book!

The altar was not very well kept, and contrary to the other figures of saints in the church, there were no candles. Either they had just found the altar and were waiting for the restoration of it or they didn't consider it very interesting.

I sat down on the floor to meditate.

Softly, softly.

Heart.

The old road – in His footsteps. Purple. The colours of the clouds. Dust. Light. The unlimited united above my head. The

Mariam and Yeshua greeting visitors outside Notré-Dame-de-Sabart

thundering sound of an unknown being flying by me. In His hand: The power to open or to close. Let the wanderer return to the beginning. I stand alone at a crossroad. Open. Closed. Down. Up. An unforgettable moment. An echo from eternity. The sound of the inevitable steps on the stairs – heard through time – and shaking me.

Awake!

> *I AM forgiveness, working here,*
> *Throwing away all doubts and all fear,*
> *Making man forever free*
> *With wings of cosmic victory.*
> *I AM the one who is calling with all my power*
> *For forgiveness each and every hour;*
> *To all life everywhere*
> *I let the grace of forgiveness flow.*

Sarangarel!

I opened my eyes. Deep inside of me I was beginning to understand the meaning of my nocturnal journey and the confrontation with the beautiful, however also very painful images. I understood that no one is a victim of apparently accidental circumstances.

No circumstances are accidental in the great game!

But why did I have to go back and look at it once more?

"You cannot get to the top of a house unless you take one step at a time. If there are one hundred steps and you only take ninety-eight of them, you'll never know how it is at the top. On the other hand, neither can you skip a step, because then you wouldn't know the way. If a well is fifty metres deep and your rope is only forty-six metres long, you'll never be able to fill your bucket with water. In the same way man must realize that as long as he cannot raise himself above the reality of the body and the senses, he shall never know anything about the reality of the higher worlds. And the prerequisite for every step is the forgiveness of any kind of judgement. You must forgive yourself."

Forgiveness. Here we go again. It was slowly getting to be a rather worn concept. I mean, the sound of the word itself was becoming quite nauseous, as it had been misused in so many contexts and had seldom been understood and practised.

The Voice immediately came to my assistance:

There is forgiveness and then there is Forgiveness. Forgiveness is not just a prayer, but the total giving up of judgement. The moment man understands the depth of these words and makes them his life, he is stepping into a totally different sphere, so totally different from anything he has known before. We are talking rebirth here. A totally new life. Give up any kind of judgement.

Every judgement is simply a projection. Do not judge anyone."

I got up, walked back and bought a candle, lit it and placed it in front of the altar to Mary Magdalene.

Sarangarel's altar.

Women's altar.

The altar to the feminine power.

I stood in silence watching the flame. It flickered slightly in the draft, but I could see that it was strong and could not be quenched. When it finally burnt out, it would continue to burn at another level.

"Forgive me," I whispered.

I then turned around and walked out.

It was not until I was sitting in the car that I felt how deeply the experience in the Notre Dame de Sabart had moved me. It was as if

The Magdalene Altar in Notre-Dame-de-Sabert.
Notice the skull and the book.

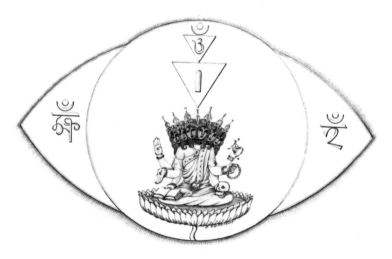

Hakini from Layayoga. Notice the skull and the book. She symbolise
the third eye. She is the moon-white sitting on a wild lotus holding in
her six arms a rosary, a drum, a bow, a skull and a book. Her hands
symbolises disintegration of fear.

(S. S. Goswami)

my ethereal body almost vibrated, as if a faint electrical current ran through it like an angel walking through a room. The veils had been pulled aside to reveal the most vulnerable part of me, the strongest part, the unconditional being; the conscious soul in the archetypal feminine centre: Mariam Magdal.

Driving along towards Foix in order to get some lunch I felt very certain that Mariam somehow had been to France. That her spirit had always been alive in the south of France. I cannot say how I knew, I can only say that it was a kind of certainty originating in the feminine part of my greater being. It was not a matter of history but the archetypal vibration sending its song through time, heralding its message of the arrival of unconditional love and its final reckoning with any kind of intolerance, any kind of abuse, any kind of power and any kind of lie.

Driving along I juxtaposed the intuitive certainty with the historical background in my mind.

During the time before and after Yeshua, Marseilles was one of the most important cities in the Roman Empire with a thriving commerce and a major concentration of esoteric knowledge. A major Jewish settlement made it more than likely that Jewish, Syrian and other pilgrims, visitors or refugees from Palestine, would come here where tolerance was greater than in many other contemporary parts of the world.

Marseilles was well known for its Athene, Diana, Minerva and Isis temples. In the city you'd see druids, Jewish mystics and Isis priests and priestesses walking freely among each other under Roman rule.

Legend has it that Mariam Magdal arrived in a boat without sail and oars with her entourage, Lazarus and Martha (brother and sister), Mariam Clophas (Yeshua's aunt), Mariam Salome (Yohannan's mother) as well as Sara the Egyptian (maid), to a small town not far from Marseilles, Les-Saint-Maries-de-la-Mer which at the time of Yeshua was called Ra or Ratis.

It is hard to say whether or not this legend should be taken literally, but there is no doubt that whatever arrived at Ra in a boat without sail and oars it was something which was going to have an enormous impact on the spiritual life of Europe.

Sara the Egyptian later became the great saint of the gypsies, celebrated once a year when the Black Madonna is baptised in the sea.

Isis, Artemis and Cybele were worshipped in Ra as early as the fourth century B.C. The first Black Madonna figures in Europe are said to come from here.

Another mystery surfaced when they started delving into this: The Black Madonnas. Who were they and what role did they play?

Writing my book about Mary Magdalene I had met these figures time and again, but without finding any answers to the questions raised by these black virgins.

However, one name kept coming up: Isis. It took me by surprise that the Isis tradition, which I, until now, had been convinced was a strictly Egyptian phenomenon, had been spread across Europe by means of the Roman advance, blending with Celtic and Teutonic traditions. And even more surprising, these heathen traditions were alive a long time after the establishment of Christianity on the European continent. They actually worshipped the Great Mother in various guises, more or less officially, up to the Middle Ages.

Not many Christians are aware that the "historical" Virgin Mary was not introduced by the Roman Church until the year 470 A.D. as a direct result of a public demand to re-establish a female divinity. The successful miscarriage of justice carried out by the Church against Yeshua's better – but dangerous – half, Mariam Magdal, had some unwarranted and, at the time, also unpredictable consequences. As a result, the feminine force had, more or less, to go underground where, nevertheless, it was able to gather so much power that it is, finally, on its way to breaking down the limitations man has accepted up until now.

It was these kinds of thoughts I contemplated on my way to Foix. This openness to the ethereal reality and its collective memory in my mind was by now so familiar that I realized that in order to keep the channel open I had to refrain from any kind of judgement or critical thought. On the other hand, there was also the demand for soberness and the courage to be totally honest in relation to the incoming information. On top of this was the question of the personal bits and pieces that should not be involved. It was a very delicate balance and in every way a great paradox, since, how do you judge something soberly without using the so-called judgement based on reason? It is simply a matter of a totally different kind, and in itself a totally inexplicable kind of certainty, where the so-called judgement, based on reason, is completely abandoned.

We are talking about a kind of certainty that not only knows about the ethereal level but also, beyond that, the astral levels. The ability to distinguish between those levels is not only a general prerequisite, but a necessity of life, if you are to keep your balance and have hopes of using the information advantageously.

There are no well-defined borders between the various levels. Everything is integrated and I know of no one who can say where one ends and the other begins. But the starting point itself, the fundamental part, the principal one, cannot be understood as long as you are solely entrenched in the earthly aspect and the earlier mentioned idea of reason.

In spite of all this, it is necessary to know the difference between the ethereal level and the astral level if you are to apply the information you receive usefully.

When man becomes familiar with the reading of the great cosmic memory he is going to wonder, well, even be shocked to see that the written history, which we have trusted until now, only constitutes part of the truth, since it is only an expression of the version of the writers of history and usually, the people in power.

You might say that the Church has been the representative of the exoteric (the external, superficial) knowledge which, successfully and for centuries, it made into dogma and historical truths, while the so called Heretics, Cabalists and Alchemists, Mystics and Rosicrucians represented the esoteric (the concealed and deeper) wisdom living a life in hiding.

The time has come, however, where everything hidden must see the light of day. And this not only goes for the collective unconscious, but for the personal level as well. Each individual must find the courage to look at his own mythology before a lasting healing may be possible. And here, perhaps, lies the greatest challenge for contemporary man.

When we wake up, we realise that there are no further escape routes. Many will continue to look for them and grasp at any opportunity to avoid taking responsibility for themselves. But this will only be a short respite. In spite of the innumerable offers of quick relief, man must realise that the promises of short cuts to freedom are just yet another illusion.

The oldest Taoists upheld the principle that the detour would always turn out to be the fastest and most effective road to the goal. I smiled to myself and thought about the scene in my book "Mary Magdalene" where Yeshua challenges every form of pharisaic self-righteousness with the words: "Only the redeemed cannot be saved."

A judgement or a sad fact?

In Foix I found the cafe in the square where the Seer and I had so many times before enjoyed a glass of pastis. It was usually here we started our work-meetings and always here that we ended them with a last aperitif. I ordered a glass of pastis and sent him a friendly thought. The sun had disappeared behind a cloud. It looked like rain. I went and sat under the awning.

Having finished lunch I thought about Sylvia's words about my journey of the Grail, "The princess is where the snake is. Find the princess and you are close to the Grail."

The Grail.

One of the oldest and most beloved legends names Montségur as the mountain of the Grail. An old shepherd told me this legend when I came here for the first time in order to meet the Seer.

This is what the old man said:

"At the time when the walls of Montségur were still intact, the Cathars, the pure ones, guarded the Holy Grail in there. Montségur was threatened. The armies of Lucifer lay outside the walls. They wanted the Grail so that they could place it in Lucifer's tiara again, from where it had fallen to the earth when the angels were expelled from Heaven. When they were in dire need a white dove came out of the sky splitting the mountain with its beak. *Esclarmonde*, the female guardian of the Grail, threw the valuable, sacred thing into the mountain. The mountain, then, closed again. That is how the Grail was saved. When the devils forced their way into the castle, it was too late. Filled with anger they burned all the pure ones at the stakes in the field below the cliffs and the castle at *camp de crémats.*"

Tradition has it that two hundred and five Cathars, men, women and children, voluntarily ran singing to the stake. According to the same tradition, they had promised to return after seven hundred years.

Montségur fell in the year 1244. Thus, the seven hundred years had passed and the time was here – now.

Esclarmonde.

Perhaps she was yet another in the series of female incarnations of the great goddess? Was she, like Magdalene, yet one more of the daughters of Isis?

Esclarmonde was the Duchess of Foix. When the Roman Church instigated the inquisition against the Cathars she became their protector and saint. She was "the Light of the World" to them.

I drove to Montségur after lunch. Once more I had the sensation that the decision was not mine to make, but that I more or less was guided along. I had actually planned a whole day for my reunion with the holy mountain. But I had started to accept the fact that the work with the ethereal reality, somehow, had a mind of its own.

The fine drizzle made mysterious filigree shapes dance before me as I spotted the mountain through the windshield. As usual, it looked like the ultimate runic letter waiting for the pilgrim who had the courage to climb it in the spirit in which it had been placed there, at one of the most open and holy sites.

I brought out my raincoat and my pilgrim's staff from the boot of the car. Apparently there were no other visitors as the parking place was empty.

My heart pounded heavily as I walked through the well-known thicket towards the meadow of Prat, the guardian of nature. For the first time in the seven years I had been coming here, I was alone and had to do what must be done without the help of the Seer.

Slowly I walked to the middle of the meadow to the spot where Prat used to be. I stuck my pilgrim's staff into the ground and took a step toward the holy spot. I closed my eyes and let go of

my nervousness. When you are standing here giving your worries to
the female guardian of the world, everything external dissolves and,
imperceptibly, you slip into the first sphere of the ethereal reality.

You, who are everywhere.

You, who are a part of me.

A fine, almost milky veil appeared in front of me. A slightly veiled
reality opened up at a point in the air where I had focused my sight,
in which the finest filigree of crystals vibrated with a purple hue.
Within this net of light I sensed a soft, feminine figure, vitalized
by beings of fire the size of sparks, which seemed to originate in an
unquenchable source of light. I assumed that the figure had to be
Prat. But before I had accepted this fact, another being appeared, and
I sensed that it was another version of what hitherto had expressed
itself through Prat.

The woman was pure light and was surrounded by the newts
of fire. Then she lifted her hands up above her head as if she was
pouring from an unknown source, and I saw that, somehow, she was
also made of water.

All the particles of my physical body, all the beings of fire in my
ethereal body, all the star material in my astral field were as compass
needles exposed to an enormous magnetic force. Everything within
and around me pointed to the centre of this radiating being in front
of me and, with one voice, asked the question:

"Who are you?"

Not that I expected an answer, since at a higher level I knew very
well that this being was at such a high frequency energy level that it
must be a higher being.

"I am Esclarmonde!"

The voice sounded like thousands flowers opening to the sun
during springtime's first vitalizing hour; a dance, dancing directly
into the centre of the heart's maze.

*"Now, as then, anyone who wants to walk the holy paths must
choose between Roma or Amor! Choose between the path of the world
or that of love!"*

ROMA – AMOR!

Esclamonde
(Painting by Peter Fich)

No compact shapes. Everything soft and pliable. Like seeing everything through a jellyfish held against the light of the sun. A mirage of milky silk and velour. But in a very clear way.

Coming back to the physical reality, the sun sent its rays through the clouds and for a long time I could still see the hectic activity of the little beings of light, sparkling like pearls in the bright air.

After the meeting with Esclarmonde I began ascending the mountain. The first part up to the stele, as usual, was the hardest part. After a short break I continued along the narrow path through the forest. Walking there, I noticed steps behind me once more. I stopped to get my bearings, but no one was there. I thought that perhaps like myself, the person in question had taken a break, but as soon as I started walking again I could hear the steps like an echo with a very slight delay, only a few metres away. I realized that, once more, it was my invisible friend on the prowl.

I stopped at all the well-known points on my way up, the ethereal openings that I had become familiar with through my work with the Seer. On the ledge where the Oracle is, you only ask the questions to which you have the courage to get the answer. The answers you get here are so direct that you are immediately robbed of any kind of illusion in which you may find yourself at that moment. Catching these answers and passing them on in the most applicable way was what made the Seer such a master in his field.

It was with a certain awe that, an hour later, I approached the entrance to the castle, the Gate of Time. It is here that you must prepare yourself for the energies activated around the Point of the Grail in the middle of the courtyard. You make yourself free from earlier incarnations and all of your old baggage in the Gate of Time. It works the same way as *The Shaft of the Soul*, as I described in *The Seer*. Images from your personal as well as the collective levels pass in front of you, and the one standing in the Gate cannot control anything at all. One doesn't always get what one wants, but always what one needs. Or: one often gets what one wants, but hardly ever in the shape one had hoped for.

I stayed in the Gate of Time until I was empty of all images. Then I stepped into the courtyard, which seemed strangely empty without the presence of the Seer. I could see him as he took over the Point of the Grail in his familiar way and prepared himself for the work of the day. It was now up to me to attempt to move the energies.

I found the Point of the Grail and drew a circle around myself with my pilgrim's staff. I then put the staff aside, opened my arms and started swirling around. I rested on my left foot while I used my right foot to propel myself around, anticlockwise. The palm of my right hand turned upwards toward the sky and my left was turned down. Slowly at the beginning, then faster and faster. Round and round until I felt the lines from the corners of the world being sucked into the centre by the centripetal force, the power of which increased with every turn.

The power was focused in the palm of my right hand. Within the centre of this centripetal force a centrifugal one was born, communicating with the external forces, so that an outgoing force was flowing from the middle of the palm of my left hand. The only way to explain this is to ask you to imagine the other side of every day reality turned inside out so that another synchronous reality becomes visible from behind the veil.

I kept on turning round and round until every kind of limitation was dissolved in a radiating being that manifested itself in the field of tension between my outstretched hands – a pillar of light, or rather a cross of light in the middle of the courtyard.

Then I let go ...

6

The wheel turns.

Round and round.

The silver string is like an umbilical cord continuing endlessly into the universe. I don't know what is at the end of it. I just see the wheel turning round and round. I am thinking that it may be the Wheel of Life that keeps turning until each and every person has fulfilled his task on earth.

I now see that the wheel is part of a spinning wheel and that a girl of about twelve to thirteen years of age is working it. She is sitting in a room without walls, totally illuminated by the sun, spinning her thread. The girl is dressed in a simple, white cotton dress. Her only adornment is a small, red fleur-de-lis embroidered on her chest. Only now do I see that it is the girl who is spinning the sunlight. This sight is devoid of sentimentality.

The image fades away and another slowly appears. A heart in a bonfire surrounded by flames. However, it is not burning on the outside. Only the eternal fire burns in the heart. The heart now changes into a fleur-de-lis. The lily burns but does not perish. The heart is burned at the stake but cannot be devoured by the flames.

Then everything becomes heavy and black.

The sun was on its way down behind St. Barthélemy on the other side of the valley as I, slightly dizzy, found my way down the mountain in the dusk.

My thoughts were focussed on the darkness I had seen in my vision.

I felt that I was carrying a burden, which was heavier than anything I had carried before. Even the rocks that I had carried up this mountain seven years earlier were nothing to this inexplicable loneliness, which had seized me and reinforced my basic loneliness more than I can say. Something inside me felt as if it was going to burst, and I felt a lump in my throat, an urge to cry which must be a thousand years old – that is how sad I was, how broken-hearted.

I realized that what had happened in the courtyard was more than I could handle by myself and in my thoughts I asked the Seer and Sylvia for help.

The pictures I had been allowed to see were harsh. But something about the way everything had disappeared into the darkness made me very miserable. The painful loneliness coming from this was impossible to explain. Perhaps it was just difficult for me to understand and accept that when the floodgates open, it is not unproblematic for a person who is not as ready to work with this kind of energy as he should be. When you want to go up, you must be willing to go down, and the heights you may reach are in proportion to the depths into which you have the courage to dive. That's the way it is. I had known this for a long time. But it is also a well-known fact that there is a difference between theory and practice.

Someone must have heard my prayer since the Voice was present once more on my way down:

"You are not alone, but you have to do this on your own."

Period.

I was shaking all over as I walked the rest of the way towards Prat's, or rather Esclarmonde's meadow. All of the Montségur-mountain had belonged to Esclarmonde in the thirteenth century. She was the Duchess of Foix and princess and saint to the Cathars. The mountain still belonged to Esclarmonde and it probably always would.

In spite of my state of mind I managed to find the point in the meadow in order to thank her for the insight I had received. Even though I didn't understand the contents of it.

Getting back to the car my legs were shaking so badly that I could hardly stand. I had to hold my car keys with both hands, that is how severely they were shaking. I was cold to the bone.

It was very difficult to get the key into the ignition. When finally I succeeded I turned the heat up all the way. I stayed like this with the engine idling until the cabin was warm and dry. A sudden inspiration made me turn on the radio and out poured the sound of a well-known voice, Leonard Cohen:

> *It was deep into his fiery heart*
> *He took the dust of Joan of Arc*
> *And then she clearly understood*
> *If he was fire, oh then she must be wood.*
> *I saw her wince, I saw her cry,*
> *I saw the glory in her eye*
> *Myself I long for love and light*
> *But must it come so cruel, and oh so bright?*

"But must it come so cruel, and oh so bright?"

In spite of the state of mind I was in, Cohen's "haphazard" comment nevertheless made me smile. Yes, dear reader, I certainly am very slow-witted. In spite of the fact that my life for many years has been filled with these wonderful and frightening coincidences, I still wonder and often hear myself repeating the same sentence over and over and over again, "how strange."

It seemed as if Cohen's song for Joan of Arc epitomized with a few brilliant words both the moment and eternity. He was truly a troubadour of love. Completely in the old, French, esoteric tradition.

And according to this tradition the troubadours were closely connected to the Cathars and the Templars. I especially remember one of the stanzas from the tradition of the Grail that I like the most, written by Arnaut Daniel in the twelfth century:

"With every day do I become a purer and a better person, because I serve the noblest lady in the world and I worship her. I say this openly. I carry in my heart the file with which I cut rare words and make them into rare rhymes because I write about an unknown being."

These troubadours were well known for the fact that their poems and songs were filled with a deep, esoteric knowledge. Influenced by the Celts and the Gnostics they worked with four levels representing the elements. The external, historical level, equivalent to the level of earth. A moral level, equivalent to water. A level of the natural sciences, equivalent to air, and finally an ethereal level of fire leading to the highest contemplation. The "unknown being", to whom they dedicated their songs, was the beloved one, the beautiful and wise Sophia in various shapes, and often incarnated as various beautiful Duchesses and Ladies of Castles. They often developed into amorous, erotic relationships between a Lady of a Castle and a troubadour, and there are numerous examples where a troubadour had to flee headlong from a jealous husband.

The afternoon's experience on Montségur kept me in thrall and at supper I was allowed to sit alone with my thoughts. The other guests at Les Conte had enough sense to notice that I wasn't interested in any kind of small talk. Cohen's song was still in my head. I knew from experience that when I was in a state of openness, nothing happened accidentally. When I turned on my car radio it was not in order to be entertained, but solely because I was meant to. In this case I clearly got an important message.

Joan of Arc.

I had been fascinated by her fate from very early in my life. Like Lawrence of Arabia, Dag Hammarskjöld and Simone Weil, Joan of Arc spoke to an archetypal level in me, which moved me deeply. All four had a very complicated and complex nature combined with a dedication, which were seen by some as pathological and by others as divine.

Most people have heard about Joan of Arc, but not everybody is aware of her unusual destiny. She was born in the small town of Domrémy on January 6th, 1412. Thirteen years old she heard a voice, which she thought belonged to the Archangel Michael. She was in her father's garden at the time, on a summer's afternoon. The voice asked her to seek out Duke Charles of Lorraine and to bring about his appointment as the rightful King of France. At the time France was occupied by the English.

Seventeen years old she was admitted to the presence of Charles and convinced him and his council that she, and she alone, would be able to lead the French troops to victory over the occupation forces, for the simple reason that she was God sent. And after one month of mental and physical examination the inexplicable happened. Charles pronounced the seventeen-year-old shepherdess leader of the French army in the revolt against the English.

It is a well-known fact that Joan of Arc succeeded in beating off the enemy and getting Charles crowned king.

On Wednesday, the 30th of May she was burned at the stake in Rouen after having been betrayed by her own people and subsequently captured by the enemy. During the proceedings of the Catholic Church the church dignitaries – a number of which hated her for her great piety and, even more so, because of the great love of the people for her – tried to get her to admit to heresy. But Joan mastered her rhetoric better than her adversaries. Her words had an authority and authenticity that swept all empty theological arguments and every hypocritical lie aside. Inevitably this lead to her death.

What makes the historical sources so extraordinarily credible is the fact that they rest on so many different statements, where both the words of friends and enemies have been written down and passed on.

What kind of power was expressed through this young woman who apparently could neither read nor write? It is reasonable to claim that she, just like Yeshua, in the course of three years went through the same as he did to get to the Christ state of mind. The difference between these two lives is that we know with certainty that Joan was a real person living in the fifteenth century. During the three years in question, she was guided by two saints; in particular St. Katharina of Alexandria and St. Margaret. They appeared as voices, which in any given situation could advise Joan as to what she should do. According to Joan herself, these voices were never wrong. The few times the promised prophesies did not come true were due only to the hesitation and ignorance of Charles' council.

Reading the historical sources, and there are many of these, one statement is repeated again and again: She was purity itself. And this purity made her the messenger of God. Everyone who met her said that she radiated such great piety that she was almost divine. No one could help being moved by her.

This was the official story. But there had to be something else. Something that could guarantee the success of this utopian project. She must truly have had special powers. But what kind, – what were they?

I let the question be for the time being.

After supper most of the guests at Les Contes were going to Carcassonne to enjoy a ballad opera about the troubadours. I declined an invitation to join them since I was too tired. Instead, I brought my tea to the fireplace. To my great surprise the Dutch mother and her son sat there already, lost in conversation. Apparently, they were not going on this excursion either.

They became silent as I entered the room and they got up smiling kindly, and bid me welcome. I immediately realized that this meeting here at the fireplace and at this time was not at all accidental. Thus, I was hardly seated before the conversation started.

"We had better greet each other properly," the woman said and offered me her hand finishing her sentence with a, "Vivien."

I answered with, "Lars," and shook her hand.

She pointed to her son who had taken a few steps backwards:
"This is my son, Roderick."

I offered him my hand, but he just took another step backwards.
"Roderick, you might at least say hello."

Her voice was not in the least reproachful. She then said to me:
"I'm sorry, but you see, Roderick has to get used to people first. It hasn't been to easy for him."

"Are you here on holiday?" I asked mainly to be polite.

Once more it was the mother who answered:

"We come here once a year. And we usually stay here for a month at a time. Roderick is of noble birth. He comes from the d'Hautpol family."

Roderick put his left hand out towards me at these words, as if to underscore his mother's words. On his ring finger he had a large ring which looked as if it was made from gold with a large, black stone in it.

"The family lost all their possessions under circumstances that I shall not bore you with, however, if you are familiar with the history of the region you'll know that the d'Hautpol family owned the old castle in Rennes-le-Château. Unfortunately, the castle is in a ramshackle state today. The family name originates in a small town called *Opoul* where one of the forefathers slew a dragon in the days of yore. But that is another story.

I looked closely at Roderick while his mother was talking. He showed no signs of emotion. But it was obvious that he was filled with a pent up anger being manifested as infantile aggression.

Certainly, I knew something about the d'Hautpols. I had seen the name several times in connection with my studies of the Cathars and the Templars. The name was also mentioned several times in connection with the, by now, world famous priest Saunière and the mystery at Rennes-le-Château.

It was obvious that the mother had told the history of the old, aristocratic family several times to strangers in the past. The question was whether or not I was considered a stranger in this context since the attitude of both mother and son was very direct. It was as if they had something tell *me*, and that somehow they wanted to get it over with.

Without further ado, I turned to Roderick and addressed my question directly to him:

"What have you experienced?"

For a moment the question hovered in the air between us. Apparently it paralyzed the mother. Then Roderick answered:

I am a so called *abductie*. I've been taken up.

"Taken up?"

"Yes, by beings from other realities."

"UFOs?"

"You may call them that. I would rather call it an abduction into a synchronous reality."

He stopped as if to give me the opportunity to collect myself. His words, however, did not make me lose my balance. I had studied both UFOs and the so-called abductions and their theories and had formed my own opinion about these phenomena. And the words of Roderick seemed to be very close to these thoughts.

His mother used the rhetorical pause to put in a remark:

"Yes, it's a family weakness, if one can put it that way. For generations we have been abducted by strange beings from other star systems who have used us as guinea pigs."

We were silent for a while.

"How did you experience this?"

He contemplated my question before answering:

"It is not a very nice story, I can tell you. What I have experienced is beyond the worst nightmares you can imagine. There is so much darkness, so much heavy matter around us and around the earth that sometimes it is difficult to understand how man can continue with life and with evolution."

"One can also question whether or not this may be called evolution? Do we not primarily still express the most primitive part of our being, although in a much more sophisticated way than we did earlier? As I see it, man is only using about a thousandth of his potential, the rest of which is allowed to stay dormant in the unconscious and is totally wasted."

He nodded.

"You are right. Perhaps the beings I know are the result of man's heartbreaking ignorance. Perhaps they are something like demons, created by us?"

"In other words, you do not think that we are talking about UFOs as such, with so called *aliens* from other planets?"

"No, not in the normal sense of the word. But I do believe that these beings manifest themselves in various shapes, according to the role they want to play in human consciousness. I believe that this is a part of the seduction. Take the Bugarach-Mountain, for example, close to Rennes-le-Château. They say that it is visited by vessels from other planets. Hundreds of people claim to have seen UFOs there."

"Have you been there?"

He nodded his assent.

"Many times. I have never had this kind of experience at Bugarach but you ought to visit the place. Something is going on there which is out of the ordinary."

Roderick's story was certainly exciting. Whether or not it was true, that was another story. I was certainly not in a position where I could decide what was right and what was wrong in this respect. I knew from my own experiences how fragile such experiences are when they are told and passed on. But there was something I had to know:

"When do these abductions happen?"

"At night when I am asleep. As soon as I pass through the R.E.M. sleep, they get me and take me to other levels. And this is not for babies I can assure you."

It sounded totally like my own nocturnal excursions. The difference being, however, that I did not experience any kind of coercion and I never felt attacked in any way. I was often confronted with difficult sights and heavy decisions, but I never felt that I was subjected to any kind of injustice or experiments. On the contrary, increasingly I had the feeling that I could move about quite freely on the other side.

"Who is abducting you, then?"

"Beings that look exactly like those described by other abductees. Little grey men without ears and noses and with big, slanting eyes without pupils. They seem to be totally devoid of feelings and in many ways quite bestial. For example they do not show any signs of compassion or sentimentality. They are not consciously evil or cold hearted. They simply do not have the same kind of sentiments as humans do. They are not human, if you know what I mean. They nevertheless seem to be very intelligent in some inexplicable way. I have had the thought that they may be some kind of robot, made by highly developed beings who do not themselves want to deal with anything as primitive as man."

He smiled at his own conclusion.

His story made me think. I couldn't help thinking that he might be right about the fact that they were artificially made. But I had no doubt at all that, whatever they were or whoever had made them, they were nevertheless something that occurs in the lower astral fields. The presence of these beings in the energy field of man resulted from conscious and unconscious manipulations with the archetypes, partly by ourselves and partly by those we had elected to manage the world and partly also by outside forces.

It is the big multinational corporations, which are managing the external world through the balance of trade and the stock exchange. Taking the risk of sounding paranoid, I suggest the possibility that these corporations have the one single purpose of exploiting all resources, material as well as mental, to the hilt, as long as mammon is the result, no matter the consequences. This doesn't necessarily mean that it is profitable, on the contrary, these institutions somehow are an expression of the collective disease on the earth level, an external expression of the internal state of mind of collective man.

I also believe that the only thing feared by these corporations is that man will wake up and see that he is not free but is kept doped by a long series of undermining activities, poisoning modern society in the shape of a cynical cocktail consisting of equal parts of fear and entertainment. To repeat this fact: these institutions are the external expression of man's collective inner fear of having to be responsible for himself.

I wouldn't be surprised at all if right now there are people working hard to find ways to buy the copyright of people's thoughts, in order to make a profit on them. Imagine a future, dear reader, where poor parents are forced, in advance, to sell the rights to exploitation of the future thoughts and ideas of their newborn child!

Do you find this improbable?

There are forces in the world, which will not stop until the last resource has been exploited and the last drop of blood has been squeezed from life itself. And these forces, again and again, are simply external signs of our own internal state of mind, which we confirm and maintain, when we feel unable to stand our ground and free ourselves from the slavery of normality.

There is so much material excess in the world today that we could reasonably quickly solve all the social, humanitarian and environmental problems of the world. The problem is, of course, that all the riches belong to very few people who do not really want to change the present imbalance of values. And as long as these few are successful in selling the illusion of free elections and democracy to the many, this imbalance will remain.

This external imprisonment, in a way, is a gift. Since perhaps it is because of this situation that one day we may understand that freedom must be found inside ourselves.

It was Roderick who broke the silence:

"Did you know that Les Contes is the twelfth *Earth Gate*?"

"Earth Gate?"

I looked at him without understanding. He nodded eagerly:

"Yes, there are thirteen superior Earth Gates on the earth and Les Contes represents Montségur, which is the twelfth."

"What does that mean?"

"It means that there is a so-called heart meridian on earth consisting of particularly open locations with access to the universe. These Gates are situated at Mt. Shasta in California, Glastonbury in England, The Temple in Jerusalem, The Cheops Pyramid in Egypt, the Chinese Wall, The Kedarnath Temple in the Himalayas in India, the Black Mountains in U.S.A., Ayers Rock in Australia, Katmandu in Nepal, Nazca in Peru, Montségur in France and Kilimanjaro in Africa."

He became silent and looked as if he lacked the right words.

"What is their function and who found these Earth Gates?"

"They constitute particularly open locations where the energies from the universe may flow freely. And the heart meridian which connects these gates constitutes in itself of a force which not only has the effect that the various gates influence each other, but also that they have an influence on the universe itself. I do not know who located the other Earth Gates, but it was a Dutch biologist and professor who formed a team of psychics who, years ago, was given the task of finding the gate that is now situated here at Les Contes. I do not know who gave them the task and I do not think that Mar or Leny knows.

It is, however, a fact that after months of intense work they found that this place was the right one. You'll be able to see it tomorrow. It is hidden at the lower end of the garden. It is a construction built to precise measurements. A rather large piece of quartz is hanging in the middle of it. Mar and Leny tell us that the energy from the gate is too much for some people while others are attracted to it from far away without knowing the cause of it. Frequently, people who are just travelling through, suddenly find themselves turning off the main road and coming here because they are drawn by a force they cannot explain."

Roderick got up and went to the big bookshelf at the end wall. He came back shortly after and placed a thin, pale yellow pamphlet on the table in front of me. The letters on the front practically radiated up at me:

The Path of Mary Magdalene and the Cathars (Earthgate expedition, Pyrenees, 1997).

There was picture of the stele, below the title, commemorating the Cathars on the Montségur-mountain.

I opened the book and looked at the first page. I couldn't help smiling. I was looking at a photo of the part of the altar in the church in Rennes-le-Château where Mary Magdalene is kneeling in a grotto in front of a book and a human skull.

A book and a skull!

The caption below the picture read: "Mary Magdalene with the *Book of Love* and the *Crystal Skull*."

The Book of Love and the Crystal Skull!

A bell with a fine, crisp, ethereal tone that spread in a field around me, cleansed the room of the heavy mood that had threatened to take over. I knew that this was a breakthrough in my search and that it was an important step in the right direction.

The three of us sat staring into the fire. Each of us had something to think about. I tucked the pamphlet under my arm, said good night and took my leave.

I found a torch in Leny's kitchen. I couldn't possibly go to bed before taking a look at the twelfth Earth Gate. Outside a storm was brewing. I turned up the collar of my coat and shivered as I followed the invisible trail in the darkness. It was further than I remembered. The soil became soft and at places even muddy before I reached the park. When I turned on the torch the cone of light caught a small gnome jumping behind a mound on which an angel was sitting cautioning the visitor to be quiet. I just stood there for moment. From all around there was the sound of water streaming down from the mountain. On the other side I could hear the Les Contes river rushing by on its way to the estuary where it flowed into the sea far away, reminding me of the journey of man. What was going on here? There was a lively commotion among the gnomes and elves which were apparently celebrating something. It was as if the grass, the bushes and the trees were being garlanded with unconditional, spontaneous and rare festoons of happiness. It was the kind of happiness, which took me by the hand and led me between the bushes towards the cosmic gate. I let the cone of light inspect the sculpture, which marked the location of the gate. It looked as if it was made to specific measurements. An enormous quartz hung in the middle. I switched off the torch and stood still until my eyes adjusted to the darkness. I felt the power of the place after a few minutes. The Gate radiated faintly like a large, ethereal heart beating slowly while it connected the sky and earth.

When I got to my room I felt immediately that I had a visitor. I couldn't see anyone but there was no doubt. The stranger, who by now was quite familiar, was present.

I lay down on the bed and leafed through the yellow pamphlet reading here and there. It seemed to consist of a series of readings made by the team of psychics, mentioned earlier, during their journey to France. Some of it seemed to be a clutter of well-known theories and unclear, occult allegories that said nothing new.

The Book of Love and the Crystal Skull, however, touched on something that I hoped the pamphlet could explain.

But I must have fallen asleep because suddenly I found myself on a beach covered with big rocks. In between the rocks are stretches of white sand and black seaweed.

I spot a boat on the horizon, which is slowly getting closer to the beach.

I can taste the air, salty from the waves beating hard against the coast.

A carpet of clouds rolls itself out in front of me.

In the same instant, I see the true face of my earlier life revealing itself in the abandoned track from the travels of my soul.

The window of time is open, the curtain of my memory is waving in the wind and everything is blue and white and green.

Now the boat, without sail or oars, touches the beach.

In the boat a black woman. At her feet a book.

The air is filled with newts.

Filled with fire.

Fire!

She is speaking through the fire:

"*My name is Neith. The Queen of Heaven.*

I am everything that was, everything that is, and everything which is to come. I am the abyss of the Universe from where the sun rose for the first time at the dawn of time. No mortal has yet been able to break through my veil. The crown I wear is red and is called Net. I am dark as the nocturnal, star-filled sky, and on its distended arch I am the gate between life and death. I am the isogenic, self reproducing virgin creating life in all the worlds. With my boat I weave the destinies of all people and all the universes. I am the goddess of magic and the incarnated, eternal, feminine principle."

7

The rain beat against the windows when I woke up in St. Francis of Assisi's room at Les Contes. I woke up with the feeling that the night had brought some kind of understanding. There was no doubt that I had reached a cross-roads and I had to take stock.

My journey had not taken me to the dragon, the princess or the Holy Grail. Instead, I was left with a handful of clues, which I couldn't fit together.

Perhaps it was time to go back to Denmark?

Although I clearly felt the presence of Sylvia I still needed to sit opposite her so that I could ask the questions which had been increasing in the wake of my journey.

"You want to come?" I asked the being standing in the corner watching me.

No answer.

I got up and showered.

Afterwards, when I was putting away my notes, a folded piece of paper fell on to the floor.

I picked it up and read it:

"Marie Périllos — Belo Bar."

I remembered the waitress at the café where I had experienced the uncanny déjà-vu. Was this yet another coincidence, that I happened to stumble on the note, which then reminded me of her? Hardly that.

I said goodbye to Leny and Mar after breakfast.

"Do come back soon," they shouted as I drove out of the driveway. This was the only thing I was certain of. I wanted to come back to this moving place very soon.

I enjoyed sitting in the car letting one beautiful landscape after the other pass me by and driving through the small villages situated like pearls on a string all the way to Perpignan. Driving through Estagel I noticed a sign saying, *"Brocante,"* – "Bric-a-Brac."

I have passed hundreds of stores like this without stopping. However, something made me park the car and visit exactly this store.

"Well, what are you up to now?" I whispered to my invisible travelling companion.

I stepped into a large hall filled with all kinds of things, – from old pieces of furniture, magazines, sculptures, paintings, flower-pots, coins and stamps – to junk that couldn't possibly have any sales value. I strolled slowly along among this explosion of things until I stopped in front of an old chest of drawers. A picture frame was leaning against the end of the chest of drawers, with the picture on the inside. As if my hand was being guided, I leaned forward and turned it around.

I couldn't believe my own eyes.

In this woven picture she was kneeling in deep prayer, in a coat-of-mail and holding a banner, which, it is said, she never let out of her sight.

Joan of Arc!

On the banner was written: "Jhesus–Marie."

Yeshua Mary. As if it was one name. Just by pronouncing the name, a power which felt as if it could move mountains manifested itself immediately. Was this the power Joan of Arc had invoked and to which she had subjected herself?

Joan of Arc

I drove into Narbonne early in the afternoon. After a couple of attempts, I soon found the small square with the "Belo Bar." I parked the car and went in. An elderly man was standing at the bar serving customers. I waited patiently. Then, finally, it was my turn:

"Excuse me, does Marie Périllos work here?"

The man looked at me, perplexed, as if he did not understand what I was saying.

"Sorry," he said, – "Who are you looking for?"

"Marie Périllos," I answered.

"Sorry, you must have misunderstood something, she doesn't work here."

He turned around in order to make a cup of coffee on a machine.

His answer took me completely by surprise.

"She is tall, dark hair and about twenty five years old."

He shook his head while knocking the coffee-grounds out of the filter.

"I'm sorry, I don't know her."

Before I managed to say anything else he disappeared into a back room. I was confused. I gave up and left the "Belo Bar." Was I going crazy?

"Please help me," I whispered to my invisible friend, but there was no answer.

When I got back to Denmark I went directly to Charlottenlund to see Sylvia. Opening the door she smiled, and I couldn't help thinking that she had known all the time how things would turn out. I simply felt like a very young soul in her presence. I really was in the company of a very mature lady.

"Come in, Lars, good to see you again."

"Just my words," I said hanging my coat on a hook in the hallway. I felt a sense of relief standing there in her living room and looking into her gentle eyes. It was like looking into an eternity of time, past as well as not yet seen, it was like looking into the teasing and unpredictable mind of a little girl, like looking into the innermost and deepest reservoir of wisdom.

I had come home.

Her golden laughter activated the ethereal game of glass-pearls, and I imagined hearing Salome's laughter the way Magdalene heard her so often then, two thousand years ago. She immediately followed me. Her attention lifted me. She saw me the way I was. She saw right through all my barricades.

"Let's get to work. It looks as if I'm only kept alive in order to finish my business with you, so let's not waste any time."

She motioned for me to sit down.

"Have you had a good time?"

It was one of those rhetorical questions where she knew very well the answer beforehand. It was more like a strange kind of politeness she felt compelled to show me in order to make me feel at home. I therefore waited with my answer, and what could I say? She sensed my awkwardness and laughed:

"I know what you mean, but let me hear about your journey."

I told her about the Voice and my invisible friend, about my nocturnal visit to the lake, about Les Contes and my night in the Cave of Bethlehem. When I had finished my story she smiled and I sensed a kind of approval in her look.

"Do you know about the mysterious birth?"

"You mean the Christian one?"

"Bethlehem symbolizes something deeper. Directly translated, Bethlehem means *The House of Bread*. What is meant here is bread or food in a divine sense. Bethlehem, then, is to be understood allegorically and may be translated with *The Location for Divine Food*. The Cave where Yeshua was born became a holy place at the moment of birth. No matter where this cave was situated, geographically, at the moment of birth it became Bethlehem. A location where the influx of a higher consciousness has maximal concentration. This happens at a symbolic level each time a person comes to understand his higher Self. When the old one dies and a new one is born. When you lay down on the stone altar in the Cave of Bethlehem it was an expression of your willingness to give up the lower for the higher. It is a ritual known since the beginning of time. They knew about it in the old religion of Zarathustra and in ancient Egypt. The three wise men, the three magi who found Yeshua in the cave came from Babylon in Persia. The three wise men represent the tripartite principle of Unity. The question now is whether or not you were visited by three magi during the ritual?"

Her gaze was both lengthy and intensely focused. It was quite clear that she wanted to guide my attention to my experiences in the cave in order to make me see them once more. I told her about Sarangarel and Oyugun. I told her about the Voice and the strange being I sensed most of the time, that had been closest on the morning I woke up in the Cave of Bethlehem. But I had no recollection of three wise men.

We sat quietly for a moment. Then she continued:

"Pay attention to the archetype of the magus. The three magi or wise men may also be three wise female magi, or three qualities in yourself. When do you leave again?"

This, however, was a question, which took me by surprise. What did she mean? I had just come back. Again she continued before I had time to think about her question:

"You see, you must find the answers to the questions you seek in yourself. But the prerequisite for that is that you go back to Montségur and find the hidden cave in the mountain."

"The hidden cave?"

I was dumbfounded.

"Well, up until now you and the Seer have only moved about on the "outside" of the mystery. You have climbed the mountain, you have found the outer point of the Grail in the courtyard itself. You might say that you have conquered the masculine side of Montségur. You have to find the feminine side *inside* the mountain."

I was about to fall off my chair, that's how dumbfounded I felt. During the six years of working with the Seer on Montségur I had never heard about a hidden cave inside the mountain.

"How do you know about this cave?"

She smiled secretively but didn't answer my question directly.

"I am asking you to go on a quest."

"Where on the mountain is it situated?"

"You'll find out. But there is an opening leading into the mountain itself. Remember the legend of the Grail about Esclarmonde who opened the mountain during the siege by the Inquisition and threw the Grail into it. Although, of course, this must be understood symbolically, a great truth is hidden here. You really ought to be able to find this truth right now and right here, but with the risk of understanding only a small part of what I'm trying to pass on to you. Your past as a magus demands that you still need the physical journey and the physical ritual, in spite of your growing abilities as an astral traveller. That is why you must go down and find the mystery yourself. Your experience in the Bethlehem Cave was not just a preliminary exercise. The cave in the Montségur-mountain is quite different. Do you want more coffee?"

She poured before I had time to answer.

"Then there is also another person I would like to talk to you about: Joan of Arc. Do you know her well?"

This was almost too much. I could hardly believe my own ears. When I had recovered I told her about my experiences with Joan of Arc. It didn't seem to jolt her at all. She just smiled and continued:

"There are a few things I must tell you so that you may understand the mystery of Joan of Arc. You know the Sophia aspect, the old wisdom aspect which through the ages has been carried by various historical persons and various, feminine archetypes? The sisters of Sophia, if one can put it that way, have had many names. To repeat it once more: there are two Sophia aspects, a higher and a lower one. The lower one has its foundations in the instincts while the higher one has its foundations on the purely spiritual level. The instincts are of course also tied to the spiritual level in a subtle way, however, at a level with a lower vibration, so to speak. There are no words to cover this or names that are sufficiently precise. That is why any attempt to explain this may seem vague and unclear. It may nevertheless be possible to get an idea of them."

She looked at me as if to make sure I could follow her.

"You may read about all the basic stuff about Sophia. I just want to underscore the fact that the higher aspect of Sophia has a name, which may not be enunciated yet. That is why you must find it yourself, which shouldn't be too difficult for you if you just follow your intuition. You neither can nor should avoid sexuality, however, as this fantastic force may be transformed. In one way you might say that the sexual force is the curse of man because it is and has always been used to created ties and to maintain the power. It is the energy, which keeps people in slavery with the strongest possible power, creating dependence, depression and pain. But it is also one, which offers fantastic potential. In this day and age, tantra has undergone a renaissance. Unfortunately, it often doesn't go much further than being a refined way of expressing your sexuality in the name of spirituality: a welcome spice with which to pep up a stagnated sex life and sexual pleasures as such. Most people must live their sexuality in good as well as in bad times, while a few people seem to have transformed it as early as the time of their birth. These are the so-called *Venus people*. They do not have to transform their sexuality but can function as sexual healers, to put it one way. This is what some of the so-called prostitute Moon priestesses were trained to be in the old Ishtar and Isis temples. These women sacrificed themselves in order to lift the man out of darkness, out of the jaws of death, in order to put him in the sky as the sun he is meant to be. As the representatives of the moon they always reflected the sun. They knew about the two shrines, the earthly vagina and the heavenly vagina. Both these shrines are protected by seven veils, each of which represents a step leading deeper and deeper into the mysteries."

She stopped once more in order to see if I was following her. She laughed at the sight of me. Probably because I looked totally enraptured.

"Practically all mystery traditions talk about these seven veils or steps. There are really fourteen; seven lower and seven higher ones. The understanding of these things is the quest you are now going on. You cannot avoid your sexuality, but remember that it is only a necessary step on the way to the higher Sophia."

My head was filled with questions I wanted answered, but I didn't know where to begin. But it didn't really matter since Sylvia so easily seemed to catch the thread I was trying to find.

"I'm sure you have noticed that Mary Magdalene is depicted with a human skull at the altar in the church at Rennes-le-Château, just like all the other altars to her in the Languedoc area. I'm sure you have been contemplating the meaning of this."

I nodded eagerly. She got up and disappeared into the next room. It took a while before she returned due to her reduced mobility. She placed a picture in front of me. It showed a man pouring water from a big pitcher. To the right behind him a small figure was stepping through a gigantic skull. At the bottom of the picture seven lotus flowers were depicted.

"As you may have seen, it is a woman walking through the mouth of the skull. The mouth symbolizes the heavenly vagina. She is walking through the throat-chakra. The man is the Water Carrier. And the seven lotus flowers symbolize the seven veils, energy centres or steps of initiation. It is the birth of spiritual love. In this connection the thymus gland behind the heart plays an important role. We are talking about transformation all the way to the hormonal level. It is the birth of the divine fire in the fifth chamber of the heart. The lower and higher Sophia are represented by eros and agape. On the external level you might say that Mount Carmel symbolizes the higher sphere while the mount of Venus symbolizes the lower one. Do you know anything about Carmel consciousness?"

"Only through my travels in Israel in 1969 and '79 as well as the spirituality which is partly communicated through the teaching of the Essenes and partly through Teresa of Avila and John of the Teaching of the Cross which ended in the founding of the order of the Carmelites in the Middle Ages."

"Good. Remember that there are three women who have played a major role in the European, esoteric tradition, and who, each in her own way, is connected to Carmel. They are Joan of Arc, Teresa of Avila and Elisabeth I of England. In the tradition in which I was initiated, *Anyahitha* is the great world mother, the embodiment of the basic principle, the unity of all things. She was the first one to postulate true monism. She is the motherly, creating principle of nature. She acknowledged the fertilising principle of the spirit of the time in the fatherhood of spirit. Progress and development is only possible through the intimate connection of both these principles, the total union of matter and spirit. What is new in our day is the

Aquarius

unity of water and fire. The old Veda of India represents the water while the Avesta writings of Persia represent the fire. The Avesta grew out of the Veda. Out of Avesta grew the Sufi, Jewish and Christian traditions."

She spread out her arms.

"I'm sorry if I'm skipping from this to that, but you must keep your ears open. There is so much to pass on."

"What was this about Joan of Arc?"

"Right, we mustn't forget her. *Jehanne* of the Arc, The Girl from Orleans, or just the Virgin. This was the traditional name for a priestess in a cult, which communicated with nature sprits, fairies, elves and the like. Joan herself, during the trial against her, told that she had received her first visions at the "Tree of Fairies." This was a gathering place for a Diana cult in her hometown Domrémy. She received a major part of her visions from St. Catherine of Alexandria and St. Margaret. The name Catherine has its origin in the Greek *cathar* = pure, which certainly has had some influence on the Cathars later on, who celebrated this saint as one of their own. The Cult of Diana had spread far into Europe when Christianity started spreading. And the Christians, especially, considered Diana to be their major competitor. They degraded her from being "the Queen of Heaven" to "the Queen of witches." In the Acts of the Apostles the total destruction of the temple of the great Goddess Diana is ordered. In the course of time, all the temples of Diana thus became the temples of Mary. The Inquisition considered Diana to be the Goddess of the heathens with whom the witches danced at night, and the church dignitaries called her the devil herself. In spite of this, they actually worshipped her until the time of Joan of Arc when she was considered the Moon Goddess. There were even places where she was worshipped in the local churches. Even today she is honoured at some places as the protector of the hunters. So you see, the great, feminine power cannot so easily be destroyed. It always finds a way. St. Margaret incarnated Aphrodite Marina, Pelagia and was called "the Pearl of the Sea." "The Pearly Gate" of Aphrodite was a metaphor for a woman's sex, like the Gate of Paradise. Her name is connected to Marga, which in Sanskrit means "the Way" or "the Gate" through ritual sexuality to Paradise for tantric male and female yogis."

"But how could it at all be possible that a young girl, overnight, seventeen years of age, suddenly found herself at the head of the French Army?"

"Well, it really didn't happen overnight. Someone had prepared her for the task."

"Who?"

She was contemplating how much to tell me.

"You'll probably find a good explanation when you revisit Rennes-le-Château and Montségur. And when you are in the village, you ought also to visit the church. It may hold some of the answers. Have you seen that?"

I hadn't. The church in Montségur was always locked when I was there. However, I had never had the thought that I should or could visit the church. By now, I recognized the ill-concealed challenge in Sylvia's voice so easily that I knew, that although it was toned down, it was her way of planting a clue in my consciousness. There was, however, one question I had to ask:

"You said at one time that where the dragon is that is where the princess is and vice versa. You said that a virgin was waiting for me somewhere out there. What did you mean by that?"

She could hardly avoid laughing. She kept me waiting for a long time before giving in:

"Don't spend too much time thinking about that. I'm sure that the Board of Directors will send you a virgin when the time is ripe."

"Send me a virgin?" I looked at her, questioningly.

She nodded:

"Well, that is how it happened for me when I was at your stage. I really thought that I was done with my sexuality, but I was wrong. My teacher, van der Stok, drew my attention to the fact that I still had something in me, which had to be transformed. One day there was a knock on my door and a handsome, young man was standing on my doorstep, and he thought that he and I had some work to do in the tantric department."

Her laughter practically opened the room so that every closed heart or stagnated mind had to surrender. When she had regained her composure, she continued:

"Well anyway, what I wanted to say is this: The ability to think is not the greatest of man's abilities. The ability to think is simply a product of objectivity contaminated by emotions. Thinking is noise. A Thought, however, is silence, because it is being certain, freed from superficial emotions. Thinking is limited by the thinker. Man is himself a divine form of thought. And when man rests here, thinking is not needed in the way we understand it. What is my point here? Well, surrender to the Thought of which you are an expression. Each and every person is a Thought from God. Each and every individual must learn how to be in it and how to fulfil the mission, which is hidden in the current form of thought. It is fine to ask questions, but it is better to be able to stay quiet and to listen. This is the only way in which to get the true answers. In this state of mind we even receive answers which are not the result of a question, because the knowledge or the certainty here is in itself a part of the individual's foundation based on his specific incarnation. We are so busy trying to get it all, and in pursuit of this we so easily miss the essential. Our lives are built on gossip, judgement and avarice. The time has come where it is no longer enough to just talk about fighting these evils, we now have to do something. If man wasn't so concerned about the physical reality he would understand that the legends and myths of the past are part and parcel of each individual's innermost being and not necessarily the historical facts. Each and every individual is affected by one or more archetypes in their current incarnation. The archetypes each represent a matrix for the various qualities in man. We must let ourselves be guided by these archetypes in our own lives, live their dramas but also remember to continue to build on to them. We carry the responsibility of our own personal mythology. This may be one of the most important reasons for our existence."

"Does this mean that everything is predestined?"

"Only to a certain extent. Man has got his free will because he is of the world we live in, which is written in many places. But nothing is written which may not be corrected. You must understand that there is a meaning to the fact that we have been reincarnated into exactly this universe. There are many other universes into which we might have been reincarnated, but we are here on earth because each of us has something, which must be transformed here. A part of us, our higher being, is also present in other universes at the same time where we are expressed through totally different shapes, identities and personalities. We are all basically a part of the divine thought-form. Each and everyone of us represents a spark from the divine fire. Remember that. The brilliant thing about myths is that they always offer wisdom, which will open that which is closed and expand the understanding of the mysteries to those initiated. And as long as the myths are passed on, their secrets are kept by those who have ears with which to hear and eyes with which to see. Intellectual figments of imagination speak to the brain; the myths speak to the heart. Dreams are personal myths. Myths are collective dreams."

She leaned back. Once more, she had transformed the room into a holy sphere in the universe.

"Well, you're something else, you are," she said smiling and shaking her head. "I had prepared to go home, and then you show up here and disturb me. Why did you do that?"

In spite of the sound of reproach in her voice she didn't look at all as if she blamed me for anything. On the contrary, I clearly felt that the cheeky meddling of destiny and the Board of Directors really suited her very well.

"Be prepared that now you'll be confronted with your past. That means that people to whom you have had close relations in the past will come and try to balance the old scores. If I'm not wrong, there'll be quite a few women coming into your life. Well, this may be difficult. Be gentle but firm."

She stressed the last few words.

"Do not get stuck in personal stuff. The images manifesting themselves for you have something to do with you but shouldn't be interpreted on a strictly personal level. Don't get caught up in the past. Your own history is only important in so far as it serves in transforming your lower self and the collective part. Forget about punishment, guilt and shame. Look at the archetypes in the collective light. Look at the overall picture."

She stopped talking. We sat for a long time. Far too long for my liking. There had been a change. The light mood which had been prevalent had now disappeared. I could see in her face that something was brewing. Something which worried her. She leaned towards me and said:

"Lars, I don't quite know how to say this, because I want to be certain that you understand the seriousness of it."

She took her time. The sudden change made me nervous. She put her hand on mine:

"Are you really aware of what it is you have agreed to do?"

There was something almost momentous in her voice.

I felt deep down that I could answer her question with a decisive yes, but just at that moment I hesitated.

"What you have undertaken involves leaving everything if that is what it takes."

I nodded.

"Believe me, I know more than most people what you are going through right now. Your "lapses," your nocturnal journeys, The Voice, the slightly too well timed coincidences and your peeks into the ethereal level. But what would you say if I told you that all this is nothing compared to what you may expect?"

It is hard to explain, but somehow I felt relieved that she finally opened the floodgates. Although it was quite frightening on one level, at another it seemed like only the natural continuation of the journey I was on. Her words did not take me by surprise. I felt that I could say yes. Also with this little part of me still feeling insecure. Perhaps it was simply the seriousness of the moment creating this feeling.

"Are you ready to surrender to what is coming? Are you ready to let yourself be surged by energies, which might kill you if you are not well prepared? Can you say that you are ready with all your heart? Look at me and you'll see someone who has experienced more than one transformation. I lost my sight, my hearing and the use of my limbs for a week a few years after my initiation at Montségur. I was lost in the deepest darkness, shut off from the world and other people. If anything may be called *the dark night of the soul*, I assure you, that this was it. This was not for beginners. I simply dissolved and was put together again. You cannot explain something like that. But would you be able to say yes to that?"

A new kind of attention showed itself. Her story had awakened something in me. It was a totally different being sitting opposite me than the Sylvia who moments ago had been pouring coffee and taught me about yet another step on my road. This was a one hundred and eighty degree change. This was the naked existence talking. She once more got up with difficulty and went into the next room. This time it didn't take long before she was sitting opposite me again.

"I'm going to give you this picture in order to remind you of what is coming." She handed me an old picture from the sixties. A woman with eyes looking as if they would be able to see through anything, sitting in a contemporary setting.

There was something totally surreal about this picture. Something sinister. The woman was clearly in a state of mind where everything which may be contained in a human being, everything light and everything dark, is on its way to the surface. It was a being who was not only human but also something else which couldn't be explained.

"This was taken one week before I caved in. As you can see, the process was already well on its way when the picture was taken. This is what a person looks like when the self is leaving them. What you see in these eyes is the same process as Yeshua went through in Gethsemane. It is the quintessence of "Thy will be done."

She leaned back in her chair but without taking her eyes off me.

I was staring intensely at the picture but couldn't recognise her. They were really two different people.

"What other options do I have?"

"Well, that is a good question. That's also what I said. When you are exactly at this point you have no choice. You think you do, but in reality you don't. Because you know very well what a "no" would mean. Knowing that, you can only say yes. On the other hand, I understand very well when someone is signing off. There are people doing that each minute of every day all year round."

"What is going to happen?"

"You are going to be taught in a way which is quite different from the teaching you have had until now. It will take you much further away from normal reality. It will be more difficult for you to relate to your everyday life and its activities. But it is a challenge to do just that."

Our meeting was about to end.

"But there is so much I would like to talk to you about. When can we meet again?"

"Remember what I told you. We are in contact telepathically. If you can let go of the little control-freak, your intellectual self, and I believe you are on the way to doing just that, then leave the rest to God. Faith, faith, faith, and then more than anything else, patience."

"Can't you give me just a single clue?"

She hesitated. Then she whispered:

"The Queen of Sheba."

"The Queen of Sheba? Give me just one more clue."

She laughed heartily. Then she became serious again:

"Hm. All right, I'll tell you this time. But it may have far-reaching and powerful consequences because it doesn't just call for a little, it calls for *everything* in order to obtain this piece of knowledge. You have asked me and the answer is, *Venus."*

We said our goodbyes in the hallway. I kissed her on the cheek. The crystal above her head radiated with a golden light like a crown of live fire. In the eternity of the blue in her eyes I saw her unconditional love and acceptance radiating out towards me, and I felt how it found its way into every cell of my body cleaning all my energy field.

"Hurry up," she said as I stepped out of her door, "I know you can do it."

She waved at me from the balcony. I waved back.

PART II

SHEKHINAH

8

Dear reader, I ask not for your patience nor your understanding. I cannot take responsibility for you. If you haven't put the book aside by now perhaps it is time to do so now. It is your choice.

What I'm going to tell you is really a pipe dream in so far as there are no words, which can describe it. And why make the attempt, you may well ask?

Because it was a task assigned to me.

What I'm going to tell you may seem confused, however, confusion is not the purpose.

Seen from our small hiding place there isn't much time. From the point of view of Heaven there is only eternity. This is the paradox of man.

The written word may seem dull. And although words may open something in us, something which gives us hope of other options, the scope of them is still limited.

Are we prepared to put aside all our regular interpretations of everything? Are we at all able to imagine an endless space in which our ideas and our measures are too small and where they do not fit in? Are we able to imagine a reality where we do not define ourselves in dualistic terms?

A person might be what we normally call clever, intelligent, well, even a genius, however, totally confused when faced with such a reality. What do we understand by the concept of "serving God?" We do not know anything. We are not capable of understanding anything at all.

The word "God" makes us clam up, and after that we do not hear anything.

When we leave language as we know it and let ourselves be dissolved by the concept "To know and to serve God," it then takes something else and something more than a learning ability and intelligence.

Even the agile intellect does not understand anything when its well-known instruments of navigation are removed from it. Instead, it immediately takes hold of the first available prejudice. The first prerequisite for approaching endlessness is the understanding that we do not understand anything. No judgement. No preconceived ideas. No damnation. No opposites.

Where are we then?

Who are we then?

I am not black because you are white. I am not happy because you are sad. I am not violent because you are a pacifist. I am not a social democrat because you are a conservative. I am not spiritual because you are not. I am not a Hindu because you are a Christian, not a Moslem because you are an atheist. I see no far reaching difference between us any more. You are carrying a seed, which is identical to mine. You may have come here from Sirius and I from Aarhus, but we both arrived here together and both of us came from the stars. We are made from the same matter. The Universe is just a small fraction in a much larger equation. The equation has been solved long ago but it is constantly in motion. You see, there were never any opposites. *Opposites are only to be found in the separated mind. And the separated mind is a result of free will which did not have the courage to be free.* Thus the eternal conflict. Man has reserved the right to be doubtful. Then he got frightened. And now, he is paralyzed by fear and caught in his own trap.

Each time we let another carry the shadow we ourselves cannot contain, another dark chapter is added to the cosmic memory. When one of us self-righteously promotes himself and only sees his own version of the truth, yet another limitation and another wound is added to the world. When a whole population is burdened by the shadow of another nation, the effects are always catastrophic. If you cannot contain your shadows and thus your whole being, you are apt to create and to maintain images of enemies. If you deny the so-called dark sides of existence you accumulate even more darkness. This is the challenge that we, the so-called spiritual people, have to face each and every day. Only by integrating our hidden aspects may we transform darkness and be able to see that it is just another side of the light. Any healing of a torn world begins with the acceptance by each one of us of the responsibility for our own mess. This takes courage and insight because you are not often able to change anything if you do not know it.

Man is a higher being. However, we may still learn a lot from the animals. We say: the animals are not as fully developed as we are. That is why we treat them any way we like. The animal within our own being, however, is out of control.

So, Sylvia was right. My life never again became what it once was. The breaking down of the old sum total, which once was christened Lars, began the day when for the first time I dared leave the bewildered mind in the hands of eternity. For a fraction of a second only, later slightly more — but even a little is not to be sneezed at, exactly because the ideas of "little" or "more" have no say in the open field of consciousness. It is only here in this world, in this mental hospital, that we need the little language.

Man and woman are seen as opposites. Man goes out and woman goes in. And still they are created for each other. The out-turned fits into the in-turned. When the two unite all opposites are cancelled out. The need to express oneself in the one is counterbalanced by the need to be quiet in the other.

Will power and the need for knowledge are the prerequisites for the possibility of having a say in the old world. In the new world I only know one single thing, which is that I know nothing.

Is that wisdom?

I don't know.

Sex and religion have for long been irreconcilable elements. When they are put together noise is usually the outcome.

The word *religion* comes from the Latin word *religio* which again comes from *religare, tying together, uniting, gathering.*

Lust is to take something.

Love is to give something.

What is the problem?

That we cannot control lust?

The Church says that Yeshua is the one begotten son. But Yeshua himself said that we are all children of God. Is the Church right and Yeshua wrong?

Does it really matter? Well yes, but only as far as it concerns the question about the maintaining of worldly power in the hands of the Church.

If we are all the children of God, do we need the Church for anything? Well, yes, but only if the Church understands the deeper meaning of the words of Yeshua: the Temple is in the heart.

Where the heart is that is where the Temple and its treasures is!

The Kingdom of God is in you and all around you!

Yeshua loved/loves Mariam Magdal. He often kissed/kisses her on her mouth. How can we know this when the word "mouth" is not to be seen in *The Gospel of Philip* because there is a hole in the manuscript at this place? We know because this is how the initiated greeted each other at the time of Yeshua.

Who was/is Mariam?

I am the first and the last,

I am the honoured one and the damned one,

I am the whore and the holy one.

Are these statements expressions of any kind of opposites?

No, on the contrary, they express the exact identity of the one with the One, and of that which no more *is* the opposite of that *which doesn't exist.* In these three sentences Mariam embraces the universe. She is *whole* and thus *holy.*

Magdal means *the elevated one* or *the one from the temple tower.* The Temple in Jerusalem had three towers. Yeshua had three Marys around him: Mari, Miriam and Mariam. The mother, the sister and the beloved one. They were three and yet they were only one.

According to the gospels, Yeshua cast out seven evil spirits from Mariam but the gospels have forgotten or left out that Mariam also opened seven gates in Yeshua.

On a Babylonian stone tablet the following inscription is to be seen: "In the depth of the sea they are seven. In the light of Heaven they are seven. From the sea (Mari) they are rising from the hidden quietness."

Would this be the two Sophia-aspects that Sylvia was talking about?

What is revealing itself here?

One allegory after the other. And allegories were the language of the initiated ones at the time of Yeshua and Mariam. And some of those who mastered this language were the Therapists at the lake of Mareotis at Alexandria.

There is a room – a secret recess of the soul – the innermost room in every human being where we hide and tend to the most vulnerable aspects of ourselves; where we hide the deepest sorrow and loneliness, where we fall to our knees and cry out in the desert.

This is where I have found Yeshua and Mariam. This is where they live in me. They have always lived there. However, under different names.

Dear Reader! You who are struggling with your own shadows! You who have no meaning in your life! You who feel Yeshua and Mariam so close. And you who do not! Here is a prayer:

Sit, stand or lie down with a straight back.

Feel your breath.

Go into the recesses of your soul. Go to your most intimate room. Place your left hand on the centre of your heart (at the middle of your breastbone).

Place your right hand on top of the left one.

Now, pull light through the palms of your hands, into your heart and out again while you silently say "I am," breathing in and "love," breathing out.

"I am love."

Stay in this vibration, sitting or lying down as long as you can or want to. That is how you get healing hands. Use them lovingly. If you are not using your hands you may use this prayer anywhere and at any time. All day long if you like.

It happened just as Sylvia had predicted. Women with whom I had had some kind of past began turning up in my consulting room and at my talks, knowing or not knowing what was really going on.

Young moslem girls began coming to my consulting room who, independent of each other, had been sent to me by a Sudanese sufi-master living in Denmark, whom I had never heard about. These girls related to the female power and they were very eager to be able to express themselves freely about deep, spiritual subjects, which they could no longer neglect. They were struggling with a sense of modesty which on the one hand was beautiful and pure, but on the other had such a limiting effect on them that I sensed that it had taken great effort to seek my help. It is one thing to visit a male stranger, but a non-Moslem one at that? That must have caused them a great deal of trouble. One of the girls was very psychic without knowing how to apply her ability. She was exceptionally beautiful. Dark with big, black, radiant and almond-shaped eyes that looked right through you. Although she was dark you could easily see the dark shadows under her eyes telling a tale about many problems, but also emphasizing the intensity of her eyes. It was during a session with her when she was presenting her situation that I saw the very being of her soul and its years of tribulations. She had neglected herself in one lifetime after the other for the benefit of others. I saw her with the men to whom she had subjected herself as well as all her incarnations as a slave and a servant. I saw the incarnation we had shared in Syria. She had been a servant at a palace belonging to a rich merchant and I a priest at a nearby temple. She was also very beautiful during this incarnation. I managed to arrange her freedom in exchange for her giving herself to me.

I saw her working in a temple in another incarnation, however, not in Babylon, Jerusalem, Heliopolis or Alexandria, but in Ethiopia.

Another image, which kept coming back to me was the boat without oars, with the Black Madonna and the book on board. The waves were beating against the beach, and I could hear the old Sufi-master's sound of *no coast*. I saw the shape of her in the fog, wrapped in a turquoise cloak, standing upright in the boat while it slowly floated into the bay of Marseilles. Her name was Sarah.

Black Sarah. Sarah the Seer!

Another moving encounter was the meeting with Sarangarel, the singing shaman who in this incarnation and apart from being one of the best sound-healers of our day and age also turned out to be a dear friend whom I had known for years. We now got the explanation of the mutual attraction between us, which made it easier to contain the feelings and to accept the fact that in the present incarnation she is happily married with two lovely children. Instead, we may work together with sound and healing.

Other women I met had been my subordinates as nuns in convents in one of my incarnations as a prelate in France while others were connected to various incarnations in Lemuria, Atlantis, China, India, Egypt, Persia, the Middle East, Spain and Germany. Women of all ages whom I have met again and with whom I have been able to form friendly and professional relationships.

For two years, more than thirty women came to me claiming to be incarnations of Mary Magdalene. How could that be? Perhaps it was just a sign of the power of the new, feminine archetype. It simply incarnated into more than one woman. Actually, it even incarnated into men.

A female artist came to me in order to show me a locket she had found at the bottom of a river in Cathar country. On one side, Magdalene's image of a six-pointed star with the heart-cross in the middle as well as alchemical symbols surrounding it. On the other side, the image of a five-pointed star engraved with star-writing and uniting the elements of fire, water, air and ether.

While I was signing books in a bookstore, another female artist gave me some postcards with two of her paintings. One was called "The Female Seer," and the other, "Blue Angel." And this happened just as I was writing this book, Dear Reader, the one you are holding in your hand.

In an old film a journalist is asking the old sage Carl Gustav Jung whether or not he believes in God. There is a long sequence of total silence where the camera dwells on an almost trance-like Jung smoking his pipe. After a length of time which on the TV of today would be considered light-years Jung lifts his head and says:

"No ... I do not believe in God."

Another long break:

"I know!"

One cannot imagine a more definite yes to the great mystery. Here is no insecurity, no dogma, no self-righteousness or self-congratulation. Here is the simple wondering, certainty and emotion.

But the *yes* of Jung, nevertheless, has its limitation. He was not able to lift it out of the field of psychology. He did not think that man was able to understand something metaphysically, only psychologically. Through his depth psychology Jung gave us a language in which to get closer to the archetypal and the subconscious. However, in the field without a language he had to keep silent.

This is where man is today: facing the wall behind which self-development, traditional astrology and depth-psychology do not have any part and are unable to help man further towards transcendence. On the other side of this wall you have to empty the cup of all acquired learning. All the usual concepts and ideas must be dissolved. We are more or less talking about self-liquidation. What is left then is the essence of the centre of the soul, the word, or the sound which was at the beginning and which is forever – the great silence. It is the decisive farewell to any kind of materialism. The personal ego or *the little self* is an extremely cunning and stubborn state of mind, which does not refrain from the use of fast, prayer and charity as a way of maintaining the image of itself as an enlightened and holy person. An ego sitting on a pillow meditating for twenty years is still an ego sitting on a pillow meditating for twenty years. Nothing else. You are not Christian, Moslem, Buddhist, Hindu or spiritually enlightened just because you say that you are.

My situation was constantly changing. However, it always was at any given time, dependent on the degree of availability I could muster towards the powers with which I was in contact. Every day I had to start all over again searching within myself for the causes of my actions. Nothing is easier than falling prey to delusions and becoming inflated. In a weak moment one may easily misunderstand one's own position and be tempted by the dream of being important. It is only human. However, in connection with spirituality, it is the mark of an infantile level. On the other hand, however, I also realized that not being willing to fulfil your role is just as blasphemous as wanting to overplay it. Behind this false modesty often lies a latent megalomania. It was more than merely a question of finding the balance between the principle of "just who do you think you are?" and hubris. This was a totally new, ethical challenge. Perhaps it is necessary to get lost in the ego's maze in order to come face to face with your own self-righteousness, judgements and hypocrisy? You either flee back on to your spiritual, pink cloud forgetting what you have seen, or you open your heart to the cleansing humour, which is able to look at the touching but also totally ridiculous betrayal of the little self.

My need for silence grew concurrently with the growing demand for my talks, consultations and courses. Signs of a kind of inflation became obvious from the fact that the borders between my private space and the public one became more and more invisible. What kind of situation was I getting into here? I sensed that I was getting in over my head. Was I losing my grip on my life or did it all result from the fact that the control of my life was being taken away from me?

Each time I tried to control something I had to recognize that the outcome turned out accordingly: the result of that limitation, which follows its own mind and acts upon it. When, instead, I let go of my worries and stepped into the flow of things, everything happened in the best possible way. It was a question of faith and trusting in certainty. But then I also received all the help I could possibly imagine. And that at all levels.

Concurrent with all this, my sense of dissolution and spaciousness became more intense, interrupted only by the feeling that I was walking a tightrope across an abyss of memories, longing and emotional wounds which didn't really matter any more when seen from a new perspective.

Had I come to my hour of Gethsemane?

"The figure ten symbolizes the consciousness we are approaching," Sylvia said when I spoke to her on the phone about it.

"The figure I is the masculine and 0 the feminine. The figure I is the individual and 0 the dissolution of the individual and the unification with the Father. The move from being to non-being. The figure I is the point at the centre while 0 is the periphery."

I slowly lifted my head and looked around. My pilgrim's cane was still lying outside the circle around me. What happened? I sat up. What span of time had passed? I looked at my watch but it didn't give me a clue since I didn't know at what time I had arrived at the castle. The sun had clouded over and it looked like rain. It had to be late in the afternoon because the cold came creeping out from all the gaps in the old castle walls.

I felt totally present and was vibrating like clear crystal. A faint note vibrated as it came out from the ethereal level:
mmmmmmmmmmmmmmmmmmmmmmmmmmmmmmmmmmmmmm
mmmmmmmmmmmmmmmmmmmmmmmmmmmmmmmmmmmmmm
mmmmmmmmmmmmmmmmmmmmmmmmmmmmmmmmmmmmmmm
I closed my eyes and let it come.

It felt like a string being tightened to its utmost point. As if the soul itself was being tuned. The note vibrated through everything. It would last forever, for the simple reason that it had always been and would never disappear.

This note is the red thread connecting everything, which is alive. It connects the past and the future to the present, friend with enemy, woman with man, man with God. It flows through each and every human being; however, only those who have ears with which to hear may hear it, as well as only those who have eyes with which to see may see.

There was much to transform. A lot of old abuse based on fear. So much that at one time it seemed boundless. There was nothing else to do but step into the circle under construction. The great subject was forgiveness. And it was during this period that I really started to understand the scope and the depth of prayer at a totally new level. All the old symptoms, the dizziness, the pain in my stomach and the back of my neck almost disappeared on that day where, undivided, I could lay a prayer in my heart. This didn't mean that I got free of physical pain, not at all, but the old pattern, which had driven me into a corner again and again didn't exist anymore.

But there was more to come, much more ...

9

The rumour had spread like wild-fire. They talked about it all over Damascus. Among princes and paupers.

They had a new Babylonian prostitute at the Ishtar temple.

Ish-a-tar.

But Ish-a-tar was not like all the others of her trade. She was fair. Fair skin and fair hair. And then she could dance with such ecstasy, they said, that no one had seen anything like it. Rumour had it that in spite of the fact that she was only nineteen years of age she was an expert in her trade. Some were offended. Others felt that she was God sent. In reality, very few had actually seen her dance.

Hashem Ben Nari shook his head. Could this be true? But the news struck a chord deep inside him. However, he waited a few days before sending someone off to find out. In matters like these it was not appropriate for a man of his standing to show too much interest. Although he had plenty of gold to buy all the prostitutes of Syria and Babylon it wouldn't do to challenge the priests.

The messenger was sent off and he couldn't wait to have his

curiosity and his lust satisfied.

But there was no reply.

He waited for two more days. Still no answer. This had never happened before.

On the third day Hashem Ben Nari went to the high priest of the temple, Sadosh.

"You must understand that Ish-a-tar is a free prostitute. She cannot be bought against her own will," Sadosh told Ben Nari " – and I have no power over her. The few men who have made her acquaintance would give everything they own for just ten minutes in the company of this divine creature."

If Ben Nari hadn't been turned on before he certainly was when he heard the words of the high priest.

"I've got to see her," he said, "what is she like?"

Sadosh shook his head.

"How should I know? Even I haven't been allowed to see the performance of Ish-a-tar. I have just seen her shadow. You see, she's got her own bodyguard. But those who have visited her during the two weeks she has been here have more than doubled the income of the temple. So, what can I say?"

Ben Nari felt faint, and the words of Sadosh only made it worse.

"What kind of power is it they ascribe to this woman. How do you know that she isn't the brood of vipers?"

The eyes of Sadosh flashed:

"She is God sent," he growled as if he was manifesting a curse.

"I suppose you mean that she has come *as if* she was sent by God?"

The two men stood facing each other. Sadosh realized that Ben Nari was challenging his credibility. This was a question of honour.

"Very well, I'll arrange for you to meet her and you may see for yourself."

Seven days later Ben Nari finally received an invitation and he immediately sent a messenger with the required down payment. His whole body vibrated in expectation when in the evening he was on his way to the temple. From the entrance hall he was led through several minor rooms where about fifteen men, most of them elderly like Ben Nari himself and also a few young men, were drinking mint-tea while apparently they were waiting to be let into the Holy of Holies where Ish-a-tar was about to dance.

Time seemed to have stopped. Ben Nari sweated profusely and to him the waiting seemed like eternity. Finally, after quite a while, something seemed to happen. A curtain was drawn aside and two temple servants came in. One of them had a sheet of papyrus in his hand, a list from which he began reading in a slow voice:

"Yakob Ben David; Salek Shalem; Melchior Zantor; Yohannan Ben Yokim."

The waiter looked up from his list and let his gaze move around from one to the other of the men gathered here as if he was looking for someone. The men whose names he had just called out were already on their feet eager like young men who enter a brothel for the first time. Ben Nari tried to catch the attention of the temple servant.

"I'm here. Ben Nari. Right here!" he said lifting his hand in the air.

The waiter, however, looked right through him.

"Paltu Nazami!"

Before Ben Nari had time to react the five men mentioned disappeared behind the curtain, which closed behind them, and a guard took up his position in front of it. All happened as if in a dream. What was this? Ben Nari had never experienced anything like it. He was not a man to whom anyone denied anything. His influence and his riches were too great for that. He just sat there, with the ten other disqualified men, feeling like a cuckold, rejected by the loved one.

Some of the men couldn't hide their disappointment. One of them felt so dismayed and cried out in such a loud voice that the temple guards came in and cleared the room. Ben Nari, however, succeeded in hiding in the shadows in a corridor where he stayed until the disturbance had died down. He could hear the enchanting music far away and he tried to imagine Ish-a-tar and her enticing dance, which could drive any man to madness. But he could not imagine the fair skin and hair of this creature. How far would she go? How daring would she be?

He disappeared into his own thoughts and slipped into a hot cave of pumping blood, which made his heart pound away to the limit of bursting. He came to at the sound of a familiar voice:

"What are you doing here?"

It was Sadosh, the high priest.

"I was passed over," Ben Nari answered, as if it were all a nightmare from which he couldn't wake up "I don't understand, I was passed over."

Sadosh looked at him thoughtfully as if he didn't understand it either.

"No one knows the ways of Ish-a-tar. No one can say what she is going to do next. With her, gold is just ordinary trivia. This is not something for which she yearns. She goes by other criteria."

"Which criteria?"

Ben Nari was desperate:

"Tell me what her criteria are and I shall do my utmost to fulfil them."

Sadosh looked at Ben Nari with some compassion and tried to find a solution. After all, Ben Nari was one of the most stable supporters of the temple. He had paid large sums of money over the years. He looked intensely at Ben Nari:

"Do you remember this Yeshua Ben Yoasaph of whom so many stories were told a few years ago? You know the one the Romans crucified with the help of Sanhedrin in Jerusalem?"

Ben Nari nodded. He himself had seen this Yeshua and heard him talk during a business trip to Jerusalem.

"Do you also remember that this Yeshua always had a woman at his side, Mariam, the one they call Magdal?"

Ben Nari nodded, and this time eagerly.

"Of course, I remember her clearly. She was very beautiful. What is it about her?"

"I know that Ish-a-tar has talked quite a lot about her. She wants to meet her. Actually, she talks about nothing else. But no one knows where she is to be found. It looks as if she disappeared completely at the same time as Yeshua."

Sadosh looked at him cunningly:

"I wouldn't be surprised if you could come before Ish-a-tar if you could help her in this matter. You with your many connections, you ought to be able to do something."

Ben Nari looked into empty space. He already saw a solution.

"Yes, I can help her. Right now and right here. Let me see her now. I have the information she wants."

"Are you sure?"

Sadosh looked doubtful. Ben Nari smiled broadly.

"Quite sure."

Two hours later Ben Nari was led through the corridors of the temple to a guarded door. The door opened shortly after and Ben Nari almost floated into a dimly lit room where he could barely see a figure sitting comfortably in a richly decorated easy chair. There was a heavy scent of expensive oils and perfumes with obvious aphrodisiac powers.

"Come forward you of whom they say that you may bring me the only gift I really want."

The voice of the woman was hoarse and broken as if it had been used too much. Ben Nari stood rooted to the spot.

"You may sit down," the woman said.

He took a step forward and sat down on the pillows which the temple servant pushed under him. The voice of Ish-a-tar sounded impatient:

"You wanted to see me. And you have something for me as well.

Ben Nari felt faint. In front of him sat the most beautiful creature he had ever seen. He had never seen a woman with such long limbs and so fair. Her breasts were bare as if this was the most natural thing. Ben Nari couldn't take his eyes from this intriguing sight. She only wore a very thin, transparent garment, which hardly covered her hips and her sex. She wore her hair down and she was warm and sweating after the dance, which she had just finished. She was sitting on her throne with her legs slightly apart looking inquisitively at him.

Ben Nari pulled himself together.

"Quite right, quite right," he stammered with a smirk, "What is it you want to know?"

Ish-a-tar pulled a scarf up around her breasts.

"I understand that you are able to take me to the Seer, Mariam Magdal. That is all I want. What do you say. Can you do that or can't you?"

"Perhaps, it depends ... "

"It depends on what?"

"Whether or not you and I may come to some agreement."

"And what do you want in return?"

"I want to see you dance."

There was a short break. Then she laughed tiredly and threw back her head.

"You are like all the others. Like a sheep running after the shepherdess. By Ishtar, if your member isn't sticking out right now like that of a young man. By Isis, I'm certain there's only one thing on your mind right now."

She was watching him as he sat twisting and turning on the pillows.

"Very well, give me your word and I shall show you something you'll only see once in a lifetime. I don't want to dance for you now, because I'm tired. You are not allowed to lie with me since I do not lie with men anymore. However, I shall grant you something which only very few have seen."

Ben Nari looked both disappointed and excited. He was bewildered, since he didn't know what this creature was planning for him."

"I give you my word. If what you are talking about does live up to my expectations, tomorrow morning I shall take you to the brother who knows for certain where you may find Mariam Magdal."

As was the custom, he placed his left hand over his heart while giving her his word. Ish-a-tar laughed at him indulgently.

"So much wealth. Such a great man and yet such a small spirit. Everything in your world is divided into exact portions. Each person you meet is nothing but a weight on your scale, a figure in your accounts. You do not believe in anything or anyone and least of all yourself. That is why your world is so small and that is why you will not understand the scope of the gift I'm about to give you. You only live in the external world. For you, the power of sight is what you see, and the more you look the less you understand. But enough talk."

She looked at him with even more indulgence. But he didn't understand anything. He only thought about her body and what he might expect to see.

"You must promise not to touch me. You may get as close as you like, but don't touch me. Do you promise that?"

He nodded eagerly.

"Give me your word."

Once more he placed his left hand over his heart and gave his word.

She waved him closer and he stepped so close to her that she could smell his heavy, garlic-infected breath.

She then leaned back into her chair while she slowly took off the transparent garment. He got very short-winded as her breasts leaped out towards him and he had to concentrate in order not to touch them. Thousands of secret scents floated towards him from her body and he was not certain that he could keep his promise. He started dribbling when she showed him her firm stomach and her hips. And it got worse when she moved her garment aside to reveal a little of her shaved sex. She held her legs together so that he only saw very little of her crack. She could hear his heart's heavy beating and she could see that he was about to lose his senses. She then opened her legs and lifted her exposed sex towards him. Her labia were red and swollen as if she had just made love. His breathing was now so heavy that she feared he might have a heart attack. But she was determined to keep her part of the bargain and show him what she had promised him. She parted her labia with her fingers and exposed her pearl of love, which was hard and purple.

"This is what I can give you," she whispered.

Her eyes caught his for a moment as if to make sure that he had seen what he was supposed to see. She then put her legs together and wrapped the garment around her. He wanted to protest but she was already on her feet and had called the guard.

"Tomorrow it is your turn to keep your part of the bargain. I'll be ready to leave at dawn."

Ish-a-tar disappeared like a shadow into an adjacent room.

Ben Nari was unable to speak and he hardly noticed that he was taken to the exit of the temple. He hadn't regained his senses as the heavy gate closed behind him.

The small caravan left Damascus the following morning. Ben Nari was silent and morose. In spite of many requests from Ish-a-tar to tell her the name of the brother dressed in white who had served Mariam Magdal, he remained silent. The experience of the previous night had turned everything upside down. He had been given a sight, which no man before him had been allowed to see. But his lust had been met by a strange, gentle and yet dispassionate attitude, which excited him but which he didn't understand. It was as if she had revealed the innermost despairing darkness of his soul with the bare nakedness of her body. As if by her act she wanted to show him how pathetic he was, and that the external world, which was his only focal point was nothing but a poor reflection of the inner world. Not in order to hurt him, but in order to show him that another reality existed. He couldn't say that this is how it was; however, this was what he felt. And in spite of the apparent apathy that this experience had made him feel, lust still burned unabated in his big body.

Ish-a-tar sat behind her veil rocking on her camel in the cool shade of the canvas. She too was silent as she looked into the horizon.

Each time Ben Nari motioned to stop she motioned for them to continue. They got to Jerusalem in the evening of the following day and they immediately rode to the Gate of the Essenes.

They found lodgings at the caravanserai outside of Jerusalem. Neither Ben Nari nor Ish-a-tar would be welcome at the house of the Essenes situated inside the walls.

Ben Nari immediately sent a message to the Brotherhood.

"We'll get an answer tomorrow at the earliest," he said to Ish-a-tar who was sitting at a small fire outside the caravanserai. However, she pretended not to hear him. He was watching this unreal being whose skin radiated as he could only imagine an angel could radiate.

"Goodnight," he said and contemplated for a moment asking her to join him. But he kept his tongue seeing that apparently she was somewhere else.

Her coarse voice suddenly cut through the night:

"If I sleep with you tonight would you tell me the name of the one who can get me closer to that which I am looking for?"

Her question struck him like lightening. But before he could react her voice changed:

"Do you think you would be satisfied with that? I wonder what you would desire after that?"

Ben Nari stood like an animal, which just caught the scent of a hunter and was now looking for an escape route. He didn't answer. Without knowing it he had already been hit.

"No matter how many times I would give my body to you, you would never be able to possess me. You would repeat an act with your genitals as if you were possessed or like a dog mating. Your senses would rejoice for a moment. Then you would want to start all over again, just like you do when you are scratching an open sore that itches and keeps itching as long you are scratching it."

She was aiming directly at him. Her words were aimed at his heart:

"Think about how many whores you have had. Think about how many times you have performed this act, which long ago changed you into a dog. You claim to be a great and important person. Nevertheless, you are nothing but a simple slave driver, more wretched than the lowest of your own servants. You are a slave to your own desires. A slave to your loveless lust."

She was silent for a few moments. Her voice was filled with pity when in a low voice she gave him the coup de gras:

"You are the poorest and loneliest soul in this God forsaken desert."

Tears were rolling down Ben Nari's cheeks. Her words had laid his inveterate heart bare and he stood in front of her, naked and unarmed like a little child. For the first time since they had met Ish-a-tar seemed to be able to see the shadow of a human being in the crying man who in his despair had thrown himself to the ground.

"I shall give you what you want," he sobbed, "the name of the man who may help you is Lamu ... are you happy now?"

He practically shouted the last words as if he might thus obtain absolution from an invisible god. Then he added in a low voice:

"If he isn't in Jerusalem the Brothers can tell you where you may find him."

Ish-a-tar got up. She moved towards the kneeling man like a gazelle. He lay there with his eyes closed. She placed a hand on his forehead:

"Blessed be you, Ben Nari. Be you blessed among sinners. May the Power have mercy on you."

Then she disappeared into the night.

The scent of incense and newly baked bread as well as the sound of bells and the shouting of shepherds filled the narrow streets as the sun sent its first rays across the roofs of Jerusalem. Ish-a-tar was standing in a passage outside the house of the Essenes waiting for a sign as the door finally opened like a miracle. A young Brother dressed in white appeared carrying a jar of oil. When he spotted Ish-a-tar he quickly crossed himself. Standing there, pale and transparent, she looked most of all like a ghost from another world.

"Who are you and what are you doing here," he said trying to regain his composure.

For a moment she considered the idea of giving another name than her own but came to the conclusion that it wouldn't make any difference to the Brother dressed in white.

"I am Ish-a-tar," she said in an almost inaudible voice, "– I'm looking for a Brother by the name of Lamu."

The man dressed in white looked at her questioningly. In a split second Ish-a-tar thought she noticed a slight vibration at the mouth of the Brother dressed in white and took this to mean that he knew the person in question. Apparently, however, he had no intention of helping her.

"Be gone, you brood of Satan!" he said harshly and tried to kick her however, he only managed to kick some sand into the air. Then a deep, soft voice was heard from the forecourt of the house:

"Why all the commotion?"

An elderly Brother appeared in the doorway. When the younger

Brother began explaining, the older one put his finger to his lips and shushed at him.

"Go in peace Brother, you have chores to do. But remember: Do not welcome a new day with your anger."

He turned to Ish-a-tar and said:

"What can I do for you my child?"

The kindness of this man embraced her the way she had never been embraced by any man. He did not want anything from her. He didn't want any quid pro quo for his helpfulness. She slowly relaxed and surrendered to this person who no doubt only wanted the best for her.

"I'm looking for a Brother called Lamu," she said.

The man smiled.

"They say that he may lead me to the holy Mariam Magdal."

The elderly brother's smile disappeared and he became serious. He seemed to look for a suitable answer for this young woman. But Ish-a-tar already knew that she was on the right track. And he knew that she was aware of that.

"What makes you think that this Mariam Magdal is holy?"

"But isn't she?"

Ish-a-tar didn't understand why he tried to dodge the question since it was obvious that he knew. Then it struck her that perhaps he knew her but didn't consider her to be holy. He didn't answer her question. Instead he said:

"What makes you think that you may find Lamu here?"

"But isn't he a Brother?"

"Yes, but not here with us. He was brought up by the Brothers at Mount Carmel but he belongs to the Nazarene Brotherhood now. You must go to their house in the Syrian quarter and ask for him there. Tell them that you were sent by Yohannan the Essene. This will make it easier for you. But you ought to be more careful. Your beauty may lead even the most dedicated Brother astray and cause many problems. Go in peace."

The smile was back on his face as he turned around and closed the door behind him.

The pain was excruciating when the rock hit Ish-a-tar on the shoulder.

"It is the white whore from Babylon!" a shrill voice shouted.

She looked around in bewilderment and saw a drunken man at a spice stand pointing at her with an accusing finger. Before anyone had time to react she pulled the shawl around her shoulders and let herself be swallowed up by the crowd and disappeared into the bazar. She tried to make herself invisible creeping along the walls but it was as if a devilish power had thrown its revealing light on her.

"It is the white whore!" another voice shouted. But she didn't turn around to see who it was.

"The white whore!"

"Where?"

"There. Right there!"

She was running now. Faster and faster. A rock missed its target and hit the wall behind her, bouncing back in the direction of the one who had thrown it. She now heard someone running behind her. Her breath was out of control and the blood was pumping around in her body. She gave up holding on to her shawl and let it slip to the ground.

"Look, the whore is already getting ready!" Someone shouted.

The cacophony of voices got closer. She turned a corner and ran through a dark and empty passage. Thoughts were whirling around in her head. Right or left?

No time to waste. She chose the passage to the left. Too late she saw that it was a cul-de-sac. She was like an animal forced into a corner.

"There she is!"

"She is right here!"

She pressed herself against the wall in a desperate, last attempt to disappear into the darkness. But it was too late. She closed her eyes as she felt strange hands all over her body.

10

They pulled her through the passageways and into one of the squares in the Syrian Quarter. Around her the men were gathering rocks for a quick execution. Ish-a-tar saw everything through a veiled, unreal haze. Then she was lifted up, up – and up above the square from where she could see the men beginning to throw rocks at a huddled figure in the middle of the square below her. She was lifted up above the roofs of Jerusalem, higher and higher, until she could see a large part of the landscape. Up among the clouds where she floated – happy and free while the the sound of fire rushed through her ethereal being:

"Forgive them, for they do not know what they are doing. Forgive them, for they do not know what they are doing."

But what was it she was supposed to forgive? She did not feel that there was anything to forgive. On the contrary, they had just freed her from slavery. They had taken a yoke off her shoulders, which she could not explain at all. She was about to let go of the last thought about the insanity going on below her when the sound of another being made the stream flowing through her change its direction:

"Your time has not come yet. You have not yet done what you came to do."

A radiating being appeared:

"Here is the power which once you were too proud to accept but which is rightfully yours. You must take the responsibility upon you and use it wisely."

A blue light floated down and united with her ethereal being. Then she was pulled back at an enormous speed, down into the figure in the square in the Syrian quarter where the men were quenching their lecherous feelings and their blood thirst.

The moment Ish-a-tar was back in her body the rocks fell to the ground like wounded birds shot in mid-air. The men stared with disbelief at the white whore who miraculously now stood in front of them, partly naked and with blood running from the wounds the rocks had torn. But she was surrounded by a light so powerful that they were forced back.

A tall man in a white coat stepped into the square and stood next to Ish-a-tar.

She was still in a dream like state of mind. He took her by the arm and led her away from the square, through the passage-ways and towards the eastern gate. They seemed to float along.

"Who are you?" she asked when they found themselves safely in a small, closed courtyard in front of a tall, narrow house.

He didn't answer but pushed her into the arms of a woman standing in the doorway who looked about the same age as Ish-a-tar:

"Take care of this woman. Dress her wounds and give her water from the holy well. Find her a place with the women where she may rest."

He then said to Ish-a-tar:

"Tomorrow we'll talk."

He began walking back towards the exit. He then turned around and smiled:

"My name is Lamu. Welcome to the house of the Nazarenes."

Then he stepped out into the light.

Ish-a-tar woke up at the sound of voices chanting a hymn, which seemed strangely familiar. She wanted to get up from the cot but was immediately stopped by a hand gently pushing her back. She hadn't noticed the sister who had taken care of her before and who was now sitting at her bed. Ish-a-tar uttered a protest:

"I must speak to Brother Lamu. It is my only chance."

The woman shook her head as if she already knew about Ish-a-tar's willpower.

"Hush. You must rest. We have given you a herbal mixture which demands that you stay calm and quiet. Brother Lamu doesn't return till this evening so you might as well rest."

Ish-a-tar realized that the sister was right, she closed her eyes and let go.

When she opened her eyes again she had no sense of how much time had passed, but she felt good and rested.

"Brother Lamu is waiting for you in the library."

The sister helped her out of bed and supported her until she found her balance. She then gave the stranger a cup with holy water.

Ish-a-tar was shown into a big room where the only source of light was two oil lamps on a large table where Lamu sat reading a scroll.

"Well, you have finally returned from the dead," he said as Ish-a-tar stepped into the room. He looked her up and down as if she was a surprise to him. However, there was no judgement in his look the way she was used to when other men looked at her.

Instead, she was looking at him with the same kind of interest, as if she couldn't believe that this was the man who had been so close to the holy Mariam.

"Where can I find Sister Mariam?" She blurted out.

Lamu smiled.

"You are in a hurry. What do you want from her?"

"I thought that would be obvious considering the fact that you know her and also know all about the wonderful things she is doing. Perhaps it isn't true what they are saying about her?"

"But what do they say about her?"

"That she is a great Prophet who raises the dead and initiates people into eternal life."

Lamu sat staring into the distance at Ish-a-tar's words. Then he looked once more at the woman in front of him. He had asked other people about her and knew of her background. But it was not a prostitute he saw in the semi darkness but a seeker, naked in more than one sense. There was a radiance around her which he had only seen once before. She reminded him of the first time he had seen Sister Mariam, when he had been sent off to accompany her from the Therapists in Alexandria.

"Sister Mariam is far away," he said in order to gain some time.

"Wherever she is, I'm ready to go there."

Lamu couldn't hold back his laughter any longer. Her eagerness was so appealing to him that he couldn't help being moved by it.

"What are you laughing at?" she asked feeling offended, believing that he was deliberately making fun of her.

He pulled himself together:

"It is not you but your stubbornness and eagerness I'm laughing at. There is no doubt that you mean what you say. Unfortunately, your wish is not that easy to fulfil. Apart from the fact that Sister Mariam is living in a strange country far away she has also withdrawn from public life. Not everyone may come before her."

"I am not everyone," Ish-a-tar answered.

"Well no, I can both see and hear that."

They stared at each other as if it was a duel to the death. He was the first to give way.

"All right, I give in. On one condition, however."

She stared at him coldly. She had heard this sentence so often that it immediately made her push her hips forward in a certain way indicating that the condition mentioned was of a particular kind.

"Tell me. I'm ready!" she said in a seductive tone of voice.

He looked at her with a surprised look on his face and then made a dismissive gesture with his hand.

"No, no, not that."

He got up from the table and went over to her. She didn't turn away when he placed his hands on her shoulders. She immediately felt the change caused by his being. It was in all his movements. In the sound of his words. There was no sensible explanation for it. It was just the way it was.

"If you really want to meet Sister Mariam you must let go of the old world."

He wanted to say more than this, but, while he stood face to face with this strange woman and looked deep into her eyes, he saw the shadow of another being totally free and unblemished, and at that moment he was seized by an inexplicable urge to embrace her. He also realized that any kind of moral preaching would be blasphemy regarding this soul which in one sense stood naked in front of him but which had been so close to re-entering the body of the prostitute. He could see both the prostitute and the pure soul. This was what made him uneasy. Before he was able to collect his thoughts, something in him made up his mind for him. It was his longing that spoke. It was his need once more to see the holy sister and, perhaps, his longing for that unknown place within himself, all of which was centred in the prostitute who was freedom itself standing right there in front of him.

"I shall go with you and show you the way," he said quietly. "However, first we must go to Alexandria in order to make the necessary preparations."

She took hold of his hand even before he had stopped talking and pressed it against her mouth kissing it. Her action made him perplexed and he lost his composure.

"It is written," he said, "it is written."

＊

I was packing my suitcase in order to go to Montségur on the quest on which Sylvia had sent me when the phone rang. I considered letting it ring but for some reason or other I decided against it and responded. Call it destiny or whatever. It doesn't make any difference.

"Hello," I said into the receiver and was met by an indefinable mixture of white noise and a mysteriously sparkling and endless universe.

"Hello!" I practically yelled. It was a call from another reality. I stood for a long time trying to sense what this both distant and very close consciousness tried to communicate to me. No such luck. Either because I was unable to understand that specific "language," or because it was a matter of two different frequencies.

To my own great surprise I heard myself saying, "No matter who you are or where you are, – I'm on my way." Instead of trying to shout my way through, I tried to listen and adjust my own voice to the pitch of the unknown one. Apparently, my efforts made a difference. The strange, white noise continued but the voice went silent which gave me the impression that someone was listening at the other end. After about half a minute or maybe a full minute the voice was activated once more. It now moved on to another pitch with a different, rhythmic stress pattern and I realized that contact had been established. However, no matter how much I tried, I didn't succeed in getting any meaning out of the sounds. Not until the voice gave up trying to "speak" and began "singing" did I give up trying to find an intellectual explanation for this phenomenon. Instead, I now opened up to the voice which then split up into several voices participating in a song which grew from a drone in a medium pitch, followed by seconds and augmented fourths and fifths in inexplicable riffs which would be heard by normal ears as dissonance. It continued like this for a few minutes. The sound was so disturbing that I had to hold the receiver away from my ear. When the voices joined in a series of pure fifths I was again able to put the receiver close to my ear. But suddenly and without warning the connection was cut and I only got the usual beep-beep-beep sound you hear when someone is hanging up on you.

Here I was with my limited faculties and perception not knowing what to make of this experience. This was something new. In spite of all my nocturnal escapades into the astral sphere as well as my growing penetration into the ethereal one, this was totally new to me.

I boarded the train in Aarhus late in the afternoon and got out again at the railway station at Foix on the following day. I had made this journey so often that by now I knew it better than the personnel at the DSB Travel Agency and the changing crew on the train.

There was a drizzle but the weather was warm when I got out

on the platform in the town of Esclarmonde and walked to the car rental at the outskirts of the town.

Foix is in itself a fairy tale. Above the town the castle looms where Esclarmonde lived until she became dedicated to the plight of the Cathars. The situation of the town, on the river, surrounded by mountains, limits its potential for external growth. Nevertheless it is a little power centre for the area that for many years was one of the poorest in France and is still considered by many to belong to the stagnant periphery. Instead, the population has developed another kind of inner power. It lies hidden in the old Cathar families and the mysterious spirit that rests on this Shangri-La. Then again, there is quite a different aura around the people of the Pyrenees than around most other people. The ethereal Akasha is much more open and accessible to me here in this area than the ethereal aura is around the descendants of the Cathars, which is much more closed. Perhaps because of the terrible destiny which befell them during the Inquisition?

I signed the lease and threw my bags on to the rear seat of the Renault Clio I had rented. Shortly after I was on my way to Les Contes along roads I knew as well as the back of my hand. As taught by the Seer, who always carried a small supply of wine, gin and canned beer as presents for hosts, which were meant to break the ice and renew old friendships, I bought a supply at the local supermarket. A tradition which I did not quite understand but which I soon learned to appreciate. These presents were simple expressions of respect and gratitude, which were direct without causing any kind of embarrassment.

I passed the Montségur Mountain half an hour later and drove through the four hairpin turns down to the village where I parked outside number nineteen, the, by now, legendary house where the Seer and I had stayed so often that I dare to call it my second home. I knocked on the door at the end of the house leading into René's workshop. René Briol is the owner of the house and a descendant of an old Cathar family. This is not only visible in his features but is also expressed in his views, the Cathar symbols in the house and the subjects that he paints.

"Ah, monsieur Lars, bonsoir!" he said as I stepped into his small studio. I had brought two cans of beer.

While we drank to each other and talked about this and that, he showed me his latest paintings. René paints in a very intuitive style, obtaining an almost surrealistic effect through his use of manneristic shadows. The subject invariably is the same, the mountain and the village.

Paintings of the mountain and the village, spring, summer, autumn and winter. All kinds of perspectives. Close up and far away. From above and from below. However, always from the outside. Never from the inside. At least this was not the feeling I got looking at them.

"You cannot paint the innermost heart of Montségur," he always said.

And I knew he was right. Any description of the holy mountain, be it in pictures or in words, will always be exactly that, pictures and words.

When we had talked for a while I plucked up enough courage to put the question to him, which I had come to ask:

"Do you know how to find the secret cave in the mountain?"

He was replacing a painting, which he had just been showing to me and looked as if he was looking for another one to show me. He didn't answer and since I took it to mean that he hadn't heard my question I therefore repeated it. Another length of time without any reaction. Then he got up and showed me yet another small painting of the village covered in snow.

"René!"

"Oui." he answered and deliberately looked more absent-minded than usual.

"Do you know anything about the secret cave which some people claim is to be found in the mountain?"

He laughed awkwardly and then shook his head:

"Well, it's the usual nonsense. You know, for some people reality isn't exciting enough and they therefore invent these kinds of figments of the mind. If you repeat such a tale often enough it soon finds its way into travel guides to the Pyrenees and before you know it, it is a historical fact."

"Come on, René, my information comes from a reliable source."

"That's what I'm saying. When you repeat it often enough there is no limit to the reliability of the sources and how far they'll go in order to make reality and fairy tales meet. I have lived here all my life. I know that this mountain is endless, but I promise you, if anyone knows this mountain it is me and I have never, repeat *never*, seen the shadow of an internal cave or heard about anyone who has. Sorry."

He placed the winter landscape in front of me like a trump to end the game.

We drank up and while René continued his presentation of his paintings I was thinking that maybe it was Sylvia who had got it all wrong. After all, it was years ago that her experiences had taken place here. Of course, it was also possible that René didn't want to take me into his confidence. I knew that these old Cathars could be quite reticent about the secrets in which the area is so rich.

I departed from René and took a stroll in the village in order to investigate further into the matter. At the hotel Costes, Gilbert and Maurisette were preparing supper. Their daughter was helping. The idea was that she and her husband were supposed to take over the hotel during the following year. The husband, Jean-Luc, also had a café in an alley across from the hotel and rumour had it that he was an expert on all the myths and legends of Montségur.

After having met Gilbert and Maurisette I found Jean-Luc in the café. I only knew him superficially but he was aware that I knew his parents-in-law quite well and that I had mentioned them in *The Seer*. I ordered a cappuccino and sat down at a table on the terrace from where I had the most wonderful view over the valley. When he brought me my coffee I decided to phrase my question differently:

"How do I find the secret cave in the Montségur Mountain?"

I noticed the small twitch in him as he placed the cup in front of me. But the question did not seem to shake him.

"You don't" he said with a big smile, "for the simple reason that it doesn't exist."

I also smiled. Either the story about the secret cave in the mountain was one big joke or it wasn't something about which they wanted to inform strangers.

"Aha," I said, indicating that I had no intention of following up on this question.

I didn't want him to think that I was desperate. Apparently this was the right tactic since he continued where he had stopped:

"Many adventurers have searched for the Holy Grail which, according to one of the many legends of the Grail, is supposed to rest in the mountain. Well, some even claim that they have been there. The marvellous reports tell about a gigantic hall and a maze of passages where you may walk for hours and eventually lose your life if you go astray. Some even say that they have seen the Grail in there."

He laughed mockingly and had an expression on his face that clearly showed his contempt for this kind of adventurer.

"Do you also believe in this kind of fairy tale?" he asked me.

I shook my head.

"No, I'm only interested in the myths, that's all. "

He nodded and looked as if he had regained his confidence in me.

"Do you want more coffee," he asked pointing to the cup, which I had just emptied.

"No, thanks, I better get on my way. Thank you."

I paid and got up, but then I thought about something:

"How come the church in the village is always locked?"

"Oh, the church. Religion is a sensitive subject here. Remember that old Cathars and former inquisitors live next to each other in the village, actually, some of them even under the same roof. If you want to go to Mass you have to go to Bélesta."

"Is it possible to borrow the key if I would like to see the church?"

"Try the tourist office." He said, wiping the table from which I had just got up.

They didn't know anything about a cave at the tourist office but I could probably get the key at the mayor's office.

When, shortly after, I knocked on the door to the mayor's office I got the same message. No cave, and the key was probably kept at the museum.

It was turning into a farce. A farce, which was enhanced when shortly after the person in charge of the museum sent me on to the tourist office. Before that he had given my dreams of a cave in the Montségur Mountain the final coup de gras:

"It's a ridiculous myth, invented by dreamers!"

It is very strange. But the more assurances and proof you get that something is impossible, the more you want to find it. Perhaps this is what I felt and perhaps I felt this way because I had the feeling that there was more to this story than pure imagination. Those people spoke against their better judgement. Or did they?

I backed out of the parking lot, turned around and drove slowly down the hill towards the valley. At the bottom I noticed a figure walking up the hill. A couple came from a side street and began walking in the same direction.

I passed the lonely wanderer shortly after. It was a young, dark haired woman who seemed familiar. I slowed down and looked in my rear view mirror. She was tall and wore a flowered dress. Then it struck me that I had really seen this woman before. Wasn't it Marie Périllos, the young waitress from Narbonne I had met the last time I was here and with whom I had the agreement to meet again?

I put the brakes on and put it in reverse. The gearbox complained loudly because I got too eager. I backed all the way up the hill but when I got to the top the woman had gone. I got out of the car to look for her. But she had disappeared.

What was going on?

"Do not lose yourself in the external journey of the Grail."

Those were the words of Sylvia. On the other hand, she was the one that sent me off on this quest. Was it all an illusion or was this the way Sylvia was teaching me? Letting me run around in circles in the old myths, which had nothing to do with form or any kind of reality? Perhaps the cave didn't exist at all. Perhaps it was Sylvia's way of telling me that the cave was within me and not in a mountain that some obscure myths happened to have named "The Mountain of the Grail?"

And what about the girl? Could I still trust my own senses? I was fed up with everything. Astral journeys, ethereal sights and voices speaking, God knows from where? Perhaps from my own strained imagination, or perhaps it was all just another construction or a colourful compensation for a normality which was both grey, sad and hopeless?

I got into the car and bowled along down the hill toward Les Contes.

Mar and Leny were sitting on the bench outside as I drove up in front of the beautiful, old building. They were sitting with their common, golden aura hovering around them and confirming their unity. I was again shown to the room of "St. Frances of Assisi," which apparently was "my room." The guests from last time had been exchanged for new ones. Roderick and his mother had also left.

I sat next to Mar at suppertime. I hadn't really planned to waste any more time on this obscure cave but something or other had other ideas. I heard my own voice, tired and dispassionate asking:

"I realize that this is probably a foolish question but do you know anything about a hidden cave inside the Montségur Mountain?"

I was lucky that I was already sitting down because his answer would otherwise have made me do it since it took me totally by surprise:

"Yes, I do."

II

Lamu and Ish-a-tar followed the route along the coast through Gaza, Raphia, Ostracine, Pelusium and further through the Nile delta to Alexandria. They rode directly to the society of the Therapists at Lake Mareotis situated some distance from the town. The news of their arrival had gone before them and they were met by a small group of women dressed in white. For the first time since they had left Jerusalem Lamu saw a smile in the eyes of Ish-a-tar. The closed, worried look had disappeared.

"How fair everything is here," she said to Lamu as if he already knew what she was talking about.

He nodded. He had also come home.

They were taken to the water tank where they washed the dust away. Then they got something to eat in the big common hall in the middle of a cluster of houses which made up this unique society where men and women worked together for the glory of God.

"What is going to happen here? Is Sister Mariam here?" Ish-a-tar asked while they were eating.

"We are here to prepare ourselves. This is the society of the Therapists where sister Mariam was initiated. When we have received the necessary education we shall continue our journey and hopefully get the opportunity to meet Sister Mariam."

They continued to eat in silence, then he said:

"Sister Mariam's personal teacher still lives here. She is a very holy woman."

"What is her name? Take me to her at once!"

Ish-a-tar put her bread down and was about to stand up when a woman's voice interrupted her:

"Mariam Salome, my child. Do not trouble yourself. I'm right here."

The voice was like balm on their hearts. A healing balm, which removed every shadow but at the same time awakened everything which had been lying about unused for far too long.

"Here, I am called by my initiation name, Salome."

Although the woman was getting old she was still beautiful with a straight and dignified bearing. She moved gracefully and almost hovered across the floor as she stepped into the room.

Ish-a-tar got to her feet and Lamu followed her example. Lamu folded his hands in front of his chest and bowed:

"I greet you, holy one." he said.

"Isn't this Lamu, the young man who was sent here long ago in order to take Sister Mariam to the Celestial City?"

She also folded her hands and greeted him. Lamu nodded his assent. He was too moved to speak. The whole scene also seemed to move Ish-a-tar. She was, if anything, even more pale than usual, but it simply made her still more strangelooking and radiant.

"And you must be Ish-a-tar," Salome said, "I have heard much about you. I'm glad you decided to come. But rest now. Tomorrow is another day and we shall start your education."

She greeted them once more.

"May peace be with you."

Then she was gone.

After the meal they were taken to the guest-house where they were each given their own room.

"Tomorrow we part," Lamu said, "you'll be staying with your teacher and I with mine. We'll meet every seven days when men and women meet at the forum. Sleep well, I hope you'll get what you want."

Ish-a-tar looked at him. For the first time she saw his innermost being. Perhaps because she was so moved that she didn't know what was up or down.

"Sister Salome is also called Mariam. I noticed that several of the women who received us are also called by that name. What does it mean?"

"You see, when you are initiated here you are given your true name. Until then, you have lived with the name you received at birth but this is only your worldly name. After the initiation you are given your heavenly name. The name Mariam signifies that the one bearing it has been accepted into the society of the Therapists. "Mari" means sea. Mariam means the sea from which the spirit of the peace of God has risen. After her final initiation, Sister Mariam got the name Magdal, "The Exalted One." Sister Salome is also called Mariam. This way the initiated ones know that one bears the same rank as the others with this name. Her heavenly initiation name is Salome, which means "The Perfect One." She is the daughter of God, the soul, dressed in sound, unity, love and peace."

"Thank you," Ish-a-tar said quietly, "thank you for bringing me here."

He smiled. He was beginning to realize that something in her being had touched his heart.

"Goodnight."

✻

"Yes," Mar said, "I know the cave very well. I was there about five years ago with a professional guide and two friends of mine."

"But are you certain that it was inside the Montségur Mountain itself?" I asked holding my breath. My tiredness had gone completely.

"Absolutely. But it is very difficult to get there. In order to get there, among other things, you must climb a very steep cliff wall. The cave itself is so well hidden that I wouldn't be able to find it again. The local people who know its whereabouts cover the entrance so that it is practically impossible to find."

"You were inside it?"

"Of course."

"What did you see?"

"Not that much. You first enter an antechamber. From there on you must crawl four to five metres through a channel, which is not for people suffering from claustrophobia. The channel opens into a large cave from which a very intricate system of passages branches out. We didn't stay for a long time since we didn't bring a proper torch. But it was a very special experience."

"How big is the inner cave?"

"It is hard to say. So big, however, that it wasn't possible for us, with our poor light, to see where it started and where it ended. But from the sound itself we were able to perceive that it has a very high ceiling. The experience, however, made me ill. I felt faint when we got out of the cave and were on our way back. After a few days I went to the doctor and he advised me to get a thorough check-up. However, the doctors couldn't find out what was wrong with me and it stayed with me for about a year when finally it subsided and then disappeared completely."

"What were the symptoms?"

He was contemplating his answer.

"I had difficulty breathing and my whole body ached. I myself was wondering about the cause of it but finally arrived at the conclusion that there must have been some stale air in the narrow channel which, according to the guide book, may be the case in caves where people and animals seldom go. I was the first one to go through it and may have inhaled the stale air which found its way into my blood through the respiratory passage."

I couldn't help thinking that it reminded me of the theories that scientists have come up with in connection with the opening of the Tomb of Tutankhamen in Egypt where quite a few people also became ill. Or it actually *was* a matter of a curse to protect the place from unwelcome visitors. No matter what, Mar's story was good news to me.

"Do you know anyone who could show me the cave?"

"Well yes, I do actually. He is Dutch and has the necessary license allowing him to work as a guide in the mountains for payment. I don't know if he is around at the moment but I'll find out by tomorrow."

It was a long night. Just as had happened on my first visit to Les Contes, I woke up to the sound of a child crying, and once more had to light a candle and say a prayer for the souls which still seemed to be held back by the place and the events which happened here. I lay for a long time and let my thoughts roam. I floated along above desolate and rugged landscapes. Then a voice announced:

"The Mountain of the Grail is the Mount of Olives!"

I let go of my resistance and felt a buoyancy in a smooth upward glide. The words were directed at me and had something to do with my quest.

"But the Mount of Olives is situated in Jerusalem in the Holy Land," I answered, "what has that got to do with the Pyrenees?"

"Jerusalem and the Holy Land will always be where man is able to see that the ethereal openings are wherever the energies are centred."

That was it. Apparently the Voice had nothing more to say and I slowly floated back to my room. I was wide-awake.

The Mount of Olives!

What was it the Voice had tried to tell me?

The Mount of Olives was the place where Yeshua ascended into Heaven. This was where they expected his second coming.

Oil! Mariam anointed Yeshua with oil.

Oil equalled initiation.

I switched on the light and found a map of the area. It was a pure intuition. I didn't know what I was doing and reacted strictly from this intuition.

It was Michelin map "344 Lokal – Aude, Pyrénées-Orientales." I was looking for my pendulum when a glance at the map, which by now was spread out on the bed, made my eyes catch the name *Col de Grail*.

The Mountain of the Grail! I could hardly believe my eyes. I immediately got down on my knees and studied the area more closely.

Then I spotted it.

I looked at the name for a long time. All kinds of doubts went through me, however, another second and all doubt disappeared.

OLBIER!

Apparently, it didn't mean anything in French. It sounded more like German. But I had no doubt that there had to be a connection to the Mount of Olives on which the Voice wanted me to focus. I couldn't find any better explanation to this phenomenon, I can only tell it the way I experienced it.

Olbier is not far from Tarascon. You pass the Church of Notre Dame de Sabart in front of which Mariam and Yeshua stand side by side greeting visitors. Then you continue to Vicdessos. And Olbier is right next to it.

Not much sleep that night. Instead, I meditated and waited for the sun to rise.

✶

They parted the next morning. Ish-a-tar just had time to wave to Lamu and then a woman took her to the house of Salome.

"I'll personally take care of you and your education," Salome said when Ish-a-tar sat in front of her, "and there is no time to waste."

She started learning the same day. Like Mariam before her, Ish-a-tar was taken through the initial lessons, day by day. She was very keen and it didn't take Salome long to find out that Ish-a-tar was made of sterner stuff. Sometimes it struck Salome how much she really resembled Mariam. But there were differences. Sometimes Salome wondered whether or not Ish-a-tar was aware what these differences would mean to her. She was poised to talk to her about it a few times but when she saw the eagerness and enthusiasm with which her student dedicated herself to the work, she postponed it indefinitely.

Ish-a-tar had to go through all the initiating steps preparing her for the real task. They were as follows:

1. Continue to repeat the name of God and become aware of the eternal Being.

2. Give up any kind of egotism and sing the praise of God.

3. Do no harm to others. Do not speak ill of others.

4. Live continuously in awareness of the Divinity in you.

5. Abandon lust, hate and greed. Do not envy the happiness of others.

6. Be true, be compassionate and practise forgiveness.

7. Abandon your doubts. Seek God, know your own true Self and see God in everything.

Ish-a-tar learned about the cycles of women. When their moon time came the women went into seclusion. Not because they were unclean but because they had opportunities during that period which were not possible otherwise.

When her holy period came Ish-a-tar spent seven days in a cave from where she had a view of the Lake of Mareotis. Her only food was drinking water, crushed sesame seeds and ripe figs. She gathered the moon blood in a pan made for the purpose. The blood was later used as a life-giving mixture, which strengthened the earth and made it holy as well as creating ethereal powers around the medicinal herbs in the garden of the brother and sisterhood.

For the first two days the moon woman had to concentrate on and invoke the archangels Uri-El, Micha-El, Gabri-El and Rapha-El.

Pain and other disturbances were, in fact, entrances to the state of mind one wanted. The practised moon woman would have eliminated any kind of unpleasantness and was able, by way of the invocations gradually to create contact to the ethereal field, which was necessary in order to see and hear the messages and visions awaiting her.

"The holy one finds the truth by abandoning delusional lust. She

*lets her thoughts unite with SHM, the holy sound, forming the stream
of life — the word, which is given her by her teacher. For two days she
intones that sound until she and SHM are one. She will receive her
true name in a vision but she does not voice it. Mind and body are
still and the fire of lust is refined until it is finally pure. This is her
true bridal gown. There is one light. It shines in everyone. Honour all
living beings. This is the true marriage vow of the bride. Accept that,
that which man calls "death" is, in truth, the door to the bridal chamber.
"Die" before you die! Forget the past and abandon your dreams about
the future. Become dust and come to Me."*

Ish-a-tar learned that the Therapists worked with metaphors and
allegories and that the more refined the language the more precisely
they would be able to communicate with the Heavenly level. The
sounding and the stressing of the words were important if rapport
was to be achieved. Everything had more than one meaning and all
beings consisted of more than one body, and each of them was in
contact with various levels of the hierarchy of the angels.

The Seraphim, the snake-fire of love, was the first order of angels.
It was under the direction of Micha-El and this angel also played
a leading role in some of the other angel choirs. Micha-El was the
angel in the burning bush who had spoken to Moses in the desert.

Micha-El was the ruler of the fire and the blue, purple flame,
which could be seen reflected on the sky in the star-formation of
Aldebaran or *Oculus Tauri*.

Micha-El was an isogynic angel-like being whose name meant
"One Who is like God." Micha-El had his origin in *Tifferet* on the
Tree of Life. The traits of *Tifferet* are compassion, beauty and divine
strength.

The appellation *"El"* simply meant *"shining or sparkling,"* which
was seen as one of God's qualities. Micha-El thus was an extension
of God Himself, a power running through the spheres, internal as
well as external, when needed and invoked. The traits of Micha-
El were divine inspiration and the power that might overcome any
resistance and barrier. In other traditions they compared Micha-El
with the Greek Hermes, the Egyptian Toth and the Roman Mercury.
When this angel was invoked with a pure heart there was no limit to

what one might do with its help.

The Therapists began their day with prayers. They turned to the East welcoming the sun, their hands and eyes turned heavenward praying that the day might be light and clear and their visions pure and true. The sun was an allegory. It symbolized the divine light behind the physical sun. The morning prayer and ritual was repeated at sunset.

The number seven played a special role for the Therapists. Seven was a holy number. Apart from keeping the seventh day holy they also celebrated the evening of the 49th day, which meant that the 50th day was especially holy.

One morning after Prayers, Salome introduced Ish-a-tar to the secret of numbers:

"Fifty is the most holy of numbers. That is what Pythagoras taught us. Fifty is the most natural of numbers and it represents the power of the right-angled triangle: (3 x 3) + (4 x 4) + (5 x 5) = 50."

Salome paused in order to let her student take it all in. Then she continued:

"Here are the three most holy numbers following fifty. Seven is the basis of any form and any quality. It first and foremost represents purity and virginity."

She paused once more.

"The Pythagoreans called 7 Lucifer's number. However, contrary to the priests of Jerusalem the Pythagoreans realized that Lucifer was the angel who brought the light into the world and gave it an ethereal form. Only the opponents of light do not understand this and thus demonise Lucifer."

She made another rhetorical pause so that Ish-a-tar had time to let the words sink in.

"It is important that you ponder these thoughts until they rest in your being. The statements about these figures have more than one meaning."

This time she paused in order to make way for new lessons:

"Now, listen well. This is a meditation, which does not ask for any questions, only reflection. You see?"

Ish-a-tar nodded.

"Good. Notice carefully what I'm telling you now. It concerns the transcendence of the three holy numbers, 7, 9 and 12."

THE TEACHINGS OF THE HOLY FIGURES

"When 7 becomes one, it is 8 at a higher level. Eight is the number of infinity and of Isis."

It was completely quiet in the room.

"The human body has 9 gates, 2 eyes, 2 ears, 2 nostrils, 1 mouth and 2 exits in the lower region. These 9 gates in the physical body have 9 parallel gates in the heavenly body. $9 + 9 = 18$. $1 + 8 = 9$. When 9 becomes one, it is 10 at a higher level. 1 is man and 0 is the universe. 1 is the masculine, 0 the feminine. 1 is the centre, 0 the periphery."

A long pause.

"The twelfth depth is the Truth from which all truths originate. This is the image of the Source (Father-Mother). This is the mirror of Creation. This is the Source of all aeons. This is *the Monad,* the One who is unknown. The Spotless One in whom all the virtues are. This is the eternal Source the incomprehensible and the unthinkable. The saving principle, *Messiah,* was born from the first thought of God (the Source), which was feminine. The feminine principle brought the son into the world and gave him the birthright of the first-born. She gave him the power over angels and archangels. She gave him twelve qualities to serve him. And she gave him a habit, clothed in which he could achieve everything. In this were all the bodies of the spheres: A body of fire, a body of air, a body of earth and a body of water. A body for each of the angel choirs: The Seraphs, the Cherubs, the Thrones, the Rulers, the Powers, the Authorities, the Princes of Power and the Magnificent Seven."

Salome made a long pause before continuing:

"The figure twelve means: $1 + 2 = 3$ which is the uppermost triad, *Kether,*

Hokhmah and *Binah* at the Tree of Life."

"When 12 becomes one it is 13 at a higher level. Thirteen is the figure of the initiated one. And $1 + 3 = 4$. Four is for the four corners of the world as well as the four elements which in this way are contained in the 13."

Another long pause.

When you add up the three transcendent figures $(8 + 10 + 13)$ you get 31. When 31 becomes one you get 32 at a higher level.

Salome stood up and went to the window and looked out across the lake giving Ish-a-tar time to take the secret of the numbers into her being. Then she returned to the table and picked up a scroll from which she began reading:

"The female dancer is the daughter of light in whom the proud clarity of kings is resting, and the sight of her is wonderful because happiness and beauty radiates from her. Her gown is like the flowers of Spring: a bouquet of seducing scents. And from the crown of her forehead the king is consolidated who nourishes those, who are founded in him, with his divine elixir. Truth is in her head and her feet dance

*with joy only. And her mouth is open and it does her good. Thirty–two
are those who sing her praise."*

Salome looked up from the scroll. Ish-a-tar sat as though
enchanted.

"Remember there are 22 paths in her gown. Twenty two paths
connecting the 10 sapphires on the Tree of Life. And 10 + 22 = 32.
When you add up 3 and 2 you get 5. The feminine power rests in the
pentagon. When 5 becomes one you get 6, which is the sun, and you
get *Tifferet* on the Tree of Life. The Hexagram, the six-pointed star,
symbolizes the melting together of the terrestrial and the celestial,
the masculine and the feminine, the lower and the higher. When 6
becomes one we have returned to 7 which has further transcended to
a totally new level where the cycle may begin all over again, however,
now with far more refined qualities."

Ish-a-tar sat for a long time and contemplated Salome's speech.
After a while she said:

""And her mouth is open and it does her good," what does that
mean?"

Salome looked surprised at Ish-a-tar as if she hadn't expected
such a question from her.

"That is a very relevant question. It tells us that the creative
principle is revealed through the gate in the neck. This is a prerequisite
for receiving visions and passing on prophesies. It all corresponds
with the various sapphires on the Tree of Life. And the powers,
which have to be activated in order to open up into these kingdoms,
are the archangels."

THE TEACHINGS OF THE ARCHANGELS

"Micha-El represents the 6th point on the tree, *Tifferet*; while Uri-El
represents the 7th point, *Netzach*, the eternal; Rapha-El represents
the 8th point, *Hod*, refulgence; and Gabri-El the 9th point, *Yesod*,
the foundation stone."

Salome went silent. Then she laughed and danced around in the
room singing:

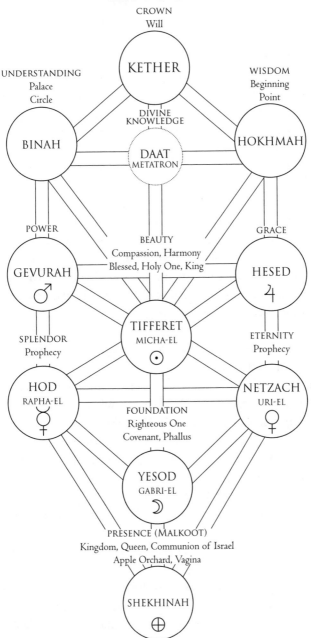

EIN SOF

CROWN
Will

KETHER

UNDERSTANDING
Palace
Circle

WISDOM
Beginning
Point

DIVINE
KNOWLEDGE

BINAH

HOKHMAH

DAAT
METATRON

POWER

GRACE

BEAUTY
Compassion, Harmony
Blessed, Holy One, King

GEVURAH
♂

HESED
♃

SPLENDOR
Prophecy

TIFFERET
MICHA-EL
☉

ETERNITY
Prophecy

HOD
RAPHA-EL
☿

NETZACH
URI-EL
♀

FOUNDATION
Righteous One
Covenant, Phallus

YESOD
GABRI-EL
☽

PRESENCE (MALKOOT)
Kingdom, Queen, Communion of Israel
Apple Orchard, Vagina

SHEKHINAH
⊕

"Everyone must become one with *Shekhinah*. She is the one getting these qualities to the level of the earth and makes sure that they get to the places where they are needed the most."

"*Shekhinah?*"

Ish-a-tar looked somewhat confused. Salome danced in front of her, took her hands and pulled her into the dance:

"Yes, *Shekhinah* is the 10th point, *Malkoot*, on the Tree of Life. This is the point closest to the physical world. This is where you find the "fallen" *Shekhinah*. The wisdom, which voluntarily floated down to the visible world in order to enlighten us and free us from our prison."

They whirled about in Salome's room.

"Don't let your speculations stand in the way of true knowledge – wisdom. Wisdom is the world of *Shekhinah*. However, she has a sister who is known by few people only, because she rarely comes down from the higher worlds and lets herself be known. Her name is secret and may only be pronounced by the one who has the key to the Holy of Holies in her temple."

During the following weeks Salome taught her student about the power of the archangels.

Rapha-El (God has healed) as the name indicates, was the carrier of the healing power of God. The angel was reflected in *Regulus* or *Cor Leonis*. Rapha-El ruled the air and the green flame.

Gabri-El (God is my strength) was the angel of compassion who ruled the waters and the mother-of-pearl-white flame. Gabri-El was reflected in *Fomalhaut*.

Uri-El (the light of God) was the angel of peace who ruled the earth and the golden flame. Uri-El was reflected in *Antares* or *Cor Scorpio*.

Ragu-El (the friend of God) was the angel guarding the other angels.

Remi-El (the mercy of God) is the angel who helped the souls to the resurrection. He is also called "The angel of judgement."

Razi-El (the secret of God) was the angel who guarded over the mysteries.

The achieuing of the Sangreal . (A. Berdsley, 1909)

"You see, Ish-a-tar, these powers are part of you. They live in you as they live in all people. However, only a few people are aware of it, and only a few people know how they relate to these powers. Study the qualities of these powers very closely. Not with your intellect but with your visionary force. 'And her mouth is open and it does her good,' you see? Empty yourself of the thoughts that will always try to keep you within the old limitations until you realize that your thinking does not take you anywhere. Instead, unite with these powers. Make them your servants. This is the only way to serve God."

They walked side by side while Salome took Ish-a-tar to the hill outside the town of the Therapists.

"When you understand all this I shall teach you about the greatest one of them all, the angel waiting for you."

They were looking across the desert as the sun set behind the horizon.

✵

When the sun was rising behind heavy, black clouds I was already dressed and helping Mar in the kitchen.

"Have you heard about the Mountain of the Grail at Olbier?" I asked him while Mar put a bowl with eggs in front of me.

"No, what do you mean? The general opinion is that it is Montségur which is the Mountain of the Grail that the various legends are talking about."

I took the bowl and placed it on a tray together with cheese and butter.

"The town is called Olbier. Do you know it?"

"No. Can you tell me more about it?"

"No, not really," I said and carried the tray into the dining room.

We were having our coffee before the guests came down from their rooms.

"About that," Mar said, "I have talked to the guide who can take you to the hidden cave at Montségur. But not until tomorrow. His name is Bart. I wrote his address down and you yourself must go and make the arrangements with him."

He handed me a slip of paper. I folded it without looking at it.

I packed a light bag after breakfast and took off in order to find the Mountain of the Grail at Olbier. It was pouring down. I drove to Tarascon and turned off at Notre Dame de Sabart and drove towards Vicdessos. I was contemplating what might be in store for me when out of the corner of my eye I spotted a human shape standing under the branches of an old oak tree, seeking shelter from the rain. It was not until I had passed this human shape that I realised that I had seen the person before.

Marie Périllos!

The young waitress I had met at "Belo Bar" in Narbonne.

I stepped lightly on the brake and looked in the rear-view mirror where I could see a dark-haired woman in a flowered dress retreating in my field of vision. I then stopped the car completely and looked after her. She looked real all right. But for how long? I slowly rolled backwards towards this woman standing at the roadside waiting with one hand resting challengingly on her hip.

12

The air was still and Lake Mareotis was bathed in a red light from the setting sun. It was the evening of the forty-ninth day, the holy evening, and the beginning of the fiftieth day where the brothers and sisters and the novices gathered in the big common room.

The women went in first and were seated to the right. A priestess lit the incense in the large thuribles at each side of the altar, then got up and began chanting:

"Holy, holy, holy – *Marmariotha* – come, come, come out of the four winds of the Kingdom, rise from the four corners of the world, come *Rukha d'koodsha*, come Holy Spirit, You who are in the deep as on high, to the right and to the left, You who ride the chariot of the breath of God. Unite the chaos of separation and tie up the dragon and all its shapes. Come *Shekhinah*, and protect your beings of light, whose gates are open and habitations are many."

Shortly after they began to sing:

AAAAAAAEEEEEEEEIIIIIIIIOOOOOOOO UUUUUUU OOOOOOO IIIIIIIEEEEEEEEAAAAAAA.

While the women were singing the men stepped into the procession and took their positions to the left.

It disturbed Ish-a-tar that she felt a stab of longing in her heart at the sight of Lamu. A priest placed himself in front of the men. The women kept singing, in subdued voices, however, in order to let the chanting voice of the priest be heard:

"Let Micha-El stand to my right, Gabri-El to my left, let Uri-El's trumpet sound in my mind, let Rapha-El rest in my heart, let Ragu-El crown my head, let Asu-El give me strength and mercy, and let Saraphu-El bless me. I call you today. Heavenly Source, Heavenly Source, Heavenly Source, Heavenly Source, Heavenly Source, Heavenly Source, Heavenly Source, Sanctus, Sanctus, Sanctus, Sanctus, Sanctus, Sanctus, Sanctus, Holy, Holy, Holy, Holy, Holy, Holy, Holy, You who rest in the holy place. You the merciful God, the invisible One and the incomprehensible One, *Marmaroulach*, *Christos*. Receive our children. Receive our song. And let us enter Your Kingdom."

Then the men sang:

"SABAOTH SABA AO, SABAOTH SABA AO, SABAOTH SABA AO."

When they had all finished they got up and carried the benches to the side of the hall. Three temple virgins came in each with their basket of twelve unleavened loaves of bread, which they carefully placed in three rows at the altar at the end of the hall, four in each row. They were followed by three young male novices carrying a large cask with unfermented wine.

Salome held the communion. A sister and then a brother would take turns and walk by the altar where they would share a piece of the bread and the wine in remembrance of *Marmariotha*, the Heavenly Source, *Rukha d'koodsha*, the Holy Spirit and *Shekhinah*, the Wisdom.

When everybody had received their communion the brothers and the sisters gathered in the middle of the hall where they quietly intoned:

Mmmmmmmmmmmmmmmmmmmmmmmmmmmmmmmmmmmmmm mmmmmmmmmmmmmmmmmmmmmmmmmmmmmmmmmmmmmmmm.

This went on for such a long time that Ish-a-tar lost all sense of time. Suddenly the closed sound dissolved into a more open one:

AAAAAAA EEEEEE IIIIII OOOOOOO UUUUUUU
OOOOOOO IIIIII EEEEEEE

AAAAAAAEEEEEEEEIIIIIIIIOOOOOOOOOUUUUUUU
IIIIIIIIEEEEEEEEAAAAAAA.

The song got more and more intense and ecstatic. Without knowing how it happened Ish-a-tar slipped into a deep and meditative state of mind where the sound was everywhere, within as well as without. When she opened her eyes she saw the most surprising sight. Around her several men and women had started turning and turning while they kept singing the holy sounds. Others were in a trance-like state of mind standing or sitting on the floor while they were swaying back and forth, still singing. She closed her eyes again and travelled along on the sound, which caught her, lifted her up, up and up until she stopped feeling her body. She was pure energy on her way into a new and foreign world.

✳

My thoughts were swirling in my head as I was backing the car in the direction of the woman at the side of the road. When I got to her I reached across the passenger seat and opened the door. She leaned towards me and smiled. It was as if I was following an invisible manuscript. The problem, however, was that it wasn't Marie Périllos, the waitress from "Belo Bar" in Narbonne as I had expected. This woman was blond and seemed taller. She looked in her middle twenties. The sight of her confused me totally. I had no doubt at all that a moment ago I had seen Marie Périllos in a flowered dress standing at the side of the road. Now, suddenly, she was wearing a pair of jeans and a short, red-striped sweater. Where did this woman come from, who was she and what had happened to Marie?

"Are you going to Vicdessos?" she asked.

It sounded more like a statement than a question.

"Well yes," I answered more confused than ever.

She was soaked and was already entering the car.

"Can I have a lift?"

"Well of course," I said moving the maps on the passenger seat.

"You can put your bag on the rear seat."

I stepped on the clutch and put it into first gear while watching her out of the corner of my eye. I was caught between my interest in looking at her more closely and my modesty, which, however, was limited by the age difference between us. Most of all I wanted to ask her directly what was going on, but at the same time I realized that she couldn't possibly know how to answer such a question. I therefore held my tongue, trying to sort out my own thoughts until she broke the silence:

"Are you going to *Montréal-de-Sos*?"

I took the opportunity of looking at her face. She was transparently pale with fine

features, which almost disappeared into the light surrounding her.

"Watch out!"

I was pulled abruptly back to reality as she took hold of the steering wheel with one hand, almost making me go into the ditch.

"You'd better concentrate on the road," she said with a smile.

"Sorry, I lost my concentration there for a minute," I said and focused on my driving, "I was on my way to Olbier."

"Good, then we are going the same way."

I sat for a while trying to find something to say. Then I began with the most obvious thing to say:

"My name is Lars."

"Just call me Ba-Bé."

"Is that your name?"

She shook her head:

"You wouldn't be able to pronounce my name anyway."

"Try me," I said flippantly.

"I don't think so," she said in a tone of voice, which put a lid on the subject. It took about twenty minutes to get to Vicdessos. We

then continued towards Olbier. The road narrowed and wound its way through the mountains surrounded by trees and dense thicket.

"This is it," she said as we turned a corner and saw the fantastic view in front of us. She pointed to the mountain lying like an island in the valley in front of us. Miraculously, the rain suddenly stopped and the sun came out behind its veil.

"Montréal-de-Sos. The Mountain of the Grail."

"Is this the Mountain of the Grail?" I asked surprised.

"Yes," she replied surprised, "didn't you know?"

"Not really, I ... "

I gave up trying to explain. It was all so certain anyway. No reason to ask any more stupid questions. What was going on? I was utterly lost and fought to regain my centre. I slowed down considerably and shortly after we drove along a very narrow street towards Olbier.

I parked the car outside of the church. We started walking into the village. Apparently she knew the way. It all seemed so paradoxical and yet quite natural. Like the air around us, she was cool and fresh and yet inexplicably present. No superfluous words. Just this wonderful presence.

We passed what must have been the smallest town square of any town. There was only room enough for two benches. Further ahead a sign pointed to the right towards "Montréal-de-Sos." A narrow passage ended in the path we were going to follow.

I followed her closely. The climb was not particularly difficult and the path was not very long. The path continued into a grotto from a ledge.

"This is the birth-canal," Ba-Bé said matter-of-factly and stepped through a Mandorla shaped opening which most of all looked like a woman's vagina, but it was high enough for a man to stand upright in. It got darker and darker and the ceiling got lower and lower the further we went into the cave. About twenty metres ahead we could see a small hole where the light was very concentrated.

"There is the exit, you don't have to worry," she said.

It suddenly struck me that she was talking to me like a kind of midwife, a maternity helper, and that in this case it was not the mother but the child, the person to be, she was trying to calm down.

And then it opened up:

A small self is floating about in an impenetrable darkness. A kind of umbilical cord is connecting it to another sphere outside, filled with light. The small self knows nothing about the radiating reality and nothing about all the other small selves surrounding it in the sphere of darkness. This small self, that is my personal identity, is recognized by a consciousness looking at the unity of darkness and light from a neutral position which may be the Great Nothingness. And the consciousness of this Great Nothingness is seen and recognized by a consciousness in another dimension, which has no name as far as we know. This consciousness sees the consciousness looking at the consciousness, which recognises the small self fumbling about in the sphere of darkness. And all of it is gathered in a single opening at the moment of birth, when consciousness is on its way through The Shaft of the Soul.

Suddenly I'm back in the cave. A drop of water has hit me in the exact middle of my forehead. Right between the eyes. It feels as if it is continuing through the chakra of my forehead, creating its own birth-canal here. At that moment I understand that the consciousness seeing the consciousness which is seeing the small self really are one

The Shaft of Re-birth

and the same, and that there has been no other separation than the one the small self has created with its separated and separating mind. At the same time I do recognize that the sphere of darkness is the sphere of possibilities and that each time a person gets a glimpse into the sphere of light it may change something in the weightier department, the known world where man is situated at this moment.

Ba-Bé supported me when I had to bend over in order to get through the stone mouth of the birth-canal.

"Welcome to the women's mountain. Or should I say *the Mount of Venus.*"

Ba-Bé had flung one of her arms out while she continued towards another grotto.

I could hardly believe what I heard: *the Mount of Venus.* This was the exact name that Sylvia had used about one of the two initiation-mountains. She had called the other one Mount Carmel.

Ba-Bé went into the grotto and disappeared into the darkness. I followed her trying to get my thoughts in order. What kind of being was she, where did she come from and what was going to be the outcome of this meeting? She wasn't particularly feminine, however, not the opposite either. She was more an example of isogynic man. She wasn't at all my type of woman. Nevertheless, she had ignited something within me to which I hadn't paid much attention for a very long time.

While I was fumbling along in the darkness, following the figure in front of me, I was contemplating the question, which she had accessed. There was nothing sexual in our meeting. Or was there? In that case it was a totally different kind of sexuality than I had known before.

The grotto was not as long as the previous one and before I knew it we were out in the open again walking along a narrow path towards the remainder of the old Castle of the Grail.

It is difficult to find words to describe the feelings I had, when we were standing side by side at the top of Montréal-de-Sos. A flock of goats were jumping down the side of the mountain when we took the last steps to the top. The sounds from the village below us sounded sharply in the clear air. Ba-Bé pointed towards the long valley cutting through the mountains to the east.

"This was the way the three Cathars from Montségur followed to the mountain carrying the secret treasure of the Cathars. There was no village then, nor any kind of habitation here. It was a desolate place which had been used by various groups of holy people in connection with a cult of the sun and as a place of initiation."

I was listening to her words but I don't know if I heard everything she said. I was far too occupied by the inexplicable radiation and magnetism surrounding her.

She was standing so close to me that I could feel her energy, which spread to me and made me feel a vibration in the side closest to her. Everything happened in slow-motion.

Slowly, slowly she turned around to face me. I closed my eyes and felt her lips very close to mine ...

☆

Salome continued educating Ish-a-tar. During the days following the great festivity Ish-a-tar felt as if she was floating along. She was both confused, happy and slightly despondent. Salome knew the kind of process her student was going through and felt that the time had come to intensify her education.

Do not lose heart Ish-a-tar. Your faint-heartedness is only natural, but do not surrender to it. When you learn how to make a holy space and how to maintain it the way you want it to be, then you'll know all that you now only feel. Feelings are usually evasive and changeable. They are rooted in the temporal. Not in eternity. In order for the queen to live she must have a space in which to manifest herself. And only a palace is worthy of a queen. Your body is not your own, it is the temple of the Great Mother.

She pointed at Ish-a-tar's heart:

"This is not *your* heart but the altar of the Great Mother. Do you understand that?"

Ish-a-tar nodded her assent. She was relieved to start working so that her thoughts had other things to do than just roam back and forth between giving up and having her most desired dream come true.

"When even the worldly embrace is a mystery it is quite clear that the embrace in which the hidden unity between man and woman is incarnated must be of another world. It is not only a reality of the flesh because the embrace about which we are talking contains a quietness, which has not been known until now. It does not originate in impulses or lust but is solely a conscious act of will. It is not darkness, it is not light. Imagine that you are embracing your own innermost being. The name of this being is *Shekhinah*. It is the holy name for the middle column of the Tree of Life. That which I may tell you in words is only a pale reflection of the certainty that you yourself must acquire through experience. *Shekhinah* is the soul of the world giving a little of itself to each and every person, male or female. At the same time she is the essence resting at the foot of the Tree of Life. *Shekhinah* is resting in her Palace while her wooers are passing by hoping to get a glimpse of the beloved one. But she only dances without veils for the one who deserves it."

Salome smiled at the sight of the concentration of her student. She continued:

"*Shekhinah* is the being with which you must consciously unite in order to receive initiation. But *Shekhinah* is not a static state of mind. She is always on the move and therefore set rules for the initiation into her spheres may not be given. Each man or woman must find the exact gate most suitable to him or her. One thing only may be given which is the same for everyone: The true *Shekhinah* hides behind seven veils."

"What are those veils?"

"The seven veils of the worldly *Shekhinah* are connected to the seven secrets of her sex, while the veils of the heavenly *Shekhinah* are woven into the seven lower sapphires of the Tree of Life. It is valid for both that the seven departments of the temple are metaphors for and represent both sides of the seven veils. The Ark of the Covenant is an allegory about the mystery. When we celebrate the seventh day and the seven by seven days, it symbolizes the cycle with which we are working. The fiftieth day thus is the beginning of a new cycle. After that we have the moon cycle of women, the four by seven days giving twenty eight days. This is the time it takes for the moon to go through its phases. Women have always been subjected to this cycle, however, just as with breathing it is a matter of being consciously present in this cycle. And breathing is also part of it. Well actually, everything in the visible world is subjected to the great, heavenly cycle."

Ish-a-tar was totally fascinated by the teaching of Salome and she couldn't keep silent when it looked as if Salome had ended the teaching of the day.

"When shall I be initiated into these secrets?" she asked, holding her breath.

Salome looked at her intensely. Then she said:

"Now, at this very moment."

She rolled up one of her sleeves, took a tablet and a piece of chalk and started to draw the shape of a vagina.

THE TEACHINGS ABOUT THE INCARNATED SHEKHINAH

"*Malkoot* represents the very incarnation of *Shekhinah* into the world of man and is symbolised by the anus. *Yesod* is the foundation stone and is symbolized by the perineum. *Hod* is the refulgence of *Shekhinah* and is symbolized by the clitoris. *Netzah* is eternity that is symbolized by the entrance to the vagina. *Tifferet* is beauty expressed through compassion and is here symbolized by the antechamber of women (the g-point at the front wall of the vagina). *Gevurah* is strength and power symbolized by the yard of Israel (the a-point at the back wall of the vagina and slightly higher placed than the g-point). *Hessd* is mercy symbolized by the altar in the yard of the priests and the priestesses (the cervix). These are the seven veils covering the Holy of Holies: *Kether*, the divine will, *Hokhmah*, the divine wisdom, and *Binah*, the divine acknowledgement, symbolized by the Ark of the Covenant (the uterus). Do you understand this allegory?"

Ish-a-tar nodded:

"Does this mean that there is also acknowledgement through intercourse with a man when both are aware of these levels?"

"Yes, this is the way of the incarnated *Shekhinah*. For the higher

Shekhinah this may be compared with a fall through the spheres into the visible world. Behind each of the levels curses are hiding which must be dissolved and transformed. Darkness hides behind *Malkoot* as an expression of the physical world. When you dwell and meditate at this point you get into harmony with the incarnations. This is the world of animal instincts, which is tied to the lust-filled world of pain and pleasure. *Yesod* is the level at which man must make a foundation of rightful being. A part of man's lower nature is hiding here. It is the level, which corresponds to the lower realm of angels (the lower astral level). By dwelling here we get the opportunity to accept the Will of God within us (the great Self) instead of staying in our own limited being (the small self). Our ignorance and intellectual resistance is hiding behind *Hod*, which tells about our limited mental state precisely because we are still caught up in the world of desires. Dwelling here and surrendering to the radiance from the clitoris may change the ignorance so that we may experience the unlimited freedom of wisdom. Here your own will is dissolved and intuition is born. The envy of death is hiding behind *Netzah* limiting any access to eternity. Dwelling here dissolves all the negative aspects connected with jealousy. Behind *Tifferet* hides the state of being caught in the body believing that it is the only reality of man. Dwell here, and all the animal-like qualities are transformed into humanity through acts of compassion. Behind *Gevurah* any kind of worldly knowledge hides. Dwell here and place the higher intuition before the written word. The poisoned wisdom hides behind *Hesed*. Dwell here, and transform all the falsity, which pretends to be the correct teaching. These three points all belong to the world of the individual which at the moment of man and woman melting together in loving certainty, may be lifted into the heavenly spheres."

She stopped in order to give her student the opportunity to take in her words. She continued after a while:

"All levels are also contained in the four letters of the holy name IHVH. Yod-Hé-Vau-Hé (Yehova). I = the Father (the masculine Origin), Hé = the Mother (the feminine Origin), Vau = the Son (the Incarnations), Hé = the Daughter (the Bride)." Salome stopped and put the tablet down. Ish-a-tar looked at her fascinated.

"What about the heavenly *Shekhinah*?" she asked, eager to continue her education. Salome laughed and all the ethereal aspects danced around them. Then she took the hands of Ish-a-tar swinging them back and forth.

"You'll have to wait a while before you meet the heavenly *Shekhinah*. But I suppose the words that I have given you will suffice for now. Take them along into the night and into your next moon time. Here you may get a glimpse of what is waiting for you."

She leaned forward and kissed Ish-a-tar on her forehead.

"But when?" Ish-a-tar whispered, "when?"

✡

I could feel her lips very close to mine.

"A heart has two sides to it."

The words of Ba-Bé practically embraced me. My field of energy united with hers and I saw with my inner sight how a new field of energy came to life above us. It was almost like two people deciding to have a child. Everything, conception, pregnancy and birth happens instantaneously in a perfect and unconditional closeness.

This pure closeness of thought form slowly floated upwards reproducing itself again and again until it formed a circle around the mountain. I then felt her lips on my forehead. At that moment a light flashed through my third eye. This time deeper than the drop of water had done in the grotto. What once I had experienced as glimpses of a distant and intangible world now opened itself and took the shape of a mandorla in which all distant and intangible things suddenly become present. It was like standing on the banks of a river tearing past at an incredible speed, but instead of water it was simply floating and radiating energy. Ba-Bé's voice seemed to come from that radiating river:

"This is the fountain of wisdom and foolishness, *the Akasha* where all the thoughts, words and acts of man are stored. Look closely at it. Here is your past, your future and the eternal now."

I saw in that moment how my own thoughts, almost before I had them, disappeared like drops into the river, which then slowed down. This then revealed a large amount of cinder-like matter mixing with the light.

"As you can see, here is both wisdom and foolishness in total turmoil. When the speed is increased all the cinders are thrown towards each other and dissolved in the light. However, it takes more than the efforts of one individual if all this field is to be cleansed and be of eternal help in the future. Concurrent with the one-sided tension accumulating because of man's present lack of empathy and ethical understanding, the river moves so slowly that the cinders, instead of dissolving, become more compact and limiting to man's exchange with light."

The mandorla folded into itself and grew smaller and smaller and slowly disappeared totally. I opened my eyes. The sight and the experience had been so moving that I simply stood there trying not to cry.

I looked around bewildered. Ba-Bé was not to be seen. I suddenly had the thought that she didn't exist in the visible world and that she either was a result of my own imagination or spoke to me from another level.

"This way!"

I turned towards the sound. Her head appeared from the ledge below me.

"Come here, I want to show you something."

She disappeared under the ledge and I started walking along the path that led to her. When I stepped on to the ledge I just saw her golden locks of hair as she disappeared around a corner further ahead.

She waited for me outside a grotto, which had a grate in front of one of its openings, apparently for safety. Her eyes glittered like diamonds. She pointed towards the grated opening:

"Do you see the cave painting on the cliff wall behind the grate?"

I moved closer while I concentrated on seeing the phenomenon to which she was referring. It took a short while before I saw a few reddish lines. I stepped even closer and now clearly saw to rows of six crosses on each side of a square decorated with smaller, equilateral crosses surrounding five drop-shaped symbols and five equilateral

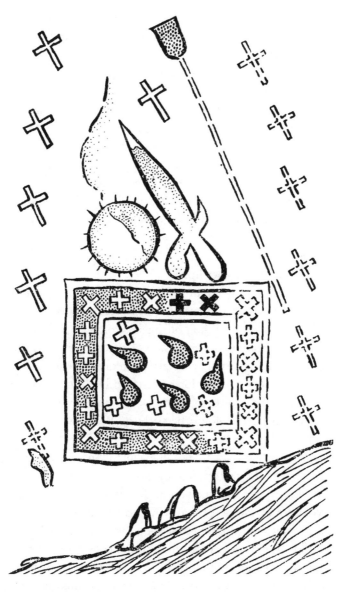

*Cave-painting at Montreal-de-Sos. The secret of the Grail
possible painted by the three Cathars who escaped the stakes at
Montségur 1244.*
(Rozekruis Pers Haalem)

crosses. Above the square a circle and a lance could be seen. Above the circle and the sword there was another cross next to a bell-like symbol resting on a
long stem that leant against the upper, right corner of the square. The whole painting did not make sense at first glance. It might be a map of positions in a landscape, which someone had wanted to pass on, perhaps a treasure map. Or it might be a kind of code containing a secret, which wasn't meant for everybody.

"Look closely at it because it is a symbolic image of the old knowledge of the Grail and isogynic man brought here by the three Cathars who got away from Montségur. Before surrendering to their destiny they hid their precious knowledge in this painting."

"But how … "

"Shush!"

She put a finger to her lips.

"No questions. Give your intellect a rest. Look, listen and learn."

Thousands of years of memory whispered their oracle answers in the wind. Like a mystical choir of timeless voices singing their message about eternal creation, the expansion of the great breath followed by the contraction, expansion, contraction in one eternal now.

I do not know for how long we stayed like this. However, when I got back to the grotto and the cave painting I was alone again. I started walking back along the path. Ba-Bé was not to be seen. I wanted to call out to her but didn't.

I saw her when I got free of the church. She was leaning against the radiator of the car, waiting for me.

"Well, here you are," she said in a neutral voice.

We drove in silence back towards Sabart. It was very strange. It seemed totally wrong having to say goodbye to her now. Nevertheless, it would be the most natural thing to do, considering the situation. But somehow I realized that there was nothing natural about this in the normal sense of the word. It nevertheless took me by surprise when she quietly stated:

"We have a common past as magicians."

13

As the tests grew harder and harder the days seemed longer and longer. At one point Ish-a-tar was losing her grip on all the knowledge Salome poured into her.

"What I'm telling you is not directed at your intellect but solely at the most elevated part of your soul. You shouldn't trouble your brain with knowledge; it is the wisdom of the heart that matters. When you understand that, the knowledge about the numbers, the letters and the holy sounds becomes manifest in your being of light as superior symbols because it is the language of angels. When your soul becomes the master of this, you'll be able to contact the heavenly powers as you see fit. Remember, that all the heavenly qualities are mirrored in you. You must trust the highest level in yourself. Have faith in the fact that your heart knows what is best for you. Know also your obligations. You gave a promise before entering this incarnation. I have read the course of your life in the Book of Life, and I'm not the one to judge that to which you have bound yourself. There are things that even I do not understand. Your road has been a hard one.

I have heard about the hard life in the Babylonian temples. Looking at you now it is difficult to imagine what you have been through. I shall have to leave you in a short while. Until now you have danced in the temples and slept with men as a prostitute. Now you must take the road of the temple virgins and the temple prostitutes, and I'm neither authorised nor do I want to witness this part of the honouring of your pledge."

Suddenly Salome looked into the distance and Ish-a-tar didn't quite understand what was behind her words.

"What does it mean to be a temple virgin or a temple prostitute?" she asked hesitatingly.

"First of all that you're not allowed to marry."

"But you are not married then?" Ish-a-tar asked.

Salome didn't answer and went over to the window and looked at Lake Mareotis, the surface of which was completely calm. She stood for long time like this before she continued:

"The difference between being a simple prostitute and a temple virgin or temple prostitute is that you now bring both your open and your goal-oriented consciousness along into your new position. Being a temple virgin is *a state of mind*. As a virgin you do not need the acceptance of others but are an independent person who is no longer dependent upon external circumstances. The virgin is independent. Taking the next step, becoming a temple prostitute, she brings this independence with her into the temple so that she may work with total freedom, without any ties at all."

"But I don't want to go back to the temples. I have had enough of the lechery," Ish-a-tar almost shouted.

Salome couldn't help smiling at the violent temper of her student.

"I know. But you are going to teach at a higher level in the future. As a Moon-Priestess you are going to help the man, who has such aspirations, out of the darkness and put him in the sky as the sun he is destined to be. You must be ready to reflect this sun to a certain degree until he finds a woman with whom he can get married and who can take over this part of the matter. Contrary to the prostitute, as a Moon-Priestess you are in equilibrium. The prostitute only has an identity through the erotic power she has over men. Beyond that she is nothing. The temple virgin, however, is a being of equilibrium. During your time as a dancer it was the unconscious side of you, the coldness of the moon and your wish for power, which was the generating force. You were able to lure and tease, but you didn't know true lovemaking. Love in the real sense of the word you didn't know at all. You reflected the innermost part of man in your own way, his unrealized bride. Your task now is to help him acknowledge this divine bride within himself by giving him unconditional love and without the desire for power. When the Moon-Priestess sets sail on her moon-boat and steers towards the sun she is uniting the feminine and the masculine aspects."

Ish-a-tar was also standing now and she ran to Salome at the window.

"But my destiny is different. I must find Sister Mariam. There are more important things in me than performing the trivialities of the temple."

"Some have come to do one thing and others another. Everyone must take upon them what is theirs to do. Until now you have followed the direction taking you here. As I said, it has been a hard road to travel but you have learnt everything about a man's way of thinking, about his needs, his dreams and his desires. You know about each and every nook and cranny of his brain and mind. It is in your power to wake him up and take him exactly where you want him to go. In your own words: You can take the animal to the trough. And here the animal will eat whatever you set before it. Up and until now, however, you have done that by giving the animal nothing but the blessings of your body. But these gifts do not last forever. One day not one single man will turn around to look at you, because the only means of power you possessed was the beauty of your body. Now, however, you have other things to offer. And this is your future task. The trough has now been filled with wisdom. You were created for this one purpose and you have made a promise in confirmation of it."

"When?" Ish-a-tar quietly asked.

"Soon."

✳

"We have a common past as magicians!"

Her words were vibrating in the air.

"What do you mean?"

"In ancient Syria and Alexandria," she replied.

She pushed the passenger seat back enabling her to place her long legs on the dashboard. Her whole being had something unspoiled, obvious, carefree and nonchalant about it. Similarly, however, I also sensed something deep and dark below this apparently carefree nature. But I also knew that this was what made her so attractive – and so dangerous.

She was surrounded by an indefinable, protective sphere, which invalidated the most natural questions about her own person. But I felt so confused that I decided to confront her with the most obvious question of all:

"Where do you come from?"

She was looking out of the side window, which became misty from her warm breath. She drew a heart with her finger. Then another one upside-down, linked with the first one. They ended in a star of Mariam in the middle while at the same time the two hearts themselves formed one. She took her time before answering:

"You need a woman to help you get to the heart of your quest. And here I am!"

I was again struck by the obviousness with which she concluded and ended the matter. All doubts were ruled out beforehand.

I refrained from any further questions and we drove on in silence. What did Ba-Bé know about my quest? Could she be the princess that Sylvia had predicted that I would meet? I could practically hear her admonitions to me before I left: "Find the princess and you have found the dragon. And where the dragon is there the Grail also is." Had I finally found the princess? I couldn't help laughing within myself since she was really the one who had found me. I realized, however, that no matter what, I had to see where the encounter with her would take me.

We drove into Foix half an hour later. I parked the car in the large square, which was filled with stalls since it was market-day. We walked between the tents. She stopped at a stall selling bric-a-brac. A table was filled with all kinds of things. My eyes had just caught a small, tarnished silver heart when she picked it up and handed it to me. Something was engraved on it. Holding it into the light I could read the word: "Jesus," on it.

"Try turning it over," she said.

I turned the heart over. Another name was engraved on the other side: "Marie."

"A heart always has two sides to it," she laughed.

I paid the three euros that was the price and attached it to my necklace. We continued to the end of the square and walked into one of the narrow passages. I walked along lost in my own thoughts when suddenly I felt her arm in mine.

Shortly after, we were in a square at the other end of town, just outside the church. She pushed me gently through the nave and I heard the door slam behind us. It was quite dark in the church. She let go of my arm and started walking down past the side altars in the aisle to the right. I followed her when she called out to me. She squatted in front of an old altar.

"Look," she said pointing to a relief where the paint was partly peeled off. It was the scene from the Last Supper. However, in this painting there was no doubt that the person next to Yeshua was a woman. In contrast to most of the paintings, the one by Leonardo da Vinci being the most well known, in this one Mariam sat to the left of Yeshua instead of to the right which is usually the case. In this painting in the church of Foix she is looking devotedly at her partner. Everyone apart from Mariam, of course, is depicted with a beard.

"It may very well be," Ba-Bé said, "that the Catholic Church in general has had its problems with Mary Magdalene however, this does not seem to be the case here in the south of France."

When we got back to the square it was cloudy and the day was fading. I then remembered the note with the address of the guide given to me by Mar in the morning. I found it in order to see where this Bart lived, the one who apparently knew about the hidden cave at Montségur.

He lived in Roquefixade, the town with the castle, which the Seer had "given" to me as an initiation gift a few years earlier. Apparently, it was now time to visit it once more.

"Do you want to come?" I asked Ba-Bé and told her about it.

"What are we waiting for?" she replied.

Roquefixade is situated about halfway between Foix and Montségur and it took us twenty minutes to get there. We had to ask for directions a couple of times before finding Bart's house slightly below the town. In the meantime the sky had changed into a taut canopy filled with rain and thunder that was about to burst.

It was Bart himself who opened the door when we finally got there. He was a tall, broad-shouldered man with a weather-beaten face. Apparently, Mar had told him about my plans and he asked us in right away and we were soon seated around a refectory table drinking tea in the kitchen. He went straight to the heart of the matter:

"When do you want to go to the mountain?"

I was just going to answer when Ba-Bé said:

"There'll be two of us."

Bart looked questioningly at her and then at me. He then said to me:

"Do you think that is wise? This is no picnic like walking the straight path up the mountain. It can be quite rough."

I don't know why but I heard myself saying:

"This is fine. There are two of us and unless you're dead against it we would both like to go."

"All right. So when do you want to go?"

Once more it was Ba-Bé who answered:

"How about now?"

At that moment lightning flashed outside followed by an ear-splitting peal.

"I'm afraid that is out of the question," Bart said.

"Tomorrow then," I said.

"Fine. If the weather clears we'll meet here tomorrow at ten."

Bart got up and went over to the window.

"We are rebuilding our house and I'm afraid we cannot offer you any accommodation for the night, but I'm sure you can get a room at Maris'."

He pointed through the window:

"He is the mayor of the town and also has a B & B. He lives in the small castle up there, you can just see the outline of it."

We said our goodbyes and ran through the rain to the car. The thunderstorm was right above us now and the flashes came more frequently and it wasn't difficult at all to see the small castle just mentioned by Bart.

The castle was really a large villa with a tower giving it a certain air of aristocracy. A narrow, steep avenue led up to a beautiful square in front of the house.

We ran as fast as we could in order to get out of the rain, which by now was pouring down with a force you only see in the Pyrenees. There was a light on the first floor. We went under the porch supported by a few symbolically decorated pillars, which formed an impressive entrance. While we were shaking the water off Ba-Bé laughingly pointed to one of the arches above us:

"Take a look at this."

A beautifully shaped, flying phallus was caught in mid air.

"And there."

She pointed to a star of Mariam hanging on a pillar next to us.

"And by God, – here as well."

"Who?" I asked forgetting all about the rain and the thunder.

"Yeshua and Magdalene!"

Sure enough and here they were, one on each side of the same pillar, just the way she had said: Yeshua and Mariam. Apparently this Mayor, Maris de Roquefixade, was no ordinary man.

I pressed a button but the thunder made it impossible to hear whether or not it was connected to a bell in the house. We waited for quite a while and were about to give up when finally the light went on in the hall. Then the door opened and a man about my own age, tall, lean with a bald patch and long hair at the back of his neck looked at us through a pair of round, thick-lensed glasses.

"Sorry about the late hour, but we are looking for lodgings and have been told you have rooms to let."

He sized us up. Then he seemed to take pity on us and stepped back:

"I see."

We went inside. The house was furnished in a classic style but I immediately noticed the books covering most of the walls. I noticed a book with an occult subject. Between the books the walls were decorated with esoteric symbols and there was no doubt that Maris de Roquefixade had an interest in this kind of thing.

"How many nights?" he asked while he still looked closely at us.

"Just one," I said.

"Double or single?" he asked.

I couldn't say why but his question disturbed me. Ba-Bé beat me to it:

"A double."

"I see."

He turned about and walked down a dark passage. We followed him. He opened a door at the end indicating with one arm that this was our room:

"At what time would you like your breakfast?"

"At nine, please," I answered.

"I see. Goodnight."

I heard his footsteps disappearing and then it was totally quiet. We stood in silence. My thoughts whirled in my head. What now? What was on her mind? Then she broke the silence by throwing herself on the double bed. She sat up and bumped up and down the way you do when you want to make sure that the bed is useful for something other than sleeping ...

✳

Lamu could hardly wait for the seventh day when men and women were to meet and sing together. However, it was quite a different song burning in his heart. The song was called Ish-a-tar.

When the day came and the men were getting close to the common room he got so impatient that he could hardly stay in his place. From inside the temple they could hear the song of the women the way the ritual demanded it. His heart was about to burst. The procession moved along very slowly and when finally they got to the room his eyes immediately looked for the beloved one. She wasn't there. He looked around bewildered. What was going on? Another woman had taken Ish-a-tar's place. This was totally unthinkable. Something must have happened. She might be ill? His heart missed a beat and he felt faint. He then pulled himself together and dismissed the thought. Meanwhile, the men took their positions. The priest had started chanting. Lamu could not concentrate. His eyes roamed from one woman to another. He spotted the tall figure of Salome. She stood there with her eyes closed, apparently, already lost in prayer.

Shortly after the rotation around the altar with the wine and the bread started. He walked trancelike, as if in a fog where he registered everything without really being present.

It was not until he passed the altar with a strange woman, with whom he received communion, that he woke from the dream and realized the painful truth that Ish-a-tar was not present.

He didn't think at all when contrary to all rules he turned to the woman at his side and asked her:

"Where is Sister Ish-a-tar?"

The woman looked at him terrified. They kept their places and continued the rotation. The seriousness in his voice must have convinced her since she whispered to him:

"In the temple of the Moon Goddess."

Then he started running.

Excited voices were calling after him. He clearly heard one of them which was the voice of a woman:

"Let him go. It is written."

It was the voice of Salome.

He was running for love. Or was it lust or both?

He was running for his life. He ran until he lay at the foot of the stairs of the shining temple of Aphrodite in the middle of Alexandria, more dead than alive. He lay there surrounded by busy men who had more than enough to think about with their own affairs: the necessary visit to the chosen daughters of the great goddess.

His lungs hurt and his legs shook under him as he climbed the stairs. Not until a temple guard brutally pushed him down the stairs again did he regain the use of his senses. He got up and bowed apologetically. The guards laughed at him and let him pass. What did a brother dressed in white want in the house of Aphrodite?

Lamu didn't notice them, just as he didn't notice that he was wearing the gown of the Therapists. He was only focused on one thing: finding Ish-a-tar before it was too late.

He followed the crowd of men and ended up in one of three queues outside three gates. He could hear from the dialects spoken that there were men from all parts of the kingdom. However, he didn't notice what they were talking about, only the excitement and the pressure towards one of the gates, which suddenly opened and embraced him like a pair of caring wings.

They were guided into a hall and one by one they passed the women who sat there in their enticing costumes, each in her own cubicle. He felt faint. There were women of all shapes. Young and old, lean and fat, tall and small, but all were overdressed to a degree that made most of them look like unreal beings or demons from another world. He saw their bare breasts and he saw the humiliation. There were women among them whose beauty was obvious and they wouldn't stay there for long. However, Ish-a-tar was not to be seen.

Before he could react he was taken to the exit where a temple guard pushed him into a blinding light.

"Better luck next time." the guard laughed laconically.

As soon as he found himself outside the building he ran to the entrance once more and this time he ran up the stairs. The guards shouted mockingly after him but let him pass. The second time he made sure that he was in the group at the middle gate. Here, however, he also only found the same grotesque exhibition of women who tried to get their temple duties over with as fast as possible. And Ish-a-tar wasn't here either.

When he walked up the stairs for the third time he felt panic seizing him. What if she wasn't in the temple at all? Then he suddenly froze hearing a few words, which struck him like lightning, "The White Whore from Babylon." He couldn't see which one of the passers-by had spoken these words. Desperately he reached out at random and took hold of a man who was on his way into the sanctuary. The man tried to tear himself away but Lamu held on to his cloak.

"What do you know about the White Whore from Babylon?"

The man looked at Lamu, frightened, surprised at the violence in his voice. Then he regained his composure:

"Take it easy brother. There are prostitutes enough for everybody. The one you are looking for you probably cannot afford anyway."

The man freed himself from Lamu's grip and continued into the darkness. But Lamu didn't let him go that easily. He ran after him and caught him again:

"Where?"

Apparently the seriousness of the situation slowly dawned on the victim because he pointed into the darkness towards an almost hidden door leading to a side chamber.

"There." he growled.

There were no guards at the door. Lamu went in. A long passage lay in darkness. Lamu stood still listening, hoping to get an indication of which way to go. He couldn't separate the sounds, which all seemed to emanate from the entrance hall from where he had just come. He touched the wall with one hand until he gradually regained his sight. He saw another door at the end of the passage and slowly approached it.

The door was ajar.

Lamu slowly pushed it open.

The dust was dancing in a ray of light coming from a small opening in the ceiling. Lamu stepped into a beautifully decorated but empty room. There was a door in each of the four walls. Standing in the middle of the room he noticed that all the worldly sounds had disappeared as if by magic. He stood still listening intensely but there was only this silence the sound of a present containing the sounds of everything from the past. And for a moment he was struck by the feeling of a time gone by or perhaps a new time rushing through his consciousness. Before he could identify with it the feeling was gone, but he felt that something within him had fallen. He felt vulnerable and unprotected in a strange way that worried him. In this strange feeling, the decision to make a choice was hiding, a decision he knew he had to make without knowing why. The door through which he had come led back to the entrance hall of the temple. The access to Ish-a-tar was behind one of the three remaining doors in the empty room, he had no doubt about that. He heard a voice from far away. As it became clearer he realised that it came from within himself.

This was also something that rushed through his consciousness like a whirlwind in an inexplicable way. He was totally concentrated and tense at the moment the voice rolled up towards the surface of his consciousness and left its ephemeral imprint before disappearing into the ethereal level:

"The door is on the inside!"

He was standing in the middle of the hall looking indecisively at the three possibilities. A set of invisible rules stemming from an unacknowledged fear told him he had one chance only. His mind was in turmoil. "The door is on the inside." What kind of statement was that? How was that to be understood?

He was looking for a solution in his mind. But his thoughts were like a hundred wild horses running in all directions. He tried to hold on to one of them but in vain. He didn't get any further than a desperate attempt to try to understand the devious mind behind this fiendish game. Which door was supposed to misguide him? Which one called for him especially? If he could find that one then there would only be two from which to choose.

But no matter how he twisted and turned the matter, another possibility always presented itself with another hidden explanation more diabolical than the previous one.

"The door is on the inside!"

Then suddenly it was as if the cone of light from above was pointing at him. He couldn't decide whether the light was an external or an internal one. But he knew that all that had been fluttering about around him moments ago suddenly gathered and found its way back to its starting point in his heart. Everything he had learned but which he had been on the point of losing: Certainty, wisdom, confidence and faith.

He slowly sank to the floor and into a lotus position.

"The door is on the inside!"

Of course it is, he thought and gave up his fear and his thought's insane spinning around.

He didn't know how long he sat like this. But he stayed in this position until the door appeared in his mind and then opened and revealed a radiating room where Ish-a-tar sat smiling and waiting for him. He then got up from his place in the hall and walked towards the middle door. He opened it slowly. A sea of secret scents met him as he went inside.

Ish-a-tar lay on a richly decorated bed, waiting for him. He approached the bed as in a dream. Getting closer he noticed that she was naked under the transparent material. He did not notice how he got out of his own clothes; all he saw was her warm and inviting smile. He slipped into bed and embraced her tenderly. They kissed as only lovers kiss. Then she whispered in his ear:

"I knew you would pass the test."

But at that moment it was very difficult for him to recognize her.

"Who are you?" he asked in the way a child might talk to an angel.

"I am *Shekhinah*," she said while slowly she let herself slide down upon him, anointing him.

Then they slowly moved into the Holy of Holies of the temple, uniting and becoming one light.

✡

Ba-Bé went to the bathroom to get ready for the night. I was slightly embarrassed and didn't quite know what to do about the situation. In an attempt to act naturally I sat down in a chair in a corner of the room and waited. It was a poignant moment but I was so full of resistance and had so many reservations that I was neither able to hear nor see what was going to happen or understand any part of the situation. Instead, I saw only seduction with all its trimmings. In a desperate attempt to create a kind of light suitable for the sleazy atmosphere, which my unconscious, hurt sexuality was arranging, I put out the light in the room except a small lamp above the bed which barely managed to give the room a faint, pale hue.

I heard the tap in the bathroom being turned off and took this as an indication that she had almost finished.

And so it was. Shortly after the door opened and she stepped into the room, naked, placing herself against the light from the bathroom behind her. I was paralyzed, gasping for air at the sight of her lithe body. Then she turned off the light in the bathroom and stood in the semi darkness of the room. I could only hear the thumping of my heart beating so loudly that I was convinced that this was all she as well could hear. Time stood still. And suddenly all the sleaziness dissolved. Like a soap bubble seeking toward the surface and exploding at the confrontation with reality, my old feelings of guilt faded like morning dew.

Then something happened which is very difficult to explain. Small vibrations manifested themselves around her body. Those vibrations most of all reminded me of butterflies dancing and being filled with light at the same time. I was so surprised at the sight of these radiating butterflies that I didn't immediately see that the light came from her. The sight of her filled me with such an inexplicable and deep sense of joy and gratitude that I cannot find words to describe it.

She was standing in the opening of the door. The chair, in which I was sitting, was situated at the other end of the room. It was therefore so much more surprising to see how the small, radiating butterflies, like the ones coming from her, were now also dancing around me.

The current around me seemed to get stronger and stronger as if there was a simultaneous charging of both my ethereal body and the butterflies. But before I could put my feelings into words I realized that the butterflies *were* my star-body like the butterflies around Ba-Bé's body were *her* star-body, which however, vibrated so fast that they became visible in this wonderful way.

She stood in front of me, totally enlightened. The butterflies were suddenly sucked into the middle of the room, and at that moment I saw her true being and origin.

This being had no face and no personality. It was nothing but pure light.

My own true being and my own true origin were also reflected in this light. This faceless being of light sending its breath into eternity was an expression of the condition, which may only be expressed by the concept so maltreated by man:

Love.

Ba-Bé / Ish-a-tar
(Painting by Francis Andreasen Østerfelt)

PART III

SALAMANDALA

14

A faint light crept in between the curtains and fell on my face. I stayed in bed dozing with my eyes half shut while I slowly found my bearings. I felt as if I had been on a long journey but I couldn't remember the destination.

Ba-Bé!

I got up and looked around in confusion but she was not to be seen. Was it all a dream or had the meeting with her taken place at another level? The covers at my side were halfway on the floor indicating that she might be more real than I thought. I took the pillow and held it to my nose to see if I could smell her scent. But where was she?

I got up and opened the door to the bathroom but she wasn't there. I pulled the curtains aside and opened a window ajar. It was impossible to mistake her golden laughter. It mixed with a man's voice, which apparently was the cause of the frivolous merriment. I immediately felt a pang of jealousy but shook it off and got dressed.

Walking through the hall I saw her sitting on the terrace on the other side of an enormous arched window that extended from floor to ceiling. Maris was serving breakfast and Ba-Bé already had a mug between her hands sitting flirtatiously with her legs pulled up under her. She was still laughing and it was quite obvious that Maris considered her to be both charming and irresistible. I stood still watching them and trying to keep my jealousy in check.

Who did I think I was? The experience of the previous evening might be just another one of a series of astral journeys which was the result of the process I was in and which I had been in for a long time. There wasn't really anything going on between us. Or was there? No matter what, – the feeling of jealousy was real. I went outside.

"Good morning. Here is the transformed prince," she laughed patting the empty chair next to her.

Her gesture made me feel like a dog or a frog more than a prince, but I accepted her invitation and sat down. Maris hardly looked at me – his whole attention was riveted on Ba-Bé. He didn't even try to hide his obvious admiration of her. She on her part, however, was totally natural. But it was exactly this openness that to my mind could so easily be misunderstood and misinterpreted by a Latin like Maris as flirtation. The fact that this was saying more about me than about him or her didn't bother me at the moment. I coughed in order to get Maris' attention. However, it was not until I knocked an eggcup to the floor that I woke him up from his infatuation and he looked at me reluctantly with regret in his eyes:

"Yes!"

"A cup of coffee would do me good," I said flippantly trying to sound unaffected and natural.

He placed a bowl with strawberry jam in front of Ba-Bé before he turned around and in an exaggerated fashion walked towards the kitchen bent over and dragging his feet. Ba-Bé laughed out loud and when Maris turned around and looked at me with a diabolical smile I realized that his little performance somehow had been an attempt to ridicule me.

He came back shortly after with the coffee and two cups. When he had arranged everything he sat down and poured the coffee. For a moment I was confused. What was he thinking? We, Ba-Bé and I were the guests and he was the host. But I didn't say anything. Instead, I sat fuming over my coffee and a piece of burned toast listening to their conversation. I felt totally overlooked and didn't hear exactly what they were talking about, only that it was about Maris and his claim to Cathar ancestry and his idea about them, the fact that he thought they were "Paulinites" or that they had adopted many of Paul's doctrines in their teaching. Instead of listening properly I tried to convince myself that I could let her go just like that. Then I heard her voice penetrating my defences and I heard say:

"But Lars knows all about that. He also writes books and is interested in the same subjects."

I looked up from my burned toast, which I tried to hide under a thick layer of jam, and caught the eyes of Maris who now looked at me with a limited amount of interest.

"What do you write about?" he asked without much enthusiasm but more in consideration of Ba-Bé.

I hesitated. How could I answer his question in a few words? I really didn't want to answer it and more than this I didn't want to start a dialogue with him. There was an abyss of resistance between him and me. The answer I finally gave him had only one purpose:

"I write about the secret of the Cathars."

He reacted promptly like a boxer who has been hit in his most tender spot: his pride.

"What secret?"

The fire was lit now. And as I was about to add fuel to it Ba-Bé pushed me in the side and pointed to the ground between Maris and me. Two newts were twisting and twirling in a fight to the death in the dust. It was the merciless battle between lizards. The battle at the same time took place in a very distant past. The sight activated something age-old, deep in my subconscious. I then realized that the duel between Maris and me was the continuation of something with roots further back, well, perhaps before the earth existed. I looked up at him but, apparently, he hadn't noticed anything. Then I gave him the coup-de-gras:

"Well, I cannot tell you, can I? It wouldn't be a secret then, would it?"

The moment I spoke the words I was painfully aware of the primitive direction our confrontation had taken, however, at the same time it was unquestionably the only way in which to solve this old problem. What surprised me the most, however, was the fact that I enjoyed every moment of it.

Ba-Bé broke the spell:

"We must go now. It's a quarter to ten."

She got up and put her arm in mine. She turned to Maris and said in the most innocent way:

"You see, we are going to have a look at the secret of the Cathars today."

✻

"I hereby give you the initiation name *El-Phatah*, 'The opener'."

The priest drew the cup with the holy fire across Lamu's chest from right to left. He took a piece of incense from the cup and made the sign of the cross in front of Lamu's heart as a sign that the eye of God had now been opened. Then he gave Lamu the cane of Mercury, the sceptre of Hermes, as a sign that the power of the man in him had been lifted into the heavenly sphere and that he now had the power to heal and to prophesy.

Finally the priest embraced him and kissed him on the mouth. This was the sign by which the initiated ones greeted and acknowledged each other.

Then Salome stepped in front of the altar. It was now Ish-a-tar's turn to get a new name.

"I hereby give you the blessing of *Shekhinah*. From this day on, your initiation name shall be *Mar-Iona*, "The White Dove of the Moon-sea."

Salome lifted the cup with the holy water into the air. She then dipped two fingers into the water and made the sign of the cross in front of Ish-a-tar Mar-Iona's forehead as a sign that the eye of the Goddess had now been opened. Then Salome gave her the Venus-ring as a sign that the power of the woman had now been lifted to the heavenly sphere and that she also from this moment on had the power to heal and to prophesy. Salome embraced Ish-a-tar and kissed her on the mouth.

"Remember," she finally said, "remember that these names must remain a secret until the day they are either confirmed or exchanged for another. It is all written. But only the one who is able to read the Book of Life shall know when the time has come."

After the initiation the brothers and the sisters sang in honour of Ish-a-tar and Lamu. The ceremony ended with a common meal after which the newly initiated ones took leave of their two teachers and went out into the world.

The rumour about this holy couple which healed and prophesied spread like wildfire. Ish-a-tar and Lamu could hardly move in Alexandria without having crowds of people following them. They did what they had been trained to do but Ish-a-tar was losing her patience. One day she heard a woman talking about Mariam Magdal and the words reawakened her deep longing to meet this sister about whom so many beautiful stories were told. However, the foreign country where Sister Mariam now lived was far away and to get there, they would have to cross the *Mare Internum* [2]. And in order to do that they had to find passage on a ship.

Summer was coming to a close and soon the first storms of autumn would make any kind of sailing perilous. But it happened that Ish-a-tar heard a name mentioned in the crowd one day when she and Lamu were in the process of healing people. At first she tried to repress it, and that made her sad, but then it struck her that perhaps the name was heaven sent. Had she really heard it? She called out over the crowd:

"Who among you has just mentioned the name of the merchant Hashem Ben Naris?"

A murmur was heard in the crowd and a black man stepped forward:

"I did."

Ish-a-tar walked right up to the man:

---

2   The Mediterranean.

"Is Ben Nari here in Alexandria?"

"He is on board one of his ships which is presently berthed in the harbour. I myself am employed on board."

"And where are you going?"

"*Melita*[3], we set sail tomorrow."

Ish-a-tar and Lamu looked at each other. This might be the opportunity they had been waiting for.

They finished the treatments and followed the man to the harbour. Shortly after they were walking up the gangplank to board the good ship "Isis" in order to meet Ben Nari. Ish-a-tar couldn't help smiling at the thought.

Isis.

How could it be otherwise?

The great Ben Nari received them in his saloon on the upper deck. He had better things to do than spend his precious time with dubious people who wanted to do business or obtain passage, just like these two Therapists who had come on board. He lay on his couch being massaged by one of his slaves when Lamu and Ish-a-tar were shown in.

"Well, what do you want?" he asked without getting up from the couch.

It was Lamu who answered:

"We are going to *Massilia*[4] in *Narbonensis*[5] and we are looking for passage.

Ben Nari dismissed it with one of his thick arms:

"We are not going that far. You must look for another opportunity."

He rolled on to his side with great difficulty while the masseur worked on his shapeless body.

They stood in silence watching the grotesque scene.

Then Ish-a-tar spoke:

"We have heard that you are going to Melita. It is part of the way and sufficient for us."

---

3   Malta.

4   Marseilles.

5   At the time a Roman province in the vicinity of Narbonne.

The big man's body jerked. Then he got up on his elbows with great difficulty. There was something in the voice of the woman, which sounded familiar.

"You!" he almost shouted when, full of doubt, he saw Ish-a-tar standing in front of him radiating a kind of beauty far above the animal-like sensuality of former days.

With an impatient movement he signalled to the slave that he wanted to get up from the couch. He practically tore the cloak from the slave's hands.

Shortly after he was sitting in a chair huffing and puffing from the exertion so that it took some time before he found his voice. He was looking at Ish-a-tar with a curious eye trying to estimate his chances with her. It was not a coincidence that he was considered to be one of the most cunning merchants in his part of the world from Babylon to Alexandria and back.

Ish-a-tar looked right through him and she must have touched something deep down in the man, which, however insignificant it might be, nevertheless made him meek as a lamb.

Ben Nari laughed self-consciously. But Ish-a-tar knew all too well that the meek lamb was a disguised jackal.

"So, you haven't found your Mariam Magdal," he smirked. "Very well, you may join us as far as Melita. From there on you must find other means of transportation."

He pointed to the slave:

"Anglus here can show you around. Go now. I need my rest. Unless of course, you, Ish-a-tar, want to stay and revive old memories?"

His laughter filled the saloon as he invitingly patted the cot with his hand. Ish-a-tar didn't respond at all but turned around and walked towards the door.

The hoarse voice of Ben Nari sounded through the wind as they stepped onto the deck:

"We leave at sun up."

✻

Paying for the B & B I couldn't help noticing the series of crystals, with a reddish-brown hue, hovering around Maris' head. But the crystals were not interactively connected. Instead, each of them constituted its own autonomous thought form which, although it bore witness to great knowledge, also showed that this knowledge was rigid, dry, separating and intellectual.

Suddenly, I felt great sympathy for him. So much so that the scene, which had just been played out between us and was reflected in the battle of the two newts, embarrassed me. In a peculiar way, I also sensed that he felt the same way.

I looked around for Ba-Bé. She was waiting by the car surrounded by an unreal light. Although the distance between us was too great for me to see the expression on her face with any certainty I had no doubt at all that she was smiling up at us. Perhaps she was the one who had caused the energy between Maris and me to change?

"You are welcome here any time. Just give me a call beforehand," he said shaking our hands in farewell. I thanked him with a genuine feeling of warmth and started walking down towards Ba-Bé.

There was an abyss between the two realities we had just experienced. Not to mention what had happened the previous evening and night. I had never experienced anything like it. At least not in this life.

It was still cloudy and in spite of the thunderstorm of the night it was foggy and humid. Ba-Bé was standing in her usual pose: hand on hip. And yet something had changed. It was as if I could see two different people in her, or rather two beings: the worldly Ba-Bé with her natural charm, who could seduce any man, and the heavenly Ba-Bé about whom nothing else could be said but that she opened and lifted everything to another sphere with her wonderful, radiating light.

As she stood there leaning against the car it was difficult to decide which one of the two was the most prominent one. But then it dawned on me that she was neither of them; she was yet a third being. A being without a name which didn't claim to have a specific personality, didn't want to claim anything at all for itself or to be treated with any kind of preference. This being simply *was* pure being.

While I was thinking these thoughts a frightening field of nothingness opened inside me. One thought said: this is how it feels when all your well-known references are taken away from you. When you are confronted with reality and you realize that most of our sense of reality, our lives and our safety are tied to false premises and ideas; then the house of cards comes tumbling down. It is all hidden in the small things and the way we judge others or the way we cling to everything. Up until now we thought that what you see is what you get. We thought that we were able to judge the contents by the wrapping.

I was watching Ba-Bé in an attempt to force my way into the mystery. But she just smiled at me. I saw the finest crystals forming a radiating ring around her head, and with a bit of imagination it looked like a crown. I had no doubt at that moment about what had happened the previous night or that she was the virgin Sylvia had talked about who would come when the time was ripe. I felt a burning desire to ask her for her own explanation. However, a strange thought told me that if I did she would disappear as mysteriously as she had come.

And the dragon?

Perhaps this was the newt within myself, which had battled with the other newt just like it?

"You took your time," she said without any reproach in her voice.

We turned out of the driveway and drove down the mountain.

Bart was standing outside his house waiting for us. He had the gear we needed in a stack in front of him. I was somewhat surprised when I saw the small pickaxes, water cans, a narrow, foldable light-metal ladder and three helmets with torches strapped on to them.

"Say, are we going mountain climbing?"

"Well yes, both outside and inside the mountain," Bart said with a sound of secrecy in his voice.

We put the gear in the boot of the car and took off.

Twenty minutes later we passed the parking site at the Montségur-mountain. I was excited to find out from which point we were going to start the ascent, but Bart didn't say anything as I drove through the hairpin bends and into the village.

"Further ahead," Bart said as I pulled to the side.

We drove down into the valley, around the bends and followed the road out of the village again. Apparently we were going up from the south, the same side I had taken with the Seer, eighteen months earlier when we took the hidden road up there. This time, however, we were to start further down as we had gone through practically all the turns before Serrelounge.

"Here it is," Bart suddenly said and signalled for me to stop the car.

Bart and I divided the gear between us and packed it in each of our backpacks. Bart took the lead, Ba-Bé followed and I brought up the rear.

Bart climbed the high stonewall which stopped the eroded rocks from breaking up and rolling down towards the road.

"Montségur is a living mountain," Bart concluded.

What looked like a piece of cake for the first five minutes soon turned out to be an almost insurmountable task. It was practically impossible to step on a rock without it immediately rolling away under you.

Although it was still foggy we could feel the warmth of the sun hiding behind the clouds. The humidity was higher than normal. After fifteen minutes of balancing on the slippery rocks I was soaked with sweat. At the same time the mountain started getting steeper and steeper until it felt as if we were climbing a vertical wall. The combination of slippery rocks, the steep incline and the humidity was insufferable. I leaned out to see how my companions were doing. Bart was moving upwards with ease ten metres further ahead and Ba-Bé was following him with just as much ease halfway between him and me. I gritted my teeth and tried to concentrate. This was quite different from my last trip on Montségur when the Seer and I had had minor problems only. However, they were nothing compared to this. I dared not think about what was in store for us. Instead, I tried to find a way to keep focused and found that the best point of focus was Ba-bé's behind moving from side to side above me. To my great surprise I suddenly experienced how my focus shifted between my struggle to keep concentrating on my climb and the struggle to control the lust, which the sight of her constantly called forth in me.

We came out of this rolling hell shortly after and into a fairy tale of a low wood of gnarled trees, hazel, nut, boxwood and birch. The surface consisted of a soft moss and it felt as if we were walking on clouds.

We paused in order to recover our breaths.

The sweat was pouring down my body. None of us could talk. We had already slipped into another state of mind.

A vibration went through the underbrush. I thought it was an animal and turned towards the sound and just spotted a small, shining being of light disappearing behind a wooden stump.

"Did you see it?" Ba-Bé quietly laughed, " – there and there ..."

She pointed here and there and to my great surprise I saw several beings of light identical to the first one slip behind some trees while I had the feeling that they were watching us the same way as we were watching them. Apparently Bart had not noticed anything since he coughed so loud that the beings disappeared as fast as they had come.

"Wait here. I must reconnoitre the area before we proceed."

He started climbing and soon disappeared between the trees. Once in a while we heard the crack of a branch breaking and a growl, which could have been a bear. But it was Bart. He was moving about in the wood with the same ease as a bear.

Ba-Bé must have read my mind for she whispered in my ear:

"Bart the bear."

He was back shortly after:

"This way."

We continued the climb.

Once in a while we passed a cairn or a *stone-man* as Bart called them. Beacons of stone set by Bart or other guides who knew the area.

We had reached a plateau where the incline wasn't as steep. At the same time I had the feeling that we were moving into a field where only a very thin veil separated the various realities. The radiating net behind everything became more and more visible the deeper we penetrated into the indescribable nothingness.

The plateau levelled out and we now moved between hazel trees only. Bart pointed to a bonfire place in the middle of an opening in the forest:

"This is an ancient site where the charcoal burners burned their charcoal two hundred years ago. You may still find personal items which they left or forgot in the area."

We continued to the ruins of the old guard tower on the rock, *Roc de la tour*, where we rested once more. I had long since forgotten how to get here. And it wasn't very important. Instead, another road was showing itself in a totally different dimension.

Soon we were on our way again. It was clear that Bart wanted to stay on the trail now that he had the feel of it.

"It can be very difficult to find the right way if you get lost and once you have lost sight of the stone-men," he said.

Not only did we balance on the edge of reality but also virtually on the edge of a ledge with the abyss, an open mouth below us ready to devour anyone who lost his concentration. And just then I felt the mountain move with a deep tremor and come alive just the way Bart had said when we started the climb. Everything was dissolving. I felt dizzy, sweaty and hypnotized by Ba-Bé's sweet behind, which was still enticing me to climb up and up, step by step. My legs felt like lead and I lost my footing once in a while, but I always managed to find something to hold on to. It is still a riddle to me how Ba-Bé could be so unaffected by the rigours of the climb.

The mountain rose up once more and became even steeper. I was just about to announce that I couldn't go on when Bart signalled for another break. Once more he had to make sure that we were on the right track. Every step was agony and every break was paradise.

I sat down on a rock resting my head in my hands watching my sweat dripping on to the rock surface. The sun came out behind the clouds and the face of the mountain was like the surface of an anvil. I imagined that I was the heavy, hard material, the steel that had to be softened in the forge in order to be reformed.

Ba-Bé stood tall and lithe looking into nothingness. I sat there watching her and wondering what she might be looking at.

It came floating down. It floated in from all sides.

A peace as soothing as a playing fountain on a bright summer's day. A transparent, radiating veil of intervals and breaks, stops and nothingness spreading over us freeing us from all burdens and any kind of worry.

A moment only.

And this was the exact moment when it reappeared, the unbelievable, vibrating sound – the song of the mountain like a humming, below, over, around and inside of me.

In front of me Ba-Bé had transformed into a totally enlightened field opening out – or was it in?

I got up and took a step toward this vibrating field.

Irresolute. Hesitating.

Then I stepped into it. Through it and out – or was it in?

It doesn't matter now as it didn't then.

I followed the path through the radiating ethereal level with its sparkling air. I walked without any difficulty. To my left a stone-man, to my right a snake. The symbolism was obvious. But by now I was so used to it that I wasn't surprised at all. And although the stone-man wanted to tell me about the antiquated and petrified parts within me, he was still a signpost. The snake was also an age-old part of me but at the same time it was newly born. It had shed its old slough and had risen like a Phoenix from the ashes.

The dragon?

A bear stood on the trail in front of me. It was standing on its hind legs, paws in the air and claws showing, blocking my way.

"This way!"

I turned around and walked toward the sound of the voice. Bart stepped out from the brush.

"I have found the cave!"

15

As the good ship "Isis", after three days sailing, found itself on the open sea and far from land, Ben Nari for the first time put forward his demand. Either Ish-a-tar danced for him and gave herself to him for one night or she and Lamu would be thrown overboard. It was all so predictable and Ish-a-tar just shook her head at this insane demand. She immediately confronted Ben Nari with the fact that neither she nor Lamu had expected anything else and they both looked forward to their deaths by drowning with pleasure rather than complying with the lecherous desires of a madman.

Ben Nari spent three more days and nights pondering this until he realised that the two Therapists didn't fear death and that he therefore had to find another way to reach the goal of his dreams. Four days later he set forth his new demand, however, this time with the added ultimatum that if his demands were not complied with two innocent slaves would be sacrificed to Neptune.

That made the difference.

Lamu fumed but Ish-a-tar calmed him with a smile:

"There are other ways."

She kept Ben Nari at bay for ten days with the excuse that she was in the middle of her moon-period.

When the long expected evening finally arrived for Ish-a-tar to dance for Ben Nari the great merchant's saloon was decorated like a Roman brothel.

Ben Nari sat heavily on soft cushions eating from all the dishes that his slaves set before him in an endless flow of food. Two Egyptian musicians were preparing their instruments, a harp and a few drums, for the event of the evening. Ish-a-tar was preparing herself thoroughly in a small cubicle. From her time as a prostitute she knew exactly what to do in order to emphasize her beauty in the most cunning ways. And especially for this event she didn't hold back but tinted the most intimate parts of her body red. In other places she underlined the shadows with black and brown charcoal. Transparent veils and small, intriguing pieces of material were fastened with thin leather straps, giving the finishing touches to the most hot-blooded and daring harlot the world had ever seen.

She let Ben Nari wait while the music played in order to build up an atmosphere.

Ben Nari turned and twisted impatiently on the pillows. He was already scarlet in the face from lecherousness and excitement.

"When does she come?" he shouted hoarsely to a servant.

The servant immediately ran to Ish-a-tar to check that everything was all right. But Ish-a-tar simply ordered the poor man to go back to his master and inform him that the White Whore wasn't ready yet but that she would soon make her appearance.

When the atmosphere was so tense that Ish-a-tar could feel it all the way to her small cubicle she walked down the passage, pulled the curtains aside and stepped into the dimly lit saloon.

Ben Nari gasped for air. He had imagined all kinds of things but this was more than any man could imagine. A being from another world was standing in front of him radiating such an intense sensuality that he immediately felt his member move. He then pulled himself together and shouted at the servants:

"Out, out. I don't want to be disturbed."

Only the musicians and the servant who had contacted Ish-a-tar were allowed to stay. His task was to operate the big fan made from palm leaves that would prevent Ben Nari sweating to death.

Slowly Ish-a-tar slipped into the rhythm of the music. The veils whirled around her like butterflies and before long it was she who conducted the rhythm and the music and not vice-versa. She was mistress of this kind of game to perfection and she allowed no one to have any doubts on that score. She hovered across the floor, round and round, so that everyone could see that her movements were worthy of a queen. However, this was just to show where dignity lay: with the dancer not the audience. When Ish-a-tar had demonstrated this impeccably, she took the dance to another level. She found a centre and started dancing around it removing the outer veils. This, combined with the intense turning, started a centripetal force moving inwards and down towards a centre in her body. She let one arm circle towards the ground while the other moved upwards as if she held on to an invisible rope connecting the terrestrial with the divine. She danced faster and faster, round and round forming a circle totally free from any kind of sensuality. Out of this intense centre a centrifugal and upward moving force was whirling, which was so powerful that it filled the saloon with a penetrating light. Everything which was untrue was revealed in its intensity. From within this ecstatic dance Ish-a-tar saw the fearful, wry face of the great merchant and his futile attempts to hide himself from the merciless light. The musicians played as in a trance. Never before had they experienced that music and dance were able to enlighten and transform space like this.

However, Ish-a-tar knew all too well that this was just a short respite. Ben Nari would continue with his demands until he got his way.

She stepped out of the whirling enchantment with ease and at that moment the light seemed to dissolve so that the saloon once more was steeped in the sleazy semidarkness of repressions. Then she started on the last dance, which she danced to perfection. She slowly led the music along into an erotic universe leaving nothing to the imagination. She resembled a bird of prey, which until now had only circled the air, watching its prey but now dived like lightning in order to plunge its sharp claws into the soul and flesh of the paralyzed victim.

She danced back and forth, provocatively and enticingly, in front of Ben Nari, who was now in a state of mind beyond understanding. Ish-a-tar wanted to get this whole charade over and done with and took the dance to its final goal. One veil after the other fell to the ground until she was standing in front of him wearing a short, transparent loincloth only. Ben Nari fell on to his side grunting like a pig as he tried to get on his feet again. His cloak opened and Ish-a-tar saw his enormous, erect member like that of a horse. The time had come. She gracefully let herself slide to the floor and took up a position on hands and knees with her bottom in the air luring him to come closer.

"Why don't you help me?" Ben Nari shouted at the servant who was just as caught up in the enticing sight and didn't notice anything else while his master was rolling around on his pillows.

Ish-a-tar knew that she was balancing on a razor's edge.

She lifted her loincloth with one hand making herself totally open and accessible. But somehow, with that gesture, she underlined the fact that it was him, and not her, that had been stripped.

Ben Nari, in the meantime, got to his feet and stood staggering from side to side like a drunkard holding on to his erect member.

"I'm yours," she whispered leaning her forehead on the floor and looking behind her between her legs. Ben Nari staggered forward with one thing only on his mind.

He wanted to get down on his knees but almost lost his balance. The servant had to support him when he slowly approached the entrance to the holy temple of Ish-a-tar with his swollen member.

The time had come for Ish-a-tar to finish her task. She quickly pulled the energies back, closed her eyes and began chanting:

"Everything that ties in heaven, everything that ties on earth, everything that ties in the air, everything that ties in the firmament, everything that ties the Pleiades, everything that ties the sun, everything that ties the moon, everything that ties the birds, by the holy ring of the Father everything that ties the seven words which Iliseus said over the heads of the holy ones the names of whom are:

Psuchou, Chasnai, Chasna, Ithouni, Anashes, Shourani, Shouranai! Let these ties be transferred to this man's member, its flesh and the soul behind it. Let it dry up like wood and turn it into brushwood which is only good on a fire!"

Then she felt Ben Nari's hands on her hips. He pushed himself against her while he roared like a wild animal. She opened her eyes and looked over her shoulder where she saw his earlier so-potent weapon hanging limp and wrinkled between his fat thighs like a nestling falling out of its nest.

He pushed Ish-a-tar away very forcefully and only because of her agility did she avoid falling over. Before he had time to react she was on her feet wearing her cloak.

"Apparently, he has lost the power of the gods," she said innocently and with fake compassion to Ben Nari who didn't know what to say. This had never happened to him before. What kind of devilry was this?

"You damned whore!" he said as she withdrew between the curtains and disappeared on to the deck.

From that evening Ben Nari had to stay in bed. He sent for Ish-a-tar every day and begged her to heal him. She, however, simply pretended not to understand. Instead, she offered to dance for him and to spend the night with him, which just made the merchant cringe in despair.

"Can't you take pity on me? Don't you have a heart?" he sobbed.

This lasted until they touched at Valetta at Melita. Here Ish-a-tar for the last time went to ben Nari in his saloon. As the weeks had passed by the big man had shrunk in size, which made him look like a real human being. At the same time he had totally changed his character and was now so compliant and grateful for any service done to him that no one could believe it.

Is-a-tar went close to the sickbed and put her left hand on the forehead of Ben Nari.

"I thank you for your hospitality, Ben Nari. From this day on you shall leave your sickbed as a new man. As of today you shall leave all your sins of the past behind. As of this day you shall never again usurp anyone since now you understand what it means to be reliant on the help of others. Do you agree to that?"

"Yes," he whispered.

"Then be you healed!" she said in a clear voice.

When Lamu and Ish-a-tar went ashore at Melita they walked straight to the holy Hypogeum in order to meet the legendary oracle who lived in the passages below the temple. Innumerable were the stories about this oracle who from the beginning of time had only had male priests but who was now serviced by priestesses. Legend had it that a complicated channel system, which communicated the messages of the oracle, in those early days, only reacted to the voices of male priests. It had been like this for centuries. But one day the unthinkable happened: the oracle went silent. For more than one hundred years the oracle of Hypogeum was silent. Until one day when a holy woman came to the island. This woman had taken the place of the oracle as if it were the most natural thing and had spoken the most amazing prophesies. The woman, however, had to travel on to an unknown place. But before leaving she had taught a few suitable women to carry on the tradition.

Ish-a-tar was impatient and hurried Lamu who was more occupied with the fact that once more they had their feet on firm ground.

She wasn't satisfied until they stood at the entrance to the holy place. A smell of burned sage and other holy herbs came up from underground. Ish-a-tar immediately began descending the narrow and steep staircase.

"Come on!" she said.

✳

"It's this way," Bart said and signalled with his hand.

I could hardly believe that we were there. Perhaps I hadn't believed that the cave was really there. The time had come to find out if the dream was real.

Ba-Bé was looking into eternity as usual. We followed Bart closely who balanced sideways on a ledge, around a sharp corner, and then, we were surrounded by gnarled trees once more.

"There it is!"

Bart pointed in between the rocks.

I couldn't see anything. There was nothing to be seen.

"Where?" I asked suspiciously.

"Come over here."

Bart took my hand and helped me keep my balance over a hole surrounded by sharp rocks. Ba-Bé followed without Bart's help.

There it was.

The entrance to the cave.

I noticed immediately that the entrance was shaped like a pyramid and that there was just room for one single person to get through at a time. It was a beautiful moment. We stood still watching the entrance until Bart handed me a helmet and broke the silence:

"Do you want to be the first one through?"

I nodded.

Having put on my helmet I approached the holy spot. I squatted outside in order to collect myself. I then took a deep breath and crawled in.

I was met by the characteristic smell of sage. It was an old smell filled with purification and mystery. It was difficult to see anything and I sat down on the floor one metre into the antechamber in order that my eyes might get used to the darkness.

I suddenly felt an indefinable hush pass through the cave. There was no doubt. Another being had made its entrance and was now also present here. I looked around. The contours of another opening into a larger cave were just visible and I couldn't help laughing at the sight. This entrance was shaped like a pyramid turned upside down. It was then I noticed that I was sitting between the two entrances the shapes of which formed the Star of Mariam.

Of course.

Naturally.

I remembered with affection the sight I had seen one year earlier when the Star of Mariam had manifested itself for the first time while the Seer and I were climbing the mountain. I was enveloped by a deep peace coming towards me from all sides. Then I felt that I was lifted from the floor about twenty centimetres.

The secret cave-entrance seen from inside the first chamber (The Chariot of Fire).

The entrance to the inner-chamber seen from the first chamber.

An electric current ran through my body with a faint vibration. At first I was frightened but before this feeling really manifested itself it was replaced by a feeling of total surrender, and I felt how everything within me unanimously agreed to what was about to happen.

I don't know whether or not I said it aloud or if it was just something I was thinking, but the question to the being in the cave came out like this:

"Who are you?"

I had hardly finished the sentence or the thought before the answer came:

"Be you greeted. I am one of the Nameless Ones."

The cave was silent. The level of vibration went up a few degrees. Everything went so fast and yet it seemed as if a whole series of options appeared before me. I could choose fear or I could surrender to this being. I chose the latter.

"Where do you come from?"

"I have always been with you. From the beginning of time and until today. However, you yourself have not acknowledged that before."

Silence.

"You have a question?"

There was something both gentle and matter-of-fact about the being. But there was no time to lose and I seized the opportunity:

"What is happening?"

There was a long break. Or rather, this is how the silence seemed to me. In this great, cosmic thoughtfulness I sensed an equally great sense of humour trying to care for me in a way that suited my level of understanding.

"Up until today, you have followed the way of water. This is the horizontal, forward moving reality run by the trinity of time, space and matter. You are now to follow the way of fire. This is the vertical, upward moving reality opening to the fourth and fifth dimensions. Up and until now everything has been conditioned by body, soul and spirit. The fourth dimension is now being opened up: the ethereal reality of the Holy Spirit."

Silence.

The being continued communicating shortly after:

"You are in the Chariot of Fire. You may travel wherever and whenever you want to."

"How does this work?" I asked and immediately felt unworthy.

But just as immediately I felt the care of the being:

"Put any kind of limitation and any feeling of inferiority behind you. Think the thought and by it you may move anywhere and at any time, whenever you wish. Try it!"

My thoughts went chaotically through my head. This opened all kinds of possibilities. But something in me collected all the threads and I was immediately aware that I should call on a dear friend who was ill and needed help. As soon as I united with this thought I felt a tickling sensation in my forehead and at once found myself by my friend's sickbed.

He was asleep but smiled at me in his sleep. I quickly put a hand on his heart and blessed him with the words: "I thank you, I respect you, I love you." Then I removed my hand and was immediately back in the cave.

I am, of course, quite aware of the fact that such an explanation is insufficient and I shall not tire you, dear Reader, in trying to explain or defend myself with words that, naturally, must sound like total nonsense. Nevertheless, my words are quite true to the degree I am in my right mind or in possession of all my faculties.

I sat in an indefinable time-space continuum in a meditative state of mind as the being continued its communication with me:

"As you see, it is not at all difficult in itself to work with fire. The only condition is that you give up every kind of judgement."

The words of this being made the joy of recognition flow through me. Since both Sylvia, the Seer and the Voice all had earlier underlined the fact that it is always man's inclination to judge everyone and everything which builds the biggest limitations. How, I wondered, were Sylvia, the Seer, the Voice and this being connected?

Once again, I had hardly had the thought before the answer came:

"Everything is connected. All beings like everything in all the universes are interactively connected. We either get closer to or remove

ourselves from each other by way of our thoughts or our actions. Each one must choose. This is the secret behind the freedom of choice. And any conscious choice is an expression of an act of will. Only the one who opens himself to this reality may step actively into it. Man is already in this reality and has always been there but only a few have had the courage to acknowledge it. And this makes all the difference. Man keeps himself away from his most supreme possibilities through his endless judgements."

Silence.

Shortly after the being added:

"Fear is the refuge of the weak."

Silence.

"If you have more questions please ask?"

Once more I was seized by panic that time was running out. But once more the being calmed me:

"There is plenty of time."

There was so much I would like to know but sometimes it happens that you are totally blank when you get an opportunity like this.

"What kind of time is it we live in. What awaits humanity?"

"Chaos!"

I felt a stab in my heart.

"Chaos?"

"Or certainty. But that is the decision of the people. Closing your eyes and leaving responsibility to others leads to chaos. Each person now must take responsibility for him or herself."

"But doesn't this lead to total egotism?"

"No! Being responsible for your own life means that you understand that you are divine and absolutely necessary for the greater picture. It doesn't mean that man should only look after himself, his own career and his material comfort. Didn't He say: "Love your neighbour like yourself." This means: "Know yourself." How can the one who knows himself do evil to others? It is impossible. The one who knows himself will gladly take his place in the great, collective transformation. Each person has a role to play. Each person has come into this world with some unique qualities. If they are not put to use chaos will arise, sickness will arise and finally destruction will come."

"What does it take for man to avoid chaos, sickness and destruction? Are we to follow the traditional directions of the old religions?"

"Man must take responsibility for himself and avoid comparing himself and his work with that of others and with their work. No one, and I repeat, no one can know the processes other people go through or why people think and act the way they do. Find your way to the truth in yourself. The old directions and guru systems are out of date. All religions have outlived their roles. All hierarchies must fall. Both the secular and the spiritual ones. Religions and hierarchies have been necessary learning aids for man to lean on. Man must now learn to stand upright without any artificial aids. Then he shall be able to perfect himself and to help others."

"What about Krishna? What about Buddha? Or Jesus? What about Jesus Christ?"

Silence.

"Let them go. The problem with all you human beings is that you always personalise everything. You worship people. We are talking about pure energy. Krishna, Buddha and Christ are cosmic forms of energy and qualities present in human beings."

"What about God then?"

"Do you want to meet ☉?"

"☉?

"Yes, ☉."

"But is ☉ the same as God?"

"Well, you might say that. The concept of God covers your limited idea of ☉."

"No human being has ever seen God."

"Do you, or don't you want to meet ☉?"

"I certainly do!"

In one flowing movement everything visible was turned inside out. Like something positive becoming negative, or vice versa. In a space between the two poles, positive and negative, a ball of light was burning intensely in all the colours of the rainbow. From all sides millions of rays of light flowed back and forth like a gigantic nerve system of light.

"Let me introduce you to: God!"

"Yes, but ... "

I couldn't say anything.

"Can you imagine that God is the result of Man's idea of God? If you stay long enough you'll find out that God, apart from being an old man with a long, white beard, also is a black woman, an alcoholic homosexual, a neurotic communist, a blind boy of five years of age, the present President of U.S.A. or who ever you have the ability to imagine."

I closed my eyes. This was more, much more than I could take in. Instead I heard myself saying:

"What is the task of man here on earth?"

"Man is the link between heaven and earth. Man is the transformer. His task is to transform darkness into light, matter into spirit. Darkness is not evil in itself. Darkness slowly becomes evil if it is not changed into light. Darkness is a series of qualities, which haven't been acknowledged yet. If they stay unacknowledged or unchanged they carry in them the possibility of what you call evil."

"How does man transform anything?"

"By exchanging the horizontal way of thinking and acting for vertical understanding and reality. By taking a vertical way of thinking man unites earthly things with heavenly things. This is the task."

"Yes, but how?"

"If you will come to us we will meet you halfway."

"Could you be slightly more specific?"

"Man must lift himself above himself. When this happens we will bow down and lift him up. But it is totally the responsibility of each individual. This is the only way for us to co-operate."

A long silence followed. I sat meditatively for a while. The being exclaimed:

"LOVE IS A HEART WHICH MAY SEE IN THE DARK."

Another long silence followed. Then I felt compelled to say:

"But many people need a teacher?"

"Today's teacher is tomorrow's student. Today's student is tomorrow's teacher. Everybody needs coaching. But people all to often

leave the responsibility to charismatic personalities who claim to have the truth. There is not one single teacher on the earth today who knows the true potential of man. Mark my words: not one! Cleverly built hierarchies and systems, seemingly logical and esoteric explanations, theories and theologies are the devilish web barring the sight of the true path. Man loves fantasies."

"But what then is the true path?"

Silence. I sensed a quiet, vibrating laughter.

"It is so simple that no one will believe it."

"Why not?"

"Because you cannot make a personal fortune or an identity through it. The truth is not a career maker. Wisdom is not for sale and may not be bought."

"What and where is the truth then?"

"Truth is a power. It is everywhere. Did He not say that Heaven is within you and everywhere around you? The message about truth sounds the purest in silence. But it is drowned by the noisy messages that are shouted from every rooftop. The political, the materialistic and the spiritual marketplace."

"But what are people who seek going to do, then, where should they go?"

"THEY SHOULD STOP SEEKING AND LET THEMSELVES BE FOUND BY ☉."

"But how? What if this ☉ cannot find man?"

"That is why man must come forth from his hiding place. Everything man longs for is, and has always been, within his reach. If he would only acknowledge this there wouldn't be anything else to look for. When this happens man will step out of his self-made prison and into reality."

Silence.

The level of vibration was now so high that I stopped shivering. Instead, I felt the light of acknowledgement flowing through me.

The being continued:

"Has it not been said that faith can move mountains? When man loses his faith in what is real he places the responsibility in the hands of dubious experts and leaders. And when these leaders only believe

*in mammon, honour and power, illness arises. Illness within society
and within each human being. And illness creates more fear. If money
is the highest power and power the highest goal and this goal justifies
the means then man has turned his back on SPIRIT. When you spite
spirit you twist everything. It is an evil circle, which can only be broken
when you regain your faith in the highest qualities and have the courage
to step out of the curse. Hasn't it been said that it isn't possible to solve
the problems of the world by the same way of thinking which made
them? Those are words of wisdom that many of you may be able to
articulate but that not one of you learn from. Positive thoughts, which
do not turn into actions become negative dead weights instead."*

There was nothing didactic or preaching in the words of the
being. They were totally devoid of sentimentality. I had a sudden
thought. Perhaps this being didn't have any feelings. As before, the
answer came promptly:

*"Feelings are an important means of expression. Control them and
become realistic or let them control you and stay within your illusions.
All emotions have two sides to them. At the other side of joy you'll find
malice. Compassion is the heart's answer to sorrow. Without feelings
man would not be able to experience empathy towards another human
being. Feelings unite people. People are baptized in water. The time
has come to baptise with fire. Only what is true will survive the fire.
Everything unclean and false shall perish."*

Silence.

"What is the Holy Spirit?" I asked hesitatingly.

*"The Doer. The Heavenly Fire. It is the new way of thinking
which does not look back."*

"If you are not supposed to look back does that mean, then, that
all that history has taught man must be abolished?"

"What has mankind ever learned from history?"

"Did millions of people die in the concentration camps in vain?
Are we just to forget that?"

*"How could you forget that? It was you who killed each other.
It was you who invented the atom bomb and destroyed thousands of
brothers and sisters. It will remain a part of you. But it shouldn't be
cultivated. It must be recognized and then let go. In this way homicide*

can never again become a solution for man."

"And we were the ones who built the pyramids, right? Should we forget all about that? What if there is a totally new kind of knowledge hidden there waiting for man to find?"

"Do not get taken in by outward circumstances. Everything the pyramids contain, you also contain. Everything — and I repeat: EVERYTHING IS CONTAINED IN MAN!"

Silence.

"What is the fifth dimension?"

"You wouldn't be able to understand it yet."

"Please, help me to understand it."

Silence.

"Compassion."

"Compassion?"

"Compassion is the fifth dimension."

"Would you care to explain that a little further?"

"As I said: You wouldn't be able to understand it yet."

"But I really want to understand."

"I salute you. We'll meet again."

16

"Who gave you permission to enter here?"

Ish-a-tar and Lamu stopped. In front of them they saw a figure wrapped in a cloak – unrecognizable in the semi-darkness. The voice was indefinable. Ish-a-tar spoke:

"We are looking for the Oracle."

"Who are you?"

"We are two itinerant Therapists from Alexandria on our way to Massilia."

The figure looked at them and at their white gowns.

"Don't you know that only the chosen ones come here?"

Ish-a-tar's answer came quickly:

"But maybe that's what we are?"

"In that case you're welcome. However, if you do not speak the truth ... you will die. But tell me now what is the secret word?"

For a moment Ish-a-tar looked in bewilderment at Lamu but he couldn't help her. She then spoke the first words that came into her mind:

"Mariam Magdal!"

The figure was visibly shocked. The sound of heavy breathing filled the room. It was obvious that Ish-a-tar had spoken if not the secret word then at least a name was not unfamiliar in this place.

The figure's voice suddenly sounded more inviting:

"What do you know about Sister Mariam?"

Now Ish-a-tar dropped all her reserve:

"She's the one we are looking for. My travelling companion here has also been Mariam Magdal's travelling companion. And we are now looking for passage to Narbonensis where she is supposed to be staying."

A sound of a suppressed surprise was heard from behind the cloak:

"You'd better come with me."

The figure turned round and started walking back along the passage from which she had come. Arriving at the end of the passage they saw an even steeper staircase than the earlier one leading to a subterranean cave branching out in all directions. Ish-a-tar and Lamu followed the cloaked one closely.

They stepped into a large room illuminated by several oil lamps.

"Wait here."

The figure pointed to a stone bench and disappeared into a narrow opening in the wall. Ish-a-tar and Lamu sat down.

They sat for a long time. After a while, however, the smell of burnt sage became more and more insistent. A delicate white smoke came up through a grate in the floor below the stone bench on which they were sitting. Shortly after the Oracle started to speak. The voice sounded as if it belonged to God himself. They could not determine where the voice was coming from, but it filled the whole room and was so powerful that Ish-a-tar and Lamu crouched and put their hands over their ears.

"*Step forward vain one and state your business.*"

Ish-a-tar got up and took one step forward. Then she said:

"We're only travelling through, but we have thought that ..."

The oracle cut her short:

"*Step forward!*"

At that moment Ish-a-tar saw a small hole in the wall in front of her. The hole was marked with red dye and she understood that she was supposed to speak into it.

"We're travelling through. We're looking for the renowned Mariam Magdal. Can you tell us where we may find her?"

The oracle hesitated before answering:

"*With the Highest One.*"

The room was now almost filled with smoke. Ish-a-tar did not understand. The answer of the oracle was no answer at all, it sounded as if it was speaking in tongues.

"But where do we find the *Highest One?*"

"*Here, there, everywhere!*"

Ish-a-tar was slowly beginning to understand how the oracle worked. Apparently, it was not possible to get a direct answer from it.

"Does this mean that she's also here?"

This time the oracle did not hesitate:

"*Of course.*"

"How am I to understand that?"

"*Who's saying that you're supposed to understand it?*"

Ish-a-tar was getting tired of this foolish game. It did not lead anywhere. Or did it? She looked towards Lamu for help, but he was totally hidden by the smoke. However, he must have sensed that she was on the point of giving up because he suddenly came out of the smoke and walked up to Ish-a-tar, saying to the oracle:

"I know that sister Mariam has been here, but also that she has left again. Please tell us how she can still be here?"

The oracle kept silent.

Lamu and Ish-a-tar, knowingly, looked at each other. Then Lamu continued:

"Please tell us what the chances are for us to get a passage to Massilia?"

The echo of Lamu's words reverberated in the silence. They were about to give up hearing more from the oracle when it spoke again:

"*You'll have obtained a passage before the day is over. You will be on your way in three days' time. There's no more to be said. Be you greeted."*

It took them some time to find their way through the smoke back to the passage and the staircase leading into the open. Not until they were standing outside the temple did they feel how dizzy the smoke had made them. They were as if bewitched and had to support each other. An image of a woman kneeling appeared in Ish-a-tar's mind. The woman was holding a human skull in one hand and a book in the other. The sound of drums and bells came up from below forming strange rhythmic patterns that followed them on their way back to the harbour.

They saw a man running towards them from the harbour and recognised one of Ben Nari's servants. When he got close to them he threw himself to the ground gasping for air and saying:

"I've been looking for you everywhere. You must follow me immediately. My master has risen from his sickbed, but we don't know him anymore and we are all afraid that we are going to lose our jobs on board. He keeps asking for you. You must come and heal my master."

Lamu could not help laughing.

"Get up my good man and go back and tell your master that we are on our way."

Having bowed and scraped and thanked them in a confusing flow of movements and words the servant disappeared back where he came from.

At the harbour a crowd of people followed the unloading of the ship. The smell of spices mixed with the pungent smell of dried hides, which were carried ashore and stacked in the long warehouses.

Ish-a-tar and Lamu were walking up the gangway to the "Isis" shortly after – for the second time.

✡

A drop of rain.

I heard the sound of it and felt it as it hit my helmet right in the middle of the crown centre. It felt like a finger from on high reaching down and knocking lightly on the top of my head.

I lifted my head in order to see where the drop came from. At that moment another drop fell. It felt like an explosion when it hit my pineal centre in the middle of the third eye.

Open.

Immediately I realized that these were the two initiating steps in a baptism to my new life. The third and last step was yet to come. But in my heart I had a clear sense of what this baptism was about and what the purpose of it was.

I suddenly understood the hidden truth about the legend of the Grail saying that the Grail was a gem, which at the dawn of time had fallen out of the tiara on the forehead of the rebellious angel Lucifer when he was expelled from heaven. This gem symbolizes the third eye and the monadic consciousness possessed by all people before they incarnate into this life. I realized that the bearer of light, Lucifer, is archetypal man who has lost his true vision, the awareness of his true origin: the certainty that we are all children of the Heavenly Source, God – or ☉. And when the old Cathar legend tells us that the saint of the Cathars, Esclarmonde, during the siege by the inquisition of Montségur, threw the Grail, the gem of Lucifer, into the mountain in order to prevent it falling into the wrong hands, then this was the Cathars' allegorical interpretation of one of the deepest and most important truths about the condition of man, his potentiality, means and purpose.

"How are you?"

Bart's face appeared in the entrance-way. My whole body felt light as a feather. I felt a lively, electrical activity around me. But I couldn't find any words to match the situation.

"You look as if you feel very well. Are you ready to continue further into the cave?" he asked slightly worried.

I must have looked silly sitting there squatting with a transfigured smile on my face and a scratched miner's helmet on my head. I pulled myself together then and tried to say something. But I couldn't find the words. Instead I sent him a thought asking him not to worry. Immediately his face also lit up in a smile and he withdrew from the entrance and left me sitting in peace. In the following silence I heard a voice whispering:

"You've found what you were looking for: the heart on your true Mount Carmel."

It was an unbelievable moment. Every cell in my body was filled with joy. I understood that each person is a sensitive field of energy, which is constantly surged by numerous kinds of powers, which it cannot always transform and recognize. And I understood that it is the degree of ability, will power or courage to acknowledge and awaken these powers, which is decisive for the way they manifest and become expressed through man. Exactly there, at that moment, I surrendered to the flow, and for the first time in my life I, more than ever before, felt in agreement with that which was real in me. For the first time ever I felt in agreement at a higher level with the task that I had taken upon myself before I was sent into the terrestrial reality. Everything the angel had told me opened up into my innermost being and sitting there in the cave I realized that the transfigured certainty within me, perhaps, consisted of this one single element:

Grace.

I silently spoke the Aramaic prayer of Heaven, thanking the angel and crawled into the open.

Outside Bart was sitting in blessed meditation. Ba-Bé was smiling at me as if she was fully aware of what I had been through. She then kissed me on my forehead and crawled into the cave.

✷

Ben Nari received them in his saloon. He looked completely different and one might think it was a stranger talking:

"The good ship Isis will be unloaded in a couple of days. It will then hoist anchor and head for Massilia with no other cargo onboard than those who are looking for the holy Mariam Magdal. It is my hope that you shall be among the travellers."

Ben Nari took a step in front of Ish-a-tar. He was not pretending when he said:

"Thanks to you a new human being was born last night. It is this human being standing in front of you at this moment wanting in all humility to give you just a fraction of all that you have given me. Without any cargo we'll be able to make the journey before the autumn storms really set in."

He knelt down before her. Ish-a-tar put her hands on his shoulders:

"Stand up, today the prayer of man has been heard by God."

✻

"Are we going any further?"

Bart stood up, came over and sat on a rock beside me.

"I don't think so," I said. "Only if Ba-Bé wants it. I have found what I came to find. What would we find further in?"

Bart was scratching the back of his neck as if he didn't quite understand why I didn't want to see it all when we had taken the trouble of crawling all the way up here. Shortly after he said:

"You crawl about five metres along quite a narrow passage. Then you enter a large room about fifteen metres in diameter and about twenty metres high. From here there are two openings, one on each side of the room, leading into an intricate system of passageways where you can walk about for hours. I've no idea how big it is or where it leads to and I don't know of anyone who does. When I have been investigating the passageways on earlier occasions, I stopped when the thread I used for security ran out. But I'm convinced that you can really get lost there."

Bart stopped talking. We were looking at the entrance to the cave waiting for Ba-Bé to turn up.

I couldn't help thinking that the innermost cave that Bart had just described was an image of man's latent need to complicate everything, a kind of matrix of our neurotic need to get lost each time we are unable to or for some reason do not want to differentiate.

I had no doubt that what I had experienced in the antechamber was the essence of everything, which I at this moment was able to contain. And I was equally aware that this experience was part of a plan to make me step out from my hiding place which up until now perhaps had kept me from being found by God.

Although I felt totally centred and rested in my heart, I also felt how sensitive and vulnerable I was. I could feel the sensitivity and vulnerability of all mankind. Thinking about what we put ourselves, and others through, and at the same time wasting all our best qualities and possibilities on nothing, made me more than sad.

I waved my sadness aside. What good was it? Instead, I followed a sudden inclination once more to try the chariot of fire. I closed my eyes, lost myself in my breathing, and briefly described my goal, which this time was a bedridden client I had worked with in Denmark for a while. I had a prickly sensation on my forehead and immediately I found myself sitting at the sickbed. My client cried out in surprise, "what are you doing here?" As though it was the most natural thing in the world I put my left hand on the chest of my client. Shortly after I heard myself saying, "I honour you. I respect you. I love you. Be you healed!" I then lifted my hand and once more I was sitting in front of the hidden cave on Mount Montségur in the Pyrenees.

My left hand was warm and the right one was cold. This was a very strange form of precision. There was no nonsense about it. And the self who spoke the words was not my own little self but something bigger and inexplicable. It had all just taken a few moments and it left me wondering and filled with gratitude. I sat for a while but then decided to contact Sylvia. Having done the necessary simple act of focussing, and having felt the familiar prickly sensation on my forehead, I was standing face to face with Sylvia. However, we were not in her livingroom in Charlottenlund in Denmark, but in shapeless floating space.

She smiled at me in acknowledgement:

"As you can see, you shouldn't play with fire."

Her golden laughter filled the ethereal space with a lifegiving electricity.

"Remember Venus," she whispered.

Shortly after she had disappeared again, and once more I was sitting on the mountain at Monségur.

Venus?

So close and yet so far away.

Where should I go from here? There were so many questions I would like to ask Sylvia, but apparently this was not the time for it. There was so much to remember and so much to understand in order to work out the puzzle. If there was a puzzle at all? At that moment I remembered Sylvia's reminder that I should also visit the church in Montségur.

Shortly after Ba-Bé appeared in the entrance to the cave. She was also visibly marked by the experience of this place.

Bart looked closely at her. Then he looked questioningly at me, and I knew what was going on in his mind. I therefore asked Ba-Bé if she was ready to crawl further into the cave. She answered immediately:

"Why? We already got what we came for, didn't we?"

Bart was confused and looked from one to the other. I couldn't help smiling at her direct ways.

"I suppose that ends the matter," I said to Bart.

We then started the descent, which was even more difficult and more dangerous than the ascent had been. The only difference was that I had much more energy now.

We came down whole, tired and sweating, but with a totally new and different kind of energy than the one it normally takes to crawl up and down mountains. We quenched our thirst with a couple of lukewarm cans of beer before driving Bart back to Roquefixade.

We paid him, thanking him for his assistance and once more set out towards Montségur.

"We now have only one problem," I said.

"And that is?" Ba-Bé asked, casually.

"How do we get the key to the church in Montségur?"

"Oh, that. Don't worry about it."

I looked at her. As usual she was sitting with her legs on the dashboard over the glove compartment looking at the landscape passing by outside.

I parked outside of René´s house. Before I could take off my safetybelt, she was halfway out of the car:

"You go on down to the church. I'll be there shortly."

Then she was gone. Standing on the road I tried to catch a glimpse of her, but she was nowhere to be seen. I started walking down through the village. The distance from René's house to the church is not very far and although I took my time, it didn't take more than ten minutes before I was standing in the little square in front of the church. I couldn't see the door which was hidden in the shadows from the trees, and I was about to sit down when I heard Ba-Bé´s voice:

"Why don't we go in?"

I squinted and could then see her standing outside the church door waving a large key in the air.

"I'll be...! Where the devil did you get that?"

"At one of the Norn's," she laughed secretively.

It was obvious that she didn't want to tell me more, but I couldn't help wondering what she knew about The Three Norns, representing past, present and future whose presence I knew all about here in Montségur. However, I didn't ask her about it.

The key made a rusty, grating sound as it was turned in the lock. We helped each other push the door open and it squeaked so much on its hinges that it was clear that it hadn't been opened for a long time. We were met by a pungent smell of chalk and mouldy wood. It was pitch-dark. I found a switch to my right, which lit a naked light bulb that turned out to be the only light in the church.

We stepped inside.

✡

One early autumn morning the "Isis" finally arrived at Massilia after twenty-six days of hard sailing.

They were not allowed to leave the ship before they got permission from one of the officials of the Roman proconsul. They waited most of the day without getting any kind of information at all. Ben Nari then sent a messenger to Herod's palace in the Jewish part of the town. This worked. Ben Nari and Herod had been involved in many business transactions over the years. They went ashore an hour later with all the necessary permits. Furthermore, Ben Nari and his entourage had been invited to dine with Herod himself who was here in order to relax.

"Would you please join me as my guests?" Ben Nari asked Ish-a-tar and Lamu.

And thus it happened that they got lodgings and were about to dine with the richest man in Massilia.

Herod was a well-proportioned man in his prime with obvious Jewish, aristocratic features. He seemed quite surprised at the sight of the re-born Ben Nari who bore no resemblance at all to his old, smirking and promiscuous self. But Herod, who could appreciate a profitable deal himself had always liked Ben Nari, if nothing else then at least because he was the most cunning and the most gluttonous of them all. Anyone in the company of Ben Nari immediately turned into a saint. Slightly insecure he embraced the great merchant who now appeared to be humility itself, showing signs of true joy. Herod was wondering what was going on, but he just didn't understand.

Ben Nari was virtue itself and if Herod had doubted his sincerity, he had to admit that the gratitude and humility which the merchant showed his two guests were unmistakable and beyond any doubt.

"Herod my dear friend," Ben Nari said. "I would like you to meet these Therapists from Alexandria to whom I owe my life."

He called Ish-a-tar and Lamu who came forward before Herod and greeted him the way you are supposed to greet a royal personage.

"I greet you, you who are dressed in white," Herod said and asked them to the table.

When, shortly after, according to Roman tradition, they lay on soft couches around a well-provided table, Herod clapped his hands and four musicians started to play softly.

"Be my guests and eat heartily," Herod laughed while he studied Ish-a-tar with curiosity.

It was clear that he had noticed her beauty. They dined in silence until Herod asked:

"What brings you to Narbonensis?"

Ben Nari answered: "A holy woman by the name of Mariam Magdal. Do you know where we may find her?"

Herod looked at Ben Nari in surprise:

"What do you want from her?"

"We really want to meet her. Do you know her?"

Herod nodded:

"I should say so, since she came to Narbonensis onboard one of my ships. But do tell me what do you want from her?"

"Well, it is really my two friends here who are looking for her. So many stories are told about this Mariam that I myself would like to meet her."

Herod now spoke directly to Ish-a-tar:

"What do you expect from Mariam Magdal?"

Ish-a-tar placed her slice of bread on the table thinking about Herod's question. After a while she answered:

"Everything. The only thing I want is to become a student of this holy woman."

Herod was feeling increasingly insecure in the company of Ish-a-tar. He was very impressed by this remarkable, beautiful woman.

"Haven't I seen you before?"

The question had an ominous ring to it. Lamu looked tense and Ben Nari had raised himself on his elbows and looked equally uncomfortable at the situation. Then he intervened with another question intending to dissolve the tension:

"I don't think so. Sister Mar-Iona has never before been outside Alexandria."

This answer seemed for a while to move Herod's attention away from Ish-a-tar, in whom he could hardly suppress his interest.

"I suppose that dancing would be inappropriate," he said. "I have some of the best female dancers in all of Gaul."

Ben Nari uncomfortably shook his head:

"No, no, there's no need for dancing. Let us dine. Now, tell us about this Mariam Magdal."

Herod got up from his pillows:

"Mariam Magdal is the most learned woman that I have ever met. As far as I know she knows more about the deepest secrets and the

Mariam Magdalene lecturing the King and Queen of Marseilles
(From painting by René d´Anjou, 1408-1480. See "Joan of Arc in Appendix C)

highest sciences than any man. Few only, however, understand her teaching which is a continuation of the wisdom of the well-known magus and messiah Yeshua Ben David. She prophesies and preaches, she heals and teaches."

"Is she here in Massilia?"

"Apparently she lives not far from here. But even I do not know where since she lives very secluded. It has been quite a while since she was seen and heard teaching. It is said that even aristocrats, rabbis, druids well, even alchemists are among her students. Some say that she lives in a castle, which has been put at her disposal by a princely vassal south of Narbo-Martius.[6] Others say that she lives in some desolate caves in the wilderness. But tomorrow I shall send out messengers in order to obtain more information about her."

---

6   Present day Narbonne.

"Is Narbo-Martius far from here?"

It was Ish-a-tar who now also sat up. Herod looked at her as if he contemplated putting aside all his inhibitions. But Ish-a-tar's white gown made him control himself:

"It is situated several days' travel from here. Narbo-Martius represents one of the largest and oldest Jewish settlements in Narbonensis in all of Gaul. I have vineyards down there, but I have never been there myself. They say it is supposed to be quite tolerable. The wine from my grapes is quite good. That is all I can say with any certainty. And for that we thank the powers in heaven. Thank God we are not and shall never be Romans. However, we do owe our safety to the power of Rome."

At these words Ish-a-tar remembered what Salome had said, "a choice is always between ROMA and AMOR."

She now had to control her impatience and wait until morning.

17

We closed the door behind us and stood in the faint light from a single light bulb, which lit up only part of the small church.

I saw her immediately. She was placed on a pedestal against a pillar to the left of the aisle.

Joan of Arc?

I walked right up to the figure and looked at the brass tag on the pedestal. As I suspected it was Joan of Arc. But it was hardly her fault that the village church wasn't being used anymore. There had to be a connection to my quest since Sylvia had both mentioned Joan of Arc and, at the same time, reminded me that I ought to visit the church at Montségur. Was there a specific connection between this saint and the village, I wondered?

I tried to remember if there were other churches where I had seen a similar figure of Joan of Arc but I couldn't remember one.

Then it struck me that I had seen a similar one once before. It happened when the Seer and I had visited Rennes-le-Château for the first time, years ago. It was placed in the small glass chapel built by the legendary priest, Sauniére, in connection with the building of "Villa Bethania" at the beginning of the previous century. The story about the priest who had found something during the restoration of the church in Rennes-le-Château which was so valuable that from that day on he became extremely wealthy, was known by most people. At least by the millions of people who had read *The Holy Blood and the Holy Grail.* In spite of numerous attempts no one has yet succeeded in solving the riddle of what it was the priest found and from where he got all his money.

The glass chapel had been built at a time when Sauniére had been temporarily suspended from celebrating Mass in the church itself because of disagreements with his bishop. According to myth, it was to this chapel that some of the great personalities like for example the diva Emma Calvé came from far away in order to participate in Sauniére's Masses. What had taken place during these Masses that was so popular?

When the Seer and I had visited the chapel several of the windowpanes had been missing and the interior clearly marked by wind and weather and the passing of time. Somehow, however, this only added to the ambience of the place. The chapel, like almost everything else in Rennes-le-Château, was dedicated to Mary Magdalene, and on the altar of the small chapel a large, beautiful sculpture of her was placed. As far as I remember, the sculpture of Joan of Arc was placed below Magdalene.

I wondered if there was a Magdalene sculpture in the church of Montségur? Or a black Madonna? According to my sources you would always find Joan of Arc in the company of either Magdalene or a black Madonna.

I walked further up the aisle but saw only the usual saint sculptures like Notre-Dame-de-Lourdes, Francis of Assisi, Teresa, Joseph as well as the mother of the Virgin Mary, Anna. I threw a casual glance at the altar and could hardly believe my eyes.

On a dais under a canopy at the centre of the altar and with three candelabra on each side was a black Madonna with child. It was pitch black and plated with gold foil. Apparently my sources had been correct. But what was the connection between the Madonna and Joan of Arc?

Sauniéres glass-chapel, Villa Bethania, Rennes-le-Château
(Notice the figurines of Mariam Magdalene and Joan of Arc)

Inside the church of Montségur

Joan of Arc, Black Madonna and Mariam from the church of Montségur

To the left of the altar I could see a sculpture of a young girl. There was no name on the pedestal. Was this supposed to be Magdalene?

I started to look more closely at the altar and to my surprise I noticed a fresco on the ceiling above the black Madonna, depicting an occult symbol: a burning pyramid with the *tetragram* IHVH within it on a pale blue background. The burning pyramid is also seen in other ecclesiastical contexts but never before had I seen it depicted like this. The figure of a black woman with a black girl beside her was painted above the left side altar. Above the right one, a white man.

No matter what had taken place in this church, one might assume that those responsible for the decoration must have worked on the basis of a specific idea. Either this, or it was the result of a bizarre sense of humour or perhaps simply religious confusion.

I continued my investigation but at first failed to find anything of interest. Only the baptismal font seemed interesting since it was shaped like the cup of the grail and was situated just inside the door. It was, however, hard to say if it was different from any other baptismal font.

Just then, I turned and looked at Ba-Bé who stood smiling behind me pointing to the stone floor. I looked down and immediately knew that those who had decorated the church had been fully aware of what they were doing.

On the floor just inside the door two diamond shapes were carved in the tiles.

They overlapped forming a third, diamond shape just as two overlapping circles form a *Mandorla*; the almond shape symbolizing Venus and the vagina.

I was just thinking that we ought to go to Rennes-le-Château when Ba-Bé said:

"Why don't we go to Rennes-le-Château?"

When we were sitting in the car shortly after on our way to Sauniére's village I was wondering why Ba-Bé had suggested that we go there at this exact moment? In spite of the fact that she was a total stranger I had only known for a couple of days, so many striking things had happened between us within those days that it seemed that we really knew each other at a deeper level. Yet she still remained a stranger to me in a worldly

The Mandorla in the church of Montségur

sense. It was a real paradox.

From where did she originate and what did she want from me?

If she was the virgin that Sylvia had talked about who would come to me, was it the Board Upstairs who had sent her? And what was it all about?

I couldn't help thinking that she might be a guide pointing to the signs I myself couldn't see as she had just demonstrated in the church at Montségur. And we were now on our way to Rennes-le-Château.

We drove through Quillan. I increased the speed as we drove out of the last curve heading towards Quiza. The answers would come soon. She couldn't go on hiding her true identity from me.

✳

They were awakened in the middle of the night. It was Ben Nari himself, dressed in his tunic only, standing outside the guesthouse where Ish-a-tar and Lamu were staying. He looked very worried:

"You must continue your journey immediately. You must leave before dawn."

"What is it that is worrying you so much?" Lamu asked slightly worried himself.

"It is Herod. I could see it in his eyes, and I know him all too well. He wants Ish-a-tar, and when he wants something he just takes it. One of my servants will take you to a person who is familiar with the area to the south of Narbo-Martius. I have already told him that you are on your way there."

"Aren't you coming along?" Lamu asked.

"No. I shall stay here and try to make Herod change his mind. I shall join you later."

The three parted in friendly fashion and before the sun had risen they had left Massilia together with a middle-aged, Jewish wine merchant whom Ben Nari had paid to lead them on their way south. They preferred to travel by lesser known paths, not only to ensure that Herod's men didn't find them, but also because *Via Domitia*, running all the way from Rome to just south of Narbo-Martius, was tough on the horses' legs.

In spite of the storm, which was quite normal in Gaul during the autumn, they reached Narbo-Martius within two days. Ish-a-tar insisted that they should continue but their guide convinced them that they should stay in the town in order to find someone who knew the whereabouts of Sister Mariam.

The size of Narbo-Martius and all its facilities were a result of the Roman presence over about a hundred years. But although the town was outside Rome itself with mainly Roman inhabitants, there was also a major Jewish community within the town's limits. This was where the wine merchant led them. The town was filled with lively activity and the inhabitants were busy with their own affairs and thus the travellers passed through unnoticed.

They found an inn where both they and their horses could be refreshed, while the wine merchant went to look for some relatives who could help them further.

They were sitting in the inn looking out at the bustle of the town when Ish-a-tar, having collected all her power in her heart to ask for a sign, suddenly saw a big, middle-aged man at the other side of the square. The man wore a gown, which very much resembled the white

robes of the priests of the Chaldeans with the characteristic signs of
the lion, bull, eagle and angel embroidered on the chest.

"When you open your heart and ask from the innermost chamber
an answer will always manifest itself," Salome had told her and she
now experienced how it worked.

"Do you see what I see?" she asked Lamu as if to make sure that
the old Chaldean wasn't a dream.

Lamu looked inquiringly at Ish-a-tar:

"The Chaldean?"

"It is probably best that you talk to him. I'm certain that he knows
the whereabouts of Sister Mariam."

Ish-a-tar stayed in her chair watching how Lamu greeted
the Chaldean priest who looked more and more worried as the
conversation progressed. When he shook his head Ish-a-tar nearly
got up and ran to the two men. Instead she took a deep breath.
"Faith, faith and more faith," that was what Salome had always said.
It was now or never.

The man looked in the direction of Ish-a-tar. His gaze felt like
pure fire burning its way into her innermost being.

✫

The gearbox moaned when I put it into second and started to climb
the five kilometres long road to Rennes-le-Château. Considering the
time of year there was more traffic than usual. When shortly after we
drove into the town and turned into the parking space I was pleased
to see that a single car only was parked there.

We went directly to Sauniéres's house, which, together with "Villa
Bethania," the garden and "Tour Magdala," has now been turned into
a museum of the mystery of the priest and his assumed treasure. I
bought tickets and immediately went up to the first floor from where
you have access to the garden and the glass chapel outside of "Villa
Bethania," while Ba-Bé saw the exhibition in Sauniére's original home
on the ground floor.

Stepping into the garden gave me my first surprise. The glass chapel had been restored with new coloured windowpanes and was totally changed. I practically ran to it and tore the door open. Inside, everything was very nice and newly painted. The sculptures of Mary Magdalene and Joan of Arc were gone. I hurried back to the ticket office and asked the woman there if she knew where the sculptures had been taken. But she didn't. She didn't even know of their existence. I suddenly doubted whether or not I had seen them in the glass chapel. But they had actually been there. Who had moved them and why? And what difference did it make? Was it at all important? When all was said and done, external circumstances interested me only to the extent that they provided delivery from or acknowledgement of inner experience. But something told me that precisely the fact that the sculptures had mattered to Sauniére and the cult he apparently had been a part of, was not a clue to an external, tangible treasure but more an important piece of knowledge about man's possibilities in the spiritual realm. I was, however, convinced about one thing: Mary Magdalene and Joan of Arc were somehow important parts of this knowledge.

I didn't need anything else in Rennes-le-Château and went back to the museum in order to find Ba-Bé. She was neither downstairs nor upstairs. I went back upstairs, through the garden to the "Tour Magdalene," but she was not in the tower or at the balustrade outside. I quickly went back through the garden and through the glass chapel to see if she was in "Villa Bethania."

She wasn't.

On my way back to the ticket office I met an elderly couple and asked them if they had seen a young woman fitting my description of Ba-Bé.

They hadn't.

At the ticket office the woman there couldn't remember if she had seen Ba-Bé passing by or not. I was getting slightly panicky.

Before walking over to the church to see if Ba-Bé was there, I asked the woman at the ticket office to tell her, should she turn up again, that I would be waiting in the car park.

Having made sure that she wasn't in the church I hurried back to the car park, but she wasn't by the car either.

I opened the door of a public toilet and shouted her name but there was no response. I ran back towards the museum to check the souvenir shop, but they hadn't seen her. Then she had to be in the bookstore. I was completely out of breath as I opened the door and almost fell down the stairs and into the shop.

"Have you seen a woman of about twenty eight years old? She is tall, slender and blond." I stuttered while trying to catch my breath. My heart was pounding and I thought that everybody in the bookstore could hear it.

The young man looked absent-mindedly at me and said dryly:

"The young woman was here just a moment ago."

I breathed a sigh of relief. Then nothing had happened to her. On the other hand, what could have happened?

He then added in a neutral voice while at the same time writing something on a note pad:

"She bought a map of *Durban-Corbiéres.*"

I thanked him and walked back to the parking place through the narrow streets. Why did Ba-Bé want a map of Durban-Corbiéres I wondered? I had never heard of the area before.

I still couldn't see her anywhere and decided to wait in the car. She was bound to appear soon.

I didn't see it until I was sitting in the driver's seat. It was tucked behind one of the wipers like a parking ticket.

The map. The sight of it worried me.

I opened the door quickly and took hold of it.

It was a map of the area Durban-Corbiéres Leucate.

I unfolded it frantically. It covered the area from south of Narbonne to just north of Perpignan. What did she want with a map of this area? And why had she left it here? I was about to fold the map again when I noticed a town, which had been circled by a pen.

Périllos.

☼

The two men said their good-byes and shortly after Lamu again sat next to Ish-a-tar.

"Good news," Lamu said, "The priest, who is not a Chaldean but a Druid and whose name is Gisbart, will take us to Sister Mariam. She is staying at a monastery to the south by the name of *Salveterra* situated at *Terresalvaesche*, a plateau outside the town of *Oppidum*[7]."

"Did he have anything else to say?"

Ish-a-tar could hardly control her curiosity.

"He is a man of few words. But you may get him to say more than I can. He undoubtedly knows Sister Mariam. He said that she had withdrawn from any worldly activity and spends a lot of time in the desert near the monastery. She regularly sees pilgrims of whom there seem to be more and more. The rumours about her are spreading and she attracts not only Jews, but also Romans, Gauls, Celts and people from the south. I do feel that we may safely put our trust in him."

"When are we leaving?"

Lamu laughed:

"You are incorrigible. We leave today. Gisbart had just one thing to do before we leave."

✶

Périllos!

Wasn't this the surname of the waitress at the "Belo Bar" in Narbonne?

Marie Périllos.

Was this a coincidence or ...?

I began studying the map more closely and now saw that a route was marked from the town of Périllos to a point not far from it, which had been marked with a red star and the name *La Caune*. The whole area seemed quite desolate. I found yet another penmarking to the south of Périllos. It was just a little more difficult to see. Next to this mark the name *Château d'Opoul* had been written.

I slowly went through the whole area on the map but couldn't find any more marks.

---

7   Present day Opoul.

It was obvious that Ba-Bé wanted to tell me something. But what? And where was she? Had she for some reason or other continued to the town on the map? The map had to be a suggestion for me to go there.

The sun was setting behind the mountains on the horizon and gave the whole landscape a red hue. While I was waiting I got the idea that I might try to contact Ba-Bé by way of *the chariot of fire*. I closed my eyes and concentrated on my breathing. "On to Ba-Bé" I whispered to myself. The familiar prickly sensation on my forehead was followed by the just as familiar, ethereal sound of hissing around me. I opened my inner eye and found myself in a totally desolate landscape. It was dark, foggy and bleak with no one in sight. There was an oppressive feeling about it all. I whispered her name once more but she didn't appear.

When I opened my eyes again I saw the last rays of the setting sun.

Had it all just been a dream? The whole meeting with Ba-Bé did seem rather unreal. And now she had disappeared as suddenly as she had appeared.

"Who are you? All of you?" I heard myself saying. "Speak to me. Show me the way!"

But there was no answer. The only other presence was the empty air. Had everything up until now been a figment of my imagination?

No, the experience in the cave at Montségur had been very real. The being that had spoken to me there had been very real, just like the experience of light with Ba-Bé had been in Roquefixade. No doubt about it.

It was too late to do anything about it now and I decided to drive down into God's valley, *Valdieu*, just below Rennes-le-Château where I knew I could find a small hotel.

✳

A few hours later they were on their way. As Lamu had already said, Gisbart was a man of few words. But that didn't stop Ish-a-tar. As soon as they got away from Via Domitia and came into a more peaceful area in the shade of some oak trees she rode up next to the Druid.

"Excuse me for intruding. I do not know anything about the faith of the Celts or the Gauls and nothing at all about the rules of the renowned Druids. I myself, however, have been taught by the Therapists in Alexandria and I sense a kinship between us."

"Hm" was all Gisbart said keeping his eyes on the path in front of him.

Such an answer might have discouraged anyone else, however, not Ish-a-tar. She simply considered his response as encouragement to continue.

"Your gown resembles that of the Chaldean priests. How is that?"

Gisbart turned his face towards Ish-a-tar. He looked closely at her and their eyes met. Ish-a-tar felt a deep sense of warmth at this meeting and she knew that she was right. Then Gisbart said:

"The Chaldean priests and we Druids have co-operated on many occasions. You ought to know that as a Therapist."

Ish-a-tar looked at him uncomprehendingly. Then Gisbart continued:

"A great deal of the Therapists' knowledge of the stars and herbs come from the Chaldeans and the Druids. And as you very well know, sister Mariam was also trained by the Therapists in Alexandria."

Ish-a-tar nodded eagerly. Gisbart now looked more obliging. Ish-a-tar almost thought that she had seen a smile in his eyes. This encouraged her further:

"Tell me, how is Sister Mariam?"

He was pondering her question for a long time. After a while he said in a low voice:

"She is different from any other person I have ever met. She is not of this world. That is all I can say."

It was very clear from the tone of his voice that he was speaking about something very special.

They were rocking along in their saddles when finally Ish-a-tar broke the silence:

"Do you think she might receive me and my fellow traveller?"

"She might. However, at the moment Sister Mariam is in the desert going through forty day's of fast. While this is going on it is only her closest sisters who may contact her. No man is allowed near her."

At these words Ish-a-tar exclaimed, not knowing where the words came from:

"But I am one of Sister Mariam's closest sisters!"

"We'll see," was the laconic answer.

✡

A giant dog came running towards me barking as I stepped out of the car in front of the hotel *Les Labadous* in Valdieu. The threatening animal was about to jump up at me when a voice called it back into the darkness. The light from the hallway shone on to the car park and a face appeared.

I booked a room for a single night and went into the dining room in order to get supper. The place was very cosy and there was a fire in the open fireplace. A small, round man about my own age was seated at the refectory table. I nodded and sat down opposite him. It would have been awkward not to. He shook my hand across the table:

"André," he said, and shook my hand again.

"Lars," I replied.

He turned one of the wine glasses over, which was placed upside down in a cluster of other wine glasses in the middle of the table.

"Would you care for some wine?"

"Yes, please, a glass of wine is just what I need."

"What brings you here," he said pouring wine into our glasses.

For a moment I thought about telling him about the disappearance of Ba-Bé but decided against it. Instead I said:

"I'm about to finish my latest book."

"Oh," he smiled almost indulgently, "you're one of the writers trying to solve the riddle of Rennes-le-Château, then?"

"No, not at all. I ..."

I hesitated. Why did I feel the need to justify myself to this person whom I didn't know at all."

"I write books with an esoteric content," I said, "and right now I'm on my way to Périllos, a small town on the coast."

He nodded approvingly:

"Have you been there before," he asked, suddenly seeming quite interested.

"Never," I said.

"It is a very unusual place with an equally interesting history. Do you know it?"

"I'm afraid not, but I would like to hear it."

Suddenly I had forgotten all about my evening meal. He got up and signalled to me:

"Come on," he said. "Bring your glass. The food will be late anyway."

Shortly after, when we were comfortably seated in a couple of oversized comfy-chairs at the fireplace, he poured more wine and started to talk:

"For centuries the area around Périllos remained unexplored for unknown reasons. Until the eighteenth century it was still marked as "white, empty space" on the map that the contemporary head of the observatory in Paris, Cassini, had made. Today, Périllos is an abandoned village surrounded by cliffs and a few, low, desert-like bushes. The last inhabitant left the village towards the end of the Second World War and moved to the village of Opoul near where several of the old families from the original Périllos now live. The whole area has always been seen as quite mystical and there is no doubt that it was once considered to be holy land. The ruins of an old castle, Château Opoul, are situated on a plateau above Opoul. This plateau was once called *Terresalvaesche*[8] , the anointed, blessed and deified land. It is also known that a chapel used to be where the castle was later built and that a small town or some buildings had been situated there at the time of Christ, and some people think

---

8   In the oldest legends of the Grail the Grail castle, *Montsalvaesche, the anointed, blessed or deified mountain*, was situated in the Pyrenees. For further information see Appendix E.

that it was a monastery named *Salveterra.*"

He stopped and lifted his glass:

"Well, we mustn't forget to drink."

His brown eyes looked happy. It was clear that he was very pleased to have found someone who was interested in his information about the area. It was quite clear that he knew something about the subject. He continued when we had tasted the wine:

"The village still looks more or less the way it was when it was abandoned. Of course the houses deteriorate with the passing of time but the people from Opoul try to keep it in order. The church is not very big but still intact and each year on the first of May they celebrate Mass there. By the way, the church is dedicated to St. Michael, St. Katarina and St. Barbe."

I leaned forward in my chair:

"Excuse me, but what was the name of the last of the saints you mentioned?"

"St. Barbe," he said, "it is short for St. Barbara."

"Yes, of course."

For a moment I thought he had said Ba-Bé, but you usually hear what you want to hear just like you usually say what is in your heart.

"Perhaps it is not very strange that the preferred saint is St Michael. There is a legend about a dragon like monster, *Babaos*, ravaging the area, which is as old as the area itself. It is told that the Babaos came up from the underworld. The ravaging of the dragon was at its peak when the master of Périllos went on a crusade to Palestine in 1270. By the way, he was also Grand Master of the Order of Malta. When he returned from the crusades he had to face the dragon in order to reinstate peace and order. It is also said that he defeated it and that it is now chained in the depths of one of the numerous bottomless pits in the area."

He lifted his glass once more before continuing his story:

"The well-known prophet Nostradamus, furthermore, has made a prophecy connected to the town of Tuchan which is situated very close to Périllos."

He brought out a piece of paper from his wallet and unfolded it:

"This is what the prophecy sounds like:

At the foot of the new sect,
The earthly remains of the Great Roman are to be found,
A shrine covered with marble shall come forth,
The earth shall shake in April, wrongly buried."

He folded the paper once more and laughed slightly embarrassed at the words he had just read out loud. They certainly echoed momentously. But what they meant was another matter.

"Do you know a place in the area called *La Caune?*" I asked him, thinking about one of the markings Ba-Bé had made on the map.

"Yes. And as the name implies it is not *any* cave. *La Caune* is simply *the* cave. As far as I'm concerned it is and has always been a very holy place. The cave has been in use for thousands of years and many interesting things have been found in it. Among others, sculptures depicting alien-like beings, sculptures which have been dated as far back as 3 – 4000 years BC. It is also in *La Caune* they found the oldest black Madonna as far as we know. Unfortunately, the shepherd who found it, painted it so that it now appears white. The shepherd however is still alive and he himself has told us where in the cave he found it and how he later gave the Madonna a "new colour of the skin.""

"Where in the cave did he find it?"

"In a small recess behind what is now called "the Altar." If you find the cave you'll soon see that "the Altar" is the holy of holies and the natural place for various rituals and initiations. Among other things the Altar has been decorated with old, equilateral circle crosses."

"Is it difficult to find the cave?"

"That must be a yes. I must also tell you that you have to find it yourself. If you find the cave it is meant to be. If you do not find it I'm afraid you must accept the fact that the time is not yet ripe for you to find it.

We were silent for a while, then he said:

"There are those who think that Périllos fits into the legend of the Grail. In one of the oldest stories of the Grail, *Perlesvaux*, it is said that the one who is seeking the Grail ought to visit the "Chapel of Périllos." The Knight of the Grail is the "Chosen One" or "Christ," who places himself in the empty seat, *The Seat Perilous*, at the Round

Table of King Arthur. When we consider that the legend of the Grail originates in the mystical figure of *Kyot*, who apparently lived in Narbonne, it is perhaps not so very strange that we are also talking about the area of Périllos."

André's tale made me dizzy.

Kyot, alias Kansbar, the old magus, who wrote the manuscript of the Grail, which the Seer had placed in my hands. Kyot, the old master, whom I had contacted in my dreams in Toledo a few years ago.

"There is more," André said looking curiously at me.

I nodded affirmatively although it was difficult to get an overview of all the information.

"Considering the mystery of Sauniére and Rennes-le-Château, new pieces of information have appeared which are also pointing towards Périllos. Before the death of the priest he ordered a plaster of Paris model of a landscape. This landscape had a very specific topography. Two tombs are shown in the landscape."

"What kind of tombs?"

"Hold your breath now," he said. "One tomb is marked down as belonging to Joseph of Arimathea and the other one as the tomb of Jesus Christ. Unfortunately, Sauniére died before the model was finished. Now, however, it has appeared from its hiding place and is becoming the cause of new considerations."

The proprietor, Yoke, came into the dining room carrying a large pot.

"Time for dinner!"

18

They rode into the interior and reached the *Salveterra* Monastery after two days of riding through almost impassable terrain. They had to leave the horses at the foot of the magnificent cliffs of *Terresalvaesche,* "*The Holy Land.*"

The monastery was only inhabited by women and Ish-a-tar was surprised that all the sisters introduced themselves with the title *Magdal* following their personal initiation names. Only a few very young novices used their first names. Apart from a short ceremonial welcome all the sisters kept silent, which created an atmosphere of contemplation and harmony.

When the travellers had washed and eaten they were quartered in a small annex where each of them got their own cell.

After the first communion of the evening, Ish-a-tar went to find the head sister. Being so close to her goal she could hardly control her impatience. But the sister put a finger to her lips indicating that Ish-a-tar should calm down. The sister was a mature woman and Ish-a-tar immediately felt devoted to her. She therefore folded her hands and silently gave her face the appropriate expression. This was met by a warm smile from the older sister who shook her head resignedly and went up to Ish-a-tar and kissed her on her forehead. She then whispered into Ish-a-tar's ear:

"Tomorrow."

Ish-a-tar twisted and turned on her couch all night long in her small cell. Several times during the night she got up on her couch looking out of the window in order to get another glimpse of "The Holy Land" which lay bathed in the mystical glow from the full moon. She tried to imagine in which direction Sister Mariam would be at this moment. She imagined what she would say to her when she stood face to face with the woman she had wanted so much to meet and for such a long time. But her thoughts wandered and she once more tried to fall asleep.

Ish-a-tar had just fallen asleep when one of the young novices woke her up again. Ish-a-tar screwed up her eyes looking into the flickering light from the oil lamp, which the young girl held in her hand. The full moon still bathed the plateau when the two figures moved across the large atrium courtyard situated like an oasis between the annex and the monastery itself. The older sister who had sealed the fate of Ish-a-tar with a kiss the previous evening was sitting in a lotus position waiting for her in deep contemplation. Ish-a-tar sat down beside her. Shortly after this sister started the ritual:

> "Give me strength to step out of all the old things,
> So that I may be re-born totally pure.
> Laying everything transient down,
> I ask for strength to dress in Your eternal gown.
> May that which belongs to the earth fall where it belongs.
> And may that which belongs in Heaven be guided in order
> to find its way home now.
> Amen."

They got up and the sister handed Ish-a-tar a cup of unfermented wine. She then said to Ish-a-tar pointing to the young novice:

"Jehanna will guide you to Sister Mariam. When you get there she'll show you what to do. Give yourself over to the care of Heaven and it shall come to pass as it must. Good-bye."

She kissed Ish-a-tar lightly on her mouth after which Jehanna and Ish-a-tar got on to their donkeys and set off.

Riding across the plateau they watched the sun, rising from the sea on the horizon, slowly lighting the white desert with its blood red fire. Ish-a-tar repeated the first lines of the morning prayer to herself:

"Give me strength to step out of all the old things, so that I may be re-born totally pure. Give me strength to step out of all the old things, so that I may be re-born totally pure. Give me strength to step out of all the old things, so that I may be re-born totally pure."

Again and again she repeated the sentences like a mantra when suddenly she noticed that the sun was rising in the east as the moon was setting to the west so that they formed a completely balanced scale, she took this as sign of the new kind of life of which she had been dreaming for such a long time and which now seriously was about to begin.

Riding down the path from the cliffs they went through the Gate of the Wind and on to a desert-like plain. While she was praying, Ish-a-tar looked at the young novice whose face radiated with an inner power, and she thought that this young girl had long ago left all the old behind in order to possess such a fine light in her. And in that face she momentarily caught a glimpse of her own face, as a fifteen or sixteen-year-old who had already tasted the rotten fruit of the world. She wondered if Jehanna had also tasted it?

They continued on the red carpet of the sun spreading out in front of them and showing the way. After half an hour's ride Jehanna turned off the path and headed for some cliff formations further into the desert. Apart from the faint wind, not a sound was heard. After a while they stopped at a low tree under which a watering trough was connected to a well.

"We are not going any further," Jehanna said in a low voice.

They got off. Jehanna untied a small bundle from her saddle and handed it to Ish-a-tar.

"Give this to Sister Mariam when you get to the cave. It is just up there."

She pointed to the cliffs not far from them.

"Just follow the narrow path there. But be careful, there are many bottomless pits in the area."

Ish-a-tar wanted to embrace the young girl, but Jehanna took one step backwards whispering:

"I'm not worthy yet."

Shortly after she added:

"I'll come back for you in three days."

Ish-a-tar watched the young girl ride back towards the path further down the slope until the two donkeys and the rider faded into the surroundings and disappeared in the red light. Then she started walking towards the cliffs.

✴

I dreamt about the great dragon, the Beast from Revelation, that night. I saw how the dragon was thrown into a bottomless pit in the desert where it was to be bound for a thousand years. And I saw it being lifted up when the thousand years had passed, and I saw a woman dressed in a purple and scarlet red gown decorated with gold and precious stones mounting the dragon. And I saw that she was the woman they called *"the great whore of Babylon"* and *"the mother of all whores."* I saw that she was really the one who, through two thousand years, had had to bear the burden of the sins that the Roman Church had given Christ the honour of having atoned for us. I saw that she was the one who had lifted the dragon, which symbolised the repressions of man, from the bottomless pit of the subconscious. Not in order to let it run wild but in order to tame it and to transform it. That is why she had mounted it. And I saw the number of the beast – 666 – written on the forehead of the dragon. And I saw that the sum of the digits of this figure – 9 – is the figure of death, transformation, resurrection, perfection and the Great Mother.

It was still dark outside when I woke up. But I was wide-awake. I clearly felt the presence of the strange being which by now wasn't all that strange any more. I prayed the Heavenly Prayer within myself. Then I got up and prepared myself for the journey ahead.

André was not up yet when I got down for breakfast, and I had my breakfast alone and wrote him a note on a postcard thanking him for his help.

I then drove back to Quillan and continued by the D 117 towards the coast. The sun was rising and gave a virgin-like, rose-coloured hue to everything. Just before Estagel I turned left towards Tautavel, through Vingrau and then headed for Opoul. There was a sign showing the way to the Château Opoul. I followed the road in that direction and caught my breath at the sight of the enormous plateau of cliffs in front of me, which had to be Terresalvaesche.

André was right. It was a bare and quite desolate landscape. But there was something grandiosely open and opening about it.

I parked my car in a gravelled space at the foot of the plateau and stepped out into the fresh air. A wooden gate indicated the beginning of the path to the castle ruins. The ascent was not that difficult, but a wind was coming up from the west and into my face when the path turned around the plateau and continued along the northern side and further up. When I got to the end of the northern side the path suddenly became steep, leading towards a natural gate between two rocks. I really felt the strength of the wind when I passed through it. It was as if it had decided to concentrate all its strength here in order to protect "The Holy Land" against intruders. I leaned against the wind for a short moment and felt how it carried me and held me in a tight grip. I really had to struggle in order to break through this "wall." The wind didn't let go of me until I had passed through the gate between the two rocks and I could step on to Terresalvaesche where once a cloister-like society by the name of *Salveterra* had been situated according to André.

If the view of the cliff as seen from Opoul had almost taken my breath away, it was nothing compared to the sight waiting for me at the plateau itself. In front of me the remains of the castle and behind it, as far as I could see, the Mediterranean and the endless horizon.

The plateau of Terresalvaesche
(Notice the almost Judean topography)

The ruins of the old château on the site of the former
Magdalenian monastery Salveterra on Terresalvaesche

To the south the peaks of the Pyrenees reached towards the sky. It was a divine sight.

I stood for a while enjoying the magnificent view and the remains of the castle ruins. Then I started to investigate the plateau in order to find out where the old monastery, *Salveterra*, had been situated. After a while I found a spot where the energies seemed to flow the most. I stood still with my eyes closed waiting for something to appear. As usual I began with the Heavenly Prayer. After a while and as I have experienced so often, I heard some fine, soft and bell-like sounds around me. This time, however, the sounds also seemed to be followed by a sweet, rose-like smell. I slowly opened my eyes and surrendered to the "far sight." Shortly after, small, flickering lights appeared and started their life-giving dance. I saw in a vision a figure resembling Ba-Bé hovering above the ground past me and into the blue air heading north. Each and every cell and each and every atom within me joined in the unbelievable song of life, which joyfully danced towards the sun.

When, about half an hour later, I walked back towards *The Gate of the Wind*, I turned around to get a last glimpse of this holy site and saw that a pure, radiating crystal pyramid hovered in the air above *Salveterra*.

✵

"III ... AAA ... OOO ... III ... AAA ... OOO ... III ... AAA ... OOO."

The sound of a woman's voice singing was heard through the low growth embracing Ish-a-tar as she got closer to the place pointed out by Jehanna. She was immediately filled with an unbelievable, joyful feeling of expectation which was incomparable but which might be described as a wave seizing you and dissolving everything at the peak of divine lovemaking.

She continued towards the sound and was lead towards an opening in the rock. A mouth seemed to open in the ground in front of her and she saw a light, which made shadows dance on the walls of the cliff further down. The smell of incense reached her nostrils. She put one foot on the first step of the staircase leading down to ...

The song stopped. Two oil lamps created small haloes in the enormous cave. She had to let her eyes get used to the faint light before she spotted the shape of a woman wrapped in a red cloak sitting in lotus position facing an altar-like formation of rocks where a thurible threw an unreal glow on to the face of the woman.

"Sister Mariam."

Ish-a-tar stood still at the foot of the stairs waiting for Sister Mariam to react. It seemed like an eternity. Slowly she opened her eyes and looked in the direction of Ish-a-tar:

"Welcome."

Ish-a-tar felt a stab in her heart at the sound of Mariam's golden voice, which was both warm and soft, clear and precise.

Ish-a-tar kept silent. She had completely lost her voice. Mariam smiled at her:

"Good that you finally got here. Come and sit down."

She pointed to the fleece in front of her. Ish-a-tar obeyed and sat down. At first she kept her eyes downcast but then slowly lifted her head and looked into the most intense eyes she had ever seen. They were like glowing mirrors burning into the eyes of the one looking into this wonderful universe. A deep, compassionate power, which made any restraint and any fear disappear. She then gave Mariam the small parcel, which Jehanna had given her for Mariam. She took it and put it next to her saying:

"Do you know why you have come?"

Ish-a-tar's voice shivered slightly when she answered, however, there was no doubt in it:

"I have come to obtain the knowledge which may set mankind free."

"It is obvious that Salome hasn't taught you in vain," Mariam answered smilingly. "Good, let us begin."

Mariam sat up and Ish-a-tar followed her example.

"I just made the initial preparations before you came. Did you hear my song?"

"Yes," Ish-a-tar said. "It is the most wonderful sound I have ever heard. It reminded me of something we were taught to sing by the

Therapists at Alexandria."

"This is true. However, the song I'm using now I learned from my beloved friend and teacher, Rabbi Yeshua. Have you heard about him?"

Ish-a-tar nodded:

"Many stories are told about him in Galilee and Judea. I have heard the most unbelievable stories about the wonders he has done. Who is he?"

"He was a true master. He was the one who reopened the women's door to the mysteries. Without him you and I wouldn't have been sitting like this. I owe him my life."

Mariam became distant for moment.

"He knew about the deepest mysteries and he knew how to unfold them for everybody, high as well as low. Never before have I known such a sensitive person with the ability to see behind any kind of foolishness and any kind of lie. He taught me about the highest of all sciences. I gave him everything that only a woman can give a man. Together we read and we wrote in *The Book of Love.*"

"What were the mysteries he taught, and what is *The Book of Love?*"

"The Book of Love" is the secret about the mystery of the fire. Yeshua belonged to the brotherhood of water and fire. Born of the lineage of David but of the order of Melchizedeck. He was raised on Mount Carmel by the Essenese but broke away and formed the brother – and sisterhood of the Nazarenes. This was what offended the priests of both Qumran and Jerusalem and turned the country upsidedown. He first came into this world as the consciousness Adam. When he ended this life he came back as Enoch. Later he came as Hermes and as Melchizedeck. Then followed the consciousnesses Yehoshua, Asaph and the master of fire, Zarathustra. The series of lives ended and it was crowned with the consciousness of Yeshua, Son of Man. He is *Metatron*, the angel who rules the seven *Elohim*[9] in the world.

Mariam's eyes were like diamonds shining in the semi darkness.

"You see, Brother Yeshua was the long awaited Messiah. He was

---

9   The seven archangels.

the Anointed One, which our world had been awaiting for hundreds of years. His earthly remains are now buried here but his spirit will always be where people invoke him. He was the master above them all. Even the seven Elohim will bow to him forever and ever. He did not want an earthly kingdom. His kingdom was of a different world."

Ish-a-tar thought that she saw a tear on Mariam's cheek and spoke in order to lead the conversation to other subjects.

"I heard in Jerusalem that some of Yeshua's disciples are forming a congregation in his honour. Some of them are building synagogues where they worship him and heal in his name. Others live celibate lives in the desert. It is said, however, that a man named Petrus goes forth with fire and brimstone attacking anyone who does not submit to the right faith."

"Well, Petrus," Mariam sighed. "I'm very sorry to hear that. Petrus has always been an ox who does not understand the deeper meaning behind the science. He has only one goal: The dream of honour and power. It is just like him to create a worldly hierarchy where he himself may sit on the highest throne."

Mariam's voice lost for a moment its golden sound and Ish-a-tar regretted having turned the conversation on to that subject. She tried once more to change tracks:

"What then is the deeper meaning behind the science?"

"The understanding of man. The understanding of the powers which are always at the disposal of the Sons and Daughters of Man."

" What kind of powers?"

"The seven Elohim. When you know the power of the seven Elohim your eyes and ears are opened and you see everything in a new light."

"What do you then see and hear?"

"You dissolve what is false and see what is true. You hear the Heavenly Sound, which surges through everything within and without. You see, the truth comes into the world naked but veiled in images and archetypes, otherwise it wouldn't be understandable. Rebirth happens through the archetype of rebirth. This is the only way to be reborn. This is the resurrection.

Entering this image, the groom is lead to the truth, which is the renewal of everything in its integrity. This is valid for those who do not just know the names of Father/Mother, Son/Daughter and Spirit, but who have also integrated them in themselves. The one who hasn't integrated these names in his innermost being, his name shall be taken away from him."

"What kind of names and what does it all mean?"

"Everything that cannot be expressed in words can be expressed in sounds and movement. The one who hasn't vitalised the true names of the Father-Mother, the Son – Daughter and the Spirit must lose his own true name. This means that the one who does not know the Power behind them must stay in front of the veil of the world and only see the external movements. Only through the knowledge of the seven abilities of the Power may man become a true co-creater in the seven worlds of *Pleromas*[10]."

Mariam looked at the young woman sitting opposite her. She contemplated the basic qualities of the woman for a while. She had followed Ish-a-tar for a while through various visions, uniting with an angel who guided her. She knew of the contrary powers which had torn Ish-a-tar's heart apart, but she also saw the simple, uncompromising yet loving power which could walk the road of untruth no more.

"We invoke the seven Elohim with sound. The angel of peace, Michael, is invoked with the sound A."

Mariam sang out the tone and signalled to Ish-a-tar to do the same. Shortly after she stopped and said:

"The angel of grace is Gabriel who is invoked with the sound of E."

The two women again sang the sound together.

"The angel of power is Raphael who is invoked with the sound H[11]. The angel of willpower, Uriel, is invoked with the sound I. The angel of truth, Raguel, is invoked with the sound O. The angel of light, Anael, is invoked with the sound Y, and the angel of healing, Saraphuel, is invoked with the sound O which in this case means Omega."

10   Cosmos.
11   Pronounced AE.

Together they then sang all the sounds in succession, AEHIOYO.

"When you are familiar with the sounds and the qualities behind them you may synthesize them all in the three sounds IAO. This holy mantra, apart from the invocation of Elohim, is also a confirmation of: I AM ALPHA AND OMEGA."

Mariam softly began singing IIIIIII. Then she changed to AAAAAAA and ended with OOOOOOO.

Ish-a-tar joined in and they repeated the mantra again and again until the ethereal level opened itself for them.

"IAO is the most effective sound with which to open the ethereal level. You may use it in connection with the seven gates of your holy Star-body. Let the sound rest in your womb and you'll activate the Snake of Fire that is curled up at the foot of the Tree of Life which has its origin there. When this is set free, be prepared, for it will tear everything impure up through the trunk of the tree, combining the seven worlds in your star-body. Only through serious preparation may you make certain that the awakening of the Snake of Fire may pass painlessly. If you cannot tame it, it'll devour you. The Snake of Fire is either creative wisdom or total destruction. Only if your motives are pure should you choose to mount the dragon. The choice is yours."

They sang all day long. Day and night became one. The holy mantra gave them strength. They needed no other sustenance than ethereal light.

They rested off and on, but not for long, then they would sing the holy mantra once more. Ish-a-tar felt how her physical body and her Star-body slowly got more and more enlightened.

Having rested, Mariam said:

"If you have any questions feel free to ask them."

Ish-a-tar sat for a while trying to think of something. There was so much she would like to know and yet she felt that it was all contained in the holy mantra.

"We met Herod in Massilia. He gave us the impression that he and you know each other quite well."

Mariam smiled:

Wisdom of the Snake
(The last painting by Maria Struzik-Krull, printed by kind permission by Hans Krull)

"Well, here is cause for gossip. You see, Herod has always appreciated the Essenese at Qumran very much. He knows about the secrets and he has been a good man for the mystery-societies. However, since he pretends to co-operate with the Romans there are many militant groups in Palestine who hate him and want him dead. But Herod is a diplomat. Without his help I had probably never reached *Salveterra*. He was also the one who arranged for the remains of Yeshua to be buried here. He owns many vineyards in Narbonensis and he helps many Jewish immigrants."

They sat in silence for a long time. There really wasn't anything to say but still Ish-a-tar's heart burned with a fire which could not be quenched. She could not hold back the words:

"Please initiate me into the mystery of the Fire and give me my true name."

Immediately the energy in the cave dissolved. It was as if a void appeared in the wake of Ish-a-tar's words. As if the invoked Elohim stepped aside to make room for something else. Was it really time? Had Ish-a-tar finally reached her goal?

Mariam got up and went over to a circle of rocks, which had been placed on the floor between two phallic looking pillars. She stepped into the circle and sat down in it.

"Have you ever heard about *Merkabah?*[12]" she asked Ish-a-tar.

But Ish-a-tar looked uncomprehendingly at Mariam.

"*Merkabah* is a chariot of fire written about by Ezekiel many years ago. When your Star-body and the chariot of fire become one you may travel in the worlds of Elohim. You may get in contact with Elohim through your breathing and the holy mantra IAO. You must throw a circle of light around you. Until you can do that by the power of your thoughts you can help the process along by making a circle of rocks around you like the one I have made here. The circle will centre you at the earthly level while the fire in you will seek upwards through you and towards the Heavenly level. You may lift yourself above everything earthly and move wherever you want to go."

She got up and made room for Ish-a-tar who sat down in the circle. Mariam continued:

"Now imagine that you are sitting between two pyramids. One upright below you and the other one upside down above you. Now, let the two pyramids unite until they form the seal of *King Solomon* and *Queen Sheba*, the six-pointed star. You activate the fire with your breath, and the fire shall move upwards from your womb and through the seven gates and into the Heavenly spheres. You may now move through any one of the seven gates. However, the higher you want to go the more gates you must open. When you can invoke Elohim with certainty, the rest is easy. The *Merkabah* is the highest wisdom. Here *Solomon* and *Sheba* become one. The radiating eye in the tiara of God."

Mariam taught Ish-a-tar everything that she herself had learned with and from Yeshua. Day and night disappeared once more. After yet another rest, Mariam continued:

---

12   Merkabah= carriage, vehicle. Belongs to the oldest part of the Enoch-tradition and the Jewish Kabalah-tradition. See Ezekiel chapter 1, verse 1 – 26 and Isaiah, chapter 6, verse 1 – 8.

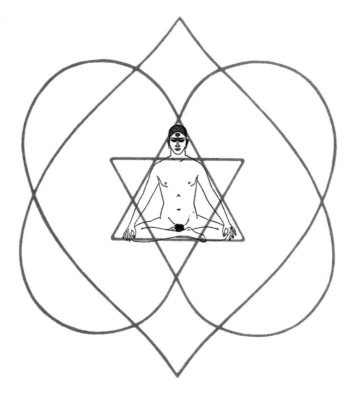

Merkabah — The Chariot of Fire

"Throughout time, Logos has been looking for Sophia the way Kether has been looking for *Shekhinah*. However, Sophia has always had more than one face. Behind them all, the great mother, *Anyahitha, the Guardian of the Heart*, is resting. She is Venus. From her came Innana, Ishtar, Isis, Hathor, Athene, Diana and Cybele as well as many, many others, known and unknown to the world. Her secret being, however, is known by a few only. She is Miriam, the precious companion and prophet of Moses, who sang *The Song of the Sea* with him. Miriam was the daughter of the water who made a fountain of miracles spout. A fountain that nourished everything and never dried out. She is *Sheba* the daughter of the fire and the black bride of *Solomon*, who sings the most beautiful song with him.

661

The secrets of the highest possibilities are hidden in *The Song of Songs*. Like a pearl in a lotus flower. *Anyahitha, Shekhinah* and *Sheba*. Together they form the threefold, Heavenly Goddess. Her number is three times six, 666. In the old writings you may read about the time when *King Solomon* received 666 talents of gold. It is the allegorical tale of the wisdom, which *Solomon* received through the union with *The Queen of Sheba*. It is the Heavenly Marriage, which must also take place in each human being. Each one of us is the bride who must prepare the bridal chamber for the arrival of the groom. As above, so below. Do you understand?"

Ish-a-tar nodded and Mariam continued:

"When Venus unites with Mercury in the sky, Pleroma offers man precious gifts and invites man to follow the example of Heaven. Yeshua was my groom and I was his bride. Together our souls reflected each other like the sun enlightens the moon and the moon reflects it. Let us now together meditate on the unification of *Solomon* and *Sheba* in our innermost chambers of the heart. Then I shall give you your true name."

Once more day and night melted into one and on the third day the two souls came back and united with the bodies sitting in lotus position in the cave.

When the eyes of the women met, the gaze of the two equal sisters united and became one revealing sight.

"As you can see," Mariam said, "the great mother, Anyahitha, and the women of the earth are heading for hard times. When, therefore, I give you your name you accept the obligation of passing this knowledge on to our sisters you meet on your way and who are mature enough to receive it. Only thus may the wisdom continue to live in the world. Only thus may the world survive. You must at any time be ready to go to the bottomless realm and lift the dragon from the depths. When *Solomon* and *Sheba* have united in you, you will possess the power with which you may tame the Beast. From now on you shall be known by the name *Mariona Magdal*. But your hidden name shall, from this day on, be BARBELO!"

Tears were running down the cheeks of Ish-a-tar who had now received the name of Mariona Magdal. Then she whispered:

"Barbelo?"

"You are Barbelo. The scarlet- and purple-clad whore from Babylon whose task it is to tame the dragon."

They each got up from their couch. Mariam took the small bundle, which Ish-a-tar had brought from Jehanna. She now unwrapped it and brought forth a milk-white crystal.

"This crystal, the first one I found in this cave, has been waiting for you at *Salveterra*. Take it. It will protect you and guide you."

They embraced, kissed each other on the mouth and departed.

"Do not look back," Mariam whispered.

Mariona Magdal turned around and began the long journey back to the world.

19

The wind became stronger and it alternately pushed and carried me down from *Salveterra*. A piece of paper whirled through the air and stuck to the windshield as I got to the parking place and was about to get into the car. I removed it and took a hasty look at it. It looked like a label from a winegrower's box with a colourful print of grapes. Below the illustration and the name of the winegrower the following line was printed in capital letters, "66600 Opoul-Périllos."

It was almost too much of a cosmic joke to be a coincidence that the postal code of the area contained the sign of the Beast, 666.

I turned the car on to the narrow road and drove towards the abandoned village Périllos and the cave *La Caune*. Ba-Bé's map lay open on the passenger seat. The landscape became more harsh and it struck me how much it resembled the topography around Jerusalem in Israel. After fifteen minutes of driving the village appeared at the end of a winding, single-track road leading up to a small mountain top on the horizon. I stopped the car and studied Ba-Bé's map. According to her markings I would find *La Caune* by following a path to the right not far from the place I had stopped. I put the car in reverse and rolled backwards to something, which might be the path. I parked, put the map in my pocket and started walking up the path with a vineyard on one side and barren, stony ground on the other. The path soon became full of holes and uneven, and at places it seemed to disappear and then reappear from the stony ground further ahead. When I reached a path that crossed mine I saw a man carvedfrom stone at the place on the map marked by Ba-Bé where I was supposed to turn left. I followed Ba-Bé's markings step by step until I reached a small open space in front of a low piece of rock. A clear path in the grass lead in between two bushes. I found the entrance to the cave on the other side of them.

I held my breath as I got closer. I stood still and took a few deep breaths; then I went inside.

If I have ever in my life experienced the feeling of being guided then it was here at this moment. How do you describe something like that? Everything around me was so quiet that you could hear the proverbial pin drop. Even the wind had dropped. A flash of light to the right. Then one in front of me. Like a spark jumping between electrical poles. The Being had entered. I stood for a moment waiting for something to happen, however, something told me that I should go on.

Although André's story was fresh in my memory nothing could have prepared me for the sight, which met me when I looked down at the holy cathedral. The size of it in itself was enough to make you catch your breath. At various places on the cliff wall, crystals shone in the light coming from a large hole in the ceiling at the other end of the cave. The hole gave a pleasant light and lit up most of the cave.

A fireplace had been built in the middle of the cave. Around it some strange, phallus-like pillars were placed reaching almost to the ceiling. I partly slipped and partly walked the rest of the way down the path, which ran at an angle down into the cave. I slowly walked around investigating everything. I finally found the "Altar" that André had mentioned as well as a small depression next to it where the old shepherd had found the black Madonna. I found the circle crosses on the Altar as well as other signs, which I couldn't, however, interpret.

LM in La Caune

*The altar in La Caune behind which a black
madonna and two 3000 year old figurines
were found*

I had finally reached my goal and slowly sank to my knees in front of the Holy of Holies. The moment was filled with an indescribable peace. There was no more to search for and no more to be found. There was only this moment. A breath. A now.

Then the being started to speak:

"Be you greeted. If you have any questions, then ask."

The voice was indeterminable. Like balm. It was, – and it wasn't. My thoughts went to the altar. I heard my own voice saying:

"What is it about this place that makes it different from other places?"

"Only the fact that you have made it special in your own mind."

"But aren't there places in the world that are holier than others?"

"No."

"Can you be more specific?"

"Places are not holy. They are just part and parcel of the great time-space-illusion. Only the conscious NOW is holy. A conscious now may only be created by a person who can free himself from the earlier mentioned illusion. This may be created anywhere and at any time you want it. It is a choice."

"But history is filled with saints, gurus and avatars who have attained enlightenment in holy places. For thousands of years pilgrims of all traditions have sought these places where some of them have actually had extra sensory experiences. The Mary revelations for example."

"It has always been important for the human mind to arrange its so-called "spirituality." For far too long it has needed to create extraordinary circumstances in order to believe. This is all right as long as the individual is able to see through the illusion. Let's call it a tool which may sometimes help to open the mind to deeper acknowledgements."

"Some people think that the energy is more intense at places where believers have practised and prayed for centuries and that this may be good for other believers."

"If this is what you think then this is how it is. However, the eternal now offers awareness irrespective of time, place and specific conditions."

Silence.

"Is it not pure fatalism to think that everything is an illusion?"

"*Only if the material reality is so important that man is unable to imagine a reality created by SPIRIT. It is not material reality but man's interpretation of it, which is twisted. It is the mind of man, which is creating the illusion. The curse lies in man's total identification with the body, his job, social status and all other external things.*"

"But why has man been placed in an earthly reality if it is an illusion?"

"*Remember that it is your own interpretation of earthly reality which keeps you ignorant, not earthly reality in itself. It simply constitutes an enormous possibility.*"

"It seems to me that human developement happens extremely slowly."

"*That depends on the position you take. Everything is and has always been accessible and open to man. EVERYTHING! But man has forced himself into a corner from where he can see no other way out than looking after number one. You have chosen a very limited interpretation of reality and that is why you see nothing but limitation. You see, there is no language, which can put this into words. Words, imagination, beings and life are all symbols. Everything is a symbol of something behind them which cannot be expressed in any other way.*"

"What is going on when I have experienced that my reality is turned inside out?"

"*You are then experiencing the other side of illusion. There may be other laws here but it is still the same illusion because you experience it as a contrast to your normal reality. But nothing is separate. Everything is one. It is simply different interpretations of the eternal now.*"

"How do you step out of this illusion?"

"*Through the understanding that there is no "outside" or "inside."*"
Silence.

While meditating on what I had learned, Mariam Magdal suddenly appeared in my consciousness and once more I heard my own voice speaking as if it came from outside of me:

"Who was Mariam Magdal?"

"*An old soul. A sister who woke up from the dream and liberated herself from her 'destiny.'*"

"Liberated herself from her destiny," what does that mean?"

"What you understand by destiny is your limited interpretation of the simple life. Mariam Magdal started her long journey from a misinterpretation of a series of lives which have continued up until now."

"What lives?"

Silence.

"If this was explained it would only give rise to more mis-understandings."

"Or it may be of value to a lot of people who are trying to break through these illusions?"

"As you wish. Sister Mariam was among the first souls. The basic identity is IO from Venus. This identity has among others been expressed as Queen Tiyi, Miriam, The Queen of Sheba, Mariam Magdal, Guinevere, Esclarmonde de Foix and Joan of Arc. It is an identity, which has always had a great personality. It has been the turning point of what you understand as good and evil. As Joan of Arc it received its baptism of fire. It was, however, not until your own time that the identity as Noor Inayat Khan completed the so-called Way of Christ. However, at the same time as it lived its life as Noor Inayat Khan the Magdal-idea also expressed itself as Helen Schucman who received and wrote the message about forgiveness and freedom from Brother Yeshua."

I contemplated these words for a while.

"I don't understand that. How can a soul incarnate in two personalities t one and the same time?"[13]

" 'Magdal' is not and has never been a personality. It is a state of mind, like your idea of Christ."

"Then there were more Magdals?"

"That is one way of putting it. The bestowed name Magdal, says something very important about the person that has it. Magdal can be compared to the Aramaic word for master, Mara, that's to say an initiated one. Mariam has both given names. She was both Mariam

---

13   Noor Inyat Khan lived from 1914 until 1944 when she died in France after having been tortured by the Gestapo. Helen Schucman lived from 1909 and died in 1981, about ten years after having finished the scribing of "A Course in Miracles," a series of channelings from Yeshua.

Magdal and Mariam Mara. The Exalted One and the Master. Where is the identity now?"

Silence.

After a while the being continued:

"*It is here. Now! Mariam Magdal is the all-dominating new female Sophia-archetype, that after more than 1700 years in the dark, has appeared out of the depths in order to regain its rightful place, on an equal footing with the Logos principle, Messiah/Christ. Since the establishment of the church its leading men have oppressed this archetype, with ensuing serious and painful consequences for mankind. Now, however, the time to put the record straight has come when the great swindle must be uncovered. The church elders were afraid of the idea that a woman could come to stand in the forefront of the new church. And rightly so. For Mariam was Yeshua's chosen disciple and his beloved equal. Therefore, she had to be eliminated, and, was, in one fell swoop, made out to be a whore. She is that wisdom that Yeshua, with the words: "Be as wise as the Snake and as innocent as the Dove," encouraged you to follow. The Dove is the symbol of The Holy Spirit, Agape and the Virgin, which represent man's 3 highest chakras, whilst the Snake symbolises Wisdom (Sophia/Hochman), Eros and Magdalene, which represent the three lowest chakras. And that is maybe the church's greatest crime against mankind, that, by condemning the Magdalene-aspect, it has made the whole life-giving foundation for mankind's incarnation on earth, sinful. Mankind has only been half present. Now it's time for you to once again be complete people.*"

I do not know if another being took over communication here, but deep inside me something told me that this was Helen Schucman speaking:

"*There are no missing links. Everything is certain. All that has been hidden will become obvious. And it happens NOW! Therefore, take all the exhibits and present them openly. The circumstances will never be better. The ideas of "Days of Yore" and "The End of the World" are limited states of mind just like "Birth and death" are. There are no such limitations in reality. The Primal Sea is without limits and the Primal Sea is identical with the enlightened consciousness. It is, however, not continuous. There are no other lives than the one within the One. We are all a part of this One Life and this is how it shall be for ever and ever. The enlightened consciousness is NOW in all of eternity. It is Eternal Life. Eternal Life embraces all forms of existence at all levels, including all temporary transitions that we erroneously interpret as stagnation and separation. Have no doubts. There is no room for doubt in healing. Unite with the light. Step into it without fear. Be it, give it and receive Eternal Life."*

My whole being was filled with quiet joy and deep gratitude and I thought that this was the creative stillness I had always sought but which I had never been able to find and unite with. In silence I sent the identity Helen Schucman my warmest greetings.

It was more than quiet. There was an openness that I had never experienced before. It was as if a large abyss appeared around me and in a moment of panic I shouted:

"Are you still there?"

Silence.

Somewhere in the cave a drop of water hit the stony ground. An answer? The great nothing? ☉?

But suddenly the Nameless One appeared again:

"Do you, from the bottom of your heart, want to be able to see and hear?"

"Yes," I replied immediately.

"If you really want to see and if you really want to listen you must accept that deep in your being you are already the eternal, unchangeable joy that you seek outside of yourself. Give up your position. Give up your special status and your dreams of it. Give up your dreams of becoming anything at all but beware that this giving up does not just open to another illusion of becoming something special. If you can manage this you will obtain a true relationship with ☉ who lives in your heart."

"You spoke last time about we, the people, hiding from God or ☉. How do we hide?"

I immediately felt that the question was naughty and that it exposed me as particularly ignorant. However, there was no judgement in the voice when it spoke again:

"Do not blame yourself for this. The hiding-place may be called:

judgements, prejudices and projections. If you let them go — and do not let yourself be seduced into exchanging them for new prejudices and projections, which will always remain what they are although they may be "ennobled" because you are now "holy" or "spiritual" — then you have made an important acknowledgement."

"You spoke the last time about the fifth dimension being Grace. What does that mean?"

"This may only be explained by way of an idea which most people know but which is only understood by very few."

"Which idea is that?"

"Forgiveness."

Once more I felt a stab of unpleasantness poking its head into my solar plexus. But I realized that there was no way around this concept which had been flogged to death in spiritual, Christian and Buddhist circles and had lost its meaning. It had been reduced to a word, a banality and an empty phrase without any meaning.

Once more I was met with empathy.

"There is only one way, and I repeat one way only, in which to understand the word forgiveness. By practising it. And while practising it, it is important to be aware that another judgement is not hiding within this forgiveness of the person or thing that is forgiven. For example, are you able to forgive yourself?"

I could feel that I was balancing on a knife's edge between fear and total surrender. The abyss around me opened into eternity.

"Be not afraid. There is nothing to be feared. But be aware that every thought, every word and every action has an impact in the cosmos. Remember that a wrong word said on one side of the globe is all it takes to create a tidal wave on the other. Step outside fear."

"Help me to understand how. Show me a way I can go."

I was losing my balance.

"Are you sure you are ready to know?"

"Yes!"

A long silence like a light-year, a free fall into endless space that made me dizzy. It was as if I was clinging to the outermost edge of the world, and of reality, with my fingertips. Then the being took pity on me:

"You yourself are the abyss opening below you as well as the bridge you must cross. You are the path you must follow. You are the mountain you have to climb. You are the cave you must find and enter. And when once you are sitting there you'll realise that you are the cloud above you in the sky, you are the Heavenly song and you are the rain falling and evaporating again, you are the drop of water uniting with the sea. No more will you have the need to know anything, because you will then be the knowledge of Heaven and the sea, the stars and the Universe. No more will you be separated from ☉."

Silence.

"In time, you may become a path that others may follow, a gate to walk through, a mountain to climb and a cave that anyone may enter."

"Is this the Grail?"

"In a way. What you call the Grail is a state of mind connected to the opening of the Third Eye, the Sapphire in the Tiara of the Forehead, the Jewel in the Lotus flower. It's a state that is directly connected to travelling in the Fire Chariot. The Fire Chariot's and Power of Thought's ranges are directly proportional to how firmly the Forehead Centre's flower is planted in the Heart Centre's earth. Just as the plant's roots must be anchored in the Sacral Centre. That is the marriage between the masculine, Thought, and the feminine, Feeling. Take note of that: Thought is the vessel and Feeling is the fuel. Thought in itself has only a limited range. Thought calculates, defines possibilities and sets conditions, before it acts, whilst the Heart immediately and intuitively knows what should be done or not done in every situation, and acts on that. The Heart has no need of any insurance or confirmation after the act. The Heart doesn't seek others' approbation. It's only concerned with one thing: to accumulate unconditional love."

It was very simple and yet very moving. And at that moment I understood that this certainty is the *Grace* that the Nameless One had spoken about earlier. And this made it easier to accept that the teaching was over for now. A sigh went through me and through the cave.

"Be you greeted. Call us when you need us. We are always CLOSE."

I saw a small milk white piece of crystal in front of me. A sign? A talisman?

I silently thanked this being, got up and began my climb towards the world outside.

The sun was shining through drizzle. I followed the path back to the car. When I turned around in order to look at the cliffs with the cave one more time, a rainbow stood like a giant gate around the place.

I parked the car shortly after outside Périllos. I walked through the narrow streets between the derelict, empty houses. Only the small chapel stood fully intact. Then I noticed the newts in various colours which were printed everywhere in the village.

A golden laughter sounded in the empty streets. It was Sylvia:

"Remember, the door is on the inside. Remember, that the key is on the inside. As of today there is no intermediate stage between man and God."

I went into the desert in the rain. The branches of the low bushes were heavy with water and here and there small puddles appeared in the depressions of the stony ground. I carried an image inside of me. It was an image of a world where man is born, lives and dies in tears and laughter, in poverty and riches, in anger and forgiveness.

This was the picture I held up towards Heaven completely sure that it would be received.

"If you will come to meet us, we shall bend down and lift you."

There was a flickering light around me in the wind:

"Heaven and earth are my parents. Consciousness is my home. Lack of selfishness is my work. Simplicity is my way. Humour my only weapon. Attention and honesty my emblem. Forgiveness, faith, patience and belief my true strength."

May the eye rest only on that which is new.
May the hand no longer take, but give.
May thought in the future be free in the service of the Exalted.
The heart is the mirror of the universe.
The heart is the true Grail.

✻

The train cut like a knife through the European dusk. The rain whipped against the windows of the compartment.

"God is peeing," a small boy said, sitting on the seat opposite me with his sister.

"Carl!"

Their mother looked apologetically at me while she leaned toward her son and wiped his mouth with a paper napkin.

"God doesn't pee," his sister answered, " – He cries."

It was not a fanfare of a statement. Just a quiet establishment of a fact with a faint exclamation mark behind it. Like a stifled breath with an immediate, checkmating effect.

"He must be very sad, then," the mother sighed resignedly with an empty look at the steamed-up window, before hiding once more behind a woman's magazine.

The girl put her head on her brother's shoulder, uncomplaining. Sitting there, they constituted the silent protest of a whole generation against the thoughtless rejection of that Holy of Holies: people's divine and frail ability to be present.

I smiled sympathetically at them and leaned back in my seat hoping to get some sleep. The old, Spanish manuscript SAN GRAL was burning in my heart.

AUM

OM

☉

APPENDIX A

AKASHA – THE COSMIC ARCHIVES

Akasha (á - ká - sha) is a Sanskrit word meaning *ether*, all embracing space, radiance. Within Indian philosophy it was originally considered to be the first and foremost and most fundamental of the five elements; the other four are called *vata* (air), *agni* (fire), *ap* (water), and *prithivi* (earth) in Sanskrit. Akasha embraces all five elements. It is the womb where everything we perceive with our senses originates and where it returns.

The Akasha-archives are the memory of eternity containing everything which is happening and which has ever happened. It is like a photographic film registering all our desires and experiences on earth.

Akasha is the level of the higher ethereal level and monadic matter. The ethereal memory of everything ever created. Every thought ever thought by man throughout time is stored here. From here those thoughts may at any time return and become expressed as archetypal material influencing man, where it either locks him into old ideas or opens him to new possibilities. For this reason alone the old traditions tell us that it is more desirable to rule over your thoughts than be under their command. Thoughts are not without cost. The energies follow the thoughts and thoughts create form, leaving their imprints on the physical, the ethereal, the astral, the mental and the causal levels. Thus, man creates the reality in which he finds himself.

We are surrounded by Akasha-reality. It is everywhere in the ethereal realm around us and always within reach. When from time to time we get a bright idea or experience the presence of a higher, intuitive inspiration it is Akasha dripping an insignificant drop of its contents on us.

Akasha is the morally neutral but intelligent universe where all information is stored. Akasha does not distinguish between good and evil. Carl Gustav Jung called the ethereal Akasha *the collective unconscious*. The Biologist Rupert Sheldrake calls it *the ethereal membrane* or *the morphic field* and appearances on *the ethereal membrane, the morphic resonance.*

The *ethereal membrane*, or *morphic field*, is the field of tension, or the field of consciousness, between the visible and the invisible. Religious revelations are seen in the ethereal membrane when archetypal images are given energy through rituals and intense worship. When people have worshipped the Virgin Mary at the same place and for centuries, it happens that the image of this archetype, which in itself is the result of man's own imagination and repeated invocation, will manifest itself on the ethereal membrane. It is the same way with the worshipping of the gods of fear. In our day and age more and more consciousness of the ethereal reality in the morph is opening up, and the number of people who actively get in contact with the great, cosmic memory in Akasha is exploding. This means that more and more people are beginning to become conscious of the connection between everything.

This, of course, gives rise to much confusion and many misunderstandings. To most of the people who do not have this kind of experience it is quite a challenge, while many of those who do often have various delusions about it. There are people who after very few experiences of the other reality will start practicing as mediums or clairvoyants without any kind of serious learning. Such limitations are examples of the thought forms of misinterpretation and fear through which the Akasha has become polluted.

Working with thought forms through creative imagination and visualization takes more than a few experiences of the divine. Many have misinterpreted such experiences as proof of a permanent possession of a higher consciousness.

A superficial flirtation with popular occultism or esoteric literature is not enough. You will only be able to establish a stable contact through devotion and intense studies of the energy values behind them. This ought to be followed by exercises where that which has been learned is used and practised. Only a well-trained seer is able to distinguish between a higher, ethereal experience and the astral images that have been created through imagination and intense desires. The trained seer has been taught to distinguish between his own personality and what is read in the Akasha-archives. Even for old souls with great understanding, however, it may be quite difficult to find and keep that balance.

Many people have been able to develop specific, extra sensory abilities while at the same time, struggling with a difficult personality. An extra sensitive perception does not necessarily entail having developed a higher consciousness throughout his or her being.

The time is ripe for a quantum leap where every single soul must allow his or her personality to be surged with the higher powers of the soul. As long we are incarnated here on earth we, of course, need the ego or our personalities. Unfortunately, time as we experience it, is running out and we shouldn't waste it. The ego is simply a tool like the body and the five senses. It must now step back and take its rightful position and let the higher potential of the soul come into its own.

This call for a change in the role of the ego and personality may be the most epoch-making message in this time of the rise of the new feminine power.

APPENDIX B

THE SACRED PROSTITUTE

In my last book I describe my meeting with the Sophia archetype, Mary Magdalene. All over the world, a wave of interest in the Magdalene is sweeping through society, making an impact in the arts, religion and politics. Individuals and groups, independently of each other, have made contact with the Magdalene energy which is just one of the many expressions of the one archetype. This archetype is the free feminine power of Wisdom which cannot remain the passive recipient of dominant masculine semen-power, the creative power which is now, both literally and symbolically, diminishing.

The time when women were regarded as nothing but child bearers, domestic servants and 'baby dolls' has now passed. The same must be said of men; no longer can they be thought of merely as sperm donors, breadwinners and gigolos. Unfortunately, far too many people have misunderstood the situation believing that equality of the sexes is achieved by men becoming 'housewives and sex objects' and women becoming bread winners and powerful macho-women.

Magdalene energy has been a growing force for some time. The rise of feminism in the twentieth century, particularly in the West, is living proof that this power can no longer be suppressed.

From earliest times this energy has been an expression of the Great Goddess. She manifested as Ishtar, the Persian goddess, who was also called Ashtoreth or Esther of the Old Testament. She was the great Whore of Babylon in John the Evangelist's Revelation. She was the goddess *Har* who called herself 'the passionate and compassionate' prostitute.

Men partook of her power and energy through her priestesses, the sacred prostitutes. She was the same Great Goddess who was worshipped throughout the Middle East under names such as Dea

Syria, Astarte, Cybele, Aphrodite, Kore and Mari. In the temple they worshipped her in her maidenly or holy virgin aspect as Mari, Mara, Mari-Anna or Miriam.

In Babylonia her name was Ishtar, the Light of the World, the Opener of the Womb, the Righteous Judge, the Law Maker, Goddess of Goddesses, Giver of Power, Lady of Victory, and the Forgiver of all Sins. These sorts of flattering attributes associated with prophecies concerning Jesus or Yeshua in the Old Testament could have been taken straight from Babylonian prayers to the goddess Ishtar.

The dark powers of the Underworld bowed down before Ishtar as she descended into the kingdom of the Underworld to save her son-lover Tammuz. Her predecessor, the Sumerian goddess Inanna, descended into the Underworld to meet her dark sister Ereshkigal, and, rising again, she sent her consort Dumuzi, Lord of the Abyss, to take her place.

Ishtar gave the following ultimatum to the guardians at the seven gates of the Underworld: "If you do not open the gate to let me through, I shall break the bolts, break through the wall and awaken the dead." The descent into the Underworld was a necessary part of the sacred drama that lasted three days culminating in the resurrection on the third day – the Day of Joy. The parallel with the crucifixion of Yeshua, his descent into Hell and his resurrection on the third day, is obvious.

Another of Magdalene's 'older sisters' is the Egyptian goddess Isis. Isis owned seven stoles instead of seven veils that were designed to keep the uninitiated from learning the secrets they were not yet ready to contain.

Ishtar and Isis were two of the goddesses of mythology who arose from the great goddess archetype. Mary Magdalene was one of the priestesses whose task it was to manifest these archetypal energies on earth.

These sacred prostitute-priestesses in the temples of the Goddess were seers, prophets, exorcists and healers. They were called 'virgins' because they were unmarried, of high social status, highly educated and learned shamans able to influence people at all levels. Even their vaginal fluids were said to have beneficial medicinal powers. On a clay tablet found in Nineveh it is said that a disease may be cured 'with the spit from a holy prostitute': an ability that was known to Yeshua.

When Christianity became an official Church institution in 325 AD, it ushered in the end of the Holy Prostitute and her heavenly powers. Thus the Feminine Divine was forced underground into the shadow of Church persecution and inquisitional crusades, finding secret expression through esoteric, occult and pagan channels. But nothing can remain in the dark forever. Everything comes to light. Whatever has been suppressed through the ages must, at one time or another, come forth from its hiding place. And that time is now.

APPENDIX C

THE INCARNATIONS OF MARIAM THE MAGDALENE

IO (before our time).
A Venusian being who carried the *Wisdom of Love* and the quality of the moon to earth level.

Unknown incarnations in Lemuria and Atlantis.

Queen Tiyi (1490 – 1468 B.C.)
An Egyptian princess, married to Amenophis III, who brought the Holy Spirit into the Egyptian dynasty and was a beloved queen who ruled with love and wisdom together with her husband who made no decisions without consulting her. Amenophis was not a weak man but he possessed no masculine and patriarchal egotism. They had a daughter, Nefertiti, and a son Amenophis (the peace of Amon) both of whom were initiated into the deepest mysteries by Tiyi herself. The brother and sister were later married to each other and ruled together over Egypt, he under his initiation name as Pharaoh Akhnaton.

Miriam (about 1400 B.C.)
Older sister of Moses and Aron by seven years, she was prophet, magus and seer. It is said that a fountain she made flow with her magical powers always followed the Ark of the Covenant during the escape of the Jews from Egypt. She worked with the concept of holy sound and composed many songs that the Therapists of Alexandria used in their rituals, centuries later.

The Queen of Sheba (1020 – 950 B.C.)
An Ethiopian princess who became the ruler of "the country to the south." She is the "Dark Bride" of *King Solomon* from *The Song*

of Songs in the Old Testament. *The Song of Songs* has always been connected with *King Solomon* but actually came about because of her. Together with *Solomon* she participated in the Heavenly Marriage (hieros gamos). The High Priestess of the true Coptic "Church" (The Wisdom of the Heart) which must not be confused with the Coptic Church of today.

Mariam Magdal (I B.C. – 76 A.D)
The elevated spirit of the peace of God.
The companion of Yeshua. Daughter of Zehar from the tribe of Benjamin and Jezebel from the tribe of Dan. Was engaged traditionally to Yeshua when she was twelve years old. The later wedding (the Wedding of Cana) first and foremost had a symbolic meaning in connection with the initiation through the Heavenly Marriage (hieros gamos). Mariam was initiated in the Isis tradition in Heliopolis and with the Therapists in Alexandria. Yeshua considered her the disciple above all disciples and she continued the impulse of the true gnostic teachings of Yeshua which differed fundamentally from the institutionalised Christianity arising from Peter's interpretation of Yeshua's teachings and doctrine developed by St. Paul. When Peter and "his church" made it impossible for Mariam to preach the secret teachings of Yeshua, she emigrated to the large Jewish settlements in the south of France. Both before, during and after the inauguration of the Church, the men of the Church went to great lengths in order to compromise her and repress her message. For many years she worked as a prophet and seer in the area around Marseilles. She probably spent the last years of her life at the *Salveterra-monastery* in the area around Opoul-Périllos between Narbonne and Perpignan. Her version of Yeshua's teachings weaves through the European mystery tradition influencing the early Celtic church, the Teutons, the Druids, the Templars, the Cathars, Alchemists, Rosicrucians, Freemasons, the Order of the Golden Dawn, Theosofists, Martinus and a large part of New Age and many others. After her death, her bones were brought back to Jerusalem and buried beside her beloved in the family tomb of Jesus.

Guinevere (about 500 A.D.)

The mystical King Arthur's equally mystical bride. Brought The Wisdom of the Heart into the Celtic world. She is the High Priestess of the mythical realm of Avalon, and is the messenger between the old and the new, and between Heaven and Earth.

Esclarmonde de Foix (1155 – 1240 A. D.)

The Light of the World.

Daughter of the Duke of Foix, Roger Bernard, and Lady Zébélia de Carcassonne. Her brother, Ramon-Roger, was a well-known troubadour who went by the nick-name *Druz, the Initiated One* or *the Pure One.* At the castle at Foix (called the Court of Love) Esclarmonde, during her upbringing and at her father's request, was initiated into the holy texts and secret words of the troubadours which were hidden in the so called Science of Joy which again was a mixture of the teachings of the Druids and the pure Christianity of the Cathars. The Cathars profited by the support of Roger Bernard. Esclarmonde married Jourdan III d'Isle Jourdain, with whom she had six children. She also founded monasteries for *Parfait*, "the perfect ones," and schools where poor children were taught *the new spirit.* After many years of preparation she herself took the initiation as *Parfait.* During the crusade of the inquisition against the heretics in the south of France she became the guardian angel of the Cathars who started small hospitals and workshops everywhere in the area. When the conflict escalated she built the last stand for the Cathars at the castle of Montségur. She herself escorted the secret treasure of the Cathars, *The Book of the Holy Spirit* or of *Love* to the stronghold of the mountain. Esclarmonde, whom the Cathars called *The dove of the Holy Spirit*, ran singing to the stake with 205 of her fellow believers after they had all refused the Roman Church's ultimatum of converting to Catholicism. She is the only saint of the Cathars.

Joan of Arc (1412 – 1431 A.D.)

Called herself *Jehanne La Purcelle, Johanna the virgin.*

Born in Domrémy she was the daughter of Jacques d'Arc and Isabelle Romée. At quite a young age, she danced with the other children around *The Tree of Fairies*, which was a sort of local form of Diana worship. When Joan was thirteen she heard the voice of God for the first time, which taught her how to behave properly. In the following years she was guided by the Archangel Michael as well as Saint Catherine and Saint Margaret, who told her that she had been chosen to save the French from the siege of the English (the evil ones) and to place Charles of Lorraine rightfully on the throne. Since Joan in her local area was considered to be of special purity and an enlightened soul she fitted the old, Druidic prophecy that said "a virgin, a daughter of God, would be sent from on High to secure the monarchy of France."

By the time she was seventeen years old word of her visions had spread and she thus became the secret protégé of the duchess Yolande de Bar. Through the son of the duchess, René d'Anjou, – who wrote the allegorical masterpiece *Le Livre du Cœur d'Amours Espris*[14] *(the Book of Love)* and also created a drawing of Mariam Magdal teaching in Marseilles,[15] – she was prepared to complete her mission as *The Female Christ*. She thus obtained permission to come before Charles with the help of the royal family *de Bar*. The rumours about her were by now so widespread that it was thought she possessed divine powers. The French army, under her command, conquered the English in the course of two years and she led Charles to a ceremony in Reims where he was anointed King. During the battle with the English her sole weapon was a banner bearing the inscription, "Jhesus - Marie." When the mission was concluded she was betrayed by her own people, captured by the English and tried for heresy. During her trial she was much more eloquent than her accusers and she showed such calm and honesty that only the bitter hate of the clerics prevented her acquittal. She was burned at the stake in the old market place at Rouen at only nineteen years of age. The young man who cleaned the site of the fire afterwards, stated that he had seen the heart of Joan in the embers, and that it was still beating. Many years later, Joan was sanctified by the same Roman Catholic Church that had executed her.

14   In the 18th folio of the book it says among other things, "Melancholy has led the knight and his page along the River of Tears until they face the dangerous passage. Pas Peril-laux." CF. the town of Périllos where this identity ended her days as the incarnation Mariam Magdal.

15   see drawing at page 627

*From 'The Book of Love' by René d´Anjou,
the spirituel brother of Joan of Arc, 1409.*

(Notice the winged hearts at the horse-armour. They are completely identical with the logo of Hazrat Inayat Khan´s sufi-momement founded in 1923. Khan was the father of Noor-un-nisa Inayat Khan, another incarnation of Mariam Magdal)

Noor-un-nisa Inayat Khan (1914 – 1944 A.D.)

Noor-un-nisa means *The Light of Womanhood*. Daughter of the sufi master and musician *Hazrat Inayat Khan* and *Ora Ray Baker*, a cousin of *Mary Baker Eddy* who founded *Christian Science*, Noor was born in Moscow but grew up at Fazal Manzil in a suburb in Paris the headquarters of *The Sufi Movement*, which was started by her father (the logo of the movement, a heart with wings, is identical to the winged heart which the spiritual brother of Joan of Arc, René d'Anjou, placed on the coat-of-arms of his heroine in *The Book of Love*). As a child she could see fairies and she possessed great poetic and musical ability. Her nick-name at the time was *Babuly*[16], which means *Daddy's girl.* From her earliest days her father taught her about the unity of all religions.

When she was thirteen years old her father went to India. The night before his departure she dreamt that "the baker flew into heaven never more to return." A year later she heard her father's voice telling her, "Babuly, from now on you must take care of the little ones." "The little ones" were her three younger sisters. They received a telegram the following day saying that their father had died in India. For the rest of her life she claimed that her father was alive and lived the life of a hermit in a cave in the Himalayas. After the death of her father her mother completely withdrew from the world. Noor, fifteen years old, thus became the head of the family taking responsibility for her smaller sisters and the day to day running of the household while at the same time going to school. She spent whatever spare time she had writing poetry and composing songs or reading old, romantic stories about knights and sacrifice. Her role model was *Joan of Arc.* She passed her exams at seventeen and started studying music with harp and piano as her major subjects as well as musical analysis and harmonics. At the same time she studied children's psychobiology at the Sorbonne in Paris. She composed some of her finest Sufi inspired works during this period, among others, *The Song of the Butterfly.* In 1939 she published *Twenty Jakata Stories* and started working on the idea of a newspaper for children, *Bel Age.* However, when the Second World War broke out, Noor and her family had to escape from France.

16   Babuly c.f. Barbelo.

Noor-un-nisa Inayat Khan, who took the name 'Madeleine', when she in 1943, as an english secret agent was operating behind enemy lines in occupied France. Her role model was Joan of Arc.

She came to England where she volunteered for the Women's Auxiliary Air Force (WAAF) in the fight against the Nazis. She became the first female agent who infiltrated into occupied France. These agents left for France knowing that no agent before them had lived more than three months behind enemy lines. In spite of the fact that she was deemed unfit as an agent, Noor became the most valuable agent and the one to last for the longest time. The Gestapo was constantly on her track, knowing her only by her cover name *MADELEINE* (the French version of Magdalene.)

Unfortunately, she was finally captured by the Gestapo having been betrayed by a French woman. At that time she had been operating as an agent for about a year. The interrogator was impressed by her quiet courage. She refused to give her real name and to reveal any of her fellow conspirators. The men of the Gestapo, who held her capture, tried to protect her as long as possible, but she denied everything and even tried to escape twice. In November 1943 they were forced to send her to the notorious Gestapo prison at Karlsruhe. Here she was chained and tortured. She was considered especially dangerous and uncooperative. She was taken to the concentration camp of Dachau and once there immediately taken to the crematorium and shot.

After her death she was awarded *the English George Cross MBE* and the French *Croix de Guerre* with a golden star. A close friend of hers in 1950 described her thus, "She gave new light and new life. She had the most beautiful heart you can imagine. Her presence was a great comfort to those who suffered. The sight of her was like a thousand suns. In her presence everything became clear. She knew how man might lift himself above any kind of trouble. She spoke to those she met with her beautiful, quiet voice, and her power was great. She never worried. She loved nature and was able to communicate with the trees, the leaves, the snow, the flowers, the birds ..."

✡

Not a direct incarnation of MM; but one of the MM taught barers of the Magdal-principle:

Helen Schucman (1909 – 1981 AD)

The channel for the receiving of *A Course in Miracles*, dictated to her by Yeshua. Daughter of Sigmund Cohn, who was half Jewish, and Rose, who was Lutheran. Helen was introduced, by her baby-sitter, to Catholisicm. As a 12-year-old she visited *Lourdes* in the French Pyrennees, and was strongly affected by the experience.

For most of her life she was split between to identities, which mutually excluded each other. In a vision, that preceded the writing down of the Course in Miracles, Helen saw herself kneeling before a very holy priestess, that was also a symbol of her higher Self. For a long time she wasn't able to look at the priestess' face, for fear of the condemnation she was sure she would see in it. In the end she looked directly at the priestess: "When I did that I broke down in tears. Her face was gentle and full of compassion, and her eyes were past description. She knew nothing about me that deserved judgement. I loved her so much that I literally fell on my knees in front of her."

She married *Louis Schucman* in 1933. In the years after she took a doctorate in psychology. During that period she suffered from depression and, at the same time, had a series of extra-sensory experiences. She became the leader of a research unit at Columbia-Presbyterian Medical Centre, where meeting *William Thetford* was decisive in the writing down of the Course.

In that period Helen had a vision of a scroll in a cave by the Dead Sea. The text on the scroll said: GOD IS. During a journey to Israel she visited, together with *Bill Thetford* and *Kennet Wapnick*, the Essenese's caves by the Dead Sea. It was an earth-shattering experience when they suddenly found themselves in "Helen's cave", where she, in her vision, had seen the GOD IS scroll.

Helen felt especially attracted to *Mariam Magdalene*, and was closely connected to *Yeshua* all her life.

Before, during and after the writing down of *The Course in Miracles*, she wrote poems, *The Gifts of God*, which were collected and published after her death. She was, right up until her death in 1981, in constant conflict with the message she was the spreader of.

APPENDIX D

THE INCARNATIONS OF YESHUA THE NAZARENE

IAO (before our time)
"I am Alpha and Omega."
The first identity of Creation carrying *the Being of Compassion* and the qualities of the sun to the earth level. The oldest brother.

Amilius (the first Adam)
Atlantis.

Adam
The second Adam, created by God and Amilius as a guardian of the Garden of Eden.

Enoch
The chosen One, the Son of Man.
Not born by a woman. The scribe who was lifted by *the seven Elohim* and shown *the seven heavenly spheres* and then wrote it all down in what today has been passed on as *the first and second Book of Enoch*.

Hermes
The Guide.
Known by the Egyptians as *Tehuti, The scribe of the Gods*. Known by the as *Trismegistos, the Threefold Great*. By that they meant that he was the greatest of all philosophers, the greatest of all priests and the greatest of all kings. In the old Gnostic writings he was considered to be *Logos, the Word* and by that they meant *Christ*.

Melchizedek
The King of Justice, Messiah and King of Salem (Jerusalem). Without

a father and without mother. Like Yeshua he was a priest, ordained by God and representing a dimension high above worldly law. Like Yeshua he was called *The Prince of Peace*. When he received Abraham at the gates of Jerusalem he inaugurated the holy communion.

Yoasaph (Joseph)
(Forgiveness and new life).
Son of Yacob and Rachel. Yacob's other sons became jealous of Yoasaph and decided to kill him. Instead, they threw him in a well and later sold him as a slave. This is how he got to Egypt where he became a servant to one of Pharaoh's employees. Here he was accused of having seduced his master's wife although he had declined all her approaches. Through his ability to interpret dreams Yoasaph was freed from the jail and allowed to go before the Pharaoh who had been looking for someone to interpret his dreams. On the basis of these, Yoasaph predicted that seven fat years would follow seven lean ones. Therefore the Pharaoh had Yoasaph make store rooms for grain and other food produce so that the country would be safe when the seven lean years came. Thus Egypt was spared a famine. Yoasaph became the right hand man of the Pharaoh and married the daughter of the sun god, Aseneth. When hard times fell on the land of Canaan his brothers came to him for help. Yoasaph forgave them and they returned to Canaan carrying new seeds and new life.

Yehoshua (Joshua)
Prophet and mystic. A leader under Moses and his successor after the Jewish exodus from Egypt. He was the one to lead the Jews to *The Promised Land* by dividing the waters of Jordan to the north of the Dead Sea. He went to Gilgal where he established Passover and circumcision. Shortly after, the Jews took Jericho, under his leadership, by breaking the town wall down using the sound of ram's horns and carrying *The Ark of the Covenant* in front of them. He was responsible for the writing down of *The Books of the Pentateuch* and *The Book of Yehoshua*.

Asaph

Prophet, magus, musician, singer and healer at the court of King David.

The author of a series of the psalms in *The Book of Psalms.*

Elisha, *El-Isha*

Prophet and healer. Pupil of Elijah (an earlier incarnation of John the Baptist), who became his successor. Raised the dead, performed provision-of-food wonders and many other miracles. With his cloak Elijah parted the waters of the River Jordan and made them *flow back towards their source,* a metaphor for the inner process he introduced Elisha to – exactly as John the Baptist, hundreds of years later, initiated Yeshua in the mystery of baptism in the Jordan. Apparently, before Elijah's ascension in *The Chariot of Fire,* Elisha also received, besides Elijah's cloak, two thirds of his spirit. In this incarnation Elisha was subject to Elijah, whilst, later, the roles were reversed, when John, through the baptism in the Jordan, acknowledged Yeshua as his successor.

Zarathustra (about 7th century B.C.)

Persian, Chaldean prophet and *Ahura Mazdas* messenger. *The Good Shepherd and Master of the Fire.* Just like Yeshua, he was born under strange circumstances and was bid welcome by three magi. Many attempts were made to take the life of that child but in vain. Was taught by the famous teacher *Burzhin-kurus* from his seventh year. During his upbringing he showed great skills and understanding of other people and their needs. He dedicated himself to prayers and severe asceticism in a cave in the Ushidarena mountain. Then followed seven years of total silence and for twenty years he lived on goat's cheese only. This is how he prepared himself for his life as a prophet. When he was thirty years old he left his cave. Zarathustra had visions where he saw God surrounded by a choir of angels.

He wrote the holy writings *Zend Avesta* using many of the sentences, which the identity Yeshua later developed! For example those about baptism, circumcision, the holy communion with bread and wine as well as the knowledge about the workings of the Holy

Spirit. His prophesies also included the coming of a Messiah.

Yeshua (Jesus) (born 7 B.C. under a Venus/Mercury conjunction)

The Nazarene, The Initiated One, The Son of Man, The Good Shepherd. The First Born and the Oldest One. The Melchizedichian Messiah and The Cosmic Christ.

Prophet and healer. Son of Yoasaph and Miryam. Trained by the Essenese on Mount Carmel. Journeys to India, Persia and Egypt. The identity in this life combined all his former lives and thus completed his mission as the incarnated *Messiah-Christ aspect.*

Established *The Church of the Burning Heart* here on earth. Never wanting to create a hierarchic institution or a church of stone.

Predicted the coming of *The Holy Spirit* before he himself left the earth level. Yeshua and the Seven Elohim operate through it forever.

APPENDIX E

THE MYTH OF THE HOLY GRAIL

The Christian myth tells us that the Grail was the cup that Christ used at the Last Supper and in which he poured wine, saying, "This is my blood" (Math. 26:28). After the crucifixion *Joseph of Arimathea* collected the blood of Yeshua in it and brought it to *Glastonbury.* Later it disappeared.

This myth appeared for the first time in the south of France during the 12th century. The original Grail myth, however, wasn't Christian but heretical. It originated in Moorish Spain. Like the Chauldron of Rebirth of Celtic mythology, the Grail may have represented the blood filled womb as symbol of rebirth.

The Grail was kept in a magnificent temple guarded by Queen *Rapense de Joie (the spreader of joy)*, an ancient name for *the holy whore*. The bards and troubadours said that her husband was a Moor and that her son *Johannes* founded the Templars, a group of holy warriors dedicated to the Grail and to the defence of women. When *the lady of the manor* or a *maiden* was in distress the knights of the Grail like Galahad, Parsifal and Lohengrin received a message as a burning sign engraved in the edge of the Grail to come to their rescue.

The Spanish Grail myth placed the Temple of the Grail at *Montsalvaesche (The Holy or Blessed Mountain)* in the Pyrenees. This temple was a model of the universe, crowned with a gigantic ruby symbolising the motherly heart of the earth, *The Holy Rose.*

Just like their Arabian predecessors, *the Hashishim*, the Templars waited for the chosen knight, a *Mahdi*, to come forward to save the world from tyranny and establish the right order of the Grail. The alternative would be the fulfilment of the prediction of *the Waste Land*, symbolised by the barren desert. *The Waste Land*, thus, was the direct result of man's violence towards *the Goddess.*

The Temple of the Grail was sometimes called *Montjoie (the Mountain of Joy)*, just like the castle *Joyous Gard* where *Queen Guinevere* retired with her lover. It was also like *Mons Veneris (Mount Venus)*. The sexual symbolism served the heretical cause as a weapon against the anti-sexual church. The old myth further tells us that the battle cry of the Grail-king was *Amor (love)*.

The Grail was for the first time transformed into a cup of Christ by the poet Robert de Borron some time between 1180 and 1199. Originally the Grail was a jewel in the crown of the Devil. Three thousand angels gave it to Satan while he was still in Heaven. During Satan's descent into Hell the jewel fell from his crown and on to the earth where it was found and changed into a cup. Joseph of Arimathea acquired the cup and gave it to Yeshua for his use at the Last Supper. It was also the *The Heavy Cup of Destiny* about which Yeshua in a weak moment prayed to God, *"Father, if this may be possible, let this cup pass me by."* (Math. 26: 39).

A number of poets from the 12th century have worked with the old Grail legend, among others, *Chrétien de Troyes* and *Wolfram von Eschenbach.* The final Christianisation of the myth was done by a monk from the *Cistercian order*, founded by *Bernhard from Clairvaux.* As a child he received a miraculous gift of mercy, when standing in front of *the Black Madonna* in Châtillon when he saw three drops of milk dripping from her breasts. This revelation had an impact on him for the rest of his life and also had far reaching consequences for the legend of the Grail. His order built hundreds of monasteries where the arts and the sciences blossomed. He also wrote the rules of conduct for the Templars, and both his uncles were members of the order. Bernhard was a remarkable man who succeeded in keeping the female principle alive within the Church, and he wrote many psalms and sermons for the Virgin Mary. He also wrote about three hundred sermons about *the Song of Songs*, this remarkable, female message of love in an otherwise very strict and patriarchal Old Testament. In the Song of Songs we meet *Sulamit (the Queen of Sheba)* who is the bride of both *Solomon* and Christ. Her cry, "I am black and yet lovely, daughters of Jerusalem" is also seen in the cult around the Black Madonna. It was the monks of the Cistercian monasteries who wrote the Vulgata-cycle of which *Queste det San Graal* forms a part. However, the great mystery about Bernhard himself is the question of the role of Mary Magdalene. In *Vézelay*, on Easter Saturday 1146, Bernhard held a sermon for the participants in the 2nd crusade. It is of importance that among the 100.000 participants were *Louis VII of France* and his young queen *Eleonora* who later married *King Henry of England* and founded the tradition of "the Courts of Love." Vézelay was at the time the most important centre for *the cult of Mary Magdalene*. The building of the great Magdalene basilica had been started fifty years prior to Bernhard's sermon.

There must have been something special about Vézelay. In 1217 *Saint Francis of Assisi* founded the first monastery of *the new order of St. Francis* there. It is also of importance that the Franciscans at Cordeliéres as well as the *Capuchins* traditionally considered themselves as the protectors of the Black Madonna.

There have been hundreds of these Black Madonnas all over Europe and although most of them are difficult to date with any accuracy, they belong to the oldest of the Madonna statues. Wherever you find a statue of a Black Madonna, you'll also find a thriving Mary Magdalene cult. A remarkable number of the Black Madonnas, which are more than three hundred years old, are said to have miraculous, healing powers.

Since the Legend of the Grail became more and more Christian and turned away from the subject of passion and love, it gradually lost its popular appeal.

The history of the Grail, however, goes back much further than the 12th century. It is not a coincidence that it was made public in the Marseilles area at that specific time, where almost contemporaneously, information about the *Kabalah* appeared. There were several old, Jewish settlements in both Spain and France in the 12th century. In towns like Toledo in Spain and Marseilles in the South of France Jewish magi and Arabian alchemists were seen side by side. The Moors ruled in Spain and it was through them that the age-old knowledge contained in both the Kabalah and *The Legend of the Grail* was brought to European mystics from Persia and the Far East. At first to Toledo then to Marseilles by someone as special as a Jewish Sufi master, *Kyot*. This man Kyot was also known under the alias *Kansbar*. According to him, the principles, which were later invested in the Kabalah, were the same as those necessary for alchemy, a state of mind which is an expression of the Grail.

Thus the Kabalah is knowledge handed down about the transcended state of mind – the awakened pineal centre which is symbolized by the Grail.

CLARIFICATION OF TERMS.

Akasha: See *Appendix A.*

Astral plane: A psychic plane which is just above the physical level and which cannot be experienced through our physical senses but only through clairvoyant sight. Human consciousness operates at this plane during sleep and after our physical death in the astral body. This is where feelings, projections and lust are at home and are expressed. In Sanskrit it is called Kâma-Loka, the world of desires. But there is also a higher, psychic/astral plane, where among other things we may experience great, transforming dreams, certain forms of clairvoyance and vision as well as a prophetic sense. It is also on this plane that we may move beyond time and space. *Bi-location*, the ability to appear in two different locations at the same time, also belongs to this plane.

AUM: The cosmic, vibration from which the universe and everything alive has been created and in which all sounds and all vibrations are contained. The three fold in the One. The divine mantra. The Absolute as sound.

Aura: Within the esoteric tradition aura has for many years been understood as the many fine bodies, ether, astral and mental bodies, which all together form the aura of an individual. It is visible only to clairvoyant and visionary people. According to the Seer an individual has twelve auras plus a thirteenth supreme aura. 1st aura: the body's radiating power (ether). 2nd aura: psyche (astral). 3rd aura: dreams, imaginations about a serene life or the escape from it. 4th aura: the mind (mental). There is no radiation from the body in the following auras, but from the head instead: 5th aura: the planets and the stars. 6th aura: electromagnetic fields, the gods. 7th aura: gravitation. 8th aura: Earlier incarnations. 9th aura: the aura of the soul. The remaining auras have not yet been set free except for the 13th aura:

the Grail. Only the part of the aura belonging to the radiation of the body (the ethereal body) may sometimes be seen by the physical eye as a slightly glowing, greyish purple fog reaching about two inches away from the physical body and lined with fine, radiating lines, the direction and clearness of which depend on the health of the person in question.

Chakras/energy points: The seven primary energy centres each of which emanates from a point in the ethereal counterpart of the human being. The chakras are: The Root centre that emanates from the perineum and is about life power, instinct of self-preservation, family and tradition. The Sacral centre emanates from a point between the pubic bone and the navel and is about sexuality and reproduction. The Solar Plexus emanates from the centre of the stomach and is about the emotional, the centre of feelings. The Heart centre emanates from the chest and is about love, empathy, interdependence and spirituality. The Throat chakra emanates from the neck and is about creativity, state of mind and tangible thought. The Forehead centre emanates from a point just above the eyebrows and is the co-ordinating centre managing abstract thinking and is the bridge to the higher world. The Crown centre emanates from the top of the head and is about synthesis-forming and is the centre of transcendence, the crowning element. All seven centres are mutually connected.

Clairvoyance: French: *vision*. The ability to see super sensory things and to see regardless of time and space. There are many degrees of clairvoyance. Most of them at the ethereal and lower psychical (astral) levels, which is the case with many born clairvoyants. Clairvoyance is not necessarily the same as being at a higher spiritual level. Clairvoyance is an ability, which is dormant in all people. In order to reach a higher degree of clairvoyance the personality must be trained since a high, ethical level is required if you are going to obtain and maintain the ability. You may only be able to move from the lower levels to become a real seer after many years of intense, spiritual and ethical education.

Dharma: Sanskrit: duty, justice, law, taking the right attitude, furthering your abilities and doing what must be done according to your karma and the universal laws in order to further the spiritual development of humanity.

Ethereal membrane: An invisible wall between physical and ethereal realities upon which archetypal images from the Akasha archives become visible when given enough energy through for example prayer.

Ethereal plane: The ethereal is the matter that penetrates space with spiritual essence, the form of energy that controls, decides and determines the outer physical shape. The binding force of the universe. The ethereal body is a life giving and maintaining subtle body of light that is the counterpart of the physical body.

Ephatah: Aramaic: from the Egyptian ptâh. Activates the power to open up. As an invocation or conjuration: open up, remove any obstacle, soften whatever is rigid, set that free which is locked, let yourself be penetrated by the energies of the universe, which give and receive all sound, hearing and speech! This invocation which has an opening effect on all the dimensions of the universe and which, furthermore, has a connection to name, hearing and sound, was used by holy men and women, mystics and healers from the Middle East. It is later to be seen in the Arabic Fatah, "The One who opens the Way," which is one of Allah's nine and ninety names and qualities. It is still used today to chant this word in the same way as did Yeshua (see *The Gospel of Luke*).

Gematria: A literary tool involving the use of numerical values of Aramaic, Hebrew and Greek letters, making it possible to calculate sums reflecting specific symbolic numbers and proportions according to the holy writings of Pythagorus.

The Grail: See *Appendix E.*

Ikhâl: Aramaic. Normally translated: *finished.* Specifically: *Completely activated, done, reinstatement of the original condition.*

Isogynic*:* Greek *isos:* the same, alike, equal. Greek *gy'ne:* woman. In this connection a condition where a human being, be they male or female, both integrates and dissolves the masculine and the feminine in him – or herself, so that the individual is both and yet none of them. According to the Seer, the isogynic individual is the human being of the future because they have left all limitations and have transcended all mistakes, emotions and diseases. Isogynic man is universal and intuitive and acts or refrains from acting from a universal point of view. It has opened up to all the latent forces: empathy, compassion, poetic, musical and prophetic gifts, clairvoyance (vision), clairaudience (clearness of hearing), the ability to heal, and a higher consciousness. From this condition the new human being is going to develop towards unfathomable heights.

Kabalah: Hebrew: received/passed on. It emanated from Jewish mysticism under this name in the 12th century in the Provençal tradition under Isac the Blind, however, it is thought to come from a much older tradition which is supposed to have been passed on to Abraham of *Melchizedek.* The Kabalah is a system of ten *sefirots* (Hebrew for sapphire) each of which expresses a specific spiritual quality. The ten points are mutually connected by 32 roads, each of which further expresses quality and possibilities.

Karma: Sanskrit: *Action.* The law about cause and effect. Is normally considered to be the law of justice. "Whatsoever a man soweth, that shall he also reap." To the Seer, karma is more a definition of the way we create our own reality. When we act in life, life re-acts according to what we do. A person's good or so-called bad karma is the collective sum of all effects that the person has caused through their own actions in this or past lives and which according to the universal law must be dealt with sooner or later. There is no such thing as bad karma, only the possibility of growth.

Kundalini: *The fire of the snake.* A power that is latently coiled up in the root centre. The energy of matter, the power of the Holy Spirit, the creating principle. A spiritual, electric and creative power which when awoken may become destructive and fatal instead of creative, if it is not guided along the right path. The kundalini experiences mentioned here and the inconveniences they caused, are meticulously described in
A Soul at Fire (Hovedland, 1993).

Mandorla: Also called vesica piscis, fish bladder. An old Christian symbol arising when two equally large circles are pulled through each other's centres. It also symbolises the female vulva, which again symbolises the gate between the celestial and the terrestrial spheres. The integration between two poles, for example the masculine and the feminine. From this obtained unity the isogynic individual may arise.

Mental plane: The plane immediately above the astral plane. The level of thought divided into two, a low level relating to the personality, the concrete level, and a higher level relating to the transpersonal and the abstract.

Merkabah: *The Chariot of Fire.* Jewish: *carriage, vehicle for transportation, travelling.* Egyptian: *Mer = light, Ka = body, Ba = spirit.* Belongs to the oldest teachings in the *Kabalah.* In *The Talmud, The Misnah, The Tosefta* and other Jewish writings *The Merkabah* tradition is mentioned more or less clearly. What is meant is a form of meditation where *The Merkabah* practitioner through breathing, yoga and prayer goes to Heaven in a *Chariot of Fire* meeting angels in the Halls of Holiness. The goal of these *Merkabah* travellers was (and still is) the state of transcendence giving access to the Throne of God in other multi-dimensional realities. The ultimate demand, thus, for any *Merkabah* traveller is the investigation of one's own reasons and a deep understanding of one's own ethics. In the Book of Ezekiel and the Book of Kings there is a tale about Elijah and Elisha, who during a walk along the Jordan river, suddenly saw a

Merkabah fire in front of them, at which point Elijah was taken up in this "chariot of fire" and disappeared out of three-dimensional reality. You may also say that *The Merkabah* is a thought form of fire which is created by *The Merkabah* traveller in order to be able to travel in time and space away from the three dimensional reality and into other conditions and dimensions.

Neutrino: A fundamental, neutral particle (antiparticle), which is not a part of specifically powerful interactions. Without electric charge at the physical level and thus very difficult to trace. May be without substance.

Rukha d'koodsha – malkoota d'shmaya: Aramaic. Rukha: breath, wind, air, energy, electricity, radiation of life. D'koodsha: The way it is supposed to be according to the universal laws. Rukha d'koodsha: The Holy Spirit. The Holy Spirit activated. Malkoota: Kingdom, human judgement and attitude emanating from the harmony between the inner and the outer. D'shmaya: Heaven, heavenly state. Malkoota d'shmaya: Transpersonal, elated state, the way it is supposed to be, desirable and harmonic state.

Sophia: Greek: Wisdom manifested as a female shape, which is honoured for being the immaculate mirror of the power of God. The Gnostics called her the wife of God. Further, she is identified as the Holy Spirit and as the Jewish *Shekhinah*, the quintessence of the refulgence of God and the holy, feminine consciousness.

Transpersonal: On the other side of or beyond the personal. Above and beyond the physical, emotional and mental personality. A universal ability seeing humanity as a whole, the goal of which is to express goodness. A plane, which includes an elevated consciousness, wisdom.

Transpersonal psychology: A branch of psychology dealing with the spiritual life of man trying to integrate wisdom from the spiritual traditions. It is therefore above the psychology of behaviourism.

Out-of-body-experience: A condition where you, awake or dreaming, leave the physical body. The state is also described in connection with near-death-experiences (cf. Raymond Moody). Plotinus (204 - 270) writes: "I have often woken up in myself outside of my body and have stepped into myself again leaving all other things alone. I have seen magnificent beauty and been convinced that I belonged to the better part. I have actually lived the best possible life and have reached an identity with the divine. After resting within the divine and getting down from this greater mind (nous) and into the reasoning mind, I was very surprised how I got down at all and how my soul got into a body as it now has shown unto itself what it really is." (Enneade 4,8,I). The out-of-body-experiences mentioned here are described more closely in "Sjæl i flammer" (Hovedland 1993) and "Skyggerejser" (Hovedland 1998).

BIBLIOGRAPHY

Barry, Kieren: *The Greek Qabalah* (Weiser 1999)

Begg, Ean: *The Cult of the Black Madonna* (Penguin 1985)

Ben-David, Githa: *The Note from Heaven*

Brunton, Paul: *The Secret Path* (London 1939)

Budge, Wallis E.: *The Egyptian Book of The Dead* (Routledge & Kegan 1923)

Davidson, John: *The Gospel of Jesus* (Element 1995)

Douglas-Klotz, Neil: *Desert Wisdom* (Harper 1995)

Douzet, André: *Perillos* (Société Perillos)

Elliott, J. K.: *The Apocryphal New Testament* (Oxford 1993)

Fuller, Jean Overtone: *Noor-un-nisa Inayat Khan* (East-West Publ. 1952)

Goswani: *Layayoga* (Inner Traditions 1999)

Greenlees, Duncan: *The Gospel of Hermes* (Theosophical Puplishing 1949)

Greenlees, Duncan: *The Gospel of the Gnostics* (Theosophical Publishing 1958)

Hall, Manley P.: *The Mystics and Mysteries of Alexandria* (PRS 1988)

Harding, Esther M.: *Woman Mysteries* (Theosophical Publishing 1955)

Hoeller, Stephan A.: *The Gnostic Jung* (Quest 1982)

Hoeller, Stephan A.: *Jung and the Lost Gospels* (Quest 1989)

Josephus: *Whole Works of Josephus* (London 1892)

Kaplan, Aryeh: *Meditation and Kabbalah* (Weiser 1982)

Kaplan, Aryeh: *Sefer Yetzirah* (Weiser 1997)

Khaboris Manuscript (The Yonan Codex Foundation 1970)

Khan, Hazrat Inayat: *Gayan, Vadan, Nirtan*

Khan, Hazrat Inayat: *The Heart of Sufism* (Shambhala 1999)

King René: *Le Livre Du Cueur D'Amours Espris* (Thames and Hudson 1975)

Krishna, Gopi: *Living With Kundalini* (The Kundalini Research Foundation 1993)

LeLoup, Jean-Yves: *The Gospel of Mary Magdalene* (Inner Traditions 2002)

LeLoup, Jean-Yves: *The Gospel of Phillip* (Inner Traditions 2004)

Lockhart, Douglas: *Jesus the Heretic* (Element 1997)

MacDermot, Violet: *The Fall of Sophia* (Lindisfarne 2001)

Mead, G. R. S.: *Pistis Sophia* (Kessinger reprint)

Mead, G. R. S.: *The Chaldean Oracles* (The Theosophical Publishing 1908)

Meyer, M. & R. Smith: *Ancient Christian Magic* (Harper Collins 1994)

Murdock, James: *The New Testament, Syriac Peshitto Version* (Hastings 1893)

Robinson, James R.: *The Nag Hammadi Library in English* (Brill 1996)

713

Sanderfur, Glenn: *Lives of the Master* (A.R.E. Press 1988)

Schonfield, Hugh: *The Essene Odyssey* (Element 1984)

Schubart, Walter: *Religion und Eros* (C. H. Beck 1966)

Schucman, Helen: *The Gifts of God* (Inner Peace 1982)

Shipflinger, Thomas: *Sophia-Maria* (Weiser 1998)

Singh, Hazur Maharaj Sawan: *Discourses on Sant Mat* (Radha Soami Satsang Beas 1970)

Starbird, Margaret: *Magdalene's Lost Legacy* (Inner Traditions 2003)

Stauffer, Edith R.: *Unconditional Love and Forgiveness* (Triangle 1987)

Steinsaltz, Adin: *The Thirteen Petalled Rose* (Basic Books 1980)

Taylor, Joan E.: *Jewish Woman Philosophers of First-Century Alexandria* (Oxford 2003)

The New Jerusalem Bible (Darton, Longman & Todd 1985)

Underhill, Evelyn: *Mysticism* (Methuen & Co 1911)

Walker, Barbara: *The Woman's Encyclopedia of Myths and Secrets* (Harper 1983)

Vermes, Geza: *The Complete Dead Sea Scrolls In English* (Allen Lane 1997)

Yonge, C. D.: *The Works of Philo* (Hendrickson 1993)

INDEX

THE ORIGINAL OIL & SALVE
OF
MARIA MAGDALENE

The famous Oil and Salve from the Bible are now available again.
Maria Magdalene used the salve/oil when anointing the feet and
head of Jesus. The anointing ritual was not only to honour and
respect kings, holy men and women, but the anointing ritual had
also a subtle elevating and purifying influence on the anointed.
By studying the Bible, the Apocrypha, and other sources closely,
Lars Muhl and Nils Erik Aamann-Christensen from Nardos A/S
have recreated the Oil and Salve. These holy remedies were used
by the Therapeuts of Alexandria in their rituals and treatments.
Nardos which was established in 1980, is named after the main
ingredient in the famous Oil and Salve.

For further information go to:
www.mariamagdalene.org

When buying the MM Oil and Salve you
support the aid organization Hearts and
Hands Denmark.
www.heartsandhands.dk